The Age of Beloveds

Walter G. Andrews and Mehmet Kalpaklı

The Age of Beloveds

LOVE AND THE BELOVED IN
EARLY-MODERN OTTOMAN AND
EUROPEAN CULTURE AND
SOCIETY

Duke University Press   Durham and London

2005

2nd printing, 2006

© 2005 Duke University Press

All rights reserved

Designed by CH Westmoreland

Typeset in Scala by Tseng Information

Systems, Inc.

Library of Congress Cataloging-in-

Publication Data appear on the

last printed page of this book.

Duke University Press

gratefully acknowledges the support

of the Institute of Turkish Studies,

which provided funds toward the

production of this book.

To Mehmet's son, Sinan, and

Walter's grandchildren, Matt, Kristin,

Katie, and Madeline Machotka and

Max Sheffield

CONTENTS

Preface ix
A Guide to Ottoman Turkish Transcription,
Pronunciation, Names, and Titles xi

1 Introduction 1
2 Beloved Boys (and Girls) 32
3 Love Scripts I, Male Bonding 59
4 Love Scripts II, Poems about Poetry about Love 85
5 Love, Sex, and Poetry 113
6 Women and the Art of Love 163
7 Seduction and Reversal 217
8 To Die For . . . : Love and Violence in the Age of Beloveds 251
9 Love, Law, and Religion 270
10 The End of an Age 304
11 Renaissance, Renaissances, and the Age of Beloveds 329

Appendix: Ottoman Sultans during the Age of Beloveds 355
Notes 357
Glossary of Ottoman Terms 389
Bibliography 393
Index 411

PREFACE

Our experience is that every book makes its author(s) anxious, yet this book has produced a degree of anxiety new to us. Not only is the subject matter intrinsically fraught with the danger of misunderstanding or giving offense, but our treatment of it is risky as well. This is a first step and could reasonably have been a small one, taken with extreme care. We chose, instead, to take a huge, perilous step in the hope of enticing others to take similar risks. Our anxiety was increased when almost everyone who read all or a part of the manuscript said something like: "There are people who will be very upset by this . . ." Our resolve was increased by the fact that none of these readers said that *they themselves* were upset or offended by it.

This book is our invitation to a broad range of scholars and thinking people to look at the Ottomans from a new perspective. It touches lightly on a lot of things that need to be looked at much more closely. It should be a wonderful opportunity for the kind of reviewer who delights in pointing out what the author of a book could or should have included but did not. Our hope is that our study will bring the Ottomans into discussions from which they have been absent and that it will serve as a springboard from which a more profound examination of Ottoman culture will emerge. It matters little to us if this examination takes the form of extrapolating on our suggestions or arguing for different directions.

All scholarly works are joint projects, the work of generations and a host of contributors. There are many people who contributed to the final form of this book, and many of their contributions, be they large or small, were crucial to our thinking. We cannot possibly mention them all, but there are a few people whose help cannot go without acknowledgment. Of course, not one of them is responsible for whatever it is that you, the reader, found upsetting. They are responsible only for the parts you liked.

We are deeply indebted to several of our Ottomanist colleagues: to Gabriel Piterberg, Cornell Fleischer, Linda Darling, Yavuz Demir, and Selim Kuru for sharing crucial sections of their as yet unpublished work; to Palmira Brummett and Victoria Holbrook for their helpful readings and support; and to Robert Dankoff and Halil İnalcık for much appreciated information. Ali Tanyeri shared his encyclopedic knowledge of Ottoman poetry. Ersu Pekin's help with illustrations was invaluable, as was the assistance of Stacy Waters and the Center for Advanced Research and Training in the Arts and Humanities at the University of Washington. Our thanks to Mary St. Germain and Ann Lally of the University of Washington Libraries for their work on our behalf and to the University of Michigan and the Seattle Public Libraries' staffs for emergency assistance with references. Walter's sister, Martha L. Andrews, did valuable and much needed editorial work on our manuscript in its earlier stages. Maria Rosa Menocal's intellectual and moral support was, as always, deeply appreciated. Patricia Fumerton and Alan Liu, who did not know us from Adam, went out of their way to lend a hand when asked. Reşat Kasaba and his University of Washington Turkish Circle provided us with valuable feedback, and Walter's student Didem Havlioğlu was generous in sharing her research on Mihri Hatun.

We are deeply indebted to Duke University Press in the persons of Reynolds Smith, who was willing to take a risk on a book about Ottoman literature; Sharon Torian, who dealt kindly with the anxieties of a sometimes grumpy author; and the other members of the Duke team who made this publication possible. Special thanks go to Joseph Brown, who did an astounding job of editing our manuscript into a readable and consistent form, and to Pam Morrison, the dimly seen presence behind the editing process. We are also grateful to the administration of the Topkapı Museum Library, the Millet Library, the Istanbul University Library, and the Turkish and Islamic Art Museum Library for their help in providing permissions for the illustrations in our book and to the Turkish Republic Ministry of Culture and Tourism for its support.

In the end, we will undoubtedly be embarrassed when we find that we have forgotten to express our appreciation to someone who richly deserves it. We ask those who were overlooked to accept our apologies and know that our oversight was unintentional and much regretted.

A GUIDE TO OTTOMAN TURKISH
TRANSCRIPTION, PRONUNCIATION,
NAMES, AND TITLES

It must be remembered that Ottoman Turkish was written in a modified form of the Arabic script. Thus, any representation of Ottoman names or words in the characters of the Latin alphabet is a transcription of a sort. In the world of Turkish studies, the most common way in which to represent Ottoman Turkish in the characters of the Latin alphabet is to begin from a base of Modern Turkish, which uses a Latin-alphabet character set developed early in the twentieth century to replace the Arabic-script characters. Ottomanists use an extension of this character set (one containing numerous diacriticals) that provides a one-to-one correspondence with the Arabic-script characters. In less specialized works, the simpler Modern Turkish orthography is used. We have chosen to use the simplest form of transcription, omitting indication of long vowels, but retaining symbols for the hamza (or glottal stop, indicated by ’ as in *Me’ali*) and the ‘ayin (an Arabic letter not pronounced in Turkish, indicated by ‘ as in *‘alem*). Words that have developed English equivalents will be spelled as they are in English (e.g., *pasha* and *ulema*). We have always chosen clarity over consistency, however.

No matter what form of transcription is employed, the relatively few pronunciation differences between Modern Turkish characters and the characters of English or other European languages can be troublesome for readers who do not know Turkish. Our solution is twofold. Here, we present a brief (and, hence, slightly defective) guide to the pronunciation of Turkish characters that differ substantially from English. In the text, we remind readers of the pronunciation of significant Turkish words and names the first time they appear (e.g., "Necati [Nedjatee]").

Turkish Pronunciation Guide

Turkish vowels are quite pure and short:

> a = *ah* (as in *father*);
> e = *e* (as in *bet*);
> i = *i* (as in *bit*) or *ee* (as in *meet*);
> o = *o* (as in *gold*);
> u = *u* (as in *bull*) or *oo* (as in *boot*);
> ö = *oe* (more or less as in German or the English vowel sound in *her*);
> ü = *ü* (as in German, or a rounded "ee" sound);
> ı = an unrounded *u* sound (there is no equivalent in English or the other European languages; hold a big smile while saying *zoot*, and you have *zıt*).

Turkish consonants are straightforward and similar to those in European languages, with a few exceptions:

> c = *dj* (the consonant sound in *edge*, which a Turk would spell *ec*);
> ç = *ch* (*çelebi* = *chelebi*);
> ğ = a glide between vowels or a lengthening of a preceding vowel (*doğu* = *dowu*; *bildiği* = *bill-diyi*; *iğne* = *eeyne*);
> j = *zh* (as in the French *Jacques*);
> ş = *sh* (*paşa* = *pasha*).

Ottoman Names and Titles

In the Ottoman Empire during the Age of Beloveds, names were much more fluid than we are used to today. Everyone had a single name, among the elites usually one of the names of the Prophet (e.g., Muhammad [often pronounced Mehmet], Ahmet, Mustafa, etc.), or of the Prophet's family or companions (e.g., 'Ali [Muhammad's son-in-law], 'Osman [one of the Prophet's immediate successors]), or of one of the early prophets mentioned in the Qur'an (e.g., Ibrahim [Abraham], Ishak [Isaac], Yusuf [Joseph]), or an Arabic compound linking the word for "servant" (*'abd*) with one of the ninety-nine names of God (e.g., 'Abdu'llah [servant of God], 'Abdu'l-baki [servant of the Immortal], 'Abdu'l-hamid [servant of the Praised]). All in all, there were a limited number of common names and no set pattern of family names to distinguish one Ahmet from the many others.

Among common people, who lived in small communities even in urban settings, simple descriptions (e.g., tall Ahmet, 'Ali the tailor) or a patronymic using -oğlu, "son of" (e.g., 'Osmanoğlu [the son of 'Osman]), distinguished one person from another. Among the elites, the practice was much the same, employing more distinguished and erudite descriptions and titles. Patronymics were created by adding the Persian -zade instead of the Turkish -oğlu (e.g., Dukaginzade [from the family of Duke Jean], Nev'izade [son of Nev'i]). Place of origin was often identified in a compound of the place with the Turkish suffix li/lı/lu/lü or the Arabic equivalent, a long ī (e.g., Taşlıcalı [from Tashlıdja], Sirozī [from Siroz]). For persons who achieved high office or some stature in the religious institution or the education system, titles were often a distinguishing feature of their common names. The highest officials (viziers, top administrators, the highest military commanders) held the title *pasha*; those in the second tier (governors, generals) were called *bey*; persons from the ulema (the learned class: professors, judges, educated people) used *çelebi* (chelebi) or *efendi*; dervish adepts and respected religious figures were often called *shaykh* (distinguished elder). Because these titles often became part of the identification of certain prominent people, we will use them regularly in the way the Ottomans did and more often than we would use equivalent titles in talking about Europeans. So you will see, for example, Ibrahim Pasha (to identify the famous grand vizier), Evliya Çelebi (the famous traveler), Hayali Bey (the poet who became a governor).

The poets all took pen names, which most often consisted of an appropriate word with a long ī added to create a descriptive abstract noun (e.g., *hayal* [image] + ī creates Hayalī [the Imaginative]). Less often a poet would simply use his own common name or some part of his name (e.g., Yahya [John] or Baki [from 'Abdu'l-baki]). The pen names were often used by the Ottomans to identify a certain famous poet.

I

INTRODUCTION

There is a story about Mehmet the Conqueror (Sultan Mehmet II, r. 1451–81) and Lukas Notaras found in the history of the fall of Constantinople by the Byzantine Greek Doukas.[1] Doukas was from an old Byzantine family of the upper classes. His grandfather had fled Constantinople during the civil wars of the mid-fourteenth century, taking up residence in Ephesus under the patronage of the Turkish emir of the ruling Aydınoğlu family. Doukas himself lived in various parts of Asia Minor and was in Constantinople at the time of its fall. He knew Turkish and Italian as well as his native Greek and was able to gather accounts of the siege and its aftermath from both the conquerors and the conquered. What intrigues us about Doukas's story—one not found in contemporary accounts by other Greeks who witnessed the siege firsthand—is the degree to which it is about love, and honor, and sexual behavior.

Love Traps

The story of Lukas Notaras and Mehmet the Conqueror is rather simple as Doukas tells it. Notaras was the high admiral and grand duke of Constantinople, the emperor Constantine's right-hand man. His father and grandfather had long been in the service of the Byzantine emperors. Notaras's father had been a court functionary and envoy for Manuel II Palaelologus, and Notaras himself had already been an ambassador to the court of Mehmet's father, Sultan Murat II (r. 1421–51), eight years before Mehmet's birth. The Ottomans were well acquainted with Notaras. Prior to the siege of Constantinople, he had covered all possible avenues and all eventualities. He held Genoese and Venetian citizenship, kept a good part of his vast fortune in Italian banks, and had sent his daughters to live in Venice, where they would wait out the siege in safety and comfort. As the Ottoman noose tightened around the city, he had served his emperor's interests by mediating between the Unionists, who in return for a crusader army would have healed the Great Schism and welcomed the authority of the Roman pope in the East, and the Anti-Unionists, who would have died first (and in many cases did). It was rumored that he had won over the Anti-Unionists by crying out: "Better the sultan's turban than the Latin miter." Many believed that he would have sold the whole city, turbans, miters, and all, to Rome for a few boatloads of defenders and worried about handing it over when the siege was lifted.

As Doukas tells it, when Constantinople fell and the youthful Mehmet (he was only twenty-one at the time) entered in triumph, he thought to offer Notaras a position as leader of the Greek community in the now Turkish city. But, when he demanded Notaras's handsome youngest son, supposedly to be used sexually to sate the sultan's perverted lusts, Notaras refused, and the merciless Mehmet had Notaras, as well as his older son and son-in-law, executed. Doukas's account polarizes the protagonists and attributes value to both sides by contrasting the love (for a son, for honor) of the Notaras family to the lust (purely sexual desire and abnormal desire at that) of the sultan.

Some people who are familiar with the history of stories about sex and love will recognize close parallels to the story of Saint Pelagius, the thirteen-year-old Christian martyr of the early tenth century, said to have been a beautiful and pious youth, who was tortured and dismembered by the Cordoban caliph 'Abdu'r-Rahman III when he refused the caliph's sexual advances.[2] It is easy to see how it could have seemed meaningful and hopeful to a Greek mourning lost Byzantium to reference the cult of Saint Pelagius, which for centuries provided spiritual energy to the Spanish Reconquista. Thus, although it is likely that Doukas's tale owes more to Saint Pelagius and a long history of attempts to portray Muslims as morally inferior than to anything that actually happened during the conquest of Constantinople/Istanbul, it is a useful story for our purposes nonetheless.

Let us imagine how we would fictionalize Doukas's fiction in a way that also accounts for what Sultan Mehmet might have been thinking had such an encounter actually occurred. It could go something like this, beginning in the aftermath of the great siege and the triumph of the Ottoman armies:

> Entering the city for the first time, the young sultan, still stunned by his incomprehensible victory, paused for a moment on the great acropolis of the Byzantines, which jutted its prow out into the convergence of the Bosphorus and the Golden Horn. Over waters glistening in the sunlight, white gulls wheeled and cried—a deceptive contrast to the city, where flocks of

carrion crows, black and gray as death or the garb of Christian monks, croaked their way through a thin haze of smoke from feast to feast, disturbed only by tired soldiers leading forlorn bands of captives into a murky future. But the gulls, now shining pure as shards of shattered diamond in the bright sky, would also stoop to the same grisly supper. Tonight, brave men would feast, and brave men would be feasted on . . . the way of this transitory world.

The sultan would need some of the old Byzantine nobility to legitimate his reign among the Greeks who remained in his dominions. If he could find Gennadius the monk, voice of the Anti-Unionists, who really did prefer the turban to the miter, he would make him patriarch of the Eastern Church, and a compliant Notaras could manage the secular affairs of the Greek community in the city of the Turks, Istanbul, which was no longer the city of either Constantine, first or last. Yes, he would see Notaras soon and woo him to his side—or at least know which way the winds were blowing. Even now the great train of wagons that provisioned his army was proceeding by another route toward the Hippodrome. This night he would feast with his army in the heart of the city, against the backdrop of the Hagia Sophia's great dome. They would put death and a bloody day behind them; on bellies filled in peace for the first time in a long while, they would transmute a thousand tragedies into the honeyed words of poets and dreams of a brilliant morrow:

I saw an angel, a sun face
    or this world's moon
Black hyacinth curls,
    smoky sighs of lovers

An alluring cypress,
    clad in black, like the moon
in night, or the Franks
    whom his beauty rules

If your heart is not bound
    in the knot of his heathen belt,
You're no true believer,
    but a lost soul among lovers

His lips give life anew
    to those whom his glances kill
Just so, for that giver of life
    follows the way of Jesus

Avnî, have no doubt,
    that beauty will one day be tame

> For you are ruler of Istanbul
> and he lord of Galata
>
> 'Avnî (Sultan Mehmet II)[3]

It was now time for Notaras. Mehmet had sealed his unbelievable victory with prayers beneath the awesome dome of the Hagia Sophia, now the grandest mosque in all Islamdom. His representative had been sent to Galata, across the Golden Horn, to calm the skittish Italians by assuring them that their economic interests—ever foremost in their minds—would continue to be served (and far better served) by the city's new masters. It was time for the first steps in waging a successful peace and creating the eternal capital of the Ottomans on the ruins of Byzantium.

Notaras's house was not far from the Hippodrome. When Mehmet arrived, accompanied only by Ya'kub the physician and a modest escort of his household janissaries, he found the house guarded by two soldiers of the feudal cavalry. One of them beat on the door with the butt of a dagger, and Ya'kub, his personal physician, spoke briefly in Greek to a red-eyed and trembling servant who emerged from the gloomy interior. After a moment, the master of the house, accompanied by his two sons and a son-in-law, all dressed in formal robes and conspicuously unarmed, appeared in the doorway and ushered the royal party into a large room.

Mehmet was shown with exaggerated courtesy to a backless sofa set on a dais that extended from wall to wall at one end of the room, whereupon the grand duke and his sons prostrated themselves before him under the stern gaze of the silent janissaries standing vigilant at his side. When Notaras proffered a coffer brimming with gems and strands of pearl and said, in a grave yet fearless voice, "This and all that is mine are at your service, my lord the sultan," Mehmet waited for Ya'kub to translate even though, having learned some Greek at his mother's knee, he understood every word. He accepted the gift with a nod to one of the janissaries, who took it from the grand duke's hand. Without looking at the coffer, he spoke to his physician-translator: "You might tell him that such a gift should have been given to his emperor, who had more need of it than I. Or you might tell him whatever you think fitting." The physician turned to Notaras and, with laconic brevity, said: "The sovereign appreciates your gift." Both physician and sultan were certain that the grand duke, on his part, held in reserve more knowledge of Turkish than he let on; the reproof and its embedded threat would not go unremarked. Let him not mistake who is in charge here.

The young sultan motioned for the Greeks to rise. As they did, he passed his eye over the four with a disconcerting deliberateness. The grand duke and his sons were tall and slender: the eldest son, a grown man like his graying father, freshly scarred by the battle they had so recently escaped;

the younger son, about fourteen years of age, slim and supple as a cypress, with dark eyes and a handsome face as white and glowing as a full moon framed in dark curls, another Jacob by name, by looks another Joseph. The son-in-law, a Kantakouzenas, was shorter and stocky, his face bruised on one side by some powerful blow. With an air of choosing his words carefully, Mehmet addressed his tautly expectant hosts: "Serve me well from this moment on, and I will restore you to the power and position you once held under your late emperor—nay, I will elevate you to power and position far beyond that in a city more glorious than you have ever known. What say you?" The physician translated, this time in full.

"My lord, we are yours to command," replied the duke.

"And your honored wife, God willing, she is well?"

"Unfortunately she lies ill in her bed. Otherwise she too would have been honored to greet you, my lord."

"Take me to her."

An instant of bewildered incomprehension . . . and then they led the sultan to the bedroom where the grand duke's wife lay. He spoke to her tenderly—he was only twenty-one and had buried his own mother not that long ago, and tenderness had not yet been wrung out of him by time and trial—"Be not afraid, mother. We will watch over you and restore to your family all it has lost. We will be pleased to see you well again, God willing."

The wish was sincere, but doubt hung between them like an early-morning mist rising from the abyss of age and faith and culture that separated the sultan from the grand duke. Could they indeed be trusted, the sultan mused? Could they ever know him well enough to be loyal? Could he know them well enough to rely on their loyalty? As these thoughts occupied one part of his mind, another part contemplated the young man holding his mother's hand on the other side of the bed.

The shape of the body and the lineaments of the face are the outward signs of inner intelligence and character, or so the respected sciences of physiognomy tell us. I would surround myself with such young men. Not only would they ever remind me of divine beauty, but they would serve me well: purity of face bespeaks moral purity; beauty and intelligence go hand in hand. Yes, he could serve, they could serve; fortune has favored me thus far, and why not in this also? I am riding the ascending arc of fortune's wheel; let those who have ridden it to its nadir now rise again with me.

They departed in a shower of formalities, the sultan riding off to feast the flower of his army, the Byzantines left behind to gnaw at the bitter ends of loss.

As the long night of feasting began in the ruddy light of sunset on garden fields of carpets laid in the great tent pavilion set amid the cooking fires and great cauldrons that dotted the great square of the Hippodrome, the grand vizier asked after Notaras and his family. "They are in good health," the young sultan said, "and I have plans for them." The vizier nodded and smiled . . . which gave Mehmet to understand that he had plans for them as well. He could not dally; he must exert himself to win the loyalty of the grand duke away from his vizier.

With an almost imperceptible nod the sultan summoned to his side the chief eunuch of his household, a huge man with large, languid eyes set in a preternaturally impassive face who stood like a shadow in the background, attentive to the sultan's every wish. When the eunuch bent to receive his command, he whispered: "Go now to the Notaras house, and bring the young man to serve at my feast."

"On my head . . . ," replied the Eunuch and departed in dignified haste with a small contingent of janissaries.

It seemed a brilliant ploy. The young man, with all his beauty and grace, and honored in the eyes of all by this invitation, would burn like a bright candle illuminating the gathering. The poets would be like moths to his flame; they would die in the incandescence of his charm and, dying, sing eloquent, impassioned staves of love, like nightingales trilling their longing for the fatal embrace of the rose. His name would be on all tongues, and, thus elevated, he would join the janissaries of Mehmet's household, where the most elite of young men were trained for positions of great prestige and power. In the janissary corps—the "new army"—everyone was a slave, conscripted from the non-Muslim population and those taken as captives in war, and from such conscripts came those who would rule the empire. As the son rose in service to the sultan, the bonds between the father and the Ottomans would grow stronger, and each, by serving his own ends and the ends of his family, would ultimately serve the interests of the sultan.

The news of this honor came like a cannon shot to the Notaras household. Without warning, the chief eunuch and his retinue appeared at the door. The summons was relayed and then repeated several times in ever simpler Turkish and then pidgin Greek until the father was sure he understood. *Understood* is, perhaps, the wrong term; he knew what was asked but could not fathom what it meant. After ushering the emissaries into a waiting room, the adult men of the family excused themselves "to prepare the boy" and gathered in one of the private inner rooms. They had lost so much this day it was inconceivable to them that this new development did not signal yet another and equally terrible loss. The father and brother sat as if stunned. The Kantakouzenas son-in-law, his face dark with rage, was the first to speak: "We know these Turkish dogs; their lust is unbridled by faith or morality or any of the nobler feelings common to civilized men. This tyrant wants the boy in order to sate his unquenchable rapaciousness. Do we send our beautiful and innocent Jacob to be the catamite of this devil? Do we next send our wives and sisters to be his whores?"

"No," the father replied, still pensive, "that we cannot do. But this sultan is a young man himself and appeared sincere in his approaches to us. Could it be that there is more to this summons than we can make out from here?"

The son-in-law: "I doubt. The wolf, I am certain, has appeared to us in sheep's clothing, father. It is a ploy to humiliate us and all whom we serve, now and in the annals of history. We may be lost if we refuse, but are we not lost in either case? Is it not a question of whether we be lost with honor or without?"

The father: "Just so. If it is true that these Turks know nothing of love and honor and obey naught but their own foul lusts, then we cannot serve them, nor can we live with honor under their yoke. Would that I knew them better or had more time to learn. But I do not. So are we agreed that we cannot comply and are willing to face the most dire consequences?"

The eunuch received them with his accustomed impassivity. When they made it clear to him that they would not send the boy and were willing to die in defense of their refusal, he turned without a word and, lacking instructions for this eventuality, made his way back to the square and the sultan. When he whispered his news in the sultan's ear, the young ruler flinched as though struck by a blow, and a flush crept up from his neck into his face. He turned to his most trusted adviser, who had returned from his mission to Galata and was seated to his left. "Notaras will not send his son to serve at our feast. We intended to honor him thus and his family with him; what does this mean?" The adviser, also angered, replied in the crudest Turkish.

"They think you mean to fuck the boy . . . right here, in front of everyone." As the sultan's red turned to purple and his lips parted in disbelief, the adviser continued in a more elegant tone: "I know these Christians. I have myself been to Venice in the guise of a merchant, and our spies have been even to the Golden Apple—Rome—where the pope has his palaces. Their heathen lusts are a public disgrace. If a highborn woman be poor through some mischance, she has no recourse but to sell herself to powerful men. She is trained in literature, poetry, music, and the arts of conversation and becomes the centerpiece of cultured gatherings, where she offers her body to the highest bidder. Such women throng the streets of Venice and even the Christians' holy city of Rome. They go about brazenly with faces and breasts exposed, finely clad, with learned men and church officials panting in their train. These men love neither their wives, whom they forsake for whores, nor the whores, whom they leave unprotected and subject to multiple rapes and mutilations. They live in a moral ignorance darker than that of the Arabs before the Prophet (God's prayers and peace be with him). How can one understand a people who know nothing of either mundane or metaphoric love?"

"Can one be so ignorant as to know nothing of love?" asked the sultan.

"They can," answered his most trusted adviser.

The headstrong boy become gardener of the realm summoned his eunuch again: "Take the executioner with you this time, and bring them here. They will come as I bid them, willing or no."

They returned their attention to the feast, but the young sultan's mood was dark on what should have been his brightest of nights. By the time the executioner and the eunuch arrived back at the pavilion with a terrible old man and his sons in tow, his mind was firmly set. To the eunuch he said: "Take the young one back to his mother." To the executioner: "As for these . . ." A simple nod was enough.

Hours later, when the feasting had ended in the dim glow of the false dawn, the ground outside the tents had already begun to smell of rotting meat.

The story told in this manner is, among other things, a story about love and the ways in which such an apparently universal human emotion can be the source of profound misunderstanding. Our story is also a work of historical fiction, which means that it follows the general curves and drift of history but adds details that history does not record and chooses from among accounts for its own reasons. As we segue into our investigation of some very intriguing beloveds and Ottoman beloveds first among them, the reasons for beginning with a fiction of this type and with this particular fiction will become increasingly clear.

From the perspective of literature, love and historical fictions about love — what we might call *undocumented emotional histories* — are crucial. It is difficult, if not impossible, to think of a literary tradition anywhere in which love is not a central issue. Moreover, from the perspective of literary history (or literary sociology), one of the crucial issues is understanding how any particular society understands love, enacts love, and parses love.

What makes love a peculiarly literary problem is the fact that there is very little historical documentation for the way in which people enact love outside stories and poems. Occasionally, when some aspect of amorous (or sexual) behavior runs afoul of the official arbiters of morality, there is a court record, the record of a punishment or fine, or an eyewitness account. Most of the time, however, people go about the business of love in private, leaving only traces of their passing in the forms of art and gossip. To be sure, there are, in Ottoman culture as in European and most other cultures, numerous treatises on love, analyzing and dissecting the kinds of love, theorizing about love, and even prescribing appropriate ways to engage in love. But our interest here lies not so much in the theory of love as in one historical instance of its practice.

What we have tried to add to Doukas's view in our openly fictional account is an educated guess about what Sultan Mehmet the Conqueror might have been thinking and how he might have been motivated had the encounter happened much as Doukas describes. Other than an emphasis on the sultan's perspective, what separates our story from Doukas's is that we assume the best about the sultan's thinking. He is not our enemy as he was Doukas's. In our story, the sultan assumes the worst about the Notaras family's thinking, and the Notaras family assumes the worst about the sultan's. This is quite normal; we tend to assume the worst without giving it a second thought. And one of the most common ways we do it is to attribute to those we do not like or do not know sexual thoughts and behaviors that are unacceptable to us.

When we talk about people and behaviors that are separated from us by difficult-to-bridge chasms of time, geography, culture, or rivalry, we can fall into a number of traps. It is easy for us to assume that the behaviors or attitudes that we notice in a few or even many members of a group are characteristics that belong to the whole. We might also assume that the meanings of the words, actions, and gestures of that group are the same for them as they are for us and, furthermore, that they have not changed over time or with place. Our attention might be caught by things that some people in a group do because they seem exotic or interesting to us, and we may come to characterize them by what strikes us about them. Once we begin to characterize and generalize in this way, we might also begin to define ourselves, our positive values and ideals, in contrast to what we imagine about those others who behave differently, and, in the end, we might come to think of them as morally, culturally, or intellectually inferior. Because these traps are as dangerous to scholars as to anyone else, the descriptions or representations of scholars have often been used in the service of projects to dominate, control, exploit, and reject groups seen as different, inferior, or unworthy. For this reason, contemporary scholars have become quite wary of such traps. They have written extensively about how we have fallen into them in the past and have invented a vocabulary for the task, words such as *racism*, *essentialism*, *idealism*, and *Orientalism*.

The areas of love, desire, and sexual behavior are important and fascinating to most people, and as such they are also especially rife with traps and potential misunderstandings. Nonetheless, it is our belief that, in order to talk meaningfully about love in a particular period, beginning with love among the Ottomans and the poems composed by Ottoman poets and consumed by their audiences from the late fifteenth century through the early seventeenth, we must explore just these sensitive areas and risk their pitfalls. So this will be a book about love, about poems, poets, and the circumstances in which they lived and made meaning, and not only about Ottoman poems and Ottoman poets. We will *not* deal extensively with the many ways in which non-Ottomans have misrepresented Ottoman sexuality, but we would urge anyone who has not yet read anything about the history of cultural traps and misrepresentations to take advantage of one of the excellent books on the topic.[4]

Ottoman Love Poems and the Natural History of Desire

European historians refer to a period running from the late fifteenth century through the early seventeenth as *the long sixteenth century*.[5] This was also the time when Ottoman Turkish culture established itself and flourished in the Middle East and Southeastern Europe with Istanbul as its undisputed center. The history of this period, as it comes to us through the stories of historians past and present, tends to focus on Ottoman military might, on the explosive growth of the empire and the development of an economy and a system of government that would administer vast territories down to the early twentieth century. To be sure, stories of burgeoning Ottoman power and influence are usually accompanied by references to a simultaneous efflorescence of art, architecture, and literature. Art objects, monuments, and literary works are often described in detail. We learn, for example, that, for the Ottomans, artistic literature was first and foremost poetry and that nearly all the poetry was love poetry. We learn of this poetry's line of descent from Arabic and Persian poetry, its rhetorical complexity, its myriad references to traditional tales, tropes, and mysticism. We know many things about Ottoman love poetry but surprisingly little about the culture, social situations, and emotional climate in which Ottoman producers and consumers of love poetry actually *loved*. One consequence of this is that the Ottomans begin to seem quite alien to us: better at things that more barbaric people are better at (war) and less good at things that civilized people, even very foreign civilized people, do (culture).

One could easily get the impression from a little reading that the Ottomans were singularly uninventive in expressing their own desires in art, finding it sufficient merely to drag the corpse of Persian desire about and occasionally stimulate a few twitches and a pale semblance of life in it by injecting a bit of the latest poetic fad from the East.[6] As old, venerable, and often expressed as this impression may be, we believe it to be false and misleading. We have said so many times in many venues and do not intend to spend many more words defending Ottoman poetry. However, some of the reasons why this misapprehension persists are quite relevant to what we are going to do, and we will discuss them in some detail in this introductory chapter. The rest of the book will avoid defending anything and devote itself to our evidence for what we think was going on. We believe that the evidence will convince open-minded readers that there is something unique to be learned about and from Ottoman culture and poetry, something that can even open our eyes to intriguing dimensions of histories and cultures we know more about. We have nothing at hand to convince or excite those who will not allow themselves to be convinced or excited.

Among the reasons why we do not know as much as we might about Ottoman poetry and Ottoman culture are many related directly to the situation of the Turkish Republic in recent times. Briefly put, some derive from the need of Turks early in the last century to distinguish a relatively small, modern, secular, democratic state from its vast, multicultural, theologically based, monarchical and imperial predecessor. Others have to do with the fact that the Ottomans were the enemies of the Europeans (we could even say *of other Europeans*) for many years and their religion (Islam) was perceived by Europeans as inimical to Christianity, although Christianity was far more inimical to Islam than Islam ever was to Christianity. Because it was, for the most part, Western European Christians and Jews who wrote the modern versions of world history, and because, at a certain point, many influential Turks wanted to see themselves as participants in the modernizing project of the West, both Europeans and modern Turks have had a stake in rejecting the Ottoman Empire and its traditional culture.

Yet another set of reasons—and the reason that interests us the most—is bound up in what we will call *the natural history of desire*. We call it a *natural* history because we do not want to argue that powers of various sorts make rational decisions about how desire (which underlies love, eroticism, and sexual behavior) is to be deployed, understood, and talked about in any particular period. And this is true even though those deployments—for example, the limits of normal behavior, what is permitted by law or custom, who can love whom and how—often seem to support, and do support, certain distributions of power. It must also be kept in mind that what we have to say about this history will be a severe condensation and reduction of many varied and complex phenomena, skewed toward introducing our readers to a particular view of love, sex, and eroticism.

From a broad historical perspective, it is generally accepted that, in the high cultures of Greco-Roman antiquity, the boundaries of permissible love for men were quite a bit less restrictive in some areas and derived from a radically different understanding than are ours today. This is strikingly obvious to us when we consider the question, To whom is it permissible (normal) for me to be attracted; whom can I love? As the historian Paul Veyne says: "The love of boys and women, as applied to men, is referred to scores of times in ancient literature: the one was the same as the other, and what one thought of one went for the other as well. It is incorrect to say that the ancients took an indulgent view of homosexuality. The truth is they did not see it as a separate problem." This is echoed by Michel Foucault: "The Greeks did not see love for one's own sex and love for the other sex as opposites, as two exclusive choices, two radically different types of behavior.... To have loose morals was to be unable to resist either women or boys, without it being any more serious than that."[7]

Foucault goes on to discuss in great detail how Western knowledge about sex and sexuality (sexology) has developed since the seventeenth century, how what we consider sexual behaviors and attractions were transmuted over time from preferences under the general heading of pleasure into "conditions" to which scientific psychological terminology and bodies of knowledge were attached.[8] This is to say that, for classical antiquity, there were no such categories as *homosexuality* or *heterosexuality*, only a range of preferences, like people in our time have for tall or short, blond or brunette, robust or slender partners. Moreover, the extremes—for example, the man who is attracted only to men or only to women, the effeminate man—were viewed with suspicion, and, for men at least, same-gender attractions were considered to be of a higher moral and spiritual order. The pleasures of sex and love were not distinguished from other pleasures and accorded a separate category. It was not assumed that a man would confine his pleasures to a relationship with one woman, and his taking of pleasure was regulated only by the avoidance of excess, immoderation being a sign of lack of control and lack of power. Thus, the masculine norm appears to have been a manly man who is erotically attracted to both boys and women, who to some degree enjoys amorous relations with both genders and leans toward preferring the company of attractive (and educated) males. The reasons why this is so are instructive (remembering, of course, that we cannot ever know *all* the reasons).

In situations where public life is dominated by men, where warfare is frequent and many men spend most of their time as warriors in the company of other men, and where men are educated and women are not, what people identified as masculine virtues—for example, strength, bravery, physical prowess, male beauty, artistic talent, eloquence—are highly valued. Being attracted to young men, loving young men, is an affirmation of those values and virtues, the very values and virtues that a man seeks in himself.[9] One may also be attracted to women and enjoy relations with them, but the relationship must always be hugely unequal in regard both to distributions of power and to the sharing of cultural expectations.

In a fascinating book on the sexual politics of classical Athens as illustrated in sculpture and the graphic arts, the scholar Eva Keuls introduces the challenging notion of what she calls *phallocracy*, which she defines as "a cultural system symbolized by the image of the male reproductive organ in permanent erection, the phallus."[10] Her invention of the term has specific reference to the situation in ancient Athens, where statues of the god Hermes, depicted with a large erect penis, were ubiquitously placed in the doorways of private homes and images of male genitalia were everywhere visible. Keuls sees these graphic representations of the phallus as overt signs of a belief in the inherent superiority of adult, free men acted out in the form of political, social, and sexual dominance. In phallocratic Athens (which she contrasts quite starkly with our romanticized fantasy of democratic Athens), the expression of power included sexual dominance over women, prostitutes, slaves, children, and younger males but was not limited to the arena of sex. It also included a high level of violence (institutionalized as torture), patriarchal structures of civic government, and imperial ambitions to forcibly dominate outsiders. Although Keuls is a careful scholar and reluctant to generalize on the Athenian situation, phallocratic distributions of power and sexual relations quite obviously continue to be the rule well into the early-modern period. For us, the attraction of Keuls's formulation and related terminology is, not only that it subsumes a whole system of power relations in the public sphere, but that it also keeps the eroticization of power relations always before our eyes in a way in which notions such as *patriarchy* and *male dominance* do not.

We must be aware that, as David Halperin points out in a seminal article, the idea of "sexuality" (as in "hetero-sexuality" or "homo-sexuality" or "bi-sexuality") "implies the existence of a separate sexual domain within the larger field of man's psychophysical nature" and "requires the conceptual demarcation and isolation of that domain from other, more traditional, territories of personal and social life that cut across it, such as carnality, venery, libertinism, virility, passion, amorousness, eroticism, intimacy, love, affection, appetite, and desire—to name but a few."[11] A large body of research indicates that, in the ancient world, sex was thought of as a (penetrative) thing that men did to others—women, boys, slaves/servants—who were (or ought to be) socially inferior. It was not thought about separately from other relations of dominance and submission, nor did sexual preference constitute an *identity* or the defining essential character of an individual any more than would any other preference: a love of hot baths or an antipathy to peas, for example. The categories and discourses of sexuality that seem so natural to us have been around only since the nineteenth century, and homoerotic behaviors were not singled out for special disapproval by the major monotheistic religions until the eleventh century at the earliest and not significantly legislated against until the thirteenth and fourteenth centuries.[12]

It is not our intention, however, to inject ourselves into the arena of significant and hotly contested arguments about the origins of sexual behavior and questions about the nominal or essential character of sexual identity.[13] Our primary interest is in sexual/love behavior and its relation to literary products and literature production, and we will consistently avoid attending closely to important theoretical issues involving sexuality, sexual identity, the politics of desire, and gender. These issues are extensively argued in many places, so much so that the sheer volume of relevant material threatens to overwhelm any attempt to break into the conversation.[14] We have, therefore, concluded that such an attempt—except in the form of occasional gestures toward major arguments—would take us far from our purpose, which is in large part to present some evidence that would allow theorizers to broaden the scope of their investigations to include the Ottomans. This said, we will add that our own position on identity and orientation could best be described as *weak nominalism*, the belief that such things as *heterosexuality* and *homosexuality*, for example, are discursive constructs. That is, they depend on the words and categories we use rather than on essential or natural characteristics. But we do not entirely discount the possibility that a broad range of inborn inclinations or preferences exists.

If a society is primarily phallocratic, if the primary subculture of males is the army or other all-male groups, if public space is male space, if there is no educational mechanism for producing shared knowledge and culture, then men and women have very different experiences and usually remain quite foreign to one another in many respects. As a result, among both Hellenic and Roman elites the assumption was commonly made that the most complete love, the love that exhibits the highest degree of mutuality and satisfaction, is the love of one educated man for another, usually younger (educated) man.

This assumption—even talking about it—is quite uncomfortable for many men (and women) in Western societies today. But its most uncomfortable aspects involve the erotic and sexual associations we make when we use the word *love* and the implications about our essential selves that we allow when we identify the gender of those whom we love. If we substituted *friendship* for *love* and said something like, "In ancient times men found it easiest or most fulfilling to be with their best (male) friends," or, "They were more comfortable hanging out with their buddies than with their wives or female friends," it is likely that a larger number of men would agree with the ancients. And this obtains right now in societies that strive to educate men and women equally, societies in which men and women share jobs, expectations, and public presence to a large degree.

In the West, this discomfort has deep historical roots, some of which trace back to the rise of Christianity as a religious and political power.[15] Christianity grew from a minor cult embedded in a vastly powerful and extensive Hellenized Roman culture. One of the ways in which it distinguished itself from the dominant culture and created its own competing or contrasting culture was by adopting a stance in regard to sexuality, sexual expression, and eroticism that in some respects redefined the boundaries of the permissible. Although this redefinition had its philosophical roots in late-classical writing, its organization into a comprehensive system was peculiar to Christianity. Thus, in general, and over time, love was spiritualized and dissociated (or seen as separable) from the erotic; sexuality (the affective and imaginary part of sexual behavior) was regarded with suspicion; sex was linked strongly to monogamous marriage and reproduction; austerity in sexual matters was highly valued; and the body was divided into sites for various manifestations of sin. Throughout the Middle Ages and early-modern period, the ethics of marriage and limits on sexual expression became increasingly codified into law. A good example is the proliferation of laws prohibiting sexual relations between males (often under the heading *sodomy*) and prescribing severe punishments, in many cases death by burning. Nonetheless, until we get into the seventeenth century, sex, sexuality, and carnal love were understood as drives natural to the body. As such, the various manifestations of physical love were talked about openly, and people were allowed rather wide leeway for sexual expression.

In the seventeenth century, the West began to break away from the notions that the body is the source and instigator of sex drives and sinful (impermissible) behaviors and that mortification of the flesh is the cure for unlawful desires. Improper behavior, which was increasingly defined by bourgeois rather than elite boundaries, shifted from being a physical problem (wrong bodily urgings) to being a symptom of a mental problem (wrong thinking). In consequence, ways of talking about and remaining silent about sex and sexuality were developed, intended, more or less consciously, to avoid stimulating wrong thinking. Deviation from bourgeois sexual norms was seen as a form of mental disease and, as such, came to be institutionalized in the available forms of dealing with wrong thinking—the asylum, the prison, the clinic, and the confessional. The advent of scientific ways of talking about phenomena meant that existing norms and deviations from them were enshrined in the language and forms of science. Love in all its manifestations became an object of study, and bodies of knowledge were developed about it—for example, medical knowledge, psychological knowledge, legal knowledge, theological knowledge—each of which had a specialized way of talking about love and sexuality using its own vocabulary, and each of which, from the clinic to the confessional, had its own way of treating mental pathology.

There is a huge difference between thinking, "My body, like everyone else's, is urging me to do things that my society (and my God) forbids," and thinking, "My mind is subject to desires that expert knowledge tells me normal, mentally healthy people do not have." Put in the simplest possible terms, premodern and early-modern thinking was more like the first statement, and modern thinking, including our own, is more like the second.

This is where we are today, Turks and non-Turks alike, looking back on the Ottomans of the long sixteenth century and their love poetry. But those long-ago Muslim Ottomans did not arrive at their attitudes and knowledge by the same route as the Christians and Europeans they encountered. Islam arose in conscious relation to Judaism and Christianity, not so much in contrast to and conflict with a Hellenized Roman culture. In fact, during medieval times, much of Greek thought was preserved in Arabic under the aegis of Islam when it was lost to the Christian world. Because Muslims consider Islam to be the completion of a history of prophecy running from Abraham through Jesus to Muhammad, it both subsumes the Judeo-Christian heritage of the lands that it occupied and contrasts itself to that heritage while at the same time adopting many of its attitudes. The history of love, sex, and sexuality in Islam leading up to the Ottomans is a vast topic, one that we will reduce to two pivotal points among a host of possibilities.

The first point involves the striking innovation of Islam in its practical concern for the status and welfare of women. In a tribal social climate where women had rights only by virtue of attachment to a family, where women who had lost husbands or fathers were usually left impoverished and helpless, where the economy provided few niches for unattached women other than slavery or prostitution, where violence against unattached women was commonplace, Islam made a huge and often misunderstood difference. Women were granted the right to inherit, and strict formulas guaranteed that right. The chance that a woman would fall outside the protection of a family was reduced by permitting and even advocating multiple marriages for men who could afford to support more than one wife. Both Islamic law and local custom protected women by reducing their exposure to public life and dangerous contact with non–family members. One result of this is that, in general, by the time we get to the Ottomans, wellborn Muslim women were not supposed to be visibly part of the public scene or public conversation, even though there were women who controlled considerable wealth and exercised great power by acting from private space through intermediaries.[16]

The second point—related to the first—is that, for most manifestations of Islam, there are unusually clear boundaries between public and private behavior. Islam is very strict in protecting the welfare of the community. Law and custom require harsh censure and severe punishments for those whose behavior undermines the moral order and well-being of society as a whole. However, in the domain of private behavior, Muslims have traditionally been accorded broad leeway. Writing by Muslims on love and sexuality is voluminous and ranges from detailed theories of love, to the theology of love, to laws involving sexuality, to the literature of love, to sex manuals, to pornography. While we could not even begin to summarize this literature here,[17] a few points are worth mentioning by way of introduction.

In the broadest view, Islamic legal practice strives to permit behaviors that people are inclined to do anyway, provided that the behaviors or their modes of practice are not harmful to the institutions of family and community. Sex and sexuality are seen as natural, God-given drives of the body whose repression can result in (socially) dangerous actions. The principle of concealment (*satr*) requires that the public punishment of private behavior—including adultery and fornication, which are strictly forbidden and punishable by death—must always be weighed carefully and avoided when making the offense public would itself be "pornographic" and subvert the moral character of the community or result in a punishment that the community would find unacceptably harsh.

We must also keep in mind that there is really no such thing as a single Islam. There are many "Islams," each determined by the practices of particular times and places, and many of the sexual behaviors common in places where most of the people were Muslims are not sanctioned by Islam and should not be thought of as Islamic, any more than the early-modern culture of prostitution in Venice should be considered Christian.

This much said, let us turn to the topic of love and love poetry in the Ottoman Empire during the early-modern period. If we begin with the question, Whom is it appropriate to love? we will find that, in general, the answer for educated Ottoman elites was similar to what we might expect it to be for educated Greeks and Romans in pre-Christian classical times and, to a certain extent, what we would expect, religious rhetoric aside, from Christian European society during the early-modern period. Some people love women, some young men; it is a matter of preference, but . . . The buts in the realm of theory include the prohibition of excess and of anything that would threaten the stability of families or undermine the welfare of the community. The Ottomans (also like the Europeans) inherit a long tradition of the spiritualization of love. This is to say (again, in painfully reductive terms) that a line of thought is broadly recognized that concludes that sexual desires or attractions are the physical manifestation of the soul's yearning for return to a divine unity from which it was separated by birth into this material world. As a result, for those Ottomans who produced and consumed high-culture literature, the love most easily recognizable as a spiritual love was that of an educated man for a younger man. Also, because of the private nature of relations with free, Muslim women, because it is offensive, both socially and legally, to express publicly one's attraction to a woman who is not one's wife (and one's wife is *never* a fit subject for public conversation), the love that could most properly be expressed as a *public* (poetic) love was that between males. Moreover, it seems to have been considered more proper (and less dangerous) for a young man to adopt the essentially submissive, self-sacrificing posture of a passionate lover toward a beloved who was male and, hence, a legitimate wielder of power in a society where men were expected to dominate in the public sphere. Beyond this, we will present evidence that, generally, the culture of the court and court-dependent elites in absolutist monarchies—both Ottoman and European—expressed itself in part as homoeroticism.

In this social and psychological climate, the efflorescence of Ottoman power and culture during the long sixteenth century to some degree manifested itself as the *Age of Beloveds*, an age in which a host of young men became focal points, not only for the desire of powerful officeholders and talented artists, but also for lavish entertainments and a rich literature of love. The thrust of this book will be, not only to point out how this culture of beloveds helps us understand and put in context some of the unique qualities of Ottoman poetry and Ottoman culture in one of its most productive periods, but also to bring forward some suggestive examples indicating that the Age of Beloveds was, not just an Ottoman, or Eastern, or Islamic phenomenon, but evident as a cultural phenomenon in late-Renaissance Europe as well. However, before we do any of this, we digress briefly to sketch in some features of the context in which Ottoman love literature has been read in modern times.

Reading (and Not Reading) Ottoman Love Poetry

The fact that no scholar has written extensively on the subject of Ottoman beloveds until now tells a lot about the psychological climate in which Ottoman poetry has been encountered in recent times. The first book to face the issue of the Ottoman beloveds head-on was originally published in Turkish in 1968 by a very well-read journalist named İsmet Zeki Eyuboğlu. The book's title, *Divan şiirinde sapık sevgi* (Perverted love in *divan* [Ottoman high-culture] poetry), is suggestive of reasons why this first book on the subject was also just about the last.[18] The long chapter from which the book's title was taken is, however, only one section of what is partly a study of and partly a polemic on the (moral) reasons why Ottoman divan poetry should not be considered an important part of Turkish literature and does not deserve its respected place in school curricula. Nonetheless, it is the unveiling of "perverted love" among Ottoman elites that seems to have been considered the book's telling argument.

Of course, *perverted love* in this case means men having erotic relations with (young) men. And, of course, Eyuboğlu is correct in saying that such relations were fashionable among the Ottoman elites, that they were an inextricable part of the poetry, and that this aspect of Ottoman poetry and poetic life has been suppressed by scholars. But, if we ask why this suppression, we will find the reasons nicely summed up in the word *perverted*. This is a term whose meaning belongs entirely to the distribution of erotic/sexual limits, permissions, and prohibitions in the modern world, a modern world dominated by Western, scientistic notions. Thus, as used today, the word *perverted* implies a normalcy grounded in scientific truth, that is, a normalcy determined by a higher order of truth than the normalcies of previous ages. What is normal now seems as if it were the standard of the normal for all times and places. If the Ottomans' conception of the normal was different from ours, it was they who were in error (or in some way morally or culturally deviant). Scholars, like everyone else, would prefer to weigh in on the side of the normal and resist appearing to praise or value the perverted.

Traditionally, and into the present, Muslims are enjoined to practice modesty as modeled by the Prophet and to avoid speaking openly of private matters, including sexual topics. In addition, Turkish scholars have been sensitive to the fact that Westerners have for many years enjoyed their own unacceptable desires by projecting them on the Orient and then reencountering them at a safe distance in stories, gossip, and even the respectable garb of social science.[19] So, until very recently, scholars have emphasized the rhetorical and aesthetic qualities of Ottoman poetry, focused on its use of love and the erotic as metaphors for spiritual states, and denied any societal referents—even after Eyuboğlu publicly let the cat out of the bag. Despite the fact that younger scholars in Turkey have begun eagerly to explore the history of love, sex, and gender, we must confess that, when we recently produced a book of English translations of Ottoman poems, we simply ducked the issue by allowing the poet who worked with us to translate the gender of the beloved as *she* when every indication is that the beloved of this poetry was most often a *he*.[20] Why, then, do we choose to do otherwise now?

First of all, we feel that words (and notions) like *perverted* have no place in serious historical or literary-historical work. They presume universal and noncontingent norms, which do not exist outside theology. They reduce complex phenomena to emotionally charged either-ors. They distort and demonize minority values, the values of foreign others, and the values of distant historical periods. Even though we recognize that it is impossible to eliminate every trace of political or axiological (valuative) argument from scholarly writing, we believe that it is possible and necessary to account for those traces that we can see.

Second, we are persuaded that a behavioral view of the normal—a view based on what people actually do rather than on what we (or they) think they ought to be doing—will show that, at one time or another, most people have strong feelings of attraction toward people of both genders. Whether the erotic nature of those attractions is recognized openly or privately, whether they are described as love or as friendship, as spiritual or as erotic, whether they can be acted out physically, depends on the taboos of the society in which one lives. For example, we believe that we can point to significant indications that, in some respects, there were in the sixteenth century only surface differences between Ottoman society, in which male elites publicly expressed their attractions to young men, and Venetian society, in which elite men paraded their attractions to famous courtesans. The differences, we will argue, lie for the most part in what was allowed to *show* rather than in what was *done*; that is, it is mostly a matter of how one is able to talk about things.

Third, we believe that it is time to face the beloveds issue forthrightly, that there is a way of reading the Ottoman elite's poetry—beautiful boys and all—that can teach us something about our own desires and expectations of love, even in an age not as comfortable with same-sex attractions as theirs. Initially, we need to recognize the obvious point that not all erotic attractions involve sexual contact. Some involve no physical expression at all, some contain minor contact (a touch, a kiss, an embrace), and some are very physical and very sexual. The biology and sociology of cross-gender attractions are apparent: society and the human genome have compelling interests in reproduction and the cohesiveness of families. The benefits of same-gender attractions are less visible, and their historical and biological roots are not as immediately apparent.

Ultimately, the Ottomans and our Greco-Roman ancestors were in substantial agreement that what was most special about same-sex (male-male) attractions and loving relationships lay, not in the mechanics of sexual satisfaction, but in the possibility of a relationship based on mutual understanding and something closer to a balance of power. As we mentioned above, it was only in a same-gender relationship that one could find a partner who was similarly educated and, thus, potentially an intellectual equal, who engaged in the same activities, who shared experiences and expectations. This kind of relationship would not necessarily be dominated by sexual intercourse and the reproductive subtext. It could be primarily spiritual and intellectual. It could include dynamic relations of power, a fluid shifting of dominance and submission, without reference to the overwhelming, culturally determined power disparity that existed between men and women.

Many modern societies have, to varying degrees, attempted to elide the disparities between male and female subcultures by providing equal opportunities for education and choice of career. We assume that men and women will, as a result, be able to have relations of sufficient equality and mutuality to make same-gender love unnecessary for any but a relatively small minority who are interested only in same-gender relations. In contrast to elite society in classical antiquity or the Ottoman Empire, where most homoerotic art and behavior was produced, consumed, and enacted by men who today might (anachronistically) be called *heterosexual* or *bisexual*, contemporary society usually relegates homoeroticism to a gay, lesbian, and bisexual community that it then takes some pains to isolate and marginalize. But, even today, the situation is not quite as clear-cut as it seems.[21]

For us today, heterosexual equality or mutuality appears possible, although to some extent unrealized; it was not a possibility publicly contemplated by the Ottomans in an age of generally phallocratic cultures. What the Ottomans produced was a literature, a language, and a subculture of love that most often explored relationships between lovers and beloveds of the same (male) gender, relationships in which power disparities were natural—that is, circumstantial (related, e.g., to age or life stage or social position) or, as the Ottomans might say, determined by fate—rather than enforced by social contracts and roles. Between males a reversal is always possible. Even though the lover may be a sultan and the beloved a slave or the lover a man and the beloved a boy, the slave can, by chance, become sultan and the sultan a slave; the boy will become a man.

In the end, however, Ottoman poetry is androgynous. The Turkish language (like Persian) does not reveal gender and, thus, allows lover and beloved to break free from a host of gendered rules and expectations. Our modern world finds a similar freedom in the possibilities of androgyny. For example, in her classic book on androgyny, Carolyn Heilbrun says: "Androgyny suggests a spirit of reconciliation between the sexes; it suggests, further, a full range of experience open to individuals who may, as women, be aggressive, as men tender; it suggests a spectrum upon which human beings choose their places without regard to propriety or custom."[22]

In the androgynous world of Ottoman poetry, the strange alchemy of hyperbolic passion can transmute a beloved boy into a sultan and even into an image of the divine and dress him in what might at first glance seem to us to be feminine characteristics—coyness, shyness, veiling, seclusion—which are, in turn, revealed as means for achieving ultimate power and reducing the most powerful lover to an abject slave.

If we look at Western literature from the long sixteenth century with an eye out for androgyny or with the assumption that homoerotic themes were not just Ottoman or Eastern, some interesting possibilities also emerge. We will bring up a number of these in what is to follow. But, for well-known examples, English speakers need go no further than the Shakespearean comedies, in which the woman dressed as a man (actually, and more telling, a boy acting the part of the woman dressed as a man) is a favorite theme. When, in *As You Like It*, Orlando, ostensibly for practice, speaks words of love to Rosalind, who is disguised as a boy—and significantly going by the name of Ganymede—might the part not have been acted, in Shakespeare's time, as if he were on the point of falling for the boy (leaving Rosalind, the woman, a bit miffed)?[23] What is the effect of the disguised-woman theme when everyone in the audience knows that the beloved woman is always, in fact, a boy, that every stage lover falls for a boy? When all the world's a stage and women are not allowed on it, then the beloved is always a boy, however dressed.

The Age of Beloveds

As we will see in what follows, a portion of that age of Europe and the West that we sometimes call *the early-modern period* or *the late Renaissance* was also an age of beloveds, an age of love and sexual activity (given that love and sex do not always overlap) to an extent that is astonishing even to us today in what is often thought of as a lax, liberal, or even libertine era. Beloveds of every sort abounded. Love was everywhere, from attachments to beloveds of the most noble and romantic sort, to the momentary quenching of desire in the arms of cheap prostitutes and the furtive groping and rubbing of young men, to the coquetries of cultured courtesans and beautiful boys who entertained the great and powerful and modeled desire for the greatest artists of the age.

Although we use the term *the Age of Beloveds* with a somewhat tongue-in-cheek and provisional air, our deeper purpose is quite serious. The terms that scholars use to generalize, describe, and segment the chronology of history, culture, and the world constitute an important heuristic shorthand that enables us to talk economically about stretches of time in relation to characteristics that seem to dominate them in certain places among certain people. Such terms are most useful when we generally agree about them, but usually even our disagreements are instructive. From the perspective of an Ottomanist writing in English, however, the problem with this shorthand is that its terms begin to take on a life and reality of their own. It becomes very difficult to talk outside the boundaries that they set and the expectations that they presume. This is because, to some degree, our terms are useful only insofar as we forget how conditional they are. We are induced to think that there really are such entities as *the Renaissance, the early-modern period, the Age of Discovery, the medieval period, the modern period, the West, the East, Christendom, Islamic culture, the Islamic world,* and so on. We forget or agree to ignore how much these terms have been shaped by the topography of our scholarly universe, how much their value for us derives from narrowing our focus and excluding things that seem to lead us too far from our expertise and interests. For example, how often do we scholars (Ottomanists included) think of Europe or the West as partially and integrally Muslim and Arabic speaking (as it was in its own west—Muslim Spain—until early-modern times), or as Muslim and Turkish speaking (as it has been in its own east from the fourteenth century), or as partially Muslim and Arabic and Turkish and Persian and Kurdish and Urdu speaking (as it is in most of Europe today)?

In this book, we want to talk about certain cultural and social phenomena as they were made manifest in the urban centers of the Ottoman Empire during a period from the late fifteenth century through the early seventeenth. But we also want to talk about those phenomena in a more general context, as if they were a part of that European period and constellation of phenomena that we call *the late Renaissance*. Our geographic scope will extend from the Ottoman Empire to Europe, focusing on Italy as representative of a broader, Mediterranean culture, and on England, as representative of cultural developments beyond the Mediterranean. As we will try to show, many of the same things were happening; similarities abounded that transcended cultural and religious differences, often making them seem no more significant than the cultural and religious differences between Protestants and Catholics in traditionally European communities. Yet the fact is that, in trying to show this, all our conventions of naming work against us. We cannot presume to start talking about the Ottomans as though they were just another European power or about Ottoman culture as though it were just another aspect of European culture. It would jar any scholar (ourselves included) to talk about *Renaissance Istanbul*. We are sure that Renaissance specialists would not particularly welcome an idea of the Renaissance that implies that they ought to know more than a little about Ottoman culture and be as familiar with Ottoman Turkish as many Ottomanists are with French, German, Italian, Spanish, Latin, Greek, and English. We are sure that they would welcome far more information than scholars of Ottoman culture have given them up to now but that they would also argue—quite rightly—that one cannot do everything. Nonetheless, the nature of our scholarly discourse (the discourse of Middle East specialists as much as that of Europeanists), the very terms that we use and the segmentations that we make, often seem to tell us to shut up and go away, to leave European terminologies alone and to stick with *Islamic* this and *Near* or *Middle Eastern* that.

So what can Ottomanists do in our position? Obviously there are a number of possible answers to this question. In our case, we have chosen to get around the terminology problem by inventing our own period, the Age of Beloveds (approximately the middle of the fifteenth century through the first two decades or so of the seventeenth), thereby capturing certain social, cultural, political, and economic phenomena that occurred during that time in a geographic area that covers a greater Europe including England on one end and the Ottoman Empire on the other. Its content overlaps in many respects with what we expect when we say *Renaissance* or *early modern* and even with our understanding of general features of very local periodization terms such as *Tudor* or *Elizabethan*. *The Age of Beloveds* is a conceptual tool, a framework in which we hope to talk about some important things from a rather unconventional perspective.

Being unconventional, this book will also be somewhat of a mongrel. Its scholarly genetics will be hazy, and both Europeanists and Ottomanists/Islamists will often find their subjects explained in simpler language and more naive detail than they are accustomed to seeing. Moreover, to borrow a concept and language from Derrida, we will constantly be reminding our readers in a variety of ways that we will be using some very basic terms *sous rature*, or, as Gayatri Spivak translates it, "under erasure."[24] What this means is that we will cross out or erase words such as *Renaissance* or *sexuality* by pointing out that they are inaccurate, misleading, anachronistic, and then continue to use them in their crossed-out form because we need them in order to communicate economically. So, if, for example, we were to mention "homoerotic sexuality in late Renaissance Europe," we would intend that it be read "~~homoerotic sexuality~~ in ~~late Renaissance Europe~~" to indicate that *homoerotic* (or *homo-* anything) and *sexuality* are words belonging to discourses that did not exist in the period under examination, that the words *Renaissance* and *Europe* pertain to the history of certain activities of certain people in certain places at a certain time and exclude the activities of other people in other places at other times even when they seem to be doing and thinking the same things. The invention of the Age of Beloveds is itself one way of putting other periodization labels under erasure.

From a slightly different perspective, we wish to move away from what the historian Rifaʿat Ali Abou-El-Haj calls *particularism* and defines in a passage that could, we believe, easily be modified and made to apply to the study of Ottoman literature and culture:

> A general look at the present state of historiography concerning the Ottoman Empire soon makes it apparent that the scholarly cost of particularism has been high, because the emphasis on the incomparability and incommensurability of Ottoman history with other histories has narrowed our perspective and has given rise to many distortions. Ottoman historians are often inclined to treat phenomena that occur throughout the world in vastly different states and cultures, such as, for instance, tax farming, as if they were the outcome of purely conjunctural factors affecting the Ottoman Em-

pire and the Ottoman Empire alone. Ottoman specialists have emphasized the "differentness" of their chosen subject to such an extent that a dialog with neighboring historical disciplines has become difficult if not impossible. We have made our field into such an esoteric one that most of the time other researchers cannot fathom what we are trying to do.[25]

What is true of Ottoman historians has been generally (but not universally) true of Ottoman literature and culture specialists. Our field has been inwardly focused, highly specialized, esoteric, and particularist (or exceptionalist) in the extreme, except as regards attending to relations within a very particularist Islamic literatures field.

If Ottomanist particularism is a problem, however, it is a problem that reflects back from the often-impenetrable surface presented to it by European particularism. In the introduction to the English edition of his seminal work, *The Mediterranean and the Mediterranean World in the Age of Philip II*, Fernand Braudel expressed his discomfort at the inability of European scholarship to account meaningfully for the Ottomans and went on to say: "Today in 1972, six years after the second French edition, I think I can say that two major truths have remained unchallenged. The first is the unity and coherence of the Mediterranean region. I retain the firm conviction that the Turkish Mediterranean lived and breathed with the same spirit as the Christian, and that the whole sea shared a common destiny, a heavy one indeed, with identical problems and general trends if not identical consequences."[26] We share Braudel's conviction and intend to present evidence in favor of it. And we are certainly not alone. In the thirty years since Braudel mused on the subject, and, in fact, in the little more than ten years since Abou-El-Haj's "general look," acceptance of the interrelatedness of Europeans and Ottomans in areas such as trade, economics, monetary trends, and even agriculture has become almost commonplace. Nonetheless, the assumption has remained that culture is a different matter. To say that Ottoman *culture* "lived and breathed with the same spirit" as European culture is to tread dangerous ground and court general disbelief.

Yet, here and there, doors and windows are being thrown open—most prominently by the brilliant and innovative work of Cornell Fleischer, which will culminate in the forthcoming *A Mediterranean Apocalypse*. In that work, Fleischer explores the burgeoning of apocalyptic thought and political prophecy in the Ottoman Empire and Europe in a period (1453–1550) that overlaps almost exactly with the height of what we call *the Age of Beloveds*. Considering that our work was never available to Fleischer and that we were only vaguely aware of the immense scope of his work until he kindly shared with us as-yet-unpublished sections from his book near the end of our writing, it is striking

that at much the same time two independently conceived studies should have
identified the same general phenomenon—a zone of convergence in which
Ottoman and European thoughts and behaviors were remarkably similar—
occurring in the same period. This concurrence appears even more striking
if one takes into account that the two studies began from widely divergent
interests and sources: the one from the literature and history of Ottoman
and European eschatological, apocalyptic, and messianic thought, the other
from Ottoman and European love poetry and the history of the beloved in the
sexual landscape of Eurasia.[27]

Fleischer's work suggests a number of reasons why such a convergence of
scholarly conclusions is all but inevitable.[28] The years immediately preceding
the turn of the sixteenth century saw the onset of great cultural, political, and
social upheavals, from the simultaneous expulsion of the Jews from Spain
and Columbus's momentous sailing at one end of the Mediterranean (1492),
to the fall of Eastern Christendom's capital, Constantinople/Istanbul, and the
burgeoning of Ottoman power at the other. In Western Europe, the appearance of a vastly powerful Islamic empire with an ambitious westward-looking
gaze aroused feverish apocalyptic and messianic speculation on the part of
frightened Christians, hopeful Sephardic cabalists, and Arabic-speaking Andalusian exiles. Lucette Valensi suggests that the biblical story of Daniel's
prophetic interpretation of Nebuchadnezzar's dream is the subtext of a Venetian suspicion that the seemingly invincible Ottoman sultan may be the final
ruler of a unified world.[29] This period, which experienced the growth of an
effervescent art and entertainment culture featuring lavish amusements and
sexual liberty, was also punctuated by the appearance of radical religious reformers—emblematized by Girolamo Savonarola's puritanical tyrannizing of
Florence—who combined a compelling vision of the imminent end of days
with a concern for a preparatory purifying of the present (including, we might
add, an imposition of strict controls on sexual behavior). In the early years
of the sixteenth century, the reforming impulse would culminate in Martin
Luther's cultural revolution, and three young men with ambitions to universal rule would almost simultaneously ascend thrones from which they would
long dominate the age: Francis I (r. 1515–47, France), Charles V (r. 1516/19–
56, Spain/Holy Roman Empire), and Süleyman I (Süleyman the Magnificent;
r. 1520–66, Ottoman Empire). The political rivalry of the now-unrivaled Ottoman and Holy Roman Empires inflamed by Süleyman's seemingly inexorable advance on Christendom in general and its center in Rome in particular
served only to heighten eschatological speculation and speed the development of messianic discourses surrounding the main protagonists. Fleischer
argues convincingly that these discourses evolved in an atmosphere of intense mutual attention, in which each side struggled to understand the other,

in which even peasant revolutionaries in Germany were aware enough of conditions in the Ottoman Empire to suggest that a true Christian life might be most freely lived among the Ottomans and to find credible rumors that disgruntled Bavarian farmers were flocking to swell the Ottoman armies.[30]

We, in turn, argue that, in this atmosphere, plowed and harrowed by cultural change, religious revolution, and political turmoil, so fecund with a variety of dreams, ranging from the birth of a robust and creative humanism, to the establishment of God's kingdom on earth in the New Jerusalem, to the advent of the Messiah/Mahdi and the Universal Monarch (*sahib-kıran*), who would establish the unified dominion of the one true religion, there emerged an intense interest in love and the beloved. It does not seem surprising to us that love, and especially the idea of an overwhelming, self-sacrificing love, should rise to special prominence in the context of absolute monarchs who wielded tremendous worldly power and were associated in the minds of many with eschatological and even incarnationist notions. Radiating out from the needs and attachments of dependent courtiers and back from the hopes and dreams of anxious commoners, desire for the attention and benevolences of the absolute ruler and an absolute God formed a turbulent confluence that generated an aura of meaning bound to the peculiar beloved of this age, not only to the ruler as beloved, but to beloveds of every sort.

It is the aim of our project to explore a resolutely nonparticularist view of this beloved. We intend to show that, in Europe and to the east, across the wine-dark sea, in the urban centers of the Ottoman Empire and especially in Istanbul, a period, especially from the late fifteenth century through the first half of the sixteenth, was an age of love and beloveds. We hope to show that this culture of love was, not only aesthetic and artistic, but also political, dynamic, and historical, that love and sexuality and poetry did not exist in a sphere divorced from the other concerns of life and livelihood. We will see that, among the Ottomans, famous beloveds were cataloged in verse, city by city. They were the centerpieces of brilliant entertainments, the stuff of gossip and tale, the companions of powerful, wealthy, and learned men. In their image, the traditional high-culture love song, the *gazel*, was rescued from a sterile Persianizing classicism and given new life in Ottoman Turkish. Poetry, poets, and parties flourished in a prosperous elite society.

The public face of this beloved was often that of a beautiful young man. This book attempts, among other things, to introduce this beloved—and his female counterpart—to our readers and to introduce him, not as a stranger representing the deviant lusts of some past or distant Oriental "others," but as a beloved of his age as familiar in his androgynous charm to the palazzi of Venice and Florence or the great houses of England as he was to the gardens and *köşks* (kiosks) of Istanbul.

Taking a slightly different perspective, we argue also that, during this period, power relations of all kinds, from the most personal (adult-child, husband-wife, lover-beloved) to the most public (courtier-monarch, patron-client, even empire-empire), were eroticized on a consistent pattern. That is, they were imagined in the forms, the language, and the metaphors of love. This is as true for Europeans as it is for Ottomans. From our perspective, it is in part the residue of this internal, discursive linking of love and power, love and dominance, that grounds the Orientalist eroticization of relations between the West and the Middle East that Irvin Schick so perceptively reveals in *The Erotic Margin*. From our point of view, it was easy for the West to eroticize its relations with the Ottoman East because that East had already eroticized its own social and political relations, in some degree through the agency of literary scripting. The erotic was everywhere available for Western scholarship and the Western imagination to discover in the East. But it seems equally true that the European West was drawn to imagining its relations with the Ottoman East in terms of an erotic discourse because the internal discourses of power in the West were similarly and as powerfully eroticized. Conceptualizing relations of dominance and submission in erotic images cut both ways. Western Orientalism had its counterpart in Ottoman Occidentalism. There is plenty of evidence, for example, that the sixteenth-century Ottomans saw their relations with Europe most obviously symbolized by sexual dominance over a "frankish boy" from the European neighborhoods in the Istanbul suburb of Galata. When critical Europeans called Venice *the Turk's courtesan*, they were imagining political relations in equally erotic terms.

We should add that our forays into Europe are not intended to enlighten Europeanist scholars of the late Renaissance on matters about which they have far more extensive knowledge than we can claim. Our goal is to suggest a framework (or a number of possible frameworks) in which early-modern Ottoman and European literatures and their social contexts can be thought about and talked about together. We hope that we will, thereby, encourage people with an interest in Europe to take the Ottomans into account, to ignore the particularisms and exclusivities projected by Middle East specialists, to use translations as a window into Ottoman culture, and to contemplate comparative and cooperative studies.

In taking a comparative European perspective, we also recognize that we are deviating sharply from the usual practice of Middle Eastern literary and cultural history, which tends to look eastward from Istanbul and to view Ottoman society and culture in the context of Persia and the Arabic-speaking world to the south, with the unspoken assumption that all this has very little to do with Europe and the West. We must say that, on the surface, the reasons for taking the eastward-looking perspective are compelling. It is true, for

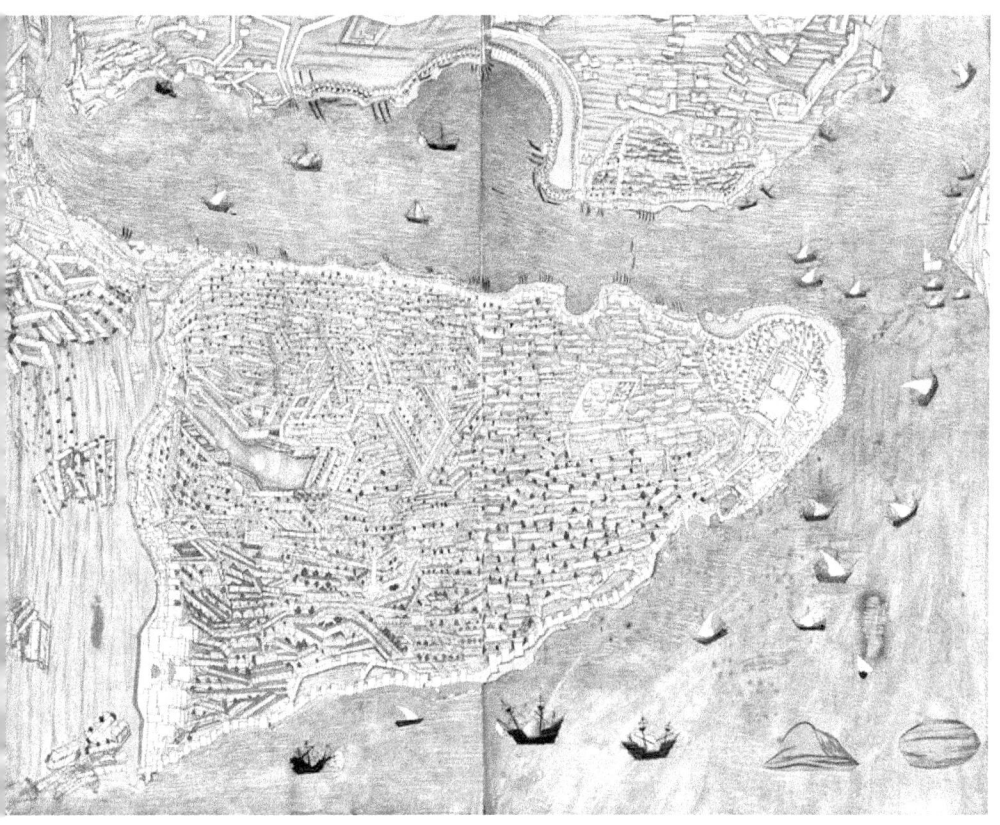

A sixteenth-century map of Istanbul. The Bosphorus Strait runs north and south. The map is bisected horizontally by the inlet of the Golden Horn, with the suburb of Galata on its north shore and the city of Istanbul proper to the south. The Topkapı Palace is on the northeast point of the city and the Hippodrome Square to the south. (Topkapı Palace Museum Library, H. 1523, "Hünernāme," vol. 1, fols. 158b–159a.)

example, that early-modern Ottoman elites saw their primary cultural influences as coming directly from Persia and the historical culture of the Arabs and that many of them complained bitterly about the favored treatment that any literarily inclined visitor or refugee from Persia received from Ottoman patrons of culture. We have only to cite the well-known couplet from the poet Le'ali to exemplify the general attitude:

> 'Acemün her biri ki Ruma gelür
> Ya vezaret ya sancak umagelür[31]
>
> Each and every Persian who comes to Ottoman domains
> Expects a provincial lordship or viziership for his pains

Early-modern Ottomans would have rejected as absurd the contention that they behaved as much like Europeans as they did like Persians. And, as we have already pointed out, it would be equally as difficult for us to assert that Europeans or Ottomans were consciously imitating one another. Nonetheless, we are suggesting that there are informative and interesting commonalities to social and intellectual life in the Mediterranean world that extend far into Europe and the Middle East and transcend perceived cultural and religious boundaries. Such commonalities do not represent "essences"—universal things that are the biological property of all human beings. Likewise, they do not necessarily depend on obvious borrowings, exchanges, hegemonies, or imperialisms, although such certainly occurred.[32] War and trade, religious conflicts, poems and stories, all are among the ways in which groups are induced to think about each other, to grow like each other, to capture and captivate each other in both concrete and metaphoric ways. However, conditions that apply globally—for example, economic and demographic conditions, weather, disease, the availability of natural resources, modes of production, general models of rule—appear to have the effect of predisposing societies to similar patterns of relationship and behavioral modes in the sociocultural sphere. So, in the end, Ottomanists and Middle East specialists will likely be as uncomfortable with some aspects of this study as Europeanists will be with others. We hope that the discomfort will be spread about evenly. If both groups are uncomfortable but find something of value in their reading, we will be satisfied.

As a final note, it is also our very tentative suggestion that the androgynous or multiply gendered beloved of early-modern times becomes a vehicle for expressing the desire of men (and women) for a new congruence between sexual desire and intellectual and spiritual companionship as well as a representation of the aspirations of women to full participation in the life of their societies. Out of the turmoil of the late Renaissance, out of the violence, the sexual oppressions, the male-centered, "phallocentric" cultures, and the eroticization of power, stumbles the prototype of a very modern beloved and the first inklings of modern thinking about relations between men and women as well as between men and men, women and women. Strange as it may seem, this is something that can, perhaps, be seen with greater clarity in the view from Istanbul, where modern (and European) assumptions about the West are constantly challenged and our vision is neither clouded by overfamiliarity nor obstructed by imaginary boundaries.

2

BELOVED BOYS (AND GIRLS)

In his 1525 *Risale-i evsaf-ı İstanbul* (Essay in description of Istanbul), the Ottoman littérateur and biographer of poets Latifi[a] includes among the condensed but verbally florid descriptions of palaces, mosques, parks, and people three sections on the beloveds of the city, entitled "In Description of the Classes of Beauties Who Are the Heart's Wish and the Soul's Desire," "In Description of the Home Life of the Mansions of Leaders and the Palaces of Commanders," and "In Description of the Inconstant Beloveds of This City." The section most interesting to us ends a description of the mansions of the wealthy and begins with a poem (which we will render in a fashion that reflects the light and occasional tone of the poem without attempting to represent any of its formal features):

GAZEL:

> 'Tis true that heavenly mansions will inspire
> In each of us and all heartfelt desire
> But replete with those whom we adore
> They must inspire affection all the more
>
> 'Tis this ornamental band that graces
> The outward aspect of all dwelling places
> Know, prude, that paradise were loved the less
> Without its glorious visions of loveliness

---

[a] For those unfamiliar with Ottoman usage, we should point out that the poets took pen names, which most often consisted of a word (in this case: *latif*, "delicate, witty") with the "relational *-i*" added to it. Thus, one gets Hayali from *hayal*, "image, imagination," the sense being "a person who can create [wonderful] images."

What, pray tell, will form and color do
Wherever there may lack a beauty's hue
Even though that mansion great may be
A China-thrilling[b] picture gallery

Let there be no trace of dwelling places
Unadorned by loved ones' lovely faces
How well it may be fashioned matters not
Such a house will still have gone to rot

With an ornamented cheek of red
The ash heap is become a flower bed
And anywhere that winsome beauties be
Is beautiful to us, oh Latifi

In Description of the Classes of Beauties
Who Are the Heart's Wish and the Soul's Desire

> According to the sense of the pleasing conceit of these witty couplets, these houses exemplify the House of Repose and rival the harem of the worldly paradise of Irem[c] with their most lovely women, exceptional beloveds, lovely faces, and moon-faced angels who would dazzle the eyes of the houris of heaven. Like the moon, every silver-bodied cypress with bejeweled and gold-embroidered clothing, with jeweled sandals of purest silver on the much-praised feet of argent-faced ones and the crescent of a golden anklet of purest gilt on a shining leg, becomes the adornment of the spheres, and, as it rises to the heavens during times of meeting and moments of conversation, ever so many crescent shapes appear and manifest themselves in the mirror-hung sky.

POETRY:

> How lovely is that silver-colored limb
> The argent pillar of a crystal dome
> Two camphor candles in parties of delight
> Making radiant the heart's dark night
> When its anklet reflects on the sky
> A new moon's face will show itself on high
> The hennaed limb as if with blood is traced
> And with it necks of lovers are embraced

---

[b] Chinese artists were considered the universal masters in Perso-Ottoman cultures.

[c] The garden-palace of the legendary King Shaddad, built to rival paradise and destroyed for the affront.

> Everyone whose neck that bow doth bear
> Though it be cruelty, receives what's fair

PROSE:

> Their necks and ears are mines of jewels, and their breasts and backs are replete with ornaments and adornments.

POETRY:

> Collar and skirt adorned with jewels
> They walk, swaying, in the courtyard
> Each houri wears a fragrant robe
> Finds ambergris, brings it to the nose
> All moon faced, dressed in Chinese silks
> All confound reason, power, and sense

PROSE:

> The narcissi of their eyes are painted with the eye shadow of coquetry, full of magic and enchantment, and their jasmine breasts are tulip red with the rouge of shyness. With this heart-beguiling comeliness, each of partridge gait and parrot-sweet speech, like the swift strutting peacock, puts its lovely body into a colorful brocade of rosy hue; some of them stand in attitudes of service, displaying their well-proportioned forms, and some sit in the seat of glory, constituting ornaments of rarity and charm, and showing their faces or displaying their cheeks.

POETRY:

> Fairy manners, angel face, houri attractive
> Pheasant-ornamented peacock charms[1]

Shortly thereafter, Latifi describes some more public beauties:

In Description of the Inconstant Beloveds of This City

> Although the heart stealers and heart ravishers of this heart-adorning city kill men with deadly, enticing glances, yet they are a people insincere in their affections who pass their days with this desire and this wish, who give their lives over to lustful lovers, and who, because their coquettish natures were created and endowed for pleasure and ease, ever are engaged in revelry and joy, social intercourse and liberality, and so receive their just deserts from this impermanent and faithless earth.

Thinking in the vein of the following couplet that

Before long the time of youth will flee
For fate is faithless, life is transitory

they are inclined to pleasure and drink, agreeable and apt to kisses and embraces. Believing that the way of the world is to love and be loved, to grant desires and be thrilled, some of them seek love, and some are sought for love, some are lovers and some beloveds; they have made love their business and affection their concern. Most of the female beloveds are attracted to a male beloved, and, when they see a good connection, they are agreeable to union.

In the mannerisms of conversation they are exceptional, and in times of union they disturb the order of the world. But they are also exceptionally flighty and utterly inconstant. They are yours until they capture your heart, and then they find another lover, after which they neither see you nor recognize you. Even if they see you again they wouldn't acknowledge you.

VERSES:

In fickleness, all smiles and winning hearts,
The boy prostitute overcame the whore of fate
To the day's elites, all charm and endearments,
The whore of the age never came on like one of these

PROSE:

And, because their entire aim is to acquire wealth and gather up material goods, they soon weary of an impecunious lover and become the darling of any vile person whom they think to be rich, preferring a grain of silver or even half a copper to a thousand affectionate hearts, a sincere friend, or a faithful lover.[2]

Sometime before he died in 1547, the poet Zati, who had a long and successful career lasting from the reign of Bayezit II (r. 1481–1512), Mehmet the Conqueror's son, to the middle of the glory years of Süleyman the Magnificent (r. 1520–66), had a conversation with the biographer of poets, 'Aşık Çelebi (Ashık Chelebi, 1520–72). In his *tezkire* (collection of poet biographies) *Meşa'irü'ş-şü'ara* (Stations of the poets' pilgrimage), 'Aşık reports it as follows:

While I was conversing with him near the end of his life, [Zati] said: "I've newly struck it rich. Every two or three days somebody's servant comes along and brings me either a few silver coins or a few of gold accompanied by some delicious food or varieties of halvah and a letter that says, 'Write me such-and-such kind of gazel [a short, roughly sonnet-length love poem] or quatrains,' and, at times, even specifies the rhyme and *redif* [a word or phrase that is repeated exactly after every rhyme in a poem].... I suppose that his master is one of the nobles or a highborn woman who is incapable of writing poetry and is enamored of a beloved. In any case, I am out nothing of my capital. The gazel goes in my divan [collected poems], and I still keep the silver, the gold, and the halvah."[3]

At about the same time, the poet Hayali Bey went to a party that 'Aşık describes in some detail. In our freely translated version, the description goes like this:

One day a beloved named Selimi Musli, who stirred the city of our day with his beauty and was loved and adored by the town for his wholesome behavior, held a circumcision feast. All the talented people were gathered, and the beloveds of the city sat in a separate pavilion. As sparks of love to moths the beloveds came together with the lovers, and each burned like a candle in the party. Those who played the *saz* [the Turkish "long lute"] or the lute and sang became all tongue from head to toe, and those who were there to listen became all ear like the rose blossom. Hayali came in half drunk, like a wine bowl on the arm of an intoxicated *saki* [wine server], shuffling his feet, his limbs like a shattered glass [goblet], and sat down. A beloved named Turak Bali was there, radiant as Mount Sinai the Illumined, and, when Hayali saw him in the gathering, he heaved a great sigh. I too was flirting with one of [the beloveds], who, in that company, was like a cypress among mere trees, brilliant as a rose among mere flowers. A guardian [*rakib*], crude, misshapen, and tall, stood watch at the door, and the beloveds were hidden by him like the sun of heaven behind a dark cloud. Under the influence of intoxication, Hayali Bey recited a few apropos lines completely revealing the secret of his attraction and pleading his desire. Because this had happened in such a company, the beloved, timid before those present and terrified by Hayali's effrontery, could not openly reveal what he felt. But, unable to content himself by communicating only with glances from a lowered head, with the knot of his curls and the curve of his brow, he spoke reproachfully, with the proud independence of the beloved, by a pouting of the lower lip and a trembling of the mouth. When Hayali thus became aware that the beloved was attracted to him, he extemporized this rhyming couplet [*matla'*] and recited it, thereby revealing his knowledge:

The beloved's reproaches give my soul a lift
How should they not, they're the unseen world's gift[4]

Cultural Scripting

As readers struggle through the intricacies of the above translations of Ottoman art prose and poetry, we hope that a few impressions will stand out above the unfamiliar rhetoric. These include the image of a society, a society of cultural elites at least, in which a host of beloveds was the center of erotic focus and of an active life of gatherings for pleasure and entertainment; a society in which the beloved was ambiguously gendered on the surface with a strong bias toward the masculine; and an erotic discourse in which the actual character of sexual attractions and relations is as much understood as expressed openly.

A careful reading of what we think of as literary sources is crucial, we believe, to understanding the social context that underlies the Ottoman literature of the sixteenth century. The reasons for this are uncomplicated. The genres and writing styles available to the Ottomans do not seem to include the kinds of accounts, personal diaries, extensive transcripts of court proceedings, and the like that we are accustomed to using when describing social life in late-Renaissance Western Europe. To date, at least, nothing has surfaced that is as detailed and straightforward as, for example, the autobiography of Benvenuto Cellini, or the casebooks and diaries of Simon Forman, or the transcripts of the ecclesiastical courts: narratives that can amplify and contextualize the supercondensed information found in official registers and accounts and ground our conjectures about the meaning and ecology of literary texts.

In this context, our arguments will often appear to be somewhat circular. We will be using a variety of literary sources as evidence for societal practices, behaviors, attitudes, and patterns of thought that, we believe, inform, structure, and help us interpret literary products. The circularity of this depiction, however, stems from the equally circular notion that societal behavior is *scripted* behavior. This is simply to say that such things as love and sex are not biological realities (in the way that reproductive sexual intercourse is). They are social constructs given form and shape by the ways they are put into language, the ways they are talked about and understood at particular times in particular cultures. The notion of cultural and social scripting is not new. It represents an attempt by social scientists and psychologists to offer a structured alternative to the biological essentialist explanation of behavior. The bare bones of the idea of scripting as it applies to sexual behavior were expressed by Gagnon and Simon in 1973: "Without the proper elements of a script that defines the situation, names the actors, and plots the behavior, nothing sexual is likely to happen." They continue: "Scripts are involved in learning the meaning of internal states, organizing the sequences of specifically sexual acts, decoding novel situations, setting the limits on sexual responses, and linking meanings from nonsexual aspects of life to specifically sexual experience."[5]

Although Gagnon and Simon are cautious about embracing the underlying nominalism implied by the word *script*—they write of "verbal and nonverbal gestures"—we are not so cautious. We take the position that cultural products, symbols such as words and pictures, are not merely *reflective* of social behavior and emotional states but actually *constitutive* of behavior and emotion in a complex set of interactions marked by mutuality of origination. To take an image from Deleuze and Guattari, this is to say that primitive biological drives are simple machines that produce a flow or an intensity of desire that becomes social reality only when captured or patterned by discursively constituted social scripts.[6] Biology creates a need for interpretation; interpretation creates our reality (including the reality of biology constituted as knowledge). Thus, in large part, it is in language—in poems and stories, legal or religious or medical or psychological texts—that we learn how and whom to love, what is normal and what is deviant, what the words and actions of love are. We must keep in mind, however, that the notion of scripting does not imply a developmental linearity or hierarchy of origins. Social behavior and interpretation exist only mutually, only insofar as they interact. Neither comes first. Language and texts are not secondary to behavior. There is no primary chicken and no primary egg. Thus, our literature-centered view of the scripting of behavior is not exactly that of Gagnon and Simon. It is similar to the perspective expressed by Louis Montrose when, speaking of *A Midsummer Night's Dream*, he says: "To the extent that the cult of Elizabeth informs the play, it is itself transformed within the play. *A Midsummer Night's Dream* is, then, in a double sense, a creation of Elizabethan culture: for it also creates the culture by which it is created, shapes the fantasies by which it is shaped, begets that by which it is begotten."[7]

The Beloveds

Referring back to the texts translated at the beginning of this chapter, we can begin to tease out a general idea of who the beloveds of sixteenth-century Istanbul were. This is not a simple task because of the generally androgynous character of Ottoman literary rhetoric and our unfamiliarity with the way in which the Ottomans categorized beloveds. For example, when Latifi is talking about beauties who live in the palaces of the great, he is careful to distinguish beautiful women from beloveds in general, referring to "most lovely women" (*hüsna* [the Arabic feminine form of *ahsen*, "most beautiful"] *duhterler* [from the Persian *duhter*, "woman," a cognate of the English *daughter*]) and then to "exceptional beloveds" (*müstesna* [exceptional] *dilberler* [heart stealers]), which is commonly used to describe young men but is ungendered and ambiguous. There is no overt way to tell whether the rest of the description refers to women or to young men. This ambiguity signals a very important point, one that we will raise again and again. Gender roles in early-modern societies are not simple binaries, as we are accustomed to expect. One cannot say, for certain, that this or that behavior, this or that role, is strictly a male or female thing. It seems to us evident that the societies at which we will be looking are predominantly phallocratic, patriarchal, and dominated by males, but this does not mean that we will not hear of women who are warriors and poets, of delicate, shy, and protected men.

When it comes to talking about the lower classes of beloveds—beloveds who are in it for both love and money or one or the other—Latifi is rather more specific. When he talks of the beloved, he distinguishes between the *mahbub*, the Arabic masculine form, and the *mahbube*, the feminine form. Descriptions of the looks and behavior of male and female beloveds are the same, in keeping with the androgyny of Ottoman erotic literature. What is striking about Latifi's descriptions and the conversation with Zati is that women were included at all. From what Latifi says, there seem to have been women who were addicted to love and who took lovers from among the beautiful boys, and this seems to be confirmed by Zati, who assumes that some of his customers for ghostwritten love poems are upper-class women who have fallen for such boys. It is also worth noting—and we will take this up in another context—that it is most commonly understood that erotic poems will, for the most part, be addressed by men to young men—only occasionally by men to women or women to men, and never *overtly* by women to women.[8]

Beautiful Boys

We can get a good idea of who counted as a beautiful boy from a number of sources. In his biography of poets, 'Aşık mentions at least thirty-five beloveds by name. In Zati's collected works, more than a hundred gazels specifically mention a beloved either by name or occupation. Several poets, including Necati (Nedjatee), Zati, and Nihali, have gazels to beloveds whose names or professions appear prominently. For example, Nihali—who, after retiring, seems to have spent many days frequenting the shop of a friend in the bazaar—has a collection of poems to and about shop boys, one of which is to a tailor (most likely a tailor's young apprentice) and begins with numerous references to the beloved's trade:

This heart became a vagabond fool for a beautiful tailor boy
Whose lovers never suffer from a dearth of cuts

My eye is [become] a thimble, my eyelashes are needles
My bloody tear streams red silken threads, oh swatch of the moon

With anguish my mouth has narrowed 'til it seems but a chalk line
And weeping has turned the black pupil of my eye to white chalk[9]

The Ottoman Age of Beloveds is also the age of the Ottoman *şehrengiz* (shehr-engeez, "city thriller"), which is most often an extended poetic catalog of the beloveds or beautiful people of a city.[10] The genre has its origins in Persia, where it was more often called *şehraşub* (shehr-ashoob, "city disturber"), which means about the same thing. The tradition of writing verses in Persian about attractive craftsmen goes back at least to Rudaki and the Samanid court (early tenth century), and a collection of verses on beautiful boys called a *şehraşub* is found in the divan of Masʿud Saʿd Salman (ca. 1046–1121).[11] The genre became quite popular in the post-Timurid period (the period after the death of Timur/Tamburlaine in 1405), and, in the 124 gazels of the divan of Sayfi, a Persian poet of the fifteenth-century court of Hüseyn Baykara in Herat, it merged with the gazels-on-shop-boys (or craftsmen) tradition.[12]

Beginning sometime immediately prior to 1512 with the Ottoman Turkish şehrengizes of Mesihi and Zati on the beautiful boys of Edirne, both the şehrengiz and the gazels-on-shop-boys traditions burgeoned in Ottoman elite culture, flourishing throughout the sixteenth century, and continuing to be popular until the end of the eighteenth century. Of the forty-six şehrengizes we know about, twenty-nine are from the sixteenth century, and these have as their topics a range of cities in the empire including Bursa, Belgrad, Vardar Yenicesi, Rize, Gelibolu, Siroz, Manisa, and Antakya as well as Istanbul and Edirne.[13]

For example, a şehrengiz by Zati was composed in honor of a visit by Sultan Bayezit II to Edirne.[14] A significant function of the şehrengiz seems to have been panegyric. Zati praises the sultan obliquely by praising one of his cities and the beauty of its inhabitants. He begins by putting erotic attraction to beautiful boys in an acceptable, cosmic context:

When this earth appeared, God be praised,
Above it all was Adam's honor raised

Before his face the angels, by rapture undone,
At his feet fell prostrate each and every one

The heavens above him spin by nights and days
And flights of angels serve him in all ways

> How splendidly the omnipotent tailor made
> A robe of honor for him of beauty's brocade
>
> That holy brocade skin a cloak of such ilk
> It makes a vagabond of the sky's blue silk
>
> The water lily in early morning freshet
> Sighs, would I were a golden button for it
>
> Whoever sees that garment proudly worn
> Will find the mantle of his patience torn

Zati then moves on to the topic of love:

> Who loves not cannot truly human be
> Was not vouchsafed the creator's mystery
>
> Allah by act of love this world made
> Then in it was a precious gem inlaid

The jewel enclosed in this world is the Prophet Muhammad, of whom the poet says:

> Allah's the Lover and the Beloved He
> This is why our world came to be

Zati then tells of his visit to Edirne and his wonder at the beautiful boys of the city, after which he begins his poetic catalog of beloveds. There are fifty-three in all, but, at the end, the poet claims that he could have included many more:

> Though stars in the sky with number and limit abound
> Moon faces of earth all reckonings confound.
>
> I have but limned some droplets from the sea
> Brought some sun motes to visibility
>
> Cypress bodies throng this city's earth
> T'would take 'til Judgment Day to tell their worth

Zati's catalog gives a good picture of who the publicly recognized beloveds were. Most of them come from the artisan, shopkeeping, and lower-level religious classes. There is a (theology) student, a merchant's son, a clog-maker's son, a cloak-maker's son, the son of a muezzin (a caller to prayer), the son of a Qur'an reciter, a silk merchant (or, as in every case in which a trade is mentioned, an apprentice), a saddler, a boot-maker, a halvah-maker, a tailor, a hat-maker, a skullcap-maker, a money changer, a butcher, a surgeon, a packsaddle-maker, a harper, an arrow-maker, a silver-worker, a perfumer, a wool-carder, a linen-draper, and a silk gauze–maker: all in all, a good cross section of the boys one would find working in the bazaar or business section of an Ottoman city. In addition to these, there are several beloveds whose occupations are not mentioned. These might be young slave-soldiers (janissaries), boys of the upper classes, or youths from among the so-called city boys (*şehir oğlanları* [shehir owlanları]), which seems to have been a palace term for young, urban, nonslave nonelites—an equivalent of the term *townies* as used in some university towns today.

The descriptions of beloveds tend to be clever references to names or other distinguishing characteristics, as in the following from the Istanbul şehrengiz of the janissary poet Yahya (d. 1582):

That King of Heart Stealers, the Falconer, Şuride [Shuride, "Love-Crazed"] Ahmet

> Şuride Ahmet, the moon face, is one
> His mouth the letter *mim* within the sun
>
> His every glance is like a deadly falcon
> His two eyelashes its wing and pinion
>
> It hunts the heart bird, so these are fitting words
> For it's a proverb: One hunts birds with birds

The Brilliant Moon They Call Safer Bali

> The janissary Safer too is one
> His brow the moon, his face the world's sun
>
> If golden headdress be this moon's attire
> Its sun-like glow would set the earth afire
>
> Wherefore is that distinguished eyebrow double?
> Two first nights to one moon's head is trouble[15]

To understand the first description, one needs to know that the Arabic letter *mim* (or *m* in the Latin alphabet) is a tiny round circle; that *mim* is the middle letter in the word *şems* (shems; written ş, m, s), which means "sun"; and that some of the vowels do not show in the Arabic script as used by the Ottomans. It is also important to know that the name *Safer* is also the name of a month (in Turkish, the word for "month" is the same as the word for "moon"). Thus, a month (or moon face) like Safer cannot have two new/crescent moons (two eyebrows like crescents) because a new month (*aybaşı*, "the first day of the month," or lit. "the head of the month") begins with every new moon (*gurre*, "first night of the new month," or "the best of a class") in the lunar calendar. To understand the second description, it is important to know that some of the janissaries wore tall hats with golden drapes on ceremonial occasions.

Beloved Women

Beloved women were certainly present—disputes between lovers of young men and lovers of women were a common theme in erotic literature—but it is not easy to discover much about them. Of all the şehrengizes that remain to us, only one is devoted to attractive women. In a society where the norm was for upper-class women (free women and slaves alike) to be kept from the prying eyes of non–family members, it was no compliment to a woman to be singled out as the object of erotic interest. For a man to be handsome was a positive attribute of his manliness. His honor could be defended by his own hand, and, if he was dishonored by his sexual behaviors, the fault and dishonor were his alone. Not so with a woman, whose honor was equivalent to the honor of her family, whose duty it was to protect her. If one loved a woman, it was prudent that any public expression of that love be veiled in impenetrable ambiguity. For this reason, poems explicitly addressed to a woman are exceedingly rare, and virtually all descriptive parts of poetry are relentlessly androgynous. Nonetheless, there were women in public view, and these ranged from foreign women, some of whom went about unveiled, if only in their own ethnic neighborhoods; to the daughters of the lower classes and slaves, who had to work to earn a living; to entertainers, whose morality was always suspect; to women who were forced into outright prostitution.

It is important to note, however, that this general societal attitude toward female sexuality and the restrictions instituted to keep it under control are not strictly Ottoman or Islamic phenomena; they were common in the same period to much of Christian Europe as well. Our tendency is to assume that the Europeans of the sixteenth century were much like we are today and that Muslims were quite different. This is an illusion as mistaken as it might be comforting to our prejudices. We take this up in greater detail in later chapters, however, and content ourselves here with giving two examples. The first is Michael Rocke's description of the situation in late-Renaissance Italy: "The defense of female virginity before marriage and chastity thereafter also played an essential role in the pervasive culture of honor, a woman's sexual behavior largely defining both her own standing and reputation and those of her family and of the males responsible for 'governing' her.... Women at lower social levels who generally lacked this powerful familial protection, had greater exposure to males and more freedom in their daily lives; for them the conventions regarding virginity and chastity were probably somewhat less rigid."[16] The second is Bruce Smith's description of the situation of a young man of the upper classes in early-modern England: "He was removed from his mother and home at an early age to an all male environment; he came to maturity in an all male household that had a sharp sense of its own identity; he married at what for us would be a late age, a full ten to fifteen years after sexual maturity; and he had extremely limited access to women of his own age and social class because of the high premium placed on female virginity."[17]

Both these descriptions could apply without significant alteration to the situation in the Ottoman Empire during the sixteenth century. To be sure, the Ottoman youth was not sent off to boarding school, as was the English youth; he moved from the women's world of the harem to the all-male environment of the *selamlık* (the male part of a home) when he reached the age of reason (about seven years). Yet the abrupt estrangement from the world of women and the subsequent bonding to an all-male environment were quite the same.

Returning to the female beloveds, the one existing şehrengiz that treats women comes from the second half of the sixteenth century. The poet, whose pen name was 'Azizi, was also known as 'Azizi Mısri (the 'Azizi of Egypt), not because he was from Egypt, but as a reference to the '*aziz* (powerful prince) of Egypt, who was the high official (Potiphar, in the Judeo-Christian tradition) whose daughter, Züleyha, fell in love with Joseph in the quranic version of the story. Our 'Azizi worked as a bookbinder and as a warder in the castle of Yedi Kule (Seven Towers) and died in 1585. One of the biographers (Mustafa 'Ali of Gallipoli) says of him: "He was a lover of women, but then only God is without fault." And of his şehrengiz: "Given it has the peculiarity of not describing beloved boys and taking that failing into account, it is still worthy of praise."[18] In the introduction to his work, 'Azizi describes the circumstances of its inception, glossing over the question of his "unusual" proclivities:

> Several friends like the breeze of morn
> That moment blew into my hut forlorn
>
> Several friends all taste and wit
> Merry of heart, troubled in spirit
>
> They came in joy and deigned to stay
> Honored my miserable home that day

One opened converse immediately
Said why sit about and silent be

Come let us waste nor day nor night
Let's down a cup, our foe to spite

When they heard his retort so fine
Their hearts boiled up like jars of wine

They made discourse in noble wise
Converse the envy of paradise

With party cup we took our measure
Of the vine's daughters took our pleasure

At times from journal and book of days
We read out works of prose and praise

Now, joy-enhancing poems we read
From city-thriller tomes we read

A city thriller was read aloud
One of the party guests avowed

You woman lovers of the day
Enslaved by lovelies, locked away

Description of beauties is a lovely form
None who recite them are left forlorn

Pray, companions, what would pass,
If in this world one described a lass?

If also women's joys were sung
As charms of pretty boys were sung

'Tis beauties who adorn the age
So why can't idols be the rage?

Those who concentrate on pleasure
Grant male and female equal measure

Oh best of friends, if this be true
Let women be beloveds too[19]

At this point, another friend interposes to say that it would take a masterful poet to carry this off and suggests that 'Azizi would be perfect for the job. After demurring modestly for a time, 'Azizi agrees to accept the challenge, takes up his "ambergris-scattering pen," and sets about describing the female beloveds of his day. The following translate two of the entries:

Adornment of the Garden of Beauty, Penbe [Cotton] 'Ayni

> One of them is Penbe 'Ayni, a jasmine breast
> Her skin, like cotton, is delicate and moist
>
> Her body is a fresh sapling in the soul's garden
> Her mouth, of purest water, is a fountain
>
> I said, Come to my breast, said the heartbreaker,
> What have fire and cotton to do together?

The Bud-Mouth Beauty Kız 'Alem

> Kız 'Alem, of lovely nature's one
> It suits her to be suckled by the sun
>
> Her hair beauty's curl flower in the heart's bower
> Her cheek you might think a little bride flower[d]
>
> True, that disrupter is a notorious woman
> But when you meet, she's a girlish virgin

The catalog of beauties described by 'Azizi often gives some indication of class. There are several women whose fathers' (or owners') occupations are mentioned. They are identified as the daughters (or slaves) of a tanner, a gimlet-maker, a candle-maker, a butcher, a chicken seller, a tailor, a teacher (*hodja*), a cavalry captain, a seaman, a table-maker, and a henna seller. A few are identified by the name of their fathers (the daughter of Kemal, of Zülfi) or mothers (the daughter of Müzeyyen) and some by their place of origin or religious affiliation ('Ayişe from Cherman, Sultan the Armenian, 'Ayni Şah from Moscow). It is impossible to tell if the women whose fathers' occupations are mentioned also worked to support the family trade and became visible in public for this reason. Only one woman—a saz player—is clearly identified by her own occupation. Several others are known only by name and appellation, as in the case of Penbe 'Ayni and Kız 'Alem, whose entries are translated above. Some of these might also have been female slaves or concubines (*cariye*).

The position of slaves and especially female slaves in the Ottoman Empire during the Age of Beloveds demands a brief digression. We know that, during the sixteenth century, Ottoman wealth and military successes brought

---

[d] A kind of poppy.

large numbers of slaves into the households of well-to-do Ottomans. To be a slave among the Ottomans was usually much more like indentured servitude among Europeans than it was like the kind of slavery that we associate with Africans brought to the Americas and other European colonies to labor in the fields. For example, Sahillioğlu cites a case brought to a *kadi* (magistrate) in Bursa in which the order of deposition was as follows: "A blonde [male] slave named Nikola appeared and stated: 'My master and I agreed [*kestik*] on a term of seven years. Now the seven years are fulfilled. He is oppressing me and does not let me have my letter of emancipation.' It is necessary now that an order be given for him to carry out the agreement."[20]

Among Ottoman Muslims, it was considered a pious duty to convert and manumit slaves. Thus, a large number of slaves moved from servitude into the free Muslim population. Women who did so were often supported with a dowry and an arranged marriage by their former owners, who would then invest in new slaves to replace them.[21] Female slaves owned by men were considered to be sexually available to their owners, and their children were considered legitimate offspring no different from the children of the owners' (free Muslim) wives.[22] Female slaves owned by women were not sexually available to their owners' husbands by law. There are indications that some female slaves were employed as prostitutes by women acting as slave dealers who would set up short-term "sales" of the women, after which the slaves would be returned to their former owners.[23]

In a fascinating article on the estates of well-to-do women in Bursa from the fifteenth century through the eighteenth, Suraiya Faroqhi documents the disposition of these women's female slaves and makes some intriguing remarks that illuminate some features of the culture of domestic slavery.[24] It is noteworthy that female slaves seem to have been exceptionally valuable—perhaps because they were relatively rare. They were generally worth anywhere from 2,000 akçe (aq-che) to a high in one case of 6,666 akçe (for the slave of a wealthy merchant), or thirteen times the 500 akçe that a male slave was worth. Elsewhere, Faroqhi presents data showing that female slaves owned by men were less often freed, presumably because some were the concubines of their owners or had given birth to children, who would be considered the legitimate offspring of the owners, at whose death the mothers would automatically be free. Although some of the manumitted slave women were provided with funds to support themselves and some even became wealthy, it seems likely that at least a few among them were left to fend for themselves and engaged in prostitution as a means of support.[25]

Another point, one that takes us back to the women mentioned by 'Azizi, concerns names.[26] Apparently, slaves and concubines were commonly (but not always) given Turkish names that differed from the names given to freeborn Muslim women. For example, quranic names or names from early Islamic history were seldom given to slaves, nor were names indicating noble birth (Faroqhi mentions Hatunbegi and Şahpasha). Slaves were often given names such as Salur (which Faroqhi suggests might be derived from *salmak*, "to let go," implying future manumission) and Devlet (meaning "good fortune," or the good fortune of becoming a Muslim) or any of a number of flower names, especially those involving the word *gül* (rose).

Taking this observation into account, we might surmise that the women mentioned in 'Azizi's şehrengiz belong to several distinct groups. The ones referred to only by nicknames—for example, Saçlı Zaman (Fate with a Mane of Hair), Meh-suret (Moon Countenance), Küçük Kamer (Little Moon), Küçük Nisa (Little Woman), Ak Güvercin (White Pigeon)—were very probably popular prostitutes. There are some who are obviously foreign and non-Muslim—for example, Divane Meryem (Crazy Miriam), whom 'Azizi describes as "the Jesus breath[e] in the monk's cell of beauty," a clear indication that she is a Christian; or another Miriam, in whose entry he mentions "Rum" twice, likely indicating that she is Greek; or 'Ayni Şah (Beautiful Eyed Monarch), who is described as being a "Muscovite" (*Moskof*). There are also names that resemble the slave names mentioned by Faroqhi (e.g., Hüma [Bird of Fortune], a name given to three women) and those that are equivocal (e.g., 'Alem [World/Beautiful Sight], a name given to several women, and Mevzun [Well-Proportioned])—are they slave names, or prostitutes' nicknames, or ordinary nicknames? In addition, there are common Muslim names—Kerime, 'Ayişe, Fahri Hatun, Havva (Eve). For many of the women with Muslim names, the father's name is mentioned too, an indication that these women are from the free Muslim population.

It is tempting to assume that these publicly recognized female beloveds were all prostitutes, the equivalent of the European *meretrice* (pl. *meretrici*). Certainly they were public women in some way, and being a public character to the extent of being mentioned in a şehrengiz would seem to compromise any woman who was not a prostitute so seriously that her family would likely complain to the authorities. In the end, however, we cannot say for sure. Some of these may simply be underclass women who were forced to work or appear in public for economic reasons.

However, with the boys, it is apparent that several, most, or many of them were not prostitutes at all. Beloveds, such as the Selimi Musli whose party was described by 'Aşık (see above), were or grew up to be respected citizens, army officers, court officials, poets, courtiers, lovers, etc. This Selimi, for ex-

---

[e] In Islamic lore, Jesus is famed for bringing the dead to life by breathing on them, as in the apocryphal story of the clay birds.

ample, was obviously a man with a household and a son whose circumcision was being celebrated. Some beloveds were of the upper classes and were loved only from afar; some, as we will see, resented being the object of someone's love. Others seem to have operated on the level of the "honored courtesans" of Italy, accepting expensive gifts and favors in return for some level of erotic relationship. Still others were clearly for sale and exchanged sexual favors for money or were associated with occupations—entertainment, primarily—that implied sexual availability. Yet we must remember that love relations did not always imply sexual relations—this is something that many poets and literate lovers took great pains to point out—and that, not only did sexual relations not always equate with loss of status, but they also in many cases affirmed status. Because in the patriarchal Ottoman society it was a given that older men should dominate young men and boys, a man could take the role of passive beloved in his youth and then, on being recognized as an adult (symbolized in the poetry by the growth of a full, dark beard), he could move into a dominant role without being stigmatized or censured in any way.[27] As an example, 'Aşık has the following entry describing the career of a poet and former beloved who went by the pen name Sani:

> He is from Istanbul, the son of a janissary. He lived in the Emir Buhari quarter. He was to such a degree the possessor of beauty that it is not known if there exists his like among the tribe of *jinn*[f] or the line of humankind. He saw his equal only in the mirror and was never accurately depicted as he is. The aforementioned's fame occupied the far horizons like the sun, and, while the Messiah's mortals were brought back to life in the heavens, the people of the world found what they desired here on earth. The appearance of his life-giving ruby [lip] made people wash their hands of the fountain of life and instead made them drink up the font of their own lives. If he took a glance into the mirror, he would say, "What do you have to compare to me?" and, for that reason, if the mirror of the fountain of life came face-to-face with him, it would be embarrassed. The heartsick lovers would come to the hospital of his threshold, and each of them gave up his life. To each for whom his lip trembled in giving a healing answer it was as if their spirits were put at ease. In order to have done with this turmoil and tumult, when his beard grew in like spirit grass [a rare healing herb], they gave up the ghost, and they thought that seeing his face once a year was better than their own lives. In this same manner, he was himself a boy chaser and was avid in making a morsel of the lips of beloveds like himself and sucking on that little goblet. He was both a poet and a seeker after skill and could read

[f] Jinn are beings with bodies of vapor and flame, thought to be especially beautiful. *Jinn* comes into English as *genie*.

and write. Although he was a janissary, in doing calligraphy he placed dots and created letters much better than those who are passionate about musket and ball; in place of a shot bag he carried a portfolio [for paper], and in place of a battle-ax he carried pen and ink case; instead of the eagle feather and the [uniform] woolens he wore a black horsetail with golden threads made of the curl of the beloved and a burning sigh filled with sparks. His companions were people of wisdom, and his intimates were the witty. I used to live in Bursa, and, at the time I came to Istanbul, I observed that he was an outstanding person:

COUPLET:

I heard of him that he was a marvelous calamity
When I saw him he was that a thousand times

And his pen name was Sani, and this couplet was the title on the page of his beauty:

COUPLET:

I heard this, that on the horizons you are second to none
When I saw you in truth it was that a thousand times over

Unbidden, I recited this couplet of Nevayi's:[g]

In whatever form splendor comes you are more splendid
They call you life itself, but surely you are more than life

The aforementioned, like the other beloveds, is a worshiper of lowlifes and drunk with the wine of beauty, and the glass of his respectability was not broken by the ill-wishers' stone of reproach. His behavior was that of a carouser, and his activity was virile. He then became a keeper of the hounds [*segban*, an irregular armed retainer] and later a mounted keeper of the hounds [*zağarcı*, a mounted irregular]; after that he became a receptacle of the glory of royal favor; that is, he was enrolled in the imperial cavalry and entered the regiment of the Sipahi Lads [Sipahi Oğlanlar, one of the six regiments of the imperial cavalry]. Nowadays his concern is for education in the sciences and perfection of his gifts. [Here is] one of his poems:

---

[g] Nevayi (d. 1501) was the master poet of Chaghatai, the literary language of the eastern Turkic dialects.

> The jugs are broken, the goblet empty, wine is no more
> You've made us prisoners of coffee, alas destiny alas[28]

What we see here is the case of a man who in his youth is a noted beloved with a host of admirers. As he matures, he becomes a lover himself, a devotee of beautiful boys and the life of taverns and (as his poem indicates) coffeehouses. He also has a very successful career as a military man, moving from a position likely as an irregular retainer to some powerful man to finally receiving an appointment to the feudal cavalry. It is intimated that his intercourse (perhaps in both senses of the term) with the artistic and intellectual crowd was the key to his success rather than a hindrance of any kind.

The situation of women is less clear, and the reasons for this—worth noting because they will underlie much of what follows—have to do with the notion of *gendered space*. All this means is that spaces in a city are associated with the gender of the people who use them, control them, and define the shape, limits, and meaning of their use. Public space in an early-modern Ottoman city was primarily adult-male space, as it was in European and other Middle Eastern cities of the age. Women and boys who entered that space did so under the protection of adult males and under the control of adult-male authority. Women especially were expected to conceal themselves from view and to behave in a modest and submissive manner. Women who exposed themselves in such spaces were presumed to be available for sexual exploitation. The situation, as described by Lisa Jardine, of women and boys in early-modern England parallels the Ottoman case almost exactly: "Outside the household, the freely circulating woman is 'loose' (uncontained)—is strictly 'out of place' and her very comeliness in conjunction with her unprotectedness (no male kin with her) signifies as availability (as it continues, residually, to do today). And outside the household the dependent boy (the 'youth') is also constructed, via the patriarchal household, as 'at risk'—more legitimately in transit on 'business', but also, in his transactional availability, sexually vulnerable."[29]

In both Ottoman and European cities, men tended to marry and establish families and careers late, so there were large numbers of young men who were living unencumbered by family obligations and unattached to any controlling institution and who gathered in public spaces. As one scholar says of Italian young men:

> In fact, young men almost seemed to have been culturally compelled to undertake both routine and ritualized forms of disruption precisely to demonstrate that they had achieved the manliness considered appropriate

to that particular stage in their life cycle. In such behavior Italian youths resembled their counterparts in German towns, who were expected to establish themselves publicly as potential civic protectors by fighting, whether over a point of honour or simply showing off their prowess. During their prolonged adolescence, created by the custom of men marrying late, Italian youths also exhibited their virility for public confirmation by indulging in excesses of "drinking, whoring, and gorging."[30]

Not only do Italian youths resemble their German counterparts, but they resemble their Ottoman counterparts as well. Several classes of such men are recognizable in the Ottoman Empire of early-modern times.[31] Among these classes are the *levends*, or unattached urban youths, many from the financially better-off classes (the term *levend* later comes to refer to a handsome, brave young man), and the *külhanbeys*, impoverished young men who formed gangs and hung about the furnaces of the bathhouses (*hammam*), sleeping near the ashes for warmth during the winter, and engaging in all sorts of petty thievery and harassment. There were also the *suhtes*, commonly youths sent by rural families to study at a *medrese* (religious school) in the hope that they would thereby attain sustenance and a career (*suhte* translates as "the burning," a reference to medrese students being "ignited" by their teachers). Some of these youths would grow up into the role of unofficial civic protectors, becoming *kabadayı* (rude uncles), who patrolled their neighborhoods, defending them against the predations and improprieties of young toughs and outsiders. We will see straightforward literary evidence of the "drinking, whoring, and gorging" of Ottoman youths in the next chapter.

The presence of such unattached, young, sexually aggressive men made public space uncomfortable, and often quite dangerous, for women. As Jardine indicates, women who entered public spaces unprotected were considered to be sexually available and legitimate targets for male sexual aggression. While public space provided a locus for male social interactions and the integration of young males into the society of men, it was also the arena in which contests for dominance were acted out, often violently. Bands of young men plagued cities in Italy. In Venice, gangs of youths fought with fists for momentary possession of one or another of the bridges. Parts of the city were turned into what Robert C. Davis calls "fairs of masculinity," complete with "challenges, muscular displays, arguments, knife fights, wagering, speech making, processions of boxers, and military-style drills." In central Italy, especially Perugia, but extending to Venice and Rome, gangs of working-class youths engaged in the *sassiole* or fights with stones that occasionally engaged hundreds of young men—and sometimes even older men.[32]

In female spaces—for example, the women's quarters of upper- and middle-class homes or the women's section of the public baths—Ottoman women could appear unveiled, in informal dress, and could act as local authorities and enforce their own social hierarchies. In general, Ottoman women were considered by the legal and social system to be of two classes. One was the veiled, chaste (*muhaddere*) or protected class, wealthier women who would either have servants do their public business for them or go out in public veiled, covered by concealing outer garments, and surrounded by a retinue that acted as a detached, mobile component of the protected area of the household (the harem).[33] The other consisted of women from the poorer classes who needed to appear in public to work or perform basic household tasks. For example, the sixteenth-century chief jurist (*şeyhü'l-islam*) Ebu's-su'ud Efendi ruled that a village woman who brought water from a spring for her family could not be considered muhaddere but that a woman who went to weddings, baths, other villages, or other quarters could be so long as she went in a chaste and dignified manner with a retinue of servants. He also delivered the opinion that this state of "chastity in public" is not limited to Muslims. A non-Muslim could be muhaddere as well.[34]

This level of protectiveness was not at all unusual in early-modern times. The Scottish traveler Fynes Moryson observed of Venetian women: "If they be chast, [they are] rather locked up at home, as it were in prison." Even the women who did appear in public—other than prostitutes, of course—were veiled and wrapped from head to toe to the extent that an Italian traveler in 1494 wondered "how they can see where to go in the street."[35]

In *Twelfth Night*, Shakespeare also makes reference to the veiling of Italian women. Viola, disguised as the page Cesario, asks an indulgence of the Duke's beloved Olivia:

> VIOLA: Good madam, let me see your face.
>
> OLIVIA: Have you any commission from your lord to negotiate with my face? You are now out of your text: but we will draw the curtain and show you this picture. Look you, sir, such a one I was this present: is't not well done? [*Unveiling.*]
> (act 1, sc. 5, lines 248–53)

In *The Merry Wives of Windsor*, two English women try to disguise the rotund Falstaff as a woman lest their husbands discover him in their presence. Female garb can be a disguise in this case because Elizabethan women commonly went about with their heads covered by kerchiefs and part of their faces concealed by mufflers:

MRS. FORD: How might we disguise him?

MRS. PAGE: Alas the day, I know not! There is no woman's gown big enough for him; otherwise he might put on a hat, a muffler and a kerchief, and so escape.
(act 4, scene 2, lines 70–74)

An interesting sidenote to this is that, for the Ottomans, the notion that appearing in public in a protected and dignified manner is a moral duty and protection against gossip or slander seems to attach itself as much to class as to gender. Males of the highest classes, from the sultan on down, were also expected to appear in public surrounded by servants in a surrogate harem (private sanctuary) of their own. For example, in an amusing anecdote about the distressing adventure of Me'ali, kadi of Mihaliç, related by 'Aşık, which we will tell in full in chapter 7 below, Me'ali decides to go off by himself for a horseback ride during which he intends a rendezvous with his beloved. His servants are appalled. As 'Aşık tells it: "No matter how often they [the servants] said, 'Riding alone is injurious to one's reputation,' or, 'You will be demeaned before friend and foe alike,' or, 'It is inappropriate,' it made not the slightest difference."[36] As we will see, Me'ali goes off alone, with disastrous consequences to his reputation: a warning to all elites of the dangers of appearing alone and unprotected in public.

When we talk of Ottoman literature, it is important to keep in mind that the gender of high-culture literature was predominantly masculine. The literature of the elites was the public form of literature production, and, as such, it both reflects and scripts the (adult) masculinity of public space. The beloved is most often male—a young male—and constitutes an ideal of male beauty. Where female beloveds are intended, or where a poem is addressed to a female, there is little, if any, gendered difference in the description of the looks or behavior of the beloved. Although we know that, like 'Azizi, some lovers were lovers of women, it is seldom possible to identify a particular poem as being about or for a woman with any certainty. This is true even for the love lyrics embedded in narrative poems where the lover and the beloved are male and female (because the subject matter most often concerns dynasties, families, and marriage) and where some of the lyrics are unequivocally addressed to a female beloved. This ambiguity about the gender of the beloved is a feature of medieval love poetry in both Europe and the Middle East. Although, in Europe, this ambiguity does not die out, it is submerged by a flood of condemnation brought about by the growth of the idea of sodomy in the late Middle Ages.[37] We will take up the issue of gender ambiguity again in later chapters.

As we have seen demonstrated in the example of Selimi Musli's party, and

A beloved boy and a beloved woman from a sixteenth-century miniature. The juxtaposition of the clothed boy and the naked woman emphasizes the carnality of relations with women and the implied spirituality of relations with boys or young men. (Topkapı Palace Museum Library, B. 408, "I. Ahmed albümü" [seventeenth century], fol. 22a.)

as we will elaborate further below, Ottoman love in the Age of Beloveds—poeticized love, or love scripted by poetry—becomes an elaborate game with its own signs and signals, its own forms of speech and dialect (the dialect of poetic vocabulary, tropes, commonplaces, and rhetoric). At the level of theory, where the range and complexity of actual desire, social interactions, parties, lovers, and beloveds are reduced to conform more or less to conventional morality, the highest forms of love could be acted out only by those who were both publicly available and intellectually prepared to play the game. And these were almost exclusively young men, who could be the objects of a love untainted by the inevitably sexual, worldly, and familial overtones of love between men and women.

Beloved Boys (and Girls) 55

Yahya even expresses a clear distaste for the traditional *mesnevis* (narrative poems in rhyming couplets), such as *Husrev u Şirin* (Husrev and Shirin) or *Layla vu Majnun* (Leyla and Mejnun), which sang of love between men and women. In the introduction to his own mesnevi, *Şah u geda* (The shah and the beggar), he says the following in response to those who praise the traditional (heterosexual) romances:

> I heard their words, how odd they seemed
> Unpleasant each and all I deemed
>
> Those, woman-chasing, lacking taste
> These, suffering, cure-less, and chaste
>
> What do they know of love's mystery
> Of the rapture of love and its ecstasy
>
> A lover true forever tries
> Making sleep unlawful to his eyes
>
> Let him love bodies like cypress trees
> Suffer, like Job, love's agonies
>
> Mirror of body and soul let him shine
> As slave to a robust boy repine
>
> Who grieves the love of a lovely boy
> Never will *Husrev and Shirin* enjoy [38]

In the conventionally coded language of Ottoman love, what Yahya is saying is that those who love women do not really understand the true depths of love and its Neoplatonic iconography. This is because the love of women implies a goal of physical satisfaction, whereas the love of boys—according to literary convention at least—implies an unconsummated (without cure) love marked by hopeless longing, sleepless nights, and a connection to spiritual mysteries far removed from sating the lusts of the body. To "polish" or "shine" the body is to make it pure by avoiding sexual contact; to polish the soul is to purify it of carnal lust and to allow it to become a mirror reflecting a pure, spiritual love. This implies that there is an intellectual, refined, and spiritual component to the love of male beloveds that is not as available in relations with women. This is a commonplace of love during the Age of Beloveds—and not only in the Ottoman Empire. The famed Italian artist Michelangelo Buonarroti could have been paraphrasing Yahya, whose preference for beautiful boys he shares, when he said (in John Frederick Nims's lovely translation):

> Not true that it's always grim with mortal sin,
> this love for a ravishing beauty here on earth,
> as long as it melts the hard heart, shows its worth
> as a target for divine love's arrowhead.
> Love shakes, wakes up the soul, grows wings that sped
> its skyward flight. Lets even fond fools aspire.
> Is the soul's first step—an impatient one—toward higher
> stairs to that heaven the sole Creator's in.
> That's where the love I speak of longs to be.
> Love for a lady's different. Not much
> in that for a wise and virile lover's trouble.
> One love seeks heaven; the other, earth's vanity;
> the soul's home, one; the other wants taste and touch,
> eye fixed on the goods of earth, its gaudy rubble.[39]

As for female poets, of whom there are several notable examples in the sixteenth century, their poems are addressed in the same terms to the same male beloved. We must take care to remember that, when women appear in public or in public roles such as that of poet, they are there on the sufferance of males and must conform to male conventions.[40] Since there appear to have been no common vehicles for recording or preserving the language and literature of female space, we have relatively little to tell us whether there existed a language and a literature in which women expressed their own understanding of love or whether women's writing was entirely scripted by public, male conventions. For all these reasons, the beloved about whom we will be talking will most often be a male beloved, but it is important to remember as well that the beloved of the poetry is ambiguous, androgynous, and could as well be a woman. Our topic is a love that does not distinguish the gender of the beloved in any meaningful way.

As we will see, the Ottomans were by no means alone in supporting a thriving culture of love. Conditions in Europe and the western Mediterranean world were similar in ways that seem to have transcended differences in religion and government. The beloveds culture of Istanbul and other Ottoman urban centers has its counterparts, for example, in the culture of courtesans in Venice, in the notoriously homoerotic culture of Florence, in the robust sexuality of society in Elizabethan England. In every case, across all sorts of boundaries, similar conditions appear to have produced similar outcomes.

Thus, as we try to imagine the social context of culture in the early-modern period both in the Ottoman Empire and elsewhere, we must keep in mind that public space at the time was male space and that male space was often violent and quite dangerous for everybody. It was vitally important to men that they form bonds of mutual interest with one another within traditional patterns of dominance and submission. If one of the ways in which such bonds were formed was by the establishing of erotic and even sexual attachments, it is not surprising; nor is it surprising that such attachments are common across cultural, religious, and social divides and exist even where the penalties are most severe and surveillance most intense. One of our tasks here is to trace the broad outlines of how responses to such conditions were scripted by literature.

3

LOVE SCRIPTS I, MALE BONDING

L'amore masculino [love between males] is solely a work of virtue, which joins males together in various sorts of friendship, so that out of a tender age come, at a manly age, worthier and closer friends.
—Gian Paolo Lomazzo, *Il libro dei sogni* (1568)

In A.D. 1627, the poet Nev'izade 'Atayi (the son of the noted sixteenth-century poet Nev'i) completed his mesnevi *Heft han* (The seven stories). This was to be the fourth in a series of five mesnevi poems (a *hamse* or "pentad") intended to match the famed thirteenth-century hamse of the Persian poet Nizami of Ganja.[1] 'Atayi's *Seven Stories* contains a number of stories about life in his time intended to warn people about immoral behavior and urge them to better conduct. Thus, 'Atayi takes the opportunity to relate numerous amusing anecdotes about various rogues, rascals, and rakes with a good deal of sexual content, much on the order of Boccaccio's *Decameron*. The seventh and last story, however, is not about evildoing or evildoers but about love and lovers who do love right and end up happy. For this reason, it provides a good starting point for a discussion of the scripting of Ottoman love and an introduction to some of the themes and social contexts that we will take up in the remainder of this study.

The story, in our prose paraphrase (with one poetic translation), goes as follows:

> Once upon a time in Istanbul a jeweler and a merchant became fast friends. As the years passed, each of them had a son. The jeweler's son was named Tayyib and the merchant's Tahir. As the children grew and embarked on their education, they made great progress in a short time. However, when

they reached young manhood, they began to interest themselves, as the young will do, in love, wine, and music.

Just at that time, the parents of both passed away, and Tayyib and Tahir became completely caught up in the wastrel's life. They roamed Galata drinking and making merry. The rush mats of Köse's Tavern they took for pillows, and there they dallied with enticing boys. They took jaunts to Anadolu Hisar and chased after beautiful lads at Göksu. Thus, they cast to the winds the inheritances they had so easily reaped and soon found themselves destitute.

However, even poverty could not destroy their friendship. Their fair-weather friends began to disappear and even to censure them. Tayyib and Tahir saw that, while it may be possible to bear a calamity, it is much more difficult to endure enmity. So, themselves penniless as dervishes, they boarded a ship for Egypt, the home of the Gülşeni Sufi order, with the idea of becoming Sufis.

Once on the open sea, the wind died, the sails hung slack, and the ship lay motionless. Thus, they remained becalmed for days. Next a great storm blew up, and the ship was tossed about on the waves like a child's plaything until it was driven aground and broken to pieces. The two friends were flung into the sea. As they struggled to stay afloat, they chanced on a drifting log to which they clung in desperation. For long they floated helpless on the ocean until, just when they had given up hope, they espied a ship. It was a mighty infidel warship filled with soldiers, ammunition, and arms. Thus, the two friends hoping for rescue found themselves captives, and for the first time in their lives they were forced to separate.

On this ship were two young and handsome noblemen named Sir John and Janno. Tayyib was taken as a slave by Sir John, and Tahir was taken by Janno. The two noblemen were good-hearted and generous to the poor, and soon Tayyib and Tahir fell in love with their masters. Their hearts were consumed in flames of passion. But love cannot help but touch the one who is loved, and so, when Sir John came to the dungeons, he saw how things were with Tayyib. Being educated, mature, and wise, he saw at a glance that the young man was ailing, and he felt sorry for him. Not wanting Tayyib to die, he set him to working in his gardens. The gardens were lovely, and the gardener, an old, experienced sage, was much pleased by Tayyib.

One day Sir John came to the garden with some beautiful young men for a gathering alfresco with food and drink. They sent for the old gardener, who entertained them with amusing stories. When the atmosphere seemed suitable, the gardener secured a place for Tayyib in the gathering. The young noblemen grew relaxed and ebullient, savoring the pleasures of the party. They called on Tayyib to tell his story and sorrowed at what had befallen him.

Every day Tayyib's love grew, and his relations with Sir John became closer. One day, presuming on their friendship, Tayyib expressed to Sir John a deep concern for his old friend Tahir. The nobleman immediately sent word, and Janno came to them, bringing Tahir with him. Bonds of affection grew among the four, and they began to spend enjoyable days together. In this they were observed by an evil, troublemaking wag tongue who made general gossip of it. The news finally reached the ears of the police commander of the town, who was a relative of the two noblemen. The consequences of this are described by 'Atayi, as follows:

But at that time the town's police official
Was a vengeful wretch, a raving infidel

Their relative he was, of noble birth
And yet a mighty blight upon the earth

When to his wretched ear these tidings came
His ire consumed him like a raging flame

In dungeons vile two noblemen once free
He ordered held in dire captivity

He brought before him Tayyib and Tahir
Commanded, Kill these two before me here

Make haste, the executioner he bade,
Give to them a taste of bitter blade

Cut loose each evil body from its head
Make them a lesson for every man to dread

The head of a disobedient fool is cut
Rebelling kings soon find their rule is cut

Seeing this, the crowd was moved to pity
The lord forthwith besought by all the city

This matter can but bring two woes, they cried
First, report of this might be spread wide

Is it meet indulging ourselves so
To foul our names in eyes of friend and foe?

If we start killing prisoners this way
Can no Muslim swords come into play?

If captives on both sides are caused to die
Who on Judgment Day will answer why?

Love Scripts I   61

> In consequence that evil hound took heed
> Put off the deaths he had of late decreed
>
> Believing love a crime, these two heartsore
> Did he condemn to slave at a galley's oar

Thus, the two friends went to sea again, chained to the oars of a galley. While at sea their ship encountered some Muslim galleys, and a battle ensued. The holy warriors of Islam took the infidel ship and made a gift of it to Tayyib and Tahir.

Meanwhile, the two nobles were shut up in prison in the company of Muslim captives, and they began to take an interest in Islam. One night as they slept, a Muslim sage appeared to them in green robes and green headdress and informed them that the gates of their desire had been thrown open. They awoke to find their chains broken and the dungeon door ajar. Thus did they escape to find the true path and accept Islam.

Sometime later they discovered a rowboat on the shore and put out to sea, not knowing whither they fared. At the same time, Tayyib and Tahir were overcome by a strange feeling occasioned by their love, which drew them in the direction of the two noblemen. Seeing the rowboat from afar, they thought it an enemy, but, when they turned to the attack, two lovers were reunited with their beloveds.

Janno was given the name Mes'ud [happy, fortunate] and Sir John the name Mahmud [praiseworthy]. They all returned to Istanbul rich and happy and there lived contented from that time on. When finally their days had run their course, they passed from this world accompanied by their pure love.

The Young Men

Among the more intriguing aspects of the story of Tayyib and Tahir are the ways in which it concerns life stages and choices within the context of erotic attraction and love as well as its manner of representing to its Ottoman readers aspects of a very typical life among the literate classes of Istanbul. We are first struck by the fact that the main characters, Tayyib and Tahir, come from middle-class backgrounds. They are the sons of an artisan and a merchant and do not come from the palace, the learned classes, or the bureaucratic-military elites, as did most of the poets.[2] They are, indeed, from the classes of young men who are described as beloveds in the şehrengiz. It is also significant that their names mean "good" (Tayyib) and "pure" (Tahir). We are certainly not meant to think ill of them at any point. Even their mistakes are understood to represent the typical and forgivable ones of their age and circumstances.

Tayyib and Tahir are bright children. They grow through childhood without trouble and do well in school. When they reach their late teens (we could guess at about seventeen or eighteen) they begin to take an interest in adult pleasures—love, wine, and music.[3] If we look at Ottoman lyric poetry in early-modern times (which we will do in some detail as we go along), we will see that love, wine, and music are fundamental features of the typical poetic gathering (or party).[4] They are intoxicants of different kinds, each capable of allowing a person to escape the confines of a mundane rationality, each also permitting the most foolish and self-destructive behavior. Escaping rationality can bestow great spiritual benefits, or it can lead directly to disaster and even death. The intoxications of the poet and his companions always hover between great danger and divine gift. In this story, we see both possible outcomes realized.

Our two protagonists may be young, naive, and inexperienced, but, as is made quite clear by the deaths of their parents, they are also adults and on their own. They have emerged from the category *emred* (beardless youths), in which they are considered sexually desirable (*müşteha*) and, in that regard, indistinguishable from women. They now fall into the class of levend (or perhaps *mücerred/ergen*, which referred to unmarried adult males living under their fathers' roof).[5] The dictionary (1780–1802) of Meninski, which represents late-seventeenth-century usage, defines *levend* as follows: "One who lacks the necessities of life and has difficulty finding them, uneducated, uninformed, silly. A freeman who goes where he wants and follows his own appetites, similarly, a free spirit. A volunteer, or a soldier of fortune, with no permanent home and obeying no commander."[6] Tayyib and Tahir certainly fit within the second definition, being young, adventuresome, unattached males with some financial resources and no institutional or family responsibilities.

Istanbul Pleasures

We see our heroes at the most famous pleasure spots of sixteenth-century Istanbul. One such place is the district of Galata, across the inlet of the Golden Horn from the Muslim city, the European enclave where the Christian and Jewish communities lived under their own laws (except in dealings with Muslims). There were found the Italian and Jewish wine merchants and tavern keepers. There pleasure lovers among the Ottoman elites kept villas where splendid gatherings and amusements were held. There were the cloisters of dervish (mystical) orders, which considered wine and love (metaphoric and nonmetaphoric) as keys to sacred rapture and union with the divine. There was the playground of poets and the presumed setting of many poems. Latifi describes Galata as follows:

> Galata, called Kalata in the common tongue, is a town filled with scenes comparable to that other high and noble town [Tophane], and it is the pleasure palace of this earth. For wine and beloved [boys] it is without peer, and it is proverbial as a place of pleasure and amusement. Every corner of it glows like sunrise with the moon-bright faces of Frankish [European] idols, yet its location and its every cranny are superior and preferable to a thousand Frankish realms.

COUPLET:

> With its idols it is filled with images
> It is all adorned with Frankish icons

VERSES:

> May God permit to me, oh saki, in this worldly home
> To sleep and rise in Galata, there drink and drunken lurch
> Oh Muslims! Wine will steal from one religion and belief
> From Allah's slave in dervish lodge, from Frankish boy in church[7]

PROSE:

> This heart-captivating town is so generous with its pleasures and so stimulating that its merriment goes on without stopping; its pleasure gatherings are continual, and its wine parties in any other place would be forbidden. Because most of its people are of the community of Jesus and the nation of the Messiah, like the ancient Shah Cem,[a] the wine cup never leaves their grip, and, because they always have a goblet in hand, worries and dark thoughts never swarm about their heads. They are sensualists and wine bibbers, worshipers of the grape and sellers of wine. Surrounded by daily cares, most of the time they are intoxicated and not in their right minds.

COUPLET:

> From fate no cruelty, from the heavens no sorrows
> Hopes fulfilled, and the cup of desire overflows

[a] Cem (Djem/gem), also known as Cemşid (Cem the Brilliant), was the first of the legendary shahs of Iran and supposedly the inventor of wine.

Because this is such an attractive gathering place and such a pleasant venue for parties, there Istanbul's pleasure seekers and revelers are by drink everywhere rendered intoxicated and ruined, witless and inflamed, stained by water and mud, their collars torn and turbans in disarray, and many a believer, shamed in his time, has this couplet on his lips:

COUPLET[S]:

> However much grief makes our faces wan, oh saki
> Pour us wine, let us drink that our cheeks again be ruddy
> Wipe away the dust of woe, with a wine cup burnisher
> Let us make the unblemished temperament like a mirror
> Adviser, don't bar the reveler from wine saying it's forbidden
> The *fetva*[b] in hand says the law of Jesus makes this licit[8]

If Istanbul of the sixteenth century seems distant from Europe and the life of European society, this is more a product of our own myopia and the blind spots of scholarship than a representation of Ottoman realities. For Ottoman Istanbulites, Europe was always just a boat ride away, and Muslims seem to have caroused with, loved, and had sexual relations with Europeans on a regular basis. As Latifi points out, European (Frankish) beauties were highly regarded and one of the main attractions of Galata. There are also a significant number of poems about Galata, for which Latifi's description serves as a gloss. For example, the following gazel is by Revani, a popular poet and notorious libertine of the late fifteenth century and the early sixteenth:

> If you are a libertine, don't turn from the cup of pure wine
> If you are wise, take your glass[c] in the direction of Galata
>
> He who wishes to see Europe in Ottoman lands
> Let him ever cross to see that city of two beauties[d]
>
> Pious one, should you see those Frankish boys but once
> You would never cast an eye on the houris in paradise
>
> I'd suppose the new moon and Pleiades conjoined
> If the lovelies[e] should board a skiff and set out to sea

---

[b] A legal opinion issued by a mufti.

[c] The word for "glass" (*ayak*) is also the word for "foot," with the obvious double meaning here.

[d] The word *ra'na* means "beautiful," but it also refers to a yellow and red rose, which is beautiful in two colors—here, Ottoman and European.

[e] In this case, the poet's party companions.

> The beloved infidel boys rob one of religion
> Oh Muslims, take care, and go not near the church
>
> Heaven's sphere is its shining palace, wherein the sun
> Has opened windows that it might observe the world
>
> Everywhere filled with paradisiacal boys and girls, Revani,
> Who enters it looks no more to the highest heaven[9]

It is an error to assume that Ottomans were ignorant of Europeans and the way they lived or, for that matter, that Europeans then were as ignorant of the Ottomans as well-educated Westerners are now. In fact, there seems to have been considerable mutual respect and even admiration. For example, in the early-sixteenth-century *Il cortegiano* (The book of the courtier), the Italian Baldessar Castiglione puts in the mouth of one of his eloquent conversationalists (Camillo Porcaro) the following anecdote (in which the exemplary courtier is Sultan Cem, Bayezit II's brother, who died in Italy in 1489 while held as a hostage by the pope) illustrating the contention that "a cutting witticism can often be facetious and have a certain gravity that does not cause laughter": "Djem Othman, brother to the Grand Turk, being a captive at Rome, said that jousting, as we practice it in Italy, seemed to him too much if done in play and too little if done in earnest. And on being told how agile and active King Ferdinand the Younger was in running, jumping, vaulting, and the like, he said that in his country slaves engaged in such exercises but that from boyhood on gentlemen learned to be liberal, and were praised for that."[10]

Venetians, especially, enjoyed close personal ties with the Ottomans. At various times in his youth, the doge Andrea Gritti spent several years in Istanbul and apparently knew Turkish quite well. There he cultivated the friendship of high officials, including, according to some reports, the sultan (Bayezit) himself. He also fathered four illegitimate sons in Istanbul, two of whom returned to settle there after being educated in Italy. His son Alvise became the close companion of Süleyman's grand vizier Ibrahim Pasha. He acquired a large fortune, built himself an Ottoman-style palace where he entertained lavishly, and died fighting for the Ottomans in Eastern Europe in 1534. It was this manner of intimate ties that gave Venice the reputation in Europe of "the Turk's courtesan."[11]

Another representative pleasure spot is in the vicinity of Anadolu Hisar, the Anatolian Keep, a castle on the Asian side of the Bosphorus built in the fifteenth century to allow the Ottomans to prevent ships from bringing supplies or reinforcements to what was then Constantinople. Hard by this castle, the stream called Göksu (Sky-Blue Water) flows into the straits amid verdant meadows and shady trees. In the sixteenth century, and to this day, Göksu

The poet Figani and a beardless boy enjoying wine and conversation in a garden or park setting. (Millet Library, Ali Emiri 722, 'Āşık Çelebi, "Meşā'irü'ş-şu'arā," fol. 267a.)

has been a popular fair-weather destination for picnickers, lovers, and poets. There were many famous destinations for outings (called *mesire*) in the Istanbul area, and Göksu is used by 'Atayi to represent them all.

Yet another famous destination is the mesire at Kağıthane. In his *Essay in Description of Istanbul*, Latifi extols the natural beauties of Kağıthane, then offers a suggestive description of some of the activities that occur there:

> In this way, because it [Kağıthane] is an attractive locale for diversion and a relaxing place to stroll, the females and males of Istanbul-town, that is, its wives and husbands, married women and their spouses, go in small boats and amuse themselves there. There do love-inclined females (to whom fate will bring just deserts) and men of low morals become a herd of gazelle bucks and does, and, after the fashion of the musk deer of Tartary on the steppes of Cathay, they scatter and roam about those wilds. Inevitably many bucks and does swarm to gather hyacinths and poppies on the skirts of

Love Scripts I 67

those hills. And, as they wander the wilds, some drop their belly scabs and some their musk bags.[12]

This passage requires a little explaining for those unfamiliar with the common tropes of Ottoman poetry. Musk, used in the making of perfumes, is contained in the scent glands from the legs of Asian musk deer (or gazelle), which were transported to and sold dried in Istanbul bazaars. The poetic tradition accounts for these glands—which, when dried, were small, hard, and black—in two related, fanciful ways. According to the first, the Chinese musk collectors set up sharpened stakes in the ground on which the musk deer scratched their bellies, either by accident or on purpose. The wounds bled and formed scabs, which later fell off, to be gathered by the collectors. According to the second, the stakes actually pierced the bellies of the deer. The bellies filled up with blood and were then collected by hunters, who killed the deer. No educated Ottoman would miss the obvious sexual symbolism of deer being pierced by sharp stakes and losing their "scabs." If we also remember that hyacinths are a standard trope for hair and the poppy (or primitive wild tulip) for the cheek, Latifi's account becomes something more like this: (Young) women and men of loose morals flock to this resort and wander out in the wilds, where the women unveil so that their lovers can touch their (uncovered) hair and kiss their cheeks; as a result, there is often sexual activity, and many women lose their virginity.

Latifi's description is not unlike Phillip Stubbes's disapproving travelogue account of English villagers' May Day excursions in his 1538 *Anatomie of Abuses*. As he reports: "Against *May, Whitsonday* or other time, all the yung men and maides, olde men and wiues, run gadding ouer night to woods groves hills, & mountains, where they spend all night in peasant pastimes; & in the morning they return, bringing with them birch & branches of trees, to deck their assemplies withall." According to Stubbes, the revelers return with a great maypole dragged behind "twentie or fortie yoke of Oxen" decorated with flowers. The pole is reared with all manner of adornments. "And then fall they to daunce about it, like as the heathen people did at the dedication of the Idols, wherof this is a perfect pattern, or rather the thing it self. I haue heard it credibly reported (and that *viua voce*) by men of great grauitie and reputation, that of fortie, threescore, or a hundred maides going to the wood ouer night, there haue scaresly the third part of them returned home againe undefiled."[13]

In his famous *Hevesname* (The book of desire; A.H. 899 [1493/94 C.E.]), the poet Tacızade Ca'fer Çelebi describes a springtime outing at Kağıthane—an excursion to the park, where he camps for at least three days—that could have been a model for Latifi's more general account.[14] While contemplating the beauties of nature, he notices a boat carrying a group of women and their servants who come ashore and set up camp. One among them is especially beautiful, and he determines to establish contact with her. She notices him noticing her and sends her servant to ask him for his divan. He has not brought it with him but manages to write out a few gazels, supposedly from memory. A mutual seduction takes place, and the woman, who is the wife of a highly placed official, consents to spend three blissful days with him, after which they part for good. This story—which we discuss more fully in chapter 6 below, providing there some translated excerpts—clearly describes love relations that far exceed what we usually take to be the limits of religion and custom for Ottomans. It may be a fantasy, but it is a fantasy that appears untroubled by fear or guilt.

For poets, there were many other popular hangouts. The sixteenth-century tezkire literature is full of descriptions of the famous taverns of greater Istanbul. The notorious and long-lived Efe Meyhanesi (Efe Tavern) was a gathering place of poets and revelers from the late fifteenth century through the sixteenth. Also mentioned are the Yani Meyhanesi (Yani Tavern), the taverns of Galata and the adjoining district of Tophane, and the numerous open-air taverns that appeared on the banks of the Bosphorus and Marmara during the summer months.[15] 'Atayi's story mentions Köse's Tavern by name, and, although we have not yet been able to find any other references to that particular tavern, it most certainly represents one of the Galata establishments of the early seventeenth century.

Late in the sixteenth century, around 1587, a courtier, historian, and littérateur named Mustafa 'Ali of Gallipoli, composed a work entitled *Kava'idu'l-mecalis* (The etiquette of gatherings), which he would later expand under the title *Meva'idu'n-nefa'is fi kava'idu'l-mecalis* (Exquisite appointments in the etiquette of gatherings). 'Ali was a talented man, disappointed in the velocity and trajectory of his career. He felt that the injustice of his situation was due to a breakdown in the proper functioning of the court and its systems of patronage. His *Etiquette* was intended to reveal and correct the defects that had crept into social interactions in the court and among high officials, courtiers, and those who served them. He dealt, not just with gatherings or salons (*meclis*, pl. *mecalis*), but with all manner of social relations, giving us a candid, if critical and somewhat self-serving, glimpse into the life of early-modern Ottoman elites.[16]

In a section devoted to wine taverns, 'Ali says that these are the gathering places and the preferred places of pleasure for two groups.[17] One consists of "sanguine youths and possessors of power who are wine worshipers, woman chasers, and boy lovers, who come to the tavern, some with their beloveds. They eat, drink, and, when evening falls, return to their private dwellings." He later describes some of this group as "eloquent speakers [i.e., the poetically inclined] from among the successful businessmen, artisans, and government officials" who come to the taverns for a cup to relax them after a hard day, after which they return home in the evening to "spread out their bolsters, mattresses, and bedclothes and take their beloveds or smooth-cheeked servant [boys] in their arms." Their drinking is seen as social, occasional, and associated with literary pursuits and the activities of love as scripted by poetry. The other group consists of "despicable black-faced Arabs and lowborn characters of Russian descent," who drink all day and waste their lives in taverns. After the manner of sots and drunkards, they consider it a religious duty to set aside each Friday evening for intercourse with women, every Saturday night for (beardless) youths and feast day eves for young (male) slaves, in the same way that the rule for wine worshipers is to go to the tavern on Fridays after prayers.

'Ali's description of late-sixteenth-century Ottoman tavern life is strikingly similar to Alan Bray's description of the seventeenth-century English "molly house" where men of many classes gathered to drink and meet with boy prostitutes. Although it was the sexual debauchery of such establishments that attracted the most outside attention, as Bray says: "Sex was the root of the matter, but it was as likely to be expressed in drinking together, in flirting and gossip and in a circle of friends as in actual liaisons."[18] This is precisely what we see in the sociability of the Ottoman tavern. Tavern culture constituted, in both England and the Ottoman Empire, a social institution that cut across class lines. Because they stood outside the accepted societal norms, both the Ottoman tavern (where intoxicants were served in opposition to Islamic law) and the English molly house (where forbidden homosexual encounters took place) became places where various classes mingled, where, in the Ottoman case, Muslims and Christians interacted, and where a certain amount of cultural diffusion took place across class boundaries.[19]

By the second half of the sixteenth century, coffee and coffeehouses had also made their appearance on the Istanbul scene, and the coffeehouses in the vicinity of the Karaman Bazaar became especially popular gathering places for poets, lovers, and pleasure seekers. Speaking of coffeehouses, 'Ali says that they appeared in Istanbul in the year A.H. 960 (1552/53 C.E.). He describes them as the gathering place for a wide variety of people looking for pleasant conversation: dervishes and people of mystical (gnostic) wisdom; homeless strangers and destitute people; silly, callow "city boys," who gossip maliciously; and *sipahis* (feudal cavalry) and janissaries from all over the empire, who tell tall tales of former glories. Among these are even some religious dignitaries who find it suitable to drink coffee.[20] The coffeehouse especially is a venue in which men of many social classes and occupations gather for conversation and a variety of entertainments, including games, music, dancing boys and girls, storytelling, poetry, and shadow-puppet performances. The historian Peçevi, one of the administrative elites from a Rumelian (European) family long in the service of the Ottomans and a firsthand observer of the empire in the last years of the sixteenth century and the early seventeenth, locates the coming of coffeehouses at about the same time (1554) and claims that they were brought by two fellows, one named Hakem from Aleppo and the other a Şems from Damascus. Peçevi went on to describe the situation in his day:

> Some pleasure-loving companions devoted to pleasure and, especially, elegant wits of the literate sort would gather there [in the coffeehouses] and would hold a gathering in [one of] twenty or thirty places. Some would read from books and beautiful literature; some would busy themselves with backgammon and chess; some would bring newly composed gazels and carry on discussions of the arts and sciences. They would spend a lot of their silver and small coins, and, by giving coffee money on the order of one or two silver pieces [akçe] to the fellow who puts together the party as a reason for close companions to meet, they would create an even more pleasurable gathering. It got to the point that, because there was no place like this where they could enjoy themselves and take their ease, regular customers such as out-of-office administrators, magistrates, professors, and those without regular jobs or wages filled them [the coffeehouses] until there was no place to sit or stand. In short, [the coffeehouse] acquired such a vogue that all the well-to-do—other than the holders of high office—were obliged to come. Imams [prayer leaders], muezzins, and hypocritical Sufis became addicts of the coffeehouse. It was said that no one came to the mosque anymore. As for the religious authorities, they proclaimed that [the coffeehouse] is a place of evil, that it was better to go to the tavern than to go there. The preachers strove mightily to forbid them, and the mufti issued legal opinions stating that any substance that achieves the state of charcoal [*fahm* or *kömür*][f] is plain and simply unlawful.[21]

About this time, a poet who went by the pen name Sa'yi moved to Edirne, leaving his comrades in Istanbul behind. During his absence, he wrote his friends a long letter in monorhyming couplets with a partly nostalgic and partly teasing, jibing tone. We discuss this letter and a response by the poet Sani elsewhere (see chapter 5 below), but, here, let us just glance at Sa'yi's rather wistful opening lines, in which he mentions some of the favorite

---

[f] The mufti is, here, referring to coffee beans, which, when roasted, look like little bits of charcoal.

Love Scripts I 71

gathering places of the intellectual and artistic elites, a passage that concluded, appropriately, with his mention of that Nev'i who was 'Atayi's father:

> What news, oh east wind, how are things in the world?
> Are Istanbul and Galata still as lovely?
>
> Do the revelers still go in troops to Tophane?
> Do they still amuse themselves with saz and song?
>
> Do the pure born still flow like water toward Molla's Bath?
> For truly it is the very lifeblood of pleasure!
>
> Is every cup worshiper still the willing prisoner
> Of a morning draught in seaside taverns?
>
> Do the beautiful ones still call at mansions and display their glory?
> Does everyone still visit the Karaman Bazaar in late afternoons?
>
> Do lovers still show themselves amiable by bargaining
> In the Cloth Bazaar for bolts of satin and brocade?
>
> Do lovers still recite adorned gazels about the beautiful ones?
> Are the wise still famed for their excellence?
>
> Do the lithe-bodied and bud-mouthed beloveds still hold
> The colorful poems of Baki the Eloquent in their hands like roses?
>
> Does Nev'i Efendi have any new poetry?
> In perfection and excellence he is a paragon.[22]

Here we have an example of a contemporary account by a participant in the life of the pleasure seeker in sixteenth-century Istanbul. We have already mentioned most of the places that Sa'yi and his friends used to visit; what remain are references to the pursuit and pursuits of beautiful boys, the boys that Tayyib and Tahir dallied with in Köse's Tavern and chased after at Göksu. Beyond the pleasures of bathing, one of the chief attractions of popular bathhouses was the opportunity to observe attractive young men, from bath boys (*dellak*) to regular customers. We need always to keep in mind that "beautiful ones" is descriptive of a range of people, from young men in general, including one's friends and contemporaries (who may not be young at all), to boys (early adolescents, for the most part) who could potentially be exploited for sex. Thus, the "beautiful ones" who "call at mansions and display their glory" are likely young, carousing poets who, according to a long-standing custom, would call at the mansions (especially the Galata vacation palaces) of the wealthy to present their poems or join gatherings in progress, in return for which they would receive presents of goods and cash.[23] This appears to have been one way to finance a day and night of partying. But the ones for whom lovers buy gifts of "satin and brocade" in the Cloth Bazaar, the ones to whom the poets often dedicate their verses, the "lithe-bodied and bud-mouthed beloveds," were the beautiful boys, often the mercenary beloveds mentioned by Latifi in the selection cited at the beginning of chapter 2 above.

One could easily spend a fortune on such boys and on the wine and drugs favored by young and wild partygoers. Tacızade Ca'fer Çelebi's son Bali Çelebi was said to be spending as much as twenty *dirhems* a day on opium, even after he became a *sahn müderrisi* (professor of sharia law) at one of the premier higher-education institutions of the age, until the drugs finally killed him.[24] The biographies tell of many men who led wild and dissolute lives as youths but went on to fill respectable positions in society as they matured. The real tragedies seem to be those who allowed youthful indiscretion to last into later life. In any case, Tayyib and Tahir are described as falling into a dissolute life typical of what would be expected of an educated, emotionally sensitive, financially independent young man of the time.

The Course of Love

It is significant that when the two young men meet with the consequences of their youthful folly—that is, when they end up broke—they decide to leave town, with the purpose of becoming dervishes (members of a confraternity of Islamic mystics), because they have become the subjects of scandalous gossip. One of the scripted principles of pleasure seeking or the life of wine and beloveds is that ultimately—as every wise person knows—both intoxication and love can be seen and experienced as metaphors for spiritual rapture and divine love. Thus, the squandering of an inheritance becomes an analogue for mystical divestiture or the stripping off of attachments to the material world. When one is down to nothing, it becomes clear that worldly wealth and passions, pleasures and intoxications, are only metaphors for something more real and more precious, and becoming a dervish—in spirit, if not in practice—is an almost inevitable consequence.

In this case, the two young men set sail for the lodge of the Gülşeni order of dervishes in Egypt. Founded by an Anatolian mystic and poet named Ibrahim Gülşeni, the order was related to the Halveti dervishes but adopted practices from both the Mevlevis—Celalu'd-din (Djelaluddeen) Rumi's successors—and the Bektaşis. In the late sixteenth century and through the seventeenth, the Gülşeni order was very popular among the Ottoman elites, and the Egyptian lodge became a popular retirement residence for Ottoman officials. This elevates Tayyib and Tahir from their artisan- and merchant-class origins and to the class of elites associated with early-seventeenth-century poets. What our story addresses, however, is neither institutional mysticism nor the life of dervishes but the question of what happens to those who live out the love script *without* devoting their lives to a mystical discipline.

Having learned one lesson, Tayyib and Tahir are abruptly turned from their mystical course by being twice captured: once by infidels (Christians) and once by love. These acts are clearly presented as destined. The young men do not choose but are ruled by weather, the sea, and a chance encounter. That they should fall in love with their captors, with people outside their religion, with enemies of their ruler, is powerful testimony to the transcendence of love. Love, in this case, ignores and makes trivial all the boundaries and barriers that commonly rule mundane lives. What is important is that the Christians, Sir John and Janno, are worthy of love, that they are kind and generous to the poor, that they are educated, wise, and mature—in short, that they display attributes valued by Muslims.

The transcendence or, one might even say, the disorderliness of love is a common theme in the literature of the medieval and early-modern period. Everywhere in the Middle Eastern and European literatures, love brings enemies together and unites people separated by class and culture. For prominent examples, we need look no further than Ariosto's *Orlando Furioso* (and the love between the Saracen [and ancestor of the Estes] Ruggiero and the Christian Bradamant or the Saracen Isobel and the Scot Zerbin), or the Provençal tale of Aucassin and Nicolette, or the story of the Persian ruler Husrev and the Armenian princess Shirin. In this context, it is almost a given that love will also ignore any social, legal, or religious construction of the normal as regards gender restrictions.

In our story, we can see a definite progression in the stages and kinds of love. In their wild days, Tayyib and Tahir love the young, lower-class boys of the taverns and parties, generally powerless boys who exploit the physical desire of their lovers to gain some advantage—usually presents, cash, or other material rewards. This love is depicted as heedless, hot, and physical. The two young men's extreme sensitivity to love in this form—attested to by the devastating effect that it has on their fortunes—predisposes them to higher forms of love, which they discover only after their worldly possessions, and even their personal freedom, have been lost. At the next stage of love, the power situation is reversed. It is Tayyib and Tahir who are powerless. They fall in love with men who are wealthy, highly placed, and more mature, men who, above all, have, as their captors and masters, complete control over their lives.

The understanding of love and the way it works that we see demonstrated in 'Atayi's story illuminates for us some aspects of the belief system lying behind highly influential structures of patronage in the early-modern period.

The first thing that we need to take into account is the situation common to the levend in the Ottoman Empire and the type of young man—possibly no longer a beardless youth and unattached to a household or an occupation—that existed in increasingly large numbers in early-modern Europe. We have mentioned above the disruptions that gangs of such youths caused for the authorities in Italy, and the same problem seems to have existed in England as well. Another aspect of this situation is a growing desperation on the part of these masterless men in the matter of finding employment at a time, especially during the late sixteenth century and the early seventeenth, when traditional systems of patronage were breaking down. This desperation translated itself into a need for a master that, on the one hand, was passionate in a way that was most elaborately and clearly scripted by notions of love and that, on the other hand, made unemployed young men vulnerable to sexual exploitation.[25] The wishful notion (reinforced by literary models) that the lover's passion cannot help but touch the one who is its object drives much of the relation between patron and supplicant at all levels. It is the supplicant's or courtier's job to love so intensely that a corresponding love will be awakened in the patron. As we see in the case of Tayyib, the first step is that the patron/beloved (Sir John) takes notice of his lovesick admirer. Then the beloved does him a favor, and a relationship is established. We see in this a conviction that the powerless, helpless, needy lover can, thereby, achieve some measure of control over a powerful and entirely self-sufficient beloved. The applications of this mode of thinking to the operation of patriarchal, hierarchical, and despotic systems are obvious.

We must also take note of the particular favor that Sir John bestows. He employs Tayyib to work in his garden. This is a significant choice of location since the garden flourishes with amorous and erotic associations in the early-modern period. In the Ottoman Empire, and in the West as well, not only is the garden a place of particular beauties of nature, beauties that mirror the beauty of the beloved, but it is also famously a place for lovers' trysts. Most homes of the period did not provide private spaces for intimate activities. Rooms in private houses were few; the inhabitants of any house tended to be many, and, in Europe, people often slept several to a bed. As a consequence, most extramarital sexual and erotic activity was carried on outside the house, at times in run-down neighborhoods, or marketplaces, or private and public gardens. Michael Rocke says of the situation for homoerotic and homosexual liaisons in late-fifteenth- and sixteenth-century Florence: "The physical layout of the medieval city plus a lack of domestic privacy, more than anonymity ... encouraged sex in public places. Many men and boys sodomized in fields outside the city gates or in the extensive private or conventual [convent] gardens that ringed the congested city center out to the walls."[26]

In his study of the casebooks of Simon Forman, an English astrologer and contemporary of Shakespeare, A. L. Rowse comments on Forman's numerous reports of sexual encounters in gardens by quoting the following from Philip Stubbes's *Anatomie of Abuses*:

> In the fields and suburbs of the cities they have gardens, either paled or walled round about very high, with their arbours and bowers fit for the purpose. . . . And for that their gardens are locked, some of them have three or four keys apiece, whereof one they keep for themselves, the other their paramours have to go in before them, lest haply they should be perceived, for then were all their sport dashed. . . . These gardens are excellent places, and for the purpose; for if they can speak with their darlings nowhere else, there they may be sure to meet with them and to receive the guerdon (reward) of their pains: they know best what I mean.[27]

Gardens are an equally prominent feature of Ottoman urban space and have similar uses.[28] Upper-class homes had attached gardens where, in warm weather, outdoor entertainments took place.[29] As we have seen in the examples of Göksu and Kağıthane, public gardens and picnic spots were abundant and very popular as places to gather.

In his pornographic masterpiece, which we will introduce more fully in a later chapter, the poet Gazali has some medical advice for a person in the throes of lovesickness:

> In that case, my lord, the medicine is this: that one abstain from all impositions of daily labor, that he repair to garden and vineyard, field and forest, with lovely voiced, lovely countenanced singers. Let him go to the rose garden and calm himself by strolling about sighing, crying out, and weeping as the nightingales begin to sing and the poppies and hyacinths open their blossoms. This is the remedy that drives away that illness and sorrow. And, if this cannot be done, let him compound the following medicine in the manner of an electuary paste: a dirhem weight of coquettishness, two dirhems of seductiveness, two of gazing, three of eloquence, four of gesture, five of excitement, six of movement, seven of song, eight of airs, and nine of embraces. Then let him purify it bit by bit of the detritus of tyranny and haughtiness, pound it in the mortar of loyalty, strain it through the cloth of purity, mix it with three times its weight of the sugar of desire, and boil it in the cauldron of affection over the flames of longing until it comes to the proper consistency. Then, after taking full measure of union, day and night, let him enter the bathhouse of the breast and there drink of perfumed crystalline sherbets and the juice of oranges. Anything else, and Plato come all the way from dusky China would not effect a remedy or cure.[30]

The beauties of the garden and those of the beloved are linked here. One is as efficacious as the other. Where the garden is, the beloved cannot be far off.

As Tayyib begins to work in the garden, the old gardener is also attracted to his physical and spiritual beauty and takes it on himself to help the young man achieve his desire. The encounter with the wise old man is a common story type, but, in this case, it happens within a complex of eroticized male-male relationships that seem to proliferate, beginning with the pure, childish love of Tayyib and Tahir for one another, then moving to primitive (adolescent) sexual attractions and encounters that, in turn, mature from mere revelry to a serious part of the business of life. As we have seen and will see, these relationships appear in the form of varying degrees of patronage, reflecting patterns of patronage in Ottoman and other hierarchical, patriarchal, and monarchical societies. Sir John acts as patron to his captive Tayyib by giving him a job. The gardener acts as an intermediary patron by advancing Tayyib's relations with Sir John, who is patron to them both.

The next significant theme is that of the garden party. This activity is so elaborately scripted by Ottoman literature that it need only be mentioned to elicit a host of associations. In 'Atayi's story, Sir John is holding a party with some beautiful young men—again highlighting the erotic character of the gathering. As is typical, the party will include delicious food, wine, entertainment, and stimulating conversation. During the course of the party, the participants gradually relax and let down the emotional defenses that protect them in the world outside the garden. They become open to one another and more intimate.[31] Tayyib becomes a focus of interest when the gardener, who has been invited to entertain the group with stories, manages to introduce him into the gathering, and the partygoers elicit the tale of his life and adventures. In their heightened (and somewhat inebriated) emotional state, they empathize with his sorrows, and the way is opened for Tayyib's love and Sir John's response to grow into a closer attachment.

There are striking parallels between the Ottoman garden party and the English banquet of the late sixteenth century and the early seventeenth. In the case of the Ottoman elites, the meclis, which involves close friends, entertainments (musician and dancers), poetry, and talk about love, moves out of the private and protected space of the home into a garden köşk. This building, usually consisting of a single open room with generous windows looking out onto a garden or pleasant vista, serves as the site for a formalized and weather-independent version of the picnic or alfresco meal or wine party.[32]

In England, as we learn from a fascinating and suggestive study by Patricia Fumerton, the traditional banquet or feast, which had commonly been eaten by large gatherings in a great hall, became increasing segmented and privatized over the course of the sixteenth and seventeenth centuries.[33] Special dining rooms were set aside, and diners often moved from room to room during the meal. The institution of the medieval and early-Renaissance void, or interlude in which sweet wine and spices were consumed standing up while the main table was being "voided" and prepared for the next course, moved first into a separate room farther in toward the private space of the house and then into special rooms, often detached from the dining area and later even detached from the house itself and contained in a special building located in the garden or park. According to Fumerton, by the late sixteenth century, every garden of any consequence contained a banqueting house or pavilion, which, from our perspective, is a very close analogue of the Ottoman köşk.[34] The trajectory of the English void and the Ottoman garden/köşk party was toward a focus on privacy, on detachment from the mundane world and the common crowd, on special entertainments (in England music, poetry, and masques, for the Ottomans poetry, music, and dancers), and on special foods (e.g., [sweet] wines; sugar creations, sugared fruits and nuts, and other confections; and highly spiced delicacies). Fumerton sees this detachment and division as compounded by features too numerous to mention here—examples would be the replacement of the medieval communal pot with individual plates and the hand with specialized utensils—and interprets it as a trend toward separating the private from the public, the self from others, anticipating, she hints (via Yi-Fu Tuan), modern (Western) alienation.[35] At this point, we have no evidence that would allow us to speculate with any confidence on possible parallels in the Ottoman situation. What we can say is that, for the Ottomans, the garden, the köşk, and the party are endowed with meaning by an elaborate cultural (primarily poetic) script and emphasize the creation of a special group of intimate, trusted, beloved friends who share a common interpretation of life.[36]

In an article on a diary written by a seventeenth-century Sünbüli dervish, Cemal Kafadar remarks on the lack of interest that the diarist shows in his professional, spiritual, and literary life. Instead, Kafadar reports: "By far the majority of entries in the diary relate the social occasions in which our diarist took part. Among such occasions, dinner parties with fellow Sünbülis obviously constituted the highlights of his social life." Throughout the diary, food and the sociability surrounding food are foregrounded as integral features of private life, even to the extent of appearing to intrude on intimate tragedies, such as the death of the diarist's beloved wife.[37]

Thus, when, at Tayyib's request, Sir John seeks out Janno and Tahir, the four come to constitute that circle of close intimate friends united in love that is one of the required elements of the party as scripted by Ottoman poetry. In other studies, we have detailed the evidence for the tight linking of erotic attachment and close friendship.[38] Here, we will note only, for example, that

On the left, one of two banqueting pavilions in the garden of Montacute House (ca. 1590), Somerset, England (photograph courtesy Alan Liu and Patricia Fumerton). On the right, an Ottoman style *köşk* (kiosk) from a late-sixteenth-century miniature showing Sultan Murat III in the Kandil Garden with dwarves, attendants, and his sons to the right. (Topkapı Palace Museum Library, B. 200, "Şehinşehnāme," fol. 98b.)

the common poetic words for "beloved," *yar* and *dost*, are often used in their (Persian) plural forms (*yaran, dostan*) to represent the dear friends who gather at the poetically scripted party.

At this point, we have been able to identify most of the essential elements of the typical poetic gathering: the lover and beloved (Sir John and Tayyib, Tahir and Janno); the circle of close friends (the four together); entertainers (the old gardener as storyteller); the setting (Sir John's garden); food and wine. Next, we are introduced to the outsiders who define the interior space of the gathering and its meaning by standing outside it and misinterpreting its significance. The first of these is the gossip. In Ottoman society, gossip or slander was a very serious business. A person's standing in the community and before the law was directly tied to a reputation for morally upright behavior. As Leslie Pierce points out in a study of one early-modern Ottoman court, the legal status of being *töhmetlü* (suspicious) or *töhmetsiz* (without suspicion) seems to refer equally to persons convicted (or not convicted) of illicit sexual behavior and to those only suspected of such behavior. Being publicly suspected of illicit behavior strongly and negatively affects the credence given to one's testimony in court. Moreover, people accused of sexual misconduct are

Love Scripts I 79

usually immune to conviction if they lack a prior *töhmet* (i.e., if one is *muhsan/muhsana*, "an upright man/woman in the eyes of the law and the community"), but the accusation itself can bring a töhmet and imperil the accused should another action be brought at a later date.³⁹ In the story, it is the actions of the gossip that turn private relations into public talk, bringing the group of friends to the attention of the authorities, and, subsequently, resulting in severe punishment and mortal dangers for them all. We will examine how this works in more detail in chapter 9 below.

The actions of the city police authority have multiple implications in relation to the Ottoman situation. The official himself takes the role played by the *zahid* (the religious precisian/ascetic) in the poetic script. He is rigid, angry, vengeful, self-righteous, and, above all, oblivious to the true (anagogic) meaning and value of love. Ottoman poetry is full of verses censuring the puritan and citing his ignorant admonitions. In this case, the setting is suggestive. In Ottoman society, sexual or erotic relations between men or men and boys were seldom punished, especially if they were carried on in private, and homoerotic relations were in a much less serious class of crimes than illicit sexual contacts with women, which could, in theory, result in death by stoning. However, the situation in Christian Europe was quite the reverse. In Europe, what was termed *sodomy* was subject to severe penalties, which increased in severity throughout the fifteenth and sixteenth centuries and very often mandated death or even death by burning; yet adulterous relations and even rapes of women, while morally condemned, were looked on with some tolerance and were often punished only by fines or a coerced marriage.⁴⁰ This is among the reasons why Ottoman culture tends to be freer in talking about erotic relations between males and European culture in talking about male-female relations. There is, however, no evidence that the disparity in what can be talked about in public or semipublic media such as poetry or stories represents a similar disparity in who loved whom. In fact, in both cases, the more severe the punishments for sex crimes, the less likelihood that they would be administered, especially to the elites.

Two benefits of setting the story in Christian Europe come immediately to mind. The first is that this allows the imposition of the death penalty, which heightens the tension in the story and points out the unreasonableness of Christians and their misprision of the true nature of love—the police official acts "believing love" (i.e., true, spiritual love between men) "a crime." The second benefit is that 'Atayi can refer to a problem of his own place and time without directly confronting powerful social factions.

The late sixteenth century and the seventeenth see the waning of the Ottoman Age of Beloveds and the rise of puritanical, revivalist, and anti-Sufi/dervish groups, most prominently the followers of Birgili Mehmet (d. 1573) and his popular spiritual successor Kadizade Mehmet (d. 1635), whose followers, called the Kadizadeli, became a powerful social force.[41] Throughout the sixteenth century, and especially in the latter half, as the first millennium of Islam drew to a close, waves of religious puritanism washed across Istanbul, driven by the oratory of such revivalist preachers and their adherents. The flourishing culture of wine and beloveds, taverns and gardens, intoxication and sex, bound as it was to the spiritual (Sufi) interpretation of love, became a favorite target, and, from time to time, the authorities bowed to popular pressure and attempted to suppress one or another of its manifestations. In the summer of 1562, for example, Sultan Süleyman had the Italian wine ships burned off Galata, an act that occasioned an anguished outcry on the part of poets and partygoers. This was what provoked Sani's famous couplet, one we have seen before:

> The jugs are broken, the goblet empty, wine is no more
> You've made us prisoners of coffee, alas destiny alas

Even the famed Baki, one of the Sultan's circle of companions and a noted jurist, had this comment:

> The wine-shop road it firmly barred, the sultan's sword of wrath
> 'Tween Istanbul and Galata, like water, cut the path[42]

Late in the sixteenth century, when reformist-revivalist preachers had begun to have a significant impact, Mustafa 'Ali summed up the attitude of the intellectual elites toward these puritans in his famed *Nasihatu's-selatin* (Counsel for sultans) of 1581. He exhorts the sultan as follows:

> So why is it that these kinds of enemies of the state, in the guise of reform, should prattle on and on and bring thousands upon thousands of simpleminded commoners to their gatherings, inciting rebellion by instigating a chain of disruption and disorder?
> ... And there is no doubt that this lot, while outright troublemakers, are passing for spiritual guides, that each of them is a secret Celali [Djelalee, "rural rebel"] in the Protected Domains [Ottoman dominions] and even right here in the Hereditary Seat of Rule,[g] and that their seditious speech fans the flames of disruption and disorder and their breath [which stinks] of calumny has blown [these flames] into a perfect conflagration.
> ... In addition to their being the very image of hypocrisy, if one questions them as regards their learning, it becomes obvious that most of them

[g] Istanbul.

are clearly village medrese students with the stench of *mensa* soup on their breaths and scraps of charity stew caught between their teeth and that, having learned but one or two lines of Arabic compounds, they disgrace themselves with their ignorance in the pulpit.[43]

It is important to note that the Ottoman popular preachers and official crackdowns tended to focus on the dervish orders and on intoxicants—wine, coffee, tobacco—and the public places where they were consumed. 'Ali makes in his remarks the assumption that these things are an integral part of the life of the elite, intellectual, and military classes that support the empire and its ruler, that those who assault a poetic or poetically scripted life are striking at the very heart of the state—although we should not neglect to mention that popular preaching often focused on official corruption, taxation, the funding of endowments, etc. as well as on the supposedly corrupt social and sexual practices of the elites. 'Ali also draws a clear distinction between the commoners and the elites, the villager and the urbanite, the simple and the subtle, the literal, surface reading of Holy Writ and the esoteric (mystical) reading, the ignorant and the educated classes. This is where the battle lines were drawn, and it should not be assumed that the elites held all the weapons. It was not always clear where the loyalties of the common soldiery lay, and even the most powerful officials, at times of greatest stability and centralized power, were threatened or destroyed by the fury of the mob. 'Ali speaks out of a sincere belief that the power of his class—more or less the educated, non-slave, courtier class—is crumbling and the mob gaining ascendancy.[44] And, by the early seventeenth century, when 'Atayi tells the story of Tayyib and Tahir, the situation is far more acute, and the palace itself will be invaded by an angry mob and a sultan—the ultimate earthly beloved—deposed and executed.

'Atayi's story avoids confronting puritanical religious reformists in his own backyard. But it does also reflect a bemused Ottoman view of European prudery, which condemned something as common and natural as erotic attractions and sexually charged relations among men (an activity as common and natural to Florence, e.g., as it ever was to Istanbul) while ignoring the consumption of wine (again, an activity as common to West as to East, one that, as we have seen Latifi claim [see chapter 2 above], left Christian Europeans befuddled most of the time). At the same time, the story strikes out harshly at the prudish official whose attitudes and rhetoric parallel those of the Ottoman religious puritans of early-seventeenth-century Istanbul and in a way that would be hard for a contemporary audience to miss. This "Frankish" official, who appears to function in the role of an Ottoman *muhtesib* or *subaşı* (officials who police public space), is called "a vengeful wretch," "a raving infidel," "a mighty blight on the earth," an "evil hound," and it is pointed out that the common people are offended and dismayed by the extremely harsh punishments that he proposes. We should also note in passing that it is precisely the distaste of the common people for extreme punishments that Ottoman legal scholars cite as a rationale for mitigating or avoiding some of the harsher penalties designated for some serious moral offenses.[45] Thus, it is likely that 'Atayi is making his own thinly disguised attack on the conservative opponents of a poetically scripted life, perhaps even suggesting that those precisians who believe that love is a crime are acting more like fanatical Christians than true Muslims.

The notion that Islam is the true religion of love rises to the surface in the rest of the story. The two Christian noblemen, already possessed by love, are incarcerated with Muslims and begin to find Islam to be compatible with their present emotional and spiritual state. What follow are a series of miracles of love. Psychologically prepared for conversion, Janno and Sir John have a dream in which they are visited by a Muslim sage dressed in green robes and turban. Green is the Prophet's color and also the color of the popular saint Hızır (the "green" man, the word *hızr* meaning "green" in Arabic), who is thought to bring the dead to life and rescue heroes from impossible situations. Here, the holy man/dream visitor is presented as the agent of love and the embodiment of the principle that love (done right) will be a powerful and unerring guide.[46] From this point on, the lovers and beloveds are portrayed as having abandoned rational choice. Janno and Sir John put out to sea in a rowboat with no idea where they are going, while Tayyib and Tahir are aimlessly roaming the waters themselves. The four are drawn together by the power of their love, which creates an invisible, mystical connection. The underlying theme of the story, which might be characterized as love's transcendence, is summarized in the moment when Tayyib and Tahir turn their ship to attack an enemy and instead find a love that transcends all worldly enmities. In the final victory of love, the four return to Istanbul, the Christians convert to the religion of love (a conversion symbolized by their taking the Muslim names Mes'ud [happy] and Mahmud [praiseworthy]), and all live successful (happy and praiseworthy) lives that end with each following his love presumably to paradise, the eternal abode of universal love.

Looking back on the story and our interpretation of it, a number of themes emerge, themes that we will take up as topics for the rest of our study. The most prominent of these is the life history of love, which can be seen as a naturalized cycle or spiral of reversals. The youth begins as a beloved, as the passive object of affection and sexual relations. He then becomes a lover, himself taking other younger men as the objects of his love. As he matures, he again becomes the submissive partner in patronage relations—until he becomes a patron himself. The final stage, attained only by some, recognizes that the ultimate love relation is one with a dominant, beloved deity. However, an aspect of this life history that we often tend to overlook is the extent to which life during the Age of Beloveds was open to the expression of sexual and erotic desire and how this affected the content of literary works and was, in turn, shaped by them. In much of Ottoman literature, and in many of the European literatures as well, there is an easily observable tendency to dwell on metaphoric (Neoplatonic) interpretations of love. Yet an overwhelming preponderance of evidence indicates that metaphoric love became fashionable to some extent because it was so firmly grounded in down-to-earth sexual love. Actual, physical love was everywhere—in the home, the garden, the field, the marketplace, the artisan's shop, the tavern, the convent, the cloister, the dervish lodge, the palace. A distinguished early-modern Ottoman jurist seriously entertained the question of whether a beautiful boy should be forbidden to pray in the front row lest the view of him prostrating himself should take the minds of those behind him off their devotions.[47] An Italian convent became so notorious for sexual misconduct that it was closed down by the pope in 1474.[48] If the literary expressions of sixteenth-century love at times seem conventional, ethereal, and insipid to us, it is most likely because we are out of touch with the core of sexual desire and sexual activity that gave them power.

In what follows, it is our intention to do with love and love poetry what we have done with the story of Tayyib and Tahir. That is, we will indicate how the literature of love is engaged in what is happening in the Ottoman Empire and the rest of Eurasia during the period that we call the Age of Beloveds. We will begin by talking about what Ottoman poets and Ottoman poems of the period have to say about poetry and the beloveds of the day. We will discuss the beloved and sexual relations and the international culture of the beloved. We will also explore the dangers of love, its reversals, and its relation to the law and to the economy of culture production.

4

LOVE SCRIPTS II, POEMS ABOUT
POETRY ABOUT LOVE

Güzeller şi're hep mayil müsahib olmaya kayil
Be hey Zati bu demlerde niçün hamuş ola şa'ir

The beauties all like poetry and want to be conversant
Oh, Zati, at a time like this why should a poet be silent
—Zati

Because we want to make an unusual argument—unusual for Ottomanists, at any rate—because we want to argue that early-modern Ottoman love poetry serves as a script for the acting out and interpretation of actual Ottoman love (among other things), we are going to begin by taking a closer look at what Ottoman poems and poets themselves have to say about the business of poetry.

Poetry in the World

Distant as we are from Ottoman Turkish poetry of the sixteenth century, it has been easy for scholars to separate the gazel from its embedding in the day-to-day occasions of peoples' lives. We have been induced to think of it and talk about it as if it were composed primarily and even exclusively for aesthetic or spiritual purposes. We are often told with great authority that, because the gazel is not realistic, that is, because it does not pretend to represent the world "as it really is," then it must be purely idealistic and fundamentally estranged from the context in which it was produced. Moreover, the accepted literary history of the Ottomans insists that the long sixteenth century was the idealizing classical age of a poetry that would never truly escape its Petrarchan character as a classicizing vernacular in the Perso-Arab tradition.

This impression stems in large part from the nature of our primary sources. Often our impressions of artifacts of past cultures are determined by the ways in which they are handed down to us. We usually run across gazels in poets' divans, which are intended to be the eternal storehouse of their authors' spiritual and aesthetic capital. Remember the passage cited in chapter 2 where Zati is talking about receiving money and halvah for ghostwriting love poems? He says: "In any case, I am out nothing of my capital. The gazel goes in my divan, and I still keep the silver, the gold, and the halvah." When Zati includes a gazel in his divan, it is like money in the bank of eternity; his focus is on preserving for all time the record of his own talent. The more the focus is on him rather than on the occasion or subject of the poem, the better. So gazels are seldom identified by the roles that they might have played in the world of the poet's day. In his divan, Zati does not say, "This gazel is addressed to such-and-such lovely shop boy or handsome young gentleman and was written in exchange for a gold piece and a plate of halvah." Nonetheless, many gazels have double natures in precisely this way. They are produced both for idealistic, aesthetic purposes and for the most mundane of goals—to make a living, to attract a patron, to ask for a job, to write a letter, to celebrate an occasion, to seduce a beloved, to impress a friend. With some gazels the occasional nature is obvious: they are about a holiday, or the New Year celebration, or autumn, or spring, or a snowfall, or a party, or a particular beloved boy. But with others it is not—in part because the medium in which they are transmitted (the divan) seldom does more than preserve the ideal relation of any single gazel to an undifferentiated and overdetermined Arabic-to-Persian-to-Turkish-and-Urdu tradition of poems about festivals, New Years, parties, seasons, weather, beloveds, patrons, and so on.

It is crucial when looking at past literatures and cultures that we be aware of our own preconceptions and account for them. As modern people, we are accustomed to expect that many poems will be understood and presented in part with reference to the occasions of their writing, that we will find labels like "to his coy mistress" or be induced to speculate on such topics as who the "dark lady" and the "young man" of Shakespeare's sonnets might have been. More alien to us is the idea that a poet might want to have his or her poem remembered, not as a magnificent (unparalleled, the best possible) description of his beloved or something similar, but as the best demonstration ever that one has mastered the techniques of writing a love poem. Conversely, it is difficult for us to believe that a person so focused on technique and mastery could write a passionate love poem about a real person. But this is precisely what we want to suggest about Ottoman poetry: that the divan represents an illusion (that the techniques of poetry are universal, ideal, and eternal) and that Ottoman poetry is most interesting and, in a sense, universal when it is embedded and understood in the context of the raw complexity of Ottoman life.

There is a second level of considerations that impel an Ottoman poet toward an emphasis on the technical and self-referential aspects of poetry. The following is a description that applies well to early-modern Ottoman poetry production, a description that most experts on Ottoman culture could, we believe, readily accept: "Thus the [gazels] are witty, erotic and sophisticated poems which place great emphasis on style and invention. Apart from such technical flourish, the genre is also characterized by extreme self-consciousness as the [gazel] writers raid each other, copy each other, and continue each other's work in an ostentatious way, thereby establishing themselves as a group of poets who are instantly fashionable and instantly recognizable."[1]

The characteristics outlined here are precisely what a long tradition of Western critiques of Ottoman poetry—at least from E. J. W. Gibb's six-volume *History of Ottoman Poetry* (1900–1909) on—has taught us to understand as the "Oriental," or "Islamic," or "Oriental, Islamic, Perso-Ottoman" poetic mode.[2] The casual (and largely unconscious) racism and essentialism of this scholarly tradition aside, the gist of Gibb's and the Gibbians' message is that the Islamic East and the Christian West followed parallel paths, analogously tying their mutual Neoplatonism to the Bible and the Qur'an, respectively, until sometime in the fifteenth century, when the "Europeans" had a Renaissance and the "Muslims" did not. Since it is the Ottomans who show up as a major Middle Eastern literary power "sometime in the fifteenth century," it is easy to imagine who these non-reborn Muslim literary folk are. Put bluntly, it also seems obvious to us that both this traditional critique and the literary history that supports it are utter hogwash. To emphasize our point, we have played a little trick. The passage quoted at the end of the previous paragraph is from an article on Christopher Marlowe that describes the Elizabethan epyllion (little epic) and the school of poets who employed it, most famously Marlowe (in *Hero and Leander*) and Shakespeare (in *Venus and Adonis*). All we have done is replace the word *epyllion* with the word *gazel*.

Our point here is not so much to take a dig at what is perhaps the silliest literary-historical tradition on record as to suggest a serious point about Ottoman poetry. Georgia Brown goes on to say of the epyllion writers:

> The epyllion was developed in answer to the criticisms which had been leveled against poetry in the 1570s and 1580s. These attacked poetry on two

fronts: the moralists attacked the philosophical basis of literature and its pernicious, immoral effects on writers and readers, while those who were literature's friends often felt compelled to attack the poor quality of what was being produced. Gradually, through the pages of controversy and debate, a literary programme was discovered in response to criticism, and ways of improving the status and quality of English literature were defined. To a certain extent the critics of literature set the agenda for the 1590s and they were partly responsible for the twin focus on literary morality and literary technique which became a characteristic feature of the epyllion.[3]

Most striking to us about this statement are its parallels to what was happening among the Ottomans only a bit earlier. From the mid-sixteenth century on—at least following the execution of Süleyman's favorite, the grand vizier Ibrahim Pasha, in 1536, when the position of poets vis-à-vis the palace becomes more contested—attacks on poetry increase from the two poles mentioned by Brown. Poetry is always morally suspect and subject to attacks by defenders of the morality of the common people. In fact, as we mentioned in the previous chapter, the zahid is a commonplace among the cast of characters peopling Ottoman verse. What really counts, however, is not the existence of moralizers—they are always in evidence—but the effect that their moralizing has on powerful people who support poets. As was related in the previous chapter, in his 1581 *Counsel for Sultans*, Mustafa 'Ali cites, as one of the factors leading the Ottoman Empire to ruin, "the hypocritical parasites, the preachers of our time, who attack God's servants with all kinds of slander and gloating and abuse and insult them by way of interfering with their acts and words!" By attacking the "illustrious elite"[4] and, as we saw earlier, "attracting thousands upon thousands of simpleminded commoners to their gatherings," these preachers put pressure on the authorities to exhibit their own piety and save their own heads by cracking down on poetry and the associated life of wine, drugs, parties, and beloveds.

A good indicator of the Ottoman poets' reaction to this situation is found in the tezkire of Latifi. In his first rendition (dated A.H. 953 [1546 C.E.]), Latifi severely but succinctly criticizes the poets of his day for being unskilled and imitative (unoriginal), on the one hand, and inattentive to the moral, instructive purpose of "good" poetry, on the other. When he issued a new rendition of the biographies sometime around 1574, the criticism and moralizing sections were hugely expanded. He says, for example:

> However, as in the case of the poet *shaykhs* [poets of special mystical insight] of the past, the verses [of the moderns] ought to be possessed of double meanings and the union of opposites, and the intent and wish and heart's desire when speaking of wine and tavern, grape and glass, should

be the attractions of drunkenness with divine love and the wine worship of the glass of holy desire.

> [The poet] should not become so engrossed in poetry as to [allow it to] become an obstacle to eleemosynary deeds, and he should not neglect reading the Qur'an and [observing] the times of prayer. He also should not criticize or satirize those of asceticism and piety and praise the amusing and forbidden, thereby following the path of Satan.[5]

Taken as a whole, Latifi's criticisms are summed up by Philip Sidney when he says: "As I affirm that no learning is so good, as that which teacheth and moveth to virtue, and that none can teach and move thereto so much as poetry, then is the conclusion manifest that ink and paper cannot be to a more profitable purpose employed."[6] These are pious sentiments but, as both Latifi and Sir Philip knew well, hardly applicable to some of the most esteemed poetry of their day.

The apparent discrepancy between theory and practice is in large part explained by the politics of despotic/monarchical systems and the material conditions of those who make their living, even if just in part, writing poetry. Sydney and Latifi emphasize the aesthetic and moral virtues of poetry because poetry is under attack by moralists who command a large following among the rabble. Such attacks can make it unwise or unprofitable for the powerful to support poetry—even powerful despots cannot easily make war on their own people and are dependent to some extent on enlisting the cooperation of the masses. This situation is a clear threat to the livelihoods of courtiers and poets, who, as a result, tend to conceal the most transgressive elements of their poetry beneath a veil of rhetoric and appeals to tradition.[7] However, just because preachers and representatives of the literary establishment decry the immoralities of poetry and the powerful grow timid, poets do not suddenly become tame. As Brown points out, Marlowe departs, in his *Hero and Leander*, from his models in Ovid to engage in contemporary debates about poetry and affirm a distinctive (and unfettered) morality for the poetic imagination.[8] Beneath the simple love story and the effusive rhetoric and flights of poetic fancy are a series of digressions into forbidden avenues of sexuality, from the pavement in Venus's temple—

> There might you see the gods in sundrie shapes,
> Committing headdie ryots, incest, rapes[9]

—to the homoerotic seduction of Leander by Neptune, in which the sea god attempts to re-create Jove's abduction of the beautiful boy Ganymede. What we see in the English epyllia we also see in the Ottoman gazel. In the second half of the sixteenth century, Ottoman love poetry is under attack—from without and within. It is under attack, not because it is ornate, or inwardly, aesthetically focused, or too idealizing, or too unworldly, or overly Persianized (all of these being criticisms brought against it by modern Western literary historians), but because it is *far too* worldly.

Those of us who work with pre- and early-modern Middle Eastern literatures are accustomed to associating worldly or utilitarian motives—begging for things, or praising individuals, or complaining, or celebrating occasions—with the *kaside* (an occasional or panegyric poem in several movements) and an abstracted or spiritualized love with the gazel. However, in Ottoman poetry of the sixteenth century, such genre distinctions seem to blur. One might even say that seduction begins to overtake praise as an effective and acceptable way of gaining the support of the powerful and love comes to establish a pattern for understanding and talking about the emotional content of life. Among the points that we intend to examine in looking at poetry in relation to the Ottoman Age of Beloveds are the following:

> 1. During this period, it became unusually fashionable, especially among the Ottoman economic and intellectual elites (but not exclusively), to become more or less publicly enamored of beautiful young men, certain of whom became quite famous.
>
> 2. The gazel became the primary medium of communicating to and about these beloveds, and this became an important social function of the gazel.
>
> 3. Within this discursive regime, refined, seductive speech took on great power by being directly associated with actual desire at all levels, and the reading of *every* gazel, no matter how aestheticized or spiritual, was touched in some way by this power and association.
>
> 4. Thus, we can identify a network of mutually affecting relations in which Ottoman love poetry (gazel poetry for the most part) both scripts a large number of Ottoman social practices and is itself shaped by them.

Poems about Poetry

As we have already pointed out, it was not part of the literary tradition of the Ottomans to write extensive prose works on the criticism and practices of contemporary poetry. As we have seen and will see, there are many descriptive and critical passages about poetry to be found scattered here and there in biographical and historical works, but, as we have also pointed out, these are strongly influenced by political considerations, including the necessity of pleasing the patron for whom the work is intended. If we want to overhear the Ottomans talking among themselves with relatively little restraint about what poetry does and should do, a good place to look is in the poetry itself.

There are a number of Ottoman poems from the Age of Beloveds that we could call *poems about poetry*. In general, these poems have the redif *şi'r* (poetry) or *gazel*, which acts as a unifying and focusing element, producing the effect of a single subject, something unusual for Ottoman poetry. Let us begin with the example of a much-paralleled gazel on gazels by a poet called Nişani, who was most likely either the Mustafa Nişani from Bosnia who became Sultan Süleyman's *nişancı* (nishandjı, "royal signature inscriber") and died in 1568 or the Mehmet Nişani who was a *müderris* (canon law professor) and nişancı and died in 1541. In order to demonstrate how the rhyme and redif go, we will give the first few lines in Turkish (the rhyme is *-aze/a* and the redif *gazel*):[10]

Getürür hatır-ı dildara vefa taze gazel
Diyelüm şevk ile ol serv-i ser-efraza gazel

Şu'ara resmi durur midhat-i erbab-ı cemal
Eyüsi şa'irün oldur diye mümtaza gazel

The original gazel reminds the beloved
  of faithfulness
Then let us write our lyrics
  to that lofty cypress

To praise the beautiful
  is a poet's wont
Who best writes gazels
  writes only of the best

Who does not oppress his lovers
  is most beautiful
Who seeks perfection of his gifts,
  who reads and writes gazels

Words of love and constancy
  are words spoken well
A gazel on flirting and flightiness
  is a torment to the tongue

Praise him to the skies
  when he loving is and true
'Ware Nişani, write no gazels to him
  whose favors are but few[11]

It is a given in this poem that the gazel was meant to be written to and about beautiful young men. Its theme might be identified as "two kinds of beloveds." One of these beloveds is the best of beloveds—he is faithful, loving, refined and educated (he reads and writes gazels), and generous with his favors. The other is the worst—he flirts and flits from lover to lover; he is low-class (not of the "best") and uneducated or unliterary; he is dishonest and stingy with his favors; he torments his lovers and takes them for whatever he can get. We might even conclude that the one is good for love and companionship, the other for lust and sex. In any case, the gazel is obviously seen as one way for a person with poetic talent to attract a beloved. A couplet by the famous Mesihi (1470–1512) ends with a description of what the poet is doing when he writes:

> Mesihi writes poems in Turkish now, in Persian then
> It seems he aims to hunt that gazelle with gazels[12]

The Ottoman practice of writing *nazire* (parallel poems), which use the rhythm pattern, rhyme scheme, and key vocabulary of another poem competitively, provides us the opportunity to see what other poets would do with the idea of hunting beloveds with gazels as introduced by Nişani. For example, the poet Sani adds an idea that reminds one of both Zati's "poetic capital" and Mesihi's gazelles:

> The heart used poetry to bring that gazelle eye thigh-to-thigh
> The gazel is a wealth of capital to the boy-chasing reveler[13]

Sihri will pick up this theme in his parallel:

> And what if they all would spend the cash of their lives on my poems
> The gazel is a hoard of capital to the boy-chasing reveler[14]

And how is this capital spent? Well, it seems that some spend it profusely in the hunt for love. As Sani says:

> I sing the praises of my beloved whenever we chance to meet
> I recite a gazel to that impudent idol when I see him on the street[15]

Those of a more practical bent realized that it takes more than poems to land some beloveds. Sipahi (d. 1605) wrote:

> It takes gold and silver in hand to hunt the beauties
> Don't think a gazel capital enough for the boy-chasing reveler[16]

At least some of these beloveds seem to have been sophisticated consumers of high-culture poetry and could have been hunted with a good gazel. Zati has a collection of *letayif* (amusing anecdotes) about his own and others' adventures. In one of these he talks of a literate beloved and the practice of writing poems to attract such young men. The anecdote revolves about a couplet in which he makes a play on the Turkish verb *sormak*, which commonly means "to ask" but can also mean "to suck on":

> At one time there was a beloved called Muharrem who was respected among the people, union with whom was valued, who was a power in the province of beauty, whose lip was sweeter than sugar, and whose words were more tasty than honey. I rattled off the following couplet for him:
>
> If those sugar lips would ask how I am doing
> I'd answer, "First I would have to ask [suck on] you"
>
> When he heard it, he said, "What a pleasant couplet." I saw that he enjoyed poetry and said to him, "Muharrem Çelebi, how about if I compose a gazel for you?" He said, "As long as it's not a mishmash of other poems. It has to be an original conceit. The poems of today's poets are all a mishmash [i.e., couplets from an old poem slightly changed]." I responded, "Come, young sir, how else should we do it? It can't be done without mishmashing."[a] When that rosebud heard these words, he blushed like a rose while speaking like a nightingale and like a bud became closemouthed.[17]

The poems obviously addressed to actual beloveds appear to bear out the impression that some beloveds were a discerning and sophisticated audience. In the couplet extemporized by Zati for Muharrem, the play on the verb *sormak* is certainly not lost on the beloved. One must assume that Zati's poems were sought after (and paid for) by lovers because beloveds liked them. Yet they are far from simple, as exemplified by the following, written in honor of a beloved named Malik:

> That full moon began to speak in description of Malik
> Saying: In this Malik's heart there is brilliant speech [*kelam*]
>
> Diligently protect your heart with the panacea of respectful treatment
> Beware his changing, should such a hot-tempered one seem tame

[a] Here the poet is playing on the phrase *katma karma*, which we translate as "mishmash," referencing the idea of "getting together, embracing, etc."

> Come now, don't swear vainly [when] saying, "I feel compassion for you"
> Oh liberal lord, in the word *oath* [*kasem*] there is venom [*sem*], and it can do harm
>
> See his perfection [*kemal*], he passes his palm over my heart
> When that curl like a *lam* [the letter *l* (ل) in *kemal*] appears upside down to my eye
>
> It saw that the beloved's mouth and body are a cure for its woes
> So my heart devoted itself to him, Zati, and thus achieved its desire[18]

The anagrams on the letters of *Malik* (written *m, a, l, k*, in the Arabic script) in *kelam* (*k, l, a, m*, "speech") and *kemal* (*k, m, a, l*, "perfection") are relatively simple but demand both literacy and familiarity with the conventions of divan poetry. A less simple cleverness occurs in the final line, where the beloved's mouth and body are commonly represented by the round and small letter *mim* and the tall and straight letter *elif*. Together they spell the word for "cure" (*em = elif-mim*).

One might assume that the choice beloveds were those from the upper classes, young men whose relationships more resembled patronage than (sexual) love affairs. We must remember that, in Ottoman society and, especially, elite society, everybody scrounged for money, gifts, and jobs. And poets, many of whom were courtiers or would-be courtiers, scrounged as much as or more than most. In another of his anecdotes, Zati describes some of his own scrounging, in which he uses both the carrot and the stick:

> At one time I was in conversation with a brilliantly fetching youngster of noble birth. In the course of our companionable chat, I had let fall pleasantries of every description, and that lantern of the gathering of the spirit was quite aroused by these witticisms. On his back he wore a smoke-colored European caftan, and he said to me, "My lord Zati, this caftan is yours; come over tomorrow and get it from my room." I showed up the next morning, and he said, "It has been put away in a trunk for you, but no one is home, and my mother has the key. Don't trouble yourself to come back; I'll send a servant with it." "Lovely," I said and left. About a month passed, and I realized that he wasn't going to send the caftan. So I composed a couplet and dispatched it to him. As soon as he saw it he sent me the caftan's price. The couplet was this:
>
> Why bestir yourself so tardily in sending the cloak to us
> Had I been some donkey's dangle you'd clothe me without fuss[19]

Clever couplets with an up-your-butt theme were considered high humor among sixteenth-century Ottomans. Here, of course, the beloved is accused of allowing himself to be penetrated by every idiot, a bit of malicious gossip that, if made public in an amusing couplet by a famous poet, would make him a laughingstock and the talk of the town. The passage also reveals some of the complexity of Ottoman lover-beloved relations. The younger man is naturally the beloved and the one who is expected to be the passive partner. The older poet actively entertains him and amazes him with his wit and brilliance. The object of this seduction is, not sex, but a gift. In the case of a lower-class beloved or a less-refined seduction, the object would be sexual gratification for the lover, and any gifts would be given to the beloved as a gratuity or an inducement to comply. In eroticized patronage relations, however, when the beloved is more powerful, richer, and more highly placed, gifts are replaced by devotion and refined entertainment (*sohbet* [(intimate) conversation], poetry) and sexual gratification by material rewards of various kinds (a caftan, money, a job). Everybody did this, from the top on down. Even the sultan rewarded the pages of his palace school—the beloved boys of his court—on various occasions by having trays of coins scattered for them to scramble after.[20] This can be visualized as a system in which everybody scatters something and everybody scrambles after something.

We will take up the subject of conversation below, but first let us look at some more serious parallel poems about poetry by poets of a higher rank. We do not know which of these poems was the original to which the others are parallels, but let us begin with two gazels by Zati, who seems to rewrite or parallel his own poems quite often:

Vasf-ı la'l-i yar ile yar-ı şeker-güftar şi'r
Lafz-ı şeker-bar ile bir tatlu nazüg yar şi'r

By describing the beloved's ruby [lip]
 the poem becomes a sweet-spoken beloved
With sugar-bearing words
 the poem becomes a sweet, tender beloved

It is a subtle physician for the ills
 of lovers sick at heart
With sweet nourishment does the poem
 pleasantly provide a cure

Saying, "I know how it is with you
 so let me be merciful."

The beloved takes up my divan
>   but does not recite a poem

Oh fairy, were its page
>   made of salamander[b] feather
In homage I'd proffer the poem scroll
>   if it did not first ignite

I spoke a gazel, each couplet
>   an elegant beloved
And in all of them together
>   there was poetry

Magically, I brought together
>   fire and cotton in one place
"What is this?" I said, and the poem replied
>   "The heart is cotton, the paper flame."

Why should the tasteful currency dealer
>   not be attracted?
Oh Zati, the poem is a coffer
>   brimming with royal pearls

Vasf-ı envar-ı ruhunla matla'u'l-envar şi'r
Şerh-i esrar-ı lebünle mahzenü'l-esrar şi'r

By describing the illuminations of your cheek,
>   a poem becomes the *Dawn of Illuminations*
By commentary on the secrets of your lip
>   a poem becomes the *Treasury of Secrets*

Its opening couplet is a bejeweled crown
>   on its head
Thus does a poem of sweet behavior
>   imitate the monarchs

Whosoever sees its face
>   becomes like a speaking nightingale
For poetry is a flower bed filled with
>   roses of colorful meaning

With it the ruler of natural talent
>   conquers the dominion of eloquence

---

[b] In Ottoman poetic lore, the salamander is something between a bird and a winged dragonet. It is also associated with fire (it seems to burn without being consumed) and, hence, with the phoenix.

The poem is a jewel-encrusted sword
> that captures the land of the heart

It is a customer, oh moon, for the wise one's
> goods of union
The poem never does business
> with the tasteless and stupid

Let me say, longing for your lip,
> should you recite a poem,
Oh idol, it would bring the dead to life
> like the speech of Jesus

It is a serpent ever born
> of my magician's talent
The poem's a highwayman, oh Zati,
> that robs the wits of humankind[21]

It is obvious that these are poems in praise of poetry and the ability to produce poetry. What strikes us about them is their insistence on the *value* of poetry and the poet. There are pragmatic references to "business," a "customer," and a "currency dealer." The poem is also linked directly to the beloved; it *becomes* the beloved, with the beloved's mystical, magical powers. It can cure like a doctor or revive the dead like Jesus. It can cause the lover to spontaneously ignite like the mythic salamander. It can magically bring fire and a puff of cotton together without burning up the cotton; like Moses it can turn a staff into a serpent. It has all the powers of the monarch (the ultimate earthly beloved), symbolized by the bejeweled crown and the conquering sword. This is all put in context by reference to lines of ancient tradition and the Persian great masters of mystical poetry: Nizami of Ganja (1140–1202), a classical Persian author with Turkish connections whose mystical treatise *Mahzenü'l-esrar* (Treasury of secrets) consists of twenty discourses each illustrated by an anecdote, and Amir Husrev (1253–1325), another Persian-speaking poet of Turkish descent who wrote the *Matlaʻu'l-envar* (Dawn of illuminations) in India as a parallel to the *Treasury of Secrets*. Thus, the poem is elevated beyond the realm of worldly love and reminds the audience—an audience that always (potentially) includes a powerful patron and the sultan—that, no matter how down-to-earth the love of this moment might be, it is also always capable of guiding the lover toward immersion in love of the divine and eternal. There can be nothing more valuable, or noble, or spiritual than this. Nonetheless, since Zati made his living on gifts from the rich and powerful, he also found it advantageous to remind them what wonderful beloveds they were and how valuable the gift of a poem ought to be to them.

In this poem and its relatives, we see more clearly the Ottoman poet's defensive posture with regard to the moral status of poetry. Yes, there is a beloved to be seduced, but beyond this interpretation are transcendent spiritual and political ones. The politics of the court is never far from the poems of elite early-modern poets wherever they are.[22]

The idea of the poem as being for and about the beloved is picked up by two other poems in this cycle of parallels. One is by İshak [Iss-hak] Çelebi of Üsküb, who was born in the second half of the fifteenth century and died in 1538/39. In addition to being a well-known poet, İshak was a noted bon vivant and conversationalist in his youth and rose to high office as a müderris and, later, a kadi. His poem is as follows:

Yüzine bakmazdı almazdı ele dildar şi'r
Kendüye mihr ü mahabbet itmese izhar şi'r

The beloved would ne'er hold a poem
    nor look it in the face
Should it not reveal affection
    for him and love

Who looks in the mirror
    and his heart is not pure
Has no form, like a poem
    that makes no sense

The jeweler would not know the value
    of the word-jewel
Were poetry not the touchstone
    of the coin of adorned speech

Since excellence and grace
    tempered the April cloud
Poetry is become a royal pearl
    in the Red Sea of my talent

Who misprizes the value of verse
    will never possess a jewel
Though everyone knows a poem
    is but a pearl-bearing cloud

He has memorized *The Rose Garden*
    and learned to create verse
The rose bower's nightingale can speak
    poetry in any way

> The poem is a jasmine-cheeked, new-bearded,
>   matchless beauty
> Heart attracting, well formed,
>   sweet of speech and action
>
> No matter I renounce poetry time and again,
>   when I fall in love
> With a faint-mustached young lad, helpless
>   I must compose a poem
>
> Let me seal my speech with mention
>   of that beauty's holy book
> Oh İshak, beware, recite a poem
>   to no other beloved [23]

The other poem is by Fevri, who was a slave in his youth, captured by the Ottomans in Eastern Europe. He was educated by one of his masters and then freed, after which he became an avid student of Islamic law and rose to the rank of full professor in one of the best law schools of the day. Fevri's poem is as follows:

Olmasa ah-ı derunum gibi ateş-bar şi'r
Ahen-i kalb-i nigara eylemezdi kar şi'r

> If the poem were not ablaze
>   like the sigh deep within me
> It would have no effect
>   on the iron of the beloved's heart
>
> Oh, you with brows like a bow,
>   if its letter *'ayin* were not like your eye,
> The poem could not be a sight
>   for those of sublime vision
>
> Do not think them spots on its face
>   they are the bloody tears from its eye
> Ever does the poem weep blood for my state
>   when I am parted from you
>
> Is it any wonder that my divan
>   is a holy text for the masters of love
> The panegyric is a sixtieth part
>   and the poem a section of ten verses
>
> Each of Fevri's couplets
>   is a lovely new-bearded beloved

> On each one of whose hands
> are written poems[24]

İshak's poem contains many of the same themes that we see in Zati's poems, which is why it is difficult to tell who is paralleling whom, especially because the two poets are rough contemporaries. İshak points out that a poem is for influencing the beloved. He emphasizes that it is a thing of value, first by invoking the business of valuation (the jeweler, the touchstone), then by relating a poem to a pearl and the idea (current at the time) that pearls are created when oysters rise to the surface to take in raindrops, which they then convert. Then a venerable tradition of valued poetry is brought into play by mentioning the famed *Gülistan* (Rose garden) of Sa'di (d. 1292), one of the legendary classical Persian poets. Nonetheless, the beloved is always paramount, and all the abstractions seem to collapse into the moment when the poet sees a beautiful young man and helplessly utters verses despite his renunciation of poetry. Love in action cannot be rationalized or controlled.

Fevri's poem departs from both Zati's and İshak's in that it is shorter and addressed more directly to the beloved. It is also, from our perspective, a bit more arcane. The poem here is the analogue of a sigh, the exhalation of an internal fire that serves to melt the iron of the beloved's heart. The poem has an "eye" because the middle letter of the word şi'r is 'ayin, which in Arabic is both the name of the letter and the word for "eye." Also, when 'ayin appears medially, it looks like an eye. In the hyperemotional world of Ottoman love poetry, a lover's eye always weeps bloody tears, and, in this case, even the "eye" of the lover's poem weeps tears that fall on the page and form the dots that distinguish some of the Arabic-script letters.

The word şi'r (poetry) in Arabic script (*right to left*: shin, 'ayin, ra).

At first glance, Fevri's last two couplets might seem almost sacrilegious. They compare the poet's divan to the Qur'an, the longer kaside to a *hizb* (a sixtieth part of the Qur'an), and the love poem to an *'aşr* (a section of ten verses), most likely because one of the standard lengths of a gazel is five couplets or ten hemistiches. This raises a point that we mentioned in the previous chapter and will take up in some detail in chapter 11 below. For those Ottomans whose ideas were scripted by poetry, the relation between love, even very worldly and physical love, and what they perceived as the true/anagogic meaning of Muhammad's message was obvious and natural.

There was no contradiction, no hypocrisy, and no sacrilege in comparing profane and divine love.

Let us now move from poetic commentaries on poetry and return to poems written to particular beloveds. 'Aşık has a little anecdote about Zati and a bath boy named Ni'met (Blessing/Gift). We need to keep in mind that one of the duties of bath boys was to shave their customers. The anecdote and the poem that it introduces go like this:

> Once he was in love with a silver-bodied, quick-witted bath boy named Ni'met and with the razor of passion cut off attachments to everyone else. Over and over he would say, "He's done me a personal blessing (*ni'met-i zati*, which could also mean 'Zati's Ni'met')." He wrote a gazel about him:

There was a fetching barber boy
    whom they all called Ni'met
The beauty of his perfect form
    made us all bow our heads

That's his stony heart visible
    in his slender body
Don't think that lovely one
    binds a stone to his waist[c]

Like a bathhouse, the steam cloud
    of love wreaths my head
Is it any wonder my eyes flow
    with tears like a bath basin

Ever did we kiss his feet
    without troubling ourselves
Would that our faces could become
    floor mats in his bath

We are his anchorites
    bare of foot and head
It was he who stripped us,
    Oh Zati, he who shaved us[d,25]

Zati figures in a number of the stories about goings on in the world of poets, lovers, and beloveds. This is not only because he lived a long life but also be-

---

[c] A fasting dervish tied a stone to his belly to stave off the pangs of hunger.

[d] The most extreme dervishes went about scantily clad with their beards shaved off in defiance of normal Islamic customs.

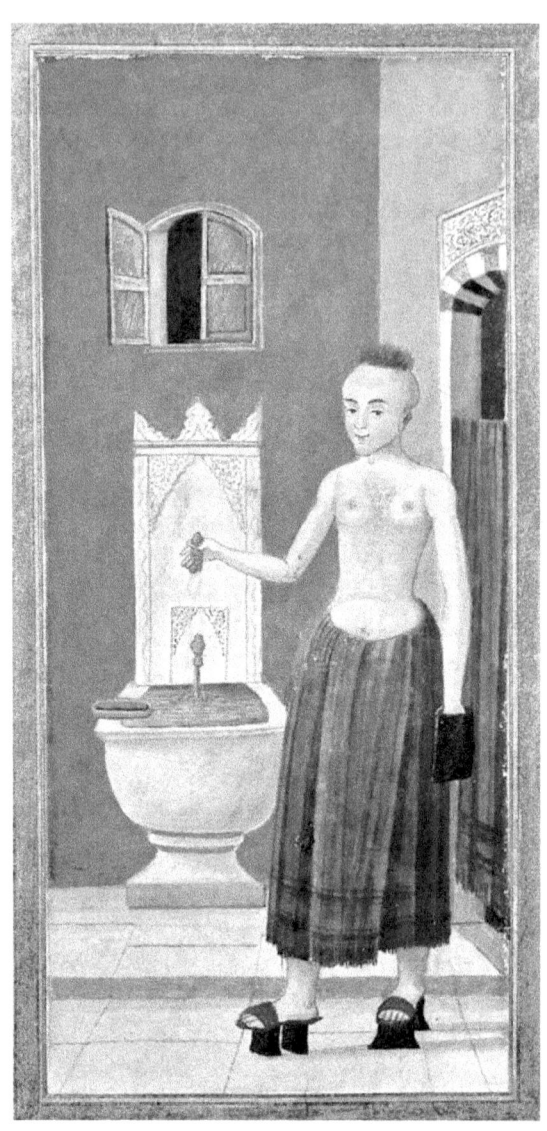

A beautiful bath boy. (Istanbul University Library, TY. 5502, Enderunlu Fazıl, "Hubānnāme-zenānnāme," fol. 175b.)

cause he was a master poet who lived by composing poetry and never took a job in the bureaucracy, as many other poets did. He was offered highly paid positions and turned them down, preferring to live off the gifts and favors that he received for his poetry from various patrons and those who benefited from his ghostwriting services. He established himself in a shop near the Hippodrome Square (At Meydanı), where he read fortunes in sand and conversed with the best poets of the day. From what we read about Zati and his activities, it appears certain that the culture of beloveds and love poetry was not confined to the palace, the homes and gardens of the elite, and the cloisters of the dervishes but was popular in the marketplace as well. 'Aşık says of him: "Some of the chief rakes among the young unattached [*şeh-levend*] artisans and those among the commoners who were famed for love and desire would, if they chanced to fall for a beloved, come to Zati and make him presents in either cash or the products of their trade. He in exchange would write a quatrain or a gazel according to the beloved's craft."[26]

There are many examples in Zati's divan of such poems, in some cases several versions of a poem, which might be the kind of "mishmashing" that the beloved Muharrem was talking about. The following is the beginning of one such poem addressed to a boy, a *ma'cuncu* (one who made a sweet medicinal [electuary] paste called *ma'cun*):

> Sitting thigh to thigh with a lovely *ma'cuncu*
>   I lose my mind
> My mouth waters at his peach
>   and I lose my mind
>
> I fear not Iskender Shah[e]
>   mid the dominion of this world
> But his doorway, worth all the world,
>   makes me lose my mind
>
> I am an exceeding strange *ma'cun*
>   in the mortar of this world
> The kiss of his mouth's vial
>   makes me lose my mind[27]

The poet and judge Vasfi, who is known as part of the literary circle patronized by Sultan Bayezit II's vizier 'Ali Pasha, has a poem about a young janissary named Memi (short for Mehmet) Shah in which there are clever references both to his sobriquet ("shah") and his occupation:

---

[e] This is Alexander/Iskender, the typal world conqueror.

Don't praise the sun or moon to me
>saying they are loved
No beauties of this world
>do I love but Memi Shah

If that moon face put on
>its cap of gold with love
The crown of the sun in the sky
>would seem too tight

Oh heart, don't think that you alone
>are fallen for him
He has stolen the wits of shah and beggar
>of officer and recruit

That shah is not unruly
>does not oppress his lover
Oh God, let the reign of his beauty
>last long and long

That shah is but a child yet
>If he kill his servant Vasfi
with the arrow of a glance
>let it be no sin[f],[28]

Poems addressed to specific beloveds were many. A popular beloved might have a large number of suitors, and the competition would run hot. For example, one collection of nazire gives (among others) fifty-six poems addressed to a beloved named Kaya. The first of these was by a late-sixteenth-century poet named Emani, who gives a good description of the qualities that are desirable in a beloved:

Oh fetching cypress, jasmine-breast flirt,
>my dear little Kaya
Oh new-sprouted child, fresh rose blossom,
>my dear little Kaya

Like the Tuba tree you walk, like the Sidre[g] stand,
>well constructed

---

[f] Children younger than the age of reason are not held accountable for crimes.

[g] Tuba is the lote tree of paradise (see Pala, *Sözlüğü*, 2:455; Onay, *Mazmunlar*, 417). Sidre is the heavenly cherry tree, which stands to the left of the throne of God and forms the boundary between paradise (the lower heavens) and the domain of God's pure essence (see Pala, *Sözlüğü*, 2:337).

Body, box-tree graceful, like a tall pine
> my dear little Kaya

Delicate waist, rosebud mouth,
> moist of lip

Merry laugh, fresh face, a new rose,
> my dear little Kaya

Head on stone I've beaten, stone on head,
> for your sake

Yet you didn't soften, oh heart of marble,
> my dear little Kaya

His head spinning, your stone threshold
> is enough for Emani

As mattress and pillow in the dust at your door,
> my dear little Kaya[29]

The competition for beloveds appears to have been fierce, and poems were often used as weapons in battles for attention. 'Aşık has a story about the scholar, poet, mystic, and translator of Persian poetry Lami'i, who seems to have been a spiritually minded, shy, and retiring person. Lami'i married early, and had a large family, but later in life was cajoled by some mischiefmaking friends into writing a poem that got him in a lot of trouble. As 'Aşık tells it:

> Near the end of his life, while he [Lami'i] was keeping himself busy with learning and worship, heart at ease, free of concern, composed of mind, and in comfortable circumstances, he wrote a gazel at the urging of some of his friends about a notorious young man called Tatar Memi. The first couplet went:
>
> His brows a bow, arrows his lashes, his glance a dagger
> In all the world is there a heart thief like Memi the Tatar?
>
> The beloved's lovers and admirers—especially the chief of his lovers, known by the name İsli 'Abdi—were incensed and tormented the late Lami'i with wild satires and vehement insults and wounded him with the stone of public reproach.[30]

For an unattached young man—a levend—chasing after beloveds was no real disgrace. As we have seen in the case of Tayyib and Tahir, it was expected that young men would lead a wild life. For an older man, however, public comment on his love life could be damaging. Lami'i was haunted to the grave by gossip and the barbs of his rivals.

Beloveds were also subject to vicious gossip and even the possibility of punishment for public lewdness. Moreover, it is clear that there was a range of beloveds, from sexually available equivalents of Venetian meretrici or courtesans, to handsome young men who had no desire whatsoever to be the focus of amorous attention. We will elaborate in a later chapter on how attention was dangerous for both lovers and beloveds. This is perhaps why few poems mention beloveds by name. As the janissary poet Yahya said in his poem about poetry:

> The poem holds the veil of script
> > over its face like Joseph
> This is its coquetry,
> > always to speak from behind a veil[31]

Poetry speaks in figurative language, both imitating and putting into words the lovers' language of gestures, glances, and emotions. Remember Selimi Musli's party and the beloved Turak Bali's reaction to Hayali revealing an attraction to him? "Because this had happened in such a company, the beloved, timid before those present and terrified by Hayali's effrontery, could not openly reveal what he felt. But, unable to content himself by communicating only with glances from a lowered head, with the knot of his curls and the curve of his brow, he spoke reproachfully, with the proud independence of the beloved, by a pouting of the lower lip and a trembling of the mouth."

Poetry and Cultured Conversation (Sohbet)

Simply speaking to (or about) a beloved, in both words and gestures, was an activity fraught with meaning for early-modern Ottomans. A form of social interaction fundamental to the society as a whole, and a central activity in the culture of beloveds as scripted by poetry, was what we would call *the party with sohbet*. *Party* in this case refers to any of a broad range of social gatherings — a dinner, or a soiree, or a garden party, or holiday festivities, or a wake, or a circumcision feast, or an outing in the country, or an evening at the coffeehouse, or a night at the tavern, or even an intimate tête-à-tête between lovers or friends. *Sohbet* is, as we have seen, commonly translated as "(intimate) conversation," but the translation does little to give people today an idea of how important conversation was and what it meant to people in early-modern times. Conversation of the sohbet type was a major source of pleasure and social bonding among people at all levels of society. In the circles of the educated elites, conversation implied wit, learning, mastery of a rhetorical style, and a general understanding of the poetic script for refined social interactions. The general outlines of that script might be sketched in as follows.

At the very least, sohbet requires two people: the lover/poet/person of learning and talent and a beloved. As the poet says:

> When the morsel of a kiss
> > and your lip's pure wine are here
> The time is right for sohbet, come!
> > all we need for a good time is here[32]
> —Revani

However, for true sohbet in the elite (and not-so-elite) culture of sixteenth-century Istanbul, more is needed, as we can see from the anecdote from Revani. There should be wine, a saki, dear friends, and music . . . even when the lover and the beloved are alone:

> Oh Necati, the wail plays music,
> > the tear serves wine, grief is a friend
> Come, for they have prepared
> > all we need for sohbet[33]
> —Necati

And the ideal setting is a garden, which is invoked even when a garden gathering is impossible:

> Whoever wants a party in the rose garden
> > let him have private sohbet
> With a beloved whose hair is a hyacinth,
> > whose face is a rose, lips a bud[34]
> —Revani

ʿAşık tells a story about the founding of a garden that came to be a favorite gathering place for intellectuals, poets, and lovers during early years of the reign of Süleyman the Magnificent. It involves a scholar called Sirkeci Bahşi who used to tell an amusing story about his retirement. According to Bahşi, during his younger days as a medrese student, he was constantly drunk and disorderly. On the night of 14 September 1510, he was drunk out of his mind at the medrese of the Mosque of the Conqueror (Mehmet II). In his words: "I was still sipping wine and throwing up when the earthquake hit." As the building shook, stone fell all about him, and the calamity destroyed the city, he climbed into the window niche and cowered there in terror. This was the Zelzele-i Sugra (the Lesser Quake), a major earthquake that destroyed large

Love Scripts II 107

parts of Istanbul. After this experience, he repented (somewhat) of his evil ways, gave up fruitless striving after power and position, and moved to Beşiktaş, which was then a village up the Bosphorus.

While he was a student and drinking to excess, Bahşi had acquired a taste for pickles, which the drinkers of the day snacked on just as today's drinkers snack on potato chips and pork rinds. He always had a couple of bowls of pickles in his rooms, where his drinking buddies would gather after a wild night to fight their hangovers with the sour snacks and the hair of the dog. So, when Bahşi gave up drinking, he turned to pickles in a serious way. In his Beşiktaş garden, one plot was devoted to fruits of all the sweet varieties, another to the sour, and yet another area to the vinegar factory from which his nickname, Sirkeci (Vinegar-Maker), came. He employed a number of 'acemi oğlans (slave pages and janissaries in training) and produced copious amounts of highly prized vinegar. The tavern keepers kept a supply of his vinegar and pickles on hand, their patrons praised him for having created a fermented drink permissible under the sharia, and, when the corsair captain Hayruddin (Barbarossa) became his neighbor in Beşiktaş, the Ottoman fleet would order barrels of his vinegar to stock their ships. Those who were dry mouthed from taking drugs—opium and *berş* (a combination drug of some sort)—would breakfast on his sweet and moist fruits, the heavy drinkers would fight hangovers with his pickles, and women would buy abundant beet and cucumber pickles for meals. Bahşi thus made a fortune.

On holidays, Bahşi's garden became a gathering place for a select group of the ulema (the learned establishment) and the choicest of beloveds. In 'Aşık's words:

> On holidays his garden was a place of pleasant conversation for the ulema and at other times a venue for pleasant companionship on the part of the most witty among the pillars of the community, the revelers among the wise, and the poet-scholars. All the mean and despicable were kept far from the skirts of this rose garden like the evil eye, and the common and ignorant were exiled from this meadow gathering like the envious gaze. But he was so pleased by a fetching countenance and anyone who possessed a share of beauty that, if a beloved appeared among the masters of sohbet, he would greet him with great solicitousness, sweeping the path before him with his white beard, and sprinkling the ground with his tears of joy until he had painted the earth at his feet with the color of his blood-scattering tears so that no wind would blow dust on him. Thus would his hue and cry make the seas reverberate and his song of desire still the host of nightingales in his garden. He would become intoxicated without drinking wine and drugged without eating opium. Now he would dance with joy and then play the harp; now, white beard that he was, he would serve coffee and then

become a bard telling tales and priceless anecdotes. He greatly loved coffee and would say that it was a thousand times better than wine. As he grew old he became envious of the young, as the hemistich says: *As death approaches, oh my heart, would you were a youth.*[35]

Because the gathering and its conversation are intimate and often erotic, it is a place for those who affirm and trust one another. Its "inside" is defined by an "outside" full of people who would prevent, disapprove, gossip, or misunderstand, not to mention "the mean and despicable" and "the common and ignorant." In the story of Tayyib and Tahir, we saw what kind of trouble disapproving gossip can cause for lovers and close friends. The story of Selimi Musli's party mentions the *rakib* (guardian) "crude, misshapen, and tall" who "stood watch at the door," hiding the beloveds "like the sun of heaven behind a dark cloud." The role of the rakib seems to be filled at various times by a number of people—a neighborhood tough, a protective relative, a rival in love, or, in this case, what seems to be a bouncer or guard who keeps the beloveds at the party from being (overly) harassed by intoxicated lovers. In addition, there are several other classes of people who are a danger to the gathering, among them religious precisians who find the gathering's activities (wine, music, love) to be immoral, those who find it unhealthy, even strangers or outsiders, who are often just people who do not understand the true meaning of what the lovers do:

> Saying he is a stranger
> > come to the meadow from the country
> They wouldn't let the wild poppy
> > into the rose season sohbet[36]
> —Necati

In the proper setting, with the right people gathered and the right people excluded, what happens is typical Ottoman sohbet. It is, on the one hand, witty and entertaining party conversation—but conversation at many levels and with many elements. There is flirtatious conversation with the beloved and talk about the beloved among the close friends. There are the production and recitation of poetry about the party and all its elements. There is a highly ambiguous conversation consisting of hints, allusions, glances, gestures, smiles, and frowns. And there are amusing anecdotes, which, like the poetry, can have the gathering as a topic and be part of the pleasures of the gathering. Thus, sohbet is also a more general kind of companionship (in the more ancient sense of the term) and includes all the things that go along with conversation.[37]

It seems impossible to overstate the degree to which the gathering/party/

sohbet was institutionalized down to the minutest details and how important it was to the participants. Even in an age when wild hyperbole was the fashion, it is difficult to entirely discount the impassioned revelations of poets:

> I stay awake the whole night long and cry 'til morn
> I'll die, for like a candle, I can't survive without sohbet[38]
> —Necati
>
> Neither garden walks for me nor the gathering with wine
> I'll die if separated from sohbet with my beloved[39]
> —Revani

Moreover, there are numerous indications that also speak to the popularity and importance of sohbet, which is tangential to the realm of poetry, in which it is most clearly institutionalized. The sultans maintained small, carefully chosen circles of multitalented companions called *musahibs* (the people with whom one carries on sohbet) who provided congenial company for times of leisure. Subgroups of such companions, including candidates being tested before inclusion in the main group, would even accompany the ruler on campaign. There is a well-known story touching on this practice about the noted legal scholar and poet İshak, whose poem on poetry we saw above.[40]

In his more naive days, İshak and his two best friends and drinking companions, Nihali Ca'fer Çelebi, kadi of Galata, and Bald Bezen, kadi of Mihaliç, being noted wits and intellectuals, were invited by Sultan Selim I (r. 1512–20) to accompany him during his sojourn in Aleppo on the way back from campaigning in the Arab provinces. Excited by the prospect, the three scholar-poets decked themselves out in unfamiliar weapons of war and made the arduous journey to the sultan's encampment. This was obviously a test to see which of the three would make good musahibs, so they had sought or were given gratis the advice of the incumbent professional companions at court. The sultan, they were told in all seriousness, likes to relax with people who carry the conversation and keep things moving along with nonstop jests, raillery, and risqué humor. So the nervous and decidedly unsoldierly would-be royal companions first committed the serious faux pas of bumbling into the ruler's presence still wearing their swords, an offense that could have seen them killed by the sultan's personal guards. Then, when it was time for relaxation and conversation, they set about to amuse the sultan by acting the fool, chattering like monkeys, and engaging in all sort of buffoonery, just as had been suggested to them. In fact, as the reigning companions knew quite well, the sultan was a serious sort who liked a good listener and a thoughtful and intelligent response. Moreover, he was inclined to be offended by foolishness and off-color humor. In the end, the outraged sultan just barely restrained himself from executing the unfortunate neophytes with his own sword and, instead, sent them packing with minimal travel expenses and insultingly small gifts. The position of conversational companion to the ruler was one of power and importance, and those who held such positions were inclined to defend them at all costs.

The greats of the empire had similar sohbet circles, circles that, like the sultan's, were also the source of substantial benefit to participants. In fact, sohbet circles often appear to correspond closely to what the Ottomans called *intisab* networks, connections of social, political, and economic patronage.

Today we have largely lost the notion that conversation (in the sense both of talk and of companionship) is itself a major art form, the mark of an intelligent and educated person, a primary form of social interaction and entertainment, a key to love, friendship, and success in life. In the sixteenth century, it was these things, not just in the Ottoman Empire, but everywhere in Europe and the East. For example, what distinguished the "honorable" courtesans of Venice and Rome from their prostitute sisters in the streets was largely a highly developed skill in the multiple arts of conversation. The English traveler Thomas Coryat described the courtesan's conversational abilities with his usual tone of prudish disapproval: "Moreover shee will endevour to enchaunt thee partly with her melodious notes that shee warbles out upon her lute, which shee fingers with as laudable a stroake as many men that are excellent professors in the noble science of Musicke; and partly with that heart-tempting harmony of her voice. Also thou wilt finde the Venetian Courtezan (if she be a selected woman indeede) a good Rhetoritician, and a most elegant discourser, so that if shee cannot move thee with all these foresaid delights, shee will assay thy constancy with her Rhetoricall tongue."[41] The "Rhetoricall tongue" used in the service of elegant conversation is presented as a sore temptation, one ranking right up there with more physical blandishments.

When the French essayist Montaigne made a journey through Italy in 1580–81, he was pained by a lack of cultured women with whom to have entertaining conversation. He says of available entertainments that, in addition to visiting beautiful gardens and vineyards (how like the Ottomans he is in this!), one can hear theological sermons and discussions and visit "some women of the public sort, where I found this drawback, that they will sell their simple conversation (which was what I wanted, to hear them talk and share in their witticisms), and are as chary of it as of the whole business."[42]

In *The Book of the Courtier*, one of Castiglione's master conversationalists says of the requirements of the consummate courtier:

> But in the end all these qualities in our Courtier will still not suffice to win him universal favor with lords and cavaliers and ladies unless he have also

a gentle and pleasing manner in his daily conversation. And truly, I think it difficult to give any rule in this, because of the infinite variety of things that can come up in conversation, and because among all men on earth, no two are found that have minds totally alike. Hence, whoever has to engage in conversation with others must let himself be guided by his own judgment and must perceive the differences between one man and another, and change his style and method from day to day, according to the nature of the person with whom he undertakes to converse.[43]

In fact, a major portion of *The Book of the Courtier* is taken up by discussion of the elements of brilliant conversation—pleasantry, witticism, rhetoric, and the like—and the impact of conversation on beloveds of various kinds, from patrons to lovers. In milieus, including that of the Ottoman elites, where, not only sexual/erotic relations, but social and political relations as well are imagined in the language of love, clever speech becomes a primary tool in the multiple "seductions" that occur up and down the hierarchy. And clever speech is most strikingly demonstrated by the language of poetry.[44] Although we will touch on the relations among love, poetry, and courtliness, work on Ottoman courtliness is only in its infancy and lacks the kind of organizing and theorizing work that Daniel Javich has done for English Renaissance courtliness.[45] At this point, we can only suggest directions for further study and point out that, while it is true for the Ottomans that, as Ann Rosalind Jones and Peter Stallybrass point out about early-modern England, the "supposedly 'private' sphere of love can be imagined only through its similarities and dissimilarities to the public world of the court,"[46] the reverse is equally as true: interactions among the elite and at court can be imagined only through a script provided by poetry and the private world of love.

5

LOVE, SEX, AND POETRY

When we read about the past, especially the more recent past (which the early-modern period is), we generally assume, without thinking much, that people then thought about basic things much as we do now, except that they did not have television, automobiles, airplanes, and computers. Yet, the deeper we look, the more surprising differences emerge, and those past people gradually begin to appear quite alien to us, with attitudes, motivations, behaviors, and moral and spiritual positions that we find difficult to understand or approve. All of a sudden, where we expected a more or less smooth transition between our ancestors (the "us" of the past) and ourselves (the "us" of the present), we encounter a huge chasm. And nowhere does this chasm seem more unbridgeable than in the areas of sexuality and the deployment of desire.

Talking about sex and sexuality is always fraught with danger and carries a large potential for misunderstanding. Talking of such things over chasms of time and culture is far more dangerous. If we are less than frank, we risk misleading our audiences. If we are frank and open, we risk offending some or many of the same audiences. It is our position, however, that, as scholars, we do much better to offend than to mislead. So let this be a gentle warning to those who feel uncomfortable with explicit discussions of sex and sexuality: in this chapter we will be touching on, among other things, explicit sexual behaviors, pornographic literature, jokes, puns, and sexual insults that many will certainly find offensive.

We are most anxious to avoid the pitfall of focusing on the sexuality of Ottoman literate elites and allowing it to appear either as representative of the sexuality of all Ottoman subjects or as something vastly different from what was common in the rest of Europe and the Mediterranean world. For this reason, we will give a general idea about some of the currents of sexuality and sexual behavior that flowed through Europe in the early-modern period before saying anything much about sexuality among the Ottomans in particular. It should not surprise our readers if, in the end, they begin to feel that the early-modern Ottomans and the early-modern Europeans were much more like one another than either group was like us today.

We must mention at the outset that it is quite a bit easier to speak with confidence about issues of sex and sexuality in Europe of the fifteenth century, the sixteenth, and the early seventeenth than it is to do the same for the Ottoman Empire, even for the very limited portion of the Ottoman Empire about which we will be talking. Where there are precious few scholarly studies that even touch on Ottoman love, sex, and sexuality, when it comes to such issues in the European context, there are thousands of articles and books by scholars in literary studies, gender studies, women's studies, gay and lesbian studies, sex and sexuality studies, history, sociology, psychology, and on and on. In fact, the greatest difficulty that we encountered in treating Western sources was choosing a few illustrative examples from among so many and deciding what interesting and informative material to leave out of our discussion. In the end, we have chosen to present a digest or review of material in a narrative that traces the trajectory of our own thinking about the Age of Beloveds. We wish to emphasize, therefore, the arbitrary nature of our choices. We could certainly, and with good reason, have chosen to use other countries as primary examples of conditions obtaining in Europe: why not, for example, Spain or France? or Germany or Holland? or even Scandinavia? What it comes down to in the end is that we could not do everything and settled for limited goals and a manageable first step.

Venice

Our journey of discovery began with an article that we were invited to write on the Ottoman Turkish gazel, an article that would end up being entitled "Gazels and the World." Our intent was to present an argument against the notion that Ottoman love poetry had nothing much to do with actual love, that it was valued only as either an aesthetic exercise or a spiritual/religious metaphor.[1] In the course of our research, it became evident that there was a pressing need to write even more extensively about the culture of beloveds that flourished in Istanbul and other urban centers of the empire during the long sixteenth century. Among the questions that came to mind as we began to study the topic were, What was going on elsewhere? and, Did any of this have relevance to what was happening in the Ottoman Empire? Or, more precisely, can we learn anything by *contrasting* Ottomans and Europeans? We began looking for answers in Venice.

The choice of Venice as a starting place might not seem obvious, but, during the period of interest to us, Venice and Istanbul often appear to be mirror images of one another. They are similarly opulent, successful, and powerful; they are imperialistic centers of political and spiritual power; they are both enemies and trading partners. The capitals of both are even adorned with appropriated monuments of ancient Byzantium. The noble sons of Venice often apprenticed in trading and diplomatic positions in Istanbul. As we have seen, the doge Andrea Gritti, who ruled Venice from 1523 to 1538, spent several years in Istanbul and, while there, fathered four illegitimate sons, one of whom, Alvise Gritti, became a wealthy jewel merchant in Istanbul and a regular in the cultural circle of Sultan Süleyman's boyhood companion, favorite, and grand vizier Ibrahim Pasha.[2] The *fondachi* (customhouses, or warehouse-hostels for merchants; sg. *fondaco*) of Venice thronged with Turkish merchants.

There are two interesting articles in a list of rules drawn up by the Venetian government in 1621 for the Fondaco dei Turchi, a fondaco for Turkish merchants established in a former dwelling of the duke of Ferrara on the Grand Canal. Articles 28 and 31, respectively, state:

> The said doorkeepers shall not allow either women or beardless persons [young boys] who may be Christians to enter the exchange house at any time, on pain of fitting punishment.
>
> Turks who are now in this city, and those who shall in future come to it, must go to live in the exchange house in full conformity with the decrees of the Senate and with that of the Collegio of 2 March last. Nobody, therefore, even if he is a broker [to the Turks], may give lodgings to Turks in contravention of the said legislation on any pretext whatsoever, on pain of those fines or corporal punishments that may be deemed appropriate by the magistrates. If any brokers infringe on these regulations, they shall be immediately deprived of their posts.

These would seem to indicate a concern to limit sexual relations between Turkish Muslims and Christians, possibly Christian prostitutes of both genders. Likewise, there is an attempt to legislate against the practice of Venetian brokers entertaining and lodging Turkish merchants in their homes. It is most likely that these rules were a response to existing relations (sexual and business) between Turks and Venetians. However, lest we think that they were especially discriminatory in singling out Muslims, we should note that they represent only a quite belated extension of rules applied to German merchants since early in the sixteenth century.³

In Venice, as in Istanbul, the sixteenth century was an age of beloveds. The tragedy of the wars of the League of Cambrai was a thing of the past. As a result of the sack of Rome by Charles VI in 1527, the culture of the *cortegiane oneste* (honest courtesans; sg. *cortegiana onesta*), which had flourished during the late fifteenth century and the early sixteenth at the papal court, shifted its center to Venice.

At the dawn of the sixteenth century, a wealthy and powerful papacy in Rome had assembled a vast entourage of celibate ecclesiastical bureaucrats and an extensive fringe of merchants, bankers, and courtiers of various stripes, drawing predators who targeted them all. The Rome of that time was largely a city of men, men who supported a thriving subculture of prostitution, at the apex of which were the beautiful, cultured, and often wealthy cortegiane oneste, who became the topics of literature, the models for art, the goddesses and mistresses of rich and powerful lords of commerce and church. Below them was the mass of common prostitutes, pimps, and procuresses. The most reasonable sources guess that, at one time, a tenth of the population of Rome was engaged in what might be called *the sex industry*.⁴

This was a sex industry employed at all levels. Johann Burchard, Vatican master of ceremonies during the reign of the Borgia pope, Alexander VI, described a party put on by Cesare Borgia for the wedding of Lucrezia Borgia and Alfonso d'Este in 1502:

> On Sunday Evening, October 30th, Don Cesare Borgia gave a supper in his apartment in the apostolic palace, with fifty decent prostitutes or courtesans in attendance, who after the meal danced with the servants and others there, first fully dressed and then naked. Following the supper too, lampstands holding lighted candles were placed on the floor and chestnuts strewn about, which the prostitutes, naked and on their hands and knees, had to pick up as they crawled in and out among the lampstands. The Pope, Don Cesare and Donna Lucrezia were all present to watch. Finally, prizes were offered—silken doublets, pairs of shoes, hats, and other garments—for those men who were most successful with the prostitutes.⁵

Rome continued to support a large population of prostitutes throughout the sixteenth century, but, after the disaster of 1527, Venice became the home of the most brilliant of the courtesans and the site of a sex industry that was famed throughout Europe. Shakespeare's Don Pedro makes a reference that his audience was expected to pick up on immediately: "Nay, if Cupid have not spent all his quiver in Venice, thou wilt quake for this shortly" (*Much Ado about Nothing*, act 1, sc. 1, lines 273–74). He means to say that, if all the (sexual) love in the world has not been expended in Venice, then Benedick (to whom he is speaking) will also fall in love soon.

Although contemporary estimates of the number of prostitutes in Venice range from the Venetian Marin Sanuto's perhaps deceptively precise 11,654 to the Englishman Thomas Coryat's 20,000,[6] again a more reasonable number appears to be the one out of ten inhabitants estimated for Rome. Even taking into account the fact that many urban centers in Renaissance Europe were heavily male—in part because of large numbers of men recruited to restore populations severely depleted by the plagues of the fourteenth and fifteenth centuries, and in part because of traveling merchants and sailors, soldiers, celibate clergy, and the like—and discounting even the lowest estimates, the numbers of prostitutes at every level in major cities are still huge and point to a conclusion that every source seems to bear out: what we call *the Age of Beloveds* was everywhere in Europe a time of almost frenzied sexual activity, to a degree that would boggle the minds of most people today.

Questions about the sexual culture of Venice and Venetian courtesans inevitably led us to Guido Ruggiero's cogently titled *The Boundaries of Eros*, a fascinating, seminal study of the sexual culture of Venice based on extensive research on court cases. In the course of discussing the seeming contradictions between very conservative and restrictive laws governing sexual behavior and an accepted culture of illicit sex, Ruggiero makes the following general remarks:

> But being the other, the outsider, this culture of illicit sexuality still developed its own defining characteristics, and one reason it is such a potentially rich concept is that with time it would gain a certain focus and become a major aspect of the general civilization of the West. From the Renaissance, parallel to the family and its Christian-based culture, another culture has developed, that of the mistress, the prostitute, the libertine, of rape, adultery, and fornication; of words with double meaning, obscene language, and pornography; of Aretino, Madame de Chatelet, and the marquis de Sade; of the exploitation of women and men, mad passions and gentler ones. This is not to argue that a culture of illicit sexuality was unheard of before the Renaissance or created in Venice, but rather to suggest that the specific forms of that culture which typify what might be seen as a modern Western tradition began to come together during the period and may be identified early on in the sexual history of Venice, a city that was to become famed for its illicit pleasure.[7]

Such questions also led us to Margaret Rosenthal's *Honest Courtesan*, a magnificent study of the life and poetry of the courtesan Veronica Franco. This book was a revelation. Rosenthal demonstrates convincingly that, in

Venice, the lives of the cortegiane oneste were bound to far more than the sex industry, that the courtesan was a social phenomenon closely (one might even say intimately) bound to the life of Renaissance high-culture literature, art, and music.

Like most women of the impoverished elites, Veronica Franco grew up with very limited choices. Because her family lacked the resources with which to provide her a substantial dowry, she could not expect to marry within her class and was faced with either the convent or prostitution. Her mother, who might have been a cortegiana onesta herself, trained the young Veronica for a career in high-class prostitution and acted as her procurer. The skills of the courtesan were many and varied—music, literature, rhetoric, and witty conversation. The courtesan was the public face of women engaged in the social arts of men. Franco herself summed up some of what it took to succeed as a courtesan in a letter to an ambitious (or desperate) mother who contemplated making a courtesan of her rather ordinary daughter:

> And if we are to further consider this matter from a carnal point of view, she really is not very beautiful, to say the least, because my eyes do not deceive me, and her conversation is so lacking in grace and wit that you will break her neck if you think that she can do well in the profession of the courtesan, in which success is hard to come by, even for those who are beautiful, charming, and wise and are proficient in many skills; so just imagine a young woman who lacks many of these qualities and is no better than mediocre in others.[8]

Veronica Franco herself had a highly successful career, with patrons among the most powerful men of the Venetian aristocracy. There was even a famous encounter with the young Henri III of Valois during a stopover on his journey from Poland to France, where he was to assume the throne in 1574. After a gondola tour of Venice and a dinner hosted by the duke of Ferrara—interestingly enough at the palace that would later become the Fondaco dei Turchi—the prince did not return home that night, and all indications are that he spent the night with Franco. Beyond her fame as a professional beloved, however, Franco also distinguished herself as a powerful and acclaimed poet, an accomplishment that won her both admirers and the enmity of some leading literary figures of the time, to whom her success represented, not just professional competition, but a more subtle challenge to the accepted canons of poetry.

The shadow of Petrarch's classicism in the Tuscan dialect stretched far and wide over the poetry of Venice, an influence perpetuated into the sixteenth century by Pietro Bembo's influential 1525 treatise on the rules of rhetoric, the *Prose della vulgar lingua*. When the literary courtesan and the female poet interrupted the private conversation of male Petrarchan poets about ethereal beloveds patterned on the likes of Petrarch's Laura or Dante's Beatrice, a dramatic change occurred.[9] All of a sudden, the beloved had a real name and face; she had her own voice and an inescapable sexual presence. In her, the world, actual love, and actual sex were returned to poetry. Rules by which a patron could judge a talented courtier and by which a talented courtier could be assured of producing an acceptable product were cast in doubt, and livelihoods were endangered. It is no wonder that the courtesan poet aroused angry and virulent responses.[10]

The impact of the courtesan beloved on the elite poetry and its social context in Venice evoked for us striking parallels to the impact of the urban beloveds on the poetry and society of the Ottoman elites. Just as Venetian poetry in the sixteenth century was heavily influenced by Petrarch and Dante, Ottoman poetry of the same era was rooted in Persian paragons and models and was always in danger of being swallowed up by a sterile, vulgar (Turkish rather than Persian) classicism. Yet, during this time, Ottoman poetry underwent a renaissance of its own, and, similar to what we described above in the case of Venice, actual beloveds became both the subjects and the authors of Ottoman poetry, infusing it with an immediacy and a sexual tension that gave it new life and power and separated it from its Persian models. It appeared to us that the parallels broke down only when we considered the gender of the beloveds. As we saw in previous chapters, Ottoman poetry was unabashedly homoerotic and Ottoman elite society largely tolerant of romantic and sexual contact between males. The situation in Venice seemed to us quite different.

Venetian poetry appears to be obviously and resolutely heteroerotic. In Venetian society, although female prostitution was generally tolerated and even officially regulated and taxed in Venice, Venetian officials, from the late fourteenth century on, promulgated increasingly numerous laws against sodomy, proscribing harsh penalties including branding, beating, and burning alive.[11] From a religious point of view, prostitution was seen as "hurtful" to God, but it was also seen as a legitimate (if deplorable) way to release the sexual tensions of unmarried young men and reduce the likelihood of assaults on respectable women. Sodomy, however, was considered an unforgivable affront to God and a sure invitation to his wrath, which had unequivocally manifested itself in the destruction of Sodom and Gomorrah. One would suppose—as we did initially—that, under such circumstances, a significant subculture of homoerotic and homosexual practices could not have grown up in Venice of the sixteenth century as it had in the urban centers of the Ottoman Empire. In this we were mistaken.

There are, in fact, numerous indications that the Venetian inclination to legislate sodomy out of existence stemmed from the increasing visibility of homoerotic and homosexual practices in Venice during the late fifteenth century and the early sixteenth. For example, a decree published by the Council of Ten in 1480 demonstrates a peculiar concern with women's hairstyles:

> The coiffure [*habitus capitis*] which Venetian women have recently taken to wearing could not be more indecent in the sight of God and men, since by means of this coiffure women conceal their sex and strive to please men by pretending to be men, which is a form of sodomy; and therefore
> BE IT DETERMINED that by the authority of this Council and the Heads of the Ten or at least two of them shall go to our Lord Patriarch and persuade him, by means of the confessors and also through an edict to be published in all the parishes, to prohibit the hairstyle [*gestamen capillorum*] which women adopt, and which they call a "mushroom" [*fungus*], and which hides the forehead; and to order the hair to be drawn and tied back behind the head, and the forehead and face to be made free of it, that they may be seen to be women, just as God made them and as was their custom before the present corrupted age: all this on pain of excommunication.

In 1509, the diarist Priuli had harsh words for the practices of some Venetian youths:

> I have yet to speak of another wicked and pernicious vice, which was widely practised and highly esteemed in this city, and this was the unnatural vice called sodomy, for which, as we read in ancient writings, the great God sent down fire upon the two cities so notorious to all. This vice was openly practiced in Venice without shame; indeed, it had become so habitual that it was more highly regarded than having to do with one's own wife. Young Venetian nobles and citizens tricked themselves out with so many ornaments, and with garments that opened to show the chest, and with so many perfumes, that there was no indecency in the world to compare with the frippery and finery of Venetian youth and their provocative acts of luxury and venery. Truly they may be called not youths, but women. . . . By the power of money these [young people] turned from men into women, and now that after this disaster [the defeat at Agnadello] money must needs be in short supply they will do far worse things in their desire to obtain it, for they have been brought up to expect these lascivious refinements which one cannot have without money and they cannot resist such things.

Priuli went on to say that those who had grown up with sodomy could be counted among the patricians and senators, many of whom were known to be addicted to the practice even to the extent of becoming the passive partners in male same-sex intercourse. He added: "However, the vice had now become so much a habit and so familiar to everyone, and it was so openly discussed throughout the city, that there came a time when it was so commonplace that no one said anything about it any more, and it neither deserved nor received any punishment—except for some poor wretch who had no money, no favours, no friends and no relations: justice was done on people like that, and not on those who had power and money and reputation, and yet committed worse crimes."[12]

As universal as sexual or sexualized relations between men were during the Renaissance, condemnations and severe repressions of the practice commonly followed disasters, both natural and man-made. The underlying theme of Priuli's railings against sodomy is that the League of Cambrai's devastating defeat of Venice at Agnadello may have been a sign of God's wrath against a city that had been permissive toward the unforgivable sin.[13] The early moderns believed that all disasters—whether earthquakes, plagues, floods, or military defeats—were examples of God chastising humankind for disobeying divine law.

What to make of all this? Frankly, we weren't sure—until we came across Ruggiero's discussion of the prosecution of homosexuals in Venice during the fourteenth and fifteenth centuries, during the course of which he says: "In this context it is interesting to note that several of these early large cases had a Florentine connection. Was the city of the lily exporting more in its humanism than republican values and a civic culture?"[14] And, thus, our gaze was turned toward Florence.

Florence

One day in the mid-sixteenth century, the master goldsmith and sculptor Benvenuto Cellini was amusing Cosimo I, the duke of Florence, by pointing out to his fellow sculptor Baccio Bandinelli and the assembled courtiers the numerous flaws and crude aspects in the hapless Bandinelli's portrayal of Hercules killing Cacus. According to Cellini's autobiography, the enraged Bandinelli finally could stand it no longer and spat out what must have been the first insult that came to mind: "Oh, keep quiet you dirty sodomite!" As Cellini tells it:

> At that word the Duke frowned angrily, and the others tightened their lips and stared hard at him. In the face of this wicked insult I choked with fury, but instantly found the right answer and said:
> "You madman, you're going too far. But I wish to God I did know how to indulge in such a noble practice: after all we read that Jove enjoyed it with

> Ganymede in paradise, and here on earth it is the practice of the greatest emperors and the greatest kings of the world. I'm an insignificant, humble man, I haven't the means or the knowledge to meddle in such a marvelous matter.[15]

Of course, Cellini was neither insignificant nor humble, and he was certainly better acquainted with the "noble practice" than he ever lets on in his autobiography. In fact, he was twice convicted of sodomy in Florence, first in 1523, then again much later in 1557. In this, he had considerable company. By Cellini's time, Florence had long been renowned for sodomy, which accounts for the reaction of the assembled nobility. As Michael Rocke points out in his *Forbidden Friendships*, a wonderful book on sexual practices in Florence, the common German verb meaning "to sodomize" was, at that time, *florenzen* (more or less "to florentize"), and a sodomite was called a *Florenzer*. Despite being unequivocally condemned by church and state, sex between males was so popular a practice in fifteenth- and sixteenth-century Florence that a special commission was created to seek it out and prosecute it. From 1432, when it was created, until 1502, when its functions were taken over by other official bodies, the Ufficiali di Notte (Office of the Night) accused nearly seventeen thousand men of sodomy and convicted some three thousand—and that in a city of only about forty thousand inhabitants.[16]

Rocke also makes it clear that, in Renaissance Italy, sexual contact between males implied nothing about lifelong orientation or preference as we are familiar with these concepts today, that men who had sexual relations with men also had sexual relations with women. Sexual contact between males was simply a normal part of—or an extension of—male social relations and was ordered along hierarchical lines that generally followed life stages and patterns of power. Older men had sex with younger men (younger men being those no older than eighteen or twenty), the former taking the active role and the latter the passive. Men who were passive participants in male-male sexual activity in their youth became active participants when they reached the appropriate age.

Moreover, close, affectionate, erotic relationships between men, even between older and younger men, were not necessarily explicitly sexual. Another passage from Cellini's autobiography is suggestive of the equivocal nature of male same-sex erotic attractions:

> While I was working hard on the Bishop's beautiful vase, I had only one small boy helping me. I had taken him as my assistant, giving in to the pressure of friends and half against my own will. His name was Paulino and he was about fourteen; he was the son of a Roman citizen who lived

on a private income. This Paulino had the most perfect manners, the most honest character, and the prettiest face of any I have ever come across in all my life. His honest way of behaving and his incredible beauty and the great love he showed me made me love him in turn almost more than I could bear. I loved him so passionately that I was always playing music for him, in order to see his lovely face, which was normally rather sad and serious, brighten up when he heard it. Whenever I took up the cornet such a frank, beautiful smile came over his face that I am not at all surprised at those silly stories the Greeks wrote about their gods. In fact if Paulino had been alive in those days he might have unhinged them even more.

We cannot say for sure that Cellini had sexual relations with Paulino—although sexual relations with a young apprentice or servant were quite common at the time—but we can say that he was obviously in love. The same is true of his relations as a young man with a fellow goldsmith, Francesco, the son of the painter Fra Fillipo Lippi. Of that relationship, compounded of close friendship, desire, and art, he says: "We came to love each other so much that we were never apart. Also his house was still full of the wonderful studies that his brilliant father had made; there were several books of them in his own hand, taken from the beautiful antiquities of Rome. When I saw these I completely lost my heart. Francesco and I went together for about two years."[17]

In another anecdote, Benvenuto distinguishes two kinds of love. While in Rome, he befriended a young man named Luigi Pulci, of whose boyhood days in Florence he said: "When this Luigi had been a boy in Florence it used to be the custom on summer evenings to gather together in the streets; and on those occasions he used to sing, improvising all the time, among the very best voices. His singing was so lovely that Michelangelo Buonarroti, that superb sculptor and painter, used to rush along for the pleasure of hearing him whenever he knew where he was performing."[18]

Gatherings of men "in the streets" were one of the occasions when Florentines courted male sex partners, often by the odd custom of stealing the boys' hats and, thereby, coercing them into submitting to sexual advances, a practice also employed by Florentine prostitutes to compel men to become their customers. Apparently, it was a public disgrace and humiliation to lose one's hat, and a person might do anything to retrieve it.[19] Cellini emphasizes Luigi's sexual attractiveness by describing him as a bright star in such gatherings and as the object of interest for Michelangelo, who was notoriously a lover of young men. After meeting Cellini, who helped him through a disease and supported him afterward, the young man entered the service of an aged bishop and attracted the attention of the bishop's nephew, a gentleman from

Venice named Giovanni. This relationship with the Venetian was not salubrious for young Luigi and caused a rift between him and his erstwhile benefactor: "It soon became only too clear that Giovanni's love for him was dirty rather than disinterested. Every day Luigi was seen wearing different velvet and silk clothes, and it was obvious that he had completely abandoned himself to wickedness and was neglecting his splendid talents. Then he began pretending not to see me or recognize me, after I had taken him to task and told him that he had allowed himself to become enslaved to the sort of bestial vices that would one day break his neck."[20]

The distinction that Cellini makes between "dirty" love and "disinterested" love has a pedigree that goes back to Plato, where the Islamic and Christian traditions of love theory converge. The Ottomans distinguish *mecazi* (metaphoric or sexual love from *hakkiki* (real) love, which has God as its true object, the idea being that any form of love can act as a metaphoric bridge to love of the divine. But it was not Luigi's "dirty love" affair with Giovanni that caused a violent rift with Cellini and "broke his neck" (got him killed) in the end; it was a triangular affair with a female prostitute named Pantesilea.

This woman, to whom Cellini was attracted against his better judgment, bore a grudge against the artist as a result of a party held by a Sienese sculptor named Michelagnolo for a social club of artists in Rome. It seems that the beautiful Pantesilea was madly in love with Cellini but that, when the invitation to Michelagnolo's supper arrived with the stipulation that each member must bring a female companion, the artist gave in to the pleas of a love-smitten friend and allowed him to escort the beautiful young woman. Pantesilea was enraged by the rejection, and Cellini was left without a companion. He was not willing to escort a less than beautiful woman and so devised a prank, one that says much about the fluidity of gender in determining sexual attractions in early-modern times. Summoning the son of a Spanish coppersmith who lived next door—a young man more beautiful, according to Cellini, than the famous bust of Antinous, the beloved of Hadrian—he dressed him as a woman, adorned him with jewels, did his hair up attractively, and brought him to the supper, where he was acclaimed by all as the most charming and lovely woman in attendance. When the ruse was exposed, the men were delighted and the women furious.[21] Pantesilea would later seek revenge in an affair with Luigi, who thus made the transition from the catamite of a Venetian merchant to the lover of a prostitute. The affair was intended to humiliate Cellini, but it ended up as a prelude to the wounding of the unfortunate Luigi in a wild melee involving Cellini and several of Luigi's friends and, later, in his predicted death as a result of a fall from a horse.

Cellini is careful, however, to inform the readers of his autobiography that he is as heterosexual in his desires as the next person and was, in his young manhood, as lusty a fellow as ever could be imagined. He reveals the following—not without an air of some braggadocio—in the course of a story about a robbery at his studio:

> As it happened, at that time, as was only fitting at the age of twenty-nine, I had taken a charming and very beautiful young girl as my maid-servant; I used her as a model, and also enjoyed her in bed to satisfy my youthful desires. Because of this I had my room at quite a distance from where the workmen slept, and also some way from the shop. I kept the young girl in a tiny ramshackle bedroom adjoining mine. I used to enjoy her very often, and although I am the lightest sleeper in the world, after sexual pleasure, I sometimes used to sleep very heavily and deeply.

Later on he fell in love with a young woman whom he planned to marry. As he tells it: "At that time, as young men do, I had fallen in love with a very beautiful young Sicilian girl; and she too showed that she felt very affectionately towards me. . . . But her mother discovered this, and began to suspect what was going to happen." The mother spirited the girl off to Sicily and, after some fruitless searching, the distraught Cellini consoled himself by "indulging in every imaginable pleasure" and took a new lover "merely to drown the other."[22]

The image that we get of early-modern Florence (and other Italian cities) from Cellini and many other sources indicates that, for young men, rituals of male bonding included both sexual relations with other males and the exploitation of prostitutes and other available women as a reassertion of culturally normal sexuality. (It also indicates just how prolonged youth or adolescence was: even into his early thirties Cellini was passing off his sexual exploits as something that "young men do.") In fact, in the late fifteenth century and the sixteenth, Florence was a leader in the movement to make female prostitution a municipal enterprise. With the stated goal of wooing men away from sodomy, municipal authorities began taking control of prostitution by regulating it through taxation, by prescribing the location and operation of brothels, and even by determining how prostitutes of various classes should be dressed and coiffed.[23]

London

From Italy we could have gone many places in the course of our survey—Valencia, Lyon, Paris, Amsterdam, Berlin. However, some cursory research indicated that closer examination of the situation in these cities would reveal few, if any, major differences. So we chose London, not only because we wished to look beyond the Continent and the Mediterranean world, but also because this is a book in English and English-speaking readers could naturally be expected to find more familiar and engaging parallels in the society, culture, and literature of England during the Age of Beloveds.

Whereas many of our sources for sexual behavior in Italy depended heavily on court records of sex-crime prosecutions, our sources for England tended instead to depend on more personal sources. And particularly important among those more personal sources were the casebooks and the autobiography of the extraordinary Simon Forman (b. 1552), an astrologer, alchemist, and physician popular among the gentry of London during the lifetime of William Shakespeare. Forman is valued by literature scholars as one of the few Elizabethans who wrote about attending some of Shakespeare's plays while the playwright was still alive. What brought him to our attention is that he was a prodigious keeper of records. As an astrologer, it was important for him to know the exact times when major events occurred in people's lives. So he maintained meticulous records of his contacts with clients, of what he learned about their lives, and of his own affairs. Among the dates and times that could be of special significance to an astrologer was the moment at which a person was conceived. As a result, he also took great pains to record the time and date of every one of his acts of sexual intercourse in the event that a child might result. Although, as the noted Elizabethan scholar A. L. Rowse says of him, he appears to have been "naive and transparently sincere" and to have regarded himself as "a moral man and even a religious man," the extent of his sexual exploits is stunning.[24]

Without the slightest hint of self-congratulation, Forman, who did not become sexually active until he turned thirty, lists encounters with multitudes of women—beloveds, clients, married women, servants, new acquaintances, old friends, and potential marriage partners. Not only did he bed numerous different women, but he also regularly had intercourse several times in a day. For example, in his laconic manner, which modestly uses the pseudo-Greek word *halek* to mean "sexual intercourse," he records the following:

> That day I was at Allen's from 10 A.M. to 8 P.M. and halek twice, in the morning and at 6 P.M. [with Mrs. Avis Allen, his true love and a married woman].
>
> 16 January, 9 A.M. halek Anne Condwell [a married client who came to him wondering whether she were pregnant]; at 12 noon, Frances Hill [his maidservant].
>
> 9 July, halek 8 A.M. Hester Sharp, et halek at 3 P.M. Anne Wiseman, and 9 P.M. halek tronco [his wife].

The 28th of February, halek Anne Nurse at 3, Ankers P.M. at 6, and Judith.[25]

He was an energetic and busy man.

In addition to notes on his own sexual experiences, Forman also records what he knows of the activities of others. Among these is an interesting note about a client named Bridget Allen, the wife of John Allen, a respectable middle-class burgher. Bridget was concerned about becoming pregnant and called on Forman often in July 1596. Forman assured her one day that she would have a child by May of the next year, and that same night her husband came home, and the two had intercourse. Two weeks later she again asked whether she was now pregnant, and the answer was that she was not but would be soon. Forman then records what the young woman did: "Next day she and her mistress went to a hot-house [a brothel]—afterwards both were exceedingly sick and like to die."[26] It appears that this activity was not unusual enough to elicit surprise or even comment from Forman, although he seems not to have approved of it for moral reasons. At least he does not ever record going to a brothel himself.

Despite his rich and varied sex life, Forman seems to have had very conventional ideas about sodomy. He does not mention sexual activity between men and rejects a candidate for marriage when her horoscope indicates a propensity for "sodomy" (the term is fluid and unclear in early-modern England; it can mean almost any nonpenetrative or nonreproductive sexual activity).[27] This does not, of course, mean that homoeroticism and homosexual contacts were as absent from Shakespearean England or heterosexual contacts as profuse as they are in Forman's records.

In an important book on homoeroticism in the literature of Shakespearean England, Bruce R. Smith contrasts two texts written by James I. The first is a "mirror for princes" treatise written for the education of Prince Henry in which the king "lists sodomy along with witchcraft, murder, incest, poisonings, and counterfeiting of currency as 'horrible crimes that ye are bound in conscience never to forgive.'" The second is a private letter to George Villiers, his royal cupbearer: "I cannot content myself without sending you this present [letter], praying God that I may have a joyful and comfortable meeting with you and that we may make at this Christmas a new marriage ever to be kept hereafter; for, God so love me, as I desire only to live in this world for your sake, and that I had a sorrowful widow's life without you. And so God bless you, my sweet child and wife, and grant that ye may ever be a comfort to your dear dad and husband."[28]

It seems that James had an equally passionate affection for Robert Carr, earl of Somerset, a handsome courtier who for some time actively returned the sovereign's regard. Exemplifying the tangled and ambiguous sexuality of the time, James's beloved Carr also became the object of an all-consuming infatuation on the part of Lady Frances Howard, the daughter of the earl of Suffolk. The love-struck lady, who had been married at fifteen to the fourteen-year-old son of the earl of Essex, refused to consummate her marriage and sought out our old friend Forman to produce a charm or philter that would bind the reluctant Carr to her. Her faith in Forman's abilities was so strong that she devoted herself to him, referring to him as her "sweet father" and to herself as his "affectionate, loving daughter." In the course of this intrigue, Forman died, but the much-sought-after Carr finally succumbed to the charms (whether personal or magical no one knows) of the countess of Essex and was aided in procuring an annulment of her marriage by the benevolence of his patron and erstwhile lover, King James. It is not untypical of high-level sexual intrigues in early-modern courts that the whole thing ended badly, with a poisoning, imprisonment in the Tower, hangings, and the ruination of the relatively innocent Carr and Forman's ever-dubious reputation.[29]

As Smith and others, including Alan Bray, have pointed out, one prominent feature of the robust sexual culture of early-modern England was its manifest refusal to restrict desire according to limits suggested by theology or ideology. For example, in his *Affectionate Shepherd* of 1594, Richard Barnfield's shepherd both recognizes such limits and spurns them:

> If it be sinne to love a sweet-faced boy,
>> Whose amber locks trust up in golden tramels
> Dangle adown his lovely cheekes with joy,
>> When pearle and flowers his faire haire enamels;
> If it be sinne to love a lovely lad,
> Oh then sinne I, for whom my Soule is sad.[30]

An interesting sidelight on this clearly homoerotic poem is that it was issued with a dedication to the notorious Lady Penelope Rich, whom Barnfield describes as

> Fayre lovely ladie, whose angelique eyes
> Are vestall candles of sweet beauties treasure,
> Whose speech is able to inchaunt the wise,
> Converting joy to paine, and paine to pleasure.[31]

Lady Rich, née Penelope Devereux, daughter of the earl of Essex and wife of Lord Rich, was a beloved of many lovers—by one of whom she bore several children. The poet Sir Philip Sidney, another of her passionate admirers, re-created her as the Stella of his famed sonnet cycle *Astrophel and Stella*, in which he extols her charms and lampoons her husband with quite blatant plays on his name:

> ... that rich foole, who by blind Fortune's lot
> The richest gemme of Love and life enjoyes,
> And can with foule abuse such beauties blot;
> Let him, deprived of sweet but unfelt joyes,
>> (Exil'd for ay from those high treasures, which
>> He knowes not) grow in only follie rich.[32]

The gender of this English beloved shifts back and forth—boy, girl, boy, girl—like the transvestite Shakespearean actor playing a girl acting a boy (who will return to being a girl). It moves from (lovely shepherd) boy to (fair) lady and back (the detritus of Greco-Roman homoeroticism, on the one hand, and medieval chivalric fantasy, on the other). The erotic ideal seems to feature both male and female beloveds. A character in Jonson's *Epicoene; or, The Silent Woman* (1620) describes the truly happy man: "Why, here's the man that can melt away his time, and never feeles it! What, betweene his mistris abroad, and his engle at home, high fare, soft lodging, fine clothes, and his fiddles; he thinkes the houres ha' no wings, or the day no post-horse."[33] The word *engle* (also *ingle*) was, according to the OED, first used in 1591 in the sense in which we find it here, that of "a boy-favorite (in a bad sense); a catamite" (*ganymede* as a synonym was also current). With such a lad (likely a young servant boy) "at home" and a mistress "abroad," a man who is rich to boot has all he can possibly desire.

There is much more to say about the sexuality of English culture and English literature, and we will mention several examples in what is to follow. But it is now time to return to the Ottomans.

Istanbul

It has been a long-standing practice in Europe and the lands of Christendom to portray the early-modern Muslim East as a hotbed of sexual license, although, as our scanty survey indicates, it would be difficult to imagine sexual activity anywhere exceeding in variety and intensity that of Christian Europe during the same period. It was not then and is not now unusual for arguments about cultural or religious superiority to refer to the relative depravity of other societies or beliefs. Elizabethan Englishmen, for example, believed that their countrymen had "caught" homoeroticism from Italy, most Europeans believed that it was most prevalent and contagious in "the East," while the Ottomans believed that their countrymen had been infected by Persians, who were the real source of the practice.

The advent of modern Western scholarship and its claims to the disinterested and scientific revelation of historical truth did little but place such arguments on a less obviously polemical footing and make it difficult to counter them without appearing to reject Western science altogether. This has been a serious problem for modernizing and modern Turks and Muslims interested in their cultural and social history. Any exploration of the sexuality of their medieval and early-modern predecessors always carried with it the danger of providing evidence for fundamentally bigoted notions and invidious comparisons. If we add to this the cultural principles — generally accepted among Muslims — that public speech and actions should be modest and inoffensive and that it is detrimental to society to make public material that could subvert the moral character of the community, it is not surprising that studies of Ottoman sexuality and even edited and uncensored primary source materials on the subject are in extremely short supply. We have for the Ottomans very few of the studies of official records, court cases, laws, autobiographies, and diaries that we used as a basis for our cursory discussion of sex in Venice, Florence, and London. What we do have are primary sources — some scattered legal decisions, many veiled and not-so-veiled literary references (which we have been interpreting throughout this study), and a few very explicit and pornographic documents, which themselves require a brief introduction.

We must understand that, for the Ottomans in early-modern times, explicit speech about sex was a private matter. When such speech was written down, it was, moreover, for the purpose of private communication among men, a cultured and literary offshoot of what today we might call *guy talk* or *locker-room talk*. It is amusing, teasing talk about sex by men and for men, conducted with men's needs and men's egos in mind. It is generally misogynistic — women tend to be depicted as objects and as at once dangerous, powerful, cunning, stupid, and weak — which contributes to its being intensely homoerotic, far more homoerotic than the society at large. And it tends to affirm the value of relations (sexual and nonsexual) between males. We must also remember that the traditional scripting of the erotic in the Persian tradition emphasized love between males and that it was important to literate Ottomans to see themselves as custodians and perpetuators of that tradition. Keeping this in mind, we can turn to the Ottoman sources themselves.

It was our great good fortune on beginning this book to have available a newly completed doctoral dissertation by Selim Kuru in which is presented, for the first time, an edited text and scholarly translation of the first and most famous of the sixteenth-century prose works about sex, the *Dafiʿüʾl-gumum ve rafi'ü'l-humum* (Repeller of sorrows and removers of cares) by Deli Birader (Crazy Brother) Gazali.[34] Gazali is a fascinating character about whom stories abound. He was at one time or another a scholar of the sharia, a law professor, a dervish adept, a courtier, and a bathhouse owner. When he wrote the *Repeller of Sorrows*, he was in attendance at the court of Prince Korkut (1467–1513), the son of Bayezit II and brother of the future Sultan Selim I. There, Gazali enjoyed the patronage of Piyale Bey, Prince Korkut's boon companion and fast friend. During the course of his relationship with Piyale Bey, he composed two major works dedicated to his patron, a religious work in rhyming couplets on ablution and prayer entitled *Miftahü'l-hidaye* (A key to the *Hidaye*), which abridged and translated an Arabic work (the *Hidaye*) on sharia law, and the *Repeller of Sorrows*.[35]

According to Gazali, Piyale Bey loved pornographic anecdotes told by the learned and asked Gazali to make a compilation of such stories. This the poet did, combining local Turkish tales with material taken from Persian and Arabic. Ostensibly, the book was to be a compendium of harmful, immoral, and immodest behaviors that should, of course, be shunned by any right-thinking person. It is, however, quite clear that many of these activities were amusing because some could be imagined as common practices and some as at least believable practices more often enjoyed than shunned. The anecdotes range from humorous stories about sexual situations and relations in everyday life to descriptions of bizarre, grotesque, and, at times, impossible sexual behaviors. Despite its subject matter and smattering of vulgar language, the book was well received by contemporary critics and continued to be copied into the nineteenth century.

The problems of using pornographic material as a source for early-modern Ottoman attitudes about love, desire, and sexual behavior are many and, for the most part, obvious. However, we are making the assumption that much of what seems humorous at any particular time must also seem, in some cases, to be possible or believable, even if exaggerated or bizarre, and, in other cases, to be impossible and unbelievable. And often, even where the hyperbole is improbably fantastic, such humor can still be understood as an exaggeration of something (even an attitude or a fantasy) that is possible, perhaps even common. Moreover, we must also be aware that the literary tradition inherited by the Ottomans has a long history of indecent or pornographic writing by the most famous poets and authors.[36] Known variously as *mucun* (impudence, brazenness), *sahf* (deficiency in judgment), *hezl* (joking, jesting, bawdy talk), and *habisat* (impure, wicked things), tales, anecdotes, and verses such as those recounted by Gazali were handed down for centuries and find their way into the most serious works.

For example, in the famous *Mesnavi* of Celalu'd-din Rumi (these days popularly known only as Rumi), often called by Westerners the "Bible" of Sufism, there is a parable about a caliph who falls in love with the slave girl of a rival ruler.[37] The caliph is so besotted that he sends his strong and virile captain to take the girl by force. The captain succeeds, but, on his way back with the girl, he is so smitten himself by her charms that he takes the opportunity to have intercourse with her. When she finally ends up in the caliph's bed, she can only laugh at the ruler's relative impotence. At first the caliph is enraged and determined to find out why she is laughing. Then he comes to his senses and regrets both his rage and the pride that caused him to covet another man's concubine. In the course of the story, Rumi makes several digressions to illuminate its theosophical point.[38]

It is in this tradition that Gazali can claim that his pornographic anecdotes are meant to be morally instructive. Many of these anecdotes are old stories of venerable ancestry, but they are brought forward because they reflect practices and attitudes that at least seemed relevant or amusing to people of the sixteenth-century present.

The *Repeller of Sorrows* begins by praising the benefits of sexual intercourse and asserting the virtues of marriage (which practically come down to not much more than providing unlimited access to licit intercourse). The discourse on marriage is, for the most part, a discussion of the sexual nature of women and the problems of married life and tends to reveal more drawbacks to marriage than benefits. According to Gazali, women are highly sexual and, if they are decent women, resistant to intercourse at the same time. As he says, repeating a traditional notion, when God parceled out sexual desire, he divided it into ten parts. One of these he gave to Adam; the other nine he bestowed on Eve. Things soon got out of hand, so God sent Gabriel to lash Eve with the whip of modesty. Ever since, women both desire sex and shy away from it.[39]

Nonetheless, a woman is always capable of bringing a strong man to his knees. In one of Gazali's anecdotes, a man once had a young son who was strong and sturdy, lusty and filled with youthful ardor. He begged his father to marry him off and, if possible, to find him seven wives. So his father found him a wife and suggested that he get along with this one for a time while he looked for six more for him. The disappointed youth resolved to make the best of things and began to have intercourse with the girl. After some time he discovered that his sexual prowess had diminished and his lust had drained from him. When his father's wife passed away, the old man began looking for a replacement, but the son stepped up and said, "Look Dad, forget about it, here is my wife, she is enough for both of us and for a hundred like us beside."[40]

Although marriage is beneficial, Gazali says, it is only so when people are good and well behaved. The world is now so evil that there is no point in marrying:

> When someone asked a wise man if it would be good to marry, he responded, "If it is your desire to go from being a complete person to being a fragmented one, then by all means marry. It is like this: A man who is a single individual with a single purpose decides to marry—why, we can't imagine. Marrying a woman, he then becomes two; he can neither be parted from her nor do anything without seeking her opinion. If she gives birth to a son, he becomes three; if she then gives birth to a daughter, he becomes four. And then what if one of them, alas, drops dead or becomes addicted to an evil practice? Then one part of him is lost, leaving him incomplete.
>
> Though marriage seems a pleasant thing
> You'll see in truth 'tis suffering
>
> You'll soon some sons and daughters breed
> Grow stingy, leave them starved, in need
>
> And if one of them should pass away
> You'll mourn until your dying day [41]

Having dealt with marriage, Gazali proceeds to the body of his text, which he introduces with a contextualizing tale about the battle of the boy chasers and the womanizers. The bias is obvious and—we should point out again— very traditional. The boy chasers, quite significantly, come in droves from the Persian-speaking lands from which the poetic tradition also came—Tabriz, Isfahan, Iraq. As we mentioned earlier, male-male love in early-modern times seems to be something virulent that is generally caught from somewhere to the east.

The boy chasers are a virile bunch: "Their arms are powerful, they make a magnificent show, and their movements are manly." The womanizers, on the other hand, appear also to have taken on some of the qualities of their beloveds. They "put on their feminine little robes, gird on their reddish little sashes, stuff gold-embroidered silk handkerchiefs in their waistbands, and wrap themselves in tasseled turbans." Weak from cowering in a "dark cave" (the vagina), they are no physical match for the boy chasers and so opt for a scholarly argument rather than a physical confrontation.[42]

Often lurking behind the praise of love in early-modern writing appears to be a fear that too much focus on women, on loving, pleasing, and praising them, will make a man effeminate. We will content ourselves here with a pair of examples. In the first, from *The Book of the Courtier*, one of Castiglione's elegant conversationalists says about the courtier:

> Many of those accomplishments that have been attributed to him (such as dancing, merrymaking, singing, and playing) were frivolities and vanities, and, in a man of any rank, deserving of blame rather than of praise; for these elegances of dress, devices, mottoes, and other such things as pertain to women and love (although many will think the contrary), often serve merely to make spirits effeminate, to corrupt youth, and to lead it to a dissolute life: whence it comes about that the Italian name is reduced to opprobrium, and there are but few who dare, I will not say to die, but even to risk any danger.[43]

The second example, from Marlowe, comes to us via Ian Moulton's "'Printed Abroad and Uncastrated,'" an article on Marlowe's *Elegies*, ten selected translations from the elegies in Ovid's *Amores*. In that article, Moulton makes the unconventional argument that the selection itself constructs a narrative of descent through love of women into impotence and unmanliness. Love makes the lover give up the manly dangers of war (as Castiglione's courtier asserts):

> He's happy who loves mutuall skirmish slayes,
> And to the Gods for that death Ovid prayes.
> Let souldiours chase their enemeis amaine,
> And with their blood eternall honour gaine.
> . . .
> But when I die, would I might droupe with doing.
> (bk. 2, elegy 10, lines 29–32, 35)

In the end, according to Moulton's reading, the lover even gives up on that organ that has betrayed him into the hands of women. He abandons to unending "drooping" this the central symbol of phallocentric culture—and, in effect, "unmans" himself, becoming woman-like in his desire to escape the domination of women:

> Like one dead it lay
> Drouping more then a rose puld yester-day.
> Now when he should not jette, he boults upright,
> And craves his taske, and seekes to be at fight.
> Lie down with shame, and see thou stirre no more,
> Seeing thou wouldst deceive me as before.[44]
> (bk. 3, elegy 6, lines 65–70)

Renaissance poets—Renaissance Ottomans included—are always ready to make the "Neoplatonic" argument in favor of homoerotic passion. In sixteenth-century Europe, the shadows of Petrarch and Dante are long, but the "spiritualized" (Neoplatonized?) female beloved of the Petrarchan tradition is giving way to a woman—a Penelope Rich or a Veronica Franco—more readily identified with carnality pure and simple, a woman who is not merely an abstract vehicle to higher consciousness but a competitor for power here on earth. The Ottoman case is different in that, for the Ottomans, the spiritualized beloved has quite often been male. But even there we see that the power argument—the argument that Gazali's tale makes that love for a woman makes a man effeminate or weak—is beginning to replace, or, at least, compete with, the Neoplatonic argument. For example, the poet Fevri laments his falling for a female beloved:

> I was a lover, and my heart was captured by this vile world's desire
> Alas, I was a man and [yet] powerless [in the hands of] a woman
>
> The troubles of the Zal of this age have bent my body double
> My twisted body has become like a *nun* [ن] beneath a woman
>
> Don't think it's the echo of his pick's blows that you hear
> It's Mount Bisütun reproaching Ferhad for loving a woman
>
> If you can reason, don't open your eyes to the woman of this world
> For eyes should not look on the sun because it is feminine
>
> Oh Fevri, the man of [true] love doesn't look at the woman of this world
> Does an accomplished man conform to one "deficient in reason and faith"?[45]

Beneath the commonplace "this world–evil/that world–good" mystical Neoplatonism that characterizes this world as a woman—the phrase *zen-i dünya* can mean both "this world is [like] a woman (this woman-of-a-world)" and "the woman of this world" (as opposed to a more ethereal woman)—lies an issue of power. What the poet says in the first couplet is, more literally, "While I was a lover ['aşık]," and "While I was a man [merd]," surfacing the two senses of the words for "lover" and "man." 'Aşık can mean either a person who falls in love or a mystical adept caught up in Neoplatonic passion; *merd* can mean just a man or someone who has the "manly" qualities (bravery, intelligence, generosity, etc.). When the poet falls for a woman, the scales are tipped in favor of the "lesser" alternative; he becomes a mere man and less "manly," a mere lover, more worldly and less "spiritual." She gains the upper hand; he is powerless.

In the second couplet, the poet compares his troubles to those of Zal, the father of the archetypal Persian hero Rüstem, whose story is found in the famous *Şahname* (Book of kings). Zal's major problem was that he was born with white hair and a white beard, which made him look like an old man. His father, Sam, left him to die on a mountain, thinking that his oddness would bring misfortune on his people. The implication here seems to be that loving a woman has made the poet old before his time and caused everyone else to abandon him. His body is deformed (by age) and bent like the Arabic-script letter *nun* (ن) "under" a woman, which not only reverses the more common male-dominant sexual position but also characterizes the woman as a (mere?) dot. There is also a suggestion here that old men are more likely than young men to prefer women. We will see this suggestion made again below.

In the third couplet, we are introduced to another of the standard characters of Perso-Ottoman literary mythology, Ferhad, a character from the romantic narrative poem *Husrev u Şirin* (Husrev [the king] and Shirin [the princess]). Ferhad's subnarrative breaks out of the classical tale during Ottoman times and becomes a popular legend in its own right. In one episode, referred to often by love poets, Shirin (Sheereen; Şirin, "Sweet") attempts to dissuade her impassioned suitor, Ferhad, by telling him that she will be his if he can perform the apparently impossible task of cutting a road through Mount Bisütun. Ferhad, who is an accomplished preindustrial civil engineer, proceeds to attack the mountain single-handedly with his pickax and, by virtue of prodigious effort, manages to complete the road, only to be told falsely that Shirin has died. The news drives him to suicide in a paroxysm of grief. Fevri evokes an image of Ferhad hearing what he assumes to be the echo of his pickax as it strikes the mountain and failing to realize that it is actually the mountain warning him that he ought not to fall in love with a woman.

The last two couplets constitute a reproach or warning—something the mountain might have said were it an educated Ottoman. The fourth couplet plays on the fact that *şems*, the word for "sun" in Arabic, is feminine (remember: Arabic has gender; Turkish and Persian do not). Employing a favorite rhetorical figure, the fantastic assignment of cause, the poet says that a person cannot look directly at the sun without damage to the eyes *because* the sun is feminine in gender and, hence, a woman. The last couplet repeats the admonition in the preceding couplet: that a man of learning and accomplishment should not be deceived by the enticing things of this world as represented by women, who are, in turn, characterized by the descriptive adage from the hadith (the Prophetic tradition) as "deficient in reason and faith" (*nāqisatu'l-aql wa'd-dīn*).[46]

Returning to Gazali's tale, the representative of the womanizers, an old, broken-down sage, makes his opening argument in favor of sex with women, and the ever-virile boy chasers are enraged. Forgetting their agreement, and still awash in martial manliness, they resolve to attack and slaughter the womanizers. The massacre is averted only by the appearance of Satan, who does not want to lose any of his adherents. He chastises the boy chasers for being hasty, for seeming incapable of developing a rational argument, and for resorting to violence immediately. Ultimately, at the devil's urging, the argument is joined by the boy chasers, and they succeed in converting the womanizers.

Told in the most vulgar language, this is still something of a morality tale, ambiguously serving both to titillate and to instruct. Beneath the surface there are references to general expectations for behavior at various life stages. The boy chasers are virile, strong, rash, and violent: all behaviors associated with the young (remembering that "the young" can be rather old by our modern standards). The womanizers have the characteristics of older men; they are weaker, vain about their appearance, interested more in intellectual disputes and rational arguments than in physical combat. As we saw exemplified in the story of Tayyib and Tahir, young men were expected to visit the taverns and dally with beautiful boys. In Gazali's story, there is an intimation that older, more mature men turn their attention to women. What makes the womanizers important to Satan is, not that they have female beloveds, but that they are promiscuous and do not confine their sexual activities to marriage. Hidden in the fact that the boy chasers win out are the forces of long cultural and literary traditions as well as the submerged notion that illicit sex with boys is more masculine and less damaging to those moral structures of society that support the institutions of family and neighborhood.

In arguing for the desirability of boys, the chief of the boy chasers asserts:

> No matter how much a person interacts with young men and is conversant with them, no one interferes, yet [the same person] can't find the liberty to get together with some old hag who has but two teeth left in her head. Beloved boys accompany you on military campaigns. They are not under someone's guardianship; so if you take one into a room alone or go out in public for a walk with one, if you put an arm around his neck and draw him to you, if you steal a kiss, rub your cheek on his, suck on his lip, if you engage him in pleasant chat, give him some wine and get him tipsy, no judge or noble lord will prevent you. Is there anything better in this world?[47]

In the course of a chapter of his *Etiquette* entitled "Describing the Smooth-Cheeked Boys Ready for Pleasure," Mustafa 'Ali echoes Gazali's appraisal of the convenience of boys as beloveds:

> In our time, the popularity of beardless youths [*emred*], smooth-cheeked boys, and well-behaved lads, whose sweet beauty is apparent, exceeds the popularity of nonmen[a] from the class of women possessed of beauty and

[a] *Nā-merd* (lit. "non-man") usually means someone who lacks the male virtues, someone who is timid and cowardly.

loveliness because a mistress from the sect of female beloveds is [only] ready [for love] in a concealed manner for fear of vicious gossip, while keeping company with a young man is a door connected to the gate of sociability, a door either secretly or openly unlocked and ajar. Furthermore, smooth-cheeked lads are loving friends and companions to their masters both on campaign and at home. But, from that perspective, those moon faces of the female gender are neither constant friends nor close companions.[48]

What we have in these passages is a description of the kind of semipublic erotic relationship scripted by Ottoman poetry and an argument for its advantages. That description bears all the features of the typical mutual seduction that we learn to associate with the erotic content of the typal poetic party. While, as we shall see in chapter 9 below, it is not strictly true that young boys did not have guardians and that no one would interfere if they were pursued sexually, it is obvious that boys old enough or independent enough to go on military campaigns would be available for romantic attachments. The military connection is also significant. The army is another place dominated by young men, a place where young men bond and where, as Gazali and 'Ali suggest, young men developed romantic and sexual relations with each other. In the case of the Ottomans and their European contemporaries, the role of the army, and the participation of a large number of men in military campaigns, is either overemphasized, when talking about political and gross historical events (forgetting that a number of part-time soldiers were also full-time artists, poets, and courtiers), or underemphasized, when talking about culture (forgetting that the poets and artists often served as soldiers as well). In such situations where hierarchies of power are clear, it seems to have been expected that younger men would be available as objects of romantic attention on the part of older men and that the penetrator/penetrated roles would shift with life stages.

A good example of how this might have worked in Ottoman society is the story about the young manhood of the famous sixteenth-century poet Hayali, whom we have already mentioned in several contexts. Hayali was born in the town of Yeniçe in the province of Vardar in the European part of the empire. At the time he was beginning to go through puberty, or, as the biographer says, "When the reflection of his eyebrow had just been cast on the mirror of his cheek and the tiny ants of dark down had just begun to swarm about his lip,"[49] he encountered a roving band of dervishes. Being out of the control of his family, he was seduced by one of the dervishes and chose to set out on the road with them. The charismatic leader of the dervishes, Baba Ali the Persian Drunkard by name and sobriquet, took Hayali under his wing and educated him in mysticism and poetry.

A beautifully dressed beloved with wine cup. This is the kind of young man who would have attracted the attention of a man sensitive to the call of love. (Topkapı Palace Museum Library, EH. 2836, "Albüm" [seventeenth century], fol. 85a.)

At this point, the future poet is represented as a young man bonded to a group through an erotic relationship with an older man—a story type that we have already seen in the case of Tayyib and Tahir. However, to the Ottoman elites of the sixteenth century, the dervishes would have seemed to be less than appropriate companions because, deservedly or not, they were notorious for seducing young men and sexually exploiting them (much as priests and monks were in the popular imagination of Europe at the same time). In Gazali's story about the boy chasers and the womanizers, for example, Satan appears between the opposing forces in the guise of a dervish and does a little dervish dance to catch their attention.

Hayali would stick with the dervishes until they reached Istanbul, where the handsome young man in the company of disreputable dervishes attracted the notice of the city muhtesib, the official in charge of weights, measures, price controls, and the general morality of the market. In an assertion of public propriety, the young man was taken from the dervishes and put under the guardianship of a respected, well-to-do citizen. This did not, however, end Hayali's career as a beloved. On the contrary, it was at this point that his career began to take off. Aided by his good looks and rhetorical skills, he was introduced to the conversational circle of the defterdar (chief finance minister), Iskender Çelebi, from there to the circle of the grand vizier, Ibrahim Pasha, and from there to intimate companionship with Sultan Süleyman himself. In his old age, he ended up wealthy and famous and retired to a lucrative sinecure as a provincial governor.

Although Hayali's was the ideal career path for a talented beloved, most beloveds operated on a far less exalted level. Much of the talk about beloveds refers to boys and boy servants or slaves who exchange erotic encounters or sexual favors for gifts of money or other valuables. In his *Etiquette*, 'Ali lists and critiques the kinds of beloveds of this sort that were available in the late sixteenth century:

> Nowadays, most of the beardless-youth kind, who serve as tasty morsels for the unmanly, are those bastard boys of Arabia and the illegitimate sons of Anatolian peasants [Turks]. Although the dancing boys of the European provinces are gentle, the large, thick-lipped slave boys of Bosnia and Herzegovina are always amenable to service. Moreover, the term of their beauty and loveliness lasts like that of [the youths from] no other country. Some of them [even] when they reach the age of thirty do not see a single disturbing hair[b] appear on the mirror of their beauty. As regards sweet loveliness,

[b] A young man became an inappropriate beloved as soon as a true beard replaced the dark down on his cheek. Sexual relations among adult males were frowned on, in part because this required an adult male to assume a passive, subordinate role.

Anatolian peasant children and the clever youths of Arabia are the most short-lived of all. By the time they have reached twenty, they are no longer fit to be love objects or to be used by lovers. But the youths of the inner provinces, the hair-waisted ones of Edirne and Bursa and Istanbul, are, from every point of view, superior to all of them in beauty and excellence. Those who are lacking something of beauty and comeliness [still] give pleasure with their made-up freshness and sweet charm, their coquettishness and fetching airs. According to the born rakes, the beardless Kurds are faultless and constrained to be amiable and abundantly obedient in whatever is proposed to them. Notably they dye themselves below the waist with henna and [thus] adorn themselves with a colorful gesture reaching down to the knees.

Those most praised are predominantly thin waisted and tall. At the moment of surrender they are said to submit with every limb. To make it short, the beloveds of the inner provinces top them all in being visibly gentle and secretly contentious. They appear as if they are submitting [however] even when engaged in sex most of them also desire to refuse. In this regard the blessing of union with them is prepared only for the nobility. Of the lovers who accompany them, they say, "It is manifest [that we have left them] disappointed, destitute, and distraught." They tell us that it is probably impossible that two [of these] youths would [ever] find an opportunity for one to take advantage of the other or for one to get the other drunk and [thereby] get the best of him. The short of it is that those who esteem the famously fair of face and wish fervently to be serviced by silver-bodied cypresses, tall of stature and elegantly moving, should not neglect to consider the boy dancers of Rumeli. Nor, God forbid, should they tire of or be sated with the Joseph-faced[c] Circassians or the musky, delectable Croats from among the janissaries. [But] even though there are also exquisite ones among the beloveds of the interior provinces, most of them are quite troublesome, unfaithful, and inclined toward tyranny and torment. Those who possess them will find ease and peace of mind to be rare indeed. Yet, as for the Albanian type, although they are worthy of stealing the hearts of lovers, this much must be said: they are also extremely impertinent and obstinate. However, the Georgians, Russians, and Gurclians[d] are the impurities among those who are available for erotic pleasures. Compared to them, the Hungarians are the most charming and reasonable of groups, for most of them will betray their masters, and everyone will see their nastiness in their actions and arrogant mannerisms. An oddity is that the Egyptian rakes prefer Ethiopians. It is said that, when it gets cold, they are human sables. They excel at bedchamber service. That is, they whole-

---

[c] In the Qur'an and the Islamic literary traditions, Joseph (Yusuf) is the paragon of (male) beauty.

[d] Gurelia was a country on the eastern coast of the Black Sea.

heartedly love to perfume clothes with incense, to arrange mattresses and bolsters. Affability is established in both the male and the female. Wherever they are taken, [behaving] with an inborn grace, their gentleness is divinely preordained.[50]

One of the things about the lower-class and enslaved beloveds that strikes most contemporary observers is how mercenary they are. The not-so-wealthy elites forever complain, as 'Ali does above, that the best beloveds reserve themselves for high officials. Gazali distinguishes three kinds of lovers in an amusing onomatopoeic classification, according to which there are three kinds of lovers: The first is the "sing-a-ling" (*sing sing*) lover, who "if he should not get his heart's desire and come together with the beloved, if he should not sit with him, have a tête-à-tête with him, if he should not see his face, say, for a month, the fire of longing will scar his heart, and he will weep with a sing-a-ling sound." Then there is the "ding-a-ling" (*ding ding*) lover, who "sets aside his honor and pride, and wherever his beloved's butt goes he goes, wherever it stops he stops, whenever his horse goes fing-a-ling he goes ding-a-ling." But the "ching-a-ling" (*ching ching*) lover trumps all the rest; "he has plenty of silver and gold; there are no throngs of rivals to oppose him; he brings [the money] with him, holds it in his hand by the thousands, makes it ring out with a ching-a-ling, and in this way hunts the beloved and achieves his desire." There is also a little quatrain that goes with this:

> Among the lovers of boys, one but weeps, going sing-a-ling
> Another just follows his love about, the silly ding-a-ling
> If in this world you would be free of all such rivalry
> You'll want silver and gold in hand singing ching-a-ling[51]

The poets and their crowd tend to see themselves in the first two categories. Much of the highly conventional hopeless longing in Ottoman love poetry may stem from traditional Neoplatonic motifs, but it is at the same time touched by the very mundane earth of beautiful but cash-hungry boys.

Shortly thereafter, Gazali mentions that one of the arguments given for preferring younger boys is that they do not bargain. They will take a few small coins and count themselves lucky, and one will find them available for sex and have money left over for a bath.[52] Others come quite a bit more dearly:

> Once there was a gorgeous beloved, a lovely boy whose violent nature and sexual purity were rarely seen in that day. One day a certain one of his lovers mentioned a beloved in his presence, saying that this boy would give it up for fifty silver pieces. The boy said, "Fifty silver pieces is no little bit; cloth like that doesn't usually fetch so much. Anyone who says, 'I'm a width of that [cloth],' can be embraced. A minaret would bend over for you if you

put fifty silver pieces in front of it." His lovers got the point, and, giving him fifty silver pieces each, they all enjoyed themselves with him.[53]

One of the things that we must keep in mind when thinking about what appear to be casual, amateur sex-for-money exchanges between men and boys in early-modern Ottoman and European societies is that this is a very common and natural outgrowth of the systems of patronage that existed at the time. Most men were enmeshed in webs of personal relations in which the weaker, poorer, and younger served the more powerful, wealthier, and older in return for valuable gifts, jobs, and introductions to people at higher levels of power. We have mentioned this before, and we will say more about it in later chapters, but, here, let us simply repeat that, from our perspective, nearly everyone in sixteenth-century Ottoman urban society seems to be frantically scrounging to reap some advantage from any and every personal relationship or contact down to the briefest service.[54] At the very top, highly talented courtiers are attempting to gain admittance to the private circles of the sultan and other highly placed dignitaries.[55] At the bottom, young men (teenagers) and boys without marketable skills or the young apprentices of artisans and shopkeepers are scrambling to augment their meager resources by exploiting the erotic attentions of older men. It was often assumed in a patronage relationship that the powerholder (anyone from the sultan or his grand vizier down to the shop owner or master artisan) would take advantage of whatever services, including the sexual, his underlings could provide.[56] Female slaves and servants both in Europe and in the Ottoman Empire found themselves in the same situation.

Mustafa 'Ali begins his *Etiquette* with a chapter entitled "About the Situation in the Palaces of the Sultans and about the Boy Servants in the Private Quarters [*harem*]," in which he points out that the sultans of the previous age (during the reign of Mehmet the Conqueror) used the sciences of physiognomy to select only morally upright and orderly young men to serve in the palace. However, according to 'Ali, in this latter and degenerate day, scoundrels had come into sensitive positions in the private service of the sultan. He admonishes palace officials, saying:

> Hereafter they [the palace officials] should not take into the harem impudent converts who rush about madly in the service of shameless lowlife types and especially not those hair-waisted ones whose hidden treasures have been shared with snakes, that is to say, those who have mingled with levends and hooligans of the city-boy class, and those notorious for going to taverns and being sold [for sex]. Let them [also] view separation from them as preferable to union, for in the likes of them manners, modesty, honesty, and faithfulness are rare indeed. Even supposing that one of them

might be an honest and faithful [beloved], the defects related to his having sold himself will become apparent. Then the class of boy slaves is generally infamous for things other than self-ruination. This is to say that they turn the irresistible snakes of their lust into deadly speckled serpents in the steaming-hot buried treasure in its coffer.[57]

It would seem that, by the late sixteenth century, even private servants of the sultan and other high officials somehow partook of the wild life of tavernhopping and sexual encounters favored by the unattached young men (levends and hooligans) of urban culture. Moreover, a slave who had become accustomed to sexual adventuring was thought, by 'Ali at least, to be a danger to a family, the royal family in particular.

As we have seen, the culturally sanctioned and scripted venue for rehearsing erotic attractions to young men was the elite gathering, or salon, or wine party. In his *Repeller of Sorrows*, Gazali mentions the wine party as one place where a beloved boy can be seduced while he is under the influence of alcohol. 'Ali's *Etiquette* does not explicitly sanction the use of the salon for hunting boys but affirms that beautiful young men and erotic interactions are essential parts of the experience:

> It is no mystery that, in a gathering intended to be a wine party, there should certainly be [young men] from among those who have beautiful voices in speech and song, especially those [youngsters] with rosy cheeks, who would serve in the role of saki and look after those at the party. And surely there must also be a popular beardless youth ready to do what he can by way of actions conforming to the temperament of the master of revels. It is preferable that the duty of waiting on foot at the table of pleasures be given to the other servants, with this condition that they be proffered a cup now and then so that their faces might grow hot and flushed and their shyness and timidity be softened by flames of wine. The master of revels should even himself give a cup to those servants worthy of flattery so that the ones thus complimented would be in some wise content not to be seated with the rest of the company. In particular [this] will assure their overlooking things that might catch their eyes [such as] unseemly actions or suggestions.[58]

One cannot have a party without a beloved, insists the dominant script for Ottoman social life, the sum of most all poems and songs, advice and admonitions. Social interactions are highly eroticized, and sex is never far beneath the surface. The contexts range from the refined and elegant salons of the elite to the tavernhopping revels of unattached young men and poets. It is, however, the poets who compose the most precious poems of love and long-

Drinking party alfresco with food, music, and female beloveds.
(Topkapı Palace Museum Library, B. 408, "I. Ahmed albümü"
[seventeenth century], fol. 33a.)

ing and praise to be recited and sung in the gatherings of the great while, at the same time, dashing off crude and vulgar lampoons that reflect low-level sexual humor and the erotic bonds of male sociability. Remember the verse letter that the poet Saʻyi sent from Edirne to his friends in Istanbul, the one we mentioned in chapter 3, beginning, "What news, oh east wind, how are things in the world? / Are Istanbul and Galata still so lovely?" Well, there was a response from one of those friends, the poet Sani, whose little biography we cited in chapter 2. This response picked up on the sometimes lampooning tone of Saʻyi's letter and attempted to top it with more vulgar humor and insult. It begins like this:

> After you packed up and left town,
>   truly, Oh Saʻyi
> Istanbul and Galata have become
>   wondrous fair

Everyone knows you fancy him
    and deserve him a thousand times over
Hasan Khan's head is up your ass
    right to the ears

If you're wondering, descriptions of your verses
    are still written
On the walls and door of the privy
    in the Molla's Bathhouse

People don't drink anymore
    in taverns by the sea
The morning draught has lost its pleasure
    since you went away

If you'd come and honor Karabash's Tavern
    with your presence
They'd all make jaunts to the seashore
    as they did of old

If only he'd come and get tipsy,
    we'd bugger him, they say
For you, friends have their cocks ready in hand,
    the heads wet with spit

If you've got the balls,[e] come
    take on the masters of verse
Parade yourself about, observe
    the heroic couplets of every warrior

If they mention you in Tahtakale,
    it's to vituperate you
The people of the Karaman Bazaar
    speak your name and curse

Both prince and pander are distraught
    since you left
Come and be the filling between layers
    of pederast and catamite[59]

This challenging, competitive, teasing, insulting verse is typical of men expressing their affection for one another in a manner that, on the one hand, is overtly sexual and, on the other, turns the sexual content of affection to humorous insult (perhaps protectively). This kind of interaction is certainly

---

[e] Literally "if you've got the ass."

as familiar to men today as it was to the early moderns. It even seems (almost) safe to say that, as soon as male interests extend beyond the immediate family, the first beloved is often—perhaps most often—another male. Such attractions have little to do with sexual orientation and usually give way to or continue alongside of heterosexual relationships. Early moderns, who lived in very masculinist or phallocentric societies, were obviously more comfortable than most men are today with the sexual dimension of their attachments to other men and repressed or inhibited it far less. (Of course, one might argue that the homophobic or heterosexist language and humor of male locker-room talk is one way men today have of thinking and talking about the sexual dimension of their own attractions to other men or boys.) This lack of repression is also far more evident in Ottoman society than it is in some European societies, where the specter of sodomy as the unforgivable sin loomed large. The tradition inherited by the Ottomans tended to permit and even value homoeroticism in the same way that the European tradition privileged heteroeroticism. The character of cultural scripting is such that a love poem in English or Italian or French, for example, is most likely to be about or addressed to a female beloved even though it was quite usual and even natural for early-modern European men to have male beloveds. The reverse is true of the Ottomans: even though Ottoman Turkish poems are overwhelmingly homoerotic, most men in the Ottoman Empire commonly and naturally had female beloveds. In a public or social context, it was easier for a European to have a female beloved and for an Ottoman to have a male, but, as we have seen, what was easy was not necessarily what was done.[60] The heart has always had its own rules.

The Beloved as a Social Category

If we step back for a moment from the various manifestations of love behavior in Ottoman culture and return to the notion of cultural scripting, we discover plentiful evidence of how the *idea* of the beloved permeated contemporary Ottoman thinking about the structure of society. The Ottomans, like all societies, categorize individuals according to a variety of often-overlapping criteria, many of which would be familiar to us today—common and noble, rich and poor, military-administrative and learned-religious, artisans, craftsmen, merchants, peasants, villagers, young women, married women, old women, young men, men with families, men without masters, and so on. What is striking about the Ottoman situation is the apparent inclusion of lovers and beloveds as significant social categories or types. As we saw in chapter 2, Latifi devotes a special chapter of his *Essay in Description of Istanbul* to beloveds of various kinds. Another suggestive example is found in the *Hasbihal* (Recounting of woes), a verse compilation completed in 1586–87 by a poet named Safi. The word *hasbihal* refers generally to a conversation or communication in which a person recounts or complains about the state of his or her life. This type of conversation is subsumed into poetry most commonly as an address to a beloved or a patron about the miseries that a little show of affection or patronage would alleviate. Safi's *Recounting of Woes*, however, is a long verse composition in forty stanzas or chapters, each stanza a separate poem with its own rhyme scheme, and each treating the woes of a typical person from one or another social group. Among the groups included are inspectors of weights and measures, scribes and secretaries, administrators of pious foundations, soldiers, cavalrymen, professors and teachers, muezzins, Sufis, boatmen, beggars and the poor, drug addicts, and people who have moved to villages. There are also sections for lovers and beloveds as well as a special section for woman chasers. Every section begins with a formulaic phrase that translates as "suppose you are a [name of a social group]," and each ends with the same one-couplet refrain. Here is the beloveds section in our translation:

The Plaint of the Beloveds of This World and the Beauties of This Time and Place

> Suppose that you're a beloved marked by grace
> An angel's form joined with a fairy face
>
> Bud lip, cypress body, cheek a leaf
> Of jessamine, you're all the lovelies' chief
>
> Within the town you've acquired much of fame
> The people without ceasing speak your name
>
> You ought never be the friend of asses
> You'd better go around with the purer classes
>
> Sighs and lamenting issue from your lovers
> When they espy your visage, each one shivers
>
> Some to see you once would gladly die
> Some, not seeing you, do naught but sigh
>
> A lowly knave who could not touch your skirts
> "I well enjoyed his favors," false asserts
>
> Thus in your beauty you live proud and bold
> On you they spend their silver coin and gold

Women all consumed with hot desire
For chat with you would let their lives expire

A day or two on transitory earth
Your hours pass with food and drink and mirth

Thus when you go about so fairy gaited
You leave humanity all devastated

Once or twice a day you change attire
Become a shining moon arrayed in fire

You live your life as chieftain of the fair
Your lovers all surround you pair by pair

One who would declare his adoration
Fears he might arouse your indignation

Some offer clothes or muslin turban bands
And some will come with ready cash in hand

Amid the luck of comeliness's sky
Well might you be the Pleiades on high

Now you hunt and then by seaside roam
For food and drink you flit from home to home

Until it chance that beauty's springtime fades
The day your beard this evil news betides

Right before your eyes those moments die
When on loveliness you could rely

Then those friends who once would die to see you
Turn away, no longer try to see you

In short, calamity without surcease
In which you take no single breath in peace[61]

Where the beloveds poem outlines the script for the type and typal behavior of a beloved, the lover poem leans on a script that should be familiar to us from many sources, from Latifi to the story of Tayyib and Tahir:

Suppose that you're a lover much oppressed
You know not a moment's earthly happiness

All things you do are for some darling dear
You're chasing pretty boys by day and year

Your mom and daddy left you quite a bundle
The cash and goods you hold are surely ample

You grow attached to certain ne'er-do-wells
Who turn you awry to elevate themselves

He's innocent, untouched, they say to you
And you suppose those twisted words are true

Do what you will, you're still entranced by him
He takes your heart, deceives you on a whim

He spends your wealth, leaves you in ruination
In heart and soul this is his inclination

If never more you see this person's face
He saw your wealth was gone without a trace

These friends were your companions silently
While knowing that your end was bankruptcy

Then they commence to denigrate and blame
To shield themselves from those who'd curse their shame

So might they say, Look, hasn't he done well
Into his hands a huge inheritance fell

But evil fortune was for him just lurking
He never got a thing by really working

At end he was deprived of a worldly life
And got himself no family or wife

The flame of his father's hearth is now extinguished
The roots of his lineage are cut and finished

Each day and night they were your company
Long ate and drank your generosity

When your beloved boy sets out to leave you
For others, they conspire to deceive you

To him they say, He's a rascal, all cash lacking
So from now on you send that fellow packing

There's a man who wants you, pockets filled with dough
So don't neglect yourself, let this guy go

Beloveds and lovers will cut you when you meet
And you'll be trodden down beneath their feet

In short, calamity without surcease
In which you take no single breath in peace[62]

In 1582, Sultan Murat III celebrated the circumcision of his son Mehmet with a ceremony of incredible pomp, ceremony, and duration. The more than fifty days of public celebration, from 7 June to 24 July, included many forms of merrymaking, among them almost daily parades of groups representing the social, cultural, and business organizations of the city.[63] The sultan and his court viewed these parades from royal loggias set up in the palace of Ibrahim Pasha on the Hippodrome Square, while other dignitaries and ambassadors, including several Europeans, watched from tiers of boxes constructed especially for the occasion.[64] The descriptions of this event and the many miniature paintings (437 in one manuscript alone) that accompanied them provide a fascinating and multifaceted glimpse of Ottoman life during the Age of Beloveds. What interests us here is the emphasis put on the display of what we have called *the beloveds* by the descriptions of these events and, presumably, by the events themselves.

For example, on the day of one parade, when all the multitude were assembled and everyone was settled according to rank or office, the gathered musicians struck up a tune and, as the chronicler records:

A sweet-voiced youth began to dance and thus graced the square:

COUPLET:

In the way of Greeks, a Greek beloved lovely as the sun
In the way of lovelocks, his locks' ringlets twisted every one

RHYMING COUPLETS:

On every hair hung a thousand hearts and souls
Every hyacinth was mussed, on account of his rose

Because of his lip, the ruby became mere stone
Because of his mouth, sugar was struck dumb

A youth [he was] of lovely countenance and smelling of musk; a tall cypress and moon face, sweet tongued and slender waisted. The Turks of Khitay [China] were bent and twisted [with envy] like hyacinths by the coils of his locks, and the [sweet] milk of Samarkand was distressed like lovers' hearts by desire for his riot-inducing sugar [lip]. The girdle of attachment to his locks was a bond to the soul, and the collar of attraction to his curls was fastened about the [neck of] the bride of the heart.[65]

A beautiful dancing boy opens the show one day at the Circumcision Festival of 1582. From a miniature by Nakkaş Osman. (Topkapı Palace Museum Library, H. 1344, Intizāmī, "Surname-i hümayun," fol. 390a.)

The following are a few more examples excerpted from descriptions of groups participating in the parade:

The Arrival of the Company of Spice Sellers

> ... And after this all the spice sellers came in good order and filled the square with beloveds. They had adorned many ornamental trees, and they walked about in circles displaying countless fruits and flowers like stars [in the sky]. Attractive boy beloveds with hair like hyacinths and faces like roses made everyone distraught, and lithe beauties with rosebud mouths caused the onlookers' hearts to cramp and their heads to spin. As they say:

> In the gathering of the soul your locks sell hyacinths to the herb merchant
> The blossom of your cheek sells roses in the gathering of freshness

The Arrival of the Company of the Old Cloth Bazaar

> ... And behind them,[f] five hundred pairs of sweet-behaved, coquettish-eyed [young men] unique in beauty, with whom one could bargain flirtatiously for love, but with great difficulty, beloveds born to tradesman families, possessed of dignity. Their many adornments and decorations were all in perfect order:

RHYMING COUPLETS:

> They were all cypress bodies, moon faces
> Blessed ascensions and fortunate stars

> Each cheek a tulip in the garden of delicacy
> Each cheek a rose in the rose bower of freshness

> The turbans of some were proud with a white star like the first of the month, and the bejeweled diadems of some were replete with pearls and gems; the waists of some were invisible beneath jeweled belts, and some would not have deigned [even] to wear the sun as a crown. The earlobes of some were conjoined with rubies and diamonds and the breasts and backs of some married to bejeweled caftans. The sun-faced ones at a glance made the sun blush red and curse, and crescent-browed calamities with graceful gait and display of shy allure made the shining moon wander into oblivion.

---

[f] Immediately preceding has been a description of the jewels and precious crafts borne by marchers.

Every pearl is pierced with envy as it looks on their teeth, and when they smile, they make rubies and garnets bloodred, and they slit the tongues of coy buds.

RHYMING COUPLETS:

Both tall cypresses and silver chins
Both partridge gait and parrot speech

The sun blushes with shame at their cheeks
Their twisty locks make the liver run musky black

Each of them has all the essentials of beauty and is alluring and flirtatious. It is the utmost calamity when one of them takes to blandishments, and each is a bareheaded disaster.

The Arrival of the European Magians Who Dwell in Galata

. . . Then came the Christian, European-born infidels of European mien who dwell in Galata, dressed in all sort of adornments and finery. Their young men, all prettied up, look like virgin girls. Their tousled locks and hair-thin waists, their delicacy, which had not a hair missing, was all in place, and they were such cruel infidels that they lacked any trace of true belief. They were dressed like beautiful women, and yet like [Christian] boy servants they were girt in [black] waistbands [that hung down in two places]. Behind them, [groups of] one man and one woman of delicate shape and wondrous form made the circuit of the happy square two by two, and, taking hands, all of them, with a thousand alluring mannerisms, made a circle and danced refined dances, and, thence, [after] reaching the portal of fortune and power, with an endless assortment of curiosities, they passed on.

The Arrival of the Company of Cooks with a Thousandfold Pomp and Circumstance

After that came the cooks. On a wagon were set up their kettles and ovens, and they cooked a variety of dishes as they marched. Their chief stewards were beautifully dressed and girded. Their beloveds were quite plentiful and beyond all measure drowned in ornaments. Their youths were incomparably hungry eyed, and in their company lovers' heads were reeling, and distraught swains, who would sacrifice their lives for a spoonful of their cooking, when faced with these moon faces found their fortunes to be wretched.[66]

The Guild of Cooks marches at the Circumcision Festival of 1582. Note the beautiful, beloved boy apprentices who carry the viands and march with the bearded masters. From a miniature by Nakkaş Osman. (Topkapı Palace Museum Library, H. 1344, Intizāmī, "Surname-i hümayun," fol. 235b.)

What we see here is an example of one way in which the idea (and scripted ideal) of the beloved is integrated within the social imagination of the Ottomans. The dramatic self-presentation of many groups has an erotic subtext supplied by cadres of attractive beloveds, in a manner not too different from that of the cheerleaders (male and female) or festival queens and princesses associated with sporting events and public parades in the United States today. What is different about the Ottoman situation is that the various types of beloveds (and lovers) are themselves seen as distinct social categories, enshrined in literary discourse, with clearly defined looks, behaviors, and roles the erotic element of which is quite openly recognized. Moreover, the presence of the beloveds creates an erotic aura that is transferred in many ways—including through the literature of praise—to the sultan in the role of beloved.

The Literary Tradition

One other significant point touching on the attitudes of Ottoman cultural elites toward sex and love that so far has been mentioned only in passing involves the influence of a long literary tradition in the Islamic languages (principally, Arabic, Persian, and Ottoman Turkish, but also the Chaghatai Turkic literary dialect of Central Asia and Urdu on the Indian subcontinent). The image of the beautiful boy has deep roots in Islamic culture. As the Arabist Suzanne Stetkevych points out, the wine party with its lovely saki and attendants (whom we have already seen described by Mustafa 'Ali) is mentioned prominently in both the Qur'an and the Arabic poetic tradition.[67] For example, in Qur'an 56:10–24, we find the following description of paradise (here in English paraphrase):

> The Foremost, the Foremost. These will be nearest [to God] in gardens of delight. A throng of ancients and few from among those of latter days, on bejeweled thrones reclining face to face. Circling among them will be immortal youths with goblets and pitchers and a cup filled with the water of pure springs from which there will be no headache or intoxication. [They will have] such fruits as they choose and the flesh of fowls according to their desires. And [there will be] wide-eyed houris like hidden pearls as recompense for their deeds.

Much the same imagery of the garden, celestial drink, and lovely attendants is employed in Qur'an 76:12–19: "He will reward them for their patience with silk and a garden wherein they will recline on couches and see neither [hot] sun nor [cold] moon. And its shadows will cover them and its fruits hang low over them in bunches. Vessels of silver and cups of crystal shall pass among them. . . . Circling among them will be immortal youths whom you would think scattered pearls should you see them."

Stetkevych argues in cogent detail that the quranic text and, as an example, the famous *Risalat al-gufran* (Essay on forgiveness) of the blind eleventh-century mystic master poet Abu'l-'Ala al-Ma'arri can be taken together to liberate a reading of the heavenly wine/drink as the producer (and not merely the symbol) of immortality, just as the "immortal boys/youths" (*al-wildan al-muhallidun*) are both "the possessors and purveyors of eternal youth."[68] She also points out that it is in the nature of Arabic poetry after the adoption of Islam to be caught up in a dialectical opposition of worldly wine, intoxication, the beloved boy, the singing girl, sex-mortality-damnation, and the culture of an age of moral ignorance, on the one hand, and the wine of paradise, the immortal youths, the wide-eyed damsels, bliss-immortality-blessedness, and the culture of the world of Islam, on the other. The imagery and language of the worldly revel, of sexual attraction and intoxication, interact with quranic imagery and language to produce an evolving and proliferating discourse of mortality and immortality, of falsity and truth, of carnality and spirituality.

The role of the immortal youth or the cupbearer of paradise becomes a fundamental trope quite early in the literary history of the cultures for which the Qur'an serves as the master narrative. The mortal, mundane counterpart of the paradisiacal youth, the archetypal worldly "witness" (*şahid*) to the divine beloved, is the magian boy. This is the servant or son of the non-Muslim—Christian, Jew, or Zoroastrian (magian)—wine-maker who sets up shop in the ruins of a conquered civilization just outside the new Muslim city in which wine is forbidden. This fundamental trope and the associated tropes attached to what we call *the wine party with beloved* persist with very little change over hundreds of years in the literatures of four different language families (Arabic, Persian, Turkish, and Urdu) in an area reaching from Spain to India. One consequence of this persistence is the tendency toward an ahistorical account of the Islamic literatures that gives the impression that identical images as used by an eleventh-century mystical poet writing in Arabic in Baghdad, a twelfth-century court poet in Spain, a thirteenth-century Persian, a sixteenth-century Ottoman, and an eighteenth-century Urdu poet in Delhi all evoke the same thing without reference to changing times and circumstances. In this ahistorical discourse, scholarly accounts converge with theological accounts that emphasize the universal and transcendent claims of Islam. As are those of other universal religions, the shared texts and rituals of Islam are seen from a theological perspective as having essential, noncontingent meanings available to all Muslims wherever or whenever they might live. And, in the area of the Islamic literatures, it is far too often the case that scholars, usually wary about making such universal claims, have assumed without question that the magian boy beloved or the wine party, for instance, meant the same thing in Isfahan or Shiraz in the fourteenth century as they did in Istanbul in the sixteenth. Let us take an example.

The following is a translation of a gazel (unusual in its unity of subject) by Hayali:

> A magian boy I chanced to see
> > in the bloom of belovedness
> A golden crown upon his head
> > and anklets at his feet
>
> Man and fairy came to him
> > enslaved to his command
> He seemed to be a Solomon
> > as he bade and banned
>
> He saw me in his gathering
> > proffered a brimming bowl
> I drained the cup and kissed him full
> > upon the mouth and lip
>
> When eagerly I downed that draught
> > from pleasure-granting cup
> Then many a day I witless lay
> > in that tavern's secluded nook
>
> Passion for that magian boy
> > in Hayali's bosom lies
> As dwells 'neath heaven's canopy
> > the monarch of the skies[69]

This is precisely the same trope, with much the same description of boy and tavern, that we see in a well-known poem by the famed Persian master poet Hafez (ca. 1320–90) that begins:

> *Duş raftam be-der-e meykede hab-alud*
>
> I came to the door of the wine temple, stained by sleep
> My mantle wet, skirts and prayer rug stained by wine
>
> The wine seller's magian boy came, in mocking tone
> Said, "Wake, oh wayfarer stained by sleep!"[70]

However, despite the persistence of tropes—a persistence similar to that of Greek and Roman mythology in the cultural tradition of the Christian West— and the fact that Ottomans were avid readers of Hafez, it should be obvious that the magian boy of a Galata wine shop run by an Italian or a Jew in the Ottoman Empire of the sixteenth century is a far different character, differently imagined, than the waiter in a tavern run by a Zoroastrian on the outskirts of Shiraz some two hundred years earlier. That this is not obvious is a consequence of the fact that the historicized and contextualized appraisal of Ottoman literature has been long repressed and is even now only in its infancy.

Those familiar with early-modern Europe will immediately recognize parallels between this magian boy and the Trojan youth Ganymede, who was abducted and raped by Jove disguised as an eagle, then rewarded by being granted immortality and transported to the abode of the gods, where he acted as Jove's cupbearer. There are two dimensions to these parallels that we feel are relevant to the discussion here.

The first dimension involves the perceived homoeroticism of the Ottoman high-culture tradition. If we look solely at lyric love poetry, it is inarguable that the Ottoman beloved is overwhelmingly identified with the trope of the magian boy (and his heavenly counterparts, the immortal youths). This epicene, wine-pouring youth or his analogues, both mundane and otherworldly, are either overtly mentioned or persist as an unseen presence in almost every love poem. One can—with some difficulty—find poems about women, but they are very few and far between. In Europe, the reverse was true. The beloved is an archetypal lovely maid, and openly homoerotic poems are relatively rare. While Ganymede is mentioned regularly, and "ganymedes" or "catamites" (*catamite* being a corrupt form of *ganymede*) in the form of sexually available youths become common socially, this is by no means a dominant or even a common poetic trope. This would seem to indicate a major difference in imagining the beloved. However, for our period, there is evidence that the differences are neither as profound nor as telling as they appear on the surface.

In his *Ganymede in the Renaissance*, James M. Saslow examines the representations of Ganymede that burgeoned in the visual arts of the Renaissance precisely during the period that we call *the Age of Beloveds*. In Saslow's view, at this time the figure of Ganymede becomes a recognized and recognizable symbol or icon of homoerotic love and, in particular, of the love of an older man for a boy. Saslow compiled a list of more than two hundred representations of Ganymede and presents them, along with a cogent analysis, in the context of early-modern culture and society, pointing out at the beginning that there are any number of other homoerotic visual images—

paintings (e.g., Parmigianino's *Amor*), drawings, sculptures (e.g., Michelangelo's *David*) — that that do not refer explicitly to Ganymede or are conflated with him.[71] What can be seen from Saslow's study is that, if one steps back from literature, from the typal Petrarchan beloved of lyric/love poetry, it becomes apparent that the European beloved is neither as clearly gendered nor as obviously female as it might seem.

This raises another question, one a bit outside the scope of this study (yet ultimately central to it, were there but time and space enough). If we take into account the fact that the Ottomans did not have a tradition of sculpture, and that painting was for the most part limited to miniatures illustrating texts, and look outside Ottoman lyric poetry, for example, toward the romantic narrative poems and their illustrations, what do we see? As Julie Meisami points out in her study of Persian court poetry — most of whose themes are adopted mutatis mutandis by the Ottomans — many of the romances feature rulers and the concerns of dynasties to perpetuate themselves.[72] Marriage and (eventually) children are important in this context, and the woman as beloved is correspondingly prominent. Because these tales are the most commonly illustrated, much of the visual art that is not directly concerned with the affairs of the Ottoman dynasty contains representations of famous scenes with female beloveds — Shirin bathing naked while a love-smitten Husrev peeks, the seven brides of Behram Gur, Shirin watching as Ferhad hews at Mount Bisütun, Leyla encountering Mejnun in the desert. We do not have a study such as Saslow's for the female beloved in Ottoman art, but it does seem likely that, if we look away from love poetry (the gazel) toward the romantic narratives and the visual arts in general, we will discover a female beloved who tempers our impression of the overwhelming homoeroticism of poetically scripted love among the Ottoman elites.

The second dimension to parallels between the Ottoman magian boy and the European Ganymede involves their roles in the iconography of Neoplatonic idealism. This is a nexus at which the Ottoman/Islamic and European/Christian intersect. We will examine this dimension more fully in chapters 9 and 11 below. We mention it here only to point out that the early-modern audiences — the primary, cultural-elite audiences — of art would have been well aware of the dual nature of both icons as representing both carnal, worldly, homoerotic desire and an intellectual, spiritualized, otherworldly response to ideal (divine) qualities.

At this point, what is missing from our account is a focused discussion of the female beloved in Ottoman culture. This gives the impression that our study is *about* homoeroticism — which it is not. Nonetheless, the relative invisibility of women in the scripting of Ottoman cultural life makes the issue of the woman as beloved more ambiguous and complex in the Ottoman con-

A lover with female beloved. (Topkapı Palace Museum Library, B. 2168, "Albüm," fol. 10a.)

text than it appears to be in the European context. In the past decade or two, the early-modern European literatures have been heavily mined for references to male beloveds, while Ottoman literature has not even been gendered to any significant extent.[73] This is to say that we have not even explored the idea of the woman as beloved in Ottoman literature to any great degree. For the most part, scholars have either treated the Ottoman beloved anachronistically and Eurocentrically as if *she* were nearly always a woman—which *he* most obviously is not—or elided the issue altogether. What this means for Ottoman culture is that the female beloved exists as a shadow presence that can be seen only dimly through a haze of homoeroticism. For this reason, we will devote the next chapter to introducing the female beloved and suggesting how she might be discerned, however vaguely, behind Ottoman cultural veils.

6

WOMEN AND THE ART OF LOVE

As is true for early-modern societies in general, most of what we know about Ottoman women comes to us in the form of documents produced by men. Throughout the world, the transmitted knowledge about women has been overwhelmingly men's knowledge adulterated by the impressions, illusions, needs, and anxieties of men. Only relatively recently has any concerted effort been made by scholars to seek out the traces of what women might actually have done and thought. And, as we shall see, this is no easy task.

PART I: WOMEN, BELOVED AND DANGEROUS

Dangerous Women

The woman as beloved is a topic far too large to capture in a chapter or two. It is a topic—a hotly contested topic—for many volumes, of which the last will never be written. The best that we can do here is to point out some patterns of thought about female beloveds that seem to us relevant to the part of the early-modern period that we call *the Age of Beloveds*. In order to do this, we start where there is the most evidence, that is, with what men were thinking about women.

One of the more striking things that we learn from looking at the broad history of men's thinking about women in the West is that such thinking seems to be dominated as much by fear as by desire. In ancient Athens, where we often locate the roots of "Western civilization," the most popular of foundational myths concerns a battle between the Greeks and the Amazons.[1] Filling in gaps in the story of the Trojan wars is a lost tale about the hero Theseus defeating an army of Amazons and their queen, Penthesileia. (It is suggestive to recall that Pantesilea is the name of the prostitute who supposedly plotted vengeance on Benvenuto Cellini.) Ancient Athens is so awash in depictions of heroes—Theseus, Heracles, Achilles—killing Amazons that it seems as though Athens saw itself as having risen to power primarily as a result of the defeat of powerful and dangerous women.

The Amazons show up prominently in Elizabethan literature as well, to the extent that Louis A. Montrose includes their legends among "the shaping fantasies of Elizabethan culture." As Montrose points out, *A Midsummer Night's Dream* begins with an "Athenian connection": Theseus's defeat of the Amazon warrior Hippolyta.[2] Here, however, the battle ends, not in death, but in marriage. Theseus says to his erstwhile foe:

> Hippolyta, I woo'd thee with my sword,
> And won thy love, doing thee injuries;
> But I will wed thee in another key,
> With pomp, with triumph and with revelling.
> (act 1, sc. 1, lines 16–19)

But there is more. From such popular treatments as the "Novel of the Amazones" in William Painter's *The Palace of Pleasure* and several accounts of travel to the New World[3] to Spenser's *Faerie Queene*, the Amazon seems most often to represent a phallocentric culture's fantasy of role reversal in which men are subjugated, crippled, dominated, and effeminized. In *The Faerie Queen*, for example, when Artegall is subdued and literally enthralled by the Amazon Radigund (who, in bk. 5, canto 5, st. 9, is described as wielding a sharp scimitar, a weapon usually associated with Saracens and Turks), she subjects him to a peculiar humiliation:

> Then tooke the Amazon this noble knight,
> Left to her will by his owne wilfull blame,
> And caused him to be disarmed quight
> Of all the ornaments of knightly fame,
> With which whylome he gotten had great fame:
> Instead whereof she made him to be dight
> In womans weedes, that is to manhood shame,
> And put before his lap an apron white,
> Instead of Curiets and bases fit for fight.

Artegall's shame is matched by that of other captured knights, who are forced to work

> Spinning and carding all in comely rew,
> That his bigge hart loth'd so uncomely vew:
> But they were forst, through penurie and pyne,
> To doe those workes to them appointed dew;
> For nought was given them to sup or dyne,
> But what their hands could earne by twisting linnen twyne.[4]

This episode is quite similar to one in Ariosto's *Orlando Furioso*. Written and revised between 1516 and 1532, *Orlando Furioso* was immensely popular and provided both a model for and a challenge to Spenser, who composed his *Faerie Queen* between 1579 and 1594. In Ariosto's tale, a group of knights led by Astolfo and the warrior woman Marfisa are driven ashore by a storm on the coast of a land ruled by murderous women who enslave or kill all who venture into their land. The only escape is first to defeat ten men in single combat and then to satisfy ten women in bed the same night. The person who did this would become the prince of the land and could free his fellow captives. The knights arrive "confident of their weapons" (of both kinds) and find a host of women riding about with their skirts hiked up, "tilting at each other like Amazons." Those of the few menfolk who were not away laboring in the fields or among the herds were busy "at their shuttles and spindles, their reels, combs, and needles." And, as they spun and sewed, they were dressed "in feminine attire falling to their feet."[5]

These are examples of what might happen when, as Spenser says, women cease to "obay the heasts of mans well-ruling hand" and forget that "they were borne to base humilitie" and their cruel natures are, thereby, unleashed.[6] They are also further reminders of something that we mentioned in the previous chapter: that the love of a woman puts a man in great danger of being emasculated and effeminized. Of course, we cannot trace the whole history of powerful and dangerous women. Let it be noted, however, that their defeats were, apparently, neither complete nor permanent.

The Ottomans themselves were not without models of strong women. For example, in the well-known classical narrative *Husrev and Shirin*, the Armenian princess Shirin is first encountered by her lover, Husrev, while refreshing herself with a bath in a forest pool after having killed a lion single-handedly in the course of a hunt that she had undertaken alone. In the Persian *Book of Kings*, the rendition of traditional stories about the kings of ancient Iran versified near the turn of the eleventh century by Abu'l-Kasim Ferdevsi (Firdawsi)—a book so respected by the Ottomans that the court supported a Persian-speaking "Şahname writer" who wrote the history of the Ottoman sultans in the style of the original—we find the story of the female warrior who, shamed by the cowardly behavior of a Persian hero defeated by the invincible Sohrab, determines to avenge the insult:

> ... she a woman was who like a knight
> Had gained renown in war, and who was called
> Gordafarid—for in her time there was
> No mother who had born her like—she found
> The conduct of Hojir so shameful that
> The tulips in her cheeks turned black as pitch.
> She wasted not a moment, but bound on
> The coat of mail a horseman wears to fight.
> She hid her hair beneath that coat of mail,
> And knotted on her head a Roman casque.
> Then lionlike she raced down from the fort,
> Girded for battle, and seated on the wind.[7]

The Turkic oral tradition contains a story from among the legends of the Oğuz Turks (the tribe of Osman), recorded in the *Kitab-i Dede Korkut* (Book of Dede Korkut), which appears in written versions during Ottoman times. It tells the story of Bamsi Beyrek and his beloved, Banu Çiçek. Although Bamsi Beyrek is a handsome and virile young prince, Banu Çiçek is not about to accept him without testing. So, pretending to be her own servant, she says to the young man, who has asked to see her, " 'She is not the sort of person who would show herself to you. But I am her nurse. Let us go hunting together. If your horse can run faster than mine, you can beat her horse too. After that, let us shoot arrows. If you can shoot an arrow farther than I, you can beat her in this, too. Then, we shall wrestle. If you can defeat me at that, you can defeat her too.' "[8] A woman worthy of marrying a hero is confident and capable of doing whatever a man can do.

Where women appear in literature outside the classical (Perso-Ottoman) romances and legends, they are often depicted as dangers: not in the guise of armed Amazons fighting with warrior heroes or aiming weapons at male genitalia, as in the art adorning so many ancient Athenian ceramics, or as subjecting men to cruel servitude, but as powerful and ruthless adversaries nonetheless. They are witches, and hags, and beautiful but insatiable beloveds wielding magic, and cunning, and, above all, the mysterious power of female sexuality.

Imagined Women

Among the Ottoman elites, the common, official mythology concerning women depicted them as so weak in reasoning power that they they constantly fell prey to their animal natures and were, therefore, in need of being controlled by men. In his *Etiquette*, Mustafa 'Ali summarizes the reasons why:

> Men's failure to concern themselves with the protection of women opens the way to each [woman] succumbing to her animal nature and following the desires of her own heart and to their interacting with outsiders, thereby rending the curtain of modesty and shamelessly shredding the veil of chastity. This necessitates letting loose the monster of animal passion, which holds them in thrall beneath its feet, and their failing to distinguish good from evil while demeaning themselves by [their] desire to couple. For the wise are in agreement that not taking control of them and then expecting them to be chaste is like pleading, "Don't ejaculate," after a man has placed his organ in a woman's vulva and, in a dominating and distinguished manner, has engaged in some sugar-sweet movements. Or it is like a thirsty man who, after several days in the burning heat, obtains a swallow of water and satisfies himself with washing his hands instead of drinking it. For example, if the amber-like genitals of matchlessly beautiful women and the straw-like, hasty organ of [male] desire are both present, saying to the one, "Take care, don't attract," and to the other, "Beware, don't be attracted," is meaningless speech and babbling without sense or empathy.[a]
>
> They say that in the lands of China there is an herb called ———. It sprouts only at a certain time every year. Whenever the scent of it affects the noses of women, all have the uncontrollable desire to mate. Without doubt, each and every one of the people of that land, because they know the situation and know it well, locks his wife up for a month and, if he can, makes it right with her by having intercourse day and night as often as possible. For if they didn't protect them, it is certain that the whole nation of women would make their sexual honor one with the dirt. So you see, it is known from this that they protect their women assiduously because [if] the reins of control over women are dropped, they will necessarily desire, willing or no, to sleep with any man they run across.
>
> It is necessary to keep women always covered and veiled
> For every part of a woman is a private [sexual] part

---

[a] In Persian, amber is called *keh-rūbā* or "straw attracting" in reference to its property of holding an electric charge, which attracts small bits of chaff.

> The Prophet said about his wives
> The woman herself is a private part [a part that should be covered]⁹

This fantasy of the woman as a sexual being lacking rational self-control—as though she were under the influence of an aphrodisiac herb—appears to be more than merely a pretext for male domination of women. From the notion of a woman as a "private part," that is, as a body part that causes arousal in others, it follows naturally that rational beings—men—will be inadvertently aroused by the sight of a woman and that women, being prey to their animal natures, will themselves be uncontrollably excited by the sight of an aroused male. Thus, if women are visible and unsupervised, everyone will be in danger of losing control, and the moral fiber of family and community will be at risk.

We must mention here that the notion of men as essentially unable to resist women or women's beauty is not strictly an Ottoman or Muslim notion. For example, in concluding early in the *Astrophel and Stella* poems a catalog (one couched in very architectural terms) of the beauties of Stella's face, Sir Philip Sidney also hits on the comparison to amber: "Of touch [i.e., amber] they are, and poore I am their straw."¹⁰

The fantasy of an out-of-control woman is part of a complex of fantasies perhaps stemming in some degree from actual physiological differences suggestive of female sexual prowess—for example, the ability to bear children, the lack of a refractory period after intercourse—in addition to male anxieties about the mysterious nature of female sexuality. Much of the humor involving women in Gazali's *Repeller of Sorrows* is based on anxieties that even time, social change, and modern-day sex education have, apparently, done little to erase. We have already mentioned the insatiable-woman fantasy in which the man is helpless before the woman's apparent ability to have (and enjoy) intercourse an infinite number of times. Hidden in this fantasy are the fears that no single man can satisfy a woman and that every man is in danger of being found inadequate by his beloved.

For example, a number of Gazali's anecdotes also exploit age-old male anxieties about penis size.¹¹ Ignorance about the physiology of female sexual response leads to the fantasy that women achieve sexual pleasure in direct proportion to the size of a man's penis. Thus, we find stories such as the one about a princess who, on attaining (sexual) maturity, asked her father to marry her to the man with the world's largest penis. The father's spies and envoys finally discover candidates in the three sons of a far-off monarch (and obviously a Christian monarch at that). The oldest of the sons had a penis so large that he used it as a bridge over a river wide as the Danube. The middle son used his as the clapper for a great church bell. But the eldest did not want to give up doing his pious duty to the community, and the middle son had committed his member to the religious foundation that supported the church. So the youngest son, with the largest penis of all, agreed to the match and had his member loaded onto a thousand camels for the journey to his intended. He was so virile that, when he heard a description of his future wife's charms, his erection lifted all thousand camels from the ground. Nonetheless, after the wedding night, the sultan asked his daughter how she liked the groom, and she responded, "He is fine, and I thank you for it, but I wish they had brought the one who uses his for a bridge and the one with a clapper so I could try them as well."[12]

Or there is the story of the villager who took his wife to the city for the first time. When she noticed the minarets of the great mosques in the distance, she asked what the upright things were. Her husband answered that they were the penises of the city, used by city women, and he asked her whether she thought she could accommodate them as well. "My God," the woman replied, "what a band of whores these city women must be; I could take in only the head, and, if there were no head, I could accommodate only half the rest."[13]

Then there was the woman who sued her husband, claiming that he did not have regular intercourse with her, as the law requires. When asked about this by the judge, the man said, "Every night I have intercourse with her five times; I come back from my shop in the heat of noon to give her a fuck, then once again before I return to the shop." The woman replied, "Come on, dear sir, look here, this madman is counting his teensy-weensy thing [as a fuck]!"[14]

Such supposedly instructive stories are not limited to marginal works such as pornography either. In the mainstream mesnevi entitled *Kitab-i usul* (The book of religious fundamentals), the janissary poet Yahya, who, as we mentioned earlier, does not consider women to be suitable beloveds, includes the following anecdote about a rich young widow:

> There once was a woman who became the heir
> To goods and money and a mansion fair
>
> All day and all night she was pleased to abide
> In luxury's lap like a blushing new bride
>
> But her only concern for the rest of her life
> Was the hope of becoming a nobleman's wife
>
> Yet foolishly everyone's suit she opposed
> Rejecting all of the men who proposed
>
> Then one of the bankrupts hears of her case
> Conspires to see her surrender take place

Off to his concubine forthwith he hastens
Teaches her tricks and misrepresentations

To the moneybags widow the concubine goes
Serenades her with weeping and wailing and woes

Says, You who are power and glory's possessor
In exile help me, be my intercessor

With a tyrant don't leave me in captivity
Buy me and free me in sweet charity

My master has sex with me ten times a day
And only wants more without pause or delay

Like the stump of an arm is this fellow's cock
As big as a sturdy tree, hard as a rock[15]

He goes day and night the servant related
If a person were iron he could not be sated

With wails and laments to the woman she cried
'Til appetite burgeoned to fill her inside

For five or ten days the concubine called
'Til the poor widow's hunger could not be forestalled

So she married the bankrupt by choice in a trice
Paying no heed to contrary advice

The profligate's fortunes took a turn for the best
The community gathered, their wedding was blest

That night when they met to couple someplace
"May evil strike you," she cursed to his face

For she'd seen his tool, a pinky-sized freak
A thin, slimy slug all flaccid and weak

It's a proverb: The guest doesn't dine as expected
And the unseen calamity can't be detected

The poor woman's dreams turned out a bust
She fell to the carpet weeping from lust

By that unmanly man was her peace put to flight
She became a consumptive and died of her plight

Her inheritance all went to him in a flash
And the impotent bankrupt was rolling in cash

A man can't say no to a woman's deceit
And men in deception aren't easy to beat[16]

These anecdotes all contain a phallocratic fascination with a grotesquely exaggerated (or minimized) penis (even to the extent of eroticizing—and phallicizing—the urban landscape by describing the minarets, which dominate the horizons of major cities, as the city's penises). Although the hyperbole of these tales is likely protective—this is so absurd that it can't really be real—at the same time the preoccupation with this particular symbol of male dominance reveals, at its core, the essence of some very primitive male anxieties: I can't do it enough to satisfy her; she would really be happier with someone who has a larger penis. In contrast to the ancient Greek myth in which the ancestral warriors defeat the Amazons (usually, and significantly, by stabbing them), in this Ottoman fantasy the woman is capable of accommodating even the largest penis and wishing for more. All things being equal, in sexual combat the Amazons win.

A crushing blow to the authority of the phallus, however, is the awareness that it can have its substitutes. "Some women," Gazali says, "cannot find a penis to their liking, and neither can they run around uncovered like whores, so they make do with dildos and satisfy their needs with them." In talking about dildos, Gazali opens the door a tiny crack onto what appears to be a forbidden (or unthought) topic in early-modern Ottoman discussions of sexuality. He relates stories about sexual practices of every sort: men loving and having sex with women and with men and boys; even men and women engaging in intercourse with animals from elephants to fleas. But there is not a single reference to women loving other women. And there is only one mention of women having sexual relations with women, and that only in the context of sex for sale or barter: "In the great cities there are famous dildo women. They wear caftans [like men] and mount horses like cavalrymen. For pleasure they ride in covered wagons [koçi/koçu]. Wealthy noblewomen invite them [into their wagons] and offer them chemises and [other] articles of clothing. They [then] strap dildos about their hips, oil them with almond oil, and set about the business in the usual manner, working away dildoing the cunt."[17]

There is some recognition here that sexual activities among women did take place, in this case when women went out for excursions in koçi, which were private rooms (harems) on four wheels, covered wagons with simple exteriors, grated windows, entry ladders at the back, and decorated interiors comfortably appointed with velvet and damasked cushions and pillows.[18] It is likely that the images of dildos wielded by "masculine" women, described as wearing male clothing and riding horses (the male mode of travel), serve to reassure the author's male audiences that sex among women is only a less-than-satisfactory substitute for the real thing: a man and a penis. As a consequence of either willful masculine ignorance of female sexual physiology or simple repression of something too frightening to contemplate, the idea that women might obtain sexual pleasure by means that have nothing to do with men or male organs or substitutes for male organs is never openly entertained.

There are numerous examples of early-modern discomfort (and, perhaps, fascination) with the idea of women loving women. In *Orlando Furioso*, we find the very suggestive story of Bradamant and Fiordispina. Briefly told, the story goes as follows: The warrior woman Bradamant is wounded in the head by Spaniards and is forced to cut her hair to keep the wound clean. She falls asleep in a forest glade, where she is discovered by the beautiful Spanish princess Fiordispina, who falls hopelessly in love with her, thinking that she is a young man (another example of the open androgyny of the early-modern beloved). When Bradamant gently reveals to her that she too is a woman and describes her career as a warrior, Fiordispina remains incurably enamored. Bradamant's "face seemed no less beautiful for this, her eyes, her movements no less graceful; she did not on this account retrieve mastery over her own heart." Having allowed a woman to have a woman as beloved, Ariosto seems obliged to assert the impossibility and uniqueness of this circumstance and reestablish the natural order. The distraught princess bewails her plight and its painful difference from other loves, saying: "Neither among humans nor among beasts have I ever come across a woman loving a woman; to a woman another woman does not seem beautiful, nor does a hind to a hind, a ewe to a ewe."[19] Fiordispina is rescued from her dilemma—that she has made actual an impossible love—by the appearance of Bradamant's twin brother, who is able to manifest all the qualities (primarily visual, in the manner of Petrarchan commonplaces) that occasioned Fiordispina's initial attraction, with the unspoken addition of the missing organ.

Ariosto's seems to have been the prevailing view in early-modern Europe. Thus, Gazali's reticence about sexual relations between women (when he is squeamish about little else, including rapes, bizarre forms of masturbation, and all sort of sexual adventures with animals) is not at all unusual. In her introduction to an account of the ecclesiastical trial of an Italian nun who loved another woman, Judith Brown points out: "Among the hundreds if not thousands of cases of sodomy tried by lay and ecclesiastical courts in medieval and early modern Europe, there are almost none involving sexual relations between women."[20] We have not been able to locate a single instance in the Ottoman legal literature of a woman being accused of illegal or immoral sexual relations with another woman.

Among the few extant European cases is an anecdote from Montaigne's travels through France—taken by both Stephen Greenblatt and Valerie Traub as a text—in which it is reported to him that, in a certain town, several women conspired to dress and live as men. One of the women even set herself up as a weaver, fell in love with a woman, and married her. The two lived together satisfactorily for some time, but, when this usurpation of male identity was discovered, the transvestite was condemned to be hanged "for using illicit devices to supply her defect in sex."[21] In this case, it is not a woman desiring another woman that creates a legal problem. It is the use of a "device" to impersonate a man and to penetrate a woman that is illegal. In Gazali's Ottoman text, the use of a device is not described as exceptional (in keeping with the fantasy that all women desire to be penetrated), and there is even a story about a woman who orders a dildo from a woodturner.[22]

Apparently, during the Renaissance, it was seldom considered possible that women could be attracted to women (and it was considered impossible that, in sexual relations with another woman, a woman could do anything but imitate a man). This kind of desire is simply not thought about, and, if it does occur, it is not "native." Fiordispina, in the extremity of her hopeless infatuation, spends a night in prayer "to Mahomet and all the gods, asking them to change Bradamant's sex for the better by a clear and self-evident miracle."[23] If a woman is going to love another woman, she must be a Muslim—or at least someone, anyone, other than "us." It is not terribly surprising, then, that, late in the Age of Beloveds, the first steps toward a discourse of lesbianism in English sources will occur in accounts of the Ottoman Empire. From the travel accounts of Nicolay (1585), Sandys (1610), and Purchas (1613) to historical works such as Grimeston's 1635 translation of a 1626 French account of life in the Ottoman saray or Rycaut's influential *The Present State of the Ottoman Empire* (1682), English writers openly recognized the existence of female same-sex desire/sexual activity and located its center in the Ottoman East, associating it directly with social conditions thought to be peculiar to Muslims and Ottomans.[24] For example, in his *Navigations into Turkey*, Nicolay says of Ottoman women in the Turkish baths:

> [They] do familiarly wash one another, whereby it commeth to passe that amongst the women of Levan, there is very great amity proceding only through the frequentation & resort to the bathes: yea & sometimes become so fervently in love the one of the other as if it were with men, in such sort that perceiving some maiden or woman of excellent beauty they will not ceasse until they have found means to bath with them, & to handle & grope them every where at their pleasures so ful they are of luxuriousnes

& feminine wantonnes: Even as in times past wer the Tribades of the number wherof was Sapho the Lesbian which transferred the love wherwith she pursued a 100. women or maidens upon her only friend Phaon. And therfore considering the reasons aforesaid, to wit, the clening of their bodies, health, superstition, liberty to go abroad, & lascivious voluptuousnes, it is not to be marvelled at that these baths are so accustomably frequented of the Turks.[25]

Same-sex love and sexual relations among women were interpreted as being the results of an imagined Muslim tolerance of same-sex love (at best a misreading of the quranic verses mentioned in the previous chapter), the strict separation of the sexes, and the natural wantonness of women distorting "natural" Neoplatonic love into the carnal and "unnatural." English writers seem to be as squeamish as Gazali about the thought of "their" women loving women, but they are perfectly willing to dwell lasciviously on the matter when it is dissociated from their own circumstances and projected onto the Ottomans.

If we set aside the idea that Ottoman or Muslim practices of covering or guarding women were somehow unique to them, we begin to see that the notion that an unrestrained woman is likely a promiscuous and dangerous woman seems to have been commonplace among early-modern men. For example, Coryat, the traveling English prude, approved of the restrictions imposed on elite Venetian women: "For the Gentlemen do even coope up their wives alwaies within the walles of their houses for fear of these inconveniences.... So that you shall very seldome see a Venetian Gentlemans wife but either at the solemnization of a great marriage, or the Christning of a Iew, or late in the evening rowing in a Gondola.... For they thinke that the chastity of their wives would be the sooner assaulted, and so consequently they would be capricornified [i.e., cuckolded]."[26] And Renaissance conduct books and sermons invariably treat the woman as a recalcitrant animal to be tamed until "shee submits herselfe with quietness, cheerfully, even as a well-broken horse turnes at the least check of the riders bridle, readily going and standing as he wishes that sits upon his backe." The methods used for such breaking—including violence and mental cruelty—are compared to those used "to tame lions, bulls, and elephants."[27] Lions, bulls, and elephants! Quite a menagerie of large, ferocious, and dangerous animals is used to describe a gender considered to be inferior in part because of its weakness.

The men in Elizabethan audiences would surely have had few qualms about applying to all women Claudio's rant against his once-beloved Hero or the hapless Ford's opinion about his wife's trustworthiness:

CLAUDIO:

> You seem to me as Dian in her orb,
> As chaste as is the bud ere it be blown;
> But you are more intemperate in your blood
> Than Venus, or those pamper'd animals
> That rage in savage sensuality.
> (*Much Ado about Nothing*, act 4, sc. 1, lines 58–62)

FORD:

> ... Page is an ass, a secure ass; he will trust his wife; he will not be jealous. I will rather trust a Fleming with my butter, Parson Hugh the Welshman with my cheese, an Irishman with my aqua-vitae bottle, or a thief to walk my ambling gelding, than my wife with herself: then she plots, then she ruminates, then she devises; and what they think in their hearts but they will effect.
> (*The Merry Wives of Windsor*, act 2, sc. 2, lines 313–22)

In *Much Ado about Nothing*, the misogynistic antilover Benedick expresses a terrible anxiety about powerful women as represented by his sharp-tongued adversary Beatrice:

> She speaks poniards and every word stabs: if her breath were as terrible as her terminations, there were no living hear her; she would infect to the north star.
>
> ... [S]he would have made Hercules have turned spit, yea, and have cleft his club to make the fire too.
> (act 2, sc. 1, lines 255–58, 260–62)

Without going into the obvious symbolism of Hercules's "club" or giving further historical examples of early-modern men's misogynistic anxieties about women's "savage sensuality" and sharp tongues, we will go on to look more closely at the female beloved as she appears in the predominantly homoerotic context of Ottoman elite culture. But first some additional background.

One thing that we mentioned earlier (in chapter 2) is the fact that while the love poetry of the European Middle Ages is homoerotic—having been produced (in Latin and Greek) predominantly by the literate members of all-male religious orders—it does not describe young male and female beloveds as different in any significant way. For example, in an article on the medieval boy beloved, Thomas Stehling cites two Latin poems by Marbod of Rennes

(1035–1123)—who served as master of the cathedral school in Angers, where he was born, and later as the bishop of Rennes—one containing the description of a beloved girl, the other that of a beloved boy:

> *Egregium vultum modica pinguedine fultum*
>
> An extraordinary face enhanced by a slight plumpness,
> Shining whiter than snow, blushing redder than the spring rose;
> A starlike gaze, a smile promising tenderness,
> Slightly swollen lips like fiery offerings;
> Good straight teeth, shining white,
> Strong limbs, guileless good manners—
> All these has the girl who wants to unite herself to me. . . .

> *De puero quodam composuit Horatius odam*
>
> Horace composed an ode about a certain boy
> Who could easily enough have been a pretty girl.
> Over his ivory neck flowed hair
> Brighter than yellow gold, the kind I have always loved
> His brow was white as snow, his luminous eyes black as pitch;
> His unfledged cheeks full of pleasing sweetness
> When they flushed bright white and red.
> His nose was straight, lips blazing, teeth lovely,
> Chin shaped after an appropriate model.
> Anyone wondering about the body which lay hidden under his clothes
> Would be gratified, for the boy's body matched his face. . . .

Stehling also points out that Marbod's student, Baudri of Bourgueil (1046–1130)—who ended his career as archbishop of Dol in Brittany—wrote most of his 255 poems about men (only fifteen are about women). In his work can be found similar idealized descriptions of a young man and a young woman:

> *Forma placet, quia forma decet, quia forma venusta est*
>
> Your appearance is pleasing because it is proper and handsome;
> So too your delicate cheek, your blonde hair, and modest mouth.
> Your voice, sounding as sweetly as the nightingale's,
> Caresses and soothes our ears.
> It could be a boy's or a girl's;
> You will be another Orpheus, unless age injures it—
> Age which distinguishes girls from boys
> When young men's cheeks are first clothed with down
> And a strong nose enhances their faces and looks.

Your bright, clear eyes touch my breast and heart,
For I believe those crystalline lights truly are a double star.
Your milky flesh and ivory chest match them;
The touch of hands plays over your snowy body. . . .

Non rutilat Veneris tam clara binomia stella

The clear double-named star of Venus has not so rosy a glow
As those two clear, luminous eyes of yours.
When I look at your hair I think that gold has a less tawny sheen
Your neck shines brighter than lilies or new fallen snow.
Your teeth shine whiter than ivory or Parian marble.
Lively charm breathes on your lips.
Your lips swell a little and I am warmed, set afire by them,
Though only a decent warmth heats them.
I say your tender cheeks should by rights be preferred to roses
Since red and white and all beauty clothe them.
To treat the composition of your body briefly:
It is the kind of body to fit such a face. . . .[28]

Both poets find it necessary to point out that, from the standpoint of ideal beauty, the boy and the girl are very much the same. Marbod sings of "a certain boy / who could easily enough have been a pretty girl," and the voice of Baudri's boy could have been "a boy's or a girl's."

For the early-modern Ottoman literate classes, the beloved has much the same androgynous character. For example, Gazali describes a female beloved as follows: "She is a queen of beauties, her body is a swaying cypress, her hair a hyacinth, her moles are like peppercorns, her cheek a rose, her lip like wine; her teeth are pearls, her mouth a signet seal, her form like Tuba, the lote tree of paradise; her cheek is a shining moon, her hair like the darkest night; her face is the remotest destination, her body is the most sublime aspiration, in the body is a fresh, young spirit, a houri of paradise, sweet tongued, bow browed, like the sultan of the world."[29] He describes the ideal boy beloved in this manner:

> The master exemplars of wisdom and possessors of insight mention the essentials of beauty. An exquisite lad and attractive heart stealer stands out among the lovely and is worthy of the name *beautiful* when he has a cypress body, a tulip cheek, a rosebud lip, an apple chin, a moon face and a crescent brow, when his moles are like peppercorns, his hair like the hyacinth, his face smiling, eyes shadowed, his glance like a falcon's, his gait bobbing like a partridge. And likewise they say he must be endowed with noble qualities and should be renowned for, accustomed and habituated to, praiseworthy

morals. But the truth of the matter is this: Whomsoever the heart desires is beautiful.[30]

As we have already pointed out, it appears evident from a number of sources that, from medieval times into the Age of Beloveds, the (elite) male imagination did not distinguish in any practical way between boys and girls/women where the erotic was concerned. The genders blend one into the other. Each one can act the part of the other in an erotic script. Anyone who can be dominated and penetrated can be the object of sexual desire. On the Elizabethan stage, boys played female roles—in part because it was considered indecent for women to appear as actors. In the poetry of the Ottoman elites, the role of the beloved was played by an epicene youth—in part because it was considered indecent to imply that a particular woman was the object of desire (i.e., that she was "unguarded/uncovered") or that a "poetic" (platonic, intellectualized, spiritualized) love could properly be directed toward the class of women available for public attention. There is a stage of youth where the girl and the "barely bearded" boy can change gender by changing clothing, as is the case with several of Shakespeare's very young male and female protagonists. Nonetheless, there are some suggestive asymmetries.

Hidden in the descriptive "could be a boy's or a girl's" or the Ottoman act of giving a boy the nickname Kız Memi (Girl Memi) or Sürmeli Kadın (Eye-Shadowed Woman) is the implication that the beautiful boy is in some degree a transvestite, a girl in boy's clothing (rather than the reverse, which is the usual case).[31] Entertainments during the Age of Beloveds featured both dancing girls (*çengi*) and similarly dressed dancing boys (*köçek*), about whom, when talking about the sorts of available beloveds, Mustafa 'Ali says: "In short, those who have a yen for famous lovely faces and are entirely desirous of summoning into their presence elegantly swaying, tall, and silver-bodied cypresses should not neglect the dancing boys [*köçek*] of Rumeli."[32] We might argue that, in patriarchal (phallocentric) societies, the transvestite object of desire is woman-plus, a woman with certain possible advantages. The girl-boy as a beloved was simply more available to younger men without households of their own.

Among the Ottomans, for example, older men with households had sexual access to their wives and female slaves/concubines, just as established and married Venetians had access to high-priced courtesans. The customary late marriage, the lack of contraception, and the number of unattached boys in need of a master or patron also contributed to the convenience of same-sex attractions. As a result, a relatively large number of young men, many of whom would be exclusively heterosexual later in life, had amorous or sexual relations with other men. Because sex roles most often changed with life stages, these men knew, in an emotionally transparent way unavailable in relations between men and women, what it was to be both the lover and the beloved of another man. Moreover, for a male to love a male affirms self-love (it is, in this sense, masturbatory); it also affirms the value of masculinity and supports a patriarchal culture, insofar as the possibility of a boy dominating a man made vulnerable by love does not threaten patriarchal structures to the same extent that a woman dominating a man might. In this context, it is not surprising that, among the elites at least, the cultural scripting of love favored a young male beloved.

Nonetheless, all such arguments considered, the fact that we do not know much about Ottoman female beloveds does not mean that there were none or that women were as invisible and passive as they appear to be on the cultural surface. Although evidence is scanty—in large part because it has never been sought in a systematic way—there are some hints that we can gather from sources mentioned elsewhere in this study. For example, as we saw in chapter 2, Latifi makes a passing reference to "female beloveds" (*mahbube*) in the course of describing "inconstant [male] beloveds," and Zati ghostwrites love poems for "highborn" women. Several poets are mentioned in the tezkires as having the "peculiarity" of being attracted to women rather than young men. In his entry for the poet Sunʿi, ʿAşık mentions one of the poet's beloveds and cites a poem:

He Fell in Love with a Greek Woman Named Sultane in
Gallipoli and Wrote the Following [Poem] about It

> A Greek sultan has brought me to the affliction of love
> > Oh my sultan, Allah, bring me remedy for this trouble
>
> That tyrant, my heart, has made me prisoner of an infidel
> > Help! Set a Muslim free from an unbeliever
>
> I am a candle that burns all the way to the church
> > Since I saw in her countenance all the lights of faith
>
> There is no hope of union with her by means of sultanis[b]
> > Quick, take the hem of the priest if you wish to embrace her
>
> Today we are slaves of the sultan, oh Sunʿi, in love and affection
> > Oh sir, she is my monarch, this Greek sultan[33]

[b] The sultani was the first Ottoman gold coin based on the standard of the Venetian ducat (see Pamuk, *Monetary History*, 61).

Similarly, as we saw in chapter 3, in his *Book of Desire* Tacızade Ca'fer Çelebi tells the story of an affair that he (supposedly) had with a highborn woman during an excursion to Kağıthane. This is a story that seems worth looking at in greater detail.

The Book of Desire itself exemplifies something of the nature of Ottoman literary style, which tends to be very self-conscious about what it is doing and usually combines seemingly disparate purposes in a single work. It begins with the usual religious verses in praise of God's unity and the Prophet, followed by a prayer in which Ca'fer admits that thoughts of love are with him even during his devotions:

> In my fancy taper, wine, and youth
> The heart does long for leg and arm in truth
>
> When I set out to pray with "God is great"
> It is my love the heart will supplicate
>
> Why is't, when e'er my face to the prayer niche turns
> My heart for the curving arch of an eyebrow yearns
>
> And then when e'er to Mecca I turn my face
> The soul's eye opens to my beloved's place[34]

This prayer is followed by a prayer for the sultan, then a poetic description of several Istanbul buildings, including the tower of Galata, the royal palace, the royal bathhouse, the Hagia Sophia, and the Mosque of the Conqueror and the attached medrese, public kitchens, and hospital, then the story of the establishment of the Mosque and Tomb of Eyüp (Eyyub). This paean to God, his Prophet, the sultan, and the capital city—or the story's spiritual, government, and physical context—is followed by the story behind the story that is to be told.

This segment is quite typical—up to a point. We see in it many features familiar from the tale of Tayyib and Tahir. The author describes his life, which is filled with learning, close friends, and parties for which he writes lyrical poems. One day, at a party, some friends suggest that he compose an original narrative poem, but he demurs, saying that such pursuits are not suitable for a true scholar and a waste of his time. He then explains to his friends his views on literature and its previous practitioners, pointing out that even the greatest among them (Şeyhi and Ahmet Pasha) were little more than imitators of the long-standing Perso-Arab tradition. He is finally convinced to write his own mesnevi and sets about finding a topic. In the end, failing to be inspired by the traditional themes, he decides to tell the tale of a personal experience with love. It is this fiction of personal experience together with the gender of the beloved that makes this a striking departure from the traditional.

Ca'fer precedes the actual narrative with a short passage pointing out that the true purpose of mecazi, or metaphoric, love is to lead one to hakkiki, or real/ideal (i.e., Neoplatonic), love of the divine—after which mention of the divine effectively disappears. The story itself begins with a description of Kağıthane in the spring. Ca'fer and some friends have traveled there on an outing to camp for several days. While he is watching the river, he notices a boat approaching and chances to catch a glimpse of his future beloved:

> As I watched the vessel, it came to the verge
> Fragments of moon I saw emerge
>
> Each so alluring, in beauty arrayed
> Each one's robe of gold-thread brocade
>
> Each a princess in domains of beauty
> Attending to each watchful servants on duty
>
> Though each one was lovely and captured the heart
> One there was matchless and clear set apart
>
> Arrow-lash icon, brows Bow-like fair
> Scorpio Moon and Hyacinth hair [c]
>
> Gemini idol, though sun of clear weather
> Leo eyes, Lamb breath, Fish body together
>
> Though weighty truly seems her head [d]
> For a waist she has a hair instead
>
> A houri she is, fairies the rest
> This one a parrot, those pigeon breast
>
> So wore that moon of auspicious mien
> The sky of a gold-worked robe of green
>
> When from her beauty its desire grew
> The robe, upon her, did gold pieces strew

---

[c] These next couplets are an extended play on astronomical references: the Arrow (*tīr*) is also the planet Mercury (the eyelashes are like arrows), the Bow is Sagittarius, the Hyacinth is Virgo, the Lamb is Ares, and the Fish is Pisces.

[d] The term *ser-giran* (lit. "heavy of head") means an intelligent, serious person.

Suppose her body a candle green tinted
Upon it golden foliage imprinted

The green brocade so tightly fit
That rosebud could scarcely fit in it

In golden knots from head to toe
Wild rosebuds decked the meadow so

That lithe disruption girt her waist
In a lovely sash with silver chased

That waist has made folk impolite
The sash, for this crime, has bound it tight

It made the beloved even sweeter
Her sapling shape a cane of sugar

A lover wrapping it in his arm
The turn of fate[e] keeps her waist from harm

Golden slippers upon her feet
With nails of gilt in every cleat

You'd think it gold with silver blended
That water and fire's war had ended

She rose, and when she showed her face
Heaven appeared, resurrection took place

When into the field that beauty strayed
It spread at her feet a green brocade

She walked the greensward with a sway
As damask roses laughed on her way

Where golden cleats on the ground did rest
Mad earth burnt cleat prints on its breast[f]

Saw hobnail stars and made a hole
In its breast for each, in place of a soul

---

[e] The word *devran* means "going around" and here is used to mean both a cycle of time or fate or the heavens (which are now favorable to embracing) and the arm going around the waist.

[f] A practice of distraught Ottoman lovers was to burn themselves with rolled tubes of paper or felt, which would leave semicircular brands, like cleat prints or horseshoe prints.

Women entertaining themselves on a picnic. (Topkapı Palace Museum Library, B. 408, "I. Ahmed albümü," fol. 66a.)

When it saw her foot touch earth, the sky
"Oh would that I were dust" did cry.[g]

Gleamed her cheek in meadow vale
As in the Yemen, the star Suheyl[h]

Rays from her cheek to all sides shone
Carnelian made of every stone[35]

What we have here is a party of upper-class women traveling alone and setting up camp in a beautiful natural setting. They are not, strictly speaking, uncovered or unenclosed (i.e., they are not what in English were called *loose women*) because they have a retinue of servants with them. It does seem, however, that they are not aware of being observed; at least the beloved removes her veil ("She rose, and when she showed her face," "Gleamed her cheek"), acting as if she were in the privacy of her home. Having removed the drab outer covering worn by Muslim woman going out in public, this beloved is dressed in a lovely gold-worked brocade, bound at the waist by a silver-embroidered sash and so tight fitting that she seems ready to burst from it.

This passage is an especially effective example of the Ottoman poetic practice of re-creating the beloved and nature (the sky, the land, the flowers) as mirrors of each other, each coming to subsume the other until the beloved inheres in the vision of nature and nature in the beloved. To Westerners, this style often seems to reduce nature to a mere stylized reflection and to suppress its actual (and cherished) profusion and diversity, but it also profoundly sensualizes and eroticizes the natural world to the point that the sensitive, poetic Ottoman's relation with nature seems surprisingly (even excessively) personal, emotional, and erotic.

In any case, the poet is immediately smitten and seeks out a go-between, who in this instance turns out to be the woman's maidservant, most likely a domestic slave. (The servant as intermediary for lovers is a commonplace of Ottoman culture over a long period and in many sources from elite poetry to shadow-puppet theater. Recall, e.g., Yahya's story of the bankrupt and the rich young widow, in which the slave concubine acted duplicitously as a go-between.) When the servant tells her mistress of the poet's interest, the woman sends her back with a request:

Go thou, she said, to him and meet
With pleasant chat and converse sweet

[g] In Islamic lore, this is what those who have gone astray will cry on Judgment Day.

[h] In this couplet and the next we must remember that, in traditional lore, carnelian is formed when the star Suheyl shines on ordinary stones in the Yemen.

> Ask of him his divan for me
> His mine of precious jewelry
>
> If he doesn't have it with him here
> Then things he's memorized, my dear
>
> Say, Write a few gazels, at least
> A morsel for our soul-feeding feast[36]

Here, we have a narrative incorporating the notion that one "hunts gazelles with gazels." If this beloved is going to have a love affair, if she is going to consent to be a beloved, she wants to be courted with poetry and to see what kind of talents and intellectual gifts the lover has to offer. She is not described as ignorant, frivolous, or lacking in wit. In fact, she is described as being intelligent and serious (*ser-giran*) and as a parrot, which implies wit and verbal (poetic) skills. Her intelligence is considered to be one of her attractive features. It is assumed that she can appreciate a high-culture love poem and tell good poetry from bad.

So the servant goes to the lover and makes her request:

> A few gazels write out as a favor
> That reading them the lovelies might savor

And the lover, perhaps because he is young and does not yet have a divan, responds by saying:

> What's a divan when you have my soul
> Whate'er you command, you're in control
>
> That it would be a necessity
> And find such popularity
>
> I couldn't guess so left it behind
> But those gazels caught in my mind
>
> I'll write them out as they appear
> Pearls to adorn my lovely's ear
>
> I took up paper, cut a pen
> Began to speak like a parrot just then
>
> The black of my pupil with tears I stirred
> Wrote out some gazels word for word[37]

The poetry is effective, and the two begin an affair consisting of several meetings, some very poetic suffering, and exchanges of love poetry. (The fact that some of the poetry is presented as composed by the beloved would appear to indicate that the idea of a woman writing poetry is not all that strange. It is also in keeping with Zati's claim that he ghostwrote poems for women to send to their beloveds, the presumption here being that women who could write their own poems did so.) When the idyll in the countryside ends, the beloved re-covers herself in a black robe and veil bound by a scarf over the head and under the chin for the journey back into public space:

> That lord of beauty from her tent like the sky
> Appeared as glimmering sunlight on high
>
> She donned a black cloak, and the gloomiest nights
> Grieved for the loss of their moon shining bright
>
> Hidden in this is a sign; you'll remark
> That the fountain of life is concealed in the dark[i]
>
> Over her cheek a veil of dark musk,
> The sunshine was turned by a cloud into dusk
>
> Then that pure vision bound up her head
> Across dimpled chin with a scarf of dark red
>
> The face of the sun in a dark veil is hidden
> And the red of a dawning tints the horizon[38]

The affair continues briefly with a few letters but no further contact. The risk to the beloved's reputation is too great and the consequences of discovery too severe.

Of course, this is a story told primarily for aesthetic and artistic reasons. Even the assertion that it is a true account is subject to doubt, for such assertions are commonplaces of literary style. Nonetheless, it is a depiction intended to convince its audiences—Ottoman consumers of high-culture literary art—that it could have been an accurate representation of a love affair between a young man and a young woman of the elite classes. That is to say that an Ottoman audience would have accepted that an encounter like this could have taken place and that the behavior of the Ottoman lover and his female beloved was reasonable under the circumstances. What this and much other evidence indicates—although the point is nowhere stated overtly—is that the garden or natural setting is a special kind of space, one where the rules of normal (public) space do not apply. We know quite a bit about the

---

[i] In the legend of Alexander/Iskender, the fountain of eternal life is found in a land of eternal darkness.

official restrictions on women's public behavior in Ottoman society. It was considered a communal duty to police sexual behavior, including the behavior of women, and there were officials, most prominently the muhtesib and the subaşı, who were charged with chastising those who offended communal norms. We also know about some private spaces in which women were free to interact openly and uncovered (both unveiled and unsupervised by men)—for example, the harem of a private home, the public bath. But we know very little about other spaces in which the usual forms of public surveillance were relaxed or did not take place, except that we suspect that there were some.

Women and Society in the Age of Beloveds

In a fascinating discussion of the prosecution of *zina* (fornication/adultery) centering on court records from the provincial city of Aintab in southeastern Anatolia during the mid-sixteenth century, Leslie Peirce brings up an interesting side issue. Intrigued by the unusually large number of cases of young women accused of zina brought to official attention in a single year, Peirce casts about for environmental factors that might account for what seems to have been an anomalous situation. One of the factors that strikes her is a relatively sudden population surge.[39] This population surge is attested to by numerous sources, but it is by no means limited to Anatolia.[40] As we have seen, population growth in the Mediterranean world and beyond led to a sharp increase in vagabonds (mostly men), unmarried young men still living in their fathers' households (called *mücerred* in the Ottoman Empire), men of more or less levend status, and young married men without households of their own (Ottoman: *bennak*).[41] The dynamics of population growth and the accompanying internal migration (in search of economic opportunity) meant that vast numbers of young men flocked to towns and cities to which they had no social ties. Because many, perhaps even most, marriages were then arranged between families who were acquainted with each other, there was considerable pressure on young men to form liaisons with women outside the traditional social structures of arranged marriage and a corresponding increase in opportunities for young women to defy their parents and attach themselves to men from outside the network of family acquaintances.

As we have already pointed out, the social climate of the Age of Beloveds, heavily affected by the presence of large numbers of young men, was highly eroticized. In many places, the sexual energies of young men were directed toward increasingly municipalized forms of female prostitution.[42] In others, including, for example, Istanbul, Florence, and London, cultural scripting and official tolerance favored or permitted more or less open homoerotic liaisons. But, even in the case of Istanbul, where the protection of women—and the protection of male society *from* women—was considered an official priority, there is some evidence that women were the objects of widespread erotic interest to an extent that demanded the attention of the authorities.

Clearly, the degree to which women were watched over and their movements and activities restricted in Ottoman urban centers depended in large part on class and religion. As we mentioned in regard to 'Azizi's şehrengiz, women who were publicly identified as beloveds were usually concubines or from the lower classes or the non-Muslim communities and might in several cases have been engaged in some form of prostitution. We must remember that, in early-modern times, a woman who was unattached to a household or impoverished for some other reason had very few options for supporting herself. It appears that public and private support systems for unattached women were far more comprehensive in the Ottoman Empire than in Europe, where the numbers of "vagabond" women, unsanctioned pregnancies, and out-of-wedlock children were huge and constituted a major problem.[43] Nonetheless, it also appears that a number of impoverished women took advantage of the relative anonymity of Ottoman urban centers to trade sex or companionship for money.

For example, in a fetva issued in a court case that we will discuss in more detail in chapter 9 below, a group of women are mentioned in connection with "entertaining" men in a house owned by one of them.[44] These women are known by nicknames very similar to some of those we saw in 'Azizi's şehrengiz (see chapter 2 above).[45] The house owner is known simply as 'Arap Fatı (Fatima the Arab/Black), another of the women is known as Narin (Shining/Elegant), and two others are mentioned both by given name and by nickname: Kamer (Moon), known as Giritli Nefise (the Delectable One from Crete), and Balatlı 'Ayni (Ayni from Balat), known as Atlı 'Ases (the Mounted Watch/Police). Names such as Shining and Delectable have obvious and obviously sexual connotations (although what the Mounted Police refers to in a sexual context one can only guess). 'Arap Fatı, who seems to have been the madam or procuress, is described as "the wife of a janissary," which suggests that she is carrying on a business to support herself while her husband is on campaign (or even missing in action, a common source of impoverishment among the wives of lower-class janissaries). We have no information on the status of the other women (except for references to their hometowns).

In another case also discussed in detail in chapter 9, a group of non-Muslim women are accused of "disturbing the peace" for congregating in certain shops and orchards in the vicinity of the Eyüp Mosque complex and entertaining themselves in public. The "immoral acts" mentioned in the complaint are playing the flageolet [pipe], dancing, and conversing with men who are not their husbands while gathering in shops under the pretext of eating "clotted cream" (*kaymak*).⁴⁶

During the same period, the boatmen (*peremeciler*) who carried passengers across the Bosphorus between the Asian and the European sides and across the Golden Horn from Istanbul proper to Galata in rowboats (Greek: *prama*/Ottoman Turkish: *pereme*) were strictly warned not to allow young men (*levends*) and young women (*taze avretler*) to travel together and to prevent young men from jumping into boats containing women.⁴⁷

In a 1575 order to the Istanbul kadi forbidding wine houses from being opened in the houses of non-Muslims in Muslim neighborhoods or near bathhouses or mosques, the following offenses are mentioned: "Drunks are constantly laying hands on ladies going to the bath." "Some evildoers come out of the wine houses, enter the [women's] baths, and molest the women, and one time a drunk even took hold of a woman in the inner private room; when the women were unable to rescue her, a large group of the community came and freed her."⁴⁸ In this same vein, one of the earliest shadow-puppet plays, mentioned by Evliya Çelebi in the mid-seventeenth century, depicts the antihero Karagöz sneaking into a women's bath, getting caught, and being led out on a rope tied to his exaggerated phallus.⁴⁹

Most likely, these are not unusual cases. We can also add to them mention of other groups of women who were visible in public — for example, entertainers (musicians and dancing girls, both often gypsies), women who worked in shops and artisans' workshops as part of family businesses, female servants running errands, women who could not afford servants and had to do their families' public business (e.g., bringing water from a fountain or shopping for food) themselves. Although, we have no evidence of the actual numbers of women in these (publicly visible, uncovered) categories, it is certain that there was a regular circulation of women through Ottoman public space.

In 1614, a young Italian named Pietro Della Valle traveled to Istanbul and, in his account of his stay, had the following to say about casual encounters with Ottoman women during visits to the bazaars:

> We from elsewhere often go along [to the bazaars] to look at the Turkish ladies who flock there either to buy or, as I believe, to be seen, insofar as this is allowed by the veils covering up their faces: these, however, do not always hide the eyes nor entirely prevent them from being able to make themselves known to whom they want. They go along stiff and straight as posts, thrusting their hands to conceal them into the slits in their gowns, which they use like our muffs, and crooking their arms at their sides so that they look like jug-handles. When they encounter any of us strangers, with whom they know they can take more liberties, they jostle us with their

elbows as if forced to do so by the crowd, and, if they are pretty, we do the same to them, and we burst out laughing. Sometimes we do not fail to exchange pleasant, teasing questions, and flirt in other little ways, and so, gently, gently, friendships are formed.

Della Valle also describes women riding the swings, which were a popular feature of the carnivals held on the major feast days (*bayram*, '*id*), and watching others ride.[50] We do not know how Ottoman women perceived the attentions they attracted on the part of wealthy young foreigners, but it is clear that some were visible in public and willing literally to "rub elbows" with strangers.

In the previous chapter, we touched on the depiction of beloveds in the descriptions and illustrations of the great Circumcision Festival of 1582. The accounts found in some of the *sūrnāmes* (festival books) highlight two incidents involving women engaged in audacious public acts, the first evidently approved, the second tolerated, by the Ottoman elites.[51] In the first instance, found in a versified account by Mustafa 'Ali, a woman is engaged in an occupation usually associated solely with men:

A Lady with Gauntlet and Hawk Enters the Festival Arena

> Then a woman appeared for all to see
> Who hunted souls with falconry
>
> On her arm she a manly gauntlet bore
> Took up a hawk and came to the fore
>
> She said, Do not think that I am a coward
> What matter that I am no man of power
>
> Do not all whom he-lions lions name
> The she-lion call fierce lion the same
>
> I'm a champion hawker in every way
> I capture more than my share of prey
>
> Womanhood is purest shame to me
> I lack no man's sense of dignity
>
> I seek, like a swordsman, though I'm a dame,
> To be ever a warrior in honor's name
>
> Thus saying, as tribute she made her display
> Performing her act like child's play
>
> Gauntlet and hawk she showed, 'tis true,
> A kingly hawk taking prey she flew

> Then the world's monarch gifts to her granted
> Made lawful to her whatever she wanted [52]

It is especially interesting that ʿAli, who is usually very critical of breaches in decorum and as casually misogynistic as other Ottoman elites, tells the tale of the female falconer with no hint of censure and some attention to the sultan's fulsome approval. Moreover, in some manuscripts, the rubric to this anecdote refers to the falconer by the title *hatun* or "lady," commonly reserved for women of respectable and elite families.

The second instance, again taken from ʿAli, hints more generally at the participation of women in public events. As ʿAli tells it:

A Woman Appears Concealed in the Festival Ground

> When the fervor of festival season grew
> Which merry folk were dying to view
>
> There occurred an event both rare and strange
> When the times underwent an aspect change
>
> 'Twas known as the fame of this gathering spread
> That elites don't give way to the lowly bred
>
> So a picture fair did change her weeds
> To become a horseman upon his steed
>
> In the garb of a cavalryman she dressed
> In the guise of royal yeomanry dressed
>
> This wench, a fine saddlecloth cape on her shoulder
> Became a splendid police officeholder
>
> Her hair to the top of her head she drew
> Beneath a turban concealed it from view
>
> Once woman, now man, this cheeky lass
> Her horse to the square like a swordsman let pass
>
> As she rode about in a manly way
> A stranger saw one of her locks gone astray
>
> Among the onlookers a churl quite crass
> Among the spectators an ill-favored ass
>
> It is someone I know, he chanced to recall
> Revealed her secret to every and all

Women and the Art of Love

The reins of her mount were taken by force
Like a drunk she was tumbled down from her horse

He brought her thence to the high seat of rule,
To that candle in modesty's gath'ring was cruel

Before the epoch's king she was haled
Holy law that day required her jailed

Next day the legal inquiries took place
Not clear from her were the points of her case

She said she had heard that all, high or low
Open or hid to the festival go

But people there gather in thronging masses
That would rend the veils of thousands of lasses

Determined myself to do this "sweet" deed
A horseman I was on a "red-roan" steed[j]

That I might, as a man, tour the festival field
In cavalryman's guise, my secret concealed

Little did I know that an ignorant snoop
Would cause the high wind of precaution to droop

The times are full of the wise, I know, yet
With a bridle in the hands of a dolt I met

But I'm a veiled woman of modesty
I am glad of the curtain of chastity

This was my wish, not some wanton act
Many women watched, not just me, in fact

Excuse me, oh judge, but my only sin
Was the mannish disguise I clad myself in

They saw she had spoken perfect sense
And so completely forgave her offense

Since truly the party of joy is this fest
To give no one grief is certainly best[53]

Again, the great sympathy with which ʿAli treats the woman, as opposed to the man who exposes her, is striking. There seems to have been some care

---

[j] "Sweet" is the translated name of Shirin, who rode a famous horse named Gülgun (Red Roan).

taken to point out that there is a difference between a woman who appears in public for immoral reasons and one who simply wants to participate in a public event. Defiance of custom on the part of the former is treated as intolerable (and worthy of punishment), but such defiance on the part of the latter is treated as tolerable (and worthy of forgiveness). Even the experts in Islamic law are unable to come to a definitive conclusion in the case of the horsewoman and end by letting her go. Certainly, her exculpatory assertion that many women attended the festival is borne out by several illustrations of the festival that show ordinary women in the crowds of onlookers, ordinary women who seem originally to have been depicted unveiled and only later retouched with black rectangular veils.

As we have seen, public spaces in Ottoman and other European cities were dominated by young men, and unprotected women were always in danger of being assaulted or harassed. The woman who rode to the festival in male clothing claimed that she did so out of modesty, to protect herself from unwanted attention or contact with men. But the fact that public roles and public spaces were dangerous to women does not mean that women were necessarily cowed or unwilling to appear in public or to take visible roles, including roles usually associated with men.

PART 2: WOMEN AND THE POETIC INSCRIPTION OF LOVE

Women Writing—Women's Speech

Ann Rosalind Jones begins an essay on the early-modern European women poets Louise Labé and Veronica Franco by saying: "A study of two women poets should open by acknowledging that to be a woman writer at all during the sixteenth century was to be an exception."[54] It is certainly true that the woman writer/poet was exceptional, but it is also true that the early-modern period was a time of burgeoning interest in those women who did write and had written in the past as well as in the potential of women to engage meaningfully in literary and intellectual pursuits usually associated with men. In Europe, including the Ottoman Empire, the medieval tradition rested heavily on ancient and misogynistic foundations, foundations that provided ample proofs, both "scientific" and religious, for the physical and intellectual inferiority of women. Yet, by the late Renaissance, such theories, however dear they may have been to the classicizing humanists, were seriously challenged by some decidedly noninferior women and some men who began to question the received wisdom.

The bitter conflict between ancient wisdom and modern experience in this regard is already apparent in some aspects of the work of Giovanni Boccaccio (1313–75). For example, in his younger days, his *Elegy of Lady Fiammetta* (ca. 1343–45), a novelistic account of the psychology of betrayed love, is composed in the first-person voice of a woman who claims to be speaking only to women.[55] This represents a clear break from the tradition of Petrarch and Dante, in whose poetry the woman is a mere topic of description, an unattainable object residing on the margins of verse, made present only by the words of the talented poet. Setting aside the transvestite (or androgynous) actuality of a male author playing a woman's part, Boccaccio allows Lady Fiammetta to speak for herself, thus giving her a reality and depth of character that the Lauras and the Beatrices lack. But, some ten years later, the same Boccaccio would author the *Corbaccio*, an attack on women that Causa-Steindler calls "one of the most virulently misogynous writings of all times."[56] Then, in 1361, Boccaccio would follow this exercise in misogyny with an apology, the *De claris mulieribus*, one of the first examples of early-modern defenses of women, and one of few that goes beyond praising "feminine" virtues such as patience, faith, morality, and gentleness to argue that women might just have a significant role to play in public, civic life.

The contradictions in Boccaccio's work and thought seem to reverberate down through the early-modern period. As we come to the sixteenth century, significant works by women and writings by both men and women arguing against the putative inferiority of women were matched (or more than matched) by a spate of antiwoman and antifeminist tracts and essays.[57] This conflict itself is evidence of a growing interest in the actualities of women's lives and women's roles in an age when women were growing more visible on the public cultural stage.

The problem women's visibility presents for early-modern culture stems in part from the widespread notion that a woman's virtue resides precisely in her invisibility and silence, expressed as modesty. For example, one of the better-known early-modern conduct books, the *De re uxoria* by Francesco Barbaro (1398–1454), admonishes women concerning speech as follows: "When place and occasion offer, let them speak to the point so briefly that they may be thought reluctant rather than eager to open their mouths. By silence indeed women achieve the fame of eloquence." Barbaro also links a woman's speech with a woman's body when approving the actions of a Roman noblewoman who concealed her bare arm from the sight of a man: "It is proper, however that not only arms but indeed the speech of women never be made public: for the speech of a noblewoman can be no less dangerous than the nakedness of her limbs."[58] This is precisely parallel to the Muslim notion of a woman as *'avrat*, or "private [part of the] body that is required to be covered," the voice being considered here a body part. *The Mirrhor of Modestie*, Thomas Salter's 1579 plagiaristic translation of Giovanni Bruto's 1555 *La institutione di una fanciulla nata nobilmente*, also advises young women on proper womanly reticence: "In this wise shee shall make election and choise of that whiche she ought to keep silent setting a lawe to her self, to do the one [i.e., listen] and exchue the other [i.e., speaking], for she ought to know that the use of the toung is to be used soberly and discretly, for to that ende nature, that wise woorkewoman ordained the toung to bee inclosed as with a hedge within twoo rowes of teeth."[59]

Certainly, the societal imposition of cultural veils was not limited to the Islamic East. In fact, it is the absence, invisibility, and *silence* — the veiling, to be exact — of the actual beloved that grounds the Petrarchan re-presentation of her as a (carnally inaccessible) paragon of beauty and virtue.[60] Where the beloved is both present and speaking, where she acts in the same cultural arena, where she argues for her own self-presentation, it becomes difficult, if not impossible, to maintain the dominant fictions of a Petrarchan beloved. In a sense, the woman stands naked (uncovered) and obviates the need for description or representation.

Ottoman Women Poets

Although we have often included the Ottomans when talking about European social trends, there are surface differences in culture production that make literary comparisons appear unprofitable or unfounded. It is obvious, for example, that Ottoman poetry could not be truly Petrarchan because Ottomans did not read Petrarch. In fact, if we must generalize, Ottoman poetry can be said to be "Hafezan" in that it looked to Persian models (among which the poetry of the fourteenth-century master poet Hafez stood out, although not nearly to the extent that Petrarch does among European models), adapting them to its own purposes. Nonetheless, there is a perspective from which Ottoman poetry (and Hafezan poetry in general) can be seen to be an extreme form of "Petrarchism" (just as Petrarchan poetry can be seen as a mild form of "Hafezism"). Ottoman (and all Hafezan) poetry takes the marginalizing, distancing, and abstracting — not to mention Neoplatonizing — view of the beloved one step further by entirely dissociating the beauty and allure of the beloved from the realm of gender. This is to say that the poetic re-presentation of the beloved's veiled image does not associate that image unequivocally with either gender and, in actuality, tends to suggest a male beloved, which can be understood as a second level of veiling more stringently protecting the invisibility/silence—the ideal virtue—of the (absent) female beloved.

Thus, the problem presented by women poets for Ottoman (male) cultural elites is twofold and similar in kind (although possibly not in degree) to the problem faced by European cultural elites in general when women show up on the public cultural scene. On the one hand, for a woman to write poetry makes the woman visible; it introduces her into the public arena, removes the double layer of veils that protects her virtue (and every woman's ideal virtue), and distances the actual woman from the idealized poetic beloved. On the other hand, writing poetry, and especially love poetry, means speaking, revealing a sexual presence, taking an active role in a competitive cultural arena, moving from being the re-presented absence to being a self-fashioning presence. In a sense, this abandonment of silence and invisibility is inseparable from the abandonment of virtue. For this reason, it was, perhaps, easier for Europeans to accept as poets female cultural actors, such as the bourgeois Louise Labé, who did not threaten the moral ideology of the aristocracy, or the highly educated and talented courtesans from Tullia d'Aragona to Veronica Franco, who had already given up pretensions to physical, sexual virtue—than for Ottomans to accept the notion that a virtuous woman could also write poetry. This is not to say that European women who ventured to express literary ambitions were not also, and quite similarly, pressured to write in a religious or Neoplatonic vein, one in which the language of love was immediately interpretable as allegorizing the progress of the soul toward union with the divine.

As an aside, we must mention that there does exist a level of cultural scripting that allows for Ottoman women writing poetry. From early on in the Ottoman tradition of mesnevis (romantic narrative poems in rhymed couplets), a tradition that had been inherited from the Persians, it became a common practice to include gazels, often presented as an exchange between male and female lovers.[61] (Indeed, we saw the same sort of exchange of gazels in Ca'fer's Çelebi's *Book of Desire*, discussed earlier in this chapter.) In this context, both heteroeroticism and the notion of women as poets are scripted and, to some extent, naturalized. However, in keeping with the lyric conventions, the contextually heteroerotic poems do not appear to be noticeably gendered or to be in any other way different from the rest of the poems in the tradition. And, in the end, as the audience knows quite well, even the "woman's poem" in these narratives was written by a man.

Tezkire Writers and Women Poets

In the Ottoman tezkires (poet biographies), which originate as a popular genre among the elites during the Age of Beloveds, there are few entries for women—usually only two, to be exact. What is surprising, however, given the erotic character of Ottoman poetry and what we now imagine as the traditional protectiveness of Islam toward female virtue, is that there are any entries for women at all. The first of the tezkires, the 1538 *Heşt behişt* (Seven paradises) of Sehi, contained a special subsection entitled "On the Subject of Women Poets" that began with the statement: "In this age there are two women poets. Because their poems are beautiful, their couplets matchless, their gazels popular, and their fame considerable, they have been included in this biographical collection."[62] There follow entries for Zeynep Hatun[k] and Mihri Hatun, both of whom became recognized as poets in the late fifteenth century. The entries themselves are quite sparse, recording only a few lines of verse, and mentioning that Zeynep was well educated and skilled in music and that Mihri was from the Anatolian town of Amasya and wrote poetry dedicated to Sultan Selim I and Prince Ahmet.

The second of the Ottoman tezkires, that of Latifi, which first appeared in 1546, expands the entries for these two women, removes them from the ghetto of a special section, and obliquely surfaces some of the concerns aroused by women's participation in literary pursuits.[63] Latifi begins his discussion of Zeynep (d. ca. 1473), who, he claims, came from his hometown of Kastamonu, by insisting that her public presence as a poet had not sullied her in any way: "She was talented in the extreme and from this point of view unique in our age; she was highly worthy, sinless, virginal, and a paragon of virtue." He then goes on to describe her intellectual abilities and educational attainments:

> Her inborn intellectual charm amazed the ordinary people of the world and astounded the discerning people of the age. Her father saw ability in her nature and brilliance in her intellect and educated her in all manner of sciences and all sorts of arts, instructing her from the poem collections of the Persians and the odes of the Arabs. After she had done gathering wisdom and acquiring ability, according to the Persian saying, "When all the conceits [that go into poetry] have been gathered, then being a poet is easy," thus equipped with a talented poetic incisiveness, she composed a collection of poems in Persian and Turkish dedicated to Sultan Mehmet [II, the Conqueror].[64]

[k] *Hātūn* carries the sense of the English *madam, mistress,* or *lady.*

Latifi on Mihri Hatun

Latifi on Mihri (d. after 1512)[65] is more expansive, most likely because more was known about her, her poems having been received and rewarded at court. (The entry is also clearly tinged with envy, Latifi himself being a poet whose aspirations to palace recognition never really materialized.) He begins with an assessment of her talents in grudging double negatives bordering closely on the rhetorical device known as *damning with faint praise* or, in the Ottoman rhetoric inherited from the Arabs, *blame that resembles praise*. He says: "In the art of poetry, she was not without rank and dignity, in the essentials of wisdom she was not of little worth." He then goes on to provide a commonplace description of her poetry personalized by metaphoric references to her gender: "With colorful, rose-colored verses, her poetry-adorning natural talent was the hairdresser of the bride of speech and the adorner of the virgin of imaginative ideas." Having raised the issue of gender and made a gesture toward the issue of virtue/virginity (presumed to inhere in a bride), he makes a more direct assault on the main problem: "Although the coquettishness of her poems and the mannerisms of her speech are feminine, in burning and being consumed [by passion] she is like a [male] lover, and in the expression of passion and pleading [to be loved in return] she is masculine."[66]

Here, Latifi sets out clearly the problem that the woman poet presents for both Hafezan and Petrarchan poetry. The beloved's power is always what the early-modern (male) poet perceives as feminine—no matter what the beloved's actual gender. That power lies in withholding, denying, inaccessibility, veiling, spirituality, silence, modesty. The beloved acts, if at all, only in the most subtle and ambiguous gestures—the shy glance, timid coquetry. Active love is the masculine role. It is passionate, suffers publicly, speaks aloud.[67] It reveals the beloved and creates the beloved's image by tearing away veils of modesty with gusts of description, making the beloved present to the gaze of the world. Thus, unless the object of her passion is God and, by extension, her own (holy) virtue, the woman poet is taking a man's part and leaving the male poet in a quandary. Either becoming a poet is the same as abandoning the (supposedly) female virtues, or presumed gender distinctions and categories no longer hold.

Latifi appears to be torn. For him, Mihri is canonized by time, general popularity, and the approval of sultans. It cannot, therefore, easily be said that she has abandoned virtue because doing so would imply that both the community and its leaders had overlooked her sinful behavior. In fact, Latifi is drawn into relating (on the authority of unidentified others) an extended defense of her moral purity. He says (in what for an Ottoman are quite explicitly sexual terms):

> They tell that, while she was so much a female beloved who worshiped beloved [men] and was so familiar with love and carnal passion, the hem of her modesty and the train of her chastity were clean of any stain of suspicion [töhmet], and she was a fearlessly pure person to whose shins the waves of the sea never reached. They go so far in [describing] her modesty and chastity [as to say] that she guarded the sanctuary of her presence from people outside her family and her hidden treasury from the [most poisonous] snake, that neither was the silvery nacre [of her oyster] swollen by droplets from the April [showers] of [sexual] union nor was her colorful [rose]bud watered by dew from the cloud of conjunction; in short, no one tasted of her two-part pomegranate, and no one cast a fish into her silver pool.[68]

Obviously, this defense is highly ambiguous. Its descriptions of sexual intercourse are ornately metaphoric in the Ottoman mode, but they are also quite graphic and fulsome in a manner that is unsubtly assaultive. A woman who was modest and concerned for her own and her family's reputation might presumably have been shamed by even such a refined and poetic depiction of her genitalia and the association (even the negative association) with explicit sexual intercourse. There is a warning here: this is what a woman can expect who ventures into the realm of poetry. However, in this passage, we also see the surfacing of a fantasy, and an attendant problem, that troubles early-modern writers far beyond the confines of the Ottoman Empire. We might call this *the problem (fantasy) of the perpetual (and powerful) virgin.*

Certainly, the most prominent example of "powerful virginity" in early-modern times is that of Elizabeth I. Elizabeth was faced by the daunting prospect of being, as Louis Montrose puts it, "the female ruler of what was, at least in theory, a patriarchal society." Her situation is, at least in kind, not too different from that of the Ottoman woman, a Mihri, who attempts to make a name or identity for herself in the male-dominated world of poetry. Each woman, the queen and the poet, was, as Montrose puts it, "a cultural anomaly," and "this anomalousness made her powerful and dangerous."[69] The anomalousness in both cases resided in the simultaneous coexistence of adult identity and virginity. As Leslie Peirce points out in the Ottoman case: "For the female, the watershed in [adult] identity was marriage." The premarital, supposedly (but not necessarily actually) virgin state was indeterminate and undifferentiated; it was a hiatus between childhood and the defined stages of adult sexual identity that began with marriage and the imposition of male mastery and social controls.[70]

Montrose expresses much the same understanding in discussing Theseus's approach to the problem of Hermia's disobedience in *A Midsummer Night's Dream*: "Theseus has characteristically Protestant notions about the virtue of virginity: maidenhood is a phase in the life cycle of a woman who is destined for married chastity and motherhood."[71] Hermia has choices: she can either marry—and fall under the social controls established for the married woman—or die or live in a nunnery. There is no place for a perpetual virgin in the normal business of life. Her unregulated sexuality is simply too dangerous and too uncontrolled. In some manner, the sexuality of the perpetual virgin—even that of the early-modern nun—is as liminal as that of the Venetian courtesan, who assumes the sexual activity of a married woman without the constraints of marriage.[72] It is the extension of this intermediate, unregulated state into a unique (anomalous) form of adulthood that Elizabeth manipulates to enhance her power without threatening the core structures of patriarchal society. She remains dangerously and powerfully *unmastered*, sexually visible and desirable, while insisting on a fundamental uniqueness that does not set her up as a potentially disruptive model for other women.

From the perspective of the male poet, Mihri seems to present a similar problem. By remaining a virgin and never marrying, she takes on a role for which there are no defining structures. She is free of both the controls imposed by accepted social formulations and those imposed by a husband. She remains a *kız* (daughter) in relation to a father who does not force her into a socially normative role and a *kız* (virgin) beyond the age when such an appellation makes much sense. This contrasts her with Zeynep, the other canonical woman poet of the Ottoman Age of Beloveds. After a brilliant poetic debut, Zeynep stepped out of the liminal hiatus of virginity into the culturally scripted role of wife. She gave up poetry and disappeared into virtuous silence. Not so Mihri. From her anomalous position and the freedom that it permitted, she chose to speak aloud in the voice of poetry, which injected her into the realm of male speech and male sexuality. On the balance point between sexuality and virginity, she was able to carve out a niche as a poet.

Much of the rest of Latifi's entry can be seen as an attempt to locate Mihri's position somewhere within the accepted limits of Ottoman (poetic and female) sexuality. A verse in which she references the legendary Alexander/Iskender's search for the fountain of eternal life (found in a land of eternal darkness) is cited: "Since Mihri attained the water of eternal life, she will not die until the Resurrection / For in the dark of that night she saw that Alexander clearly." Latifi reports that this couplet stemmed from her affection for Iskender (Alexander), the son of Sinan Pasha, and was the cause of a töhmet (suspicion) that she had engaged in illicit contacts with him. He adds that, when the poets and wits of Sultan (Prince) Ahmet's court in Amasya hinted at this with clever bons mots, Mihri shut them up with an apropos verse again referencing Alexander's search: "The sweet water of my ruby lip sent many Alexanders / In search of water and sent them back still thirsting."[73] The anecdote reminds us, nonetheless, that, no matter how pure its origins, an erotic poem is always subject to a shameful interpretation.

The arena of poetry is not only sexual but also tough and combative. Latifi points out that Mihri admired the poet Necati and wrote parallels to several of his verses. But he also cites a short fragment by Necati scathing an unnamed imitator and claims that it was addressed to her. The bit goes:

> Oh you who would parallel my verses
> Beware of stepping off the path of decency
>
> Don't say, My poems in rhyme and rhythm
> Are just the same as Necati's
>
> There being five letters in both words
> Are *skill* and *error* the same?[74]

The only evidence that we have that these lines do, in fact, refer to Mihri is in the tezkires, which often pass on unsubstantiated gossip, or invent contexts for poems, or imaginatively adapt poems to the contexts of existing stories. What we can say with relative certainty is that Latifi uses this fragment to suggest that Mihri was attacked by her beloved paragon and that the best of poets had little sympathy for women meddling in the business of men.

'Aşık on Mihri and 'Ayişe

The next major tezkire was the *Stations of the Poets' Pilgrimage* of 'Aşık, completed, after many years of work, in 1568–69.[1] 'Aşık was a bon vivant, partygoer, and raconteur who was acquainted with most of the leading literary lights of his day. His biographies are filled with stories, gossip, and personal adventures. They represent the accumulation of a lifetime spent in elite literary circles and are very much the richest source of anecdotal material for the social life of the elites in the urban Ottoman Empire during the height of the Age of Beloveds. We have referred to him often and will continue to do so.

'Aşık has two entries that we will consider in detail in this section: an extensive entry for Mihri and a less-detailed one for a woman named 'Ayişe,

---

[1] In fact, 'Ahdi's *Gülşen-i şu'ara* precedes it but is limited both in scope and in the character of its entries.

to whom later biographers refer by her pen name, Hubbi (the Affectionate, from the Arabic *hubb*, "love, affection"). The entry for Mihri begins as follows:

> Her name and pen name were both Mihri. The sun [*mihr*]^m of her appearance was [in] the sky of Amasya; for that reason she was the compatriot of Afitabi [he of the sun]. Although she is a woman, that unmanly [*na-merd*] person gave a mule's kick to ever so many men of war. Even as she often alluded to Necati, [once, in response to his] saying:
>
> So let there not be a single atom of benevolence in earth or sky
> All Necati requires for blanket and mattress is a mat of reeds
>
> Mihri said:
>
> You, oh Necati, want a reed mat for a mattress
> For Mihri a simple place on the beloved's threshold is enough⁷⁵

'Aşık brings up the gender-competitive aspect of a woman's entering the field of poetry right from the beginning. What is more, he represents Mihri as an adequate, or more than adequate, player in the poetry game. He plays on the word *na-merd*, a Persian compound that means "nonman" but has the usual sense of "unmanly, cowardly, timid" in contrast to the soldierly virtues of the *merd-i meydan*, or "man of the battlefield," to whom this "nonman" gives a two-footed kick. (Remember, a virtuous woman is supposed to be "timid," or shy and modest, protecting herself from the gaze of strangers.) This is followed by the verse examples in which Mihri one-ups Necati in hyperbolic willingness to sacrifice all for love.

In the next section, 'Aşık continues situating Mihri as a virtuous woman succeeding in the practice of an immodest art:

> According to [the Arabic saying], "The woman is all a private part [which should be covered up]," that protected one was veiled, but the voice of the beauty of her talent's bride ascended [like a star] from the veil of modesty's horizon, and her poems, like her beauty, became famous. That gazelle, with the lasso of poetry and the bow and arrow of the ambergris-scattering pen, made the valleys of eloquence her hunting [ground] and made the meaning [of the Arabic couplet] "Being feminine is no shame to the name of the

---

^m It is usual in Ottoman high-culture art prose for the author to make plays on peoples' names. Throughout, 'Aşık will play on the fact that the word *mihr* can mean both "sun" and "love" and that the letters of Mihri's name—*m, h, r*—can be differently voweled to mean "seal" (*mühr*) and "dowry" (*mehr*).

202   Women and the Art of Love

sun / Being masculine is no glory to the crescent moon'"[n] her refuge and castle. Even as she said:

> They call women *the deficient in reason*
> So whatever they say should be excused
> A female is better if she be competent
> Than a thousand incompetent males

she made the adornment of the virgins of meaning her own with the dowry [*mehr*] of verse and brought them to her bridal chamber of [carnal] pleasure. In the lovely poems [where] she describes beautiful beloveds there is the virginal quality of Joseph.[o] While the male poets had a craving for virgins of meaning, being a woman [herself] [they] came cheap. Although in her poetry there are some indecent words, that [kind of] menstrual fluid comes from the male gender, and they [women] see [morally] deficient expressions and, being of the class that needs guidance, are affected by this influence.[76]

The biographer's dilemma is apparent in this passage. By the rules of custom and tradition, a woman should not be as exposed to public scrutiny as a poet necessarily is. So what emerges is not Mihri's physical self but her voice, what is exposed is not her physical beauty but the beauty of her natural ability. The metaphoric context of the next sentence is blatantly ironic. Mihri is described as a gazelle, an animal known both for its beauty (especially the beauty of its large brown eyes) and for its popularity as the prey of hunters. Accordingly, the gazelle is commonly used as a metaphoric substitute for the beloved. However, in this case, the gazelle is the hunter, not the prey. She wields the lasso and bow, roams the wilds in search of prey, and takes refuge in her castle (by night). Although there is perhaps an allusion here to the legendary Armenian princess Shirin, who was both hunter and beauty, the sense of role reversal (and, perhaps, the incongruity of such a role reversal) is made quite apparent.

'Aşık's presentation of Mihri as an active combatant in the arena of poetry, giving a "mule's kick" to her male rivals, or as a "gazelle" hunting with lasso and bow is anomalous and perplexing in the context of men writing about women writers during the Age of Beloveds. In both Europe and the Ottoman Empire, the business of poetry was for the most part carried out by

---

[n] In Arabic, the gender of the word for the sun (*şems*) is feminine, and the gender of the word for the crescent moon (*hilāl*) is masculine. Neither Persian nor Turkish indicate gender.

[o] In the quranic tale and subsequent legends, Joseph was the paragon of both male beauty and male chastity.

groups of men who imitated and rewrote each other's work and the work of past poets.[77] It was in many ways the activity of a special community from which women were generally barred. Nonetheless, we do see that Mihri (and Zeyneb) were included in the sohbet circles of powerful men, as were such European women writers as Pernette du Guillet, Louise Labé, and Veronica Franco. However, where Labé and Franco present themselves in active roles by describing themselves as contesting with men for a place in the world of poetry (Franco even presenting herself in the role of a duelist), there is only a little evidence that Mihri does the same.[78]

The fact that 'Aşık seems at times to be attempting to make Mihri's case as a contestant or combatant reinforces an argument made by Jones in the context of a discussion of the position of women writers in Renaissance Europe. Jones argues that hegemony (in Gramsci's sense) is not imposed by a dominant group but, rather, *negotiated* by means of a series of compromises calculated to win consent from a variety of less powerful groups. The problem is not to impose hegemony but to make the majority accept or even *desire* hegemony. Accordingly, this opens up "the possibility that woman poets were drawn into, even cultivated in, their particular urban or national cultures, rather than uniformly censored by a monolithic, male-dominated literary establishment."[79] Regarded in this light, 'Aşık's cultivation of Mihri (a posthumous cultivation that we might see as directed at his immediate female contemporaries) takes on the character of an attempt to co-opt women with literary aspirations to the task of winning (elite) women's consent to the dominant (and misogynistic) project of Ottoman elite poetry and Ottoman public love. Beyond this, we might recognize parallels to the ways in which the Ottoman state strove to win the passionate compliance of its intellectual elites by negotiating a certain amount of tolerance toward their amusements, which included antiestablishmentarian poetry, drinking, carousing, and sexual adventuring.

Yet 'Aşık still seems not quite to know what to do with Mihri. He quotes a pair of couplets in which she displays the satirical wit for which she was famous. According to 'Aşık, in one couplet she can be understood to assert: "If you [men] are going to go around quoting the Prophetic tradition, which says that women are deficient in reason, then I can say whatever I want, and you must excuse me. After all how can someone who cannot reason properly be blamed for saying something that seems unreasonable? So I will say that one capable woman is better than a thousand incapable men. And what can you say to that?"[80] On the one hand, Mihri is portrayed as tough and combative; on the other, 'Aşık seems to feel the need to excuse her and emphasize her femininity.

Following the assertive couplets is an extended series of figurative flourishes playing on the image of virgin brides and vocabulary associated with women. 'Aşık ends this passage, clearly intended to emphasize Mihri's status as a woman, with another interesting reversal. Continuing the use of vocabulary associated with women, the indecent language of poetry is described as a menstrual fluid (*hayz*).[81] But, in this case, it is not the menstrual fluid of women, which pollutes them to the extent that they cannot pray or engage in intercourse while menstruating. It is the menstrual fluid of men, which pollutes poetry as well as the language and modesty of women who presume to write poetry. This may excuse a woman and a woman's poetry, but it also returns primary agency for women's behavior and women's honor to men and emphasizes the masculinity of the poetic arena.

In the next passages, 'Aşık emphasizes the ways in which a woman poet's reputation can also be polluted by tales and gossip:

> On the whole she is not ignoble, her poetry is middling good, her writing is like a woman's embroidery, and her prose is wanton. [According to the saying,] "The male lion is a lion [i.e., it has the attributes of a lion—strength, bravery, ferociousness, etc.], but is the lioness not a lion too [does she not have the same attributes]?" she was not entirely free of boy chasing. When Mü'eyyidzade [who would eventually rise to the position of chief military magistrate (*kadı'asker*)] was young and a resident of Amasya, he first became acquainted with her and then acquired a glow by virtue of love. There was affection on her part [too], and, later, when Mü'eyyidzade had taken the pen name Hatimi and became chief military magistrate, Mihri for a time persisted [in her affection]. The late [Mü'eyyidzade] made reference to the affair with innuendos and allusions, [so] Mihri composed this couplet and sent it to him:

> You lied, Hatimi, when you played the lover with Mihri
> By God, Mihri loves you [more than] any boy [would]

> Her relationship with a beloved named Iskender is [also] well-known. One early morning, when he appeared to her gaze, she wrote this gazel:

> I opened my eyes from sleep, and suddenly
>   raised my head
> There I saw the moon-face of the love-thief
>   shining

> [My star of good luck had risen—I was thus
>   exalted
> When in my chamber I saw this Jupiter rise
>   to the evening sky]

He appeared to be a Muslim but by his dress
> an infidel
And divine light poured from the beauty
> of his face

[I opened, then closed my eyes, but he had
> vanished from my sight
All I know of him—he was an angel
> or a faery]

Now she knows the water of life,
> Mihri will not die until the Judgement Day
For she has seen that visible Alexander
> in the eternal dark of night[82]

She was also a contemporary of the late Güvahi, and the two of them competed with one another in [exchanging] pleasantries. Mihri wrote the following fragment and sent it to Güvahi:

By God, in this world, oh Güvahi,
> May the divine afflict you with a beloved

Let him bind the rope of his curl about your neck
> And make a dimple pitfall for you in his chin

Let the lip of him whose neck is like a decanter['s]
> Remind you of his cup of wine in the gathering

Finally, let a sultan from a dominion of beauty
> Hang you at the tip of his forelocks

If you wonder what the sense of this poem is
> You'll ask, What was Güvahi's sin?

It is this: Why don't you mention Mihri
> In a couplet or two every now and then?[83]

The assessment that 'Aşık gives of Mihri's poetry at the beginning of this passage may seem grudging, but it also seems accurate. Her poetry is good, just not as good (in Ottoman terms) as the work of the best of male poets. In fact, 'Aşık seems to work hard at praising her and refrains from repeating Latifi's story about Necati's criticisms. Following the lion/lioness saying—a commonplace that seems to turn up whenever a woman is depicted as active in affairs usually reserved for men—Mihri is described in the poetically scripted role of an active lover. She has beloveds of her own whom she woos and chides with poetry. She even has at least one close male companion, a fellow poet with whom she exchanges pleasantries. This part of the entry is precisely what one would expect of an entry for a male poet, right down to the male beloveds. It is as though the lion/lioness saying introduces a parenthesis, inside which she will be treated like any other poet. And poets are expected to have a special susceptibility to the urgings of passion. The parenthesis closes with a return to the subject of Mihri's supposedly lifelong virginity.

This discomfort with the idea of a woman writing poetry appears to be widely shared among early-modern males. Jones points to the case of the Lyon poet Pernette du Guillet's "irreproachably Neoplatonist" 1545 verses addressed to Maurice Scève. In his preface to the poems, the publisher Antoine du Moulin in effect apologizes for publishing them at all, saying that he did so only after du Guillet's death and at the insistence of her mourning husband. du Moulin also published them, as Jones says, "hedged . . . around with epigraphs commemorating her life-long chastity."[84] This is the same redemptive (and powerful and dangerous) "life-long chastity" that the Ottoman biographers insist on in the case of Mihri:

> Although she was such a boy chaser, like the world-woman[p] no [man] got what he wanted from her, and, other than the cup of love, no strange foot/cup[q] entered the sanctuary of her respectability, and the hand of no greedy miser touched her hidden treasure. Other than a woman's necklace or amber strand, no arm was thrown about her neck. She came into this world a virgin and a virgin left it. [At one time,] when they spoke of a suspicion [töhmet] that she had done something forbidden with Iskender, she said:

COUPLET:

> The pure water of my lip has sent many Alexanders [Iskenders]
>   To water and brought them back thirsty

> At that time, the professor of Eyüp,[r] Pasha Çelebi, asked for Mihri's hand in matrimony, and [the poet] Zati wrote the following verses:

> We heard the pasha's asked for Mihri's hand
>   Should she submit to such a man?

[p] The world is often described as a woman (or hag).

[q] The word *ayak* means both "foot" and "drinking cup." 'Aşık is using it in both senses here: "no strange cup but the cup of love" and "no strange foot" (the foot of no person outside the permitted degrees of relationship).

[r] The college associated with the Mosque of Eyüp, the companion of the Prophet (who died during the first Muslim siege of Constantinople and whose grave was miraculously discovered immediately prior to Mehmet the Conqueror's final assault on the city).

> That poor thing fasted for so long
> > Should she now feast on a donkey's dong?[85]

In this final passage (which is followed only by some examples of verses by Mihri), 'Aşık defends Mihri, lets her defend herself, and then cites an indecent verse in which Zati (who was a leader among the poets of his day) supposedly defended her with a bit of lampooning that disapproves (however much tongue-in-cheek) the fate suffered by her fellow woman poet, Zeynep: marriage and subsequent withdrawal into invisibility and silence.

'Ayişe

As ambivalent as his entry on Mihri appears, we would emphasize the fact that 'Aşık allows her a voice and an active role in the business of poetry and its social context. This is striking—and even more so in the light of his entry on the woman poet 'Ayişe, a contemporary of 'Aşık's (1520–72). (The entries on 'Ayişe in subsequent biographies by Kınalızade Hasan Çelebi and Mustafa 'Ali appear under the pen name Hubbi.)[86] Again, it is worth looking closely at the language of the entry.

'Aşık begins by situating 'Ayişe among the elite families of Istanbul: "'Ayişe Hatun [Lady Ayishe] was one of the children of the late Shaykh Ak Şemsüddin, the grandson of the late Shaykh Yahya. She was the wife of the late Şemsi Çelebi, who was tutor to our sultan while he was still a prince, and she was the daughter of his [Şemsi's] maternal aunt." This terse genealogy is followed by a brief preface in which 'Aşık argues—in the common mode, one larded with citations from the religious and profane traditions—for the naturalness of women's participation in cultural and intellectual pursuits:

> It is not hidden from the masters of learning that a person is superior to other animals by virtue of containing all the excellences peculiar to human beings. From this perspective, [both] men [and] women who manifest this perfection are superior to the beast of burden species [binü nev'inden]. His lordship the Expounder [of the Qur'an][s] said, "He [Muhammad] does not speak whimsically," with reference to this notion when interpreting the hadith, wherein he [Muhammad] said of the Blessed 'Ayişe,[t] "Her submission to your religion was more than [that] of any of these donkeys," which is a clear proof of our assertion.

[s] Ibnu'l-'Abbas, the Prophet's first cousin.
[t] Muhammad's youngest and dearest wife.

Those manifesting eloquence, who possess the treasure [referred to in the saying,] "Allah has treasures beneath the throne, and the keys to them are the tongues of the poets," [also] establish this notion and confirm [the following] claim:

COUPLET:

Being feminine is no shame to the name of the sun
Being masculine is no glory to the crescent moon

Is it not a proof of this that the great ones have said: "The male lion is a lion, but is the lioness not a lion too?"

The intent of this prelude is to say that, although there are many of the female gender who compose poetry, there is no poetess as capable of natural rhythm, beauty of versification, delicacy of expression, and poetic fluency as the aforementioned.[87]

Ending with two maxims that he also uses in the entry for Mihri, 'Aşık delivers a rationale for women poets in a style that imitates the introductory sections of serious treatises. What he seems to be doing is writing a mini-tezkire and history of women poets in the Perso-Ottoman tradition:

Among the women poets of Iran are Cilayi (the Burnished), who, with purity of inborn talent and brilliance of mind, polishes the tarnish from the mirror of eloquence; and Afaki (She of the Horizon), who, with the dawning of the sun of poetry, is a sun of perfected speech arising from the horizon of eloquence. The former quit this world in fear of her ['Ayişe's] advent, and the latter, thinking, "I shall be destroyed by the rising of her sun," just by dying took up residence in a nook of the tomb. Cihan Hatun (Lady World), crown on the crest of the world, is in all aspects inferior to her. Dilşad Hatun (Lady Merry-Heart) was made sad by her joy-granting poems. Mihri was one of the poetesses of Rum, dowry [*mehr*] of the bride of virginal ideas approved by the holy spirits, mark of the admiration of masters of sociability, seal [*mühr*] on the treasury of poetry. Had she arrived during this one's ['Ayişe's] era, with love [*mihr*] she [Mihri] would have become her servant, carrying her gold-plated washbasin on her head like the wheel of heaven, both the sun and a woman named Felek-naz (Allure of the Heavens) would have become her Marya.[u] Likewise, if Zeyneb, who was the hairdresser of natural talent who adorns the new brides of poetic speech, who, in the lands of verse unveils the faces of [all] kinds of beauty, came to serve her ['Ayişe], she would be as humble in the ranks of poetry

[u] Marya was a Coptic woman who was given as a gift to Muhammad.

as indigo dye,ᵛ as black faced as eye shadow,ʷ as shattered as curls, and as familiar with knots as the comb.ˣ, 88

Perhaps the most fascinating aspect of this passage is the fact that, beneath the conventions of fulsome praise, it situates 'Ayişe within a history of women poets. This removes the woman poet from the general category of unnatural events and strange creatures and naturalizes her presence within a history that resembles and intersects with that of male poets. We believe that a contemporary Ottoman would have understood that the appearance of two or three entries for women among the biographies of noted poets represents only a few of many women who were writing poetry (as 'Aşık says), just as it was understood that most would-be male poets never achieved any level of public recognition. It is likely that, as we examine more unedited manuscripts, more women poets will show up. Already, Mehmed Çavuşoğlu has discovered several poems by a woman who wrote under the pen name Nisayi during the reign of Sultan Süleyman. She was probably a woman of the royal harem; her verses were copied down in one of the many unedited and often unexamined private journals or chapbooks (*mecmu'a*) found in Turkish libraries. It is mentioned in several places that Tuti Hanım, the wife of Baki (granted the title "Sultan of Poets" during the reign of Süleyman), was also a poet of some skill.⁸⁹

In addition, it should be noted how 'Aşık attempts to create in this passage a rhetorical context for talking about women poets. As he did in the entry for Mihri, he employs figurative language aimed at invoking the context of a woman's life: the servant carrying a gold-plated washbasin as she accompanies a highborn woman to the bath; the dresser combing a woman's hair, applying makeup, adorning a bride. This may be for the most part another example of an Ottoman author showing his rhetorical mastery over any and all aspects of life, including women's lives, but it does have the effect of figuratively contextualizing women in the same way that men were contextualized by tropes having to do with war, trade, and life at court.

ᵛ The reference here is to the dye called *waşm*, which was used by nomadic Arab women to tattoo themselves. It was likely thought to be a nonurban, Bedouin practice and, therefore, low-class.

ʷ Being black faced means being ashamed (here, of one's inferiority). The eye shadow (*sürme*) is black.

ˣ We are not confident about the sense of these last two images. The curls/locks of hair "curls" (or locks of hair) could be "shattered" (or broken) in that they are disheveled, and the "knots" can be both knots in the hair—which are combed out—and the knots of trouble (or even the state of being tongue-tied) that 'Ayişe's superiority causes for Zeyneb.

What follows is a straightforward description of ʿAyişe's poetic output, followed by a few citations from her poetry:

> She [ʿAyişe] worked at every genre of poetry and tested her talent on each of them. She has gazels and *muʿamma* [enigmas], kasides [panegyrics] and mesnevis [rhyming couplets]. She has an affecting mesnevi entitled *Hurşid u Cemşid* [Hurşid and Cemşid] of more than three thousand couplets, treasured up within which are many excellencies and delicacies. This is confirmed by the citation of just a few couplets. At the beginning she describes her weaknesses and failings, begs pardon, and excuses herself:[y]

POEM:

Every year a host of people live and die
    But when a person goes, there is no returning

If you ask after our ancestors, noble or common
    It is either their names that remain or their speech

As I think on this, I emit a sigh
    And say, "Perhaps God will do me a favor"

I did not mend that I might be remembered
    That people might gladden my soul with a prayer

Yet I do not have wealth to endow a charity
    So they'll remember me till the Resurrection

Since children are founded on the wind
    How can a person be remembered by them

Fortune belongs to that person who composes
    Who is capable of putting together a book

In [composing] I was no scholar of the age
    That I should compile Traditions or elucidate the Qurʾan

Nor is it my place to [write] admonitions
    If I were to admonish, it would be shameful

I am incapable, miserable, and mean
    Weak and poor and impoverished

And she also comforted herself from this perspective:

---

[y] This is a commonplace show of (usually false) modesty found in the introductory sections of many mesnevis.

> Is this necessary, that you be a lord of learning?
> > That you be wiser than everyone else in the world?
>
> Since you are one of the "deficient in wit"
> > Your word need not be the most beautiful
>
> If the intellectual says no to what you say
> > No woe be to you, it is he alone who errs
>
> This is the custom since this world began
> > A person only and ever talks with peers
>
> Because in your time the talk of women is simple
> > It is not equal to the sociability of men
>
> By this notion, if a superior should mingle with you
> > It would be a point of pride for you and a shame for him
>
> Will the intellectual be harmed by this?
> > If an accomplished one treats you as an equal.[90]

We cannot say for sure where this citation came from. So far as we know, none of ʿAyişe's major work—neither a divan nor the *Hurşid and Cemşid*—remains. But it is likely that the cited fragments come from her long narrative poem and, more specifically, from the *sebeb-i te'lif* (reason-for-writing) section of the preface. If this is, in fact, the case, it is significant because it means that, while ʿAşık could have chosen any of "more than three thousand" couplets, he chose to transmit a piece in which ʿAyişe speaks in her own voice about the reasons why a woman might decide to write and the problems that she would have in doing so. The reason-for-writing section is the one place in all their works where poets speak unequivocally in their own voices about their own situations. It is difficult to escape the impression that ʿAşık, who seems unabashedly liberal in his views on poetry, poets, sexual morality, and strong drink, is interested in letting a woman speak her own words and make a reasonable (and virtuous, nonerotic) defense of her decision to write poetry.

Ottoman men assert over and over again in their works that they write in order to make their names persist in the world beyond death. That a woman should want the same thing seems reasonable, and that it should be exceptionally difficult or risky for her to achieve such immortality is poignant. When ʿAyişe says, "I did not mend that I might be remembered / That people might gladden my soul with a prayer," she expresses the same longing that a frustrated Latifi reveals in his complaints about the degeneration of patronage in his day: "If [all] you want from composing [something] is to [leave] one good work in the world and a reason for prayers of goodwill because you produced such a work, how much a possessor of name and fame are you going to be [these days]?"⁹¹ In talking about Italian intellectuals of the late Renaissance, scholars confidently associate an emphasis on worldly fame with humanism. For example, when talking about Louise Labé and Veronica Franco, Jones says: "Both poets challenged the terms of masculine discourse by claiming a place for themselves amidst humanist glorification of worldly fame, by refusing the restriction of that fame to males." Elsewhere, in a discussion of the "honored courtesan" Tullia d'Aragona's poetry in praise of contemporary male poets, Jones says (quite suggestively): "Although few of Tullia's sonnets are love poems, in nearly all of them she courts fame."⁹² It is difficult to see 'Ayişe as doing anything less. If there is such a thing as "Ottoman humanism" during the Age of Beloveds, it is most clearly evident in the same, often-expressed desire for fame—and for fame as both a form of persistence after death and an adjunct to particular worldly rewards within official and unofficial systems of patronage. As much as Ottoman intellectuals speak this longing openly, it is masked by literary conventions that induce the poet to adopt the role of a dervish (mystic) and reject all illusions of permanence in this world. One might even argue that conventional mysticism masks both the humanistic tendencies and the overt eroticism of the Ottoman poetic milieu during the Age of Beloveds.

As 'Ayişe points out, a woman is effectively barred from the education necessary to produce a scholar; what is left for her to write but poetry? Her contemporary, Louise Labé, finds herself in the same situation, but, while lamenting that situation, sees, in Lyons at least, the dawning of a new age of educated women. In the dedication of her poems to Clémence de Bourges, she has the following to say: "Since the time has come, Mademoiselle, when the harsh laws of men no longer prevent women from studying the arts and sciences, it seems to me that those who have the ability should take advantage of this honorable right to learning which our sex formerly wanted so much, and show men the wrong they did us by depriving us of the pleasure and honor which could have come to us from study. And if one woman succeeds to the extent of being able to set her ideas in writing, let her do it carefully and not reject fame."⁹³

That this dawning was, for many women, more conjectural than actual is exemplified, sometime after the Age of Beloveds, by the case of poor Mary Wroth, an Englishwoman who ventured to publish a romance entitled *Urania* in 1651. It seems that a certain courtier, one Lord Denny, took offense at an episode that he believed to be a thinly disguised reference to his own participation in the forced marriage of his daughter. He subsequently composed some nasty verses in which he assaulted Mary, in part for being a grossly defective woman:

> Hermaphrodite in show, in deed a monster
> > As by thy works and words all men may conster[z]
> Thy wrathful spite conceived an Idell book
> Brought forth a foole which like the damme doth look.
> . . . leave idle books alone
> For wise and worthyer women have written none.[94]

A woman who writes, the angry courtier asserts, has become in part a man or at best a fool in woman's garb. However, the fact that she is described as a "hermaphrodite" and a "monster" appears to go beyond the notion that she is a transvestite and to suggest that, by taking up the pen, she has taken on the phallus and has become a creature that is neither woman nor man.

Part of the problem is that the poetic milieu is highly competitive. The fringes of poetry bristle with harsh and often obscene lampoons, satires, and vituperations. Moreover, there is no way of opting out or stepping aside. As Kemal Silay points out in an article on women in Ottoman poetry, there is no "other" sphere of high-culture poetry outside the standard forms and conventions of a tradition that implies a male voice. If a woman speaks, she must speak with a man's words and in his forms and genres.[95] Entering the arena of poetry means taking men on with their own weapons in battles whose stakes include power, position, and livelihood. The Lord Dennys are looking for assailants everywhere because their assailants *are* everywhere, and they strike back viciously because that is how it is done in the mortal combat of life at court.

Where Mary Wroth takes up the pen and, to one man at least, seems to grow a phallus, Veronica Franco takes up another prominent phallic symbol, the sword.[96] Entering the field of poetry, she is attacked by several men, to one of whom she responds:

> You found me defenseless, alone, off my guard
> fainthearted and never practiced in combat
> and strong, fully armed, you wounded me sorely

Unlike Mary, who withdrew her book from publication, Veronica (who has no reputation for modesty to uphold) chooses to fight back:

> though a woman born to milder tasks;
> > and blade in hand, I learned warrior's skills,

---

[z] That is, "construe," or to judge or infer from evidence. The OED gives the following example, which is very similar to Lord Denny's lines: "DANIEL *Compl. Rosamond* xxxii, A sinful monster, As by her words the chaster sort may conster."

so that, by handling weapons, I learned
that women by nature are no less agile than men.
 So, devoting all my effort to arms,
I see myself now, thanks to heaven, at the point
where I no longer fear harm from anyone.[97]

'Ayişe's social situation is much like Wroth's and not at all like Franco's. She is from the intellectual aristocracy, a family of scholars, interpreters of the Qur'an and the hadith, and canon law jurists. Her hypermodest and self-deprecatory style is just that: a style. This is the way inferiors presented themselves to their superiors, the way elite writers presented themselves to their audiences—audiences that were always presumed (or wishfully imagined) to include the monarch. The writer is always "the poor and miserable" (*hakir, fakir*).

When we take this conventional stance into account, 'Ayişe's plea to be taken seriously begins to appear as brave and confrontational as Franco's or Labé's (even in 'Aşık's representation). She plays on the "deficient in reason" hadith in much the same way we saw Mihri doing, with obvious irony in a context where, as everyone knew, not every man or even many men could manage a decent couplet, much less a decent poem. She admits that, in general, the conversation of women may be simple and untutored in comparison to the cultured discourse of educated men. But left unsaid and yet looming large is the knowledge that she is educated and widely read in the Arabic and Persian classics and that she is, even in the course of her self-deprecation, demonstrating her mastery of the language and rhetoric of the Ottoman elites. If she were to be treated as an equal, she asks, what harm would that do to an educated and intelligent man? For an Ottoman woman of good family, this runs hard against the grain. Like Mary Wroth or a Venetian woman of the same social class, she would have been expected to remain invisible, covered, modest, silent, and private.

We have seen that, among men in the Ottoman Empire and elsewhere in Europe at that time, being a friend or conversational companion meant also being a beloved of sorts. An erotic dimension to friendship was recognized as normal. Men accepted that love of a friend could be (even should be) passionate and intense and appropriately expressed in the language of erotic verse. The boundaries between the erotic-emotional and the erotic-physical/sexual were understood, and the actual social penalties for breaching them were either nonexistent or relatively light. But in this network of scripting, unspoken understandings, and conventions—what the sociologist Pierre Bourdieu called *the habitus*—there was no place for a woman.[98] Perhaps the simplest way to put it is to say that, as far as it appears to us today, *for elite males* there was no cultural script that, in the case of a woman, allowed for clear boundaries between friendship (with its erotic dimension) and sexual activity. However, we say, *as far as it appears to us today* to point out that we cannot really be sure that what is visible to us is what was actually going on. There are hints, suggestions, that make us wonder. How did Mihri, for example, interact with Mü'eyyidzade during their Amasya days? She is described as having been in some way "in the circle of" Sultan Selim I and Prince Ahmet when they were serving as governors in Amasya, and 'Ayişe is said to have been a musahib of Selim II (r. 1566–74) while her father worked as his tutor. Did this mean nothing more than sending them poems? Were there other kinds of contact? Were there actual conversations? Under what circumstances? What kinds of social contacts could "premarried" women have with men?

In talking about early-modern Ottoman women, Leslie Peirce mentions suggestively: "While virginity was valued, it is interesting that adolescent girls appear to have circulated with greater freedom than their married older sisters." Peirce also points out that the norm was for women to marry "upon physical maturation so that the awakening of sexual desire occurred within marriage." What the case of a woman whose virginity persists into (and throughout) mature adulthood might be is not clear. Peirce's analysis suggests the possibility that a permanently "presexual" or nonsexual woman would, like the "postsexual" woman, be seen as unthreatening to the honor of a family and the paternity of children. This would allow her greater mobility and contact with men as well as a measure of respect.[99] 'Ayişe's poem, which asks right out for the opportunity to converse with educated men, would seem to indicate that such a conversation was thinkable. 'Aşık's transmission of her plea and his lack of comment also seem to suggest that what she is asking for is not all that outlandish. In his entry for Zeynep Latifi says: "Zeynep was married and was under the control of her husband; she withdrew from poetry and conversation [*musahibet*] with men."[100] This seems to imply that, before marriage, she was able to have some sort of sohbet relations with men. We have much left to learn about the activities of Ottoman women during the Age of Beloveds.

7

SEDUCTION AND REVERSAL

The minor poet Me'ali was a kadi who died in 1535/36, having risen in his profession as far as the judgeship of Istanbul during the reign of Bayezit II. Me'ali was notorious for being a lover of boys, and the biographer 'Aşık tells an amusing story about him in this regard, although he refuses to attest to its authenticity. We have no opinions on the story's authenticity either, but we find it a fascinating—even if fictional—point of entry into some issues involving relations between highly placed lovers and lower-class beloveds, issues that have implications for our understanding of love as enacted and imagined by courtiers or court-dependent elites in early-modern authoritarian monarchies. Our translation of the story goes as follows:

> While Me'ali was living happily as kadi of Mihaliç and the people of that district lived content with his judgments and directives, he engaged himself in a bout of flirtatiousness and amorous advances toward a saucy-eyed, sweet-faced, ravishing beauty of a boy, the son of a janissary and the pride of every local urchin. They say this beloved was as disruptive as his oh-so-disturbing eye and the source of catastrophes as numerous as his twisted ringlets. He was a beauty who for sheer impudence would swipe the cap from John Doe's head and wipe the very eye shadow from a proud rogue's eye.
>
> The wretched kadi would beat his breast and cast languid, loving glances at his beloved in mosques and public gatherings, and, as he grew increasingly distraught, his beloved would display all manner of tempting airs, coquettish tricks, and come-hither glances. Now giving him an angry look, next a smile and a sweet chuckle, then again making the love-smitten jurist blush red with favors and kind treatment, he caused the miserable kadi to cast all resistance and firm resolve to the winds and raze the dwell-

ing of his steadfastness, building in its stead the unshakable palace of his love.

Me'ali became as unstable as a handful of air and realized that the affair had struck him to the quick, the dagger had pricked him to the bone. Now in scrolls of verse, now in missives of prose, like a pure white candle he flamed with love for that fiery-cheeked darling, and then again, in message and disposition, he revealed his every hidden desire. Meanwhile, that rogue and thief of hearts, on his part, would alternately look on Me'ali with compassion and then ridicule his sparse beard. In the end, the honorable kadi could no longer content himself with mere observation, but longed for communion and pleasant companionship, or even hoped, perchance, for a kiss, an embrace, a moment sitting side by side.

At this point, the beloved sent him word saying: "Submission to His Eminence's command is incumbent on us in every respect, on the one hand, because he is the official arbiter of our town and a learned man and on the other hand, because he is a person of talent who knows Persian and is possessed of wisdom and every virtue, a man of noble lineage, of delicate disposition, of a pleasant and unworldly mien. Would that all our time were spent in his service and that the capital of our life were expended on companionship with him. Would that we were a gleaner at the harvest of his excellence and a gatherer of crumbs at the feast of his learning. If only the coin of our beauty could be this well spent and the merchandise of our love thus find favor in the marketplace. However, the folk of our town are unsophisticated, and beardless youths are everywhere. They are finders of fault and censorious. If we were to carry on our companionship openly, they would wildly shoot off their mouths, inventing charges such as, 'He went to the kadi's house in the evening.' What reputation and what honor we might possess we would sacrifice without question for his sake; our goal is only to protect his good name. However, if His Eminence were to command a secluded rendezvous, we would hitch up our skirts and make haste at his bidding to brighten our cup in his gathering. We are prepared to flame up, to roast with passion like a candle, and to be as fervent of heart as a censer."

When His Eminence the Kadi heard this thrilling news and these glad tidings from the messenger, his excess of ardor caused him to faint away, stunned by amazement. When he had, after a time, regained a measure of consciousness, agitatedly rising up and sitting down he wept with joy, and, according to the saying, "First of all, give what is due for that which just arrived," he poured forth at the feet of that bearer of glad tidings the pearls of his tears in quantities never before seen by the eye and scattered thereupon jewels of language the likes of which the ear has never heard.

A COUPLET BY THE AUTHOR:

If you wish gold, you'll find it, pleased to say, upon my face.
If rubies, pearls, or corals, these this pair of eyes replace.

And the kadi sent a reply saying: "Our only motive is to have the honor of a rendezvous. Upon us too is it incumbent to protect the reputation of both parties since our class is known the world over as suspected lovers of boys. Our desire is that, in the company of that candle of beauty, we ignite one another from the flame of love and that, before the chess master of fate moves the pawn of death and cries out 'checkmate' to the soul, we sit together on the same game mat and chat agreeably about the chess game of deep affection. When he is with us, what do we care about the world, and, when the love of our life is absent, what does life in the world mean to us? With him a barren mountaintop is a garden, and by the light of his loveliness each bit of common stone is a brilliant gem. Only he who swiftly gives swiftly obtains his desire; those who are aware say of he who makes the first offer, 'We have seen him in paradise!' Our hope is that the desire for union not turn out to be a deceitful promise, that we not be destroyed by being made to wait, and that he not suffer the evil consequences of this destruction."

The beloved responded and said: "We stand by our promises; we live and breathe faithfulness and honesty! A meeting in town would be difficult, but we know of a tumbledown dwelling resembling a farmhouse on the outskirts of the city. Even though it is neither a pleasing building nor an agreeable atmosphere, nonetheless like the lover's heart it is a journey of a thousand days removed from the eye of the enemy, and like the domain of faithfulness it is protected from stones of reproach cast by either friend or foe. If it should seem proper to him

Since traveling's a blessed act at dawn
Let him at dawn upon his way be gone

Let him deign to exit the city gates alone and repair to such-and-such hamlet; there let him see his humble servant by his stirrup like a shadow at his bidding."

His Eminence rejoined, "Upon my oath I will!" And that night he could not sleep for eagerness but remained awake until morning, like the stars in the sky never closing his eyes for his ardent longing. He saw the moonlight, thought it dawn, and so proceeded to do his ablutions. Realizing that it was not morning, and not wanting his ablutions to be wasted, he did a supererogatory late-night prayer. He was so distraught that in the course of two ritual prostrations he made three or four errors. He was about to wring the neck of the cock for being late in crowing and was determined to fire the muezzin, thinking that the man couldn't tell time. Three or four times he told his servants to saddle up, and finally they saddled his horse and loaded up the pack animal. His Eminence then indicated that there was no need of either pack animal or attendant, of companion or servant. "I merely had a frightening dream," he said. "And since they say, 'The back of a horse is blessed,' therefore, have the groom saddle the blessed horse, and I will, by myself, circle the town, coming and going without delay." No matter how often they said, "Riding alone is injurious to one's reputation," or, "You will be demeaned before friend and foe alike," or, "It is inappropriate," it made not the slightest difference. He donned his most elegant turban and a clean garment, breakfasted joyously, and mounted himself on his horse. In his ardor, he threw all restraint to the winds, now spurring on his horse, now making it leap.

Thus he arrived at the agreed-on way station and there saw his darling awaiting him, all bold and saucy. The youth greeted His Eminence with a laugh on his lips and heart-ravishing glances, and the two proceeded together, smiling and chatting. The young man completely stole the heart of the kadi with seductive wiles and flirtatious airs, leaving him sitting there on his horse, a lifeless shell of a man. As the two romanced each other verbally with plaints of loneliness and separation, of union and faithfulness, all of a sudden there appeared before them one or two buildings. Each of them was darker and more cramped than a jealous heart, more ramshackle and run-down than the generosity of a miser. The roof of each was lower than the aspirations of the vile, its timbers more broken than the hearts of lovers, and over them all hung a pall of smoke like clouds over a mountaintop.

As it so happened, this place was a leper colony and a stopping place for every poor and helpless wight. As they drew near, the darling boy spoke: "The air of this village is unhealthy, and its water is exactly like bathwater. It is oppressive from the ground up, and the atmosphere there is excessively warm. However, it has this particular property, that, although its air is insalubrious, it is also sexually stimulating. Although its water is warm as a bath, it at the same time incites carnal desires. If you would deign to proceed slowly, allow me to go on ahead, and empty out a grain bin, and spread it with whatever mats and carpets they might have."

The kadi gave him leave to go, and thus the boy proceeded to the village and called together the imam of the lepers and those of some repute in the colony, saying:

"Glad news! Your fortune's day has just begun,
And all here shall be exalted like the sun!

"Do not suppose of me that I am here on a fool's errand; I am a royal servant come at the bidding of the monarch. One of the companions of Sultan Selim [I], Lord of the Seven Climes, has by divine disposition become afflicted with your disease, in the remedying of which the physicians are helpless. They have made me his companion and sent him here; however, neither is he himself aware of what is taking place, nor is he resigned to the situation. I went to no end of trouble in bringing him here and assured his arrival at your village with a thousand clever deceptions so that you might attend him and entertain him and he might grow content and learn to prefer your company. He is a man of quite substantial means, capable of endowing ever so many charitable trusts. God willing, he will surely establish a number of philanthropic institutions here and will undoubtedly spend large amounts on your hungry and needy. Moreover, the sultan will hear of this and will likely grant you official rewards, putting an end to your poverty. He may indeed grant you the revenues of a number of villages that you might go no more to the plow, nor into servitude, that you might renounce poverty and have done with destitution! However, until the matter is completed and he is settled in and has sent me away, neither show yourselves nor make the slightest advertisement of your existence."

When the lepers heard this, they were delighted, and in transports of joy they disappeared like weasels, each into his own den or subterranean burrow. The beloved then located the front room of a granary and, insofar as possible, decorated it with pieces of ancient reed matting and bits of cloth left behind by the lepers. He made a couch of a bit of felt and a bolster of a saddlebag filled with stale bread crumbs.

He then went out to meet His Eminence with profuse apologies and manifestations of helplessness and shame at the ugliness and harshness of the place. Dropping a man dead at his feet with every step, and stealing the wits from a sage with every word, all seductive blandishments and romantic enticements, he said, "I am tormented by shame in your presence for having fallen short in doing you service. My goal was to enjoy the honor of your company and accept the opportunity to wait on you. You must forgive my shortcomings and conceal my failings beneath the veil of discretion." And, holding the kadi's stirrup, he helped him down, taking him by the arms.

As he was helped to dismount, Me'ali chanced to sniff his darling's neck, their cheeks fleetingly brushed, and the poor gentleman collapsed swooning into his beloved's arms. For a time he remained stunned by the scent of his darling's musky locks and for a period was struck dumb, incapable of speech. Then the kadi said, "My dear little sir, what occasion is there for excusing anyone's shortcomings? The only disaster would be the disaster of delay. 'The honor of a habitation,' they say, 'is in its inhabitants.' For myself the pleasure is solely in this, that we come together in fact rather than in fantasy.

What I desire is your beauty, all else is pretext!

And then, the darling boy in the lead and His Eminence hard on his heels, they ascended by a ladder as terrifying as the shrouds of a ship and as fraught with fear as the tightrope of an acrobat. At first, they were revolted when they saw this place with its frightful atmosphere, this dwelling flimsy as the web of a spider that was to be their sitting spot. But on the way up the ladder His Eminence espied "that which is desired" and the long locks reaching down his beloved's back. So he reached out his hand that he might touch the "hidden treasure." His darling at once turned sour faced and irritable, saying:

The goods of communion come not without bother
A ladder is climbed one rung, then the other

When His Eminence heard him mention the scent of communion, he forgot the evil odor of the place, and, when he saw the tender freshness of its inhabitant, his heart was distracted from the harsh staleness of the habitation. Once again, the greedy honeybees of lust swarmed about him and covered him from head to toe like his robes. He saw before him a waist—so-called but lacking all substance—and hips so substantial that they could not fit in an embrace. He determined to give him a kiss and a hug, throwing an arm about his neck as his ringlets were thrown, clasping him firmly about the waist as he was clasped by his belt. He whet his appetite for setting to the kissing of his hand, readied himself for casting aside all formalities as one casts aside the skirts of modesty and for taking the matter in hand, handling it by laying a hand to the drawstring of his darling's pantaloons. In order to induce his beloved to show compassion, he would alternately whisper plaintively and plead aloud. Meanwhile, the darling boy made his brows an attractive single line with seductive looks and laughter; he gave twist and curl to his locks with coyness and reproaches, with coquetries and enticements.

"My dear sir," he said, "have patience, restrain your hand! To make sweets from green fruit requires patience. First, amiable conversation, then getting to know each other better so that friends and casual acquaintances alike not reproach us. To insist on having one's way before we have looked each other over, before bashfulness has been driven away like a stranger by the hand of joyous ease, is no more than crude lust and is forbidden even among the devotees of love. More appropriate is this: that you calm yourself. For if you again act wildly, you will have me as your companion only in your imagination. In the meanwhile, I, your humble servant, will engage myself in preparing the yellow judge—what they call the flagon—that is found in your saddlebag. On the other side of that low pass over there is a village of non-Muslims. They make a distilled wine of such great purity and potency that whoever, like an alchemist, places a dram of it on the scales of his grief sees his whole life turn to gold and whoever possesses a jar of it becomes the finder of kingly treasure by the jugful and possesses the wealth of Korah. If you would turn the matter over to me, I will go now by your leave, fill the yellow judge, and be back in the wink of an eye, at which time I will be prepared to serve you as you desire.

"We will raise a glass or two, then cast the turban of modesty and the robe of gravity, like the cloak of hypocrisy, into the all-encompassing sea. If we do not get enough during the day, we will stay the night at it, the while letting modesty be dispelled and companionship prevail without formality or anxiety, now partaking of brimming bowl and delicious viands, now sipping the lover's toast of communion from the hand of passion, and after you will eat as you please of the fruits of union with me. Now, intoxicated by the wine of couplet and verse, we'll let our pleasure seeking become reckless, now we'll let my kiss be the toothsome morsel, my lip the wine, my love the wine pourer. Now you'll study my breast, my bosom in the moonlight, now suck on my lip, kiss my face, smell of my locks, stroke my neck with your cheek. In sum, we'll let the gates of merriment be thrown open wide and the cup of pleasure be raised on high. And when it comes time for the intoxication of sleep, time for the onset of the flood of wine's victory over the senses, should you be troubled by lack of pillow or bolster, we'll let my silver-skinned forearm be your bolster and my musky locks your soft cushion, and you'll let me serve you until morn by stroking your hands and feet. Finally we will slumber, holding each other tight, and keeping one another warm. Let us pay no heed to the muezzin's morning cry nor listen to anything but the voice of the nightingale. Let us grow into oneness, let our spirits mingle one with the other, let us add sweet to sweet. If the shirt tries to come between us by even so much as a hair's breadth, let us take it by the hand, pull it over the head, and have done with it. And at dawn, even as the heavens take in hand the drinking bowl of the sun, let us ward off the effects of drink with a morning cup, mayhap becoming again so intoxicated that we do not recover for three days!"

When the wretched gentleman heard these exhilarating words and this inspiring message, he completely surrendered himself. He emitted a heart-rending sigh, looked on his beloved, and responded in verse:

"So pleasantly you've tuned your lute, so sweet the key
Should you not break a string upon this melody

How well you know to give afflicted ones relief
Should you not with laughter ridicule their grief"

The beloved immediately disappeared from view like a ghost or the new moon that appears on the first night of the month. He mounted his horse and made his way home, becoming as though he had never been. Behind him the kadi was, for a time, left gaping like an open-mouthed corpse from which the soul has just fled. Later he was beset by demons of confusion, fright, and horror. He cast his eyes about him and everywhere saw mounds upon mounds of dirt and, in them, yawning pits like cavernous fissures. He hesitated a moment in thought, then looked again and noticed that each of them resembled a mouse's nest or the burrow of a mole. And, before he could do more than wonder what this was, suddenly, out of each hole, like a tortoise emerging from its shell, there appeared a head, and, gradually, following on the faces, the forms of people became visible. However, their voices could not be rightly heard but seemed to be hoarse and suppressed so that one could not make out what words they spoke. They gathered about him, all in a group, some with broken earthenware bowls of bread and cheese in their hands, others holding small wooden platters of onion and garlic, which they offered to him. As they approached, he became aware that they were lepers. Their faces were covered with pustules, their hands with sores, and their feet were scrofulous. At first glance, he thought them to be beggars. Saying, "All right! It is now obvious why you wish to approach me," he reached a hand into his pocket so as to extract a silver piece and give them alms. But still they gradually advanced on him. How could it be that not one of them would withdraw! When he saw them thus continuing to move closer, he thought, "These hapless wretches, it can only be that they have a lawsuit; they recognized that I am a kadi and must have come for that reason. What an unfortunate stroke of luck!" "Muslims!" he said. "We did not come here to do business. If you have pending litigation and are in need of a judgment, would you come to my court instead!"

This too profited him nothing. The lepers climbed the ladder with the intent that they all meet together, the greater among them seated, the lesser standing. "Don't bother to sit," he cried. "Just tell me what it is you want!" Now cringing back, and now holding his nose, according to the saying, "What pleasure is there that time does not wither nor age destroy," he forgot the erstwhile imagined delights of communion. Becoming irate, he addressed them, saying, "You fellows, what is it you want? Tell me, but make it snappy!" "Dear sir," they responded, "our intent is only that we may look on each other eye to eye. What they say animals do by sniffing one another, and humans do by conversing together, we here do by gazing into one another's eyes."

The kadi's mind clouded; his eyes glazed over. He cried out, "Oh you fellows! Taking precautions against mingling with your kind has been common practice for generation upon generation since doing otherwise is an invitation to destruction. If you wish only that which is your due, then you will get what is coming to you. 'Everyone's daily bread will be put within his reach.'" And, thus saying, he counted out a few silver pieces.

However, this too brought him neither relief nor escape, nor did the lepers accept his counsel. They squatted around him, brought their bowls, and placed them in the center, saying, "First food, then conversation. . . . In the name of God, please begin. Let us dip our hands into one bowl; let separateness grow into unity. The creator who made you also made us, and, in the end, he made some of us healthy and some of us diseased.

Whatsoever comes from God, he commands in everything
What he decrees none escapes, neither slave nor king.

"They say that 'tragedy calls on the prophets and torment visits even the saints.' We hear from scholars such as yourself that on the day of resurrection our faces will be as pure and shining as the full moon. And, more particularly, the Messenger of God (on whom be peace) is said to have stopped and lingered with our kind, giving aid and comfort. Thus to be disgusted by us, to be so distressed by our company, befits neither your learning nor your maturity, neither your customary behavior nor your age."

The kadi replied, "There is nothing in what you say that is not well-known. Nonetheless:

Every kind with its own kind shall flock
Pigeon flies with pigeon, hawk with hawk
Where illness should a healthy man infect
To set him off apart would be correct

Just supposing that you are well; then you are indeed well, and I am well away from here!

Avoid troubling others no matter the cost!"

They answered him saying, "Dear sir, it is appropriate that a person resign himself to his fate. Before Job was stricken by disease, he had not earned the epithet Most Grateful Servant, nor had Abraham been confirmed in the honorific Most Excellent of Servants before he had patiently endured tribulations. This world is a place of weariness and torment, and at the end of it all is annihilation. For a few short days of life, what matter suffering and illness; indeed, what matter jewels and worldly wealth!

In this world the goal is but to get along
The jewel of health cannot be gotten for a song

"There was a time we too were healthy like you. Today we are getting along as you see us. Like other folk we sweat and strain. But in the afterlife we will enter paradise many thousands of years before those who lived in health, and before them we will see the face of God. Supposing that you too were stricken, what then could you do? All we want is that we might enjoy ourselves together for a few days, pretend that our hunger is attributable to our vigor, and take our ease for a while. Having it come easy is worth nothing to a man and, on the contrary, must need teach him to be worthless. He who is the most self-sufficient after a few days longs for the company he once despised. If you become heartsore from loneliness, the poor little daughter of our imam has only just become a leper. Her eyes do not yet resemble boils, nor does her nose yet look like an eggplant. There is no rasping yet in her voice, nor is her breath noisome. Grant permission for a marriage; let us put on a wedding ceremony, and you enter into wedlock. It is ultimately in the hands of God, but it may be that progeny will issue from the two of you to cheer our hearth and brighten our lamp."

The kadi was beset by such a rage that the revolving dome of the heavens seemed but a grain of millet to him. "Oh you savages," he cried, "oh you wild asses, you don't make something beautiful by force! Nor does a rose lose its beauty by falling on a dunghill. What nonsensical drivel you speak! Go on, get out of here! Go away, and converse with your own kind! Why is there no sergeant at arms here?"

And they replied, "Dear sir, alas, when doom comes to call, precautions avail us not at all! Don't struggle so obstinately against it. Don't turn on us and bite us like an adder. We fear for our very lives. We cannot, with our sons and daughters, become prisoners and targets for the executioner's sword just because of you! This is happening by order of the ruler; a royal servant delivered you into our hands by the sultan's decree. He told us that you had become one of us and that the sultan, on the recommendation of his physicians, had ordered that you be added to our company; he let us know exactly what we should do. We will tie you up by main force and bring you along willy-nilly, no matter what!

HEMISTICH:

Whether your heart is open to it or closed"

When the kadi heard these words, he said, "What a heap of nonsense and a pack of lies! Damn you all, and damn any leper wherever he might be, and damn that vulgar disgrace, that promiscuous, passive prostitute of a catamite with the tattered anus who claimed to be a servant of the sultan!" And with this he arose that he might descend by the ladder, mount his horse, and head back for the city.

But the lepers cried out, "One must first look out for his own life and only then look out for others. Better your mother weep for a bit than all our ancestors weep for all time." And they threw themselves on poor Me'ali, rolling about on the floor in an attempt to hold him, and wrapping their arms about his neck trying to pin him down.

When the rancid odor of their putrid armpits and misshapen bodies and the stench of their bestial faces reached his nostrils, he became nauseated, his stomach heaved, and he vomited for a bit. Then for a time he lost his wits and fell in a swoon. The imam of the lepers then took his head on knees covered with a thousand sores.

When the kadi opened his eyes, he took refuge in God and wept a few tears of bitter regret. The leper's carrion crow of a face seemed to have perched on his life like the raven of doom, and the bird of his soul seemed to have fled its fleshy nest for the wilderness of annihilation. He saw that there was no way out but to apply the saying, "Verily, the truth shall set you free." There he was in the midst of his enemies without a succoring friend, so he told the truth, swearing oath after oath, making vow after vow.

"I am that unfortunate, ill-starred one they call Me'ali, the kadi of Mihaliç. But—and only the divine is without fault—I am a devotee of catamites and a boy chaser. This tempter flaming with seductiveness, this deceiver with his collection of devious stratagems, trapped me in the snare of his deceit, the while promising himself to be trapped in the snares of this material world. His aim seems to have been to display his artistry in deception and enchantment and perfidious sorcery. For God's sake, send a man, have him go to the court! Let them know that I am well and receive abundant gifts and presents for bringing the good news."

When they heard this, the imam and the notably intelligent among the lepers said, "Dear friends, the gentleman does not appear outwardly to be like us. His face and eyes are sound, and what he says seems from the way he speaks to be sound as well. Let's send someone to the town and see if what he says is true."

The kadi, his mind reeling, his life fading, languished there weak and sick, half dead and full of terror. Meanwhile, their man set off smartly toward town. On arriving, he saw that the kadi was not in court. He then asked those present where he might be, and they said, "He stayed at home today. . . . He has business in his private chambers. . . . He even took a medicinal draught. . . . He has an ailing constitution. . . ." The man then met with the kadi's steward, who said, "The gentleman went out for a horseback ride. Call again some other time."

The fellow replied, "Let me tell you something about your master. Aren't his face and form like this . . . and his turban and dress like that. . . ? He has only one or two hairs on his chin and is so thin that he resembles a shadow puppet. His nose looks like an eggplant grafted on a beet. He has neither slave nor manservant with him."

"Hah! Those are exactly the characteristics of the gentleman," they said. "You can see on his face only one or two hairs! Pray tell, what palace or villa might he be in, in what garden or vineyard?"

And the messenger said, "He lies in the village of the lepers, suffering and ill, his ribs shattered by vomiting. If you make haste, you may get there in time to save his life, or at least in time to be blessed at his last breath!"

Their hearts leaped into their throats, and they mounted their horses and rode off. They found the kadi in a pitiable state and sprinkled rosewater on his face as they sprinkled tears at his feet. When he had come to his senses, they bowed before him, and he signaled to them that he had neither the ability to speak nor the strength to make his condition known and that they should take him home. So they loaded him on a pallet and rushed him homeward.

For an exceedingly long time, Me'ali lay ill and would regale his friends with what had happened to him. Whenever the affair of the lepers came to mind, he would start with terror. However, this situation resulted in his asking forgiveness of God for his drunkenness with the cup of lust and his worship of passion. And, thereafter, he walked in the paths of righteousness. May God eradicate his evil acts and cast off his errors![1]

Love and the Court

That, even on the surface, the story of Me'ali tells of seduction and reversal is obvious. In fact, it is but one variant of a number of early-modern anecdotes in which a highly placed man falls prey to the wiles of an unscrupulous lower-class boy or woman. This example is very Ottoman. The seduction, with poetry and ornate prose, with tears, mournful supplications, and the boy's sensual description of a night of love, is precisely as scripted by Ottoman poetry. Nonetheless, the core of the story has analogues in many places, and, as we will argue, it has a special significance in the context of absolute monarchies during the Age of Beloveds.

Elsewhere, one of us (Andrews) has pointed out that Ottoman gazel poetry can be seen as a nexus where four discourses—love, religion, politics, and psychology—intersect in a complex ecological relationship.[2] However, rather than beginning with the Ottomans, we broaden our focus and modify the thrust of Andrews's earlier argument by adopting a perspective suggested by Ann Rosalind Jones and Peter Stallybrass during the course of a reading of Sir Philip Sidney's sonnet sequence *Astrophel and Stella*, which was first published in 1591, five years after Sidney's death, and dedicated to the famous beloved Penelope Devereux Rich. For our purposes, one of the most pertinent facts about Sidney is that, during the late sixteenth century, he was famed less for his talents as a poet and scholar than for being the model courtier. In the course of contextualizing their reading of Sidney's sonnets, Jones and Stallybrass make the following statement, which we believe could apply, with only the slightest, inconsequential alterations, to the Ottoman love poetry of the court-dependent elites: "The structure of the lovers' relationship is a variant *not* of the actual relationship between men and women, which was one of female subordination to father or to husband, but of the relationship of the courtier to his prince, or the suitor's to his patron. Even the silence of the sonneteer's beloved has more in common with the prince's silence, in which his or her every look must be interrogated for the slightest sign of favor or disfavor, than with the forced silence and obedience of daughter and wife."[3]

If we expand the gender of the beloved to include beloved boys and take into account that in the Ottoman Empire—and in England and Italy, for that matter—young boys were nearly as subordinate and protected, and considered as vulnerable to sexual exploitation, as young women, there is nothing in this statement that would distinguish the gazel poet from the sonneteer. What Jones and Stallybrass argue is that, *for the court-dependent elites*, the relationship to the monarch and the patron is primary, that there is no private sphere where the ground of poetic, Petrarchan, Neoplatonic love resides, that, "even within the poems, the supposedly 'private' sphere of love can be imagined only through its similarities and dissimilarities to the public world of the court."[4] This notion is also prominent in Stephen Greenblatt's work, most noticeably when he says of the early-sixteenth-century English poet Sir Thomas Wyatt: "I would suggest that there is no privileged sphere of individuality in Wyatt, set off from linguistic convention, from social pressure, from the shaping force of religious and political power. Wyatt may complain about the abuses of the court, he may declare his independence from a corrupting sexual or political entanglement, but he always does so within a context governed by the essential values of dominance and submission, the values of a system of power that has an absolute monarch as head of both church and state."[5]

What we would like to suggest is that what is true for the Petrarchan poetry of Western Europe is also true for the Ottoman poetry of Eastern Europe. In an article on the Ottoman kaside, Andrews says in the same vein:

What I intend to convey is that for the Ottoman elites the garden of desire is the palace and the palace is manifest in each and every garden. Power of any kind—temporal, divine, the power to incite desire—is a garden tended by the sultan and beneath the sun and sky of his domination:

> The lord Bayezit is that sky of dominance in whose
> Garden of power ever so many roses shine like the sun
> —Necati

And, with reference to the couplet by Hayali

> Were it not, once a year, to bow its head in the dust at his feet,
> The rose would not have bejeweled its ruby crown with pearls of dew

which evokes the ceremony by which officeholders renewed their fealty, Andrews goes on to remark: "There seems to be an almost transcendent appropriateness to this figurative centering of the monarch, a kind of Neoplatonic emanationism by which the qualities of the ruler are responsible for the character of the material universe. This is the reason for absolute loyalty in the context of absolute power. For the petitioner/lover, the universe *is* constituted by the ruler; what the world is, what it means is ever determined by its relation to the monarch."[6]

The brilliant Turkish Ottomanist Ahmet Hamdi Tanpınar had, in his seminal study of nineteenth-century Ottoman literature, already come to a similar conclusion: "In truth, all these various elements [of Ottoman poetry]—perhaps with the exception of those works that are obviously religious or mystical—seem to us to be a wide-ranging, grand metaphor for the palace."[7] If it is also true that the relationship between the court-dependent elites and the absolute monarch transcends apparent cultural boundaries, as is indicated by the similarities between the observations of Jones, Stallybrass, and Greenblatt on English poetry and the independently derived conclusions of Andrews and Tanpınar about the Ottoman situation, then the simple story of reversal in which the lowly boy dominates and makes a fool of a powerful man becomes complex and takes on additional layers of meaning. This complexity and multivalence derive in large part from the primary situation in which relations with the monarch constitute a script for understanding and expressing love.

At court, every seduction is directed upward. The less powerful attempt to win the attention, support, and favors of the more powerful, and at the top of the seduction pyramid is the absolute monarch, who is, in theory, a supplicant only to God. In this context, most love poetry implies a reversal on the surface. Simply put, where the poet is an elite male, the ostensible beloved—

boy or girl, young man or woman—is an inferior. The surface fiction of the love poem is a private seduction directed downward (on the social and power scales), while the dominant pattern of relations demands a public seduction upward. In the context of the poem, the actual balance of power is reversed, and the powerful man cedes power and submits to a dominating beloved who exerts control by being inaccessible, unmoved, and silent.[8]

In the Ottoman situation, fundamental similarities between the monarch and the beloved of elite literature are strikingly close and consistent. The monarch is as protected as any beautiful boy or elite woman; he seldom emerges from the sanctuary of the palace and is seen only on rare and usually ceremonial occasions, when he is accompanied by a retinue of guardians. The silence of the sultan and his court inspired fear and awe in European observers. In the inner courts of the palace, no one spoke in the presence of the sultan; no one spoke even when the sultan might by chance be present. The slave pages of the palace school and the servants of the inner courts communicated by sign language in areas that might be visited by the sultan. This terrible silence reigned even when thousands were gathered on formal occasions. As a member of a French embassy in 1573 recalled of one such event: "We looked with great pleasure and even greater admiration at this frightful number of Janissaries and other soldiers standing all along the walls of this court, with hands joined in front in the manner of monks, in such silence that it seemed we were not looking at men but statues. And they remained immobile in that way more than seven hours, without talking or moving. Certainly it is almost impossible to comprehend this discipline and this obedience when one has not seen it."[9]

Moreover, Italian embassies report that, beginning with Süleyman, sultans received important visitors seated, immobile, and silent on the throne—like an idol, according to several European observers—without ever responding to what was said, saying anything themselves, or acknowledging others. For the Ottoman courtier/official, beyond this posed or theatrical silence lay its terrifying objectification in the form of the shadow presence of the executioner deaf-mutes of the inner courts. When palace dignitaries were summoned into the presence of the sultan in the Chamber of Petitions ('Arz Odası), their futures down to their very lives were at stake. As Gülru Necipoğlu says in her marvelous study of the Topkapı Palace: "During the presentation of petitions in the chamber the head gatekeeper, the head treasurer, and several mutes stood by behind the gate, ready to execute the guilty dignitaries when the sultan stamped his feet on the ground as an indication of his displeasure."[10]

A powerful subtext lying behind the ominous distancing and silencing of the monarch is the eschatological and messianic themes brought to our attention by the studies of Barbara Flemming, Cornell Fleischer, and Lucette Valensi. The early years of Süleyman's reign are tinged by speculation, based on astrological calculations, geomancy, and apocalyptic histories, that he was the foretold Universal Monarch, or even the Messiah/Mahdi, whose coming would signal the end of days. The impetus of Süleyman's early reign was seen as directed toward provoking the "final battle" for universal dominion with the Holy Roman Emperor, Charles V, whose sack of Rome in 1527 was seen as an attempt to merge mundane and spiritual rule and, thereby, position himself to challenge Süleyman for the role of Universal Monarch. In a context where some Muslims believed that Jesus would return as the Messiah/Mahdi and some Christians and Jewish (and Christian) cabbalists determined that Süleyman himself might be the true Messiah, it is no wonder that the Ottoman monarch would wrap himself in an aura of mystery and pregnant silences and that the image of the silent beloved would take on tremendous significance. Moreover, this prevalent sense of eschatological, apocalyptic foreboding and the underlying (and mostly unspoken) suspicion that the monarch may be an incarnation of the deity, or at least the deity's agent, linked heaven and earth in a new way for early-modern individuals.[11]

Ottoman poetry, generally and over a long period preceding and following the Age of Beloveds, linked the sultan (often in the role of Sufi master, as dictated by the Persian, Hafezan tradition) and the divine. But it is our contention that the peculiar climate of widespread apocalyptic speculation obtaining during the latter part of the fifteenth century and the early sixteenth drastically changes the meaning of traditional imagery and forges bonds between mysticism, the occult sciences, Sufism, and terrestrial rule that shift the course of Ottoman poetry's meaning core away from its historical (and continuing) surface referencing of Persian masters. The Ottomans' is a new beloved of a new age.

The powerful silence of the beloved is expressed in its most extreme and abstract form in the ceremonial of the palace. In the language of poetry ultimately presumed to reach the monarch's ears, this profound reticence and seclusion is depicted as the beloved's shyness, coyness, coquetry, modesty. As we see in the story of Me'ali, the coyness of the actual beloved is perhaps of a different degree but of the same order. The beloved rascal communicates at first in a language (a sign language?) of "tempting airs," "angry looks," "a smile and sweet chuckle," that recalls Selimi Musli's party and the actions of Hayali's beloved Turak Bali, who, "unable to content himself by communicating only with glances from a lowered head, with the knot of his curls and the curve of his brow, . . . spoke reproachfully, with the proud independence of the beloved, by a pouting of the lower lip and a trembling of the mouth" (for both Selimi Musli and Turak Bali, see chapter 2 above). The attentiveness of the lover to this form of gestural communication and his fluency in reading its language are precise parallels to what Jones and Stallybrass term the courtier's *interrogation* of the prince's every look and gesture and are far from what actually would be necessary in establishing a relationship with a beloved boy of the lower classes.[12] It appears that the beloved—here the rascally beauty— is invested with the power and character of a monarch and, thereby, with the power of gestures hyperbolically reflecting the monarch's terrible stamping of a foot. And therein lies the peril, the abyss into which the careless love addicted are in danger of falling: being mastered by a ruthless boy (or woman) who wields the power of life or death.

In a sense, the court- or patron-dependent elites are conditioned to fantasize being mastered or dominated by a powerful beloved representing the monarch. But, in fact, as Beier has shown for England, being mastered (having a master) was seen, in early-modern times, as a requirement (increasingly inscribed in law) of good citizenship for dependents at all social levels, from boys to women to household servants to soldiers to courtiers.[13] This more general enshrinement of being mastered as a positive value shows up in the beloved's response to Me'ali's cultured importuning:

> Submission to His Eminence's command is incumbent on us in every respect because, on the one hand, he is the official arbiter of our town and a learned man and, on the other hand, he is a person of talent who knows Persian and is possessed of wisdom and every virtue, a man of noble lineage, of delicate disposition, of a pleasant and unworldly mien. Would that all our time were spent in his service and that the capital of our life were expended on companionship with him. Would that we were a gleaner at the harvest of his excellence and a gatherer of crumbs at the feast of his learning.

On the surface, this response indicates (however duplicitously) the beloved's willingness to be mastered by the highly placed lover. We should note that the reason for this willingness has two parts: First, the lover is powerful and holds a respected social position (he is "learned," which puts him in the privileged class of ulema), and being mastered by such a person affirms the duty of the inferior to the superior. Second, the lover (Me'ali) is talented, knows Persian, is educated, virtuous, of noble lineage, of subtle disposition, and pleasant mien—all things that would recommend a courtier to the favor of a prince and affirm the duty of a prince or patron to favor only the most qualified of men. The beloved's position is complex here and combines the dominance of the prince with the submission of the supplicant. Unlike the prince, however, this beloved has only erotic and physical favors to offer. But is *only* appropriate in this field of hyperbolic desire? To the love-addicted jurist, this makes him no less powerful. Both parties express an equal desire to be mastered by a dangerous love, and both parties engage in a dance of mutual seduction, to the counterpoint of the kadi's vague and quickly repressed sense of the danger he is in—the danger of being mastered by an unscrupulous boy to whom he has ceded the role of monarch in the hope of gaining a temporary erotic liaison. The boy cedes nothing. He takes the power he is given and uses it to deliver Me'ali over to the mastery of a village of lepers and the society of the lowest of the low. In the end the boy is triumphant and the kadi abject. The kadi's danger is objectified by the most frightening and loathsome of early-modern diseases, and his degradation and moral shortcomings are highlighted by ironic contrast to the obedience and righteousness of the leper community.

Nonetheless, the story of reversals does not end with a laugh at poor Me'ali or the warning to all men who would play with unscrupulous boys. It is not quite so simple. Stallybrass and Jones call the elite love poem "a complex displacement of the ideological pressures of the court."[14] Part of that complexity derives from the fact that the ideology of the monarch as a distant, ideal, Neoplatonic beloved exists in tension with the actuality that a monarch can act with all the arbitrary, casual cruelty of Me'ali's rascal boy. In addition, the "ideological pressures of the court" are not just unidirectional. The monarch, as the ultimate patron of literature and, at times (in the case of several Ottoman sultans), as a producer of literature, is not immune to conceiving of himself or herself as re-presented by both the Petrarchan/Hafezan beloved and that beloved's shadow presence, the rascally and cruel girl-boy. Sidney as Astrophel threatens his Stella, and by extension his monarch/patron, with the obverse of his talent for praise:

> You then ungratefull thiefe, you murdring Tyran you,
> You Rebell run away, to Lord and Lady untrue,
> You witch, you Divill, (alas) you still of me beloved,
> You see what I can say; mend yet your froward mind,
> And such skill in my Muse you reconcil'd shall find,
> That all these cruell words your praises shall be proved.[15]

There is a complex series of embedded reversals here: the poet of praise becomes or threatens to become a purveyor of blame; the monarch/beloved becomes a thief, a tyrant, a rebel, unfaithful, a witch, and a devil (an "antimonarch"); the "cruell words" display the potential to revert again to praise. To someone who works with Ottoman poems, it is striking how familiar each of Sidney's epithets is and how commonplace their reversals. In the divan of Necati (d. 1509), for example, we find on the tyrant:

> *Geh cefası hükm ider mülk-i dile gahi gamı*
> *Ol iki zalim bu bir timara düşdi müşterek*

> At times his torment rules the heart's domain, at times his grief
> These tyrants two have joined to fall upon this single fief

On tyranny and unfaithfulness:

> *Geh cefa geh cevr geh naz oldı çün kim hu sana*
> *Bi-vefa dil-dar imişsin ey sanem ya hu sana*

> Tyranny, torment, coquetry, they're all your nature's part
> Oh idol, woe to you, the untrue holder of my heart

On the thief:

> *Dil sevinür yanagunda hat-ı hoş-bu olıcak*
> *Ugrınun güni dogar ay karanu olıcak*

> *Dostum böyle yabanlar mı gözetmek yaraşur*
> *Gamze-i mest harrami gözün ahu olıcak*

> The heart rejoices when your cheek
>   by perfumèd down is clouded
> The sun of the robber does brightly shine
>   when the moon by dark is shrouded

> My beloved friend, to eye the wasteland stranger
>   suits you well
> When like a thief with drunken glance
>   your eye is a wild gazelle

On the witch:

> *Ne gönül kodı ne göz hal-i ruh-u-'ariz-i dost*
> *Oda yanmaz suya batmaz nice cadudur bu*

> The mole upon the beloved's cheek
>   neither heart nor eye lays down
> What a witch this is who will neither
>   burn in flame nor in water drown

On the devil:

> *Yüzüni göstermesün agyara zülfün key sakın*
> *Mar olan şeytana cennet kapusın derhal açar*

Your lovelock ought not show your face to strangers, 'tis not wise
It opens the gates of paradise to Satan in a serpent's guise

On the rebel:

Nice kez ol serv-i serkeş[a] *gördi ayaklar rakib*
Dimedi bir kez ki el çek derd-mendümden benüm

How often did that rebel cypress see me trampled by my foe
And did not once speak out to say, Unhand my love who suffers so[16]

On the one hand, the evil behavior of the rascal boy (or the unavailable woman of "absent presence") that we see so starkly exemplified in the story of Me'ali is transmuted (or transmutable) by these relationships to an object of praise. On the other hand, the same behaviors stand as a double threat. Where relations to the monarch are ever foremost in the mind, the courtier is warned that the monarch can always turn cruel, and the monarch is warned that the language of cruelty turned to praise can always be reversed and employed in the service of satire. This is the threat that Me'ali's story dramatizes: to place a rascal boy in a position of (erotic/sexual) power by succumbing to love means falling under the control of a person of questionable morals—for who but a rascal would stoop to becoming a love-addicted jurist's catamite? Like the monarch, whose whims and motives are neither ruled by ordinary concerns nor subject to ordinary restraints, the discourse of cruelty and oppression that flatters the beloved by exalting his or her power over the submissive beloved can be dangerously actualized in the case of a beloved who ignores the conventions of polite romance. When the power ceded by the lover is wielded in the service of cruelty and humiliation by an unscrupulous beloved, the lover is in terrible danger. And this goes for the monarch as well—perhaps even more so. At the highest levels, the monarch rules by ceding portions of his (or her) power to various beloveds, who carry out the actual business of the state. In every case, treason and treachery are possible. In every case, the ruler must depend to some extent on relations of loyalty and obedience, which the court imagines in the language and rhetoric of the discourse of love.

If we accept the contention that the court and the widespread networks of patronage that radiate out from the court are primary factors in the shaping of scripts for imagining and enacting love among the court-dependent

---

[a] The term for rebel here (*serkeş*) literally means "tossing the head" and refers to a horse that rebels by pulling against its bit. The beloved is compared to the cypress, which sways from the top in the wind like a horse tossing its head.

elites of the late Renaissance, then certain things follow that are perhaps more clearly visible looking westward from Istanbul.[17] The first among these depends on the unremarkable observation that the Renaissance court is a patriarchal, all-male institution. From this it follows that the object of the courtier's desire is always another, more powerful man and, furthermore, that, when political patriarchy is eroticized (and the erotic politicized), the *normative* situation is homoerotic (and violent, insofar as a beloved patron really can destroy the lover by neglect, cruelty, or outright execution).

A Tale of Two Slaves:
Love and Power in the Ottoman Court

One of the dangers in our taking a broad view of the Age of Beloveds is that we are drawn to focus on commonly overlooked similarities and to elide significant differences. In this regard, we should point out that the situation in the Ottoman court diverges from that in (other) European courts in one very striking way, a way that makes the issue of reversal especially relevant. In European courts, courtiers and high officials overwhelmingly came from the ranks of the hereditary nobility. Both the qualities that define the courtier and the right to share in the monarch's power are seen as natural, as inhering fundamentally "in the blood." In contrast, in the Ottoman court, the only "blood" that counted was that of the line of Osman.[18] Power in the palace and, increasingly, in the empire at large was controlled by the *kul* or elite slaves either bought or given as gifts, or taken as the sultan's one-fifth share of captives in war (*pencik*), or, for the most part, recruited in their early teens from the non-Muslim population of the empire. Among these, some were selected for their talents (and physiognomy, as we saw in the excerpt from ʿAli in chapter 5 above) to become part of the palace family and trained for high office in the palace school. In our period, the Ottoman court as an institution was inimical to hereditary claims. The custom by which each sultan ordered the execution of his male siblings on taking the throne meant that there ought to exist no hereditary claims to the monarchy outside the immediate descendants of the reigning monarch. To be sure, there were families of noble (but not royal) descent among the intellectual classes (the "people of the pen," *ehl-i kalem*) whose members staffed the powerful judicial and education systems and from among whom many of the social companions of the ruler were chosen. There were also great families with military retinues and hereditary claims to lands and loyalties outside the capital, but these were commonly treated with suspicion or co-opted by the court and were always subject to domination by highly placed kuls.[19]

As a result, the Ottoman system embodied a fundamental reversal in which power and prestige emanating from the center (the court) was more and more often vested in men recruited as boys from the lowest and most peripheral classes—non-Muslim villagers, prisoners of war, and purchased slaves. Moreover, even within the inner sanctuary (the harem) of the palace itself, it was increasingly the case that the powerful women—the favorites and the mothers of princes and sultans, who controlled significant fortunes—were also slaves. Then we should take into account the fact that, among the elites, including the elite slaves (the kuls), the intellectual elites, the military elites, and the economic elites (wealthy merchants, tradesmen, fiefholders, and manufacturers), it was customary for slaves to serve as domestic servants, laborers, and concubines. Thus, at the higher levels of society, everybody (even the kuls) owned slaves, men made love to slaves, and everybody was in some degree dominated by slaves. To what extent this Ottoman "slavery" was similar in structural ways to English forms of indenture and requirements of service institutionalized in the vagabond laws we cannot say with any certainty. But it does seem clear that the discourse of slavery in Ottoman society and culture during the Age of Beloveds has a peculiar character scripted dramatically in Ottoman poetry.

The Age of Beloveds in the Ottoman Empire is dominated by the almost half-century reign of Sultan Süleyman I—the Magnificent to Europeans, the Lawgiver (Kanuni) to Ottomans—and that reign is dominated by the shadowy subtext of the sultan's love for two slaves: Ibrahim and Hurrem. We turn first to Ibrahim.

For the first sixteen years of his reign, Süleyman's relationship with the kul Ibrahim takes center stage.[20] Ibrahim, who would come to be known as Ibrahim Pasha, the Favorite and the Slain (Makbul u Maktul), was born near Parga on the Greek coast in 1493 or 1494 and was in some manner taken as a slave into palace service. During the period of his education and training, he became the personal servant, friend, and companion of the then Prince Süleyman. Ibrahim was brilliant, ambitious, and said to be handsome and an excellent violinist. Certainly, Süleyman was devoted to him, and, when he succeeded to the throne, Ibrahim accompanied him in his rise to power. He was first appointed as the chief chamberlain, and, in the second year of Süleyman's reign, a great palace, which still stands, was built for him on the Hippodrome Square. In 1523, Süleyman ordered that Ibrahim, at the young (for a highly placed kul) age of thirty, be given the position of grand vizier (*sadr-ı aʿzam*), the highest secular official in the empire, disappointing several worthy, experienced, and long-serving candidates. The next thirteen years saw the former slave page elevated to a degree of power unprecedented in Ottoman annals. In 1524, Ibrahim was married to Süleyman's sister. He was

Süleyman's commander and surrogate on campaigns in Europe and Persia. Everywhere, he spoke with Süleyman's voice and exercised the sultan's powers.

At the height of his power, Ibrahim was the central beloved of the empire, in some respects overshadowing the sultan. He controlled vast wealth and spent liberally. He was a generous patron of poetry, scholarship, and the arts. To be in his circle of sociability was to achieve the pinnacle of success and to open doors to the attention of the sultan. Latifi praises him (posthumously) without restraint: "He was an Asaf,[b] renown adornment of the warrior's ranks and chief minister with the dignity of Djem[c] and the attributes of Husrev.[d] In the days of the Ottoman shahs, no vizier of superior patronage, no distinguished lord or noble grantor of desires, has ever come to the pillar of viziership and the seat of grand viziership who was his equal or equivalent. He was noble of spirit, the soul of bounty, and a natural Hatem[e] in whom there were traces of the most generous of ancient kings."[21]

Yet, like the typal beloved, Ibrahim could turn harsh and cruel to his poet lovers. There are many stories. For example, our old friend Deli Birader Gazali (the legal scholar and pornographer) wheedled a munificent retirement bonus out of the viziers and dignitaries at court and built himself a charitable complex in Beşiktaş with a mosque, a dervish lodge, and a magnificent bathhouse that was his pride and joy. Staffed by the most beautiful and compliant of bath boys, and presided over by the handsome son of the Sufi who was master of the dervish lodge, the bathhouse, with its unusual large round pool, became a center of social life for lovers from all Istanbul and its environs. But the other bathhouse owners rankled at Gazali's success, which threatened them with a devastating loss of income. So they went in a body to complain to Ibrahim Pasha. Now, the pasha had reason to be unsympathetic toward Gazali. At one time, Ibrahim had a boyfriend named Çeşti Bali to whom he was quite devoted, and Gazali had poked fun at this relationship in a teasing couplet with some serious implications:

Ne mahkum arada belli ne hakim
Düğündür ki çalan kim oynayan kim

It's not that clear who is ruled and who rules these days
It's a wedding feast, so who is dancing and who plays[22]

---

[b] Asaf was the legendary grand vizier of Solomon.

[c] Cem was the legendary founder of the line of Iranian kings.

[d] Husrev, or Chosroes, was another famed Iranian king. The word *husrev* is also used to mean "the sun," as in the monarch of the heavens.

[e] Hatem of the Arab tribe Tayy was legendary for his hospitality and generosity.

The suggestion that the mighty pasha is under the spell and control of a beloved boy is one thing, but the embedded reference—intended or not—to widespread murmurings about Ibrahim's influence over Süleyman and his assumption of the sultan's authority was more perilous than funny. So Ibrahim took the side of the bathhouse owners and sent a troop of *'acemi oğlans* (slave pages in training) to tear Gazali's bathhouse down, breaking the poor poet's heart.[23]

Gazali got off easier than some. When Ibrahim returned from a spectacularly victorious campaign in Hungary (1526), he brought back with him as booty statues of Apollo, Hercules, and Diana, which he set up in front of his palace. As time passed, the populace's grumbling about Ibrahim's ascendancy and supposed sympathy for his non-Muslim roots grew, and a couplet went about the city from tongue to tongue, attributed to the youthful Figani, who had already achieved considerable fame as a poet. The couplet contained a play on the name Ibrahim (Abraham) and on the story, popular among literary Muslims, about the young and ferociously monotheist prophet Abraham destroying the idols in a pagan temple:

> Into this world two Abrahams appeared
> One idols broke, the other idols reared[24]

The implication that Ibrahim had polytheist (pagan) leanings was apparently too much for the beleaguered grand vizier to bear, and Figani, who may not, in fact, have authored the couplet, was taken to the docks and hung.

Zati had several run-ins with Ibrahim and was twice rebuffed. The first snub was occasioned by a lampoon written by Zati's friend Kandi (the Candyman) and directed at the poet Hayali, who was a favorite of both the pasha and the sultan. Kandi, as was his practice wherever he lived, had opened a candy shop in the bazaar, where he displayed all manner of beautiful sugar confections. Enraged by the lampoon, Hayali had downed a bottle of wine and, loading his skirts with rocks, proceeded to unleash a barrage of stones on poor Kandi's shop. The shopkeeper-poet barely escaped with his life, and the shop was ruined. As a result, Zati, with a delegation of poets from Kandi's circle, went to Ibrahim demanding that Hayali be punished. The pasha only laughed and fobbed Kandi off with a small cash gift, while Hayali emerged unscathed.

Zati was again snubbed when he and some friends went to beg for the pardoning of their companion Keşfi's brother Hasbi, who had been caught diverting public funds to his own pocket. The pasha's justice could be neither stayed nor diverted. Hasbi ended up being tortured (briefly) and thrown in prison, at which time his pen name was changed from Hasbi (more or less "The Distinguished" and/or "He Who Complains") to Habsi (He of the Prison).

A crowded Ottoman bath with a round pool similar to Gazali's. (Topkapı Palace Museum Library, B. 408, "I. Ahmed albümü," fol. 79a.)

What makes these accounts of Ibrahim's nobility, generosity, harshness, and arbitrary exercise of power especially poignant is that they are told from the perspective of a second stunning reversal. The Christian slave who comes to rule an empire and, in some minds, to dominate a vastly powerful monarch caught in the toils of love is the first reversal. The rest of Ibrahim's tale constitutes the second.

Customarily, when a slave page "graduated" from the inner service of the palace and took a position in the world at large, he never came back to the sanctuary of the inner courts—except for Ibrahim. He had his own room in the harem, to which he would occasionally return to spend nights and continue his intimate companionship with the now sultan. The pasha was at the height of his power and prestige when, one night in mid-March 1536, without a whisper of warning, the deaf-mutes came to his room in the palace and strangled him. It was so sudden and so complete a reversal.

The Ottoman poets (and non-Ottoman poets) often seem obsessed with the imagery of heaven's turning wheel, the astrological mill wheel that inexorably raises men up and grinds them down. The conviction that reversal is built into the very structure of the universe is rooted in the conditions of court-dependent elites. Everyone is subject to unexpected reversals of for-

Seduction and Reversal 241

tune—courtiers, ministers, wives, children, queens, and kings. Every commitment of love and loyalty may bind one to a falling star or a treacherous beloved. All were aware of astronomy's realities and were sincere believers in religions that plotted a linear path through the relatively trivial ups and downs of a brief life from birth to death and on to an eternity of paradise or perdition. Yet, compared to the day-to-day, year-to-year confirmation, in the form of harsh experience, that people's fortunes turn as the stars turn over their heads, astronomy and religion are distant and abstract. This is what made astrology such a powerful metaphor—and more than a metaphor. Simon Forman was able to wade knee-deep in the intrigues of the Elizabethan and Jacobean courts in part because he offered up the promise of knowledge and control through readings of the heavens and magical manipulation of events on earth. The head astrologer (*müneccim başı*) was a high official in the Ottoman palace, and no enterprise was undertaken but at the most astrologically propitious moment. As we have mentioned, Süleyman himself was often referred to as the *sahib-kıran*, "the possessor of a fortunate conjunction [of heavenly bodies]," the Universal Monarch who would lead the Islamic world into its second millennium.[25]

In what we might call *the love chronicle* of tales about Süleyman's reign, one of the reasons given for the abrupt fall of Ibrahim the Favorite was the rising star of another favorite slave, the sultan's beloved concubine and eventual wife Hurrem Sultan, known as Roxelana to the Europeans. The story of the harem and a sultan's private life and loves is always hazy at best—a few indisputable facts and dates inextricably tangled in a mass of gossip, speculation, and outright fabrication. For this reason, we find it most useful to talk about the story of Süleyman and his beloved slaves as if it were a piece of historical fiction, more significant for what it tells us about the motivations and thoughts of its authors and audiences than for anything it can tell us about the reality of life in Süleyman's harem.[26]

Hurrem was not Süleyman's first female consort. While he was serving as governor in Manisa, he fathered two sons by a woman named Gülfem (Rose Mouth) and one by a woman named Gülbahar (Rose Spring). When Gülfem's sons died soon after Süleyman ascended to the throne, Gülbahar, as the mother of the eldest son, Mustafa, became Hasseki (the Special/Elite) and a power in the harem second only to the sultan's mother, the Valide Sultan (i.e., the royal mother), Hafsa. Hurrem was a slave—"sold meat" Gülbahar would call her in a moment of fury—said to be from Poland, a slight woman of no outstanding beauty but obviously possessed of tremendous charm and determination.[27] She enchanted Süleyman from the early days of his enthronement in Istanbul—quite literally bewitched him, if some angry detractors are to be believed. She bore the sultan a son in 1521 and at the same time began to eclipse the power of her rival, Gülbahar. By 1530, she would bear the sultan a daughter and three more sons, including Selim, who would eventually become the second Selim to sit on the Ottoman throne. Süleyman's passionate attachment to Hurrem shines in his poetry, especially in the following well-known verse letter written under the sultan's pen name, Muhibbi (the Affectionate/Lover):

> My solitude, my everything, my beloved,
> > my gleaming moon
> My companion, intimate, my all, lord of beauties,
> > my sultan
>
> My life's essence and span, my sip from the river of Paradise,
> > my Eden
> My springtime, my bright joy, my secret, my idol,
> > my laughing rose
>
> My happiness, my pleasure, lantern in my gathering,
> > my luminous star, my candle
> My oranges bitter and sweet, my pomegranate,
> > the taper by my bed
>
> My green plant, my sugar, my treasure in this world,
> > my freedom from woe
> My Potiphar, my Joseph, my existence,
> > my Pharaoh in the Egypt of the heart
>
> My Istanbul, my Karaman, my lands of the Byzantines
> My Bedakhshan,[f] my Kipchak Steppes, my Baghdad,
> > my Khorasan
>
> Mine, you with hair like vav [و], brows like ya [ى],
> > my languid and seditious eye[g]
> If I die my blood is on your head, so come to my aid,
> > my non-Muslim[h]
>
> As if I were a panegyrist at your door, I sing your praises,
> > I wish you well
> My heart filled with grief, my eyes with tears, I am your lover,[i]
> > you bring me joy[28]

---

[f] Bedakhshan was noted for its mines of precious jewels, especially rubies.
[g] The letters *vav* and *ya* together can spell *vey*, a shortened poetic form of *vay*, "alas."
[h] This is a play on the usual cry for help, "Muslims, come to my aid!"
[i] He actually says, "I am your Muhibbi [his pen name]," which means "I am your lover."

The story of Hurrem's ascendancy parallels that of Ibrahim's. And the two stories together constitute what is nearly a parable of the "life-stages-of-love" progression that we have seen from one end of Europe to the other. A young man, hot-blooded and somewhat wild, is first devoted to the love of other young (or younger) men; then, as he ages, he turns to women and the life of family and children. In the phallocentric context of early-modern times, this progression is imagined as a movement from a very virile, manly period, in which the erotic focus is on the masculine, toward a more effeminate period, in which the erotic focus is on the feminine and a man turns to a more contemplative, sedate, and inactive life. We have, in chapter 5 above, already seen clear traces of this perceived progression of life stages in the sociology of Florentine life, in Gazali's pornographic battle of the boy chasers and the womanizers, in Castiglione's *Book of the Courtier*, and in Marlowe's *Elegies*. A subtext of the "stages" story is the life of a man in physical decline succumbing to the superior sexual prowess of women and falling under their domination. This is precisely what we see in the story of Hurrem: a metaphor for struggles to determine who will control the Ottoman state. Who will be the lover and who the beloved? Will power be ceded to a beloved woman or a beloved man? Will the core of the state be feminine or masculine?

From the moment that she became the mother of a prince, Hurrem marched inexorably toward domination of the harem and the center of power. In 1530, the heir apparent, Mustafa, and his mother, Gülbahar, were sent to Manisa, where he assumed the governorship of the province. In 1536, Ibrahim, who supported Mustafa and Gülbahar, was executed under mysterious circumstances. The stage was set for the next major move. Up to the reign of Süleyman, the harem of the Topkapı Palace had been a male sanctuary, the residence of the sultan, his sons, his slave pages, and his personal servants. The harem of women was in the Old Palace, which Mehmet the Conqueror had built on the site of the fourth-century Forum Tauri of Theodosius I near the center of the city. But, in January 1541, a great fire raged through parts of the Old Palace, and Hurrem, with her retinue, decamped to take up residence in the Topkapı Palace.

What was probably seen at the time as a temporary expediency had far-reaching consequences for the story of the Ottoman state. Once in the new palace, the most powerful women never left it, and, there, if the tales are to be believed, they schemed and dominated sultans and viziers for the next hundred years. Whatever the truth of the matter, the notion of a "sultanate of women" that began with Hurrem was, at least, a topic of general gossip that would mature and grow into a "historical fact" by modern times.[29]

It seems remarkable to us how closely this story of the growth and development of the Ottoman state also follows the sociobiological life-stages-of-love pattern. The state itself is imagined as having a youthful period (up to 1536 or 1541), when its center is exclusively masculine, literally phallocentric, and consequently homoerotic, insofar as both the lovers (courtiers) and the objects of desire (the sultan and his surrogates) were exclusively male. In this period, the state is also seen as virile, war-like, strong, brave, successful, and growing. The empire is widely assumed to be the launch point from which the Universal Monarch would establish his dominion over the whole globe and usher in the last days and the appearance of the Messiah/Mahdi. The story of the second period is marked by an intrusion of the feminine into the center. In the courtier's imagination, the execution of Ibrahim was connected to Hurrem's intrigues in favor of her own sons against the heir apparent, Mustafa, and was characterized as a battle for the affections of the sultan. In the end, the female favorite overthrew the male favorite and, subsequently, established herself in the formerly male center. The erotic focus shifted, and the marriage of Süleyman to Hurrem came to symbolize an increasing heterosexuality—which early-modern males tended to read as contamination by female domination and effeminization—of life at court. As we can see in Latifi's encomium to Ibrahim Pasha, there is a clear argument that, with his death, support for the circle of poets and their youthful, unconventional, carefree, masculine, and homoerotic sociability was ended or greatly diminished.

Latifi references the whole story of Ibrahim's assumption of royal power and the consequences of his fall in a few paragraphs of adorned prose:

> To [his] position of vizier was added and appended the office of commander of commanders, and his power and exaltation were [thus] multiplied and redoubled. In affairs of the commonweal, kingly power revolved about him, and to the aforementioned [Ibrahim belonged] sultanic rule, and, because, in the conferral of offices and assignment of ranks, matters of appointment and dismissal and particulars of granting and taking away were pendant on and bound to his beneficence-filled person, people in need and those with anxieties found their wishes and needs [fulfilled] at his desire-granting threshold; and to all people and everyone, either noble or common, he performed kingly acts of patronage, and took monarchical pains to give aid, and granted to every disappointed one his wish and heart's desire. In the days of his good fortune, the hours of the people of this world were gladdened and propitious; and the times of earth dwellers were praised and praiseworthy. His lofty patronage reaching to the sky was higher than the Cepheid stars, and in expending his beneficence and generosity he was superior to Hatem of Tayy. He was liberal and favor granting to such a degree

that, to a beggar who proffered a fresh leaf,[j] he would give a handful of gold, and the time was [briefly] when he would grant [gifts of] rubies and pearls like the most generous kings of old.

COUPLET:

However much this base world has abandoned talent
Do not suppose getting one's hands on wealth to be perfection

He was [a man] of exalted favor and patronage like the bird of fortune; the felicity of his concern and the seemliness of his care raised up ever so many poor and miserable people from the shoe rank[k] and raised so many possessors of precedence and joy from the humility of abasement and made them lofty in power; also, ever so many fallen orphans did the sun's rays of his care send from earth to the heavens like pearl drops of morning dew. Insofar as he was inclined toward a complete preference for people of talent and patronized people of perfection to the utmost degree, he did justice to the pillar of viziership and the seat of grand viziership.

[POEM] BY THE AUTHOR:

The wheel of heaven has a thousand eyes
    that gaze from place to place
But never has it seen someone like him
    whose favor is like the bird of fortune

PROSE:

In his happy day, the poets had [a share of] power and patronage, and, in his blessed age, the people of excellence and talent were tended and desired. From the origins of the Ottoman sultanate down to the time of the aforementioned, the poets of Rum[l] received an annual stipend from the Ottoman royal treasury and were granted their share of royal awards, [in return for which] some of them wrote [poems of] praise [to the sultans] and others versified their victories. After the late and divinely forgiven [pasha] left the grand viziership, the honors and awards of the above-mentioned

---

[j] *berg-i ter*, or "fresh leaf," has the idiomatic sense of "the beggar's mite" but, here, also has a secondary relation to Arabic *varak*, or "leaf," meaning a "page," which gives the sense of a poor poet or writer proffering a newly completed page to the patron.

[k] The "shoe rank" is the place outside the threshold where people left their outdoor shoes on entering someone's house. To be left there is similar to being left out in the cold.

[l] *Rum* (Roman territory) here refers to the central Ottoman lands.

group were completely cut off, the power and popularity of the masters of verse and prose were annulled, and the society of their company was broken.

The sympathies of poets certainly lay with Ibrahim, in opposition to the supporters of Hurrem, especially Rüstem Pasha, who succeeded Ibrahim. Latifi refers to these successors with a comparison: "Neither was he [Ibrahim] mean-spirited and of evil gaze,[m] like those who followed him, nor was he [like them] addicted to gold and silver."[30]

The story of Hurrem not only subsumes a gender conflict—whose love will control the aging sultan—but also touches on a generic generational conflict between the older and the younger man. As we have pointed out, the typical lover and beloved are culturally scripted as hot-blooded, virile young men. The young man appears, in early-modern times, to concatenate the strength, virtues, cleverness, and physical features that constitute complete beauty and erotic attractiveness. The death of a young man at the hands of the old is seen as a fundamental reversal of natural progression as well as an offense against beauty and love. And it is precisely this kind of a death that Hurrem's machinations engineered next.

Süleyman's eldest son, Mustafa, was tremendously popular among the army, the literati, and the masses. He seems to have possessed in great measure the "beautiful warrior/knight" characteristics so prized by the age. But the politics of reproduction in the harem of women was such that the success of Mustafa meant certain death for Hurrem's sons, according to the rule of succession established by Mehmet the Conqueror, and exile to a life of powerlessness and obscurity in the Old Palace for Hurrem herself. However, should one of her sons succeed Süleyman, Hurrem would become the Valide Sultan, the most powerful woman in the empire. So, as the story goes, Hurrem plotted and schemed diligently and long. Finally, in the fall of 1553, Prince Mustafa was executed in Eregli in the presence of his father, accused of plotting a rebellion aimed at supplanting his father, who was said to be too old and feeble to lead.[31] Other deaths would follow as Hurrem pursued her aims, but it was the death of Mustafa, the beloved prince, and the cruel reversal of his fortunes that occasioned the greatest outcry. The army was outraged, and Hurrem's supporter, Rüstem Pasha, was dismissed from the grand vizierate as a sop to their anger. The poets also expressed their displeasure in an amazing series of elegies (*mersiye*) that excoriated the sultan in the harshest

---

[m] There is a play here on the word *nazar*, which means both "gaze" and "the favor of the great (in the sense of 'looking out for someone')." So the same phrase can mean both "evil eye" and "evil or malicious favors."

terms. It seems that, in the face of widespread rage, even the most powerful of despots was helpless when it came to controlling a literary outpouring of grief.

Many examples of mersiyes on Prince Mustafa by the most famous poets have been preserved.[32] However, for our purposes, one of the more interesting examples is from a distant periphery far from fame. Its author is one Nisayi, a woman of the harem—already an oddity since so little poetry by women is preserved at all—who, at the time of writing, must have been elderly (she apparently knew Süleyman as a boy) and in the retinue of Mustafa's mother, Gülbahar. We know nothing more about her. She had no public life, and her name appears in none of the biographies or mentions of poets. But what she says seems certainly to contradict our usual image of the subservient, dominated harem woman:

> You were tyrannical, treated that young man with exceeding injustice
> You bound the garrote about his neck and punished him [by taking] his life
> Knowing that compassion is part of the faith, you did not fear God
> What has the merciless Monarch of the World done to Sultan Mustafa?
>
> You allowed the words of a Russian witch into your ears
> Deluded by tricks and deceit, you did the bidding of that spiteful hag
> You slaughtered that swaying cypress, fruit of life's orchard
> What has the compassionless Monarch of the World done to Sultan Mustafa?
>
> You are Lord of the World, yet the people [now] hold you in contempt
> No one is inclined to have sympathy toward you anymore
> And may God's mercy never reach the mufti[n] who approved this
> What has the merciless Monarch of the World done to Sultan Mustafa?
>
> When you were young, you acted with equity and justice
> In every circumstance you gladdened the hearts of one and all
> So why, in your maturity, do you now act with tyranny and injustice?
> What has the compassionless Monarch of the World done to Sultan Mustafa?
>
> How did you come to see spilling innocent blood as a good thing?
> Did you think that a monarch will never be called to account?
> With what pretext will you give answer to the Lord God?
> What has the merciless Monarch of the World done to Sultan Mustafa?
>
> Don't you know that this transitory [world] does not last for anyone?
> By killing your own young son are you [now] going to escape death?

[n] The mufti is a high-level legal scholar who issues opinions on canon law. In the case of the execution of a prince, the opinion would likely be issued by the highest legal authority in the land, the şeyhü'l-islam.

Seduction and Reversal

You possess this world, [yet] in the end won't you [too] be transitory?
What has the compassionless Monarch of the World done to Sultan Mustafa?

Let him come under the protection of a great lord, the Prophet of God
May he be accepted at [the divine] court in the presence of God's Prophet
Don't you fear that the straight road for you may be the road to perdition?
What has the merciless Monarch of the World done to Sultan Mustafa?

His throne and lineage were destroyed by suspicion and surmise
What did that pearl drop do, oppressed and innocent as he was
His mother burns like Jacob [with grief] at separation [from him]
What has the compassionless Monarch of the World done to Sultan Mustafa?

That lady writhed in [an agony of] separation with the patience of Job
In the dwelling of this transitory earth, she suffered the torments of hell
Let him see the dread demons of the pit who torture and torment her
What has the merciless Monarch of the World done to Sultan Mustafa?

This woeful Nisayi cried out and wept blood
The soul in her body wept from the pain of [her] longing
Angels in the seven-layer heavens wept and humans wept on earth
What has the compassionless Monarch of the World done to Sultan Mustafa?[33]

It is difficult to account for the fact that, in a climate where a Figani can be executed for an ambiguous couplet, one of the least powerful of the sultan's subjects is able, in this instance, to describe him as a hell-bound, merciless tyrant, his beloved wife as a Russian witch, and her supporters as demons of the pit—and get away with it. It would appear that, although it is in some wise acceptable for the lover to die for his or her love, the murder of a beloved is another story. It is the unimaginable tragedy—and, in the case of a sultan's son, a tragedy that also bereaves the killer. This bereavement is a possible key to understanding the Ottoman mersiye. A cleavage occurs by which the sultan as bereft father is split off from the sultan as murderer of his son. By permitting the angry mersiye and, thereby, participating in the general rage and grief, the father-sultan distinguishes himself from the murderer-sultan and, thereby, redirects and dissipates the dangerous negative feelings of the populace. If, as in this case, the redirection is toward an ultimately expendable slave (a Rüstem Pasha) or concubine, so much the better.

Hurrem does not live to see her final triumph, the accession to the throne of her son Selim. The end of her story takes us back on a winding road to some of the themes of reversal with which we began in the story of Me'ali and the rascal boy. The language of Nisayi's mersiye demonstrates Astrophel's point that the poetic language of love is easily reversible; the tyrant of love can quickly become a tyrant despised; the lover/poet's praises can smoothly slip into blame; the most subservient of courtiers can of a sudden grow teeth and bite; even the ruler must quake in the face of an angry mob supported by the army and incited by verse. The (hi)story of two slaves (Ibrahim and Hurrem) shows how a foreign slave can come to control an empire, how the female beloved can take the place of the male beloved, how even the most powerful man can come to be dominated by love. The world of the court and courtiers—of female courtiers (beloveds, concubines, wives, queens, courtesans, and ladies-in-waiting) as well as male—is a dangerous one, scripted by the poetry of a dangerous love with many dimensions. The courtier and the courtesan are *addicts* of love. They quite literally cannot *imagine* their lives outside the metaphors and actualities of love. For them, love is primary, passionate, and precarious. In the next chapter, we will further examine the precariousness and danger of love in the violent social context of early-modern times.

8

TO DIE FOR . . .
Love and Violence in the Age of Beloveds

There is a famous story from sixteenth-century Istanbul about a poet named Ferdi who was fabulously handsome and one of the noted beloveds of the age. The story is told in some detail by 'Aşık and is related in a slightly different version in the first half of the seventeenth century in a narrative poem of advice and tales by the poet and biographer Nev'izade 'Atayi, the author of the *Seven Stories*, from which we took the story of Tayyib and Tahir related in chapter 3 above. 'Aşık's version tells the tale in the voice of Ferdi himself in an "as told to the author" style. The bulk of our telling will freely translate this version, but 'Atayi begins by describing Ferdi's situation, and we will begin with his paragraph:

> When Ferdi was a young man, he was widely known in Istanbul as a handsome and attractive beloved. But he was, at the same time, unruly, quick-tempered, and given to rages. At one point he was pursued by a man who seems to have taken the hyperboles of poetry seriously. As Ferdi told it:
>
> Once there was a fellow who was enamored of me. Although it was plain to see that he was "a city boy" and not one of the elites, he was rather elegant and had some education. However, he was idle—a layabout, like the dregs in a cup of wine—and somewhat bored with living. He could not content himself with merely observing me from afar as one observes the moon in the sky. When there was a gathering with candles and wine and I was absent, he could not take his ease. During the day, he would follow me about like my own shadow. At night, from dusk to dawn, he would plant himself in my path. Even when I was at home, I could not rid myself of him. If I drove him from my door, he would drop in through the chimney like a moonbeam. If I were invited someplace, he would hear of it and go there on his own, unbidden. If I went on an outing, he would arrive before

me, and I would discover that, no matter where I looked, there he would be, standing and waiting.

One day I could finally endure no more. I went into a rage and beat him severely, splitting his head and blinding him in one eye. But this too did little to dissuade him. He would merely say, "I have no need to look on this transitory world with two eyes. Moreover, if you will be so kind as to knock out my other eye, then I will be able to see you always in my imagination. If you won't let me stare at you, let me see you just one last time among the other beloveds and then make an end of it."

Still, whenever I looked, there he was, across the way, gazing at me with his one lovesick eye. It seemed as if he courted blindness purposely. Although he could hardly see, every time I went somewhere for pleasant conversation, there he was, doing as he pleased. Then he began to make violent oaths, vehemently swearing, "Whatever the case, either you will kill me, or I will kill you." It got to such a point that I would wake in the night thinking I was alone in my room and there he would be, standing by my head with a sharp dagger at his side. I couldn't tell how he had gotten in. It seemed as if he had just slipped in through the window like a ray of moonlight.

Then one day I woke from my slumbers at dawn and saw him there, sitting on my pillow with a sharp sword in his hand as if he had been sent to kill me. For a moment, I thought that Mars had fallen through the roof! However, I soon came to the realization that, things being the way they were, he was right. If I didn't kill him, he would, in the end, kill me. So I became resigned to the notion that, just as I had removed a source of his vision by taking his eye, I would have to remove the entire source of his existence in this world by taking his life.

We had a talk and agreed that we would go together to Shaykh Sinan Village, a popular spot for outings, on the outskirts of Istanbul. The fellow was overjoyed. He performed the major ablutions and dressed himself in plain white burial clothes. Then, as a dying man will, he forgave any and all debts, material and spiritual, owed him by his friends and made his farewells to everyone. Then, crying, "Now for our holiday!" he danced with joy and merriment.

[There follows here a very long description of autumn, nearly as long as the story itself, which can be summarized as follows: It was autumn, and the park at Shaykh Sinan was resplendent in fall colors. Winter had not yet touched the grass, and all was green earth, gold and red foliage, and blue sky softened by a cool haze. The trees had just begun their divestiture in anticipation of winter's reminder that the beauties of this world are only for a season and quick to pass.]

Amid this glory we walked over hill and dale until we came to the wide and pleasant meadow known as the Dervish Lodge Springs. This clearing was surrounded by great trees whose roots reached down to the fish on which the earth rests and whose trunks reached to the twin stars that we call the Fishes. Their branches and leaves were all entwined like Sufis dancing hand in hand or wrestlers grappling for a hold. At the place of honor in this gathering of loveliness was a fountain to gladden the heart of any who saw it. It would grace all according to their merits and bestow gifts on all according to their spirits. It would wash away the cares of the world, the troubles of life, the heat and the chill of living.

The rest is short and uncomplicated. Near the foot of this fountain was a deep streambed, and to that place the two of us repaired. Out of the breast of his cloak, he drew an amulet, which hung about his neck, and, from his collar, he unsheathed a deadly dagger. He spoke to me, saying, "If you do not kill me now, I will kill you without hesitation." And I saw that I had no choice. The religion and its law allow one to kill a murderer in self-defense and to repel one's attacker by force.

So I bound his hands. He knelt, and I looked into his face and wept. "Come," he cried, "no matter how you take it, killing me is a needful thing. It is an undisputed fact that sooner or later one of us will kill the other." And he pointed to that knife sharper than the legendary dagger that they call Bringer of Sudden Death. Helpless, I took it up and, without dwelling further on the matter, slit his throat. He surrendered his soul to the eternal realm while gazing into my face. Thus did he become a victim of the bitter blade of love and achieve his ultimate desire.

I wept for a time, sighed some, and finally dragged his earthly remains off by the clothes and stuffed them into a deep fissure in the ground. I then turned my face in the direction of town and went on my way. As I retraced our steps, I recited the opening sura of the Qur'an many times for the peace and salvation of his soul.[1]

'Atayi's version goes on to say that Ferdi was so distraught that he died not long after and that the two were buried side by side in the meadow by the fountain. These tombs, it is said, became in time a place of pilgrimage for true lovers. 'Aşık tells no such story and seems to indicate that Ferdi, now known as Ferdi the Lover-Killer, went on living and became a poet worth writing about.

Deadly Beloveds, Violent Love

The story of Ferdi is by no means unique. It is of a type more often told from a perspective more sympathetic to the murdered lover. For example, Latifi's entry for the poet called Helaki (the Destroyed) relates the following account of the poet's death:

He was from Rumeli and the province of Dobruca, a dervish by nature and of the sect of illuminati [ışık]. He was a lover at heart, a worshiper of beloveds, and preoccupied with affection. Alive or dead, he would [still] find a beloved. He could get along without bread and meat before he could manage without a loved one, and he used to fall for [any] tall, tender-bearded beloved and cypress-bodied darling. He was destroyed by any such lover-killing, hasty beloved, and his breast was rent by any dagger-drawing glance, in accordance with which he took the pen name Helaki.

In the end, he was affected by the influence of this pen name, and, one day, at a wine gathering, a coquet whose wont was cruelty, in rage and anger, without hesitation drew the dagger of oppression and the sword of cruelty and destroyed that sincere lover Helaki, shredding his breast like a [wild] tulip flower with a thousand cuts.[2]

Some of the beloved boys were tough teenagers, armed street ruffians, and even young janissaries. Importuning them for love, and implying that they should be available as passive sex partners was dangerous business. It was clearly dangerous even to cross some of them.[3]

In the divan of a well-known poet from Bursa called Cinani, there is a chronogram (a poem in which the numerical values of some of the letters add up to a date, usually the date of someone's death or a momentous event) about another beloved, one 'Ali Bali, who killed his lover, Mütevellizade. The little poem and its introduction translate as follows:

> The chronogram for [the date on which] a young man who went by the nickname "Liver Stitcher [Piercer]" killed his lover.
>
> Mütevellizade, while his wailing lover,
> Without cause, sore reprimanded 'Ali Bali
>
> When he ['Ali] killed him with the liver-stitching sword
> They spoke his chronogram, "Killed by the sword of 'Ali"[4]

The letters in the phrase *killed by the sword of 'Ali* (*küşte-i seyf-i 'Ali*) add up to the date A.H. 986 (1578/79 C.E.).

As we have mentioned before and will bring up again in a later chapter, the Age of Beloveds was an age of young men, many of whom lacked steady employment and the opportunity to marry and establish a stable family. Moreover, throughout Europe, men of the upper classes often went about armed with daggers and swords and occasionally with firearms, especially when traveling outside the safer confines of major cities. Wars were frequent, and young men were commonly recruited as temporary soldiers and released to their own devices when the need for cannon fodder waned. The Englishman Simon Forman records in his diary: "This year [1599] was the great muster in August at St. James's. I bought much harness and weapons for war, swords, daggers, muskets, corslet and furniture, staves, halberds, gauntlets, mails, etc."[5]

In England, the mustering and dismissing of soldiery—there was no standing army—left a residue of armed young men, accustomed to combat, often with more time on their hands than money or employment. This was true even in the Ottoman Empire, although the Ottomans did maintain and support a large standing army—which drew professional soldiers from as far away as England[6]—and were assiduous in attempting to enforce public tranquillity in major cities. However, the situation seems to have been quite the reverse of today's, in which violence seems to increase in direct proportion to economic deprivation. As Beier mentions in an aside to a discussion of the violence perpetrated by English vagabonds during the late sixteenth century and the early seventeenth: "It would be misleading, however, considering the limitation of the evidence, to underplay or to stress the dangers presented by armed vagabonds. All classes of society were likely to go armed. The poor, if anything, were less violent than the rest. The list of aristocratic violence is so extensive that it could be 'indefinitely repeated'; in Essex, crimes of violence in fact diminished as one descended the social ladder."[7]

An outstanding paean to the culture of violence among the elites that permeated late-Renaissance Europe is found in the extravagantly self-fictionalized life of Benvenuto Cellini that we encounter in his autobiography. In the guise of a realistic account, Cellini portrays himself as a paragon of male virtues. He is the consummate artist in several media, an omnisexual lover of prodigious capacity, a brilliant conversationalist, an accomplished musician, a daring and heroic combatant, a swordsman and marksman without peer. His violent encounters usually find him face-to-face with a crowd of armed adversaries, whom he routs with deadly skill, audacity, and wit. For example, when his longtime rival and enemy Pompeo de Capitaneis gathered a gang of ten well-armed ruffians about him and threatened Cellini, the noble (and superhumanly courageous) artist, fearing that some of his innocent friends might be injured, resolved to avoid a confrontation and handle the matter when he could do so single-handedly. So, when the unfortunate Pompeo a short time later emerged from a chemist's shop into the company of his band, Cellini acted. As he relates it:

> I grasped my little sharp-edged dagger, forced my way through his guards, and put my hands on his chest so coolly and swiftly that none of them could stop me. I aimed to let him have it in the face, but he was so terrified that he turned his head and my dagger struck him just under the ear. I followed

this up with only two stabs more, for at the second he fell dead; not that that had been my intention, but, as they say, there are no rules in war. Then I retrieved the dagger with my left hand, while with my right I drew my sword to defend my life. At this, all those ruffians crowded round the dead body, and did not so much as make a move against me.[8]

Perhaps Cellini's most audacious assertion (amid a host of audacious assertions) is the response that he reports as having been made by his patron, the former Cardinal Farnese recently become Pope Paul III, when told that the artist was in hiding because of the murder of Pompeo. The pope immediately ordered that he be given a safe-conduct and, when told that it would be unwise to issue a pardon so early in his papacy replied (according to Cellini): "You don't understand the matter as much as I do. Men like Benvenuto, who are unique as far as their art is concerned, are not to be subjected to the law—especially not him, for I know what good cause he had."[9]

There is an assumption in the words that Cellini puts in the mouth of the pope that the artist is somehow above the laws that apply to ordinary people and subject only to a higher law, a law far more lenient toward excesses of passion and desire. In the Ottoman context, a similar belief underlies the common understanding among the intellectual elites that the poet/mystic community, the "people of the tavern" (*ehl-i harabat*) or the "people of the heart" (*ehl-i dil*), should be able to commit or contemplate even the mortal sins (crimes against the limits imposed by God) of wine drinking and fornication with impunity because of the higher-level, spiritual purity of their motives. As Hayali says of the drinkers:

Bir 'aleme ermişdürür erbab-ı harabat
Kim düşde dahi görmez anı ehl-i münacat

Mey telh olıcak halet olur anda ziyade
'Aşk ehline yeter bu kadar keşf-ü-keramat

The people of the tavern have attained a revelry
The pious in their dreaming can never hope to see

When bitter is the wine oft they reach an ecstasy
That serves for revelation to love's community[10]

Beneath the surface violence of love rhetoric in the Age of Beloveds—the language of war and self-defense, of swords and daggers, bows and arrows, musket balls and cannon shot—lies a subtext of sexual violence. In both Europe and the Ottoman Empire, where it was common for mature men and youths to seek sexual relations with quite young boys and women, sexual violence was widespread. Speaking of the situation in Florence, Rocke says: "Unsurprisingly, the greater strength of youths or mature men and the stress on proving their manhood meant that sodomy with boys all too often involved intimidation, threats, or outright violence. Cases of rape represented only a fraction of the thousands of homosexual encounters revealed to the courts, but men bullied and assaulted boys frequently enough that this inherently domineering relation was invested with a constant threat of violence." Rocke also points out that it is unlikely that court records accurately reflect the frequency of forced sodomy since it was common for young adolescents to be employed as apprentices or servants and to be sexually exploited by their employers, whom the boys would be reluctant to accuse.[11]

Ruggiero points out that, in Venice, the sexual exploitation of women in prostitution was so widespread that heterosexual rape was customarily addressed with relatively mild punishments except in the case of child victims. Rape of a prostitute was not considered a crime, and the literature touching on courtesan culture is full of accounts of famous gang rapes and mutilations organized as vengeance on uncooperative professional beloveds by rejected or disappointed lovers.[12] For women already victimized by prostitution, mutilation of the face threatened them with loss of livelihood, gang rape with uncontrolled exposure to disfiguring and deadly sexually transmitted diseases. The rape of young women of marriageable age was treated as trivial, and punishment was often forgone if the rapist agreed to marry his victim.[13] As for England, Simon Forman's casebooks are full of accounts of female servants made pregnant by their masters—for example, Forman recorded that a certain "Joan, Mr. Borace's servant, of Radcliffe" was "pregnant by her master; he hath given her some ill medicine and gone to somebody to bewitch her that she should die"—and Forman himself regularly records intercourse with his servants.[14]

Among the Ottomans, our old friend Gazali's *Repeller of Sorrows* has a number of humorous anecdotes about buying boys, coercing boys, and outright raping boys. For example, in one story, an old lecher, unable to win his beloved of the moment with money, took the boy to a gathering and plied him with cup after cup of wine, in the end getting what he desired while the boy was unconscious.[15] In another story, a beautiful boy drank so much at a gathering that he passed out. When the rest of the revelers saw him in this state, they pulled down his trousers and had their way with him. When he woke in the morning, the boy said, "The wine would be just dandy—if only it weren't such a pain in the butt."[16]

We need to be clear here that Gazali's is a work of pornography. Because we are not discussing it in the context of European pornography of the same period, it may give the impression that the Ottomans were somehow cruder, more depraved, or more explicit in talking about sexual matters than Europeans. This is most emphatically not the case.

However, it is true that actual sexual violence (as opposed to the symbolic or displaced violence of the stories) was a problem in the Ottoman Empire as it was in the rest of Europe. There are a significant number of court records that refer to violent acts against both women and boys. For example, among the cases that were sent to the famous sixteenth-century jurist Ebu's-su'ud was the following:

ISSUE:

> Their company commander, Zeyd, sent 'Amr and Bekri off,[a] ordering them to bring to him at once the beardless boy Beşr. They forcibly removed him [Beşr] from the home of his neighbor, Halid, where he had fled to take refuge, and sent him [to Zeyd]. Zeyd took the youthful Beşr to a desolate spot and—God forfend—committed the act of the people of Lot [sodomy] with him. What is the canonical thing to do?

RESPONSE:

> It is canonically permissible to execute Zeyd even if he is not married. If he is not executed, a severe flogging and long prison term are required, and he must be dismissed from his post. People with judicial authority who witness this order have no excuse before God [for not carrying it out], and no [contradictory] response to it [is permitted]. 'Amr and Bekr must be severely punished and serve long prison terms.

Nor were women safe from assault:

ISSUE:

> [The man] Zeyd enters the house [of the woman] Hind, desiring to use her carnally by force; Hind, being unable to drive him off by other means, strikes him with an axe and wounds him. If Zeyd dies of his wounds, what should be done to Hind?

RESPONSE:

> She has been a warrior in defense of Islam.[17]

---

[a] Zeyd and 'Amr are the two John Does of Islamic legal language. Hind is the Jane Doe.

258 *To Die For . . .*

Scripting Sexual Violence in *Hero and Leander*

At this point, let us digress slightly, examine some of the less obvious aspects of sexual violence, and gather up, from brief mentions in previous chapters, a few relevant points, concerning the mutual relations among literary scripting, "real" love, sexual behavior, and violence during the Age of Beloveds. We take as our text Marlowe's famous epyllion *Hero and Leander* and use it to suggest our reading of an episode that has become a standard example in discussions of English Renaissance sexuality.[18] The episode occurs in the second sestiad, when the love-inflamed Leander resolves to swim the Hellespont to Hero's island tower, there to be reunited with his love. He strips and, naked, dives into the sea, where his youthful male beauty attracts the amorous attentions of the god Neptune:

> Whereat the sapphire-visag'd god grew proud,
> And made his capering Triton sound aloud,
> Imagining that Ganymede, displeas'd
> Had left the heavens.[19]

What is to become a homoerotic seduction scene is introduced by a reference to the myth of Jove and Ganymede, which, as Saslow argues very convincingly, can be considered one of the foundational myths of homoerotic love in the late Renaissance.[20] The myth also suggests a reading of the Leander-Neptune episode and raises several points that touch directly on the theme of this chapter. First, the Ganymede tale is most simply the story of abduction and rape. Second, it is traditionally pedophiliac in that it tells of an immensely powerful male (a god, and a ruler of gods at that) exerting sexual dominance over a mortal boy. Third, insofar as Ganymede is granted immortality and a job as cupbearer to Jove in return for sexually satisfying the god, the notion that a boy's sexual submission can have very practical rewards is affirmed. We should note here that the "reward" obscures the intrinsic violence inhering in both the mythology and the practicalities of pedophiliac sexual relations. The boy (or girl) does not (and is not expected to) receive sexual pleasure. In fact, a boy who enjoys the passive role in sexual relations with a man is suspect and thought to be in danger of continuing to seek out "childish" or "feminine" pleasures as an adult—a predilection generally considered reprehensible by both Ottomans and Europeans. If the boy is to gain anything from the relation, it must be some sort of material reward—money, jewels, clothes, a position. There can be no other kind of mutuality or exchange in the relation.

To continue Marlowe's tale, Neptune attempts to reenact Jove's abduction of Ganymede and drags Leander down to his realm in the depth of the sea, where the god sits amid impressive treasures that he disdains to value. This display of power and limitless access to wealth seems intended to subdue the youth and to suggest rewards for compliance:

> Where kingly Neptune and his train abode.
> The lusty god embrac'd him, called him "love,"
> And swore he should never return to Jove:
> But when he knew it was not Ganymed,
> For under water he was almost dead,
> He heaved him up, and, looking at his face,
> Beat down the bold waves with his triple mace,
> Which mounted up, intending to have kiss'd him.
> And fell in drops like tears because they miss'd him.[21]

Here, the power disparity and its dangers are most starkly displayed. The mortal beloved dragged down to the depths is on the verge of death. It is only the god's mercy that keeps the god's lust from killing him. Yet even the waves lust after the boy, and their love would kill him as easily as would the god's. But the amorous waves are quelled by a display of the god's almost ludicrously phallic "triple mace"/trident. Meanwhile, Leander, back on the surface, begins to swim, pursued by the impassioned god. He cries out, begging that he be allowed to see his beloved again, and the god grants him a token that protects him against the sea. As the youth swims, the god continues his seductive assault:

> He clapped his plump cheeks, with his tresses play'd,
> And smiling wantonly, his love bewray'd;
> He watch'd his arms, and, as they open'd wide
> At every stroke, betwixt them would he slide,
> And steal a kiss, and then run out and dance,
> And, as he turn'd, cast many a lustful glance,
> And threw him gaudy toys to please his eye,
> And dive into the water, and there pry
> Upon his breast, his thighs, and every limb,
> And up again, and close beside him swim,
> And talk of love.[22]

The god's attempted seduction is of a type and very near Me'ali's approaches to his beloved boy:

Once again, the greedy honeybees of lust swarmed about him and covered him from head to toe like his robes. He saw before him a waist—so-called but lacking all substance—and hips so substantial that they could not fit in an embrace. He determined to give him a kiss and a hug, throwing an arm about his neck as his ringlets were thrown, clasping him firmly about the waist as he was clasped by his belt. He whet his appetite for setting to the kissing of his hand, readied himself for casting aside all formalities as one casts aside the skirts of modesty and for taking the matter in hand, handling it by laying a hand to the drawstring of his darling's pantaloons. In order to induce his beloved to show compassion, he would alternately whisper plaintively and plead aloud.

The distraught Leander, who has more heterosexual goals in mind, cannot be diverted and replies, crying out, "You are deceiv'd; I am no woman, I."[23] But Leander is a naïf. Of course, in all respects (but one) the young man subject to being physically/sexually dominated by an older, more powerful man *is* a woman—especially if we ignore physiology for a moment and take *woman* to represent a position in the sociosexual power structure. As we have said many times, there is plenty of evidence that early-modern love did not distinguish significantly between young men and women. Although there was considerable attention paid to sodomy, which at the time meant any kind of "unnatural" or nonprocreative intercourse with men or women, there existed no discourse of homosexuality or heterosexuality—in fact, no discourse of sexuality at all. The gender ambiguity of the beloved seems to be very much on the surface of thought during the Age of Beloveds.

One indication of this is the theme of the identical twin brother and sister, which seems to be ubiquitous. As an example, we need only recall Viola and Sebastian of Shakespeare's *Twelfth Night*. At one point, Viola, disguised as a boy, is asked by the duke to be his emissary in the wooing of his beloved. When she demurs, the duke contradicts her and points out that her "womanish" characteristics will put the shy beloved at ease. As he describes the lad, he reveals at the same time his own eroticized attention to the womanly (or sexually interesting) characteristics of what he believes to be a boy:

> Dear lad, Believe it;
> For they shall yet belie thy happy years,
> That say thou art a man: Diana's lip
> Is not more smooth and rubious; thy small pipe
> Is as the maiden's organ, shrill and sound,
> And all is semblative a woman's part.
> (act 1, sc. 4, lines 29–34)

The duke's interest in Viola as an attractive boy will be echoed by Olivia's interest in her as a man—a complex situation that overtly asserts the interchangeability of the woman and the young man. And we see this same theme everywhere: in *Orlando Furioso,* where we saw poor Fiordispina deceived by Bradamant's boyish look and rescued by the appearance of her beloved's twin brother; in the Italian *commedia erudita,* perhaps most famously Bibbiena's *La calandria* (first performed in 1513), where the identical (male) twins theme of his classical model (Plautus's *Menaechmi*) is complicated by using disguised twins of different genders. Even Leander is described by Marlowe, who says: "Some swore he was a maid in man's attire, / For in his looks were all that men desire."[24] Thus, in the context of early-modern attention to a fundamental ambiguity in the gender of the beloved, Leander's cry ("I am no woman, I") can be seen as an amusing (and satiric) referencing of the many dramatic situations in which a beloved throws off his or her disguise, reveals a "true" gender identity, and sets the "natural" order aright.[25]

But is Neptune put off by Leander's revelation? Not in the least. Like any worldly English aristocrat, he has not been deceived. He knows a beloved boy, a ganymede, when he sees one. Unabashed, he continues his seduction:

> Thereat smil'd Neptune, and then told a tale,
> How that a shepherd sitting in a vale,
> Play'd with a boy so lovely-fair and kind,
> As for his love both earth and heaven pin'd;
> That of the cooling river durst not drink,
> Lest water nymphs should pull him from the brink;
> And when he sported in the fragrant lawns,
> Goat-footed Satyrs and up-staring fauns
> Would steal him thence.[26]

Here, Neptune, like a good English poet of Marlowe's time, evokes the pastoral mode. Leander stripped to his "ivory skin" and compared to the shepherd boy dangerously beloved of the nymphs recalls Barnfield's affectionate shepherd who sinned "to love a lovely lad" with "ivory white and alabaster skin" whom "the nymphs bestird them-selves / To trie who could his beautie soonest win."[27] Coupled with the god's importuning, Neptune's little unfinished pastoral also reminds us of Marlowe's own famous and often paralleled and answered song about an importuning shepherd that begins: "Come with mee, and be my love." Indeed, not only does the sentence "Come with mee, and be my love" sum up Neptune's pleading, but the rest of the song parallels the god's attempts to win the unwilling beloved by offering gifts of various kinds. In discussing this poem, James Mirollo points out that there is a long tradition, extending from Boccaccio at least, of describing the elite female beloved as a nymph—the embodiment of natural forces—a tradition that casts the beloved boy as the object of desire for powerful women as well as for powerful men and boys who appear in the roles of satyrs and fauns.[28] Neptune's abortive tale makes the danger of this power disparity overt. For the beautiful boy, the natural world is charged with the threat of abduction, rape, and death. The fate of Ganymede is ever present to an attractive lad. The nymphs could drown him; the satyrs could carry him off. Everywhere lurks the threat of sexual violence, for Neptune's is at bottom a threatening tale.

But, before the god can finish his story, Leander sees the sun reflecting off Hero's tower and, with a last effort, comes almost to the shore. And the god is not pleased:

> Neptune was angry that he gave no ear,
> And in his heart revenging malice bare:
> He flung at him his mace; but, as it went,
> He call'd it in, for love made him repent:
> The mace, returning back, his own hand hit,
> As meaning to be veng'd for darting it.

When the boy exerts his only power—the limited power to refuse and choose another love (or another patron and protector)—the implicit violence of the encounter becomes explicit. Neptune casts his phallic triple mace, symbolically acting out a rape attempt, and then relents. In calling back the mace and, thereby, rejecting the application of force, the god/lover wounds himself. Ironically, what is described as an act of love (renouncing force) deprives the lover of the beloved, to whom he has (by renouncing force) granted the power of resistance. At precisely this point, the god's situation intersects with that of the typal lover in early-modern cultures. He is faced with a beloved whom he cannot sway by show of power or wealth, or by entreaties, or by the application of force. He is reduced to mistaking the beloved's laudable sensitivity and compassion for the beginnings of love and making the usually faulty assumption that only by suffering can he attract sympathy and, then, passion:

> When this fresh-bleeding wound Leander view'd,
> His colour went and came as if he ru'd
> The grief which Neptune felt: in gentle breasts
> Relenting thoughts, remorse, and pity rests;
> And who have hard hearts and obdurate minds,
> But vicious, hare-brain'd and illiterate hinds?
> The god seeing him with pity to be mov'd,
> Thereon concluded that he was belov'd;

> (Love is too full of faith, too credulous,
> With folly and false hope deluding us;)
> Wherefore, Leander's fancy to surprise,
> To the rich ocean for gifts he flies;
> 'Tis wisdom to give much; a gift prevails
> When deep-persuading oratory fails.[29]

By this stage, Marlowe has reduced the once-potent god to a deluded old man rushing off to find something of value in the vain hope that his beloved boy can at least be bought. We see an obvious parody here: of the courtier helplessly watching his prince for signs of sympathy that can be read as love, of Me'ali, the aging pedophile, in pursuit of an indifferent (or hostile) boy. Neptune's intent, related as Marlowe's wisdom ("a gift prevails / When deep-persuading oratory fails"), recalls Gazali's "ching-a-ling" lover who, as we saw in chapter 5, hunts the beloved with a handful of gold. But, in mocking Neptune's failure, Marlowe also implies a contrast both with the actions of Jove, who did not hesitate to carry out his rape, and, as the story unfolds, with the actions of Leander, who finishes his swim and completes his assault on the maidenhood of his beloved Hero.

Sexual Violence in Ottoman Poetry

Ottoman poetry tends to conceal beneath a surface reversal the implied violence that resides in the power disparity between the older, highly placed man and the younger, subordinate boy. In the universe of the poem, the boy has all the weapons; his glances are arrows, his lashes are daggers or darts, his eyebrows bows or curved swords:[30]

> *Yardım içün gamze-i hun-rizine ol katilün*
> *Bir yana hançer turur şemşir-i bürran bir yana*
>
> To aid that murderer's blood-shedding glance
> Here lies a dagger and there a keen-edged scimitar
> —Fevri

> *Fevriyi öldür diyü bilsem günahum n'oldı kim*
> *Tig ile hançer nigarun yanına takıldılar*
>
> What is my sin that they should gird the beloved
> With sword and dagger to murder Fevri
> —Fevri

> *Tir ü hançer çekme gamzenden Necati kasdına*
> *Bir karınca katline lazım degül bunca yarag*
>
> Don't draw arrow and dagger from your glance to murder Necati
> That much weaponry is hardly necessary to kill an ant
> —Necati

> *Gerçi çeşmün bi-muhaba öldürür 'aşıkları*
> *Gamzenündür suç ki mestün destine hançer sunar*
>
> Truly your eye kills lovers without compunction
> Your glance is guilty for putting a dagger in the hands of a drunk[b,31]
> —Necati

Even the garden of love and the private sanctuary of the home are penetrated and transformed by the beloved's murderous weaponry:

> *Taze dagum kırmızı gül zahm-i tigün susenüm*
> *Bülbülüdür bu gülistanun fegan-ü-şivenüm*
>
> *Hane-i kalbüme hüsnün pertevi düşsün deyu*
> *Dag-ı sinem cam olubdur zahm-i tirün revzenüm*
>
> My [love] burns are crimson roses, your arrows' wounds the iris
> My wails and [pleading] blandishments this garden's nightingales
>
> So that the light of your beauty['s rays] will shine in the house of my heart
> The burns on my breast are [rosy] glass, your arrow wounds are windows[32]
> —Hayali

The lover is cruelly murdered by the indifferent beloved time and time again —when he does not just weep and pine his way to death:

> *Atından inse küşte-i 'ışk üzre n'ola yar*
> *Üstine nur inermiş anun kim şehid olur*
>
> What matter if the beloved step from his horse onto the murdered
>   lover['s body]
> Divine illumination descends upon the [dead body of a] holy martyr
> —Fevri

> *Yüri hey çeşmi katil hali zalim bi-aman afet*
> *Lebi kanlar içici gamzesi navek-figen dilber*

---

[b] The languid eye is commonly described as a drunk.

> Come on, you with the murdering eye, the tyrant mole, you merciless calamity
> You! Beloved with the blood-drinking lips and the dart-blowing glance[33]
> —Fevri

The boy beloved is cruel, a murderer and tyrant, because he (or his beauty) is guilty of causing the man's attachment to him; he is responsible for the lover's suffering because he refuses to end it by submitting. The actual situation is reversed, and the relatively weak and powerless boy is portrayed as dominating and tormenting the older, stronger man. This seems very much like a rhetorical attempt to even out the power disparity and inject some mutuality into what was more properly a rape or a contemplation of rape. There is an irony in this fiction, grown stale with repetition, and rescued to a certain extent by ostensibly real-life tales of actual murders by beloveds wielding, not deadly glances, but what Beier calls "the inevitable knife."[34]

As we outlined in the previous chapter, the apparent contradiction in the rhetorical power reversal is a consequence of a complex situation in which relations at court—political relations—structure relations within the poem. In the context of the court and the court-dependent elites, the beloved (the desired object) is more powerful in an ascending scale up to the ruler and God. The poetic script tends to naturalize this powerful boy by using him to embody or manifest the power of love itself. The Western European tradition often does this through the image of Cupid, who is often conflated with Ganymede, and who has the same dangerous and bloodthirsty characteristics that we saw above in the Ottoman's beloved boy. Love/Cupid shoots arrows that cruelly wound the lover:

> Not at first sight, nor with a dribbled shot
> *Love* gave the wound, which while I breathe will bleed
> —Sidney, *Astrophel and Stella*

Love is the beloved's killer glance, hidden like an assassin behind dark lashes and brows:

> Flie, fly, my friends, I have my death wound; fly,
> See there that boy, that murthring boy I say,
> Who like a theefe, hid in darke bush doth ly[35]
> —Sidney, *Astrophel and Stella*

The beloved may be a woman, but her glances and the love that her beauty arouses are embodied as a boy.

For the Ottoman poet, it seems to be expected or even required that the beloved—a real, poetic beloved—will be murderous, violent, and vengeful. As Hayali says:

> The beloved, they say, should bear malice
> > toward the one who loves him
> His wont and his art should be to murder his lover[36]

In the world of court society, this hyperbolic devotion of the lover to a powerful and often indifferent or even cruel beloved is valuable as an attention getter. Being noticed by the beloved is the first step toward arousing the beloved's affection, and with affection goes power and position. (That suffering can be a prelude to attracting love is Neptune's delusion.) Yet this is precisely what we saw as an effective strategy in the story of Tayyib and Tahir. Young Tayyib's lovesickness attracts the attention and, then, the sympathy of Sir John. Once attention is gained, another reversal is induced. As we mentioned above, the beloved is held responsible for the lover's plight. The beloved becomes cruel, murdering, and tyrannical, not by doing anything, but simply by being so attractive that the lover cannot help himself. This is how both the helpless boy about to be raped and the powerful patron about to be asked for something can be conceived of in the same rhetorical context. Impelled by the power of his lover's need, the Christian nobleman rescues the Muslim youth from prison and gives him a job in his gardens, where he can be near his beloved. From there, the beloved nobleman's sympathy turns to affection, his affection to love, culminating in a series of reversals from which the lovers and beloveds emerge into a new, more equal distribution of power: Christians become Muslims (everybody is a Muslim); captives become capturers (everybody has been both captive and capturer); Europe becomes Istanbul (everybody is an Ottoman); the powerless become powerful; and despair turns to joy. From one perspective, the story of Tayyib and Tahir allegorizes the career of a successful courtier or member of the court-dependent elite. In the end, the poetic script proclaims, love will bring the kind of sharing of power—albeit a *dangerous* sharing—that we see made into "history" in the story of Ibrahim Pasha and Sultan Süleyman.

At the level of actual social/sexual/erotic relations, even though the poet takes a subordinate, supplicating role, there is an understanding that this is a rhetorical stance required by the idealizing nature of the poetic universe and that actual power and authority run in the opposite direction. For the Ottomans, this understanding is subsumed in the idea of *vefa* (faithfulness), which comes to mean both the usual kind of lover's faithfulness (you shall have no other lovers but me) and faithfulness to the conventions of poetically scripted love (you [the beloved boy] will not betray me by acting as though my rhetorical stance and the dictates of my desire define power relations in the real world). This double understanding is illustrated by the kind of betrayal or lack of vefa that we saw in the previous chapter in the story of Me'ali, where the older, powerful man was made helpless and endangered by an unscrupulous boy who used the poetic script to trap his prey. It also appears to us significant that, in this story, the boy turns the tables by pretending to be a servant of the sultan, taking on, however duplicitously, a role that returns us to the situation at court and its deployment of power relations.

At this point, we would like to make clear where we stand on one important issue. Our insistence on returning the discussion of love to a focus on the court stems directly from a core hypothesis that we have referred to indirectly several times in the preceding chapters: that terms such as *love* (and the associated feelings) have no content, no meaning, outside particular historical, political, social, and cultural circumstances. Certain emotional clusters, including even physiological responses, may be in some manner universal; that is, they may be experienced by all or most human beings. Although assessing the truth of this assumption is beyond our expertise and interests, we do believe that there is abundant evidence indicating that there is nothing universal or ahistorical about the meanings that we attach to those clusters and responses. Whatever the biology of love may be, the *meaning* of love is historical and contingent. Accordingly, we are raising the possibility that the widespread similarities that we see between love and the beloved in the Ottoman Empire and in the rest of Europe during the Age of Beloveds result, neither from biology, nor from direct influences or borrowings, but in some degree from similarities in the way existing political and social systems structured relations among groups and individuals.

In this chapter, we are trying to suggest that the character of absolutist authoritarian despotism/monarchy expressed as love is violent and pedophiliac. The overarching power structure sets a pattern of dominance and submission that repeats itself throughout the spectrum of social relations, with lessening effect the further- one gets from the court. Down through the hierarchy, the weaker are induced (by the implied violence of absolute authority) to offer themselves to the domination—political, social, and sexual—of the stronger: the courtier to the minister or king; apprentice to master; wife to husband. Returning to an example mentioned above in a different context, remember what Benvenuto Cellini said in response to a fellow artist who accused him of being "a sodomite": "I wish to God I did did know how to indulge in such a noble practice: after all we read that Jove enjoyed it with Ganymede in paradise, and here on earth it is the practice of the greatest emperors and the greatest kings of the world. I'm an insignificant, humble man, I haven't the means or the knowledge to meddle in such a marvelous matter." In Cellini's mind, it is a given that love, sex, homoeroticism, and power go together and that making the connection constitutes a good argument against the condemnation of sodomy. From our perspective, because the absolutist monarchy, and the society that it rules, is also phallocentric, its pedophilia (placing the object of desire in the role of child, either actually or structurally) is also fundamentally homoerotic (the hierarchy of domination is male on top of male). In consequence, at this level of abstraction, the absolutist monarchies of early-modern times can be seen to generate very similar deployments of desire and very similar cultural products.

9

LOVE, LAW, AND RELIGION

It is not our object in this chapter to give a comprehensive account of the legal aspects of sexual behavior in the Ottoman Empire during the Age of Beloveds. In the first place, the scope of our study limits us to summarizing general knowledge and citing a few pertinent examples in a situation where there is precious little general knowledge about the actualities of Ottoman sexual practice to summarize. In the second place, we must mention that the field of sex crime is distant from the realm of desire, eroticism, passion, and the tender feelings of affection, the proper topic of our study. The problem is that, when we attempt to examine points at which the fanciful realm of literary love intersects with the enactment of love in the world, we are abruptly brought up against the fact that most love behavior belongs to the very private domain of thoughts and feelings, interpreted glances and gestures, passions never acted on, and dreams never fulfilled.

Except for Leslie Peirce's study of the court records from Ayntab in eastern Turkey, we have no rigorous study of Ottoman sexual practice to help us and nothing remotely like Guido Ruggiero's seminal study of sexual behavior and the law in Venice, *The Boundaries of Eros*. The title and contents of Ruggiero's book suggest that the application of law at any moment is useful in defining the actual limits of permissible sexual behavior and making visible extensions of behavior beyond those limits. In the absence of such a study for the Ottomans, we have nothing but snapshots and educated guesses about what the actual limits and transgressions might have been. Consequently, we will be doing what we have been doing all along: examining what might be called *the fringes of eros* in the context of poetry. This is a significant point. If, as we have said, the heart of eroticism lies in the world of the mind and the most private personal interactions (as it must), then what we use as nonliterary evidence of erotic behavior—historical accounts, court cases, legal opinions, etc.—is evidence only of the bare fringes of erotic behavior, the relatively rare moments when erotic behavior intersected with public awareness in a way that resulted in a written record. Even when, at some future time, all the available historical evidence is taken into account, the result will still be no more than an account of the barest fringes. The heart of the matter will still be accessible only by means of the ambiguous, abstract, and often ahistorical evidence of art and literature. The difference between the documented fringes and the interpreted heart will always define a fundamental difference between the study of history and the study of literature. That much said, let us return to love and the law.

PART I: BELOVEDS AND THE LAW

According to Islamic law—both the sharia and the sultanic law (*örf/kanun*)— the only licit sexual relations between adult men and women occur within the confines of marriage. The most serious sexual transgression, the crime of zina (fornication or adultery), is considered to be among the crimes of *hadd/hudud* (limit/limits), that is, crimes considered offenses against the limits imposed by God, whose punishments are "rights or claims of God" (*hakk Allah*). The notion that God's relation to human beings was personal— in the sense that God can be harmed or have legal rights violated by human agents—seems to have been common in our period. Ruggiero, talking of Venice, has an interesting passage in which he describes a relation to God that is in many ways similar to the relation that underlies the notion of hadd crimes: "Sex crimes against God reveal a subset of sexual criminality curious to modern eyes. But the vision of these crimes turned upon a central perception of Renaissance religiosity. God was a deity close to man, personally involved in this world and personally touched by human actions. When those actions involved nuns, priests, monks, ecclesiastical settings, or Jews, God was thought to be personally injured, and the government stepped in aggressively to restrict such deeds. In a way, then, Venice was prepared to protect God much as they assumed, or at least hoped, God was prepared to protect them."[1] What particular acts constitute "sex crimes against God" may be different in Venice and Istanbul, but the notion that God can be offended against in such a direct and personal way is arguably the same—a circumstance that might well expand our understanding of the boundaries of Renaissance religiosity.

In Islamic legal theory, not only can hadd crimes not be pardoned, but their punishments are set and cannot be mitigated by civil authorities.[2] This class of crimes includes, not only zina, but also drinking wine and committing theft and highway robbery as well as false accusation of zina. Because fornication is punishable by stoning to death (*recm*) when it is adulterous (committed by a married Muslim and, therefore, zina), false accusation of zina (*kazf*) itself belongs to the most serious class of crimes (crimes against the limits set by God), and the guilty party is subject to the same punishments as are required for someone who commits zina. In other instances of forbidden sexual conduct (e.g., fornication by the unmarried, with a non-Muslim, with a slave belonging to one's wife, with a woman who is being divorced, or among slaves), the punishments in Ottoman times involved severe and damaging floggings ranging from one hundred lashes (for respectable Muslims) to fifty (for slaves). Penetrative sexual relations with a boy were, in theory, equivalent to relations with a woman and subject to the same punishments, usually less than stoning or death (by means other than stoning), except in the case of rape. Because of the severity of the punishments and the absence of official discretion, the usual requirement that a crime be witnessed by three upright (male) Muslims is expanded to require a fourth witness when zina is involved. In addition, confession to zina must be repeated on four separate instances (the equivalent of the four required witnesses), and the magistrate is required to question the suspect to be certain that he or she understands the crime that is being confessed. According to Islamic law, fornication or adultery requires penetration (usually described in terms such as *like the eyesalve pick into the bottle* or *the rope into the well*).[3] Anything less falls short of being a crime of limits (hadd) and is subject to discretionary punishment.

On a theoretical level, that part of the sharia that touches on the most serious sex offenses has two striking characteristics. On the one hand, it disapproves mightily of illicit intercourse with respectable and married Muslim women. It imposes severe punishments and removes such matters from the discretion of civil authorities. On the other hand, it also shows extreme reluctance to convict and impose the obligatory punishment for zina. As a practical matter, it seems highly unlikely that an act of sexual penetration would be witnessed by four upright members of the community, let alone four upright community members willing to risk severe punishment if their accusations are found to be false or mistaken. It is only slightly more likely that a penitent adulterer would confess on four separate occasions to a crime punishable by death, given several chances to think things over. Moreover, it was a principle of the Ottoman understanding of the sharia that a Muslim is not required to come forward and witness against someone who has violated a claim of God (a crime for which a hadd punishment is required), and failure to inform the kadi of such a crime was not punishable as it was in the case of crimes against persons (for which the punishments were "claims of man"). Uriel Heyd suggests that "the Ottomans even regarded it as humane not to assist in such cases in the conviction of a fellow Muslim." He also points out that a Muslim could be fined for not reporting a case of theft, for which retribution is *both* a claim of God (God's right to set the punishment for hadd crimes) and a claim of man (the right of the victim to have his property restored to him).[4] The surest sign of the reluctance of the Ottoman legal establishment to prosecute zina and punish offenders by stoning is the fact that there is no evidence of an execution by stoning at any time during the Age of Beloveds. The first attested case occurred in 1680 and involved a non-Muslim man engaged in sexual relations with a married Muslim woman.[5]

Reluctance to apply the hadd penalty in cases of adultery and fornication does not mean that other punishments were not meted out for sexual misconduct. In the Ottoman case, there were two classes of administrative punishment (not determined by the sharia) that were carried out at the discretion of the civil authorities: *siyaset*, which involved severe corporal punishments ranging from death to castration, branding, and slitting the nose, and *taʿzir* or *teʾdib*, which involved chastisement such as caning, flogging, or bastinado as well as imprisonment, compulsory servitude at the oars of galleys, monetary fines, and exposure to public ridicule. In the case of public ridicule, for example, there are several reported instances of a sexually misbehaving woman paraded about seated backward on a donkey with rotting offal draped over her head.[6] This sort of punishment by humiliation was also common in Italy. John Brackett records that, in Florence during the sixteenth century, "the offender was mounted on a donkey and then led through the city with a black miter on his or her head, on which the crime was described."[7] In fact, overall, we find the same punishments imposed for similar sex crimes in Italy and the Ottoman Empire, with only minor differences: the Venetians burned offenders convicted of sodomy, the Ottomans occasionally executed sex criminals by hanging them on a hook; the Italians amputated the hands of those convicted of sex offenses, the Ottomans amputated the hands only of those convicted of theft. There are also numerous Ottoman legal opinions upholding the right of parents or family members to kill a female child for engaging in illicit intercourse and to kill her lover if the two are caught in the act. In practice, however, the Ottomans instituted a system of fines for sex offenses that existed alongside the more violent punishments. Leslie Pierce summarizes the situation as follows:

> Both religious and sultanic law gave the court a number of options in punishing illicit sex. While Süleyman's law book did not entirely dissociate itself from violent solutions (it sanctioned honor killing and never explicitly suspended the punishment of death by stoning, prescribed by religious law for Muslim adulterers), the punishment most explicitly and fully articu-

lated was imposition of a monetary fine. Fines were calculated according to the civil and socio-economic status of the offender: adultery was penalized more heavily than fornication, free persons were penalized more heavily than slaves, Muslims more heavily than non-Muslims, and wealthy persons more heavily than persons of middling or little wealth. In addition to de-emphasizing violence, the state's justice was relatively cheap.[8]

Generally speaking, the practical application of Islamic law in our period of interest appears to have a strong bias toward protecting the peace, security, and values of the Muslim community. It is very responsive to the concerns of local communities; it is flexible and pragmatic and avoids imposing punishments (even prescribed punishments) that would offend or seem oppressive to upright citizens. Where actual love or sexual behavior seems to contradict what we know, or think we know, of Islamic law, it is important to keep in mind this pragmatic and communalist bias.[9]

Love, Sex, and the Law in Practice

At this point, let us turn to a few examples of the Ottoman legal system in action. The first—one that we have mentioned earlier (see chapter 6 above)—is from a 1565 order sent to a kadi by a mufti. In this case, it appears that the mufti was responding to a kadi's request for an opinion regarding the public nuisance caused by a certain group of women:

DECREE TO THE KADI OF GALATA:

> You sent a document to my auspicious portal to the effect that the people of the mosque of the (late) Sultan Gir outside Galata came to the sharia court saying, "Women of our quarter named 'Arap Fatı [Fatima the Arab/Black] and Narin [Shining/Elegant] and [two] named Kamer [Moon] and Balatlı 'Ayni [Ayni from Balat] who are known as Giritli Nefise [the Delectable One from Crete] and 'Atlı Ases [the Mounted Watch/Police] are notorious for misbehavior; when a man was invited in [to her house] and allowed to see 'Arap Fatı, this caused gossip, and, when the other [women] came [to the house] and were face to face [with men], the Muslim community said, 'They are mischiefmakers,' and some of the people of the quarter—Müderris [Professor] Mevlana Muhyiddin, Katib [Clerk] Mehmet Ilyas, Sinan Halife, and other Muslims—witnessed this; and even before this, in order to control the situation of the above-mentioned [women], the imam [prayer leader], the muezzin [caller to prayer], and the community gathered in front of her house and cursed her, saying, 'This is an insult to your kadi, your

imam, and the sharia,' and, prior to this, she was caught in the Kalafatçı Quarter with a man who was not her husband, and, in addition, the aforementioned 'Arap Fatı's home was also observed with a strange man in it, and this is an evil assault on the morals of the quarter, so we request that her house be sold and she be removed from our quarter." When you informed me of their saying this, I commanded that, on receipt of this noble decree of judgment, the house of these women should be forcibly sold and they should be driven from the town; the foulmouthed wife of the janissary should [first] have her faith renewed [by punishment] and then be imprisoned until her husband returns.[10]

In order to understand what lies behind some of the condensed descriptions in Ottoman legal decrees and behind this decree in particular, there are a few principles of Ottoman urban social organization that need to be mentioned. In Ottoman cities, the most intimate social unit outside the family was the *mahalle*, or "quarter." The quarter was usually organized around a local mosque or, in the case of quarters inhabited by non-Muslim minorities, around a church or synagogue. Some quarters were predominantly inhabited by members of one guild or adherents of one religion, but there is evidence that, in many or most quarters, the members of various trades and religions mingled.[11] We see, for example, a number of official complaints that involve sexual relations between Muslim and non-Muslim neighbors as well as cultural clashes arising from differences in what was considered permissible behavior among religious groups residing in the same quarter. The quarter was considered a social and administrative unit by its residents and seems to have been treated as such by the authorities. In many instances, the main street could be closed off by gates at night or in times of unrest.

The representatives and administration of the quarter appear to have been unofficial and customary (the central government did not appoint administrators of the quarter as such). Certain upright citizens recognized by the residents as having special status—for example, the imam of the local mosque, a teacher, a wealthy and educated man—acted as spokespersons for the quarter and carried its business to the proper authorities, who recognized their quasi-official status and considered them responsible for overseeing the moral climate of the quarter.[12] As we will see, the morality of the quarter was enforced primarily by local pressure to conform. Only when things could not be resolved at the local level did residents bring their problems to the attention of the authorities. This, then, is the general atmosphere in which the decree to the kadi of Gatala was produced.

Wading through the hypotactic verbiage of Ottoman official decrees, what we find is, evidently, that a woman named 'Arap Fatı, who was married to a janissary then off on campaign, moved into a certain quarter known by the name of its mosque, which was, in turn, named after the man (the late Sultan Gir) who most probably had built and endowed it. This woman had come to the quarter allegedly after being expelled by the authorities from her previous place of residence. This means that she came with a töhmet, a suspicion of improper behavior, which would make it difficult for her to defend herself against subsequent accusations of the same sort of behavior.[13] It seems obvious that she either recruited or brought with her other women and opened a house of prostitution in which she and the others entertained male clients. However, this is not what is actually alleged in the complaint. There is no overt mention of sexual activity, only the assertion that these women were observed interacting unveiled and unprotected with men outside the permissible degrees of relationship (i.e., men other than a husband, a father, grandfathers, and brothers) and that this caused gossip (likely the voiced suspicion that illicit sexual behavior was taking place) and, therefore, threatened the moral climate of the neighborhood.

As we have mentioned above, in order for a charge of zina to be brought, there must be witnessed or confessed contact involving penetration. The complaint mentions only two of the four required upright male witnesses by name and occupation—a professor and a secretary or clerk—which indicates that the crime does not involve an allegation of zina and falls more properly under the general category of disturbing the peace or offending the morals of the Muslim community. The complaint also mentions steps that were taken at the community level to rectify the situation. The officials of the mosque (imam and the muezzin), who were expected to monitor the morality of the community, are reported to have organized a kind of charivari in which inhabitants of the quarter gathered outside the home of the offending woman to shout insults, imprecations, and admonitions. Only when this had no effect did they make a complaint to the kadi, who then asked the mufti's advice as to the disposition of the case.

It is clear that a woman ('Arap Fatı) had opened a house of prostitution, where she served as procuress, in the quarter of the complaining witnesses. It is also evidently common knowledge that she had been expelled from another quarter for doing the same. By identifying her as the wife of a janissary who is away on campaign, the document appears to suggest a mitigation or explanation for her behavior: she is trying to make a living in the absence of her husband and, perhaps, his income, and, in any case, she lacks a male protector to control her behavior. The disposition of the case reflects a primary concern for remediating the social disruption caused by the prostitutes as opposed to punishing their behavior severely. The house is to be taken away, the women (other than the procuress) to be expelled from the neighborhood (as

ʿArap Fatı was in a previous instance), and the procuress to receive a refresher course in Islamic morality (most likely with some blows of the cane) and to be held awaiting the return of her husband. This suggests that neither the inhabitants of the quarter nor the legal authorities are interested in making a case for outright sexual misconduct and applying harsh punishments to the offending women.

Much the same ambivalence about behavior with sexual overtones is seen in another case, this one from 1573, also mentioned earlier (see chapter 6 above):

DECREE TO THE KADI OF EYÜP:

> You sent a letter informing me that Muslims told you that, in most of the shops, bakeries, and orchards located in the Grand Mosque Quarter near to the now rebuilding Noble College of Eyüp and next to the Noble Primary School, there are those of the non-Muslim community who do immoral things; they play the flageolet, dance, and are an obstruction to the business of the quarter and the [ability of] innocent people to read the Qurʾan and hear the call to prayer; and, in some of the clotted cream [*kaymak*] shops, some women enter under the pretext of eating clotted cream and then sit about meeting with men who are not their husbands and behaving in a manner contrary to the sharia. At this time, the most important business of the law is to eliminate conditions such as this, which exist in contravention of the sharia. Neglect is not appropriate in this case. I have issued the following order—may you be solicitous in this regard: from now on do not allow non-Muslims in the previously mentioned shops and gardens; remove them, send them elsewhere, give the places to Muslims, and get rid of this problem by insistent, severe warnings to the shop owners that they should not allow females to enter under the pretext of eating clotted cream. If, after being warned, the females enter a shop once again and the shopkeeper does not remove them, you should first bring in the actual owner of the shop and harshly remind him of his limits; you should exhibit great zeal in carrying out my noble order and avoid neglecting it. It is required that this letter containing these particulars be noted. Thus, an apology will not be accepted if these particulars, which you submitted, are not ameliorated as required by my noble decree, and you will be censured. Know this. In this manner make this a priority, and lose not a moment in attending to it.[14]

This case indicates that the quarter surrounding the Grand Mosque in the district of Eyüp was inhabited by a mixed population of Muslims and non-Muslims. Apparently, non-Muslim women (and men?) were accustomed to appear in public and to amuse themselves in shops and gardens by playing

An Ottoman house of prostitution. The owner is being reprimanded by an Ottoman official. (Istanbul University Library, TY. 5502, Enderunlu Fazıl, "Hubānnāme-zenānnāme," fol. 280b.)

music, dancing, and eating clotted cream. This kind of gathering parallels quite closely the poetic prescription for a gathering of lovers and beloveds, with the result that, in this case, the women are cast as objects of sexual desire. That this was intolerable to some of the community is evidenced by the complaint itself. That it was a tolerable condition to others is implied by the language of the response. Many decrees of this sort end with standard admonitions to the local kadi requiring him not to neglect application of the order. This practice may have been an official recognition of the popular impression that all lower-level kadis were open to bribes as inducements to overlook certain offenses. Here, however, there are clear indications that the mufti had reason to believe that his order might not be carried out and, indeed, that this may not have been the first order issued concerning this matter. The admonitions to the kadi are repeated throughout, and detailed instructions are given for remediation. This suggests that the higher authorities may have taken a dimmer view of this behavior than did many of the residents of the quarter in question, including the local kadi. There is also the suggestion that the presence of women and the amusements that they provided were good for the business of the local shopkeepers and that, as soon as official scrutiny waned, everyone would go back to business as usual.

Our old friend Gazali tells an obscene little anecdote that points to a popular understanding of the way in which the legal system actually worked:

>Once upon a time, in a certain city, there was an attractive young woman. She was an extremely agreeable and elegant companion, but she chose to be a whore. She arranged to pay protection money so that no one would interfere with her. Taking a hundred gold pieces for a single act of intercourse, she obtained the wealth of the high and mighty, making them low and humble, and she left several rich men bankrupt and impoverished. But there was one rich man who was exceedingly greedy and miserly. She couldn't get him to fall for her, nor could she get even a few gold pieces out of him. One day this miser said to some people, "Last night I had an orgasm with her in my dream and thereby got for nothing what others paid a hundred gold pieces for." The puss immediately hauled the miser up before the kadi and said, "Look, you're taking my money [as a 'tax in lieu of fines'], and this miser had an orgasm with me in a dream. He took his pleasure and savored it. Now order him to pay me my fee!" The kadi was subtle and made a sign asking that she give him half the fee. The puss demurred, saying, "Why should there be a bribe added on [to what I already pay]. So the kadi turned and, with a wink at the miser, said, "What'll you give me if I get you out of this?" The miser was willing to go for fifty gold pieces. So then the kadi took a prosecutorial role and said, "Bring me a mirror!" And

they brought it. [Whereupon] the miser counted out the gold. The kadi then said to the puss, "Open your hand." And to the miser, "Take these [gold pieces], and strew them over the hand in the mirror." The miser did as the kadi asked and placed the gold on the hand in the mirror. The kadi then awarded the gold to the miser and dismissed the puss from the session, saying, "This is the kind of fee appropriate for that kind of fuck." And so, with this trick, he managed to do the miser out of a few gold coins.[15]

This is a good story only if it is also a plausible story. We know that the Ottoman legal system permitted (although not without some controversy) what was called a *kesim* or a fine paid in advance of an offense in the form of a regular tax.[16] Although the word *kesim* usually refers to moneys collected by the muhtesib from shopkeepers in anticipation of fines that they would surely have paid, a lawbook entitled *The Lawbook of the Gypsies in the Province of Rumelia* contains the following item: "The gypsies of Istanbul, Edirne, Plovdiv, and Sofia pay a fixed tax of one hundred akçes per month for each of their women who perform acts contrary to the sharia." These punishable acts seem to have been dancing and entertaining male audiences.[17] Evidently, it was quite conceivable to Gazali's audiences that a kadi too would collect protection money from a prostitute in the form of a kesim as a substitute for the fines usually exacted for sexual misbehavior. What the prostitute objects to in the story is, not the payment of the kesim, but being asked to pay a bribe on top of a bribe.

The historical record indicates that issues of prostitution (both male and female) and illicit intercourse (including rape) that come to the attention of the courts are only a tiny, visible sign of a much larger problem for local authorities all over Europe. A matter that pops up wherever we look during the Age of Beloveds is the problem of large populations of unmarried and underemployed young men. On the basis of a 1543 cadastral survey of villages in southeastern Anatolia, Leslie Peirce makes the following observations on a situation strikingly similar to what Beier describes for England and Rocke for Florence during much the same period:

> One marked aspect of family structure in [the villages of] Hiyam and Keret, as in the other more populous villages, was the large number of bachelors living with parents or elder brothers. In coming decades, the proportion of bachelors to married men would rise dramatically in Hiyam and Keret. Because marriage was essential to achieving adult social identity, these bachelors most likely remained unwed not out of choice but rather because they encountered economic or social obstacles to forming their own households. Young men may have found it difficult to accrue the resources necessary for establishing a marital household, particularly if the

growth of population outstripped the capacity of the village to provide full employment. An influx of younger men into the village may also have created a gender imbalance that would make it difficult for a young man, particularly a newcomer to the local society, to find a bride locally.[18]

In places with large populations of young men at their most libidinous, there must have been tremendous sexual pressure on society as a whole. This represented a quandary for those charged with keeping public order. Official responses typically had two faces, each of which contradicted the other in significant respects. On the one hand, at the urging of religious authorities, who perceived a need to define strict limits, new laws were promulgated, carrying increasingly harsh punishments for sexual misbehavior, and increased attention was devoted to the policing of sexual activities.[19] On the other hand, there is copious evidence that both secular and religious authorities recognized that tightening the lid would only increase pressure to the bursting point, with serious consequences for women, families, and public tranquillity. Thus, the theoretical legal crackdown was accompanied by a pragmatic tolerance of activities that provided (relatively) controlled outlets for the sexual desires of young men.

For example, in Florence, the duke Cosimo I de' Medici, apparently in response to an earthquake and a lightning strike on the cathedral, promulgated an unusually harsh law against sodomy in 1542. Although there followed a flurry of condemnations of sodomy in the 1540s, subsequent decades saw a falling off to negligible levels after the 1550s. One eighteenth-century historian attributed the decline to the severe social disruption that prosecution caused and the economic consequences of an exodus by citizens and artisans.[20] Venice, which considered itself the godliest of cities, made prostitution a municipal enterprise, collecting taxes from its practitioners and regulating them down to the clothes they could wear.[21] Sodomy was also, according to Priuli, rampant in Venice, where it was tolerated at least among the elites, while, in Florence, the authorities attempted to deflect young men's interests away from sodomy by importing prostitutes from Northern Europe and instituting prostitution as a municipal project.[22]

Lacking any even remotely adequate general study of sexual practices and the law in the Ottoman Empire, we have been able only to point quite tentatively to scattered sources that suggest Ottoman attitudes. The official attention given to suppressing prostitution and drinking in urban centers during the latter half of the sixteenth century would seem to indicate that these were common problems. In a 1567 decree, Sultan Selim II ordered that the millet-beer (*boza*) halls, wine shops, and houses of prostitution in the district of Eyüp be closed. The decree contained the following language:

> I have commanded that the quarters in the aforementioned town [Eyüp] be diligently and exhaustively inspected, that the drinking of wine and brewing of Tatar beer [i.e., boza] be prohibited, that, if there are prostitutes in [the quarter's] rooms, they should be expelled, and that those who commit immoral acts should receive their just deserts according to the noble sharia; therefore, when this order arrives, let the imams, the muezzins, and the *kethuda* [bailiffs] of the quarters thenceforth be warned that, as this order requires, they should give continuing priority to this matter, they should restrain those who drink wine or brew Tatar beer, and they should arrest those prostitutes they discover so that from this day forth in [these] quarters no one be tolerant of immoral persons, prostitutes, and beer-makers, so that [such people] be opposed and driven out, and so that those who are not restrained [from doing these things] be reported to the proper authorities.[23]

However, it appears that, when houses of prostitution were closed, some women simply added sex to other services provided to unattached young men.

Shortly thereafter came the 1570 decree directed at women who took in washing, including that of men who did not live with their families or who lived in bachelors' quarters and had no women to wash clothes for them. Many public institutions in the Ottoman Empire were supported by endowments, under the terms of which buildings, markets, and other income-producing properties were administered to benefit a mosque, or a hospital, or a soup kitchen, or an educational institution. This particular decree targeted administrators of pious endowments renting space to women who were ostensibly taking in washing but were also (at least suspected of) engaging in prostitution on the side:

DECREE TO THE KADI OF ISTANBUL:

> Because it has been reported that washerwomen have appeared in some shops in the aforementioned city and that some unattached young men go to the shops for that reason and are the source of ever-so-many depravities, I have ordered and commanded that from now on that [kind of] washerwoman should not be found in shops and should be suppressed; therefore, on the arrival [of this decree], let it summon the administrators of both sultanic and common endowments found in the aforementioned city and strenuously warn each of them accordingly, [saying] that, if there are washerwomen in these endowed properties, they should be expelled immediately and that, henceforth, shops should not be given out to women.[24]

As does Selim's 1567 decree, this one concludes with strict admonitions to the endowment officials and warnings that they could face punishment if washerwomen are again found in possession of their shops.

Among the legal decisions of the great jurist Ebu's-su'ud is a similar case involving the coffeehouses that sprang up as an alternative to the legally vulnerable wine shops and boza breweries (note in particular the shift in objects of sexual desire mentioned in this case):

ISSUE:

> If it so happens that, although his lordship, the monarch, refuge of the faith (shadow of God on earth), has time after time [ordered] the prohibition of coffeehouses, they are [still] not prohibited and some people of the hooligan sort, in order to make a living, keep coffeehouses, take on beardless apprentice boys in order to warm their gatherings, organize and set up entertainments and amusements such as chess and backgammon, gather those of the city who are addicted to love together with [beloveds] of pure, shining faces and evil deeds, eat electuaries of *bersh* [a combination drug], opium, and hashish, and, on top of this, drink coffee, occupy themselves with the duplicitous arts, and also neglect the prescribed prayers, what is the canonical thing to do to the kadi who is in a position to prohibit and eradicate the aforementioned merchants and coffee drinkers?

RESPONSE:

> Those who engage in or abet the aforementioned unseemly [activities] should be prohibited and restrained by [means of] severe punishment and long imprisonment. Kadis who go easy in their chiding [of these] must be dismissed from their posts.[25]

The impression that we get is one of a situation in which the authorities apply pressure in one area—say, wine shops and boza breweries—and something similar—a coffeehouse serving drugs, for example—pops up in another. Prostitutes are driven out, only to be replaced by beautiful boys. Although there was obviously concern on the part of the legal authorities for the sexual exploitation of young boys, young men and boys were far more common in public roles than were women, and they were subject to far less public scrutiny.

As we have mentioned in several places above, boys served as apprentices in various trades, waited on customers in taverns and coffeehouses, cared for men's needs in public baths, and accompanied armies on campaign. This made them widely available as objects of romantic desire and as companions in romantic liaisons. Mustafa 'Ali's *Etiquette* describes several venues in which beautiful boys were used to attract customers. There were wine shops where "wine-loving men of substance who are woman chasers and lovers of boys come sometimes with their beloveds" and certain public squares where lower-class men work as acrobats, tricksters, jugglers, and *kasebaz*, the latter being known for their sweet voices and mastery of song, entertainers who "dress up in colorful clothing bewitching monarchs of popularity and exceptional youths with silver countenances and camphor-candle-like necks set off by golden rings." These beauties were sent out to work the crowd, where, with their fetching ways, they "bring ever so many masters of asceticism and hypocrisy to the neighborhood of disaster" and "make avid pederasts out of men who never [before] in their lives were attracted to a beloved."[26]

When the poet Gazali built his famous mosque complex with bathhouse (later destroyed by Ibrahim Pasha; see chapter 8 above) in the suburb of Beşiktaş, one of the first things he did was to fill the place with beautiful bath boys to entice and entertain bathers. Among the buildings he planned was a dervish retreat (zaviye), and his choice for master of the zaviye's dervishes came with a special bonus:

> He made an ecstatic dervish named Ateşi [the Fiery] master of the zaviye. [This dervish] had a smooth-faced son called Memi Şah, and whoever saw him would involuntarily become an 'Alevi.[a] Birader became a moth to the flame of his beauty, a ruin [concealing] the [buried] treasure of love for him, and a madman in the chains of his twisted locks. And so, sickened by loving him, he made the flame of his beauty a candle by his pillow. First of all, he finished the bathhouse and staffed it with bath boys each of whose bodies was a silver cypress. Because it had a pool, he named it "The Spa." Ateşi's son [Memi Şah] he set up as the [love] idol of the gathering; he [then] made himself the bathkeeper and so took his ease. The beloveds of Istanbul streamed to that bath from all directions, and the lovers came, burning hotly in fires of separation [from their beloveds], and in that bath they enflamed the wild horses of their hasty desire in the waters of lust. The most elegant of both noble and common, when they failed to find room [in the bath], climbed up on the roof and looked on through the windows. Birader filled casks with silver bullion; the [other] bathhouse keepers, [overcome] by desire, put on bath towels [and joined in], and the bath boys stuffed their purses.[27]

---

[a] *'Alevi* refers to those dervishes who are devotees of Muhammad's son-in-law 'Ali, but *'alev* means "fire," so *'Alevi* could also mean "one who is burning [with passion]."

Although the beautiful boys were at the foundation of Gazali's short-lived success as a bathhouse proprietor, the authorities, at least occasionally, took a much dimmer view of the boys in some bathhouses. The following is from an order sent to the kadis of Bursa in the name of the sultan:

> I [previously] issued a decree that smooth-cheeked young men should not be in the bathhouses in order that nothing contrary to the sharia might issue from them. It has recently come to my attention that there are again boys in some bathhouses and [that] they are engaged in all manner of [morally] disruptive activities. Therefore, I have sent the conveyor of royal commands, 'Amr Aga, in order to decree that each of you should see to the inspection of the bathhouses under his jurisdiction and that, if such boys are found [therein], they should be chastised; you should take care in this regard to manage this [situation] and to reprimand the vile youths. . . . Cemadi I, [890 A.H. [1585–86 C.E.].[28]

There is an apparent ambivalence in the official tolerance of high-level administrators for establishments like Gazali's. What the record seems to indicate, however, is that the authorities—at least some of whom were customers and social intimates of Gazali's, as they were of other highly placed bathhouse owners—were inclined to tolerate the sexual subculture of the bathhouses until direct complaints and moral outrage on the part of local residents forced them to act. In telling the story of Gazali's bath, 'Aşık adduces a wonderfully complex cluster of possible reasons for its destruction by Ibrahim Pasha: the pasha was angry at Gazali for a couplet intimating that he was dominated by his beloved and the accompanying suggestion that he himself dominated the sultan; the bath was so popular that it caused an economic crisis for other bathhouse owners, reducing the income of some important people, and throwing a number of people out of work; the other bathhouse owners complained (hypocritically) to the pasha that Gazali's bathhouse was a hotbed of immorality.[29] We must note, however, that 'Aşık's tale is told by one member of the intellectual elite about another. There is no suggestion that the love behavior at Gazali's bathhouse is actually immoral in 'Aşık's eyes. For reasons we will take up in more detail below, the charge of immorality is seen as no more than a pretext for the acting out of personal enmities, either Ibrahim Pasha's or the bathhouse owners'.

In general, the availability of beardless youths as objects of desire rose to the level of a public, legal problem only when it led to rape and other forms of sexual assault or when it was seen as subverting the moral character of society. There are in the legal literature a number of cases involving boys or youths being raped. Take, for example, this opinion by Ebu's-su'ud:

ISSUE:

> If Zeyd confirms that Bekr—God preserve us!—committed the act of the people of Lot [sodomy] on his [Zeyd's] beardless son, 'Amr, what should be done to Bekr?

RESPONSE:

> If he [Bekr] is a proved transgressor, it is canonically lawful to execute him with the permission of the imam. Determining whether he is an upright, [married] citizen is not necessary, just as in the case of zina.[30]

What is noteworthy about this decision is that the rape of a boy is not treated as one of the hadd crimes (crimes punished as a claim of God). The case is tried by a magistrate (a kadi), the decision is approved by the local religious leader (the imam), and the punishment is by siyaset, or severe corporal punishment (including capital punishment), carried out by the civil authority. Although this may have been an accepted procedure, the more common procedure seems to have been the imposition of a fine. Leslie Peirce points out that the Law Code of Süleyman required a cuckold tax on men whose wives were involved in adultery and punishment for fathers whose young sons yielded to pederasts.[31] There is also evidence that, in certain instances, punishment in cases of sexual assault was at the discretion of a local administrative authority. One example of such a case is found in the popular story of a poet who went by the pen name Sihri. The story is found in the biographies of both 'Aşık and 'Ali and goes like this (in 'Ali's version):

> He [Sihri] was of the class of city boys from Istanbul. He was widely known by the name of Kız Memi [Mehmet the Girl]. In connection with his having joined the ranks of the eunuchs when he had arrived at graying middle age, he was also referred to as Sihri-i Bi-haya [Sihri the Shameless]. He was a fellow of the scribal service, a composer of chronograms, a beloved of elegant tyranny, and much given to romance. When he went with Sirozi Hasan Çelebi to Aleppo, Sihri served as secretary of the Horse Bazaar. He thought that he could mount any animal he got behind and so one day took a beardless youth to his rooms. All through the night, he gave the youth abundantly to eat and drink, until finally he caused [the boy] to pass out. The next day the youth awoke sleepy headed and hung over. He found the tie of his *shalvar* [pants] broken and his shirt and underwear torn. The devout Muslims from among his relatives went to the council meeting of Kubad Pasha, the beylerbey [governor general, lit. "lord of lords"] of Allepo. They complained that Sihri had defiled this young man. It so happened that there had been a long-standing enmity between the pasha

and the defterdar [i.e., the finance minister, Sirozi Hasan] and [the pasha] longed to punish and humiliate [the defterdar's] adherents. He who lacks the power to beat the donkey beats the saddle. So he brought in the Secretary of the Horse Bazaar, the wretched Sihri, and pruned his testicles, making a public spectacle of him.[32]

Again, we have a member of the poet class writing about another poet. Even though Kubad Pasha acts in response to a complaint by upright Muslims, the implication is that there is no real crime here, that Sihri would not have been punished had there been no grudge on the part of the beylerbey. Underlying this reluctance to condemn are significant class differences inscribed on the legal system and the resulting perceptions of relations between social class and permissible behavior. Formal learning was, in the Ottoman Empire, religious learning, in large part because Islamic law was religious law—in the sense that even laws promulgated by the monarch were subject to review by learned interpreters of the sharia. Ultimately, this meant that the learned class was accorded great respect in the eyes of the law, in large part because the interpreters of the law were also members of the learned class and were not shy about defending it against the claims of other powerful groups. (For example, Heyd points out that, out of respect for the religion, the ulema were subject to neither siyaset nor taʿzir: if they were convicted of a crime that called for punishment by siyaset, they were subject only to dismissal from office; if they were convicted of a crime that called for punishment by taʿzir, they were subject to no more than a stern reprimand.)[33]

Colin Imber cites a fascinating legal decision by Ebu's-suʿud that gives some insight into the ulema defense of its own claims. He translates the decision as follows:

> Zeyd is a man of learning. He is betrothed to the Muslim Hind, the daughter of ʿAmr, and sends some of the advance dower. Before they are married, can ʿAmr, with her consent, give Hind not to Zeyd, but to the wealthy Bekr?

ANSWER:

> It is unworthy of a Muslim that they should prefer anyone to a man of learning.

And there was a follow-up question intended to determine how far this might apply:

IN WHICH CASE:

> What in law should happen to ʿAmr when he prefers the said Bekr on the grounds that Zeyd is poor?

Love, Law, and Religion 287

ANSWER:

> Zeyd's learning is better than 'Amr's worldly goods. He should prefer learning.[34]

The opinion is straightforward: 'Amr's action is technically legal but reprehensible because it does not recognize the superiority of learning and the learned classes. This decision, and the attitude that it implies, is a significant indication of a more general pragmatic principle that might seem strange to us today (although, perhaps, it should not). In early-modern times, the law is not conceived of as applying equally to all classes of people; the lower the class, the less discretion was allowed in behavior, and the more dangerous misbehavior was considered. The educated and aware classes were accorded more leeway, in part because, as superior people, they could be expected to have better reasons for their actions and their private behaviors would have little chance to disrupt the peace and tranquillity of the masses. Because formal learning was religious learning, respect for the learned derived—in theory at least—from respect for their subject matter: Holy Writ and canon law. Because many of the poets were also trained in the sharia, the literary community took pains to suggest in their verses that religious learning and literary learning were equivalent and worthy of the same special status.[35] And this is not just an Ottoman belief. We already saw Cellini make much this same claim in his autobiography when he quotes the pope as excusing the murder of Pompeo by saying: "Men like Benvenuto, who are unique as far as their art is concerned, are not to be subjected to the law—especially not him, for I know what good cause he had." The intimation here is that the highest religious authority grants special status to artistic talent because art is in some way divinely inspired and intended for the greater glory of God.

PART 2: LOVE, THE BELOVED, AND RELIGION

The subject of the authority of religious learning and the respect paid to its possessors in the Ottoman Empire leads us into what is, for us, the most difficult and perilous area of our investigation. Any discussion of religious matters is rife with possibilities for misunderstanding and giving offense. When religion and carnal or worldly love are brought together in the same discussion, the possibilities only multiply. For this reason, we want to be exceptionally clear about the boundaries and limits of what we intend to do in what follows. First of all, our primary topic is neither religion (Christianity, Judaism, or Islam) nor religious poetry, *except* where religion and religious poetry (including spiritual, mystical, Neoplatonic poetry) overlap with actual beloveds and worldly love. There is a large body of work on the spiritual dimension of Perso-Ottoman poetry, and we do not aim either to expand on it or to summarize it (except in passing). In addition, we are aware that some very knowledgeable people sincerely believe that there is no such area of overlap, that spiritual poetry from Dante to the Ottoman Sufis has no significant relation to worldly love. While we respect their opinions, we do not share them, and we hope that our arguments will be understood as referring to but one aspect of the historical practice and interpretation of religion by human beings and not as an assault on the fundamental beliefs of any of the religions we touch on. Just as the application of divine law to the practicalities of life in early-modern times demanded all manner of compromises, interpretations, negotiations, decisions, contestations, and struggles for authority, so is the area where spiritual and mundane love overlap an irresolvably messy, complex, and contested place, one where, as we will argue, the erotic generates emotional power and immediacy within people's quests for spiritual authenticity and connection to the divine.

The Spirituality of Love

If the subject matter of this chapter had to be reduced to a few lines of verse, the following from Sidney's *Astrophel and Stella* would do quite well:

> And not content to be Perfection's heire
> Thy selfe, doest strive all minds that way to move,
> Who marke in thee what is in thee most faire.
> So while thy beautie drawes the heart to love,
>   As fast thy Vertue bends that love to good:
>   "But ah," Desire still cries, "give me some food."[36]

Here we find the spirituality of the beloved in the Age of Beloveds stripped down to its barest essentials: The beloved is perfection; perfection is beauty. This perfection is the legacy and image of divine perfection. The beloved's (perfect) beauty draws people to love perfection. The beloved's virtue (resistance to carnal desire) turns the lover from carnal desire to a purified love of (divine) goodness.[37]

But, the poet says—and the domain of this *but* is the proper topic of this chapter—desire still seeks its food. The notion of food brings us back to the body, to the quintessentially bodily functions of ingestion, digestion, and elimination, suggesting the other primary bodily function: reproduction. Human love cannot be wholly spiritualized because it can exist only in a body and the body has its own imperatives, its own needs. Among the famous ascetics of Islam, one (Juneyd) preceded Sydney in saying, "I need sex the way I need food," by which he affirms the idea in the hadith that one cannot lead a wholesome and godly life if one's mind is always on sex.[38] Hosts of early-modern poets, from London to Istanbul, have preserved, in their verses, the notion that spiritual love alone, spiritual desire ungrounded in worldly, bodily love, is starved and thirsty.

It is a more recent, post-Enlightenment consciousness that sees a clear demarcation between spiritual and physical desire and passion and finds hypocrisy in the sexual activities of divines, religious leaders, theologians, monks, and nuns. For Ottoman poets, hypocrisy was the ascetic's—any kind of ascetic's—denial of the body and insistence that there could be spiritual love and intoxication without an actual beloved and a cup of wine. Real (hakkiki) love may be love of the divine or passionate desire for return to the primal unity of all existence, but such a love is not accessible to humans except via the bridge of metaphoric (mecazi) love, love of beauty manifested in a very physical, this-worldly beloved. Physical love is justifiable, even laudable, when its metaphoric character is recognized. And this is not just an Ottoman belief. Remember Michelangelo on a beloved boy:[39]

> Not true that it's always grim with mortal sin,
> this love for a ravishing beauty here on earth,
> as long as it melts the hard heart, shows its worth
> as a target for divine love's arrowhead.

In the introduction to her 1547 *Dialogo della infinità d'amore* (Dialogue on the infinity of love), the courtesan poet Tullia d'Aragona (speaking in the voice of her Tullia character) says:

> Leaving all possible subdivision aside, let me say that love is of two types. We shall call the first "vulgar" or "dishonest" love, the other "honest," that is to say, virtuous. Dishonest love—which is found only in vulgar and low-minded individuals, that is, in those whose souls are low and vile, who lack virtue or refinement, whether they come from noble or insignificant stock—is generated by a desire to enjoy the object that is loved, and its goal is none other than that of common animals. They simply want to obtain pleasure and to procreate something that resembles themselves, without any further thought or concern. . . .
> Honest love, which is characteristic of noble people, people who have a refined and virtuous disposition, whether they be rich or poor, is not generated by desire, like the other, but by reason. It has as its main goal the transformation of oneself into the object of one's love, with a desire that the loved one be converted into oneself, so that the two may become one

or four.... And as this transformation can only take place on a spiritual plane, so in this kind of love, the principal part is played by the "spiritual" senses, those of sight and hearing and, above all, because it is closest to the spiritual, the imagination. But, in truth, as it is the lover's wish to achieve a corporeal union besides the spiritual one, in order to effect a total identification with the beloved, and since this corporeal unity can never be attained, because it is not possible for human bodies to be physically merged into one another, the lover can never achieve this longing of his and so will never satisfy his desire.[40]

Tullia's arguments are, for the most part, commonplaces of late-Renaissance love theory and found in a number of similar dialogues on love—most prominently Leone Ebreo's *Dialoghi d'amore* and Pietro Bembo's *Gli asolani*—that incorporate Ficino's influential theory of Platonic love as expounded in his commentaries on the *Symposium*. However, it is worth noting one of the distinctions made by the Tullia character, a distinction between the acts of vulgar and noble individuals according to which natural, animal acts can be transformed into spiritual experiences and acts that would be reprehensible in most circumstances are made praiseworthy. Thus, it is possible for love, even love expressed physically, to be a different thing for a certain group, a group that shares an intellectualized and spiritualized interpretation of emotional and sensual experience. The notion of an emotional/intellectual elite, which we mentioned above, is borne out by the actual Tullia's experience. When she was accused by the Florentine authorities of failing to obey the sumptuary laws, which required courtesans to wear a yellow wrap, the duke Cosimo suggested that she be "exonerated in consideration of her being a poet," and the compliant authorities exempted her from the law on the grounds of her "rare knowledge of philosophy and poetry."[41]

To us, there seems to be a touch of irony in the dialogue's Neoplatonism. When the fictional Tullia's interlocutor, Varchi, demurs at her contention that love of youths is reprehensible and argues that Socrates and Plato, for example, "did not love them [youths] the way that people commonly interpret" and were interested, not in sexual (penetrative) activity, but in generating "beautiful souls," we cannot quite forget—as none of Tullia's readers could have forgotten—that the real Benedetto Varchi was widely suspected of having sexual relations with his young (male) students and was arrested in 1545 for raping one of them.[42] In a way, this parallels the case of Tullia herself, who makes her living in large part by satisfying the physical, sexual (vulgar) desires of her customers while taking on the role of a beloved with all the talents and attractions that an ideal beloved should have.[43]

We say *to us* because this is an irony and an appearance of hypocrisy that would, we believe, be lost on many early-modern elites. It appears that, among the intellectual elites, Ottoman and European alike, many held the sincere conviction—and we would hesitate to say who was sincere and who was not—that the moral quality of sex acts depended entirely on their motivation and the perspective from which they were interpreted. A Varchi could see himself as being attracted to beauty in a youth, and, because beauty was the outward image of the good, he could, therefore, understand himself as being attracted to the good and desirous of uniting with it—hardly a reprehensible act. As for the courtesan, she is engaged in making a living in one of the few ways open to her. Her behavior is pragmatic and amoral; a lover's behavior is vulgar or spiritual depending on his own spiritual state. In neither case, however, is the physical aspect of love, even of honest, spiritual love, denied or censured. As Rinaldina Russell points out, by the time of Tullia's *Dialogue*, there were already several treatises on love that argued for the natural necessity of an actual beloved and actual sensual fulfillment.[44]

Arguably, the master trope of Ottoman poetry is the notion expressed by the Tullia character: that, in addition to spiritual union, honest love seeks a corporeal union that can never be achieved and, consequently, brings with it an inevitable separation, longing, and profound melancholy. If there is a point at which Ottoman and European, Hafezan and Petrarchan love intersect completely, it is in the taste for melancholy as a dominant theme. We are not the only ones to have noticed this. For example, in discussing Wyatt's lyrics, Stephen Greenblatt mentions in passing that "melancholy was fashionable in the late sixteenth century," going on to say: "In the absence of a fully articulated celebration of married love, in a cultural milieu dominated by a ruthless despot and pervaded by intrigue and envy, it may not surprise us that court entertainments habitually express disillusionment, frustration, menace, hostility to the very women who are courted, and craving for a security that erotic love cannot offer."[45]

With the possible substitution of *beloved boys* for *women*, this passage could as well have been describing the culture of Ottoman courtiers. For the Ottoman, what gives the melancholy born of this situation a direction and a vocation is a context in which the beloved of this world has, as an underlying reality, a divine beloved who promises absorption into the universal unity beyond the multiplicities of this material world. As the poet says:

> Loving you the heart gave up its life and went into exile
> It found no peace in multiplicity and passed into unity[46]

Thus, the lover's melancholy is naturalized as an appropriate response to the swarm of painful separations—from beloved, patron, wealth, power, security, etc.—that living in this world entails. The poet says with a very conventional anguish, an anguish no less deep or heartfelt for all its conventionality:

> Since God exiled me from your light, oh moon face
> Today in earth and heaven for me there is no place
>
> Beloved, the cup of separation is a thousand times
>   more bitter than death
> Yet better a thousand times dead than exiled once
>   from your door[47]

We must remember that, for the early moderns, this world was *essentially* and incorrigibly confusing. As Baki, a prominent jurist and scholar granted the title "Sultan of Poets" during the reign of Süleyman, put it:

> The people of this world have always been
>   a muddle
> Some laugh, some weep, and some
>   just wail
>
> Some of them nightingales moaning
>   for the beloved's cheek
> Some of them moths to the candle of
>   the beloved's face
>
> In the end, monarch and mendicant
>   are alike
> Trampled beneath the hooves of fate's
>   camel wheel
>
> To some this world is a pavilion
>   of sweet delights
> To some a prison of terrible
>   torment
>
> Oh Baki, in the mystics' retreat of this
>   perplexing world
> Everyone who arrives is bewildered
>   by this secret[b,48]

---

[b] The word for "secret" here is *esrār* (lit. "secrets"), which also has the sense "opium, opiate." This gives a second meaning: the attempt to understand this world is like a drug in that it befuddles people and makes them incapable of seeing the spiritual truth, the real reality.

There is no sense here, just people doing every which thing, ruled by a fate that is as blind, capricious, and dangerous as a berserk camel. Only the links binding this world to a consistent, meaningful, and unary elsewhere make real sense. The power of the poem, then, and the power of sexual desire, lies in the transference made from this beloved (on earth) to the other (spiritual) beloved. The hotter and more hyperbolic the desire, the more the accretions of this world are burned away. Love in the world always intersects with religion.

Ottoman Spirituality and Love Poetry

We do not have to go far into Ottoman poetry to find points at which religious spirituality and sexuality intertwine. For example, Zati, whom we have seen extolling very real beloveds both for his own amusement and and for profit (as a ghostwriter), has the following striking gazel about a beloved, adorned with the rhetorical complexity (which translation is helpless to transmit) and sparkling hyperbole that mark Ottoman love lyrics:

> When that moon raised the veil from the sunshine
>   of his beauty
> He filled eighteen thousand worlds[c] end to end with
>   light
>
> You would think his brothers had abandoned Joseph[d]
>   in the pit
> But he only sank into the earth, put to shame when he saw
>   that moon face
>
> Top to bottom these nine spheres dance with love
>   for him
> The earth lies there, drunk on the wine of passion
>   for him
>
> Whenever they begin to read from a chapter in the book
>   of his beauty

[c] In the popular imagination, the whole of creation consists of eighteen thousand worlds. The number is arrived at by adding together the "universal intelligence" (the active principle, ʿakl-i küll), the "universal soul" (the passive principle, nefs-i küll), the nine spheres of the heavens, the four elements (air, earth, fire, water), and the three states of matter born of the four elements (animal, vegetable, mineral, al-mawālidu'th-thalatha) for a total of eighteen and then multiplying them by the "infinite" number, one thousand (see Şentürk, Antoloji, 237).

[d] In traditional Islamic lore, Joseph (Yusuf) is the most beautiful of all humans.

Roses bloom, and grief is shut off from those who
> hear it

God! May Zati rise with him at the gathering of souls
> on the Last Day
Let him be risen in joy and spared the torments
> of hell[49]

This gazel is included in a magnificent anthology compiled with copious illustrations and detailed notes by Atillâ Şentürk, one of the most knowledgeable explicators of Ottoman poetry in our day.[50] Şentürk mentions that it was not unusual for Ottoman poets to make the first poem in each rhyme-letter section of the subgroup of gazels (for this is how Ottoman divans were customarily divided, by genre, then by the last letter of the rhyme) a love poem in praise of God or the Prophet. He goes on to say that Zati's love poem is one such. He also points out that this would be easy to miss and draws our attention to the fact that the metaphors and images used to describe the Prophet are in this case (as in most others) no different than those used for ordinary, very worldly beloveds. For example:

They say of love: the heart one day fell prisoner to a king
Whose command held sway in eighteen thousand worlds

Did you see the moon and sun? Well, in the banquet of your beauty
The spheres of heaven took two tambourines in hand and danced

The boy's beard does not write out the book of your beauty without reason
To fix a reading it writes commentary on the margins of the holy text[e, 51]

Most often, in the end, we cannot know, and are not meant to know, whether a poem is secular or religious. We continually find ourselves poised on the cusp of an ambiguity, not because the early moderns loved ambiguity—which they did—but because they did not see a clear separation between the religious and the secular. Hayali, the mystic, courtier, and lover (of women and boys), has two poems that begin with very similar images and then head off in quite different directions. The first is as follows:

The beloved is known to return affection
> with malice
His art and custom are to slay his lovers

---

[e] Here, the face is compared to a copy (*mushaf*) of the Qur'an and the dark, soft down of the early adolescent to commentary, written in tiny cursive in the margins, with the intent of determining the correct voweling of the Arabic script.

Let love for his boy's beard make ambergris
    seek exile
Let the musk bag of China be the poor, scented
    lover of his curl

Let the new moon bow before his two
    crescents
Let the Pleiades for him be made of moles
    on his lunar cheek

If the puritan of the town pass without seeing
    his curl and cheek
I fear he will have got neither religion nor
    belief

Oh Hayali, I hope the Lord of Rum
    will again approve
This poem in the lovely style of Hasan[52]

From an image of the cruel and dangerous beloved, the poem moves to a series of descriptive hyperboles: the beloved's hair is sweeter smelling than ambergris; it turns the source of musk—the black dried scent gland of the Asian deer—into another destitute and helpless lover; the very heavens are put to shame by the beloved's beauty, which resembles and outshines theirs. Then the poem moves abruptly—in Ottoman poems, most transitions between couplets seem abrupt—to a matter in which the Ottoman elites did see a clear separation. The *zahid*, here translated as "puritan," represents the precisian, who devoutly follows the outward, apparent (*zahir*) rules and admonitions of Islam. The precisian contrasts at every point with the lover, who follows the inner, esoteric (*batin*), hyperreal rules of Islam conceived as the religion of love. We need to be clear here: The zahid does not deny spiritual love, the love of God or divine unity. What he does deny is the absolute necessity of the *actual* beloved, the need for enlisting primal, sexual passions in the service of enlightenment. Without an actual beloved, the zahid never sees beyond the surface to the true (esoteric) meaning of religion and belief.

Although we might be tempted to interpret this poem as taking a religious or spiritualizing turn at this point, it is, in fact, doing quite the opposite. It returns us to the actual, this-worldly beloved. The final "signature" (*tahallus*) couplet despiritualizes the poem even further by surfacing the poet's role as courtier and poet. The second hemistich contains plays on the words *husrev*, which can mean either "lord or sultan" (as in our translation) or the name of a famous Persian poet (Husrev of Delhi), and *hasen*, which either means "lovely" or references the name of Muhammed's panegyrist (Hasan ibn Thabit). Thus, the line can have a range of senses, from "I hope that a poet as famous as Husrev would approve my verses, which are like those of Hasan, Muhammad's favorite poet," to "I hope that the Ottoman sultan [Süleyman] will approve my lovely poem." The "Lord of Rum" here is the sultan, the beloved as ultimate patron.

It seems likely that the resistance of elite Islamic mysticism to entirely spiritualizing the beloved and relations with the beloved stems from a significant difference between Islam and Christianity. For Christianity, the divine was "made flesh" in the person of Jesus, who is uniquely a bridge between the material and the spiritual realms. Love for Jesus is unmediated love for God. It does not need to pass through an actual beloved. Although this is a bit simplistic—Christian mysticism is replete with stories of mundane beloveds (Héloïse and Abélard, Tristram and Iseult)—it highlights a contrast with Islam in which the divine is never made flesh, is "neither born nor gives birth" (Qur'an 112:3). The ultimate this-worldly beloved is Muhammad, who is special but fully human, holy but not divine. Muhammad has a human presence; his activities are exemplars for the devout to emulate, but they are human activities. He eats and sleeps, is angry and joyous; he lives in the world, loves in the world, and is a sexual person. From one perspective, he is the pinnacle of a series of worldly beloveds ascending from the beloved boy or woman to the patron or mystical master to the sultan-caliph (shadow of God on earth).

Hayali's second poem takes us in a quite different direction from a starting point in the same cruel and murderous beloved:

> The art of the beloved's eye is first to please
>   and then to rage
> Oh heart, beware, else that tyrant glance
>   will run you through
>
> In the gathering of the select we are laid
>   waste by a wine
> That makes this world's vintage seem but
>   vile dregs to spill
>
> Ah burn scar! When my heart cooks on a luckless
>   night in flames of woe,
> That sleeper in bathhouse ashes could pass
>   for a candle
>
> This world constructed of mud
>   is an eternal bridge

> Over which pass soldier and captain,
> > destitute and well-to-do
>
> That he might rub his face in the dirt at the feet
> > of the adepts
> Hayali has spent years in the dust at the
> > Gülşenis' door[53]

Although it begins with the beloved, this poem is a meditation on the mystical perspective. It references the two master tropes of the theosophical tradition: the beloved and wine. Just as there are two beloveds—in Tullia's terms, the beloved of vulgar love and the beloved of honest love, sexual pleasure as an end and sexual attraction as a bridge—so there are two wines and two intoxications. For the select, wine is the means to an intoxication that entails abandonment of ordinary rationality and mirrors the ecstasy of the lover-adept, in whom the cruelty of this world's beloved (the impossibility of physical union) has ignited a conflagration of desire that burns away all mundane attachments and makes possible reabsorption into the unity of all existence. This lover is no longer interested in this world and material attachments. He is become like the lowest of the low, the külhanbey, the homeless, impoverished young ruffian who sleeps in the ashes of the bathhouse. This identification with vagabonds and beggars is one of the commonplaces of the poetic tradition. As one decidedly well-off poet, Lamiʻi, said:

> We are such companions as are without fortune
> > and without woe
> Now ascetics and now drunks, as happy hooligans
> > we go
> For the wealth of this vile globe, we give
> > not a straw
> We're spendthrift rascals who freely squander
> > the coin of life[54]
> —Lamiʻi

Hayali ends his poem from the position of a mystic. First, he dismisses this world and all its distinctions. Then, where in the previous poem he returned in the signature couplet to the role of courtier-poet, in this poem he identifies himself as a follower of the Gülşeni dervishes, one of the more popular dervish orders among Ottoman intellectuals and bureaucratic elites during the Age of Beloveds and the one that the destitute young profligates Tayyib and Tahir were running off to join (see chapter 3).

The existence of a script (a generalized mystical, Neoplatonic script) that values passionate love done right or done in the correct interpretive context creates a high degree of ambivalence on the part of those responsible for maintaining public order and religiously prescribed morality. On the one hand, we see powerful, court-dependent elites and an artistic community supported by them indulging in the continuation and development of a spirituality of passionate love closely linked to a social culture of actual beloveds. On the other hand, we see, during the sixteenth century, increasing attempts to control public sexual (and love) behavior. Thus, in Florence, for example, we see initiatives by the authorities to limit and control both sodomy and prostitution at the same time as the court is striving to make the city a cultural center by supporting artists and intellectuals such as Cellini and Varchi, who were from time to time arrested for immoral (sodomitic) behavior.

The Ottoman poets constantly reference a generic, artistic mysticism (Sufism), nearly indistinguishable from the writings of full-time mystics, that looks beyond the surface meaning of Holy Writ and the Prophetic tradition (the bases of Islamic law and practice) toward esoteric meanings that affirm the transcendent values of love.[55] There is only a fuzzy and shifting line between what is acceptable and what is to be suppressed in acting out attachments to the physical, material referent for spiritual love (or the spiritual referent for physical love). In the following case, the mufti makes no bones about his condemnation of activities that a host of elite intellectuals, muftis among them, script and praise in their poet personae:

ISSUE:

> In the mosque of a dervish lodge, while various persons mingled with carnally desirable boys and praised God's unity with all sort of chants, changing the prayer of unity now to say "my heart" and then [to say] "my life," now reciting [the couplet] "You are a great sultan, the [spirit of] life among lives / When I saw you manifest, the portal [of life] was [no longer] hidden," and then [the couplet] "The paradise they call heaven is [only] a house with a few houris / Give it to those who desire it, you [alone] do I need . . . you," while they [thus] beat their breasts and engaged in all kinds of strange behaviors, if some persons from among the residents of the quarter asked Zeyd, master of the aforementioned dervish lodge, "Why do you allow and countenance this kind of behavior?" and Zeyd answered, "So what? God said, 'Verily I created humans and djinn that they might worship [me].'" What should be done to Zeyd according to the sharia?

RESPONSE:

> In addition to the behavior and speech being utter depravity, the evil words spoken about paradise are obvious blasphemy, [therefore] killing them would be permissible. The apostate who is their master, in addition to being an infidel because of his saying about the speech and actions reported [to us], "If they go on with this [sexual] behavior, so what?" is twice an infidel for considering those disgusting things to be a form of worship and citing a holy verse as proof of this. If he does not renounce this kind of worship, it is obligatory that he be executed.[56]

The "prayer of Unity" is the part of the witness that says, "La ilaha illa 'llah" (There is no God but God). The dervishes are saying, "There is no God but my heart [my beloved]," and by this identifying the beautiful boys as manifestations of the divine. This is reinforced by citing lines of poetry, including verses containing the commonplace assertion that the mystic no longer dreams of a future in paradise because "the people of the heart" have achieved a spiritual union with the divine all that transcends the fleshy (and, hence, merely metaphoric) pleasures of the paradise that "people of the surface interpretation" imagine. For a member of the educated classes to attack as "obvious blasphemy" beloved-centered (or tavern-centered) interpretations of common religious symbols, stories, and practices and rejections of the surface reading of Holy Writ is for him to pretend, at least, to ignore a major portion of the literary culture of his class.[57]

Such statements are everywhere in the poetry; there are very few love poems that do not contain one or several. For example, a poet of the learned classes says, quite unremarkably:

> If you take that lovely body of yours
>   into the place of prayer
> Though it be a feast day[f] for all others
>   it is the Last Day[g] for me
>
> My greatest fortune would be to sit happy
>   in the shade of your cypress
> Else, God knows, a bough from paradise's tree
>   is a rod to beat me with

---

[f] These are the *bayrams*, the religious feast days, most prominently the Feast of Sacrifice ('Īdu'l-adhā) and the Feast of Fast Ending ('Īdu'l-fitr) following Ramadan.

[g] The Day of Judgment, or, in Ottoman Turkish, the (day of) Kıyamet. *Kıyamet*, which means "rising," is derived from the same root as *kamet*, "stature, body": thus the common association of the beloved's body with the Day of Judgment.

Or (on the beloved's hair):

> Those two locks became a crown on the moon of loveliness
> One is the Night of Power and one the Eve of Ascension[h]

Or (quoting directly from the Qur'an):

> On your forehead, beneath your brows is writ:
>   "Say he is God the One"
> What a gracious gift and matchless beauty is
>   "God the Eternal and Absolute"[i]
>
> Oh cypress body, to mime your way of walking
>   here on earth
> Let Sidre[j] of the seventh heaven raise its head
>   a thousand times to the wheel[58]

There is an apparent contradiction in a situation that appears to indicate cultural tolerance of certain activities—for example, sexual relations with boys or with women outside marriage, wine drinking and tavern culture, and the linking of these to revered religious symbols—and, at the same time, occasions active official disapproval and widespread moral condemnation. This is similar to the situation in Renaissance England that troubled Alan Bray, who asked: "How are we to square the profound, the metaphysical fear of homosexuality they express with its complex elaboration throughout society in a variety of forms? How is it to be reconciled with the tacit acceptance of homosexuality in the household and educational system?"[59]

Bray assumes that European Christianity was unique in its theoretical intolerance of homoeroticism: "There was no civilisation in the world at that time with as violent an antipathy to homosexuality as that of western Europe."[60] While this may be so, it does not mean that Ottomans or Muslims in general were as tolerant as the prurient interest of Western travelers makes them out to be.[61] Undoubtedly, the old fallacy of comparing what "we" *believe* to what "they" *do*—our theory to their practice—plays a significant role here. Certainly, the mufti's response to dervish practices and official attempts to end sexual activity in bathhouses and taverns is an indication of violent disapproval by powerful societal factions. So from what perspective do we reconcile theoretical condemnation with practical acceptance?

---

[h] The Night of Power is the night of Muhammad's birth. The Eve of the Ascension is the night of the *mi'rac*, when Muhammad ascended to heaven on the steed Burak.

[i] The quotations here are from Qur'an 112:1–2, known as the Ihlas (Purity).

[j] The poet here says that the heavenly tree has to strain to the limits of the rotating heavenly spheres (the *eflāk*) in order to match the tall beauty of the beloved's body.

In approaching this issue, Bray makes a few telling points that we believe apply equally to the Ottoman situation. In theory, both the English and the Ottomans strongly disapproved of excessive or unusual sexual behaviors, classifying them with other kinds of debauchery, including, most often, drunkenness. (As we have seen, Islamic law has no separate category for unlawful sexual intercourse, including it with drinking wine and theft.) The English authorities may have been relatively more tolerant of the public sexual exploitation of women and the Ottomans of boys, but in neither case was the tolerance great. Furthermore, as we can see in both Bray's work and our own survey of Ottoman attitudes, what is actually done is not done, for the most part, by theoretical people whom we do not know; it is done by our families, friends, and neighbors in contexts that obscure relations to our theoretical moral concerns. In societies that were not heavily urbanized or, when urbanized, were highly compartmentalized, people had most of their contacts with people they knew quite well.[62] The apparent conflict between societal pressures and individual desire is resolved because, as Bray says, "the individual could simply avoid making the connection; he could keep at two opposite poles the social pressures bearing down on him and his own discordant sexual behaviour, and avoid recognising it for what it was."[63] In the same way, outright hypocrisy aside, a member of the Ottoman educated class could contextualize his sexual behavior and that of his intimate friends within a traditional, culturally supported interpretive framework that provided a consistent, fully elaborated alternative to the moral norms of society, to which he could also quite sincerely and wholeheartedly subscribe. Where the Renaissance European cultural elites could find a socially acceptable alternative to Christian morality scripted by the less-restrictive moral universe of the resurrected Greco-Roman ancients, their Ottoman equivalents had at hand the traditional moral universe of the Islamic mystics, whose metaphors had always been subject to materializing in behavior.[64]

Returning to the Ottoman mufti's legal opinion, we must take care to understand that not all mystical (dervish) practice was the same and had the same status. Dervish practices and beliefs permeated Ottoman society at all levels and, to some extent, provided a generalized script and vocabulary for charismatic, emotional religious experience that transcended class differences and facilitated the diffusion of elite cultural elements throughout society. But the manifestations of mysticism were many and varied, far too varied to encompass in a few paragraphs. The intellectual elites indulged in a generic Sufism (what might be called *the Islam of the poets*) and were commonly adherents of staid and thoughtful orders such as the Mevlevi—the order founded by Celalu'd-din Rumi—whose refined whirling dance contrasts starkly with the wilder ecstatic practices of other groups. Mehmet the

Conqueror's son and successor, Bayezit—popularly known as "Sufi Bayezit" —was attached to the Halveti dervishes, who were widely suspected of conniving to poison Mehmet and assure Bayezit's accession to the throne.[65] The various companies (*ocak*) of the janissary corps had Bektaşi adepts as their spiritual guides.[66] During the reign of Mehmet II, rural dervishes inspired a major populist revolution in Anatolia most often associated with the name of Shaykh Bedruddin—a revolution that continued to trouble Ottoman rulers into the sixteenth century, when Anatolian peasants were heavily propagandized by adherents of the Ottomans' most dangerous Muslim rival, the dervish-adept Shah Isma'il Safavi of Iran (r. 1501-24), known even to the Europeans as the Great Sufi. Extreme antinomian orders such as the Kalenderis attracted unattached young men who wandered the countryside dressed in bizarre outfits, rejecting all the outward forms of Islam, begging, and occasionally robbing fellow travelers.[67] Although the Age of Beloveds in the Ottoman empire, especially the reign of Süleyman, was a relatively good time for dervish orders—after all, Sufism is at its core the religion of the beloved— the latter part of the sixteenth century and the dawn of the seventeenth saw increasing hostility toward dervish practices on the part of the legal establishment and the followers of puritan religious reformers.

The intent of this sketch is to suggest some idea of how charismatic popular religion, cultural scripting, and conflicting desires for autonomy and control manifested in a generalized cult of the beloved that contained within itself many, if not all, of the tensions present in Ottoman society at large. It is precisely these tensions—between absolutism and antinomianism, between the practices of legally sanctioned religion and unorthodox, ecstatic, charismatic practices, between communalism and individual inwardness, between the order of marital sexuality and the disorder of extramarital, often homoerotic, sexuality, between the cultures of home and mosque and those of tavern and coffeehouse—that, we believe, power the renaissance of traditional Islamic culture under the Ottomans. In a time when large-scale economic, demographic, and perhaps even climatic trends (which we will suggest in the next chapter) inclined a number of societies toward an age of beloveds, the cult and culture of beloveds, including beautiful boys, public women, and their impassioned lovers, grounded a reinterpretation and revitalization of traditional Islamic literary symbolism in the Ottoman Empire. And it is in poetry that the Ottomans brought most closely together the seemingly antithetical areas of sexuality, religion, and worldly authority, transferring some of the hot emotional character of sexual desire to the experience of religion, and endowing sexual feelings with a transcendent spiritual dimension.

10

THE END OF AN AGE

In this chapter, we intend to draw together some truncated or broken threads of history and historical speculation that we have taken up in the previous discussion. When we began talking about an age, however heuristically and lightheartedly, we made or implied the claim that, in a certain period, there were significant characteristics of life common to certain classes of people inhabiting a broad area reaching at least from the central Ottoman lands to the British Isles. This is a huge claim, larger, in truth, than our study can possibly cover or our expertise comprehend. We make the claim nonetheless, in part because we see it as a challenge, and in part because we have good company. As Rifaʿat Abou-El-Haj says in a passage that we will echo in our own way: "Given the present dearth in knowledge, the Ottoman problems of the seventeenth century constitute too large a task to be tackled by a single researcher. At this stage of inquiry, the question that must be raised is simply why there were major social and economic upheavals at this particular time. Any attempt to explain these upheavals shows that they form part of a pattern, and that Ottomans and Europeans of the seventeenth century experienced comparable economic and political dislocations, which can be regarded as symptoms of a far-reaching transformation."[1]

The Socioeconomics of the Age of Beloveds

This chapter will be a sketch—a sketch of some historical currents whose outlines have not even been established. We will focus speculatively on a few of many economic, demographic, social, and political trends, and we will do so from a perspective that demands a brief introduction. History has traditionally been the history of the state, in large part because the state keeps the records on which later historians base their accounts and itself has a compelling interest in telling and promoting the story of its own continuity. Literary history, in turn, has traditionally been seen as a subset of this history of the state and has presumed a continuous history of organic change (growth, decline, health, disease) more or less parallel to that of the state. There are a number of things that follow inevitably from this kind of history, both general and literary, including: (a) the assumption that the state is an essential entity that persists over long periods and is not a superficial ideological and rhetorical construct whose apparent continuity or self-identity is used to mask profound discontinuities and changes in the distribution of power; (b) the parallel assumption that the meanings of words and symbols are similarly essential and persist over extended periods and that the apparent continuity of words and symbols does not mask profound changes in meaning; and (c) the assumption that the behaviors and desires of masses of people and the deployment of words and meanings do not profoundly affect the shape and behavior of the state.

A number of perceptive historians these days adopt a somewhat different perspective and arrive at different conclusions. Among other things, they argue that the state is constructed in large part by the descriptions of those who have a stake in the business of the state and, as such, have investments in telling the state's story in ways that further their own interests.[2] They also realize that the impact of the gross activities of the state (such things as war, economic policy, and taxation) on the daily lives of masses of people is mingled with issues such as love, and sexuality, and marriage, and families, and reproductive politics—the kind of issues that are mediated and scripted by art and literature. We will adopt from this perspective the premise that, because literary history relies on the self-descriptions and documents (i.e., poems etc.) of cultural communities, it can be seen to reflect low-level, local economic impacts and changes that may not be represented in the official documents of the state.[3] Obviously, it is beyond the reach of a single book to argue from a comprehensive overview of the state of the Ottoman Empire and Europe during the long sixteenth century, but we believe that it is possible to give a few examples in support of our main arguments.

A Point of Rupture

The title of this chapter is intended to focus attention on a period in the late sixteenth century, from approximately 1550 to 1622, in which contemporary historians locate the beginning or ending of a wide variety of significant events in Ottoman history, including (but not limited to) unrest among the peasants and revolts in Anatolia, economic crisis and price revolution, the transformation of Ottoman provincial government, expanded trade with Europe, the rise of Anatolian towns, the profound bureaucratic changes at the center recounted by Mustafa 'Ali and other Ottoman critics, religious revivalism, the roots of change in taxation practices and the power structure of government, and so on. We also want to draw attention to similar and equally profound changes and disruptions occurring in Western Europe at the same time. Our understanding of this period assumes that, from both the Ottoman and the Western European perspectives, this was a period of rupture during which a new intersection of trajectories in libidinal and economic investment becomes visible to observers—both contemporary, internal observers and present-day historians.[4] This is to say, from the viewpoint of this book, that the culture of love and the cult of the beloved peculiar to the long sixteenth century are affected by a multiplicity of nonliterary trends and events to which literary scripting, in turn, gives form and meaning. The issue faced by literary historians in comprehending this period requires first that we recognize and find ways to talk about a shift to a new plane of consistency among a vast number of microevents. Then we must assess the impact of that shift, not only on the lives and livelihoods of poets and the content of their poetry, but also on groups of people of all classes as they are affected by literary scripting.

In greater Europe (i.e., everything from Ottoman Eurasia to the British Isles), the transformative events of the latter part of the sixteenth century occurred in the context of cultural trends that peaked in the last decades of the fifteenth century and the early years of the sixteenth. Therefore, our Age of Beloveds covers the last decades of the late Renaissance and somewhat beyond. In its later decades, it represents the momentum of Renaissance culture carrying a residue forward into a post-Renaissance age.[5] In the Ottoman Empire, contemporary observers often trace the roots of change in the situation of poets and society in general back to the death of Ibrahim Pasha, the Favorite and the Slain, in 1536. They intimate that his death marks the beginning of a change in patterns of patronage and the literary life—changes significantly for the worse from the viewpoint of the literary community and the court-dependent cultural elites. As we mentioned in earlier chapters, in his tezkire, Latifi specifically laments the death of Ibrahim in a special section and attributes the subsequent decline in the fortunes of poets to the somehow related elimination of stipends traditionally granted by the palace to large numbers of them.[6] However, because Latifi's tezkire was originally completed in A.H. 953 (1546 C.E.), we might get the mistaken impression that this recognition and explanation of a decline in poetic fortunes were more or less contemporary with the event. In fact, the modern, printed text of Latifi's tezkire published by Ahmed Cevdet is a pastiche of versions.[7] The tezkire was rewritten at least once and probably more than once, and Cevdet simply combined older and later versions in his text. The section on Ibrahim Pasha (the *Risale-i evsaf-ı İbrahim Paşa* [Essay in description of Ibrahim Pasha]) does not appear in the early versions, and the critiques of the age in the introductory and concluding sections of the early versions contain only commonplace complaints: for example, that nowadays there are too many poets and too many bad poets, that patrons do not have any critical sense, and that poets are too greedy for money.[8] It is only in versions completed sometime between 1562 and 1575 (and most likely after the death of Süleyman in 1566)—well within the rupture period—that the Ibrahim Pasha section appears together with an extensive expansion of the concluding section and its critique of the age.[9]

From the same general period come the three most detailed and anecdotal tezkires of the sixteenth century: the *Meşa'irü'ş-şü'ara* (1568–69) of 'Aşık Çelebi; the *Tezkire* (1586) of Kınalızade Hasan Çelebi; and the poet biographies of Mustafa 'Ali's *Künhü'l-ahbar* (The essence of history) (1592–99). 'Aşık's tezkire is a striking case. With its copious anecdotes and rich descriptions of persons and places, it seems clearly to be a memorial, the affectionate and nostalgic obituary for a departed age. In contrast, Sehi (writing before 1538) and the early Latifi (writing before 1546) are relatively spare in their entries—perhaps feeling little need to flesh out the milieu in which they lived their everyday lives and that, it might have appeared, would go on as it was forever.

What 'Aşık describes in his 1568–69 retrospective is, for the most part, the cultured Ottoman's experience of the Age of Beloveds, a period in which the palace, wealthy *'askeri* administrators,[a] and members of the ulema supported a relatively large, active, and even brilliant culture of gatherings with food, music, poetry, scintillating conversation, and a host of beloveds (*dilberler* [heart thieves], *mahbublar* [beloveds], *huban* [beauties]) whose origins seem to cut across class lines from the youthful elites, to the lower-level janissaries, to artisans' apprentices, to shop boys, and to professional boy (and female) prostitutes.[10] This is the same culture that Latifi depicts, albeit more fancifully, in his 1525 *Essay in Description of Istanbul*.

---

[a] The 'askeri were members of the military-administrative branch of the state.

The Economy of Love

One feature of the culture of love that concerns us in this chapter is its expense (and that it was expensive is an assumption that we believe to be well founded). Latifi points out that the beloveds were, in many cases, ruthlessly mercenary and would attach themselves to a lover with more regard for the state of his purse than for anything of substance about him. As we mentioned before, Latifi says much the same of most poets. In this period, the poet Zati, for example, was able to refuse official patronage appointments and make do quite nicely on gifts and favors from wealthy admirers, awards from the palace, and payment for ghostwritten poems. Deli Birader Gazali was able to hit up the high functionaries at court for a retirement package sufficient to build a mosque, a zaviye, and a bathhouse in Beşiktaş. The impression given is of a lot of people chasing a lot of money, money in addition to and likely far exceeding the state stipends of poets and other literati.[11]

A simple question that, in other forms, has been crucial to historians (and, perhaps, not crucial enough to literary historians) is, Where does the money supporting a lavish entertainment culture come from early in the sixteenth century, and where does it go by the end? Our interest in this question stems from the fact that the livelihood of poets and the conditions of possibility for a culture that supports poetry are dependent on investments of both libidinal energy (desire) and surplus funds. More controversial is the observation—which runs against the grain of the general aestheticizing and universalizing tendency of literary study—that even the content of poems and other art forms is strongly affected by the economy of investments (of both desire and cash) by artists and audiences in a particular time and place.

If we are correct in assuming that Latifi's most pessimistic moments come after the middle of the sixteenth century, he certainly has ample company in modern historians. The crisis of the sixteenth century and the early seventeenth is everywhere a historical given even though the exact character and causes of the crisis are matters of dispute. Generally, it is in the late fifteenth century and the early sixteenth in Western Europe—and somewhat later in the Ottoman Empire—that we see the beginning of a dramatic upswing in economic activity driven by the penetration of European traders into the Far East and the New World and a rise in population that continued well into the second half of the sixteenth century. However, this broad tendency brought with it the seeds of a widespread disruption that shows up in the confluence of a number of events none of which by itself was enough to stand as the origin of the perceived crisis. Among the trends that contributed to this crisis are several that we have referred to in passing as having had a direct impact on the sociocultural phenomenon that we call *the Age of Beloveds*. Let us look briefly at a few of these.

The Economy and Demographics

In his *Economic Life in Ottoman Europe*, Bruce McGowan summarizes the demographic situation during the sixteenth century as follows:

> The brave new world of exploration and trade which opened up in the sixteenth century was a world with swiftly changing demographic proportions. In Western Europe the traumatic plague-related losses of the fourteenth century had long since been effaced, and population densities in most areas were edging upwards to unprecedented levels. An older tendency toward a concentration of population in the northwest reasserted itself; population density in the Low Countries became two or three times that of less populous parts of Europe. To the east, the Ottoman territories—like most of Eastern Europe—remained relatively far less populous in terms of density, even though evidence of flourishing Ottoman towns persuades us that the populations under Ottoman rule—in line with populations on the western rim of the Mediterranean and in Europe generally—were also growing dramatically throughout the sixteenth century.[12]

The population of Venice, for example, rose steadily throughout the sixteenth century, from 115,000 in 1509 to a high of 170,000 in 1563, after which the plague epidemics of the 1570s caused a decline that lasted well into the seventeenth century.[13] The population of Tuscany increased by a sixth between 1552 and 1627, and the area experienced several famines in the last decade of the sixteenth century and the early years of the seventeenth when population growth outpaced food supplies.[14] At the same time, Tudor England also saw substantial growth in population, a trend that slowed only briefly with the great influenza epidemics of 1556–58.[15] As population pressure increased and large numbers of unemployed men and women became a visible problem, critical opinions of poverty became popular, and laws targeting vagrancy were enacted by the English authorities.[16] As for the central Ottoman Empire, M. A. Cook's data, studies by Barkan and İnalcık, and much recent work suggest that population pressure in rural Anatolia may have increased substantially over the same period.[17] Population pressure in the provinces and artisans brought in for building projects certainly increased the flow of immigrants into Istanbul and prompted the authorities to issue a number of edicts intended to stem the tide.

One of the effects of increased population densities in Western Europe was a growing tendency toward local agricultural insufficiencies and the need to import food staples. This, combined with European prosperity and, according to some, the influx of precious metals from the Americas, meant that the Ottoman Empire, which was less pressured by increasing populations, initially found lucrative markets for its goods and experienced a prosperous period, the resulting substantial revenue flows allowing the central government to finance, among other things, the conquests, lively culture, and great building projects of Süleyman's reign.[18] However, in the Ottoman Empire, as in Europe, one of the results of prosperity and rapid economic growth was inflation. What is called *the price revolution* of the sixteenth century is a much vexed and dangerous territory for literary historians, yet, as we will see, it is territory that we cannot avoid. Şevket Pamuk lays out the situation as follows:

> The Price Revolution of the sixteenth century has been the subject of one of the most enduring debates in European historiography and more recently in the historiography of the world economy. That European prices, expressed in grams of silver, increased by more than 100 percent, and in some countries, by more than 200 percent from the beginning of the sixteenth century to the middle of the seventeenth century has been well established and broadly accepted. It is also clear that not all prices rose at the same pace. Increases in agricultural prices outstripped all others. In countries which experienced currency debasements during this period, overall inflation was proportionally higher, reaching, in some cases, 600 percent or more for the entire period.[19]

In both the Ottoman Empire and England, expensive military adventures and palace expenditures were financed, in part, by inflation and debasements of the coinage.[20] Among the English, the pound was steadily debased beginning with the 1522 French wars until, by 1551, it had fallen from the equivalent of thirty-two Flemish shillings to thirteen shillings, fourpence.[21] Among the Ottomans, Mehmet the Conqueror's policy of financing state projects by successive debasements of the akçe had been so repugnant to the standing army (the janissaries), whose fixed incomes were diminished by the inflationary effects of debasement, that, following Mehmet's death in 1481, there were no significant debasements until 1585–86, when the akçe lost some 44 percent of its value.[22] According to recent work by Pamuk, much of the inflationary impetus in the Ottoman Empire was a result, not of debasement, but of a populationwide increase in the use of money (monetization), increased velocity in the circulation of money, and the influence of Western European price increases transmitted through trade.[23]

The Literary Economy

Keeping in mind that our focus in this chapter is on providing a historically grounded glimpse of the literary economy of the Age of Beloveds, let us for a moment redirect our attention back to the situation of poets and cultural elites. From the perspective of the state, as contemporary commentators from Latifi to Mustafa 'Ali point out, support of learning and the learned was seen by the Ottomans as one of the duties of government, enjoined by Islam, and traditionally practiced by Islamic rulers. For example, Mustafa 'Ali lists the following as among the primary requirements for successful rule: that a ruler be pious; that he care for his subjects; that he mix with philosophers and wise men and avoid idiots; that he study history and the lives of ancient rulers; that he avoid violence and aim for justice; that he not allow fools, dwarves, mutes, and party companions, who are "the Magogs of sedition and disruption," to have a voice in affairs of state when there are accomplished men available, men who are like "sound coinage"; and that he "especially show favor and condescension to the wise ulema and accomplished persons of perspicacity, who are the pillars of the council hall of faith and kingship, the sound limbs on which stands the edifice of dominion and nation." After also mentioning the importance of supporting the military and tending to the destitute, 'Ali goes on to the second set of requirements, first among which is "an eloquent and cultured conversational companion of rare qualities . . . an excellent prosodist and poet of sweet speech."[24] Beneath the "you really need someone like me" surface is the understanding that support of literature production (including poetry production)—and, by extension, support of the milieu in which poets function—was one of the duties of a properly functioning state. As a result, the state history—written by the literate class—tells the story of the fulfillment or nonfulfillment of such duties as a function of the moral and economic health or malaise of the continuing state.

In the early sixteenth century, the palace and the royal courts of princes in the provinces, far from being unique, were models for the courts (and courtiers) of highly placed pashas. On the one hand, the theoretical duties of the government or the ruler to support literature and learning were diffused among a number of centers and central individuals. On the other hand, the culture of love associated with the poetic life can be seen as crucial to the fortunes of individuals whose positions (and lives) were dependent on the affection and goodwill, not only of the ruler, but also of those whom even the ruler had some reason to fear: the standing army and the populace of the capital.

This point demands some explanation. As we argued above, in the sixteenth century, the poetry of the Ottoman elites is embedded in a lived culture of homoerotic love. The poetry in a sense becomes productive of a patterned, metaphoric flow that conducts libidinal energy back and forth from the handsome young man directly at hand to a beloved patron and, on another level of abstraction, to the ruler and the divine. In the despotic or absolutist state—England, or France, or the Holy Roman Empire as much as the Ottoman Empire—it was important that love be associated with the despot.[25] The despot needs to be loved as well as feared, and, beyond this, he (or she) needs to be the signifying center or the center of a primal love relationship that gives meaning to all other relations of love. In the period that we are examining, it seems to have been worth substantial investments on the part of the despot's representatives to present themselves as focuses of love. If the despot's representatives were loved in an acknowledged and public way, this love was transmitted through them to the ruler, who was understood to be the ultimate object of love. Indeed, one aspect of the power of poets is their ability to present a subordinate powerholder as either worthy or unworthy of love and, hence, indirectly as an enhancement of or a danger to the status of the ruler as love object. Thus, we argue for recognition of a dominant *form of semiosis* (meaning production) during the Age of Beloveds that implies a direct link between entertainment—the party (tavern, coffeehouse), intoxication, sexual excitement—and the maintenance of power, between the şehrengiz and the kaside, the erotic and the panegyric. We even suggest that the link between power and eroticism is a significant feature of the masculinization of the erotic in Ottoman elite culture.

We have also pointed to evidence that much the same general relation between the court and courtship, between patriarchal absolutism and homoeroticism, obtains wherever we look in Europe. Even the case of Elizabeth, a powerful woman in the position of ruler as beloved, presents itself more as a problem for the dominant cultural perspective than as evidence of a countertrend. Elizabeth's femininity is often occluded by a focus on what might be called her *hypervirginity*, which foregrounds a combination of sensuality with an absence of typical female, reproductive sexuality. Moreover, it was common in Europe to represent a dominion or an empire as female. Although such representation usually occurred in the context of territory dominated by a male monarch, thus ultimately affirming the values of the patriarchal family, a female monarch would, at first glance, seem to unite the gender of the ruler and the ruled territory in a single person and restore a culturally normative heterosexuality to the relations between courtiers and the courted royal beloved. Indeed, the iconography of Elizabeth's reign appears to emphasize this congruence.[26] For example, the famous "Ditchley portrait" by Marcus Gheeraerts the Younger, in which the queen stands possessively on a map of the world, is, quite suggestively, the gift of a courtier, Sir Henry Lee, who had fallen out of favor with the queen for falling under the spell of another woman—a rival beloved. The background shows a black cloud (of the beloved queen's jealous wrath) parting to show the sun (of forgiveness for the errant lover).

Although the female public beloved is normative for English society, the problem of Elizabeth derives in large part from her contradictory position in a patriarchal (phallocratic) political context according to whose assumptions the monarch cannot be seen as having a master other than God and a woman cannot be tolerated who is not mastered by some male.[27] In other words, the model of dominance and submission governing relations at court is that of an all-male society—a homoerotic society—in which the hierarchy of domination does not admit of a woman dominating a man at any point and the beloved of the courtier's world is a dominant beloved.[28]

After Elizabeth, the homoerotic subtext resurfaces along with the patriarchal in the rhetorical universe of the early Stuarts. An excellent example is found in the letter (cited in chapter 5 above) from James I to his beloved royal cupbearer, George Villiers, in which the king describes his and Villiers's relation as a marriage, himself as both "dad and husband," and his beloved as "child and wife." As we have pointed out again and again, for the court-dependent elites, the erotic (sexual) dimension of life is always modeled on relations at court. Thus, the drive to impose patriarchal ideology (however homoeroticized) on society as a whole appears to us to be evidence of a perceived need to restore English absolutism to a more normal state, one that, we would also suggest, resembles—beneath the rhetorical surface—the state of absolutism in the Ottoman Empire.[29]

In examining what happens to the situation among the Ottoman elites that substantially reduces investment in this culture of love and its semiotic universe, we intend to marshal an economic explanation that contrasts with the personal explanation favored by contemporary Ottoman accounts and the present-day general histories that follow them. The personal explanation asserts, simply, that the decline in the fortunes of poets, or anyone or anything else, was attributable in large part to weak sultans and other powerholders who failed to appreciate either learning and talent or the essentials of a properly functioning ideal state.[30] The economic explanation, on the other hand, has no simple form. It can only point to densities and patterns of coalescence within an irreducible multiplicity of microevents—an economy of interests, investments (of cash and desire), self-preservative decisions, etc.—each of which may be problematic in its own right. Accordingly, the weak sultan can be seen not so much as the primal cause of anything as a consequence of a power shift resulting from a host of individual decisions/investments made by administrators, bureaucrats, military leaders, and palace (especially harem) powers.

In her book on Ottoman sea power, Palmira Brummett points out that the protectionist economic policies of the sixteenth-century Ottoman state—meant to assure adequate provisioning of the capital with foodstuffs and raw materials—did not prevent wealthy functionaries of the ʿaskeri class from responding to market forces and the opportunity for quick and substantial profits by investing in the speculative trading of officially protected commodities such as grain. Brummett also quite insightfully points out that we need not be surprised by the apparently contradictory situation in which powerful individuals could carry out the premercantile protectionist policies of the state and, at the same time, engage in private capitalist ventures of their own.[31] A good example of such a venture, in the legally permissible area of luxury goods, is the lavishly adorned European-style crown produced by Venetian goldsmiths and speculatively financed by the highest Ottoman ʿaskeri officials, the defterdar Iskender Çelebi and the grand vizier Ibrahim Pasha, working with their frequent party companion the Venetian doge's bastard son Alvise Gritti, a jewel merchant who acted as a middleman.[32] Another example is Süleyman's grand vizier Rüstem Pasha, who invested in "one of the burgeoning Thessalian fairs, the port town of Tekirdağ-Rodoscuk, in the central district of Istanbul, and also in the south-east-Anatolian town of Malatya."[33] It seems quite likely that, despite theoretical formulations that insist on their uniqueness, such projects fit a pattern of wealthy government officials privately investing the income from agricultural lands to which they held title. This brought substantial returns to wealthy individuals and enabled them to support huge expenditures on a culture of love, literature, and entertainment that, in turn, supported the talents of a large number of poets.[34]

Although Ottoman literary culture and its purveyors were bound closely to the palace, central administrators, and the capital, the economic conditions that determined the fate of both originated largely outside the capital and outside the control (or in opposition to the control) of the state. Let us mention a few things that stand out. As Daniel Goffman indicates in his book on the rise of Izmir, the success of speculative investment by the elites in world markets had, by the last half of the sixteenth century, stimulated similar investments at the local level. Products that were officially reserved for the provisioning of Istanbul and the palace were hoarded locally to wait for price increases on the world market. That this strategy succeeded despite the opposition of the state is attested to by the burgeoning of Izmir and other towns in Anatolia.[35] Thus, as the population of Istanbul grew, in part because of an influx of artisans and laborers brought in to support the lavish building projects and military ventures of the mid-sixteenth century, it became increasingly difficult to assure adequate provisioning of the city.[36]

The inflationary pressure of more cash chasing fewer goods seems to have caused wide discrepancies between the officially set prices (*narh*) and returns obtainable on the unofficial market. Foodstuffs, including meat on the hoof, that once traveled from Anatolia and Rumeli to Istanbul were siphoned off on the way, heightening the artificiality of the official price structure. A good example of the consequences of this situation is given by Faroqhi in her discussion of providing meat for the capital and the forced recruitment of wealthy Anatolians to serve as butchers in Istanbul, where official pricing made the occupation a venture certain to lose money.[37] Instead of raising official prices, the administration ordered provincial magistrates to require artificially low costs on the grounds that "Istanbul was inhabited by many prominent officials, important ulema, illustrious descendants of the Prophet, and other distinguished personages."[38] But it turns out that, in this instance at least, the learned classes were privileged more in theory than in practice since the administration also restricted the amount of meat that high officials (including distinguished personages) could purchase in order to ensure an adequate supply for the general populace, whose dissatisfactions were always a danger.

We see quite the same situation in both Venice and England.[39] Throughout the whole period under consideration, Venice struggled with the problem of assuring a regular supply of grain from the *terrafirma*, with only limited success.[40] Attempts to secure regular meat supplies for the urban center in the mid-sixteenth century were strongly opposed by mainland cities. The sixteenth century saw a number of different initiatives aimed at regularizing the provisioning of Venice and increased interest in investment opportunities in terrafirma agricultural land.[41] In England, the voracious appetite of London for foodstuffs kept wages and food prices high in the adjacent counties, favoring agriculture, and gradually driving industry to more distant areas. Concern for the provisioning of the city caused authorities to try a number of measures even including attempts later in the seventeenth century to discourage the country gentry from moving to the city.[42]

In all the areas we examined in our survey, inflation, large disparities in prices from one area to the next, differences in population densities, and localized shortages encouraged significant numbers of people with financial or commodity resources to invest in the trading of staples. This trend blurred somewhat the usual class distinctions between merchants and nonmerchants and expressed itself variously as the employment of middlemen, or as smuggling, or as entrepreneurship on the part of government administrators and bureaucrats. One of the consequences of this appears to us to have been a major alteration in the perceived relation of the courtier (palace-dependent elite) class to the monarch. When the elites—the wealthy slave administrators of the Ottoman Empire and the nobility of Europe alike—were under financial pressure and the palace was unable to meet their needs through the usual avenues of direct remuneration (the granting of offices and gift giving), when they found that even their traditional income from the sale of influence and outright bribery had become inadequate, they appear to have turned, not to the palace or the despot (both had their own financial problems), but to markets of various kinds. In such circumstances, relations with culture production also seem to have changed in complex ways. This much said, let us return to our summary of selected historical trends.

Breakdown

Among the other consequences of the increasing investment-mindedness and inflationary pressure in the Ottoman Empire was a similarly increasing avidity for cash at the center. From the early sixteenth century on, there was a growing tendency to favor cash over in-kind payments of taxes even though this was contrary to the theoretical policy of the state.[43] One result of such a tendency was the gradual deterritorialization of agricultural land and agriculture as well as grazing land and herding. Thus, relations to the land and its products changed. Simply put, the relation land ↔ food product ↔ eating was profoundly altered by the interjection of cash. This is to say that reterritorialization based on a cash ↔ food relation (in a sense replacing nutritional value with cash value) alienated the land and processes of food production from the basic need to eat. Although the trend toward deterritorializing (and reterritorializing) Anatolian and Rumelian lands had significant effects on the lives of people in the Ottoman Empire, other changes had similarly profound consequences.

As Leslie Peirce discusses in her comprehensive study of the Ottoman harem and the reproductive politics of the palace, the latter years of the sixteenth century and the early years of the seventeenth saw dramatic changes in relationships within the palace and among the palace, the administrators of the empire, and the people of the provinces.[44] From the early days of the Ottoman Empire, it had been customary for Ottoman princes to be assigned to governorships in the provinces, a practice that not only trained future sultans in the practicalities of rule and engaged rival claimants to the throne in a survival-of-the-fittest contest but also established important personal connections between the palace and provincial powerholders. Beginning in the reign of Mehmet III (1595–1603), the sons of the sultan were no longer sent out to the provinces but remained enclosed in the palace and under its direct control. They were still assigned governorships, but stewards from among the highly placed kul administrators were appointed to fulfill their duties.

As indicated by Metin Kunt's study of the elite servants of the monarch (the kuls), the appointment of kuls to replace princes in the provinces was part of a broader tendency to appoint powerful ʿaskeri officials from the central administration to governorships in the provinces, where they dominated or replaced local administrators. These trends resulted in a withdrawal of the palace from direct contact with the broader populace and redirected the focus of the palace from the empire to its own internal politics.[45] Anxieties about preserving the Ottoman bloodline led to the abandonment of the rule of fratricide (by which the brothers of the new sultan were executed). Battles for succession were fought via intrigues in the narrow arena of the harem as seniority replaced perceived fitness to rule as the deciding factor in determining who would take the throne on the death of a sultan. Frightened sultans executed sons who seemed too popular or capable. Powerful queen mothers began to dominate the politics of the palace as personal relationships with the sultan began to diminish in importance. The alienation of the palace and the increased reliance on central kul administrators meant that the power of provincial elites gradually diminished.[46]

In addition, the last decades of the Age of Beloveds saw the beginning of a gradual decline in the timar (prebend) system, according to which members of certain military classes—traditional provincial military families, the great *akıncı* (raider) clans, powerful volunteers, and kuls emerging from the palace school—were granted control of lands. It was from these lands that the timariots extracted their pay (and a set amount for the government) through taxation (in kind and cash) of the local peasant population. In return for these grants, they recruited, armed, trained, and supported a predetermined number of mounted retainers who, in times of war, formed the provincial cavalry known as the *sipahi*.[47] In the mid-sixteenth century, the sipahi formed the core of the Ottoman army, and 30–40 percent of military expenses were collected from the timars.[48] By the late sixteenth century, however, a number of factors combined to make the sipahi increasingly obsolete. Inflation substantially reduced the value of the set incomes derived from the timars, new military technology emphasized firearms over cavalry, fiscal administrators at the center achieved savings by recruiting *sekban* (irregular musketeers; sometimes *segban*) in times of war and dismissing them when they were no longer needed (the model that had been widely applied in Europe for some time), and tax farming was introduced as a more efficient means of extracting cash—cash needed to pay the regular (and irregular) army—from the peasant population.[49] The other response to advances in military technology was to increase the janissary corps, which nearly trebled in size in the seventeenth century. This exacerbated financial pressure on the central government, which passed the pressure down to the rural population in the form of taxes, an action that had a destabilizing effect on traditional agriculture and contributed to the monetization of agriculture and agricultural entrepreneurship.[50]

Broadly considered, these changes in the Ottoman system, often lamented by traditional historians as harbingers of decline or evidence of breakdowns, appear more realistically to be (in Metin Kunt's terms) "modernizing" movements responding to the need—occasioned, in part, by population pressure and increased urbanization—for increased efficiency in the collection and dispersal of revenues and in the production and distribution of agricultural products.[51] However, it is also clear that the alienation of agriculture and the concomitant evolution away from the peasant smallholding and local control are not just Ottoman phenomena. For example, the movement in England toward *enclosure*, by which the institution of common or communal village land shared by small landholders, was replaced by individual holdings demarcated by fences, thereby making smallholding unprofitable, consolidating agricultural land, and turning large numbers of formerly independent farmers into wage-earning farm laborers.[52] A huge expansion of the textile industry also resulted in engrossment, the widespread conversion of arable land to pasturage for sheep, further driving farmers from the land.[53] Moreover, the late Tudors and the early Stuarts had adopted a practice (common all over Europe) of replacing the wellborn military careerist (an occupation considered noble and even chivalrous) with irregular mercenaries recruited in times of war and, afterward, demobilized and left to their own devices, a practice similar to the growing use in the Ottoman Empire during the late sixteenth century of sekban to replace sipahis.[54]

The consequences of these tendencies are many, but a few are especially pertinent to our argument. In England, displaced farmworkers, unemployed laborers, and cast-off mercenaries swelled the ranks of masterless men— vagabonds and beggars—already found throughout the country.[55] Groups of angry commoners rioted or tore up hedges in response to attempts by landlords to enclose or overgraze common lands. Food shortages brought out mobs demanding that grain be sold at fair prices. In 1536 (a fateful year for more than just Ibrahim Pasha, it seems), bad harvests and oppressive taxes roused the north in the massive protest rebellion—with religious overtones —that came to be called the Pilgrimage of Grace.[56] In the Ottoman Empire, similar disruptions had similar impacts at all levels of society.

In Ottoman practice, the *re'aya* (the nonmilitary, nonadministrative "flock") classes were required to remain within strict class boundaries. Peasants were required to remain on their farms and were subject to a punitive tax called the *çift bozan resmi* (farm-breaking tax) should they abandon their land. As a result of some combination of demographic pressure, the increase in rural unrest, demands for taxes, and the breakdown of traditional agricultural practices, men left the land and fled to the cities and towns in such numbers that the authorities were unable to stem the tide either by taxation or by coercion. These now masterless (and landless) men formed the core of three groups that had a profound influence on the shape of Ottoman society at the end of the Age of Beloveds: the sekban; the suhte; and the mendicant dervishes.

The sekban were, as we have seen, irregular mercenary musketeers who had begun to replace the sipahi. They were recruited out of the rural population into the households of the great pashas and military commanders in times of war and summarily dismissed when their services were no longer needed. Left to their own devices, some of these men—known as *levend* (armed mercenaries) or *sarıca* (mounted irregulars)—gathered into armed bands and sustained themselves by harassing, intimidating, and outright robbing local villagers and peasants.[57]

The suhte were, as we saw in chapter 2, young men, many of village or peasant origin, who were sent by their families to the urban medreses with the idea that they would eventually find careers in the religious institution. In the late sixteenth century and the seventeenth, when the numbers of suhte increased because of population pressure and agricultural dislocation, the medreses were unable to accommodate all applicants, and there were not enough employment opportunities in the religious institution to accommodate all graduates. One consequence was that the traditional practice of *cerr*, by which impoverished religious students would go out to the provinces for a time and provide religious services and instruction to villagers in exchange for room and board, was transformed into an occasion for intimidation, with bands of violent young students compelling reluctant villagers to support them.

Antinomian mendicant dervish groups also burgeoned with an influx of unattached young men. These groups rejected the outward practice of Islam and the conventions of society in favor of devotion to an esoteric truth. This rejection manifested itself, not only in wildly unconventional dress, obnoxious behavior, and rituals designed to offend the traditionally devout, but also in occasional episodes of obtaining "donations" by intimidation or compulsion, behaviors that closely resembled robbery.

As we have suggested in earlier chapters, population increases and a demographic bias favoring young men seem to have been among the conditions that gave the Age of Beloveds its unique character. In the rupture period, however, growing demographic pressure combined with severe economic dislocation to bring the Age of Beloveds to an end. Outside the capital, the deterritorialization of agriculture, the inability of the central administration to deal with conditions in rural Anatolia, and the availability of numbers of disaffected, unemployed, and armed young men resulted in continuing unrest and opposition to the state usually known as *the Celali revolts* and characterized by Karen Barkey as *banditry*.[58] In the capital itself, some of the same disaffected young men would, by the end of the 1620s, swell the ranks of the Kadizadeli movement, a popular reformist religious movement that took its name from its intellectual leader, the fiery orator Kadizade Mehmet who, from Istanbul pulpits, decried the degeneracy of the ulema and their deviations from the purity of the Prophet's age. Inspired by Kadizade Mehmet and other popular preachers, mobs of puritanical reformers physically assaulted social institutions that had come to symbolize the entertainment culture of the Age of Beloveds as scripted by Ottoman poetry and enacted in the poetic life: primarily the tavern, the coffeehouse, and the dervish lodge.[59] There appear to be clear parallels between Ottoman and English puritanism. Allison Wall cites examples of London mobs, aroused by Shrove Tuesday celebrations, being incited to attack brothels and theaters (which the authorities also condemned) in a manner resembling the raids of Kadizadeli supporters on Ottoman entertainment establishments.[60] At the same time, Italy saw increasing suppression of the courtesan culture and the homoerotic indulgences of young men in Florence and Venice.[61]

The activities of all the groups under discussion here had a negative impact on the economy of the governing elites as well as on the tranquillity and provisioning of the capital. However, as Faroqhi and Goffman point out, the result may well have been the growth and prosperity of provincial towns and better living conditions for a large number of ordinary people outside the capital.[62] We should note that the negative consequences of unrest are often part of the (hi)story as told from the perspective of the central administration. It is not possible to be sure, for example, whether the reports from Anatolia about unrest, Celali banditry, the depredations of sekban and suhte (religious students), etc. are accurate or reflect the unwillingness of local areas to send their products (and tax money) to Istanbul. Moreover, in response to the increasing frequency of assaults, the peasants and villagers of Anatolia began to arm themselves with muskets and actively defend their communities, once more against the policy of the central government, which restricted possession of firearms to the military classes.[63] Thus, in a number of ways, the provinces grow increasingly independent of the capital, retaining their own resources, and looking to local powers for protection.

Returning obliquely to the situation of literary communities, we suggest that the reduction in personal relations to the land and its people on the part of the monarchy and its representatives also diminishes the importance of personal relations at the meaning-producing center of the state. At times when the financial situation at the center seems precarious, the powerful and wealthy make self-preservative decisions about where to invest time, money, and interest. As the sixteenth century progresses, it also becomes increasingly risky for high officials to support what might at some time be seen as an affront to popular piety and, thereby, open themselves to scapegoating on the part of a morally outraged public.[64] Thus, even though poetry may retain some of its value as an enhancement to the status and reputation of the great, the poetic life—the synthesis of pleasure, profit, and a structured semiotic universe that linked pashas and shop boys in the late fifteenth century and the early sixteenth—begins to give way to something else. The contraction of the dynasty and the elimination of the satellite courts of princes and high officials reduced the opportunities for poets. High officials and the economic elites no longer invested as much in the poetic life. Poets increasingly held jobs in a much more regularized scribal service and bureaucracy.

This latter point requires some expansion. In a detailed and nuanced discussion of the situation of Ottoman poets in the seventeenth century, Walter Feldman shows how, from the mid-sixteenth century on, the increasing bureaucratization and regularization of both the scribal service and the religious/education profession gradually reduced the possibility of a talented poet from outside the medrese system of the capital finding work in either.[65] Moreover, as the population of medrese students rose, the number of positions available to graduates at the very highest levels of the system became inadequate. In the 1560s, Süleyman responded to the situation by restricting the granting of paid appointments—the equivalent of a doctorate—to once every seven years. The cumulative effect of these trends was that there was less social mobility and poets began to emerge much more often from the established families of the educated classes. They moved through regular channels into jobs in the religious/education institution and, failing that, in the similarly regularized and bureaucratized scribal service. These poets had their own support and patronage systems, were less lavishly patronized, and were, consequently, less dependent on the patronage of powerful 'askeri administrators. For many of the same reasons, they were less inclined to seek their primary social relations in the salons of the kul elites, turning to the Sufi orders as a venue for sociability and the poetic life.[66]

The impacts of a multiplicity of economic and social conditions on poetry production seem to have been profound and not limited to a rupture period late in the sixteenth century, instead gradually increasing throughout the century and into the next. When times were good and the essentials of life relatively easy to come by, moral objections to conspicuous consumption and the behaviors associated with poetic partying—wine drinking, homoerotic passions, beloved chasing, dancing, music, tavernhopping—were relatively rare. But, when the general populace of the capital was troubled—by plague, or food shortages, or economic hardship, for example—the perceived malfunctioning of the protectionist state was seen as a consequence of moral decline. And public dissatisfaction in the capital was always a direct threat to the palace and to highly placed administrators. In such a climate, attachments to poets and the poetic life (including its mystical-religious dimension) became, not just unproductive, but downright dangerous.

Taking a broader look at some of the trends that we have touched on, what seems to be happening at the end of the sixteenth century is a shift in balances of power. The movement in England from late-Tudor absolutism to an increasingly limited monarchy under the Stuarts is well defined and widely accepted. In the Ottoman Empire, there appears to be a parallel to the English case in the double enthronement (1618 and 1622) of the mentally incompetent Mustafa I sandwiched around the deposition and regicide of (Genç [the Young]) Osman II.[67]

This series of events certainly brings to the surface a struggle among palace functionaries—for example, the Valide Sultan, harem agas (the eunuchs who oversaw and administered the affairs of the private quarters of the palace)—religious bureaucrats, and kul commanders for control of a substantially diminished sultanate. From the perspective of poetic scripting alone, the death of Osman II can be seen as a watershed event. As we have seen, the death by sorrow or even the murder of the *lover* is a commonplace everywhere in the literature of the early-modern world. But the murder of the *beloved* (by those of the lover class) is a rare and immensely disruptive symbolic act. It is disruptive psychologically as well as politically because it breaks the symbolic bond that links the absolute monarch on earth with the supernatural absolute. It is this bond that scripts in erotic and emotional terms a theoretical political notion most often subsumed under the phrase *the divine right of kings*.

The bond is, in fact, more than the granting of a divine right to rule; it is the equation by analogy of the monarch with God, of earthly rule with heavenly rule. As we have seen, apocalyptic and messianic responses to a changing world had made this theoretical bond more real and visible during the early years of the Age of Beloveds. When this bond no longer holds, when the beloved as God and the beloved as monarch are no longer as self-evidently identical, then the perception of power has already undergone a dramatic change. In a symbolic sense, absolute love for an absolute beloved here on earth is no longer as possible, and a fissure opens up between the world of absolute truth and the ordering of this world, a fissure that even has some of the underlying characteristics of the very modern notion of the separation of church and state.

Why movements toward limitations on monarchical absolutism are seen as an advance in the one case and as a decline in the other we will leave to nonliterary historians to thrash out. What we would like to emphasize is our contention that the character of poetic (and artistic) scripting during the Age of Beloveds is bound to a broadly imagined (but not imaginary) absolutism in which an all-powerful monarch (the shadow of God on earth, if not the incarnation) stands as the ideal beloved and grounds the meaning of all other beloveds, actual or fictional, spiritual or carnal, male or female. Yet, absolutism in theory does not mean absolute power in fact. The early-modern absolute monarchs certainly did not enjoy absolute security. As Allison Wall says in regard to the Tudor and Stuart monarchs: "The difficulty of securing both the life of the monarch and obedience to him or her lay partly in the lack of formal coercive force. In early modern England there was a small central bureaucracy, no regular army, and no organised police force. Kings and queens could be very vulnerable, and they knew it. So how could they establish their authority, how could they persuade the nation to accept and abide by it?"[68] Wall's answer emphasizes a rhetorical (and an iconographic) style that insists on a divine right to rule, to which we would append the notion of literary scripting, in which the ruler is identified with the beloved.

On the surface, the Ottoman case seems quite the opposite of the English. The Ottoman ruler had a powerful standing army, a large central administration, and a relatively effective policing power. However, the security provided by these was also equivocal and, in the end, left the sultan not much better off than the English kings and queens. Certainly, the standing army secured the ruler from provincial rebels and the mob in the capital. But this security held only so long as the army itself did not see its interests threatened. Ottoman history is replete with instances in which army factions or powerful administrators engineered the retirement of sultans in favor of popular sons or supported one claimant to the throne over others. Even the immensely powerful Süleyman ordered the execution of his son Mustafa in part because the son was reported to have induced members of the standing army (the janissaries) to prefer him to his aging father.[69] For the Ottomans as well as for other European monarchs, what tilts the balance in favor of the monarch is the existence of a discursive universe in which the monarch stands between God and the beloved, between agape and eros, and draws power from analogies to both.

When the discursive script is violated and the beloved falls victim to the lover, the absolute power of the sultan is called into question, and enough little things change that, in time, nothing is quite the same anymore. The language and culture of love is no longer as directly bound to the palace. There are still poets, beloveds, parties, and patrons, but there is a fundamental semiotic shift: this beloved at hand no longer, as simultaneously and as automatically, recalls a party, a patron, and a ruler. More and more often, love conjures up a mystical master, a dervish ceremony, and a relation to the divine. The ruler is more often bypassed. By the middle of the seventeenth century, the primary target of puritan religious revivalism is the *tekke* (dervish lodge) and its version of a poetic life, not the poetic life of the sixteenth century as symbolized by the party and the tavern.

A Tale of Two Poets

It has been our custom in this book to begin each chapter with a story. Here, we will end with a little story, one that, we would suggest, can be taken as the late-sixteenth-century Ottoman literary community's symbolic representation of the fissures that appeared in the synthesis that had marked the Age of Beloveds.

The story involves the poet Hayali, whom we should know rather well by now. Hayali was a freeborn Muslim from the provinces and a dervish also. In this, he exhibits important characteristics of one pole of Cemal Kafadar's "schizoid mental topography" inhabiting the master narrative of the Ottoman Empire: exterior (*taşra*) origins, born Muslim, with an antinomian dervish rather than an orthodox religious/mystical perspective.[70] We have already described his rise from scruffy mendicant dervish, to courtier, to conversational companion of Sultan Süleyman, to provincial governor. We have also mentioned in passing the many enemies that he made on his way to the top.

The story also involves the janissary poet Yahya, whom we have also already met. Yahya represents the opposite pole. He was an Albanian slave from a land that seems to have grown rocks better than anything else, for which reason he was sometimes called Yahya from Taşlıcalı (Stoneland). At other times he was known as Dukaginzade, which referred to his purported descent from a Norman crusader named Duc Jean. He had gone through the usual janissary training, and kind patrons nurtured his considerable talent for poetry, inducing him to yearn for promotion to a position in the kul administrative hierarchy.

'Aşık Çelebi, who claims to have known them both, makes it clear here and there in his chatty biographies that the two were longtime enemies. While Yahya traveled with the Ottoman armies, risking his life in defense of Islam and the empire, Hayali lived the life of a famous beauty and beloved in the salons of the great and the taverns of Galata. While Hayali enjoyed a rapid rise to the highest levels of patronage, Yahya composed sheaves of poems and five extensive mesnevis and still struggled—ultimately in vain—to find a patron who would reward him with the kind of position he sought.[71]

As Hayali became a fixture in the entertainments of the highest courtiers and administrators, he continued jealously to guard his position against other potential companions. One day, both he and Yahya were in attendance at the conversational gathering of the great Kemal Pashazade, the famed jurist, historian, and poet, with whom Yahya later claimed to have studied. At one point, Yahya rose resplendent in full janissary regalia and recited a kaside in honor of his host. When he was done, the noted poet İshak Çelebi made some approving comments on the poem, only to be interrupted by the defterdar, Iskender Çelebi, who gave a flattering and skillful interpretation of the opening couplet. Only Hayali, who was in attendance in the company of Iskender Çelebi, his patron, had negative things to say, but, much to his chagrin, he was soon quieted by the opposition of the others.[72] And, from this time on, Hayali and Yahya were bitter rivals. Hayali was ever protective of his position—perhaps because he lacked either the advantage of belonging to an ulema family or that of being one of the elite slaves—and Yahya felt it terribly unjust that an effete dervish, who had most likely worked his way to the top by his good looks and possibly by granting sexual favors, would be more successful than a soldier who had fought for the sultan.

Hayali seems to have been able to walk the dangerous road of royal companionship with great skill. However, the situation changed dramatically when Ibrahim Pasha went from being "the Favorite" to being "the Slain" on the night of 14 March 1536—a shift of but two tiny dots in the Arabic script and a disaster of major proportions for the community of poets and companions (not to mention for Ibrahim). The poets had already lost a generous patron in the defterdar Iskender Çelebi, but the loss of Ibrahim resulted in a substantial diminution in the patronage flowing from the palace itself. The yearly salaries, the guaranteed awards granted to worthy poets and companions, had, apparently, become the base livelihood of a large number of talented artists. As we have already seen, Ibrahim's successors, Ayyas Pasha and Rüstem Pasha, cut off these awards and left the poets to find individual patrons and compete for government positions, which, by the second half of the century, seem to have been given out only to those with powerful connections, for exceptional service, or for an extraordinarily worthy performance.

The poets were livid. Poems of complaint were everywhere. The courtier poet Emirek (Little Prince), or Mirek-i Tabib (Little Prince the Doctor), wrote a gazel with the redif *ca'ize* or "reward." It begins and ends like this:

The End of an Age 325

> The beloved would not give his candy lips to the lovers as rewards
> Yet over and over again he grants my hopes to others as rewards
>
> . . .
>
> Oh God, cut off the life of the cutter off, for he did the deed
> While on all my dear friends were established their rewards[73]

From this time on, Ayyas Pasha's name is mud. He is seldom mentioned without reference to the regrettable deed of cutting off payments that had been customary since the time of the Prophet, or a snide remark, or an outright insulting description. He becomes characterized as an anticompanion, entirely lacking the talent and sensibility that marked the in-group of poets and wits. Where the poets/companions are refined, learned, and possessed of delicate natures, he is a brutish, uncultured, Albanian swine. Where the poets carry on ethereal, sensitive romances with lovely young men, he is so perverted that he prefers sexual relations with women and so lustful that he fills the palace with cradles. The vengeance of poets and conversationalists could—as was well-known—haunt a perpetrator far beyond the grave, and Ayyas Pasha's name was forever associated with whatever the truly intelligent and discerning were not.

Rüstem Pasha also partakes in the general disapproval directed at post-Ibrahimian grand viziers.[74] However, the targets of criticism seem to vary. Latifi, for example, has nothing good to say of Rüstem and seldom (if ever) mentions Ayyas Pasha. 'Aşık brings up Ayyas everywhere and always to insult him. In any case, it appears that there was constant underground warfare between the new powerholders—Ayyas Pasha and Rüstem Pasha, the harem clique, and the established companions.

Yahya prospered for a brief time as a result of this conflict, and his assaults on Hayali continued. For example, one day, when Hayali was spotted wearing a white skullcap, he extemporized the following verse:

> That Hayali Bey with yellowed face and speckled eyes,
> When he dons a skullcap, seems a poppy on a dunghill[75]

In 1548, on the occasion of the second Iraq campaign, Yahya composed a panegyric with the following couplets:

> Had there been granted me
>   the honors shown Hayali
> God knows, I'd have made fresh verse
>   like licit sorcery

> Beneath me as my shadow,
> > this flaming dervish
> Taking the sun's place above me
> > is a sure calamity
>
> Bare as a dervish he runs about
> > and I a soldier on the day of war
> He an impotent mystic
> > while I am the sword of bravery[76]

Rüstem Pasha seems to have liked this and was, perhaps, inclined to prefer a solid janissary to an influential and rural-dervish-minded courtier companion anyway. In any case, he rewarded Yahya with five lucrative endowment trusteeships, which left the poet quite content for a time.

But prosperity did not last for Yahya. When, in 1553, the harem faction of Süleyman's wife Hurrem engineered the death of the popular prince Mustafa, Yahya was among the poets who wrote heartfelt elegies intimating that the sultan had made a terrible mistake. When Rüstem was ousted from the grand viziership in 1555—belatedly scapegoated for the Mustafa affair—several people, Hayali among them, pointed out to him that Yahya had criticized the sultan's decision and, by extension, his grand vizier's wisdom. So, when Rüstem returned to power, Yahya lost his trusteeships and was subjected to a searching audit. In a poem sent to Rüstem, he complained in vain of his sorry state and the treachery of his rivals. In the following excerpt from that poem, we see one of those rivals, Hayali, depicted as a drug-taking dervish:

> What has it come to for me?
> > Alas for me and woe!
> That the wicked are thought good
> > and the good thought wicked
>
> My advancement's sun is veiled
> > beclouded by some nobodies
> Sons of nobodies, addicts
> > of opium and hashish

And on the subject of his grueling audit:

> There among strangers by auditors
> > I was brought to ruin
> So even the bricks pitied me
> > and cried out

> Though I emerged from their hands
>   still straight as an arrow,
> The judges twisted me
>   and bent me like a bow[77]

Yahya never made it back into the good graces of the court. He begged and pleaded in verse after verse—but to no avail. In the end, he turned to mysticism and left the capital for provinces, where he died in 1582. Hayali, however, continued to have a close relationship with the sultan. But he seems also to have foreseen a bleak future. Süleyman's longtime companions were under siege; it was a dangerous time for the poet community, and dervishes were falling out of favor. So Hayali begged the sultan for a district governorship (*sancak beyliği*) in the provinces, which he was finally granted. This allowed him to distance himself from the court and its intrigues and made for a comfortable (and relatively safe) semiretirement from public life.

This little tale encapsulates one of the major subtexts of 'Aşık's tezkire, a subtext running through anecdotes and entries strewn throughout the volume. It tells of two talented poets of widely divergent backgrounds, neither from an ulema family. One was a beauty, a beloved, and a lover, the other a soldier and a scholar; each achieved fame during the height of the Ottoman Age of Beloveds. In the end, at the waning of the age, one satisfied, the other hugely disappointed, they both depart a capital that they could no longer trust to support them. It is difficult to avoid the conclusion that 'Aşık is acutely aware that something has happened in the latter years of the sixteenth century and that these anecdotes from the lives of the poets are his way of expressing the same nostalgia for something lost and the same uncomfortable feeling of existing in the midst of fundamental change that Mustafa 'Ali tried to theorize in his volumes of advice.

Beyond the ending of the Age of Beloveds, it seems no more reasonable to argue for a substantial continuity in the language and semiotic universe of poetic love than it does to argue for the continuity of the fundamental economic principles and practices of the later seventeenth century and the eighteenth with those of the early sixteenth century. Allowing for the possibility of substantive discontinuities in the history of Ottoman poetry makes it possible to revise our perception of that poetry and, especially, its relations to the history of the society in which it was produced.

II

RENAISSANCE, RENAISSANCES, AND THE AGE OF BELOVEDS

Historically, the discussion of Ottoman literary culture has focused on obvious continuities with Arab and Persian literature, on the esteem with which Persian predecessors were regarded, and on the apparent reluctance of the Ottomans to depart from traditional literary norms. What has been missing is even the slightest suggestion that the Ottoman experience may have been a renaissance—comparable to the European Renaissance—of Middle Eastern, Islamic culture, a revitalization of traditional forms and themes and not just the last gasp of a moribund tradition. After all, the dominant literary culture of the late Renaissance in Europe *could*, on the basis of ample evidence, be described as a sterile imitation of classical Greek and Roman models as mediated through the unique genius of Petrarch, an unimaginative succession of idealized beloveds, of ancient gods and goddesses, of amorous shepherds and shepherdesses, all given the barest semblance of life by the literary genius of Italian poets, authors, and playwrights severely limited by Bemboist vernacular neoclassicism. This *is*, in fact, how Ottoman literary culture has been described—just replace the Greek and Roman models with Arabic and Persian models, Petrarch with Hafez, the classical gods, goddesses, and shepherds with the Leylas and Mejnuns, the Husrevs and Shirins, of the Islamic tradition.

There are a number of reasons why this has happened, prominent among them a situation in which the history of Ottoman culture was written, both inside and outside Turkey, from a Western, modernist perspective (or retrospective). One consequence of this is the notion that the Renaissance in Europe *must* have been a time of vital intellectual ferment, a rebirth of the powers attributed to the great Western civilizations of the past. This must be true because of what follows—the Enlightenment, the Industrial Revolution, and the rise of Europe as a dominant world power. That such a thing cannot have happened to the Ottomans was (self-)evident from the fact that, at the time when the first authoritative modern cultural histories were written, the Ottomans were not doing well and the Europeans were. Everything about the Ottomans had to be different from the Europeans—and different in ways that accounted for the so-called decline of the Ottomans and the success of the Europeans. This is a formulation with considerable explanatory power, enhanced by an often-unspoken subtext that attributes European success to intellectual and moral superiority.

Historical notions that both explain everything and flatter their primary audience have tremendous momentum, and so it is with the history of Ottoman culture. Arguing for a revision of this history often inspires the feeling that one is lying down in the path of the juggernaut. Nonetheless, the situation is not as apparently hopeless as it once was. Prominent Ottomanist scholars are arguing for a revision of the simplistic view of Ottoman decline.[1] They are chafing at the particularism of Ottoman studies.[2] They are even suggesting that we trespass on European notions, the idea of the Renaissance prominent among them.[3] As we see it, a large part of our contribution to this revision will be to make visible some texts, some relations between texts, some interpretations of texts, and some translations of texts underscoring similarities that can, we feel, both broaden and revitalize our understanding of the Renaissance. From the perspective of historians, the notion of renaissance as manifested in *the* Renaissance has been losing much of its former specificity, coming now to reference, not a particular European cultural movement, but a period in which a number of similar events, movements, and trends are visible on a global scale.[4]

It seems to us that an approach that to some extent globalizes the Renaissance also divests it of European particularism and allows the notion to open out productively into broader questions, including those surrounding issues of political economy and social change. What we have tried to do in the preceding pages is to demonstrate with examples how literary scripting, or, more generally, the literary aspects of meaning production, interacts with global forces such as politics, economics, and demographics to influence both social change and social stability. From our perspective, it makes no more sense to argue that there is a sphere of Ottoman literature separate and isolated from a global context than to argue that there are similarly isolated spheres of Ottoman economics, politics, demographics, climate, etc. In this chapter, we intend to tease out of our many specific examples some of the broad literary issues and comparisons that we have hitherto only suggested in passing. We are not economists, or sociologists, or even historians pure and simple; we are literary historians, and the literariness of our project lies, not just in our choice of texts (and our calling texts *texts* rather than *documents*), but in the way in which we look at texts (and contexts). Ours is most often the story of ambiguities and contradictions, the knowledge that a word, or a phrase, or a literary work, or a movement can always mean something and its opposite, and the realization that it is just this lack of resolution that generates utility and power. That much said, let us turn to a brief restatement of some literary issues that have been lurking at the fringes of the previous discussion.

Language: Classical-Vernacular

In the previous chapter, we described the later decades of the Age of Beloveds as representing the momentum of Renaissance culture carrying a residue forward into a post-Renaissance age. At this point, we will suggest that, in part, the Renaissance represents a wave of medieval culture washing up on the shores of modernity. This serves to suggest also that the periods (Renaissance, early modernity, etc.) that we have referred to as though they had some meaningful specificity and easily recognizable characteristics are all contaminated by other periods, are all of indefinite duration, and are all distorted by retrospection. As María Menocal argues in *Shards of Love*, her fascinating exploration of medieval culture and its affiliations to what we now call *postmodernity*, the Renaissance is largely an attempt to re-create the imagined unity and grammaticality of the classical languages in a world fragmented by the medieval vernaculars. Menocal evokes the ambiguity at the core of the Renaissance through a handful of symbols: Fray Bartolomé de Las Casas rewriting—in the newly invented Castilian of Nebrija's 1492 Spanish grammar—Columbus's own vulgar (and ungrammatical) account of his decisive voyage; Petrarch's ambivalent drive to "clear the rubble" of the Middle Ages in preparation for the master narrative of classical purity to be reborn in what would come to be known as *modernity*. Menocal's call is for a redirection of our attention to what has been elided in the post-Petrarchan narrative of modernity with its focus on the origins and primacy of the unary and grammatical nations and national languages:

> Indeed, let us tell the story from an aesthetic posture that is not horrified by cacophony (as Petrarch was, and as Bembo would be, and as medievalists will be). Let us instead take pleasure from fragments and the riotous pluralities and often-chaotic poetics that made much of the medieval world so resistant to that smooth narrative. In fact (and this too carries almost unbearable poignancy), Petrarch himself is, famously, the most divided of men; his fear of the violence and the ruptures of different kinds of chaos

lives in querulous intimacy with his fascination with that same apocalyptic threat. And then he writes those wonderful love songs in a vernacular. He is Columbus and Las Casas, but we have let the Las Casas tell us how to read Columbus.[5]

The late Renaissance, our Age of Beloveds, is an arena in which the struggle to write the master narrative of the classics and their rebirth is still hotly contested. Bembo's attempt to enthrone Petrarch as the model of a vernacular classicism and to anoint the Tuscan dialect as the national language of Italian culture runs up against the claims embodied in the passionate verses of other robust dialects, just as the classicizing idealism of Petrarch's beloved is challenged by the very real erotic, sexual presence and poetic talents of the Tullia d'Aragonas and Veronica Francos. The rebirth of classical culture was not a rebirth of classical languages; it was the first, tumultuous stage in the classicizing of the vernaculars and the elevation of the largely oral (and sung) languages of troubadours, minnesingers, and Turkish nomads and villagers to a level at which they could translate and rewrite the classics of Latin, Greek, Arabic, and Persian. The Age of Beloveds was not a time of tidy languages. Dictionaries and grammars were rare. Shakespeare had no dictionary of the English language at his disposal, nor did the sixteenth-century Ottoman poets have a dictionary of Ottoman. It was not even clear where English and Ottoman began and left off. Even the boundaries between languages were flimsy and permeable. Steven Mullaney describes the situation of Elizabethan English as follows:

> The vernacular was not a fixed linguistic system so much as a linguistic crossroads, a field where many languages—foreign tongues, local dialects, Latin and Greek—intersected; as the vernacular transposed and assimilated words and phrases from other languages, it came more and more to be a "gallimaufray or hodgepodge of al other speches." The medieval world had been structured around a dual language hierarchy: on the one hand a stable and monolithic Latin for learned and official society, and on the other, the metamorphic, plural, and largely oral vernacular, a plethora of local dialects, idioms, and jargons that was the province of popular culture. As that hierarchy broke down, however, the linguistic worlds that had formerly been held apart, as distinct and separate entities, come into increasing contact with one another. The European vernaculars came to inhabit the boundaries of other languages, to import values, concepts, and ideologies from strange tongues both foreign and domestic. The literary and linguistic vitality of the Renaissance was born in the space of such contact and assimilation.[6]

Mullaney was not talking about the dialects of the Turkic peoples who inhabited the Middle East from the eleventh century on and their transformation into classicizing literary languages—Chaghatai, Azeri, and Ottoman Turkish—but he could have been. The renaissance (and Turkification) of Middle Eastern culture had its beginnings in the fifteenth century on the eastern Iranian and Central Asian peripheries of "Islamdom" during the reign of the Timurids (the successors of the great conqueror Timur, known to the East as Timur-i Lenk [Timur the Lame] and to the West as Marlowe's great autocrat Tamburlaine).[7] With the rise of the Ottomans as a world power at midcentury, the Turkic cultural revival spread to both the eastern and the western boundaries of Islam. During the Age of Beloveds, the weight of cultural renewal shifted to the west, where the language of the Ottoman elites was emerging out of a chaos of Turkish, Persian, Arabic, Greek, Italian, Ladino, and all the many languages and dialects of the empire. Mullaney cites an incisive passage from Bakhtin's *Rabelais and His World* (talking about the French of Rabelais, who by himself could have added a chapter or two to this book had we "but world enough and time"): " 'The primitive and naive coexistence of languages and dialects had come to an end; the new consciousness was born not in a perfected and fixed linguistic system but at the intersection of many languages and the point of their most intense interorientation and struggle. Languages are philosophies—not abstract but concrete, social philosophies, penetrated by a system of values inseparable from living practice and class struggle.' "[8]

In both England and the Ottoman Empire, the battle lines were clearly drawn (although not without some ambiguity on the part of individual combatants). In his discourse on the construction of identity (self-fashioning) during the English Renaissance, Stephen Greenblatt associates the poles of contrastive self-understanding ("I" in relation to an alien other) with irreconcilable differences that existed between Sir Thomas More and William Tyndale. It is clear from Greenblatt's exploration that one of the crucial matters (if not *the* crucial matter) at issue was one of language. More clung (to the death, we might add) to the universality of the Roman Catholic Church, to the primacy of that church's authority (over the rulers of secular states), and to the Latin Bible and the Latin language (as the universal text and language of the rule of truth). Also a martyr to his beliefs, Tyndale held equally firmly to the reformed church of Luther, to the priesthood of the individual, and to the word of God translated into the vernaculars of common people, echoing the desire of the great Renaissance humanist Erasmus, who said: "I disagree very much with those who are unwilling that Holy Scripture, translated into the vulgar tongue be read by the uneducated. . . . I would that even the lowliest women read the Gospels and the Pauline Epistles. And I would that they were translated into all languages so that they could be read and understood not only by Scots and Irish but also by Turks and Saracens."[9] The battle here swirls about the issue of whether the unified, universal languages of Holy Scripture and classical literature would retain their authority over a similarly unified Christian world or be overtaken in a fragmented Christendom by local dialects, spoken by the uneducated and educated alike, given power and a claim to dominion by vernacular translations of Scripture. It is about language, but it is also about class and social power, about states and empires and the dominion of the church, about the power of princes and popes, about whose rule represents the will of God.

Among the Turks and Saracens, the situation is and is not the same. There can be no question of translating the Qur'an. God's message to Muhammad is insistent that this was an Arabic text sent to an Arab prophet: "Verily We have sent it to you as an Arabic Recitation [Qur'an]."[10] This grants a spiritual authority to the Arabic language, privileging it in a way that resembles but exceeds the privileging of Latin by the Roman Catholic Church. Although Islam does not—cannot—fracture along the fault line of translation, it fissures very early on the issue of authoritative interpretation: the question of whether the scientific, philological methodology of the Sunnis or the Shia's reliance on the prophetic, charismatic understanding of inspired individuals would dominate. Although the Sunni/Shiite split is institutionalized in Islamic history, it is overlaid by another split with somewhat similar characteristics but different deployment. This is the fissure that divides Islamic orthodoxy from an increasingly institutionalized mysticism (Sufism). Mysticism had long been available as a source of personal, emotional, ecstatic religious experience to Sunnis and Shiites alike, but, by the Age of Beloveds, it had acquired a popularity that dramatically altered both its character and its social role. Just as the Reformation rewrote (literally, translated) Christianity and its texts in the languages of daily life and popular culture, tearing them away from the scholars and the hierarchy of the Catholic Church, so did popular Islamic mysticism step aside from Arabic and its scholastic tradition and reinscribe the emotional inspiration of Islam in Persian and Turkish and Urdu.

Mysticism became a spiritual springboard; from it the Turkic peoples of Central Asia entered the mainstream of Islam; and from it that mainstream first began to seep into Byzantium and Europe. Arabic remained the language of ritual, of theology and canon law, but, by the mid-fifteenth century, it seemed that almost everyone in Ottoman lands was a mystic of one sort or another; these mystics' texts were poetry and hagiographies, their languages Persian and Ottoman Turkish. Sufism ignored the Sunni/Shiite divide but, if anything, favored the Shia, which had a ready-made bias toward the emotional experience of religion and knowledge of the divine. When, in the early sixteenth century, Shah Isma'il Safavi rallied the Turcoman tribes of eastern Anatolia and Iran around the banner of Shiite Sufism and established himself as the ruler of Iran, the supreme Sufi master, and (possibly) the Mahdi, the Ottomans were in a quandary. In one form or another Sufism was everywhere; people of all classes imbibed it, as Rypka said of the poets, with their mothers' milk. The empire would necessarily remain Sunni—one cornerstone of the Ottoman sultanate's legitimacy was the fact that, since early in the sixteenth century, Istanbul was also the locus of the caliphate, the Sunni line of successors to the Prophet's role as leader of the Islamic community. Nonetheless, despite its affinities to Shiism, Sufism was attractive. By the end of the fifteenth century, the mystical orders had become a central and powerful social and political as well as religious force.

Mehmet the Conqueror was enamored as a youth; his son Bayezit II would be called Sufi Bayezit in his dotage; Selim I wrote mystical verses in Persian in which he presents himself as a mendicant dervish; Süleyman doted on the dervish Hayali. Posing the ruler as a dervish adept and spiritual beloved had its advantages, as we have pointed out, but what makes this possible and effective is the part that Sufism played in re-creating the vernaculars—Turkish and Persian and Urdu—as languages of religion. Sufism elevated vernacular poetry—from Rumi's voluminous *Mesnevi* to popular lyrics in simple Turkish—to the level (or nearly to the level) of Scripture; it gave Islam a language of emotion that speaks to a broad audience of nonelites and evades the linguistic authority of Arabic and the ulema. Sufism, as it existed in the Ottoman Empire from the sixteenth century on, did not represent a reformation, but it did do for Islam some of the same things that the Reformation did for Christianity. It broke the hegemony of the privileged language and diffused religious literacy (including oral literacy) across class and education barriers. It weakened the grip of the traditional religious authorities and multiplied the rituals and metaphors of religion. Moreover, as Shah Isma'il (like Henry VIII) understood well, it cleared space among the institutions of power for a monarch who did not have the backing of orthodox religious legitimacy.

Despite the appearance of effects that resemble those produced by the Reformation in England, the reaction of Ottoman religious authorities to the growth and diffusion of popular Sufism near the end of the Age of Beloveds was closer in practice to that of the Italian Counter-Reformation. Stung by Reformation criticisms of its corruption, immorality, and unconcern with the sufferings of the common people, the Catholic Church took steps to display its concern with orthodoxy, decency, and decorum, tilting away from its (at least tacit) support of the liberal standards of late-Renaissance elite art and literature and toward a simpler, more common morality. The Council of Trent (1563) took pains to promulgate standards for sacred art. The supererogatory male nudes in Michelangelo's *Last Judgment* had already been painted over, and, in 1573, Veronese was called before the Inquisition to answer for what were deemed the "inappropriate secular elements"—a jester, a dwarf, and a dog—in his *Last Supper*.[11] It is also worth noting that the jester, dwarf, and dog were typical adjuncts to the royal courts of European monarchs (and to the courts of the Ottoman sultans). Obviously, the parallel drawn between the monarch's court and that of the Son of God, which apparently seemed natural to Veronese, was too blatant for the Inquisition, which demanded that the painting be retitled *Feast in the House of Levi*.

The assault, however, seemed to be directed for the most part at erotic portrayals, which had always been viewed with some suspicion, the outstanding example being the suppression of Giulio Romano's early-sixteenth-century illustrations of Aretino's sonnets on the sexual positions. That Aretino was still defending the sonnets and illustrations in the second half of the century is an indication of the appearance of a new and more stringent morality. The beloved too was under attack. In Venice in 1580, the honored courtesan and poet Veronica Franco was accused of witchcraft by the disgruntled tutor of her children, whom she suspected of stealing from her. Only narrowly did she evade the fate of the public prostitute Emilia Catena and the honored courtesan Isabella Bellocchio, who in the late 1580s were publicly whipped and forced to wear miters inscribed with their crimes for an hour on the very public Rialto Bridge.[12] The heyday of the courtesan was drawing to a close, but, overall, the repression was ambivalent. The Council of Trent had also affirmed the importance of sacred art, but religious authorities still left a certain amount of leeway for the erotic so long as it did not trespass overtly on the realm of the sacred. In Venice and Florence, prostitution remained as a lucrative municipal enterprise.

In the Ottoman Empire, the response of religious authorities to the moral liberality of the Age of Beloveds was, as we saw in chapter 9, also ambiguous. Their main options were either co-opting the dervish orders by privileging the most orderly and compliant of them or denouncing dervish practices as immoral and heretical. They did both. The elite, intellectual orders such as the Mevlevi, the Halveti, and the Gülşeni were gradually folded into the cultural life of the educated class. Other practices and practitioners were condemned and repressed. Puritan, moral revivalist movements (e.g., the Kadizadeli movement and its intellectual precursor in the writings of Birgili Mehmet) were more orthodox than the dominant ulema on issues of doctrine and social practice. They were also violently anti-Sufi and condemned the cultural institutions of the poetic universe. Internal reforms of the legal system and its bureaucracy also took on a conservative hue. In the latter years of Süleyman's reign, the jurist Ebu's-suʿud not only regularized access to the religious bureaucracy but also attempted to systematize the law and put a stop to the more extreme examples of mystical heterodoxy—a restatement of the law that would win for Süleyman the epithet of the Lawgiver. Yet the conservative reformers considered even Ebu's-suʿud to be a dangerous liberal on account of actions such as his defense of the practice of endowing charitable institutions with cash or movable goods, which was seen as an unwarranted transgression of the quranic prohibition against usury.

What we observe seems to have been a general reaction to or retreat from the synthesis of urban entertainment culture (tavern, coffeehouse, literary salon), love in the world (the beloveds and their lovers), the emotional religion of love (Sufism), and the court (the sultan as beloved) that marked the Age of Beloveds. As we have said before, all these elements would remain alive in Ottoman society—but in a more fragmented form—until the early eighteenth century, when the palace would attempt to revive the synthesis. In general, the Ottoman case is paralleled by features of the Puritan revolution in England, which, in turn, reflected a widespread Protestant puritanism in Europe and the more restrictive moral climate of the Counter-Reformation. The Age of Beloveds was a period of extraordinary creativity and dramatic change in the way in which people saw themselves and their place in the world. It was a time of great promise and great turmoil as the world gave birth to modernity amid a cacophony of emerging languages, the infancy of national states, and the lowering of barriers to social mobility. The retreat and reaction was only a pause, a moment for the world to catch its breath.

In both Europe and the Ottoman Empire, however, mysticism was the other, dissenting, antireactionary response to fundamental change. Michel de Certeau has a lovely passage on the role of mysticism in sixteenth- and seventeenth-century Europe:

> But the mysticism of that age is connected as much to the collective history of a transition as it is to inaugural "wanderings." It is the story of the Christian "Occident." It came in, it seems, with the setting sun, but vanished before morning, announcing a day it never knew; the "retreat of mystics" coincides with the dawning of the century of the Enlightenment. The project of a radical Christianity was formed against a backdrop of decadence and "corruption" in a world that was falling apart and in need of repair. It borrowed the vocabulary of the Reformation, applying it to a biographical context: schism, wounds, etc. The end of a world was the experience sought by every spiritual poet. Their daring and luminous paths streaked a night from which they were later extracted by a piety greedy for mystical traces;

they inscribed themselves on its black page, and it is here we must relearn how to read them.[13]

As Fleischer's work on the shared apocalyptic, eschatological vision of Eurasia during the early sixteenth century indicates, the end of *a* world—the perception of dramatic change—was widely interpreted as a sign of the impending end of *the* world. This sense of living in the final days was productive of two contradictory impulses, one stemming from the conviction that out of the absolutist monarchies of the time would emerge the Universal Monarch, who would unite the world under the one true faith, the other from a determination to escape the domination of earthly powers, both secular authority and the church and its doctrines, and seek salvation through direct experience of the divine. In both Islam and Christianity, there existed a distinction between God's power as revealed historically through the choices that he made in communicating his will to human beings (in Christian theological terms, the *potentia Dei ordinata*; in Islamic theological terms, the power inherent in the sharia) and God's absolute power to do whatever he wills (*potentia Dei absoluta*).[14] In the belief that it is possible to find salvation in a direct appeal to God's absolute power, mysticism fundamentally evaded the institutions of control that had emerged historically to enforce what God had ordained. This created a zone of freedom and dissent distinct from and opposed to the domain of secular and religious authority.[15] It also held out the hope of healing the multiple alienations, both spiritual and material, that marked the crisis period of the late Renaissance. For a brief time, at least, the power of mystical ideology, fed by abundant streams flowing out of medieval Christianity, Islam, the Jewish cabala, and Neoplatonism, was great enough that even secular powers strove to co-opt or participate in its alliance of poetry with the metaphors of love, beauty, and eroticism.[16] The result was a historical moment in which the beloved took center stage, a beloved who, even at his or her most powerless, carnal, and mercenary, was linked in some degree to the beloved monarch and the absolute presence of God.

Ottoman Poetry, Mannerism, and the Late-Renaissance World

We are certainly testing, if not exceeding, the limits of audacity to bring up the terribly vexed issue of literary mannerism. The two books that convinced us of the usefulness to our project of considering the concept of mannerism spent their first seventy-one and forty-seven pages, respectively, just outlining the scholarly history of its definitions.[17] Traditionally, mannerism has been seen as a tendency in the visual arts characteristic of an intermediate period between the Renaissance and the Baroque that resembles not so much a geographic layer (as Braudel described the baroque) as a transition zone between layers.[18] However, it is our belief that, if we are going to presume to do what Braudel regretfully did not and suggest similarities in patterns of culture and literature production between the Ottoman Empire and Europe, mannerism is a productive place to start.

The reasons for this are as straightforward as the concept of mannerism is elusive. Simply put, when we attempt to describe the general characteristics of Ottoman literature (which is heavily weighted toward poetry) in the language of traditional European cultural theory, the terms and clusters of terms that we come up with seem to match up with mannerism better than with anything else. Of course, this does not mean that the Ottomans were mannerists in any reasonable sense of the term. They could not possibly have been. *Mannerism* signifies a particular configuration of European art and artistic sensibility during a certain period with very specific origins, consequences, and internal relations. Our contention is only that there is a brief period of convergence during which European art (both visual and literary), while on a journey of its own, one with a distinctive starting point and a distinctive destination, takes a path very similar to that of Ottoman art. The Europeans and the Ottomans came from different places and would soon take different roads, but, as we have already argued about a number of cultural and social phenomena, a complex multiplicity of conditions during the so-called Age of Beloveds nevertheless produced a host of similar behaviors apparently unmotivated by the usual means and modes of sociocultural transmission.

Our foray into mannerism will be regrettably brief and limited to exemplifying some of the more prominent points of similarity, our primary purpose being to assemble into a coherent argument some of the propositions encountered here and there in the previous chapters. Specifically, we will focus on certain characteristic features of mannerism that we find to parallel features of Ottoman poetry.

One set of features has to do, in general, with the relation of artistic products to art and the history of art, or, otherwise stated, the artist's consciousness of himself as a producer of art, not only imitating nature, but also imitating other art. James Mirollo says, in this regard: "This is why, for example, and again in contrast to the baroque, so much sixteenth-century love poetry courts mannerism by eschewing thematic expansion and settling for stylistic refinement or modulation, with the inevitable mixed results that range from the merely mannered and stylized to the more effective and appealing kind of mannerism we take up below. This is why, also, literary mannerism is so often sought in those literary phenomena, such as Petrarchism, where there is parodic juxtaposition to, even a parasitic dependence upon, a thematic and stylistic model."[19] The other set of features is more specifically stylistic and is taken from Paul Castagno, who says, in general: "I recognize in Mannerism a style that is typically exaggerated, distorted, lacks compositional unity, substitutes rhythmical effects for harmony and balance, obscures spatial relationships, utilizes figural crowding, sprezzatura, *effetto meraviglioso* [magical effects], and other definable traits." Among the "other definable traits" Castagno includes *mescolare* (the mixing of incongruous elements), *discordia concors* (the juxtaposition of opposites), preciosity, *bizzarrie*, ornamentation, and eroticism.[20] Our conclusions, however, will build more directly on the more global contextualization of mannerism found in Arnold Hauser's pioneering *Mannerism*.

As examples of how an overt awareness of mannerism might inform a reading of an Ottoman poem, let us consider a pair of poems from the center of the tradition and the height of the Age of Beloveds. The first is a well-known poem by the most famous poet of the later years of Süleyman's reign. If anyone represents the typical Ottoman success story, it is the poet and jurist Baki (1526–1600). He was the son of a relatively poor man, either a tender of lamps in a mosque or a saddler (depending on whether one reads the Arabic letters s, r, ā, j as *sirāj* [tender of lamps] or as *sarrāj* [saddler]). Education was free and open to Ottomans of every class, and Baki was apparently a brilliant student. He pursued his education through the university system and embarked on a career in the religious institution, finally reaching the position of chief military magistrate of the Anatolian and, then, the European provinces. His talents as a poet were unmatched, and he became a favorite at court and the conversational companion of Sultan Süleyman, who recognized his mastery by granting him the title "Sultan of Poets."

The poem at which we will be looking is famous primarily for its third couplet, one of the most often cited couplets in all of Ottoman poetry. The other lines are seldom remembered and are most often thought of as if they were no more than the setting for the one exquisite couplet. We find them more interesting than that. In our translation, the poem goes something like the following (although, as can be seen by the transcribed original of the opening couplet, the line breaks in the translation do not represent the appearance of the Turkish and are intended only to give a sense of the syntactic rhythms of the original). The rhyme is in "a" with the redif *imiş*, which is the third-person reportorial mode (i.e., "he/they say or report that . . ."). Our translation goes as follows:

Zülf-i siyahı saye-i perr-i hüma imiş
Iklim-i hüsne anun içün padişa imiş

His black lovelock, they say,
    is the shadow
        of the bird of fortune's wing
And for this, they say,
    in the clime of loveliness
        he is become the king

As it bowed down
    the cheek of the sun
        turned itself to gold
A wondrous alchemy
    they say, is the dust
        at the beloved's door

Cast your voice loud
    into this world
        like the psalmist David
For 'neath this dome
    naught remains, they say,
        but a pleasant echo

Our eyes, failing
    to see the beloved
        see nothing of this world
The mirror of his beauty
    they say, is the glass
        wherein the whole world shows

Oh my love,
    Baki the wretched
        is in thrall to your locks
Addicted, they say,
    to the toils
        of calamity's rope[21]

The first couplet is an example of the tremendously popular rhetorical figure called *hüsn-i ta'lil* (beauty of cause, or fantastic assignment of cause). The background is this: According to popular Ottoman-era beliefs, there is a little bird—without legs in some versions—that flies high, invisibly, and ceaselessly about the world. If the shadow of this tiny bird chances to fall on someone as it passes overhead, that person will be blessed by good fortune and rise to a position of wealth and power. Here Baki says that his beloved is the king of beloveds *because* he has been touched by the shadow of the *hüma* (bird of fortune). Do you see it? The shadow is still there, on the cheek, resembling a (wing-shaped) lock of hair.

In this first couplet, there is a concatenation of the bizarre, the hyperbolic, and the magical, creating the kind of distortion of reality that foregrounds the couplet's status as poetic *art*. In mannerist terms, what gives this artifice power is its interior design (*disegno intero*), which we might characterize as the *idea* of a real-world structure of relations that underlies the artifice and, in a sense, makes it natural. In Baki's universe, the beloved *is* the monarch, and the role (or one of the roles) of poetry is to re-create the powerholder as the object of love. Moreover, in a situation where a lamp tender's son or a lowly slave can rise to power and position and the most powerful dignitary can be executed on the monarch's whim, one would quite naturally entertain the idea that rising or falling in this world is, ultimately, dependent on arbitrary, aleatory events, not unlike happening to be brushed by the shadow of a tiny, unseen bird.

The second couplet continues the rhetorical theme of beautiful/fantastic causes. Here, the poet accounts for the commonplace fact that the sun's disk often looks as though it is made of gold. The setting sun is personified by describing it as a petitioner bowing before the ruler or as a Muslim touching his brow to the ground in prayer. For a Muslim, one of the most natural and common acts is the obligatory five-times-a-day prostration in prayer, an act of humility and submission as timed and regular and inevitable as the setting of the sun. For the courtier, prostration before the ruler was equally a sign of humble submission and, by analogy, a recognition of the ruler's mandate from God. Even the ambassadors of foreign monarchs were escorted into the sultan's presence by two magnificently clad eunuchs, one on each arm, who would rather roughly force them to bow before a silent, immobile, and haughty ruler.[22]

One of the defining features of the Ottoman manner is its unrestrained indulgence in testing the outermost limits of hyperbole. Here, the notion that the sun—commonly referred to as *the monarch of the heavens*—would bow to the beloved is one way of saying that everything, every power in the material universe, is subordinate to the beloved. The only way to account for this notion without pushing hyperbole into the realm of sacrilege (i.e., without putting the beloved in the place of God) is to be aware, as the audiences of Ottoman poetry were, that love for the beloved boy at hand is just a metaphor for real love—love of the divine power to which all things are subordinate. And we have not even gotten to the beautiful cause yet! As it bows, the sun's face comes in contact with the dust at the beloved's door (the dust of the courtyard or street in front of his or her house). When touched by the beloved, this dust, the lowliest of substances, is endowed with the legendary property so widely and vainly sought by medieval science: the ability to turn base metals to gold, the power of the philosopher's stone and the ultimate goal of alchemy. Hyperbole on hyperbole. And, in them, the courtier's view of the sultan as the ultimate source of riches and power re-creates the ruler as a bird of fortune in whose shadow the lowly are exalted and imagines him as the source of a power so great that the very dust at his threshold is transmuted into the dream of alchemy and the source of limitless wealth.

As this little explication indicates, one of the consequences of writing within the confines of conventional themes and composing in relation to influential predecessors and models is that it becomes possible to cram a bewildering array of ideas into very few words. In this, the fullness of many early-modern Ottoman (and European mannerist) poems comes to resemble the *horror vacui*, the abhorrence of empty space that we see in mannerist painting. Where the painter seems to dread leaving a space untouched by his talent, the poet shrinks from the impression of having left a possible thought unthought and unspoken. In this, what leaps to the surface everywhere is *art*. Art is both the arena in which battles for dominance are fought and the weapon wielded by the combatants in a struggle whose prize, in the end, is *survival*. Whose poem, whose name, will live on in this world where all else is mortal and soon forgotten? This, then, is the theme of the famous third couplet.

Admittedly, a large part of what makes this couplet famous is precisely that it makes a straightforward claim about the enduring and universal qualities of artistic expression. Those who cite the verses of poets are likely to be persons—other poets, scholars, biographers, literati—who have compelling interests in the immortality of great art. So this kind of confirmation by a recognized master poet is right up their alley. Beyond this attractive claim, however, the couplet appears simple, especially following the extravagant, lush, and even bizarre hyperboles of the previous two couplets. And perhaps it *is* simple. This too might be part of its appeal today. There are few lines in Ottoman poetry that have an appropriate message and that can also be cited without extensive explanation. But such considerations aside, let us look more closely at the matter of the couplet's apparent simplicity. The Ottomans inherited from the Persians the concept *sehl ü mümteniʿ* (the simple and complex), by which is meant the highly valued art of creating an expression that on the surface is straightforward but on closer inspection reveals surprising complexities. A simple and complex couplet is also emblematic of the larger goal (vital to both Ottoman and European mannerist poets) of manifesting what the Italians called *sprezzatura*, demonstrating one's superiority by doing the difficult effortlessly. In this context, let us look more closely at Baki's famous couplet.

It is not hard to imagine this world according to the conventional cosmology of Ottoman poets as existing beneath the solid blue dome of the heavens. Nor would an ordinarily sensitive reader of poetry miss the connection between a loud voice echoing from the dome of a great building and the echoes of poetry reverberating down through time under heaven's dome. Nonetheless, a good deal of the complexity of mannerist art (including the Ottoman version) is just this referencing and commenting on its own status and devices. Baki is renown for his playfulness with language. Seldom does he miss a chance to exploit the multiple meanings of a crucial word. In this couplet, the most obvious example—a mere throwaway for someone as skilled as Baki—is a play on the poet's name. It does not show up in translation, but, in Turkish, the phrase that more literally translates as "that which endures" is *baki kalan*. Moreover, the name Baki is also one of the ninety-nine divine names, "the Everlasting/Immortal (Baki)." So the second hemistich can read "that which endures in [beneath] this dome is a pleasant echo" or "what remains of Baki beneath this dome is a pleasant echo" or even "what remains of the Everlasting beneath this dome is a pleasant echo" (the poem as an intimation of the divine, which, in turn, inheres—echoes—in the physical world). Here, we have art using artifice in praise of art. And that is not all.

In the first hemistich, the word for "world" is ʿalem, which can also mean "a drinking party." This brings us back from all the hyperbole and preciosity of art on display to the tavern, the drinking party, the beloved, and the reveler's ecstatic cry. This world is just a party in which we recite a poem at the top of our lungs and move on, leaving nothing but an echo behind. But this is no little thing, for Baki takes us back, before all the models and paragons of Islamic literature in Arabic, Persian, and the Turkic languages, and conjures with the name of David, the psalmist, the lover and panegyrist of God. That the memory of David, the poet-king, still reverberates through the world in Baki's day is sure proof that a poet, who knows the spiritual meaning core of love and intoxication, can survive the body's certain demise.

The fourth couplet affirms the centrality of the beloved and the essential truth of the lover's vision. If the lover is not gazing on the beloved, he is gazing on nothing, for nothing in this world is really real except the beloved/the divine. The beloved's face is a mirror because—and this too is a commonplace—it is absolutely pure in the way of a mirror made by polishing metal until it is free of rust or scratches or any kind of blemish. And purity of countenance must reach beneath the physical surface to the moral center. Those who behave in a shameful manner find their evil written in black on their faces. Then the mirror is described as ʿalem-nüma (world displaying), and the Ottoman audience immediately recognizes a reference to the legendary mirror of Alexander, in which the world conqueror was said to be able to view whatever was happening anywhere on earth. The magical mirror and its counterpart, the all-seeing cup of the legendary Persian king Cemşid, are never far from the consciousness of Ottoman poets because, for them, poetry is that very mirror, that very cup, in which is reflected—if only you have the wit to see it—all that is meaningful about the world. Poetry is, not the mirror of nature (as some will claim in a later age), but a mirror that perfectly reflects the *idea* of nature.

The final couplet—by the rules of the gazel genre a "signature" couplet—returns us to the name of the poet and the very common situation in which the poet addresses or refers to himself (or herself) by name. There is a doubling here that parallels the real-world circumstances of many talented persons, such as a man named 'Abdu'l-baki (Servant ['abd] of the Everlasting [al-Baki]). 'Abdu'l-baki is a quite distinguished official in the legal/religious bureaucracy, a friend of the sultan, a scholar and arbiter of law and morality at the highest levels of the state. He is also a poet who, playing on his given name, took the pen name Baki (the Immortal) and, as such, sang the praises of dubious young men, extolled the virtues of the drinking party, and, in his youth at least, may well have given himself over to love and a lover's melancholic pursuits. In the final, signature couplet of the gazel, the two personae often speak to or about each other. 'Abdu'l-baki looks compassionately on his wretched alter ego and attempts to enlist the sympathies of the beloved on his behalf. "Look at him," he says to the beloved. "He is miserable yet, like an addict, happy in his misery. He is bound, caught up in the lasso of a terrible calamity." The poet knows better, however. What the man of the world thinks he sees is not what the ehl-i dil, the man of the heart, knows: that the rope is no more than a curling strand of the beloved's hair; that the only calamity (*bela*) here is addiction (being *mübtela*, from the same root letters as *bela* and, hence, "caught by a calamity"); and that addiction to the beloved's locks is no tragedy. The terms reverse themselves. Calamity is the greatest fortune; being an addict is the path to happiness; being bound like a prisoner is the greatest success. This is the Sufi's logic and, strangely, the courtier's too. To be bound, mastered by a worthy ruler is all that can be hoped.

The second poem is by Hayali, the dervish-beloved-lover-courtier-governor with whom we are already familiar. As we have seen, Hayali was both valued and derided for being a dervish, and his poetry is always open to a mystical interpretation, one that we will pass over in favor of a more worldly reading emphasizing stylistic features and parallels to mannerist art:[23]

> *Serv ile gül çemende ki durub oturdular*
> *Bu kadd ü bu 'izarı sende gördüler*

> Cypress and rose in the meadow stand and sit
> That same body and that cheek, they see in you

> The rose sent a leaflet to the bulbul flying
> Borne by the footman breeze to say,
> > we'll not blossom without you
>
> Wine is a substance famed for its efficacies
> But in the era of your lip, they spill it at their feet
>
> The torrent dug his grave, the north wind came
> > and the east wind,
> They bore him thence, when he died—Mejnun,
> > bereft and lorn
>
> When the sea touched Hayali's tears with its tongue
> The clouds gathered above him and praised him
> > from the skies[24]

In this poem we will find, perhaps even more starkly than in Baki's, traces of what we might call (for lack of anything better) *Ottoman mannerism*. The lack of compositional unity and the focus on exaggerated, fantastic imagery is obvious, but the effects that are the most mannerist (or mannerist-like) are those that make the poem untranslatable in many places. That we have translated an untranslatable poem is no miracle; it is only a sign that we have left out almost everything of importance.

The opening couplet is one of the more translatable ones. Its only difficulty lies in appreciating the *attention* to every word that the Ottoman poet demands. The setting is the ubiquitous Ottoman poetic garden, in which we find two of the major features: the cypress and the rose. The bulk of the line personifies these two. They "stand and sit" insofar as the cypress *stands tall* to show off its slender, swaying body, while the rose sits, bowed down by the weight of its blossom. But, in this poetic universe of concentric contexts, the garden elements are, not only beloveds themselves, but also parts of a compound beloved of which the rose is the cheek, the cypress the body, the hyacinth the hair, the narcissus the eye, etc. So, when the garden sees the beloved, it recognizes itself reflected—to perfection—in him or her. Herein lies the *preciosity* of the Ottoman manner: the production of subtle and often minute variants on a commonplace image, variants that to the educated eye stand out sharply, delighting those who know and escaping the unrefined gaze.

The second couplet continues the garden imagery but recontextualizes the garden as the household of the ruler or some other wealthy and powerful beloveds. Here, the beloveds are depicted as sending a message via a footman or messenger to the lover. As we mentioned above, when an important Ottoman man or woman went out in public, he or she would do so surrounded by retainers. Among the retainers accompanying the sultan (and other dignitaries) were the footman-messengers known as *peyk* or "satellites," who ran alongside the royal personage. In the garden, the footman is the east wind, a gentle breeze. The lover is always the bulbul, the eastern nightingale, who sings of love to the rose and, embracing the ever-dangerous beloved, is pierced by thorns, either dying or being terribly wounded (as evidenced by the red marking on the bird's breast). The roses send a message—the "leaflet," more exactly "a paper" (*kağıd*)—blowing on the breeze: the verb for "to send" here is *uçurmak*, which also and more literally means "to make fly." But to send a piece of paper flying would be unacceptably incongruous according to the standards of Ottoman poetry. Even though the poet needs the two long syllables to fit his rhythm scheme, a piece of paper has no place in the garden; it would be trash and the lines too. What rescues the couplet—and makes it even more precious—is that we know that, here, "paper"/*kağıd* (the common Turkish word) is just a variant of a more common *poetic* word, the Arabic *varak*, which means *both* "paper" and "leaf." The message of the roses also contains a commonplace double meaning: the verb translated as "[to] blossom" (*açılmak*) is more literally "to be open," and, while in the garden context it can refer to the opening of the rosebud, it more usually has the sense of someone relaxing, smiling, laughing, and enjoying a social occasion. This attention to the ornamentation of every possible word, leaving almost nothing unadorned, nothing simple, is another feature of mannerism Ottoman style.

Yet another feature of the *maniera turca* is its unconcern with extended thematic development and smooth passages (or any passages at all) between couplets. As Hauser says of the European mannerists: "The most striking feature of mannerist anti-classicism, however, was its abandonment of the fiction that a work of art is an organic, indivisible, and unalterable whole, made all of a piece."[25] The only difference is that, for the Ottomans, the abandonment of the whole had occurred in a distant and invisible past and represents a continuity rather than a break. For example, from the garden, Hayali makes what feels like an abrupt and disconcerting jump to the drinking party. Most educated observers of Ottoman poetry have commented on the apparent rule that the couplets of an Ottoman poem should stand alone and need not have any discernible connections or transitions. While this may, indeed, be true, it is also true that the supercontextualization of the poetry, its constant referencing of models and conventions, often makes overt connections and transitions excessive and, to Ottoman audiences, tedious. Of course there is a drinking party in the garden; of course the smiling and laughing beloved is the center of the drinking party. To what else are the roses inviting the lover/bulbul?

In the third couplet, translation begins to fail spectacularly. There is no way to represent this couplet except precisely as it is. This is the magical effect of Ottoman poetry, the counterpart of the effetto meraviglioso of the mannerist artist. The artist in words uses the inherent ambiguity of language to make a few words conjure multiple images (perhaps the counterpart of the mannerist artist's exaggerated use of perspective). Hayali says that wine is a substance (*meta'*, lit. "material goods of commerce") known for its beneficial effects. Wine had many medical applications in early-modern times in addition to its mood-altering potential. Nonetheless, Hayali says—and this is where things get out of hand—in the "era" (*devr*) of your lip they just pour it out at their "feet" (*ayak*). But here is the problem: both *devr* and *ayak* have multiple meanings, and every combination of those meanings is relevant to the context of the couplet. *Devr* means "turn" or "cycle" as in "the turning of the cup around the circle of drinkers at the wine gathering," it means "cycle" as in "era or age," and it means "circle" as in "the little circle of your lips." And *ayak* means "foot" in common everyday Turkish, then and now, but to the Ottoman poets and revelers it also meant "cup, wine cup."[26] So what we have as possibilities for the hemistich are these (at least): "In the era of your lip [when your lip is there to sip] people just dump their wine on the ground [even considering how valuable a commodity it is]"; or "As your lip goes around the gathering [for us all to kiss] we just dump [forget about] the wine, etc."; or "When your lip is there [as your lip goes round] people fill their glasses [because then it is a real party]"; or "Faced with your lip's [amazing] little round circle the people at the gathering [are so bewildered that they] spill their wine [or they pour it into their glasses]." And of course it means all these things, and that is the magic of it. A good Ottoman poem, like a mannerist work of art, "is always a piece of bravura, a triumphant conjuring trick, a firework display, with flying sparks and colors."[27]

The next couplet is exquisite and another imaginative leap, seemingly unanchored in what went before—except that, in Ottoman poetry, as it is with Petrarch's "long deceased woes," the beloved is never available, and the mood always runs to melancholy. Mejnun is arguably the archetypal lover in the tradition inherited by the Ottomans. Enshrined as the putative author of a cycle of Arabic love poems, narrated in the romantic narratives of, among others, Nizami (1140–1202) and Amir Husrev (in Persian Amir-e Khosrow; ca. 1299) in Persian, Nevayi (1441–1501) in Chaghatai Turkic (ca. 1483), and Fuzuli (mid-sixteenth century) in Azeri Turkish, and recalled in thousands of love poems, Mejnun is everywhere the spokesman of hyperbolic melancholy. His name means "crazy" in Arabic and is the sobriquet bestowed on him by his school friends in the early days of his consuming passion for his beloved Leyla. His was a life constructed around anguish and separation from the beloved. He tried and failed to possess her—until she came to possess him internally to a point where nothing of him remained. Mejnun is the icon of the self-sacrificed lover and equally a metaphor for the mystic divested of all selfish and worldly desires.[28] In his last days, he wandered the wastelands in the company of the most timid and fierce of wild creatures, unable to interact with humans, weeping, wandering, and alone.

In Hayali's couplet, we see the natural forces of the wasteland providing for Mejnun at his demise just as the wild animals had watched over him in his mad roaming. The torrent (of rain, but indistinguishable from the torrent of his tears) gouges a watercourse through the waste, digging his grave. The desert winds that, in more hopeful days, delivered his messages to Leyla carry his body, now emaciated and worn and light as a leaf, to his burial. Here, we are far from the garden with its gentle streams, compliant messenger breeze, enticing roses, and musical bulbul/lover. At the final level of love, that of mystical transcendence, the landscape is harsh and barren, stripped of all surface beauties and redolent only of death—the death of the self. Yet, at this point, the opposites—garden and desert—are conjoined. In the conventional mysticism of poetry, the outsiders, the common folk, the puritans and ascetics of the spiritual surface, mistake the garden of paradise, with all its exaggerated earthly delights, for the true paradise of union (or reunion) with the divine. But, in truth, to the people of the heart what seems like a desert is the ultimate garden.

The closing, signature couplet presents another insurmountable problem for translation. The first hemistich could be said to have the literal (and erotic) reading "when the sea stretched out its tongue to Hayali's tears." But, as Mehmed Çavuşoğlu points out, *-e dil uzatmak*, which we translate as meaning "to stretch out the tongue to," commonly means "to criticize, denigrate," which would give the sense "the sea belittled or criticized Hayali's tears." Then again, the word for "tongue" (*dil*) can, in the context of the sea, also mean "a tongue of ocean" or "a gulf." This reverses the "critical" reading and introduces the image of the sea stretching a (sympathetic?) gulf to meet (the river of?) the poet's tears.[29]

Çavuşoğlu also points out that the verb of the second hemistich, *uçurmak*, has several very different meanings: "to ridicule"; "to make something disappear from view"; and "to praise effusively."[30] It is used here to repeat the rhyme word of the second couplet, but it is also used in a different sense, which makes its repetition an ornament rather than a fault. So, again, the meaning of the couplet hangs in an indeterminate space between possibilities. The couplet could be saying: "The sea criticized Hayali's tears, and the clouds gathered above him and ridiculed [them] from the sky" (with the sense that he cried neither quite as much as the sea nor as copiously as the rain). This is certainly consistent with the rhetorical principle of congruence (*müra'atü'n-nazir* or *tenasüb*), which would suggest the reading "criticizing" for both verbs. But the same principle would also argue for understanding the couplet as saying, "The sea made a gulf to [accommodate all of] Hayali's tears, and the clouds gathered above it and hid it from view," which gathers all the vocabulary into the same image. This preserves the congruence between the sea and the clouds and also completes the "beauty of origin" figure by explaining that the gulf or inlet is covered by clouds in order to hide Hayali's abundant tears from those who would gossip about his love affair. Then too, it might be that the sea criticizes his tears and the clouds gather to praise them from above.

Since no reading dominates, we are forced to consider them all.[31] The result highlights—and exaggerates to the point of distortion—the ambiguity and multidimensionality of language wielded by a master artist in, again, much the same way as the mannerist artist plays with the rules of proportion and perspective. This is the *discordia concors* of the rhetoricians of mannerism, the conjunction of opposites, a trope based on "the permanent ambiguity of all things . . . the impossibility of attaining certainty about anything."[32]

If we also consider the eroticism implied by the language and imagery of attraction and seduction and add to that the erotic contexts (parties, love affairs, etc.) provided by biographers and commentators, the overall tendency of sixteenth-century Ottoman love poetry begins to resemble the spiritualized eroticism (and especially homoeroticism) that Saslow, among others, saw in the mannerist works of Italian artists such as Parmigianino.[33] However, any and all of the stylistic similarities that we have pointed out would, taken by themselves, be no more than mildly interesting instances of simultaneous (and chance) occurrence could they not be seen in the same way in which we have attempted to visualize many other social and cultural phenomena—as part of a global response to global conditions.

Although the whole discourse of mannerism implies a broad European context in which the characteristics of mannerism became meaningful to artists from a wide variety of linguistic cultures working in a variety of artistic media, we need to go back to the work of Arnold Hauser to find a Braudelian attempt at a comprehensive social, psychological, and historical contextualization of mannerism as a cross-cultural phenomenon. (Calling European mannerism *cross-cultural* assumes, of course, that we do not take Europe to be a single culture.) Beginning with his 1951 *Social History of Art*, and continuing with his 1965 *Mannerism*, Hauser developed the general argument that mannerism represented a break with the High Renaissance and with the supernormativity and utopianism of classical models. In his view, the social crisis of the late Renaissance and its affective, psychological consequences resulted in a deep anxiety that manifested itself in a sharper focus on the spiritual (and mystical) aspects of religious experience, an exaggerated intellectualism (accompanied by a reactive anti-intellectualism), and a taste for elegance and subtlety.[34] Even in the masterpieces of the Italian Renaissance—the work of Leonardo, Raphael, Michelangelo—he saw traces of the crisis out of which mannerism would arise:

> Something terrible must have happened to that generation, something which shook it to its core and made it doubt its highest values. However, the crisis must have been in part rooted in the nature of Renaissance classicism itself, for symptoms of the breach with classical principles appeared even before the destructive forces to which that crisis could be attributed made themselves felt. In spite of the masterpieces produced by the Renaissance, the sense of harmony, the eternal values attributed to its creations and its absolute standards seem from the first to have been a dream, a hope, a Utopia, rather than a certain possession which could be passed on without question to succeeding generations. Apart from brief episodes, the complete harmony between subject and object, form and content, characteristic of antiquity and the Middle Ages, was never reached again. . . . They [the works of Leonardo, etc.] were products of a great Utopian art, not of a harmonious world. Sooner or later the fiction was bound to collapse, and before it collapsed cracks appeared in the edifice, signs of doubt and uneasiness and declining power.[35]

Hauser's vision is expansive. The mannerist impulse is, not only traced throughout Europe, but also located in literature as well as in the visual arts. But this vision is cut off abruptly at the borders of purely European thought. Hauser is able to talk about Cervantes and the *Quixote* without the slightest mention of the heterogeneous Hispano-Arabic culture of Andalusia. He can discuss Marlowe's *Tamburlaine* and never mention the Ottomans, who certainly must have played a significant role in the anxieties of sixteenth-century Europeans and likely shook their faith in their core values.[36] We mention this not to denigrate Hauser's work—he would have had precious little to go on if had he wished to include Ottoman Europe. We do want to suggest, however, that our work seems to indicate that Hauser's vision is expandable to the Ottoman East, that the crisis, the anxieties, and even the impact of these on the character of literary art can be observed in an Ottoman context.

It seems clear to us that there are traces of a crisis of confidence and crumbling ideals even at the height of the great Golden Age in the early years of Süleyman's reign. In the tezkires, especially the later Latifi, 'Aşık, and Kınalızade Hasan, and the advice works of Mustafa 'Ali and many others in the seventeenth century, there is a sense that the Golden Age—the Renaissance, the Age of Beloveds—has already become the object of narration and interpretation. This appears quite similar to the case of Vasari, the biographer and artist who, unwittingly, invents mannerism in an attempt to narrate, interpret, and, thereby, discover what is going on in a world troubled by change and disintegration. In the second half of the sixteenth century, for the Ottomans as for the Europeans, relations to classical models (Persian and Arabic models in the Ottoman case) had become more problematic. Art had begun to feed on itself, to imitate art and the art of contemporary poets. The chaotic world outside was growing less interesting—or more threatening—than the internal world of the artistic ideal.

By the seventeenth century, the impulse identified as European mannerism had become recognizably the baroque, reducing mannerism to the status of a transitional phase. For the Ottomans too, the passage from confidence, exuberance, and synthesis to disillusionment, anxiety, and disintegration was paralleled by a dramatic change in literary products. The late-sixteenth- and early-seventeenth-century changes in patronage, employment, and social affiliations that we summarized in the previous chapter combined with a new wave of stylistic innovations emanating from Persia to alter the literary landscape profoundly.[37] As Walter Feldman's work on seventeenth-century Ottoman poetry is beginning to show, the new discourse (*taze-guyi*), strongly influenced by the Indian style (*sebk-i hindi*) of the Persian poets who had thronged to courts of the Mughals, shows a tendency toward metaphysical obscurity marked by novel and strange metaphors that break from the naturalistic idealism and dominant rhetorical principle of congruence of the Age of Beloveds.[38]

The character of this break and its abruptness can be encapsulated in a comparison of the opening couplets of Hayali's gazel (discussed above) and a signature couplet by the poet Na'ili written in the mid-seventeenth century:

> Cypress and rose in the meadow stand and sit
> That same body and that cheek, they see in you
>
> The rose sent a leaflet to the bulbul flying
> Borne by the footman breeze to say,
>   we'll not blossom without you
> —Hayali

> *Ey Na'ili nihal-i siyeh-bag-ı bahtdan*
> *Ne gonca-i emel ne gül-i arzu kopar*
>
> Oh Na'ili, from the sapling of fortune's
>   black garden

> Sprouts neither the bud of desire nor
> > the rose of longing[39]
> —Na'ili

From a garden in which nature mimes the beloved, in which the beloved's every gesture is a sign or message of hope and desire, we are cast into the black garden of despair, unlike any garden of the world, an inner garden of the psyche, wherein the blossoming beloved has been replaced by a barren sapling that offers nothing of this world. Everything has been distanced. The rose is no longer the beloved or the beloved's cheek; it is now the image of the poet's inner state (longing) in relation to the beloved.

In an exchange with Feldman on the topics of the poetry of this period, this couplet in particular, and the collapse of what he calls *the system of cosmic similitude*, we had the following to say:

> In the later poetry, however, this visualizing [of a cosmic synthesis] loses its force. The poetry cuts loose from its grounding in material actuality and begins to indulge in rhetorical questioning and de-centering of that grounding. This seems to be Na'ili's role. He seems to abandon any notion that material actuality can be rescued by interpretation, that the consistency of relations between actuality and its metaphoric extensions has any significance, and that grounding in the actual has any importance at all. Thus, we see the diminution in the role of the beloved (the beloved may be like other wielders of power but that likeness ceases to signify by itself), and with the beloved go the wine and the garden and all the symbology of the past. The words remain as signs for positions in relation to various concepts but their structured, grounded (actuality-grounded) metaphoric universe has been destroyed. Then one can have the image contrary to fact, the black garden, which in its contradictoriness bespeaks despair at the ability of language, through metaphor, to heal the disjunction between this world and that, between the actual and the real (which is the ruling belief of the previous age).[40]

To this we would add only that from our perspective—the perspective of love and the beloved—the long sixteenth century was a historical moment when Europe and the Ottoman East appear to walk much the same path. As the Age of Beloveds wanes, they again diverge, each on the trajectory of its own particular modernity. But it should be some comfort, in this latter age when we are haunted by seemingly insurmountable difference, to know that East and West were once so close, that, at the dawning of the modern world, Muslims, Christians, and Jews were united in a desire for a unique and powerful beloved.

APPENDIX

Ottoman Sultans during the Age of Beloveds

    Mehmet II, 1451–81 (second reign)

    Bayezit II, 1481–1512

    Selim I, 1512–20

    Süleyman I, 1520–66

    Selim II, 1566–74

    Murat III, 1574–95

    Mehmet III, 1595–1603

    Ahmet I, 1603–17

    Mustafa I, 1617–18 (first reign)

    Osman II, 1618–22

    Mustafa I, 1622–23 (second reign)

NOTES

Unless otherwise noted, all translations are our own.

1 Introduction

1 The story of Mehmet the Conqueror and Lukas Notaras as told by Doukas can be found in Magoulias, trans., *Decline and Fall*, 234–35. The information that follows about Doukas's life is taken from Magoulias's introduction. Other sources used for the story of Mehmet and Notaras include Sphrantzes, *Fall of the Byzantine Empire*; Barbaro, *Diary of the Siege of Constantinople*; and Dirimtekin, *İstanbul'un fethi*.
2 Jordan, *Invention of Sodomy*, 10–28.
3 A version of the Ottoman text can be found in İsen and Bilkan, eds., *Sultan şâirler*, 75–76.
4 Perhaps the most relevant to our study are Irving Schick's *The Erotic Margin* and Matar's *Turks, Moors, and Englishmen*.
5 See, e.g., Braudel, *Mediterranean World*, 2:892–96.
6 For English-speaking readers, a good introduction to the tradition of scholarship can be found in Gibb, *History of Ottoman Poetry*, 1:3–32, 125–36. For critiques of this tradition, see also Andrews, *Poetry's Voice*, introduction; and Holbrook, *Unreadable Shores of Love*, chap. 1.
7 Veyne, "Homosexuality in Ancient Rome," 26; Michel Foucault, *History of Sexuality*, 2:187.
8 See Foucault, *History of Sexuality*, vol. 1, passim. For a critique of Foucault's view of "Eastern" sexuality, see Pflugfelder, *Cartographies of Desire*, esp. 1–8. Pflugfelder is dealing with Japan, but his material (see esp. 23–145) has many intriguing parallels with the picture presented in our work.
9 See Tripp, *Homosexual Matrix*, esp. chaps. 4–5.
10 Keuls, *Reign of the Phallus*, 2.

11 Halperin, "Sex before Sexuality," 41.
12 Jordan, *Invention of Sodomy*, 29–66.
13 For those who are interested, we would recommend a series of three articles in Duberman, Vicinus, and Chauncey, eds., *Hidden from History*, that set out the arguments for the major positions with exceptional clarity: Boswell, "Revolutions, Universals, and Sexual Categories"; Halperin, "Sex before Sexuality"; and Padgug, "Sexual Matters."
14 For a brief but cogent theoretical overview that seems especially pertinent to our study, Sedgwick, *Between Men*, 3–48.
15 Here, we are attempting a massive reduction of an extremely complex topic, our purpose being simply to set the stage for what is to come. For those who wish to explore further, we suggest Foucault, *History of Sexuality*, vol. 1; and Boswell, *Christianity, Social Tolerance, and Homosexuality*.
16 A good example is the wealth accumulated by harem women and the ways in which wealthy harem women exercised power in the outside world (see Peirce, *Imperial Harem*, esp. 132–36, 186–218).
17 Readily available secondary sources are few, but there are some outstanding overviews of the history of love and sexual relations in the Islamic Middle East. Among the best are the essays contained in al-Sayyid-Marsot, ed., *Society and the Sexes*; and Wright and Rowson, eds., *Homoeroticism in Classical Arabic Literature*. In addition to these, we would suggest Giffen's *Theory of Profane Love*, the examples and notes in Sprachman's *Suppressed Persian*, and the translation of Gazali's *Dafi'ü'l-gumum ve rafi'ü'l-humum* (Repeller of sorrows and removers of cares) in Kuru, "Deli Birader."
18 Another book, Murat Bardakçı's *Osmanlı'da seks* (Sex among the Ottomans), was published in 1992. It is a compendium of translations from Ottoman works on sex, lacking any scholarly apparatus or identification of sources, and apparently intended mainly for the titillation of its readers.
19 For a full discussion of this practice, see Schick, *The Erotic Margin*.
20 See Andrews, Black, and Kalpaklı, eds. and trans., *Ottoman Lyric Poetry*.
21 A recent example is a thriving short fiction genre called *slash* fiction. How something can be a "genre" and be "thriving" and still be unknown to most people is a function of the tremendous reach of the Internet; it is truly worldwide, so a few people here and a few there add up to a significant audience. Slash—the name refers to nothing more sinister than the slash, or solidus, character—has developed into a type of homoerotic short fiction based on erotic encounters between the male characters of popular television shows, e.g., "K/S" stories, referring to Kirk and Spock, the main male characters of the original *Star Trek* series. What is most relevant about slash for us is that it is most commonly written by (and for) heterosexual women, with the goal of exploring love relations between persons for whom the power disparities inherent in male-female relations do not exist. See Bunn, "The X-Rated Files."
22 Heilbrun, *Androgeny*, x–xi.
23 All quotations from Shakespeare will be taken from, and all references keyed to,

Rowse, ed., *The Annotated Shakespeare*, with act, scene, and line numbers given in the text. The reference here is to act 1, sc. 3, line 27 of *As You Like It*.
24 Derrida, *Of Grammatology*, xii–xviii.
25 Abou-El-Haj, *Formation of the Modern State*, 2.
26 Braudel, *Mediterranean World*, 1:14.
27 We are deeply indebted to Cornell Fleischer for sharing his as yet unpublished work (both *Mediterranean Apocalypse* and "Mahdi and Messiah"). A striking indication of the divergent origins of our similar conclusions in some areas can be seen in a comparison of the sources listed for each study, in which overlap is nearly nonexistent and limited mostly to the work of Fleischer himself.
28 In addition to Fleischer's *Mediterranean Apocalypse*, see also his "Seer to the Sultan," "Lawgiver as Messiah," and "Mahdi and Messiah."
29 Valensi, *Birth of the Despot*, 45–53.
30 Fleischer, "Mahdi and Messiah," and *Mediterranean Apocalypse*. For Venetian accounts, see also Valensi, *Birth of the Despot*, 17–20.
31 İsen, ed., *Künhü'l-ahbâr*, 143.
32 For concrete examples of borrowings and influences, see Mack, *Bazaar to Piazza*.

2 Beloved Boys (and Girls)

1 For an edited and transcribed version of the original text, see Pekin, ed., *Evsâf*, 44–45. Pekin's text contains many errors in transcription, which we corrected by comparison to the original Arabic-script manuscript before attempting our translation.
2 Ibid., 49.
3 Meredith-Owens, ed., 'Âşık, fol. 279b (lines 3–9). Citations from 'Âşık's tezkire will be referenced according to Meredith-Owens's text. However, all citations have also been compared with the text in 'Âşık, "Meşâ'iru üş-su'arā," and corrected accordingly.
4 Meredith-Owens, ed., 'Âşık, fols. 273a–273b.
5 Gagnon and Simon, *Sexual Conduct*, 19. For their understanding of scripts as they apply to sexual psychology and behavior, see ibid., 19–26.
6 See Deleuze and Guattari, *Anti-Oedipus*, chap. 1.
7 Montrose, "A Midsummer Night's Dream," 87.
8 It is important to note here that Ottoman rhetoric eroticizes affectionate relationships of all kinds. Therefore, poems written to or about friends (to honor a visit, or to offer condolences, or to celebrate some occasion) will often situate the friend as a beloved without implying a sexual component to the relationship.
9 Meredith-Owens, ed., 'Âşık, fol. 143a (lines 19–21).
10 The standard work on the Ottoman şehrengiz is Levend, *Şehr-engizler*. See also Stewart-Robinson, "A Neglected Ottoman Poem"; and Öztekin, "'Şehrengizler ve Bursa.'"

11 See Sharma, "Poetics of Court and Prison," 132–43.
12 Sharma, "Generic Innovation."
13 See Stewart-Robinson, "A Neglected Ottoman Poem," passim.
14 The translations that follow are based on Zātī, "Edirne şehrengizi."
15 The Ottoman text of these verses can be found in Çavuşoğlu, ed., *Yahyā Bey: Dīvan*, 255.
16 Rocke, *Forbidden Friendships*, 151–52.
17 Smith, *Homosexual Desire*, 84.
18 İsen, ed., *Künhü'l-ahbâr*, 316.
19 The full transcribed text of 'Azizi's şehrengiz (from which our examples are translated) can be found in Levend, *Şehr-engizler*, 119–38. Gibb (*History of Ottoman Poetry*, 3:179–86) also translates several entries.
20 Sahillioğlu, *Studies*, 115–16.
21 The data on slavery in this section are taken from ibid., 105–73; and Faroqhi, "From the Slave Market."
22 For background on sexual relations with slaves in Islamic tradition, see Bürgel, "Love, Lust, and Longing," 101–5.
23 Refik, *İstanbul hayatı*, 42 (no. 8).
24 Faroqhi, "From the Slave Market," passim. See also Faroqhi, *Ottoman Men and Women*, 133–39.
25 Faroqhi, *Ottoman Men and Women*, 141–42.
26 Ibid., 8–9.
27 For a discussion of the legal and sociosexual discourse of male adulthood, see Peirce, "Seniority, Sexuality, and Social Order," 174–75.
28 Meredith-Owens, ed., *'Āşık*, fols. 258b–259a.
29 Jardine, "Twins and Travesties," 28. Where sixteenth-century English uses the term *loose* for women who are publicly available or visible, the equivalent popular term for the opposite in Turkish (in the sixteenth century as today) is *kapalı* (covered), which implies both containment and veiling. An "uncovered" woman is a "loose" woman.
30 Strocchia, "Gender and the Rites of Honor," 51 (see also n. 22).
31 The Ottoman terminology of male life stages is discussed in Peirce, "Seniority, Sexuality, and Social Order," 176–81.
32 Davis, "Geography of Gender," 25 (see also 23–31). In a section suggestively entitled "Making the Streets Male," Davis points out that organized male violence in public spaces was often a way of "purging the streets and public spaces of women" (25). On the companies of young men who organized disorderly and often violent carnival events, see Muir, *Civic Ritual*.

In Ottoman Istanbul, the amount of attention paid by the legal system to controlling the public behavior of women (see the examples presented in chapters 6 and 9 below) appears to indicate that women were publicly visible in urban society at least to the extent that this created a problem for male authorities. We are persuaded, however, that it may be premature to make the argument (which we see in, e.g., Yılmaz, "Mahremiyetin sınırlarına dair") that village women had far more public presence than did urban women because they worked in agricultural production.

33 Peirce, *Morality Tales*, 157–61; Düzdağ, *Ebussuūd*, 55 (no. 153).
34 See Düzdağ, *Ebussuūd*, 55 (nos. 154, 155, 156).
35 Moryson and the Italian traveler are quoted in Davis, "Geography of Gender," 21.
36 The Ottoman text of the story is found in Meredith-Owens, ed., *'Âşık*, fols. 113a–117a.
37 See Jordan, *Invention of Sodomy*, passim.
38 Cited in Çavuşoğlu, "Yahya Bey'in İstanbul şehrengizi," 76–77. For a discussion of Yahya's views on sexuality as understood from his poetry, see also Kaya, "Cinsellik."
39 Nims, trans., *Michelangelo*, 131 (no. 260).
40 For a discussion of Ottoman female poets, see chapter 6, part 2, below.

3 Love Scripts I

1 Most of the material in this section on the life of 'Atayi and on his hamse is derived from Kortantamer, *Nev'ī-zāde Atāyī*. We have paraphrased and translated liberally from Kortantamer's prose précis of the *Seven Stories* in producing our own prose-narrative version of the story of Tayyib and Tahir. An edited text of the story of Tayyib and Tahir can be found in Karacan, *Heft-hvân*, 317–44 (couplets 2408–2726).
2 İsen, "Meslekî konumları."
3 For an excellent overview of the social structuring of life stages in the Ottoman Empire during the Age of Beloveds, see Peirce, "Seniority, Sexuality, and Social Order," esp. 179–81 (on the perceived unruliness of unattached young men).
4 These themes are analyzed in detail in Andrews, *Poetry's Voice*.
5 Peirce, "Seniority, Sexuality, and Social Order," 174–75.
6 Meninski, *Lexicon*, 2:4210.
7 These verses are from the divan of Helaki. See, e.g., Çavuşoğlu, ed., *Helâkî: Dîvân*, 166 (no. 126, couplets 1, 3).
8 Pekin, ed., *Evsâf*, 57–58. For a detailed view of the population and character of Galata during the Age of Beloveds, see İnalcık, "Galata."
9 Çavuşoğlu et al., eds., *Revānī dīvānı*, "Gazeller," no. 7.
10 Castiglione, *Book of the Courtier*, 165.
11 Valensi, *Birth of the Despot*, 18–20.
12 Pekin, ed., *Evsâf*, 59–61.
13 Quoted in Mullaney, "Strange Things," 76.
14 Erünsal's *Ca'fer Çelebi* is the outstanding source in English for Tacızade Ca'fer's life. Erünsal (ibid., xlvii–lxii) discusses the *Hevesname* but does not give a full text. The text has not yet been edited and published; a version of it can be found in Ca'fer, "Hevesnāme."
15 The story of the social life of Ottoman littérateurs has not yet been told in any de-

tail. The best existing source is İpekten, *Muhitler*. For references to the taverns of Istanbul, see ibid., 243–54 (which is reproduced in Kalpaklı, ed., *Metinler*, 224–28). See also Açıkgöz, "Kültür hayatı."

16   For a transcribed and edited version of the text of the *Etiquette*, see Şeker, ed., *Kavâ'idi'l-mecâlis*, to which is appended an extensive study. For a translation into "today's Turkish," see Gökyay, ed., *Ziyafet sofraları*. The Modern Turkish version has many useful notes, but the translation is itself difficult (often less clear than the original) and is marred by the reluctance of the translator to include in his notes information about material with sexual content. Brookes's *Ottoman Gentleman* (an English translation of the *Etiquette*) appeared too late for us to consider or cite in our account. The translations herein are our own. The life and times of Mustafa 'Ali are discussed extensively in Fleischer, *Bureaucrat and Intellectual*.

17   Şeker, ed., *Kavâ'idi'l-mecâlis*, 365–66.

18   Bray, *Homosexuality*, 84.

19   Bray says of the molly houses: "The society of the molly houses did not follow class lines but rather tended to dissolve them. It did so because it was not mediated by existing social forms, of class or otherwise: it was set alongside them, a social institution in its own right" (ibid., 86). This seems to be precisely what 'Ali indicates in his description of the tavern and what we will see in general descriptions of coffeehouse culture as well.

20   Şeker, ed., *Kavâ'idi'l-mecâlis*, 363–64. The most complete source in English for the history of coffee in the Near East and its introduction into the Ottoman Empire is Hattox, *Coffee and Coffeehouses*. Hattox's pl. 6 reproduces a miniature showing some of the various groups that frequented sixteenth-century coffeehouses, including literary types and people engaged in "frivolous" pastimes such as backgammon and mancala.

21   Peçevi, *Tārīh*, 363–65.

22   Sā'yī, "Mektūb," fol. 149b.

23   See İpekten, *Muhitler*, 131–61 (esp. 140–42 [on Tacızade Ca'fer's mansion (*konak*)]) and 229–51 (on gatherings of Ottoman poets).

24   Ibid., 243. The Ottomans had no coin called the *dirhem*. This is a traditional term for an Arab silver coin. Assuming that, in this case, *dirhem* is a literary usage for the standard silver akçe, the amount that Bali Çelebi spent on drugs each day was about three times the daily salary of a janissary and twice the salary of a skilled construction worker. We are grateful to Şevket Pamuk for his expert advice on this matter.

25   On the issue of vagabonds and "masterless men" in England, see Beier, *Masterless Men*; and also DiGangi, *Homoerotics of Early Modern Drama*, 66.

26   Rocke, *Forbidden Friendships*, 153. In the Ottoman story related at the beginning of chapter 7 below, we see the sexual rendezvous taking place in a run-down village.

27   Rowse, *Sex and Society*, 55.

28 For a comprehensive overview of sixteenth-century Ottoman gardens, see Necipoğlu, "Suburban Landscape."
29 See, e.g., Andrews, *Poetry's Voice*, 150–58; and Andrews and Markoff, "Group Ethos."
30 Kuru, "Deli Birader," 187–88 (translation), 76 (text). (See n. 39, chapter 5, below.)
31 Andrews, *Poetry's Voice*, esp. chaps. 6–7.
32 For the wine party, see chapter 5 below.
33 Fumerton, *Cultural Aesthetics*, chap. 4, esp. 113–22.
34 See Necipoğlu, "Suburban Landscape," 35–41. The most comprehensive source for the Ottoman köşk is Eldem, *Köşk ve kasırlar*.
35 Fumerton, *Cultural Aesthetics*, 123.
36 Andrews, *Poetry's Voice*, 158–73.
37 Kafadar, "Self and Others," 143 (quotation), 144.
38 For example, Andrews, *Poetry's Voice*, 158–65.
39 Peirce, *Morality Tales*, 133–34, 362–63.
40 See Ruggiero, *Boundaries of Eros*, esp. chaps. 5–6.
41 For the Kadizadeli and their predecessors, see Zilfi, *Politics of Piety*, esp. chap. 4.
42 Cited in Çavuşoğlu, *Divanlar arasında*, 41.
43 Tietze, ed., *Counsel for Sultans*, 1:149–50 (text), 56 (translation). (Throughout, we have retranslated Tietze's text to conform with our style and reading of the text.)
44 The issues of systemic change as reflected in Ottoman advice literature are taken up cogently in Abou-El-Haj, *Formation of the Modern State*, passim.
45 The reluctance of Ottoman legal authorities to offend the populace by imposing harsh punishments will be taken up at some length in chapter 9 below.
46 The dream visitor or secret guardian/adviser (*hātif-i cān*) is a popular character in Ottoman poetry.
47 Peirce, "Seniority, Sexuality, and Social Order," 178.
48 See Ruggiero, *Boundaries of Eros*, 70–88, esp. 83.

4 Love Scripts II

1 Brown, "Breaking the Canon," 60.
2 E. J. W. Gibb lived, studied, and wrote at the end of the nineteenth century, which was the heyday of "high Orientalism." He was a kind and gentle man who devoted his life to the study of Ottoman Turkish literature. Although he never found an opportunity to travel to the Near East, his home became a refuge for Ottoman reformers who visited England, and he was strongly influenced by their views on the failing Ottoman Empire and its historical literature. Like his informants, he believed that the Ottomans had a glorious but fatally flawed past and that their culture could be reinvigorated by the infusion of European mod-

ernism. For a good idea of his perspective, see Gibb, *History of Ottoman Poetry*, vol. 1, chaps. 1–2, 4, and vol. 5, chap. 1 (edited after Gibb's untimely death by the Persianist E. G. Browne). Gibb's *History of Ottoman Poetry* is a monumental work that has dominated Western perceptions of Ottoman literature for the whole of the twentieth century. Because of its naive Orientalism, it is now an easy target, and we would be reluctant to criticize it were it not that its breadth and depth of scholarship has made its obviously faulty cultural perspective so long-lived and pernicious.

3   Brown, "Breaking the Canon," 60.
4   Tietze, ed., *Counsel for Sultans*, 1:148–49 (text), 55–57 (translation).
5   Latîfî, "Tezkīre-i şuʿarā," fols. 165a, 114b. Late in his life, Latifi rewrote his tezkire, elaborating the style, and adding a large amount of material. This "new rendition," which cannot be reconciled with the earlier tradition, has not been edited and exists only in manuscript form. Our translation is from the new-rendition manuscript. There exists a transcribed edition of the tezkire—Canım's *Latîfî, tezkire*—which we did not use.
6   Sidney, *Apology*, 168.
7   For a perspective on the way in which the Ottoman poets created a tradition that preserved their own interests, see Andrews, "Other Selves."
8   Brown, "Breaking the Canon," 63.
9   Marlowe, *Hero and Leander*, 17.
10 The tools for extensive monorhyme do not exist in English. Hence, our translations will rhyme only occasionally and only within couplets. For basic information in English on the genres of Ottoman poetry, see Andrews, *Introduction to Ottoman Poetry*.
11 "Mecmūʿatü'n-nezāʾir," fol. 148a.
12 Mengi, ed., *Mesîhî dîvânı*, 265 (no. 232, line 5).
13 "Mecmūʿatü'n-nezāʾir," fol. 148a (no. 1).
14 Ibid., fol. 148b (no. 5).
15 Ibid., fol. 148a (no. 4).
16 Ibid., fol. 149a (no. 2).
17 Çavuşoğlu, "Zâtî'nin letâyifi," 13.
18 Tarlan, ed., *Zatî divanı*, 2:504.
19 Çavuşoğlu, "Zâtî'nin letâyifi," 8.
20 For descriptions, see Necipoğlu, *Architecture, Ceremonial, and Power*, 117–18, 157. For an illustration from the eighteenth century, see ibid., 158.
21 Tarlan, ed., *Zatî divanı*, 1:346, 347.
22 This point will be addressed in more detail in chapter 7 below.
23 Çavuşoğlu and Tanyeri, eds., *İshâk Çelebi: Dîvan*, 176.
24 Fevrî, "Dīvān," fol. 139a.
25 Meredith-Owens, ed., ʿÂşık, fol. 283b (lines 10–16).
26 Ibid., fol. 279a (lines 2–4).
27 Tarlan, ed., *Zatî divanı*, 2:1003.
28 Çavuşoğlu, ed., *Vasfî: Dîvan*, p. 160 (no. 102).

29 "Mecmūʿatü'n-nezāʾir," fol. 163a.
30 Meredith-Owens, ed., ʿĀşık, fol. 109b (lines 3–7).
31 Çavuşoğlu, ed., Yahyā Bey: Dīvan, 349 (no. 108, line 1). See also Andrews, Black, and Kalpaklı, eds. and trans., Ottoman Lyric Poetry, 101.
32 Çavuşoğlu et al., eds., Revānī dīvānı, "Gazeller," no. 122.
33 Tarlan, ed., Necatî Beg divanı, 544 (no. 632, couplet 7).
34 Çavuşoğlu et al., eds., Revānī dīvānı, "Gazeller," no. 292.
35 Meredith-Owens, ed., ʿĀşık, fol. 294a (lines 10–23). ʿĀşık's whole entry for Deli Birader Gazali, which includes the stories of his friends (including Sirkeci Bahşi), Bahşi's orchard, and Gazali's bath (see chapter 7 below), is found in ibid., fols. 292b–295a.
36 Tarlan, ed., Necatî Beg divanı, 268 (no. 198, couplet 2). For a translation of the whole poem with notes, see also Andrews, Black, and Kalpaklı, Ottoman Lyric Poetry, 41.
37 For a discussion of Ottoman sohbet, see the introductory remarks in Kafadar, "Self and Others."
38 Tarlan, ed., Necatî Beg divanı, 290 (no. 237, couplet 4).
39 Çavuşoğlu et al., eds., Revānī dīvānı, "Gazeller," no. 295.
40 The story can be found in Meredith-Owens, ed., ʿĀşık, fols. 42a (line 20)–42b (line 16). A very similar story—one in which the main character and victim of malicious advice is Mevlānā Şemsüddin Kāmī—is told by Mustafa ʿAli (see Tietze, ed., Counsel for Sultans, 2:231–34 [text], 99–100 [translation]). The stories may or may not be true, but the story type is obviously meaningful as a warning to those who would aspire to being conversational companions to the great and powerful.
41 Coryat, Crudities, 405.
42 Trechman, trans., Diary of Montaigne's Journey, 161.
43 Castiglione, Book of the Courtier, 109.
44 It is important to keep in mind that, among court-dependent elites in early-modern absolutist monarchies, the poetry of love (and, to some extent, love itself) always has what Daniel Javich called "impure motives" insofar as it is always directed at demonstrating the skills of the courtier and his (or her) ability to be a devoted servant. See Javich, "Impure Motives."
45 See Javich, Poetry and Courtliness.
46 Jones and Stallybrass, "The Politics of Astrophel and Stella," 54.

5 Love, Sex, and Poetry

1 See Andrews and Kalpaklı, "Gazels and the World." See also Andrews and Kalpaklı, "The Ottoman Gazel in the Age of Beloveds."
2 See Necipoğlu, "Süleymân the Magnificent," 166ff. See also Rogers, "The Arts under Süleymân," 262.
3 Chambers and Pullan, eds., Venice, 352 (quotations), 328–29.

4   See, e.g., Lawner, *Lives of the Courtesans*, 4–6.
5   Ibid., 36.
6   For the Sanuto estimate, see Rosenthal, *Honest Courtesan*, 11. For the Coryat estimate, see Coryat, *Crudities*, 402. The population of Venice in 1509 is estimated to have been 115,000 (see Pullan, "Wage Earners," 150 n. 3).
7   Ruggiero, *Boundaries of Eros*, 10.
8   Cited in Rosenthal, *Honest Courtesan*, 135. The whole letter appears in English translation in Jones and Rosenthal, eds. and trans., *Veronica Franco*, 37–40 (no. 22).
9   There were several courtesan poets and intellectuals preceding and contemporary with Franco. For examples, see Masson, *Courtesans*.
10 For the response to Franco, see Rosenthal, *Honest Courtesan*, esp. chaps. 1, 4. For a discussion of the position of Franco and Louise Labé, see Jones, "City Women."
11 See Ruggiero, *Boundaries of Eros*, chap. 6.
12 Chambers and Pullan, eds., *Venice*, 123, 124, 125.
13 Ibid., 188–90.
14 Ruggiero, *Boundaries of Eros*, 137.
15 Cellini, *Autobiography*, 341.
16 On Cellini's "considerable company," see Rocke, *Forbidden Friendships*, 298–99 n. 123. On the German vocabulary of sodomy, see ibid., 3. On the activities of the Ufficiali di Notte, see ibid., 4. For a discussion of Cellini's sexuality, see Saslow, *Ganymede*, 142–55.
17 Cellini, *Autobiography*, 33, 19.
18 Ibid., 53–54.
19 See Rocke, *Forbidden Friendships*, 155.
20 Ibid., 55.
21 This story appears in ibid., 47–51.
22 Ibid., 92–93, 113.
23 Brackett, "The Florentine Onestà."
24 Rowse, *Sex and Society*, 3–4.
25 Ibid., 65, 80, 250, 294.
26 Ibid., 57.
27 Ibid., 76.
28 Smith, *Homosexual Desire*, 14.
29 For an account of this adventure, see Rowse, *Sex and Society*, 255–61.
30 Barnfield, *Affectionate Shepherd*, 5.
31 Ibid., 3. In regard to the *Affectionate Shepherd*, Bray (*Homosexuality*, 61) cites Barnfield's contentions that he was doing nothing more than imitating the story of Alexis in Virgil's second eclogue and that he had no homoerotic intent at all. Bray also points out that Barnfield also produced a commonplace book that was "robustly pornographic and entirely heterosexual." Smith (*Homosexual Desire*, 99–115, esp. 102) takes a quite different view of both the poem and Barnfield's disclaimer.
32 Sidney, *Poems*, 177 (no. 24, lines 9–14).

33 Jonson, *Epicoene*, 11 (line 23)–12 (line 2). Bray (*Homosexuality*, 34) says of the descriptions of late-sixteenth- and early-seventeenth-century English authors: "On this point they are remarkably consistent: the sodomite is a young man-about-town with his mistress on one arm and his 'catamite' on the other; he is indolent, extravagant and debauched."

34 See Kuru, "Deli Birader." A printed English translation of the *Repeller of Sorrows* exists (see Landor, trans., *Book of Shehzade*), but it is a poor-quality translation of a modern Turkish translation of a roman-font transcription of a late and defective Arabic-script manuscript. We neither use it nor cite it—for obvious reasons.

35 For further details, see Kuru, "Deli Birader," 1–10. The *Hidaye* will be mentioned in n. 2 of chapter 9 below.

36 For examples and an introductory discussion of sexually explicit writing among elite Persian authors, see Sprachman, *Suppressed Persian*.

37 For a discussion of the ambivalence of the Sufis toward actual love and its pornographic representations, see Schimmel, "Eros."

38 See Sprachman, *Suppressed Persian*, 24–43; and Nicholson, ed. and trans., *Mathnawī*, 5:245–52 (lines 3848–3964).

39 Kuru, "Deli Birader," 163 (translation), 49–50 (text).
    In this and all other instances in which we cite the *Repeller of Sorrows*, we have retranslated, using Kuru's translation as a guide, to fit our style. Accordingly, we give two sets of page numbers, the first for Kuru's translation, the second for the transcribed text, which precedes the translation. References to the manuscript folios can be found in the transcribed text.

40 Ibid., 162–63 (translation), 49 (text).

41 Ibid., 168 (translation), 56 (text).

42 Ibid., 170 (translation), 58 (text).

43 Castiglione, *Book of the Courtier*, 289.

44 Cited in Moulton, "'Printed Abroad,'" 83.

45 Fevrī, "Dīvān," fol. 139b.

46 This description, found in all the major collections of hadith, refers to the customs that a woman's legal testimony is worth half that of a man's and that a woman cannot pray in the mosque or fast during Ramadan when she is menstruating.

47 Kuru, "Deli Birader," 177–78 (translation), 66–67 (text).

48 Şeker, ed., *Kavâ'idi'l-mecâlis*, 283.

49 'Āşık, fol. 270b (lines 15–16). The whole story of Hayali's young manhood can be found in ibid., beginning on fol. 270b (line 14).

50 Şeker, ed., *Kavâ'idi'l-mecâlis*, 283–84.

51 Kuru, "Deli Birader," 186–87 (translation), 75 (text).

52 Ibid., 189 (translation), 78 (text).

53 Ibid., 206–7 (translation), 97–98 (text).

54 During the period 1554–62, Ogier Ghiselin De Busbecq served as Ferdinand of Austria's ambassador to the court of Süleyman the Magnificent. And in letters

to a friend he commented on the scrounging that went on at even the lowest levels. For example, when talking about the janissaries he encountered in the castle of Buda:

> These Janissaries generally came to me in pairs. When they were admitted to my dining room they first made a bow, and then came quickly up to me, all but running, and touched my dress or hand, as they intended to kiss it. After this they would thrust into my hand a nosegay of the hyacinth or narcissus; then they would run back to the door almost as quickly as they came, taking care not to turn their backs, for this, according to their code, would be a serious breach of etiquette. After reaching the door, they would stand respectfully with their arms crossed, and their eyes bent on the ground, looking more like monks than warriors. On receiving a few small coins (which was what they wanted) they bowed again, thanked me in loud tones, and went off blessing me for my kindness.

Or more generally:

> A man who visits the Turks had better make up his mind to open his purse as soon as he crosses their frontier, and not to shut it till he quits the country; in the interval he must sow his money broadcast, and may thank his stars if the seed proves fruitful. (Forster and Daniell, eds. and trans., *Life and Letters of Busbecq*, 87, 108)

For Venetian accounts of Ottoman scrounging, see also Valensi, *Birth of the Despot*, 43–44.

55 İnalcık (*Economic and Social History*, 47–48, 74–75) mentions how this works at the highest levels of the empire.
56 See, e.g., Rocke, *Forbidden Friendships*, 163–64. Saslow (*Ganymede*, 155–60) points out that the Ganymede image was used in classical times as a "rhetorical convention for praising beautiful slaves or servants" and that this usage was taken up by Renaissance literati.
57 Şeker, ed., *Kavâ'idi'l-mecâlis*, 273.
58 Ibid., 347–48.
59 Sānī, "Cevap," fol. 150b.
60 For examples of private loving communications between elite men and women, see the love letters written by Hurrem to Sultan Süleyman and those written by Ibrahim Pasha to his wife, Hatice (Süleyman's sister), in Uluçay, *Aşk mektupları*, 19–120.
61 Batislam, *Hasbihâl-i sâfî*, 156–57.
62 Ibid., 158–59.
63 These kinds of public celebrations were popular in Venice as well. Muir (*Civic Ritual*) presents a detailed view of attempts by Venetian authorities to harness the wild and violent aspects of public merrymaking to the more staid purposes of celebrating civic virtues. Given the close attention that Venetian observers paid to Ottoman affairs, it is not unlikely that the implied focus of Ottoman

celebrations on the sultan as beloved influenced the politicization of Venetian ritual during the sixteenth century.
64 For detailed descriptions and analyses of the festival, see Terzioğlu, "The Imperial Circumcision Festival of 1582"; and Prochazka-Eisl, *Sūrnāme*, 5–66.
65 Prochazka-Eisl, *Sūrnāme*, 92–93 (fols. 18r [line 20]–18v [line 5]).
66 Ibid., 100 (fol. 23r [lines 17–23]), 112–13 (fols. 31r [line 11]–31v [line 4]), 117 (fol. 34v [lines 1–10]), 146 (fol. 53v [lines 8–15]).
67 Stetkevych, "Intoxication and Immortality," 210.
68 Ibid., 223.
69 Tarlan, ed., *Hayâlî Bey dîvânı*, 388 (no. 90).
70 Hafez, *Divan*, 844.
71 Saslow, *Ganymede*, passim.
72 Meisami, *Medieval Persian Court Poetry*, 77–179. Meisami's study is an important resource for those who want to understand the tradition inherited by the Ottomans.
73 An example of the very tentative and unsophisticated nature of traditional approaches to the gendering of Ottoman poetry is found in a tiny vignette by Mehmet Kaplan entitled "Divan siirinde kadın aşkı yok mudur?" (Is there no love of women in divan poetry?), in Kalpaklı, ed., *Metinler*, 263–64.

6 Women and the Art of Love

1 Keuls, *Reign of the Phallus*, 44–47.
2 Montrose, "'Shaping Fantasies,'" 35–36.
3 Ibid., 36.
4 Spenser, *Faerie Queene*, 198–99 (bk. 5, canto 5, sts. 20, 22).
5 Ariosto, *Orlando Furioso*, 223–25 (canto 19, sts. 57–72).
6 Spenser, *Faerie Queene*, 199 (bk. 5, canto 5, st. 25). The whole stanza goes:

> Such is the crueltie of womenkynd,
> When they have shaken off the shamefast band,
> With which wise Nature did them strongly bynd
> T' obay the heasts of mans well-ruling hand,
> That then all rule and reason they withstand
> To purchase a licentious libertie:
> But vertuous women wisely understand,
> That they were borne to base humilitie,
> Unlesse the heavens them lift to lawfull soveraintie.

7 Clinton, trans., *Sohrab and Rostam*, 35–37.
8 Sümer, Uysal, and Walker, trans. and eds., *Book of Dede Korkut*, 46.
9 Şeker, ed., *Kavâ'idi'l-mecâlis*, 364–65.
10 Sidney, *Poems*, 169 (no. 9).

11   Keuls (*Reign of the Phallus*, 67–75), e.g., discusses the Athenian insistence that a "small taut" penis was superior to the large (and crude) organs associated with "satyrs and barbarians." This is obviously one way of approaching anxieties about penis size, one appropriate to male Athenians' preoccupation with the phallus in general and their own sex organs in particular.
12   Kuru, "Deli Birader," 232–33 (translation), 119 (text).
13   Ibid., 233 (translation), 120 (text).
14   Ibid.
15   The term that we have translated as *sturdy* is *sinirsek*, which has several meanings, including a plant (*Plantago major*) with a long upright flower stalk as well as, according to the *Derleme sözlüğü* (10:3642), "Güç kırılan, kırılmaz, sert (odun, vb. icin)" (difficult to break, unbreakable, hard [for wood, etc.]). We have chosen the latter reading, which was suggested to us by Robert Dankoff.
16   Yahyā, "Kitāb-i usūl," fol. 35a.
17   Kuru, "Deli Birader," 235 (translation), 121 (text).
18   See Pakalin, *Sözlük*, 2:286.
19   Ariosto, *Orlando Furioso*, 299 (canto 25, st. 33), 300 (canto 25, st. 35).
20   Brown, *Immodest Acts*, 6. For reference to Louis Crompton's counterargument that female same-sex sexual relations were as serious a legal concern as male same-sex sexual relations, see ibid., 166 n. 5.
21   Traub, "'Lesbian' Desire," 152–53. See also Greenblatt, *Shakespearean Negotiations*, 66–93.
22   Kuru, "Deli Birader," 235 (translation), 121 (text).
23   Ariosto, *Orlando Furioso*, 301 (canto 25, st. 44).
24   For an intelligent summary of English views, see Matar, *Turks, Moors, and Englishmen*, chap. 4.
25   Cited in DiGangi, *Homoerotics of Early Modern Drama*, 96.
26   Cited in Rosenthal, *Honest Courtesan*, 22.
27   Stallybrass, "Patriarchal Territories," 126, citing William Whately's *A Bride-Bush* and Robert Snawser's *A Looking Glasse for Married Folkes*.
28   Stehling, "Medieval Boy," 153–56. The poems from which the first three excerpts were taken can also be found under the titles "Dissuasio amoris venrei" (An argument against sexual love), "Satyra in amatorem puelli sub assumpta persona" (A satire on a young boy's lover in an assumed voice), and "Ad juvenem nimis elatum" (To a youth too proud) in Stehling, trans., *Medieval Latin Poems*, 31–33, 30–31, 38–39.
29   Kuru, "Deli Birader," 232 (translation), 119 (text).
30   Ibid., 188 (translation), 76–77 (text).
31   For Kız Memi, see Meredith-Owens, ed., *'Āşık*, fols. 151b–152a; and İsen, ed., *Künhü'l-ahbâr*, 228.
32   Şeker, ed., *Kavâ'idi'l-mecâlis*, 284. For illustrations depicting Ottoman dancing girls and boys (taken from paintings in a ca. 1590 album in the Austrian National Library), see And, *Istanbul*, 280–81.

33 Meredith-Owens, ed., ʿĀşık, fol. 220b (lines 7–12).
34 Caʿfer, "Hevesnāme," fol. 3a.
35 Ibid., fol. 39.
36 Ibid., fol. 63.
37 Ibid.
38 Ibid., fol. 120a.
39 See Peirce, Morality Tales, 367–74.
40 The issue of population growth will be taken up in more detail in chapter 10 below. For a focused overview of the issue, see Cook, Population Pressure.
41 For England, see Beier, Masterless Men, esp. his chap. 2 and 54 n. 17 (where he points to a study indicating that, in 1599, 49 percent of the population of Ealing was under twenty-one years of age). The Ottoman terminology of male life stages is discussed in Peirce, "Seniority, Sexuality, and Social Order."
42 See, e.g., Brackett, "The Florentine Onestà"; and Chambers and Pullan, eds., Venice, 126–27.
43 Beier, Masterless Men, chap. 4.
44 Refik, İstanbul hayatı, 38 (no. 1).
45 We must remember, however, that, in the Ottoman Empire, not just prostitutes but everyone had nicknames. See Kafadar, "Self and Others."
46 Refik, İstanbul hayatı, 40 (no. 5).
47 Ibid., 41 (no. 6).
48 Ibid., 141–42 (no. 9).
49 Gökyay, Evliya Çelebi, 310 (fol. 211a, line 10). On the phallus in early shadow-puppet theater, see And, Geleneksel türk tiyatrosu, 138–39.
50 Bull, trans., The Pilgrim, 11 (quotation), 23.
51 The two incidents that we discuss are mentioned in Terzioğlu, "The Imperial Circumcision Festival of 1582," 94.
52 Arslan, Surnâmeler, 469–70.
53 Ibid. 507–10.
54 Jones, "City Women," 299.
55 See Causa-Steindler and Mauch, eds. and trans., Lady Fiammetta. See also Causa-Steindler, "Introduction."
56 Causa-Steindler, "Introduction," xi.
57 For brief overviews, see Russell and Merry, eds. and trans., Infinity of Love, 1–19, 21–42; Stortoni, ed., Women Poets, ix–xxviii; and Jordan, "Feminism and the Humanists."
58 Cited in Jones, "City Women," 299, 300.
59 Holm, ed., Mirrhor, 131, 133.
60 Mirollo (Mannerism, 99–124) has an excellent analysis of the theme of veiling in sixteenth-century European art and literature.
61 See Dankoff, "Use of Ghazals."
62 Sehī, Heşt bihişt, 287–88. For the entries themselves and the introduction, see ibid., fols. 109a–110a.

63 Sehi's segregation of the female poets is due in large part to the fact that he organized his entries according to divisions by occupation, none of which would be relevant to women.
64 Cevdet, ed., *Tezkīre-i şu'arā*, 178.
65 There is no actual record of Mihri's death. All we know is that her name is not mentioned after 1512.
66 Cevdet, ed., *Tezkīre-i şu'arā*, 320.
67 Again, the characters of some female heroes of the mesnevis run against this tendency. An example is the presentation by the Azeri poet Fuzuli of the female beloved Leyla as the active force in *Leyla and Mejnun* (discussed in Andrews and Kalpaklı, "Layla Grows Up").
68 Cevdet, ed., *Tezkīre-i şu'arā*, 320.
69 Montrose, "'Shaping Fantasies,'" 47–48.
70 Peirce, "Seniority, Sexuality, and Social Order," 176 (quotation), 181.
71 Montrose, "'Shaping Fantasies,'" 37.
72 The convent may be theoretically pure, but there is evidence (e.g., Ruggiero, *Boundaries of Eros*, 71–84; Brown, *Immodest Acts*) that, especially in situations where dowryless young women were parked in convents as an alternative to poverty or prostitution, the life of those in the convent was almost as sexually active as that of the surrounding population.
73 Cevdet, ed., *Tezkīre-i şu'arā*, 320, 321.
74 Ibid., 321.
75 Meredith-Owens, ed., *'Āşık*, fol. 127b (lines 13–16).
76 Ibid., fol. 127b (lines 16–25).
77 Jones (*Currency of Eros*, 3) describes the general situation in Europe as follows: "All writers in this period presented themselves as readers; and their readers understood that the poet was alluding to, commenting on, or reworking other poems. Group improvisation, the circulation of manuscripts before they were printed, and coterie collaboration in publishing also positioned writers as audiences and producers simultaneously." This is a description that would apply equally to the Ottomans, with the exception that texts were prepared for circulation, not by printers, but by skilled calligraphers, many of whom were also poets.
78 For Renaissance female writers, see Jones, "City Women," and *Currency of Eros*; and Rosenthal, *Honest Courtesan*. For a discussion of the position of female poets in the Ottoman Empire that focuses on the imposition of patriarchal limits, see Silay, "Singing His Words." We must remember also that Mihri was writing a generation before any of the women Jones discusses.
79 Jones, *Currency of Eros*, 2–3.
80 Meredith-Owens, ed., *'Āşık*, fol. 127b (lines 20–21).
81 Ibid., fol. 127b (line 25).
82 This translation of Mihri's gazel is by Nejaat Black (see Andrews, Black, and Kalpaklı, eds. and trans., *Ottoman Lyric Poetry*, 49). 'Aşık cites only three of the gazel's five couplets. The omitted couplets are given in brackets.

83 Meredith-Owens, ed., ʿĀşık, fols. 127b (line 25)–128a (line 15).
84 Jones, "City Women," 300–301. See also Jones, *Currency of Eros*, 82–103.
85 Meredith-Owens, ed., ʿĀşık, fol. 127b (lines 16–22).
86 See Kutluk, ed., *Kınalı-zade Hasan Çelebi*, 1:280–81; İsen, ed., *Künhü'l-ahbâr*, 301–2. See also Cunbur, "İmadu'l-cihad"; and Kızıltan, "Kadın şairler," 113–14.
87 Meredith-Owens, ed., ʿĀşık, fol. 185b (lines 11–13, 13–23).
88 Ibid., fols. 185b (line 23)–186a (line 10).
89 On Nisayi, see Çavuşoğlu, "Nisāyī." For information on all the recognized female poets who wrote in the Ottoman elite style, see Kızıltan, "Kadın şairler." (On Tuti Hanım in particular, see ibid., 115.)
90 Meredith-Owens, ed., ʿĀşık, fols. 186a (line 10)–186b (line 1).
91 Cevdet, ed., *Tezkīre-i şuʿarā*, 22–23.
92 Jones, "City Women," 316, and *Currency of Eros*, 104.
93 Cited in Jones, "City Women," 307.
94 Ibid., 301. See also Jones, *Currency of Eros*, 141–54.
95 Silay, "Singing His Words," 212.
96 For an insightful theoretical view of the sword and its relation to the phallus, the pen, and the tongue in traditional Islamic literatures and cultures, see Glünz, "The Sword."
97 Jones and Rosenthal, eds. and trans., *Veronica Franco*, 161 (lines 22–24), 163 (lines 33–39).
98 Bourdieu, *Logic of Practice*, 53–65.
99 Peirce, "Seniority, Sexuality, and Social Order," 184–85, 185–86. For a discussion of postsexuality and power in the palace, see Peirce, *Imperial Harem*, 23ff.
100 Meredith-Owens, ed., ʿĀşık, fol. 83b (line 22).

7 Seduction and Reversal

1 ʿAşık's entry on Me'ali can be found in Meredith-Owens, ed., ʿĀşık, fols. 111b (line 20)–117a (line 23). The story begins on fol. 113a (line 11). The translation here was first published in a slightly different version in Silay, ed., *Anthology*, 138–46.
2 See Andrews, *Poetry's Voice*.
3 Jones and Stallybrass, "The Politics of *Astrophel and Stella*," 64. See also Javich, "Impure Motives," where it is argued that, during early-modern times, poetry has as one of its motives the demonstration of skills required for the courtier.
4 Jones and Stallybrass, "The Politics of *Astrophel and Stella*," 54.
5 Greenblatt, *Renaissance Self-Fashioning*, 120.
6 Andrews, "Speaking of Power," 293, 298.
7 Tanpınar, *XIX Asır*, xix.
8 As Jones and Stallybrass ("The Politics of *Astrophel and Stella*," 54) point out: "This is one of the paradoxes of Petrarchan poetry: although the lover depicts

himself as humble suitor to a dominating lady, he actually performs an act of public mastery, demonstrating his virtuosity in the practice of a masculine convention." This is certainly true of Ottoman divan poetry (and of Hafezan poetry generally) as well.

9   Necipoğlu, *Architecture, Ceremonial, and Power*, 118, 65–66 (quotation).
10 Ibid., 102–3, 107 (quotation).
11 See esp. Fleischer, *Mediterranean Apocalypse*; but also Flemming, "Public Opinion" (and other of her articles cited therein); Fleischer, "Lawgiver as Messiah," and "Seer to the Sultan"; and Valensi, *Birth of the Despot*.
12 Jones and Stallybrass, "The Politics of *Astrophel and Stella*," 54.
13 On the problem in England and the response of the authorities, see Beier, *Masterless Men*, passim. For an overview of how issues of mastery and masterlessness were reflected on the English Renaissance stage, see DiGangi, *Homoerotics of Early Modern Drama*, esp. chap. 3.
14 Jones and Stallybrass, "The Politics of *Astrophel and Stella*," 54.
15 Sidney, *Poems*, 215 ("Fift Song," lines 85–90) — an example used by Jones and Stallybrass.
16 Tarlan, ed., *Necatî Beg divanı*, 342–43 (no. 323, couplet 2), 153 (no. 14, couplet 1), 315 (no. 278, couplets 1–2), 415 (no. 443, couplet 2), 245 (no. 162, couplet 3), and 358 (no. 350, couplet 2).
17 Louis Montrose "'Shaping Fantasies,'" 55: "Sexual and family experience were invariably politicized; economic and political experience were invariably eroticized."
18 For a discussion of Venetian views on this topic, see Valensi, *Birth of the Despot*, 35–36.
19 See Kunt, *The Sultan's Servants*, esp. 95–96.
20 For the story of Ibrahim's life and career in English, see Jenkins, *Ibrahim Pasha*.
21 Latîfî, "Tezkīre-i şuʿarā," fol. 85a. A similar, but less complete, version of the "Icmāl-i evsāf-ı merhūm Ibrahim Pasha," the section (in the entry for Şükri 2) of Latifi's tezkire from which this passage is taken, can be found in Cevdet, ed., *Tezkīre-i şuʿarā*, 204. Another version can be found in Sevgi, ed., *İki risale*, 24.
22 Meredith-Owens, ed., *ʿĀşık*, fol. 295a (line 8).
23 The entire story can be found in Meredith-Owens, ed., *ʿĀşık*, fols. 294b (line 1)–295a (line 20).
24 Meredith-Owens, ed., *ʿĀşık*, fol. 199b (lines 18–19). The entire story can be found in most of the major sources: e.g., ibid., fols. 199b (line 13) ff.
25 Flemming "Public Opinion," 52–53.
26 For the story of Hurrem, see *Encyclopaedia of Islam* (new ed.), vol. 5, fascs. 79–80, pp. 66–67. See also Peirce, *Imperial Harem*, chap. 3.
27 For the "sold meat" story, see Peirce, *Imperial Harem*, 59–60.
28 Our translation is based on texts found in İsen and Bilkan, eds., *Sultan şâirler*, 129–30; and Muhibbî, *Dīvān*, 124. Another translation can be found in Halman, *Magnificent Poet*, 30–31. For the kinds of letters that Hurrem wrote to Süleyman, see Uluçay, *Aşk mektupları*, 19–76.

29 The best overview of the Ottoman harem in the period under discussion is Peirce, *Imperial Harem*. Peirce avoids, however, discussing the sexuality of harem life. See also the account in Penzer, *Harem*.
30 Our translation is based on both Latîfî, "Tezkîre-i şu'arā," 85a–85b; and Cevdet, ed., *Tezkîre-i şu'arā*, 204–5.
31 For this and a version of the story of Süleyman and Hurrem, see Fisher, "Life and Family," 10–15. The story of Mustafa and his tragic death was of interest to Europeans as well, as is attested to most prominently by the posthumously published play *Mustapha* by Fulke Greville (1554–1628) (see Greville, *Certaine Learned and Elegant Workes*). Our thanks to Yavuz Demir for pointing this out to us.
32 See Çavuşoğlu, "Şeyhzāde Mustafa Mersiyeleri."
33 Çavuşoğlu, "Nisāyī," 411–13.

8 To Die For . . .

1 The first paragraph of the story of Ferdi is taken from Kortantamer's summary (*Nev'î-zāde Atāyī*, 227–28) of destan 39 of the *Sohbetü'l-ebkar*. The remainder is our translation from Meredith-Owens, ed., *'Āşık*, fols. 190b (line 23)–192a (line 3).
2 Cevdet, ed., *Tezkîre-i şu'arā*, 365.
3 The violence of love was also theorized on classical models. For example, in his commentary on Plato's *Symposium*, Ficino (*Commentary*, 166) discusses the "capture" by love of persons dominated by various humors and indicates that the dangerous love of a melancholic and a choleric "consumes" the melancholic lover and provokes the choleric "to wrath and killings."
4 Okuyucu, ed., *Cinânî*, 380 (no. 14).
5 Cited in Rowse, *Sex and Society*, 296.
6 Matar (*Turks, Moors, and Englishmen*, 44–55) points out that the English custom of demobilizing troops in times of peace induced unemployed soldiers to seek employment in Muslim armies in both the Ottoman Empire and North Africa. Beier (*Masterless Men*, 93–95) mentions that unemployed soldiers swelled the ranks of the vagrant poor during the late sixteenth century and the early seventeenth.
7 Beier, *Masterless Men*, 138–39.
8 Cellini, *Autobiography*, 128.
9 Ibid., 130.
10 Tarlan, ed., *Hayâlî Bey dîvânı*, 113 (no. 3, couplets 1–2).
11 Rocke, *Forbidden Friendships*, 162–64 (generally), 162 (quotation).
12 Masson (*Courtesans*, 146–47) describes the institutionalized gang rape, called a *trentuno* (thirty-one), inflicted on a prostitute and later courtesan named La Zaffetta. Rosenthal (*Honest Courtesan*, 37–38) adds that La Zaffetta was apparently raped by eighty men on the island of Chioggia and further subjected to a

humiliating satire by Lorenzo Venier that described the episode as vengeance for refusing entrance to her home to a would-be lover.

13 Ruggiero, *Boundaries of Eros*, 89–108.
14 Cited in Rowse, *Sex and Society*, 205.
15 Kuru, "Deli Birader," 192 (translation), 82 (text).
16 Ibid., 193 (translation), 82 (text).
17 Düzdağ, *Ebussuūd*, 159 (no. 788), 158 (no. 781).
18 See Smith, *Homosexual Desire*, 132ff.
19 Marlowe, *Hero and Leander*, 50.
20 See Saslow, *Ganymede*, passim.
21 Marlowe, *Hero and Leander*, 51.
22 Ibid., 52–53.
23 Marlowe, *Hero and Leander*, 53.
24 Marlowe, *Hero and Leander*, 15.
25 The revelation of the body hidden beneath transvestite dress in English Renaissance drama is cogently analyzed in Stallybrass, "Transvestitism." Smith (*Homosexual Desire*, 136) argues that the androgyny and ambiguities of the beloved in early-modern literature "represent, not an exclusive sexual taste, but an *inclusive* one. To use the categories of our own day, these poems are bisexual fantasies. The temporary freedom they grant to sexual desire allows it to flow out in all directions, toward all the sexual objects that beckon in the romantic landscape." We agree but feel that the freedom that Smith mentions is sharply curtailed by scripts imposed by the structures of absolutist monarchy and relations at court.
26 Marlowe, *Hero and Leander*, 53.
27 Ibid., 50 (line 7). Barnfield, *Affectionate Shepherd*, 5–6.
28 See Mirollo, *Mannerism*, 163ff., esp. 165.
29 Marlowe, *Hero and Leander*, 54.
30 Ficino (*Commentary*, 159–60) summarizes the common understanding (as common to the Ottomans as to Europeans) when he says that the blood of a young man being "thin, clear, warm, and sweet" emits an especially deadly vapor that is drawn out in the rays [of vision] that are emitted by the eyes: "Therefore, what wonder is it if the eye, wide open and fixed upon someone, shoots the darts of its own rays into the eyes of the bystander, and along with those darts, which are the vehicles of the spirits, aims that sanguine vapor which we call spirit? Hence the poisoned dart pierces through the eyes, and since it is shot from the heart, it seeks again the heart of the man being shot, as its proper home; it wounds the heart."
31 Fevrī, "Dīvān," fols. 116b, 131b; Tarlan, ed., *Necatî Beg divanı*, 308 (no. 265, couplet 7), 258 (no. 184, couplet 3).
32 Tarlan, ed., *Hayâlî Bey dîvânı*, 277 (no. 16, couplets 1–2).
33 Fevrī, "Dīvān," fols. 133b, 133a.
34 Beier (*Masterless Men*, 139) uses this phrase apparently to indicate that occasions of violence usually produced a knife and a stabbing. The inevitability of the knife seems to be a feature of Ottoman quarrels and even lovers' tiffs as well.

35 Sidney, *Poems*, 165 (no. 2, lines 1–2), 174–75 (no. 20, lines 1–3).
36 Tarlan, ed., *Hayâlî Bey dîvânı*, 105 (no. 19, couplet 1).

9 Love, Law, and Religion

1 Ruggiero, *Boundaries of Eros*, 88.
2 We have used as an authoritative compilation and commentary on Islamic law: Marghīnānī's *Hidāyah*. The only English version is Hamilton, trans., *Hedaya*, originally prepared for use by British courts in India, and based on a Persian abridgment and translation. For the relevant sections on hadd crimes, see Marghīnānī, *Hidāyah*, 2:96–116; and Hamilton, trans., *Hedaya*, 175–203. For a good summary in English of the legal theory of the Hanbali school, see Baroody, trans., *Crime and Justice under Hanbali Law*, a translation of the *Manār al-sabīl* by Shaykh Ibrāhīm ibn Muhammad ibn Salīm ibn Dūyān, which is, in turn, a commentary on the *al-Dalīl* of Shaykh Marʿī ibn Yūsif al-Karmī al-Maqdisī al-Hanbalī, a summary of the latter's *Ghāyat al-muntaha*.
3 *Encyclopaedia of Islam* (new ed.), vol. 11, fascs. 187–88, pp. 510–11.
4 Heyd, *Studies*, 246. Imber (*Ebuʾs-suʿud*, 91) says, in this regard: "Highway robbery, however, is the area where the laws of the fixed penalties engage most closely with reality. Fornication and wine drinking are different since the clear intention of the jurists is that the penalties should never be inflicted. There, punishments are, therefore, not so much real as symbolic of the enormity of the offense in the eyes of God, and it is as symbols that they came to play a role in the Ottoman practice of government. They came, above all, to form a standard ingredient in the indictment of heretics."
5 Heyd, *Studies*, 263 n. 4; and Demir, "Zina üzerine," 6. Peirce (*Morality Tales*, 351–89) gives a detailed account of the lengths to which sixteenth-century magistrates would go to avoid prosecuting cases of zina. Demir ("Zina Üzerine") gives a good general overview of Ottoman legal responses to prostitution and zina, including the kinds of punishments actually applied.
6 For punishments applied to Ottoman lawbreakers, see Heyd, *Studies*, chap. 4.
7 Brackett, *Criminal Justice in Florence*, 68 (see also 116, 123).
8 Peirce, *Morality Tales*, 366.
9 For an example from al-Gazalī's *İhya'* of the theory of licit Islamic sexuality, see the chapter "The Etiquette of Marriage" in Farah, trans., *Marriage and Sexuality*.
10 Refik, *İstanbul hayatı*, 38 (no. 1).
11 Ergenç, "Mahalle," 71 and passim.
12 See, e.g., ibid., 74.
13 For a contextualized discussion of töhmet, see Peirce, Morality Tales, 133–34, 362–63.
14 Refik, *İstanbul hayatı*, 40–41 (no. 5).
15 Kuru, "Deli Birader," 251–52 (translation), 133–34 (text).
16 Heyd, *Studies*, 233–34.

17 Imber, *Ebu's-su'ud*, 45.
18 Peirce, *Morality Tales*, 369.
19 In "Politicizing Sex," Peirce points out that there had been an increasing expansion of laws regulating sexual behavior from the time of Bayezit II through the reign of Süleyman. The reforms of Süleyman and Ebu's-su'ud even went so far as to criminalize "suspicious association," thus institutionalizing local surveillance.
20 This event is related in Rocke, *Forbidden Friendships*, 233–35.
21 For documents regulating prostitutes, see Chambers and Pullan, eds., *Venice*, 126–27.
22 For Priuli, see Chambers and Pullan, eds., *Venice*, 124. For the Florentine municipalization of prostitution and the theoretical justifications for it, see Brackett, "The Florentine Onestà," passim.
23 Refik, *İstanbul hayatı*, 138 (no. 3).
24 Ibid., 39–40 (no. 3).
25 Düzdağ, *Ebussuûd*, 149 (no. 3724).
26 Şeker, ed., *Kavâ'idi'l-mecâlis*, 365, 309.
27 Meredith-Owens, ed., *'Āşık*, fols. 294b (line 17)–295a (line 1).
28 İnalcık, "Belgeler," 49.
29 Selim Kuru has pointed out to me that some of the pressure to close nonconforming bathhouses may have been a result of severe water shortages and the competition for water supplies.
30 Düzdağ, *Ebussuûd*, 159 (no. 787).
31 Peirce, "Seniority, Sexuality, and Social Order," 187. See also Heyd, *Studies*, 277.
32 See the entries for Sihrī-i Sānī in İsen, ed., *Künhü'l-ahbâr*, 228; and Meredith-Owens, ed., *'Āşık*, fols. 151b–152a. On castration as a punishment for sodomy, see Heyd, *Studies*, 267.
33 Heyd, *Studies*, 269–70, 274.
34 Imber, *Ebu's-su'ud*, 173. See also Düzdağ, *Ebussuûd*, 180 (no. 901).
35 İsen ("Meslekî konumları," 310–14) gives a breakdown of the professions of the poets who receive entries in the major biographies of poets. The largest number, 36 percent, are from the ulema class and another 6.5 percent from other religious professions. This means that a total of 42.5 percent were in fields directly related to religion. The next largest group was bureaucrats at 28 percent.
36 Sidney, *Poems*, 201 (no. 71).
37 See, e.g., Ficino, *Commentary*, 45–52.
38 See Bellamy, "Sex and Society," 31 n. 25 (citing al-Ghazālī).
39 For a seminal discussion of Michelangelo's Neoplatonism, see Panofsky, *Iconology*, esp. chap. 4.
40 Russell and Merry, eds. and trans., *Infinity of Love*, 89–90. For information on Tullia d'Aragona and the *Dialogue*, see ibid., 21–42; and Jones, *Currency of Eros*, 103–17. Tullia was born in Rome in 1510 to a mother who was herself a famous courtesan during the heyday of courtesans in Rome. Tullia was noted for her

intellect and sharp wits, was trained in music, and wrote poetry and prose, all of which made her a popular companion of the Roman intelligentsia. During the period 1535–48, as the climate in Italy for courtesans deteriorated, she moved to several cities, including Venice and Florence, where she enjoyed the attentions of the powerful and famous. She died in 1556 some time after returning to Rome.

41 Russell and Merry, eds. and trans., *Infinity of Love*, 26.
42 For the discussion of pederastic love, see ibid., 95–97. Benedetto Varchi (1503–65) was one of the leading lights of Florentine intellectual life during the period of Tullia's sojourn in that city, a scholar, poet, historian, and author of a mediocre learned comedy. He was a noted partisan of the ancients and an Aristotelian with Platonic ideas about love who became a part of Tullia's social circle, which included the foremost Florentine intellectuals of the day. The discussion of generating "beautiful souls" is paralleled in the Islamic tradition by the notion of the pregnancy of the soul (for which, see Schimmel, "Eros," 138–39).
43 See Brackett, "The Florentine Onestà," 294.
44 Russell and Merry, eds. and trans., 29.
45 Greenblatt, *Renaissance Self-Fashioning*, 138, 139.
46 Fevrî, "Dīvān," fol. 217.
47 Burmaoğlu, *Lamiʿî*, 88 (no. 3 [lines 1–2]).
48 Küçük, ed., *Bâkî dîvânı*, 247 (no. 238).
49 Çavuşoğlu and Tanyeri, eds., *Zatî divanı*, 3:3 (no. 1004).
50 See Şentürk, *Antoloji*, 236–38.
51 Fevrî, "Dīvān," fol. 132b; Çavuşoğlu et al., eds., *Revānī dīvānı*, "Gazeller," no. 174 (line 3); Fevrî, "Dīvān," fol. 130b.
52 Tarlan, ed., *Hayâlî Bey dîvânı*, 105–6 (no. 19).
53 Ibid., 144 (no. 45).
54 Burmaoğlu, *Lamiʿî*, 146 (no. 32 [lines 1, 3]).
55 For a brief schematic overview, see Andrews, *Poetry's Voice*, chap. 4.
56 Düzdağ, *Ebussuûd*, 87 (no. 353).
57 It appears that the issue here is precisely one of class. There was considerable disagreement at this time about the social status of dervishes. Some were clearly of the "educated administrative" (ʿaskeri) class and enjoyed the privileges and immunities of that class, but others were considered to be members of the common "flock" (reʿaya) and, therefore, subject to restrictions placed on that class. The problem is that the boundaries were hazy and shifting.
58 Burmaoğlu, *Lamiʿî*, 86 (no. 2 [lines 5–6]), 102 (no. 10 [line 1]), 108 (no. 13 [lines 1–2]).
59 Bray, *Homosexuality*, 57.
60 Ibid., 79.
61 For the Prophet's and Islamic theologians' views of sodomy, which seem no less extreme than those of Christian theologians, see, e.g., Bellamy, "Sex and Society," 37–39.

62　Ergenç ("Mahalle," 74) gives examples of Ottoman neighborhoods working to expel people whom they did not know well and whose morals they could not vouch for.
63　Bray, *Homosexuality*, 67.
64　See Schimmel, "Eros," passim.
65　Martin, "The Khalwati Order," 281–82.
66　See Karamustafa, "Formation of the *Bektâsîye*," passim. The most comprehensive account of the Bektaşi order in English is still Birge, *The Bektashi Order*.
67　For a theoretical discussion of the antinomian tendencies of "poetic Sufism" and their relation to the despotic state, see Andrews, "Singing the Alienated 'I,'" passim.

10　The End of an Age

1　Abou-El-Haj, *Formation of the Modern State*, 11.
2　For a cogent overview of recent trends in thinking about history and the writing of history, see Abou-El-Haj, "Theorizing beyond the Nation-State"; and Piterberg, *Ottoman Tragedy*, 135–84.
3　Using literary sources in this way is highly controversial. As Brown points out: "Literary sources can be prescriptive rather than descriptive. They tell us much about the attitudes of the literate groups that produced them and about the public that read them, but they may not correspond to social realities" ("A Woman's Place," 207). We would not disagree but would argue simply that the attitudes and circumstances of those who produce and consume literature are themselves social realities that shed light on such nonliterary sources as laws and records, which must also be interpreted—and interpreted with similar cautions about context.
4　An interesting aspect of this recognition of rupture is found in the striking change in Venetian discourse about the Ottoman Empire that occurs near the end of the sixteenth century. For a summary of Venetian accounts, see Valensi, *Birth of the Despot*, 69–87.
5　Of course, this assumes an agreement that does not exist about when the late Renaissance ends. For Italian historians, it is usually sometime around or shortly after the 1570s; for some British historians, it is not until the 1640s.
6　It is most likely that the notice on Ibrahim Pasha in Latifi's tezkire is an interpolated excerpt from a longer essay (*risale*) praising the late pasha (see Sevgi, ed., *Iki risale*).
7　See Cevdet, ed., *Tezkīre-i şuʿarā*. The textual history of Latifi's tezkire is discussed at some length in Andrews, "The *Tezkere-i şuʿarā* of Latīfī," 18–51, and briefly in Andrews, "Metin nerede?"
8　Anyone who reads much of the literature of advice and admonition will recognize that certain complaints are universal. As one economic historian laments: "So long as literary sources are being used, historians . . . can deal

with very similar questions—and tend to get very similar answers. For literary sources often have their origin in the complaints of the disgruntled or of social reformers, and the literature of economic and social protest shows an almost monotonous uniformity throughout the ages" (Fisher, *The English Economy*, 132).

9 For a discussion of the texts of Latifi's biographies, see Andrews, "The *Tezkere-i şu'arā* of Latīfī," 29–40, and "Metin nerede?" passim. The weak point in our reasoning here is that we are not certain of the date for Latifi's *Essay in Description of Ibrahim Pasha*, from which the description in later versions of the tezkire seems to have been excerpted. It is our contention that, most likely, this was done after the death of Süleyman.

10 We should note that 'Aşık says that he began writing his tezkire much earlier but that he was so put off by the appearance of Latifi's tezkire, which he claimed stole his idea of listing the poets in alphabetical order, that he set it aside for some time.

11 Examples of the kind of awards that Ottoman literati received from the palace for scholarly works and poetry presented at official ceremonies during the early years of the reign of Süleyman are found in Erünsal, "İn'āmāt defteri: Süleyman," passim. It was not uncommon for a poet of the first rank to receive a thousand akçes for a single panegyric on such occasions. About a quarter century earlier, Necati received two thousand akçes for a kaside and Mihri Hatun three thousand akçes for a copy of her divan. Three years after his death, the three sons of Necati received fifteen aspers a day from the royal treasury as a stipend. (Erünsal, "Arşivlerin değeri," 221.) The individual gifts are huge, ranging from more than half to a third of the yearly salary of a skilled artisan or professional soldier.

12 McGowan, *Economic Life*, 2. Braudel (*Structures of Everyday Life*, 32–49) gives a broad global view of population fluctuations during this period.

13 See Pullan, "Wage Earners," esp. 150 n. 3.

14 See Brackett, *Criminal Justice in Florence*, 98–99.

15 See Fisher, *The English Economy*, 151, 168–69.

16 Beier, *Masterless Men*, 3–16.

17 The evidence in Cook, *Population Pressure*, 10–15 and passim, which is cited in (partial) support of Braudel's general conclusion, is inconclusive. But the statements in Barkan, "Price Revolution," 27–28, especially as expanded and interpreted by İnalcık (*Economic and Social History*, 25–43, and "State, Sovereignty, and Law," 85–89), as well as more recent data, such as those cited by Peirce (*Morality Tales*, 367–74 [for the villages of Hiyam and Keret]) and Faroqhi (*Towns and Townsmen*, 191–205), confirm the general picture of increases both in gross population and in population pressure.

18 On the relation between demographics and work in the agricultural sector, see McGowan, *Economic Life*, 7ff.

19 Pamuk, *Monetary History*, 112. For a cogent argument for a broader than purely economic view, see Piterberg, *Ottoman Tragedy*, 141–46.

20 We should point out that inflation has a financial advantage to the state only so long as there is a lag between inflation and the demand for higher stipends or unrealistically low prices on the part of the standing army.

21 See Fisher, *The English Economy*, 85. For the effects of the price revolution on Venice, see Pullan, "Wage Earners," passim.

22 Pamuk, *Monetary History*, 47–58 (for the policy of revenue enhancement by debasement), 122–23 (for the debasement of 1585–86).

23 Pamuk, "Price Revolution," 82–83, and *Monetary History*, 127. See also Sahillioğlu, *Studies*, 27–47.

24 Tietze, ed., *Counsel for Sultans*, 1:127–28 (text), 41–42 (translation).

25 We must recognize that the term *despot* is an anachronism when discussing the sixteenth century. The word *despotic* was not commonly used to describe any form of government until somewhat later, and then it referred to a form of absolutism represented by the Ottomans, among others, in which no aristocracy or nobility existed to limit the power of the monarch. For a more complete discussion of the development of the term *despot*, see Valensi, *Birth of the Despot*. Here, we use the term, without implied value judgment, to refer to an absolute monarch, either Eastern or Western.

26 There are two famous portraits of Elizabeth associating her with the map of English territory: the 1592 "Dichley portrait," which has her standing on a map of England, and a 1598 Dutch engraving in which her body becomes the image of Europe. Reproductions of these portraits can be found in Strong, *Portraits of Queen Elizabeth I*, 75–76 and pls. XV and E32. See also Stallybrass, "Patriarchal Territories," 129–30; and Wall, *Power and Protest*, 18.

27 *The problem of Elizabeth* is our term, but the problem itself is clearly manifested in Montrose, "'Shaping Fantasies'"; and Stallybrass, "Patriarchal Territories," esp. 130–33.

28 See Andrews, "Sexual Intertext."

29 For patriarchy during the reign of the Stuarts, see Goldberg, "Fatherly Authority," passim.

30 In this, we follow the lead of Braudel (*Mediterranean World*, 2:1166), who said of the patterns of war and peace in relations between Western Europe and the Ottoman Empire: "If ever there was a pattern in history, this is one. But it is unknown territory chiefly because historians have persistently overestimated the power of individuals. They have paid little attention to deep-seated, underlying movements."

31 Brummett, *Seapower and Diplomacy*, 128, 178ff.

32 Necipoğlu, "Süleymân the Magnificent," passim.

33 Faroqhi, "Politics and Socio-Economic Change," 102.

34 See Goffman, *Izmir*, 36–49. A similar economic argument is made by some observers of Renaissance England, who suggest that the influx of rural gentry visiting in London was one of the conditions that made it possible for professional theater to thrive during the Elizabethan Age (see, e.g., Fisher, *The English Economy*, 115).

35 For the problems of provisioning growing towns, see Faroqhi, *Towns and Townsmen*, 191–266.
36 Pamuk (*Monetary History*, 11–15) cites the conclusions of Mehmet Genç to the effect that the number one priority of the government "was the provisioning of the urban economy including the army, the palace, and state officials." This conclusion seems to be accepted as a given of Ottoman economic history. See also İnalcık, *Economic and Social History*, 179–87, pointing out that the sultan had to demonstrate a personal interest in the bread supply of the Istanbul masses in order to prevent dangerous unrest in times of shortage.
37 See Faroqhi, *Towns and Townsmen*, 191–266. See also İnalcık, *Economic and Social History*, 221–41. Faroqhi (*Towns and Townsmen*), Goffman (*Izmir*, 36–49), and Brummett (*Seapower and Diplomacy*) give numerous examples of the diversion of provisions by law destined for the capital.
38 Faroqhi, *Towns and Townsmen*, 322.
39 For an example of Venetian restrictions on meat consumption among the elites, see Chambers and Pullan, eds., *Venice*, 178–79.
40 For bread and grain shortages in the Ottoman Empire and Europe, see McGowan, *Economic Life*, 34–38.
41 See Woolf, "Venice and the Terraferma," 180–87 and passim.
42 Fisher, *The English Economy*, 181–82, 196–97, and chap. 4 generally.
43 Abou-el-Haj, *Formation of the Modern State*, 14–15.
44 For this and the following, see Peirce, *Imperial Harem*, 97–112.
45 However, ties to the palace were in some degree maintained by the marriage of palace women to highly placed kuls who served as provincial authorities.
46 Kunt, *The Sultan's Servants*, 95–96.
47 See, e.g., İnalcık, *Economic and Social History*, 69–74. The term *prebend*—Weber's coinage—is intended to distinguish the Ottoman institution from that of medieval European feudalism, which it resembles on the surface.
48 Pamuk, "Price Revolution," 84.
49 There are numerous accounts from a variety of perspectives of the transformation of the Ottoman timar system. Compare, e.g., the summary formulations of Barkan ("Price Revolution," 23), Abou-El-Haj (*Formation of the Modern State*, 11–18), and McGowan (*Economic Life*, 56–58). We must also keep in mind that, as Murphey (*Ottoman Warfare*, 36–43) indicates, in actual numbers of retainers, timariot forces seem to have grown from the mid-sixteenth century to the mid-seventeenth.
50 Pamuk, "Price Revolution," 84–85. It is important, in this regard, to note the cautionary remarks on the effects of taxation policy on rural agriculture made by Murphey (*Ottoman Warfare*, 186–89), who points to a lack of adequate detailed studies of economic impacts and evidence that monetization caused little change in the impact of taxation on rural economies.
51 Kunt, *The Sultan's Servants*, 98 (cited in Piterberg, *Ottoman Tragedy*, 149).
52 See Fisher, *The English Economy*, 84, 153–54.
53 See Laslett, *World We Have Lost*, 60–61; and Beier, *Masterless Men*, 19–22.

McGowan (*Economic Life*, 38–41) discusses a similar tendency in the Ottoman Empire toward favoring wool production in areas where civil unrest made agriculture difficult or unprofitable.

54 Matar, *Turks, Moors, and Englishmen*, 45–46; Beier, *Masterless Men*, 93–95; Wall, *Power and Protest*, 160–61.

55 For a discussion of the 1524 and 1525 peasant rebellions in Germany and a comparison of it to unrest in late-sixteenth-century England, see Greenblatt, "Murdering Peasants," 14ff.

56 For the unrest in England, see Wall, *Power and Protest*, 146–62, 170–73.

57 Murphey (*Ottoman Warfare*, 190–91) argues that, while the sekban may have contributed in some way to unrest in Anatolia, their numbers (which he pegs at between four and ten thousand in wartime) were insufficient—assuming that not all were demobilized in periods of peace—to affect social conditions in the whole area, as some accounts have indicated. We are suggesting only that unattached sekban were one of several groups contributing to rural instability.

58 See Barkey, *Bandits and Bureaucrats*, which sees the rural bandit less as a revolutionary (one who intends to overthrow the state) and more as a rebel (one who uses insurrection as a means of negotiating a position in the governing apparatus). Piterberg (*Ottoman Tragedy*, 146–54 and esp. 157–60) objects to Barkey's reification and idealization of *the state*. Braudel (*Mediterranean World*, 2:749–54) sketches a more global view of the banditry problem. The standard source for the Celali revolts and the unrest in Anatolia is Akdağ, *Celalî isyanları*. See also Griswold, *Anatolian Rebellion*; and Goffman, *Izmir*, 25–33.

59 For the situation of the ulema at the end of the Age of Beloveds and later, see Zilfi, *Politics of Piety*, esp. 129–81.

60 Wall, *Power and Protest*, 160.

61 For the increase in severity and number of laws against sodomy in Florence during the sixteenth century, see Rocke, *Forbidden Friendships*, 227–35. For a fascinating comparative study of Stuart England, Ottoman Turkey, and Ming China that elaborates the kinds of parallels that we are suggesting but locates the parallel to Stuart Puritanism in Sufism rather than in the response of Kadizadeli conservatism to the artistically scripted aspects of popular Sufi practice, see Goldstone, "East and West." For an introduction to and analysis of Goldstone's work, we are indebted to Piterberg, *Ottoman Tragedy*, esp. 141–46.

62 See Faroqhi, *Towns and Townsmen*, 295; and Goffman, *Izmir*, 50–76.

63 See Jennings, "Firearms, Bandits, and Gun-Control."

64 We need to remember, in this regard, that Ottoman rulers regularly executed or turned over to the mob high officials to assuage popular dissatisfaction. For the officials, public unhappiness was a life-and-death matter.

65 Our summary of this topic is heavily indebted to Feldman, "Social Environment of the Tāze-gūyān."

66 A good example of the social life of the dervish orders is found in Kafadar, "Self and Others."

67 On the whole issue of the struggle to frame this event in historical narratives,

see Piterberg, *Ottoman Tragedy*. That there was a struggle to frame the event in historical narratives seems to be a sign that it was, as Piterberg indicates, a cataclysmic and difficult-to-interpret event for Ottoman elites.

68 Wall, *Power and Protest*, 10.
69 See Fisher, "Life and Family," 13.
70 See Kafadar, *Between Two Worlds*.
71 There are many sources for the stories of Yahya and Hayali, including the major tezkires: 'Aşık's (the *Meşa'irü'ş-şu'era*); Latifi's; and the poet biographies of 'Ali's *Künhü'l-ahbar* (see İsen, ed., *Künhü'l-ahbâr*). For a summary of Hayali's biography in Turkish, see the introduction to Tarlan, ed., *Hayâlî Bey dîvânı*, vii–xviii. Short versions of biographies of both Yahya and Hayali in English can be found in Andrews, Black, and Kalpaklı, eds. and trans., *Ottoman Lyric Poetry*, 241–44 and 233–35, respectively.
72 This anecdote can be found in Meredith-Owens, ed., *'Aşık*, fol. 96a (lines 11–20).
73 For Emirek's biography, see Meredith-Owens, ed., *'Aşık*, fols. 48b–49b (the poem is on fol. 49b [lines 9–13]).
74 See, e.g., the passage cited from Evliya Çelebi in Fisher, "Life and Family," 16. For Mustafa 'Ali's view, see Fleischer, *Bureaucrat and Intellectual*, 258–59.
75 Meredith-Owens, ed., *'Aşık*, fol. 274b (lines 5–6).
76 Çavuşoğlu, ed., *Yahyā Bey: Dīvan*, 44 (lines 38–40).
77 Ibid., 95 (lines 14–15), 96 (lines 28–29).

11 The Age of Beloveds

1 See, e.g., Kafadar, "Ottoman Decline."
2 See, e.g., Abou-El-Haj, *Formation of the Modern State*, introduction.
3 See, e.g., Fleischer, *Mediterranean Apocalypse*, esp. chap. 1. One other such exploration is found in Darling's thoughtful "The Renaissance and the Middle East," which points to a series of late-medieval and early-modern "renaissances" of Middle Eastern culture, culminating in an Ottoman Renaissance. Darling's essay was written after we were well along in our own exploration (an exploration of which Darling was entirely unaware), yet, examining different evidence from a different perspective, she comes to much the same general conclusion: that what is now often referred to as *the Renaissance* was as much a global event as a Western European one.
4 Darling, "The Renaissance and the Middle East," 55–56, 65–66.
5 Menocal, *Shards of Love*, 10.
6 Mullaney, "Strange Things," 80 (quoting from the prefatory epistle by "E. K." to Spenser's *The Shepheardes Calender*).
7 For the history of "renaissances" in the Islamic world, see Darling, "The Renaissance and the Middle East."
8 Mullaney, "Strange Things," 81.
9 Cited in Greenblatt, *Renaissance Self-Fashioning*, 106. On self-fashioning or con-

trastive self-understanding in the English Renaissance, see ibid., esp. chaps. 1–2.
10 This is the sense of Qur'an 12:2 (see also 13:37, 41:44, 42:7, 43:3).
11 Mirollo, *Mannerism*, 22.
12 See Rosenthal, *Honest Courtesan*, 153–77.
13 de Certeau, *Heterologies*, 80.
14 See Ozment, *Mysticism and Dissent*, 2ff.
15 For one analysis of how this works in the Ottoman case, see Andrews, "Singing the Alienated 'I.'" The European case is extensively discussed in Ozment, *Mysticism and Dissent*.
16 It is certainly significant that the Age of Beloveds is also the age in which the final disbursal of Andalusian culture occurred, sending the seeds of Islamic mysticism and Jewish cabalism into the rest of Europe and the Ottoman Empire. For an engaging and thoughtful overview of Andalusian culture and its impact on Europe, see Menocal, *Ornament of the World*.
17 We are referring here to Mirollo's *Mannerism* and Castagno's *The Early Commedia*. Both works cite numerous books and articles, and many of the former carry fifty- to sixty-page bibliographies on the topic. Readers who are interested in an overview of the issue of mannerism should refer to both Mirollo's and Castagno's introductions.
18 See Braudel, *Mediterranean World*, 2:827.
19 Mirollo, *Mannerism*, 68–69. We would also note the relation of Mirollo's view of mannerism to the discussion of the English epyllion in Brown, "Breaking the Canon."
20 Castagno, *The Early Commedia*, 4 (quotation), 147–53.
21 Küçük, *Bâkî dîvânı*, 234 (no. 218).
22 See Necipoğlu, *Architecture, Ceremonial, and Power*, pp. 102–3 and pl. 62.
23 For a primer on the mystical reading of Islamic poetry and numerous examples, see Schimmel, *As through a Veil*.
24 Tarlan, ed., *Hayâlî Bey dîvânı*, 129 (no. 15).
25 Hauser, *Mannerism*, 24.
26 Çavuşoğlu, *Divanlar arasında*, 35–48, discusses the *ayak* (cup/foot) and contextualizes it as a part of the Istanbul social scene.
27 Hauser, *Mannerism*, 13.
28 For a summary of the story of Leyla and Mejnun, see Andrews, Black, and Kalpaklı, *Ottoman Lyric Poetry*, 70–72. For a discussion of the transmission of the story from Persian to Turkish, see Andrews and Kalpaklı, "Layla Grows Up."
29 Çavuşoğlu, *Hayâlî: Örnekler*, 117.
30 Ibid.
31 Although it is strictly true that a mystical reading would collapse these multiple possibilities into one, there is no indication that such a unary reading was sought or valued by most Ottoman poets.
32 Hauser, *Mannerism*, 13.
33 See Saslow, *Ganymede*, 97–141.

34 Our discussion of Hauser's general position is based on Mirollo, *Mannerism*, esp. 33.
35 Hauser, *Mannerism*, 6.
36 We would point again to Valensi's reading in *Birth of a Despot* of sixteenth-century Venetian sources, a reading that recognizes Italian observers' serious doubts about the inevitability of an ultimate victory for Christianity. No one has as yet looked at the late Renaissance in the context of Hauser's crisis hypothesis to determine what the effects of the Ottoman threat might have been on the psychology of European art and literature.
37 For a marvelous picture of seventeenth-century Persian literature and its origins, see Losensky, *Welcoming Fighānī*, passim.
38 See Feldman, "Celestial Sphere," and "Social Environment of the Tāze-Gūyān."
39 The text is from Feldman, "Celestial Sphere," 207.
40 Ibid., 211 (quoting an email message from Andrews).

GLOSSARY OF OTTOMAN TERMS

'askeri: The military class of slaves (see *kul*) who administered the nonreligious affairs of the empire as agents of the sultan and those nonslaves in the administrative and military branch of the empire.

Bey (sometimes *Beg*): A title applied usually to high administrative officials.

beylerbey: "Lord of lords." The governor general of a province.

Çelebi (Chelebi): A title of respect applied to men of the educated classes, to the sons of the learned elites, and, at times, to the sons of sultans.

defterdar: A minister of finance.

divan: In poetry, the "collected works" of a poet, divided into sections usually consisting of a prose introduction, panegyric and occasional verses, verses in stanzas, lyrical and erotic poems, quatrains, and fragments.

divan poetry: Refers to the elite poetry of the Ottoman period, the kind of poetry that was collected in divans.

Efendi: An informal title applied to economic or intellectual elites.

fetva: A written legal opinion issued by a mufti (q.v.).

gazel: The most popular form of Ottoman elite poetry, a sonnet-like lyrical, often erotic or mystical-erotic poem, most often (but not always) of five or seven couplets with a single rhyme on the pattern *aa, ba, ca, . . .* , and one of a group of traditional rhythms.

hadd (limit): One of the set penalties given in the sharia for five offenses—zina, false accusation of zina, wine drinking, theft, and highway robbery. These are considered offenses against the limits set by God and, thus, as crimes against God.

harem: The private, protected area of a house or palace—an area forbidden to nonrelatives—where the women of the family live and entertain and where the family carries on its intimate domestic life.

Islamic law: The law that was enforced in the Ottoman Empire, including both administrative law (*'örf/kanun*) and religious law (sharia).

kadi: A judge who applies religious law in the adjudication of disputes and those few penal cases envisaged by the law and who also has jurisdiction over mosques and pious endowments.

kaside: A long panegyric or occasional poem with a single rhyme (*aa, ba, ca,* . . .). It is usually in the range of fifteen to thirty couplets in length, but it will sometimes have fewer couplets and occasionally more than a hundred.

kul: Literally "slave," but in the Ottoman system an elite slave taken from the non-Muslim population and trained as part of the sultan's "extended family." Such slaves held the most powerful positions in the state and were often married to the sisters and daughters of the sultans. This was a very privileged form of slavery.

levend: A young adult male, living an adventuresome life on his own, without family or master or significant attachments. In some contexts, an unattached mercenary soldier.

mesnevi: A poem in rhyming couplets (*aa, bb, cc,* . . .), a form often used for longer narrative and didactic poems, at times running to thousands of couplets.

muezzin: A mosque employee who calls the Muslim community to prayer five times a day.

mufti: A high-level judicial official trained to interpret the sources of Islamic Law and deliver legal opinions called *fetva* (q.v.). The mufti of Istanbul, known as the *şeyhu'l-islam*, was the highest legal authority in the empire.

muhtesib: An official appointed to oversee the moral behavior of the public and especially to regulate the public markets.

musahib (from the same root as *sohbet*): A person with whom one participates in sohbet. The musahibs of the sultan were an elite group of very talented conversationalists who were present at the private entertainments of the ruler and who derived considerable power from intimate contact with him.

'örf: The administrative practices and regulations promulgated by Ottoman rulers to supplement the sharia (q.v.) in the form of edicts called *kanun*.

Pasha (*Paşa*): A title given to the highest-ranking officials of the state, usually those of vizier rank.

redif: A word or phrase that follows the rhyme in Ottoman poetry.

Rum: From *Roman*, originally meaning the lands held by the Byzantines, especially Asia Minor, but often the whole of the central Ottoman lands. Hence, the Ottoman sultan is called *the Sultan of Rum*. In popular and poetic parlance it also comes to mean a person of Byzantine or Greek extraction and particularly a fair-skinned person.

Rumeli: From *Rum* + *il* (province), meaning the province of the Byzantines. The official name of the European provinces of the Ottoman Empire.

sahn müderrisi: A theology and religious law professor at the Court of the Eight Colleges (*sahn-i seman*) attached to the Mosque of the Conqueror. This was the highest level of the university system.

şehrengiz (city thriller): A verse catalog of the beautiful boys and young men of a city, usually with a stanza for each beauty. There is only one existing *şehrengiz* that describes female beloveds.

sharia: The totality of rules governing the lives of Muslims, derived from Scripture (the Qur'an) and the acts and nonquranic sayings of the Prophet (the hadith).

shaykh (also *Şeyh, Sheyh*): Meaning "elder," this title was applied to men in positions of religious or spiritual authority in both the regular and the mystical (dervish) institutions. It also refers to village elders.

sipahi: A cavalryman holding a timar in the provinces or a member of the sultan's standing cavalry corps.

sohbet: Intimate conversation as a social practice.

subaşı: A police commander responsible for law and order in the community. He works as an agent of the kadi and has various police units under his control.

Sultan: Literally "ruler." It is one of the titles of the Ottoman monarch, but it is also used, at times, to refer to princes of the royal house and to especially powerful palace women. When it refers to a ruler, it precedes the name (e.g., Sultan Süleyman); when it refers to others, it usually follows the name (e.g., the Valide Sultan).

sura: A chapter in the Qur'an.

tezkire: When it is a short form of *tezkire-i şu'ara*, it refers to a collection of short biographies of poets and littérateurs containing anecdotes about them, samples of their work, and critical comments.

timar: A fief whose revenues were granted in return for military service. Larger fiefs of the same type were called *zeamet*.

töhmet: A suspicion of previous wrongdoing prevailing in the community or a prior conviction of a similar offense.

vizier: One of the sultan's highest ministers, a member of the imperial council. The chief minister was the grand vizier.

zaviye: a dervish retreat where travelers could lodge. The main lodges of dervishes were called *tekke*.

zina: Unlawful fornication punishable by law. In the Ottoman system, this was considered most serious when it involved a married Muslim woman and less serious when it involved unmarried persons or slaves. In the sharia, the punishment for zina is death by stoning, if the person involved has been legally married, and by a hundred lashes of the whip, if the person involved has not been legally married. Death by stoning was almost never applied in the Ottoman Empire.

BIBLIOGRAPHY

Published Sources

Abou-El-Haj, Rifaʿat Ali. *Formation of the Modern State: The Ottoman Empire Sixteenth to Eighteenth Centuries*. Albany: State University of New York Press, 1991.
———. "Theorizing in Historical Writing beyond the Nation State." In *Armağan: Festschrift für Andreas Tietze*, ed. Ingeborg Baladauf and Suraiya Faroqhi, 1–18. Prague: Enigma, 1994.
Açıkgöz, Namık. "Tezkirelere göre 16. asrın sonuna kadar Türk edebî kültür hayatı." In Kalpaklı 1999, 413–21.
Akdağ, Mustafa. *Türk halkının dirlik ve düzenlik kavgası: Celalî isyanları*. Istanbul: Cem, 1995.
ʿAli, Mustafa. *Nasihatu's-Selatin*. See Tietze 1979–82.
———. *Künhü'l-ahbar* (Biographies of poets section). See İsen 1994.
———. *Kavaʿidu'l-mecalis*. See Şeker 1997.
al-Sayyid-Marsot, Afaf Lutfi, ed. *Society and the Sexes in Medieval Islam*. Malibu: Undena, 1979. A collection of essays presented by noted scholars for the Sixth Giorgio Levi Della Vida Biennial Conference at the University of California, Los Angeles, 13–15 May 1977.
And, Metin. *Geleneksel türk tiyatrosu*. Ankara: Bilgi Yayınevi, 1969.
———. *Istanbul in the 16th Century: The City, the Palace, Daily Life*. Istanbul: Akbank, 1994.
Andrews, Walter G. "The *Tezkere-i şuʿarā* of Latīfī as a Source for the Critical Evaluation of Ottoman Poetry." Ph.D. diss., University of Michigan, 1970.
———. *An Introduction to Ottoman Poetry*. Minneapolis: Bibliotheca Islamica, 1976.
———. *Poetry's Voice, Society's Song: Ottoman Lyric Poetry*. Seattle: University of Washington Press, 1985.
———. "The Sexual Intertext of Ottoman Literature: The Story of Meʾālī, Magistrate of Mihalich." *Edebiyat*, n.s., 3, no. 1 (1989): 31–56.

———. "Singing the Alienated 'I.'" *Yale Journal of Criticism* 6, no. 2 (1993): 191–219.

———. "Metin nerede? Hangi metin? Kimin metni?" *Varlık*, no. 1062 (March 1996): 46–50.

———. "Speaking of Power: The 'Ottoman Kaside.'" In *Qaside Poetry in Islamic Asia and Africa*, ed. Stefan Sperl and Christopher Shackle, 1:281–300. Leiden: Brill, 1996.

———, ed. *Intersections in Turkish Literature: Essays in Honor of James Stewart-Robinson*. Ann Arbor: University of Michigan Press, 2001.

———. "Other Selves, Other Poets, and the Other Literary History: An Essay in Three Movements." In Andrews 2001, 49–91.

Andrews, Walter G., Najaat Black, and Mehmet Kalpaklı, eds. and trans. *Ottoman Lyric Poetry: An Anthology*. Austin: University of Texas Press, 1997.

Andrews, Walter G., and Mehmet Kalpaklı. "Layla Grows Up: Nizami's Layla and Majnun 'in the Turkish Manner.'" In Talattof and Clinton 2000, 29–49.

———. "Gazels and the World: Some Notes on the 'Occasional-ness' of the Ottoman Gazel." In Neuwirth, Pfeiffer, and Sagaster, in press.

———. "The Ottoman Gazel in the Age of Beloveds: Poems about Poetry." In *The Migration of a Literary Genre: Studies in Ghazal Literature* (Beiruter Studien), ed. Angelika Neuwirth and Thomas Bauer. Würtzburg: Ergon, 2005.

Andrews, Walter G., and Irene Markoff. "Poetry, the Arts, and Group Ethos in the Ideology of the Ottoman Empire." *Edebiyat*, n.s., 1, no. 1 (1987): 28–70.

Ariès, Philippe, and A. Bejin, eds. *Western Sexuality*. Translated by Anthony Forster. Oxford: Blackwell, 1985.

Ariosto, Ludovico. *Orlando Furioso*. Translated and with an introduction by Guido Waldman. Oxford World Classics. Oxford: Oxford University Press, 1998.

Arslan, Mehmet. *Türk edebiyatında manzum surnâmeler: Osmanlı saray düğünleri ve şenlikleri*. Ankara: Atatürk Kültür Merkezi Başkanlığı, 1999.

'Aşık Çelebi. See Meredith-Owens 1971.

Baki. *Bâkî dîvânı*. See Küçük 1994.

Barbaro, Nicolo. *Diary of the Siege of Constantinople: 1453*. Translated by J. R. Jones. New York: Exposition, 1969.

Bardakçı, Murat. *Osmanlı'da seks: Sarayda gece dersleri*. Istanbul: Gür, 1992.

Barkan, Ömer Lutfi. "The Price Revolution of the Sixteenth Century." Translated by Justin McCarthy. *International Journal of Middle East Studies* 6, no. 1 (January 1975): 3–28.

Barkey, Karen. *Bandits and Bureaucrats: The Ottoman Route to State Centralization*. Ithaca: Cornell University Press, 1994.

Barnfield, Richard. *The Affectionate Shepherd*. Edited by James Orchard Halliwell. Early English Poetry, Ballads, and Popular Literature of the Middle Ages, vol. 20. London: Percy Society, 1847.

Baroody, George M., trans. *Crime and Punishment under Hanbali Law*. N.p., n.d. While the publishing history of this book is difficult to ascertain, it seems to have begun life as a ca. 1961–62 M.A. thesis at the American University in

Cairo entitled "Crime and Punishment under Islamic Law." Besides the edition that we used, which carries neither date nor publisher, there are also two Regency Press editions: we have been unable to ascertain the date for the 1st ed., published under the title *Crime and Punishment under Hanbali Law*; the 2d ed., published under the title *Crime and Punishment under Islamic Law*, is dated 1979.

Batislam, Hanife Dilek, ed. *Hasbihâl-i sâfî*. Istanbul: Kitabevi, 2003.

Beier, A. L. *Masterless Men: The Vagrancy Problem in England, 1560–1640*. London: Methuen, 1985.

Bellamy, James. "Sex and Society in Islamic Popular Literature." In al-Sayyid-Marsot 1979, 23–42.

———, ed. *Studies in Near Eastern Culture and History: In Memory of Ernest T. Abdel-Massih*. Ann Arbor: University of Michigan, Center for Near Eastern and North African Studies, 1990.

Birge, John Kingsley. *The Bektashi Order of Dervishes*. 1932. Reprint, New York: AMS, 1982.

Boccaccio, Giovanni. *The Elegy of Lady Fiammetta*. See Causa-Steindler and Thomas Mauch 1990.

Boswell, John. *Christianity, Social Tolerance, and Homosexuality: Gay People in Western Europe from the Beginning of the Christian Era to the Fourteenth Century*. Chicago: University of Chicago Press, 1980.

———. "Revolutions, Universals, and Sexual Categories." In Duberman, Vicinus, and Chauncey 1989, 17–36.

Bourdieu, Pierre. *The Logic of Practice*. Translated by Richard Nice. Stanford: Stanford University Press, 1990.

Brackett, John K. *Criminal Justice and Crime in Late Renaissance Florence, 1537–1609*. Cambridge: Cambridge University Press, 1992.

———. "The Florentine Onestà and the Control of Prostitution, 1403–1680." *Sixteenth Century Journal* 24, no. 2 (1993): 273–300.

Braudel, Fernand. *The Structures of Everyday Life: The Limits of the Possible*. Translated by Siân Reynolds. New York: Harper and Row, 1981. This is a translation of Braudel's *Les structures du quotidien: Le possible et l'impossible*, vol. 1 of *Civilisation matérielle, économie, et capitalism, XVe–XVIIIe siècle* (Paris: Colin, 1979).

———. *The Mediterranean and the Mediterranean World in the Age of Philip II*. Translated by Siân Reynolds. 2 vols. Berkeley and Los Angeles: University of California Press, 1995.

Bray, Alan. *Homosexuality in Renaissance England*. London: Gay Men's Press, 1982.

Brookes, Douglas S., trans. *The Ottoman Gentleman of the Sixteenth Century: Mustafa Âli's Mevâ'idü'n-nefâ'is fî kavâ'idi'l-mecâlis ("Tables of Delicacies concerning the Rules of Social Gatherings")*. Sources of Oriental Languages and Literatures 59 (Turkish Sources 51), ed. Şinasi Tekin and Gönül Alpay Tekin. Cambridge: Harvard University, Department of Near Eastern Languages and Civilizations, 2003.

Brown, Georgia E. "Breaking the Canon: Marlowe's Challenge to the Literary Status Quo in *Hero and Leander*." In White 1998, 59–75.

Brown, Judith C. *Immodest Acts: The Life of a Lesbian Nun in Renaissance Italy*. New York: Oxford University Press, 1986.

———. "A Woman's Place Was in the Home: Women's Work in Renaissance Tuscany." In Ferguson, Quilligan, and Vickers 1986, 206–24.

———. "Lesbian Sexuality in Medieval and Early Modern Europe." In Duberman, Vicinus, and Chauncey 1989, 67–75.

Brown, Judith C., and Robert C. Davis, eds. *Gender and Society in Renaissance Italy*. London: Longman, 1998.

Brown, Patricia Fortini. *Art and Life in Renaissance Venice*. New York: Harry N. Abrams, 1997.

Brown, Steve. "The Boyhood of Shakespeare's Heroines: Notes on Gender Ambiguity in the Sixteenth Century." *SEL* 30 (1990): 243–63.

Brummett, Palmira. *Ottoman Seapower and Levantine Diplomacy in the Age of Discovery*. Albany: State University of New York Press, 1994.

Bull, George Anthony, trans. *The Pilgrim: The Travels of Pietro Della Valle*. With an introduction by George Anthony Bull. London: Hutchinson, 1990. This translation is an abridged version of *The Pilgrim*.

Bunn, Austin. "The X-Rated Files." *Brill's Content*, May 2000, 96–99.

Bürgel, J. C. "Love, Lust, and Longing: Eroticism in Early Islam." In al-Sayyid-Marsot 1979, 101–5.

Burke, Peter. "Concepts of the 'Golden Age' in the Renaissance." In Kunt and Woodhead 1995, 154–63.

Burmaoğlu, H. Bilen. *Bursalı Lamiʿî Çelebi divanı'ndan seçmeler*. Ankara: Kültür Bakanlığı, 1989.

Candaş, Subhiye, ed. "Taşlıcalı Yahya Bey ve *Şâh u gedâ* mesnevisinin dört nüsha üzerine tenkidli neşri." Accession no. T137. Graduation diss., Türkiyat Enstitüsü (now the Turkology Research Center of Istanbul University), 1941.

Canım, Rıdvan, ed. *Latîfî, Tezkiretü'ş-şuʿarâ ve tabsiratü'n-nuzamâ (inceleme-metin)*. Ankara: Atatürk Kültür Merkezi, 2000.

Castagno, Paul C. *The Early Commedia Dell'Arte, 1550–1621*. American University Studies, ser. 26, Theatre Arts, vol. 13. New York: Peter Lang, 1994.

Castiglione, Baldesar. *The Book of the Courtier*. Translated by Charles S. Singleton. Garden City: Doubleday, 1959.

Causa-Steindler, Mariangela. "Introduction." In Cause-Steindler and Mauch 1990, xi–xxvi.

Causa-Steindler, Mariangela, and Thomas Mauch, eds. and trans. *The Elegy of Lady Fiammetta*. By Giovanni Boccaccio. Chicago: University of Chicago Press, 1990.

Çavuşoğlu, Mehmed. "Taşlıcalı Dukakin-zâde Yahya Bey'in İstanbul şehrengizi." *Edebiyat Fakültesi Türk dili ve edebiyat dergisi* 17 (1969): 73–108.

———. "Zâtî'nin letâyifi." *Edebiyat Fakültesi Türk dili ve edebiyat dergisi* 18 (1970): 1–27.

———, ed. *Yahyā Bey: Dīvan*. Istanbul: Edebiyat Fakültesi, 1977.

———. "16. Yüzyılda yaşamış bir kadın şâir Nisâyî." *Tarih Enstitüsü dergisi* 9 (1978): 405-16.
———. *Vasfî: Dîvan*. Istanbul: Edebiyat Fakültesi Matbaasi, 1980.
———. *Divanlar arasında*. Ankara: Umran Yayınları, 1981.
———. "Şehzâde Mustafa Mersiyeleri." *Tarih Enstitüsü dergisi* 12 (1981-82): 641-86.
———, ed. *Helâkî: Dîvân*. Istanbul: Istanbul Üniversitesi Edebiyat Fakültesi, 1982.
———. *Hayâlî Bey ve divânından örnekler*. Ankara: Kültür ve Turizm Bakanlığı, 1987.
Çavuşoğlu, Mehmed, with Mehmet Kalpaklı, Ali Tanyeri, and Walter G. Andrews, eds. *Revānī dīvānı*. Ottoman Texts Archive Project Electronic Edition. N.d. http://courses.washington.edu/otap/a_revpag.html. Çavuşoğlu's incomplete transcription and critical edition was completed after his death by Kalpaklı and Tanyeri and the electronic edition prepared by Andrews. The text can be found permanently at the University of Washington Digital Repository, http://hdl.handle.net/1773/1963.
Çavuşoğlu, Mehmed, and M. Ali Tanyeri, eds. *Zatî divanı*. Vol. 3. Istanbul: Edebiyat Fakültesi, 1987. This edition of Zati's divan appears in three volumes. For vols. 1-2, see Tarlan 1967-70.
———, eds. *Üsküplü İshâk Çelebi: Dîvân*. Istanbul: Istanbul Üniversitesi Fen Fakültesi, 1990.
Cellini, Benvenuto. *The Autobiography of Benvenuto Cellini*. Translated by George Bull. 1956. London: Penguin, 1998.
Cevdet, Ahmed, ed. *Tezkīre-i şuʿarā*. By Latīfī. Istanbul: Ikdām, 1896/97.
Chambers, David, and Brian Pullan, eds. *Venice: A Documentary History, 1450-1630*. Oxford: Blackwell, 1992.
Clinton, Jerome W., trans. *The Tragedy of Sohrab and Rostam*. Seattle: University of Washington Press, 1987.
Cohn, Samuel K., Jr. "Women and Work in Renaissance Italy." In Brown and Davis 1998, 107-49.
Cook, M. A. *Population Pressure in Rural Anatolia, 1450-1600*. London: Oxford University Press, 1972.
Corbin, Henry. *Creative Imagination in the Sufism of Ibn ʿArabī*. Translated by Ralph Manheim. Bollingen Series 91. Princeton: Princeton University Press, 1969.
Coryat, Thomas. *Coryat's Crudities*. Vol. 1. Glasgow: James Maclehose and Sons, 1905.
Cunbur, Mujgân. "İmadu'l-cihad ve XVI. yüzyıl kadın şairlerinden Ayşe Hubbî Kadın." *Türk tarih kongresi bildirileri*, 1988, 901-3.
Dankoff, Robert. "The Lyric in the Romance: The Use of Ghazals in Persian and Turkish Masnavīs." *Journal of Near Eastern Studies* 43, no. 1 (1984): 9-25.
d'Aragona, Tullia. *Dialogue on the Infinity of Love*. See Russell and Merry 1997.
Darling, Linda T. "The Renaissance and the Middle East." In Ruggiero 2002, 55-69.

Davis, Robert C. "The Geography of Gender in the Renaissance." In Brown and Davis 1998, 19–38.

Deats, Sara Munson. "The Subversion of Gender Hierarchies in *Dido, Queene of Carthage*." In White 1998, 163–78.

de Certeau, Michel. *Heterologies: Discourse on the Other*. Translated by Brian Massumi. Minneapolis: University of Minnesota Press, 1989.

Deleuze, Gilles, and Félix Guattari. *Anti-Oedipus: Capitalism and Schizophrenia*. Translated by Robert Hurley, Mark Seem, and Helen R. Lane. Minneapolis: University of Minnesota Press, 1983.

Demir, Aydoğan. "Zina üzerine düşünceler." *Tarih ve toplum* 169 (January 1998): 4–10.

Derrida, Jacques. *Of Grammatology*. Translated by Gayatri Chakravorty Spivak. Baltimore: Johns Hopkins University Press, 1974.

DiGangi, Mario. *The Homoerotics of Early Modern Drama*. Cambridge: Cambridge University Press, 1997.

———. "Marlowe, Queer Studies, and Renaissance Homoeroticism." In White 1998, 195–212.

Dirimtekin, Feridun. *İstanbul'un fethi*. Istanbul: Belediye Matbaası, 1949.

Doukas [Ducas]. See Magoulias 1975.

Duberman, Martin Bauml, Martha Vicinus, and George Chauncey Jr., eds. *Hidden from History: Reclaiming the Gay and Lesbian Past*. Markham: New American Library, 1989.

Düzdağ, M. Ertuğrul. *Şeyhülislâm Ebussuûd Efendi fetvaları*. Istanbul: Enderun, 1972.

Eldem, Sedad Hakkı. *Köşkler ve kasırlar*. 2 vols. Istanbul: Devlet Güzel Sanatlar Akademisi, 1969–73.

Ergenç, Özer. "Osmanlı şehrindeki mahalle'nin işlev ve nitelikleri üzerine." *Osmanlı araştırmaları* 4 (1984): 69–78.

Erünsal, İsmail E. "Türk edebiyatı tarihine kaynak olarak arşivlerin değeri." *Türkiyat mecmuası* 19 (1980): 213–22.

———. "II. Bâyezid devrine ait bir in'âmât defteri." *Tarih Enstitüsü dergisi* 10–11 (1981): 303–42.

———. *The Life and Works of Tâcî-zâde Ca'fer Çelebi, with a Critical Edition of His Dîvân*. Istanbul: Edebiyat Fakültesi, 1983.

———. "Kanunî Sultan Süleyman devrine ait bir in'âmât defteri." *Osmanlı araştırmaları* 4 (1984): 4–17.

Eyuboğlu, İsmet Zeki. *Divan şiirinde sapık sevgi*. 1968. Istanbul: Broy, 1991.

Farah, Madelain, trans. *Marriage and Sexuality in Islam: A Translation of al-Ghazālī's Book on the Etiquette of Marriage from the* Ihyā'. Salt Lake City: University of Utah Press, 1984.

Faroqhi, Suraiya. *Towns and Townsmen of Ottoman Anatolia: Trade, Crafts, and Food Production in an Urban Setting, 1520–1650*. Cambridge: Cambridge University Press, 1984.

———. "Politics and Socio-Economic Change in the Ottoman Empire of the Later Sixteenth Century." In Kunt and Woodhead 1995, 91–113.
———. "From the Slave Market to Arafat: Biographies of Bursa Women in the Late Fifteenth Century." *Turkish Studies Association Bulletin* 24, no. 1 (spring 2000): 3–20.
———. *Stories of Ottoman Men and Women*. Istanbul: Eren, 2002.
Feldman, Walter. "The Celestial Sphere, the Wheel of Fortune, and Fate in the Gazels of Nā'ilī and Bākī." *International Journal of Middle East Studies* 28 (1996): 193–215.
———. "The Social Environment of the Tāze-gūyān." N.d. Typescript. An earlier version, entitled "The Social Environment of the Ottoman Literary Avant-Garde of the Mid-Seventeenth Century," was delivered at the thirty-third annual meeting of the Middle East Studies Association, 19–22 November 1999, Washington.
Ferguson, Margaret W., Maureen Quilligan, and Nancy J. Vickers, eds. *Rewriting the Renaissance: The Discourses of Sexual Difference in Early Modern Europe*. Chicago: University of Chicago Press, 1986.
Ficino, Marsilio. *Commentary on Plato's Symposium on Love*. Translated, with an introduction and notes, by Sears Jayne. 1944. 2d rev. ed. Dallas: Spring, 1985.
Fisher, Alan. "The Life and Family of Süleymân I." In İnalcık and Kafadar 1993, 1–19.
Fisher, F. J. *London and the English Economy, 1500–1700*. Edited by P. J. Corfield and N. B. Harte. London: Hambledon, 1990.
Fleischer, Cornell H. *Bureaucrat and Intellectual in the Ottoman Empire: The Historian Mustafa Âli (1541–1600)*. Princeton: Princeton University Press, 1986.
———. "The Lawgiver as Messiah: The Making of the Imperial Image in the Reign of Süleyman." In Veinstein 1992, 159–77.
———. "Mahdi and Messiah." Paper presented at the conference "Messianism in the Age of Charles V," Seminario Fundacion Duques de Soria, Antwerp, October 2000.
———. "Seer to the Sultan: Haydar-i Remmal and Sultan Süleyman." In Warner 2001, 290–99.
———. *A Mediterranean Apocalypse: Imperialism and Prophecy, 1453–1550*. Berkeley and Los Angeles: University of California Press, in press.
Flemming, Barbara. "Public Opinion under Süleymân." In İnalcık and Kafadar 1993, 49–57.
Forster, Charles Thornton, and F. H. Blackburne Daniell, eds. and trans. *The Life and Letters of Ogier Ghiselin De Busbecq*. Vol. 1. London: C. Kegan Paul, 1881.
Foucault, Michel. *The History of Sexuality*. Vol. 1, *An Introduction*. Vol. 2, *The Use of Pleasure*. Vol. 3, *The Care of Self*. Translated by Robert Hurley. New York: Vintage, 1980–90.
Franco, Veronica. See Jones and Rosenthal 1998.
Fumerton, Patricia. "'Secret' Arts: Elizabethan Miniatures and Sonnets." In Greenblatt 1988, 93–133.

———. *Cultural Aesthetics: Renaissance Literature and the Practice of Social Ornament.* Chicago: University of Chicago Press, 1991.
Gagnon, John H., and William Simon. *Sexual Conduct: The Social Sources of Human Sexuality.* Chicago: Aldine, 1973.
Gazali [al-Ghazālī]. "Book on the Etiquette of Marriage." See Farah 1984.
Gibb, E. J. W. *A History of Ottoman Poetry.* 6 vols. London: Luzac and Co., 1900–1909.
Giffen, Lois Anita. *Theory of Profane Love among the Arabs: The Development of the Genre.* New York: New York University Press, 1971.
Glünz, Michael. "The Sword, the Pen, and the Phallus: Metaphors and Metonymies of Male Power and Creativity in Medieval Persian Poetry." *Edebiyat*, n.s., 6, no. 2 (1995): 223–43.
Goffman, Daniel. *Izmir and the Levantine World, 1550–1650.* Seattle: University of Washington Press, 1990.
Gökyay, Orhan Şaik, ed. *Gelibolulu Mustafa Âli, görgü ve toplum kuralları üzerinde ziyafet sofraları.* Tercüman Gazetesi: 1001 Temel Eser. Istanbul: Kervan Kitapçılık, 1978.
———. *Evliya Çelebi seyahatnâmesi. 1 kitap: Istanbul.* Istanbul: Yapı Kredi, 1996.
Goldberg, Jonathan. "Fatherly Authority: The Politics of Stuart Family Images." In Ferguson, Quilligan, and Vickers 1986, 3–32.
Goldstone, Jack A. "East and West in the Seventeenth Century: Political Crises in Stuart England, Ottoman Turkey, and Ming China," *Comparative Studies in Society and History* 30 (1988): 103–42.
Greenblatt, Stephen. *Renaissance Self-Fashioning.* Chicago: University of Chicago Press, 1980.
———, ed. *The Power of Forms in the English Renaissance.* Norman: University of Oklahoma Press, 1982.
———. "Murdering Peasants: Status, Genre, and the Representation of Rebellion." In Greenblatt 1988, 1–29.
———, ed. *Representing the English Renaissance.* Berkeley and Los Angeles: University of California Press, 1988.
———. *Shakespearean Negotiations: The Circulation of Social Energy in Renaissance England.* Oxford: Clarendon, 1988.
Greville, Fulke (Baron Brooke). *Certaine Learned and Elegant Workes (1633) by Fulke Greville.* With an introduction by A. D. Cousins. Delmar: Scholars' Facsimiles and Reprints, ca. 1990.
Griswold, William J. *The Great Anatolian Rebellion, 1000–1020/1591–1611.* Berlin: K. Schwarz, 1983.
Hafez. *Divan-i khvājah shams al-dīn muhammad bih tashīh va tawzīh-i parvīz nātil khānlarī.* 1943. 2d printing, Tehran: Intishārāt-i Khvārazmī, 1983.
Halley, Janet E. "Heresy, Orthodoxy, and the Politics of Religious Discourse: The Case of the English Family of Love." In Greenblatt 1988, 303–25.
Halman, Talât. *Süleyman the Magnificent Poet.* Istanbul: Dost, 1987.

Halperin, David M. "Sex before Sexuality: Pederasty, Politics, and Power in Classical Athens." In Duberman, Vicinus, and Chauncey 1989, 37–64.
Hamilton, Charles, trans. *The Hedaya or Guide: A Commentary on the Mussulman Laws*. New printing. Delhi: Islamic Book Trust, 1982.
Hammill, Graham L. *Sexuality and Form: Caravaggio, Marlowe, and Bacon*. Chicago: University of Chicago Press, 2000.
Hattox, Ralph S. *Coffee and Coffeehouses: The Origins of a Social Beverage in the Medieval Near East*. Seattle: University of Washington Press, 1985.
Hauser, Arnold. *The Social History of Art*. Translated by Stanley Godman. London: Routledge and Kegan Paul, 1951.
———. *Mannerism: The Crisis of the Renaissance and the Origins of Modern Art*. Vol. 1, *Text*. Vol. 2, *Plates*. Translated by Eric Mosbacher. London: Routledge and Kegan Paul, 1965.
Hayali. *Hayâlî Bey dîvânı*. See Tarlan 1945.
Heilbrun, Carolyn. *Toward a Recognition of Androgeny*. New York: Knopf, 1973.
Helaki. *Helâkî: Dîvân*. See Çavuşoğlu, ed., 1982.
Heyd, Uriel. *Studies in Old Ottoman Criminal Law*. Edited by V. L. Ménage. Oxford: Clarendon, 1973.
Holbrook, Victoria Rowe. *The Unreadable Shores of Love*. Austin: University of Texas Press, 1994.
Holm, Janis Butler, ed. *A Critical Edition of Thomas Salter's The Mirrhor of Modesty*. The Renaissance Imagination, vol. 32. New York: Garland, 1987.
Howard, Jean E. "Sex and Social Conflict: The Erotics of *The Roaring Girl*." In Zimmerman 1992, 170–90.
Imber, Colin. *Ebu's-suʿud: The Islamic Legal Tradition*. Edinburgh: Edinburgh University Press, 1997.
İnalcık, Halil. "Osmanlı idare, sosyal ve ekonomik tarihiyle ilgili belgeler: Bursa kadı sicillerinden seçmeler." *Belgeler* 10, no. 14 (1980–81): 1–91.
———. "State, Sovereignty, and Law during the Reign of Süleymân." In İnalcık and Kafadar 1993, 59–92.
———. *An Economic and Social History of the Ottoman Empire*. Vol. 1, *1300–1600*. Cambridge: Cambridge University Press, 1994.
———. "Ottoman Galata, 1453–1553." In *Essays in Ottoman History*, ed. Halil İnalcık. 273–376. Istanbul: Eren, 1998.
İnalcık, Halil, and Cemal Kafadar, eds. *Süleymân the Second and His Time*. Istanbul: Isis, 1993.
İpekten, Halûk. *Divan edebiyatında edebî muhitler*. Istanbul: Millî Eğitim Basımevi, 1996.
İsen, Mustafa, ed. *Künhü'l-ahbâr'ın tezkire kısmı*. Ankara: Atatürk Kültür, Dil ve Tarih Yüksek Kurumu Atatürk Kültür Merkezi, 1994.
———. "Tezkirelerin ışığında divan edebiyatına bakışlar: Divan şairlerinin meslekî konumları." In Kalpaklı 1999, 310–14.
İsen, Mustafa, and Fuat Bilkan, eds. *Sultan şâirler*. Ankara: Akçağ, 1997.

Jardine, Lisa. "Twins and Travesties: Gender, Dependency, and Sexual Availability in *Twelfth Night*." In Zimmerman 1992, 27–38.
Javich, Daniel. *Poetry and Courtliness in Renaissance England*. Princeton: Princeton University Press, 1978.
———. "The Impure Motives of Elizabethan Poetry." In Greenblatt 1982, 225–38.
Jenkins, Hester Donaldson. *Ibrahim Pasha: Grand Vizier of Suleiman the Magnificent*. Studies in History, Economics, and Public Law, ed. Faculty of Political Science of Columbia University, vol. 46, no. 2. 1911. New York: AMS, 1970.
Jennings, Ronald C. "Firearms, Bandits, and Gun-Control: Some Evidence on Ottoman Policy towards Firearms in the Possession of *Reaya*, from Judicial Records of Kayseri, 1600–1627." *Archivum Ottomanicum* 6 (1976): 229–58.
Jones, Ann Rosalind. "City Women and Their Audiences: Louise Labé and Veronica Franco." In Ferguson, Quilligan, and Vickers 1986, 299–316.
———. *The Currency of Eros: Women's Love Lyric in Europe, 1540–1620*. Bloomington: the University of Indiana Press, 1990.
Jones, Ann Rosalind, and Margaret F. Rosenthal, eds. and trans. *Veronica Franco: Poems and Selected Letters*. Chicago: University of Chicago Press, 1998.
Jones, Ann Rosalind, and Peter Stallybrass. "The Politics of *Astrophel and Stella*." *SEL* 24 (1984): 53–68.
Jonson, Ben. *Epicoene; or, The Silent Woman*. Edited, with an introduction and notes, by Aurielia Henry. Yale Studies in English 1. New York: Henry Holt, 1909.
Jordan, Constance. "Feminism and the Humanists: The Case of Sir Thomas Elyot's *Defence of Good Women*." In Ferguson, Quilligan, and Vickers 1986, 242–58.
Jordan, Mark D. *The Invention of Sodomy in Christian Theology*. Chicago: University of Chicago Press, 1997.
Kafadar, Cemal. "Self and Others: The Diary of a Dervish in Seventeenth Century Istanbul and First Person Narratives in Ottoman Literature." *Studia Islamica* 69 (1989): 121–50.
———. "The Myth of the Golden Age: Ottoman Historical Consciousness in the Post-Süleymânic Era." In İnalcık and Kafadar 1993, 37–48.
———. *Between Two Worlds: The Construction of the Ottoman State*. Berkeley and Los Angeles: University of California Press, 1995.
———. "The Question of Ottoman Decline." *Harvard Middle Eastern and Islamic Review* 4, nos. 1–2 (1997–98): 30–75.
Kalpaklı, Mehmet, ed. *Osmanlı divan şiiri üzerine metinler*. İstanbul: Yapı Kredi, 1999.
Karacan, Turgut. *Heft-hvân mesnevisi*. Ankara: Sevinç, 1974.
Karamustafa, Ahmet T. "*Kalenders, Abdâls, Hayderîs*: The Formation of the Bektâsîye in the Sixteenth Century." In İnalcık and Kafadar 1993, 121–29.
Kaya, İ. Güven. "Dükaginzāde Taşlıcalı Yahyâ beğ'in şiirlerinde cinsellik." *Journal of Turkish Studies* 14 (1990): 273–81.
Keddie, Nikki R., ed. *Scholars, Saints, and Sufis: Muslim Religious Institutions since 1500*. Berkeley: University of California Press, 1972.

Kellogg, Stuart, ed. *Literary Visions of Homosexuality*. New York: Haworth, 1983.
Keuls, Eva C. *The Reign of the Phallus*. New York: Harper and Row, 1985.
Kınalızade Hasan Çelebi. *Tezkire*. See Kutluk 1989.
Kızıltan, Mübeccel. "Dîvân edebiyatı özelliklerine uyarak şiir yazan kadın şairler." *Sombahar* 21/22 (January/April 1994): 104–69.
Kortantamer, Tunca. *Nev'î-zāde Atāyī ve hamse'si*. İzmir: Ege Üniversitesi Edebiyat Fakültesi, 1997.
Küçük, Sabahattin, ed. *Bâkî dîvânı*. Ankara: Türk Dil Kurumu, 1994.
Kuehn, Thomas. "Person and Gender in the Laws." In Brown and Davis 1998, 87–106.
Kunt, Metin I. *The Sultan's Servants*. New York: Columbia University Press, 1983.
Kunt, Metin, and Christine Woodhead, eds. *Süleyman the Magnificent and His Age*. London: Longman, 1995.
Kuru, Selim. "A Sixteenth Century Scholar Deli Birader and His *Dāfi'ü'l-gumūm ve rāfi'ü'l-humūm*." Ph.D. diss., Harvard University, 2000.
Kutluk, Ibrahim, ed. *Kınalı-zade Hasan Çelebi: Tezkiretü'ş-şuarâ*. 2 vols. Ankara: Türk Tarih Kurumu, 1989.
Landor, Robert, trans. *Book of Shehzade: Dafiü'l gumûm, rafiü'l humûm*. By Mehmed Gazalî [Deli Birader Gazali]. Edited by Stuart Kline. Istanbul: Dönence, 2001.
Laslett, Peter. *The World We Have Lost: Further Explored*. 1965. 3d ed. London: Methuen, 1983.
Latifi. *Evsâf-ı İstanbul*. See Pekin, ed., 1977.
———. *Tezkīre-i şu'arā*. See Cevdet, ed., 1896/97.
Lawner, Lynne. *Lives of the Courtesans*. New York: Rizzoli, 1987.
Levend, Agâh Sırrı. *Türk edebiyatında şehr-engizler ve şehr-engizlerde İstanbul*. Istanbul: Baha, 1958.
Levin, Carole, and Karen Robertson, eds. *Sexuality and Politics in Renaissance Drama*. Lewiston, N.Y.: E. Mellen, 1991.
Losensky, Paul E. *Welcoming Fighānī: Imitation and Poetic Individuality in the Safavid-Mughal Ghazal*. Costa Mesa: Mazda, 1998.
Mack, Rosamund E. *Bazaar to Piazza: Islamic Trade and Italian Art, 1300–1600*. Berkeley and Los Angeles: University of California Press, 2002.
Magoulias, Harry J., trans. *Decline and Fall of Byzantium to the Ottoman Turks by Doukas: An Annotated Translation of* "Historia Turco-Byzantina." Detroit: Wayne State University Press, 1975.
Marghīnānī, 'Alī ibn Abī Bakr. *Hidāyah fī sharh al-Bidāyah*. 4 vols. Kū'itah: Maktabah Habībīyah, 1985.
Marlowe, Christopher. *Hero and Leander*. New York: Covici-Friede, 1934.
Martin, B. G. "A Short History of the Khalwati Order of Dervishes." In Keddie 1972, 275–305.
Masson, Georgina. *Courtesans of the Italian Renaissance*. London: Secker and Warburg, 1975.

Matar, Nabil. *Turks, Moors, and Englishmen in the Age of Discovery*. New York: Columbia University Press, 1999.
Maus, Katharine Eisaman. *Inwardness and the Theater in the English Renaissance*. Chicago: University of Chicago Press, 1995.
McGowan, Bruce. *Economic Life in Ottoman Europe*. Cambridge: Cambridge University Press; Paris: Editions de la Maison des Sciences de L'Homme, 1981.
McLuskie, Kathleen. "'Lawless Desires Well Tempered.'" In Zimmerman 1992, 103-26.
Meisami, Julie Scott. *Medieval Persian Court Poetry*. Princeton: Princeton University Press, 1987.
Mengi, Mine, ed. *Mesîhî dîvânı*. Ankara: Türk Tarih Kurumu, 1995.
Meninski, Franciscus à Mesgnien. *Thesaurus linguarum orientalium: Turcicae-Arabicae-Persicae. Lexicon: Turcico-Arabico-Persicum*. 5 vols. Facsimile reprint, with an introduction by Mehmet Ölmez and elucidation and Turkish index by Sanisław Stachowski, Istanbul: Simurg, 2000.
Menocal, María Rosa. *Shards of Love: Exile and the Origins of the Lyric*. Durham: Duke University Press, 1994.
———. *The Ornament of the World: How Muslims, Jews, and Christians Created a Culture of Tolerance in Medieval Spain*. Boston: Little, Brown, 2002.
Meredith-Owens, G. M., ed. *Meşā'irü üş-su'arā or tezkere of 'Āşık Çelebi*. London: Luzac, 1971.
Mesihi. *Mesîhî dîvânı*. See Mengi, ed., 1995.
Michelangelo. See Nims 1998.
Micklewright, Nancy. "'Musicians and Dancing Girls': Images of Women in Ottoman Miniature Painting." In Zilfi 1988, 153-68.
Mihri Hatun. *Dīvān*. Edited, with an introduction, by Elena Mashtakova. Moscow: Nauka, 1967.
Mirollo, James V. *Mannerism and Renaissance Poetry*. New Haven: Yale University Press, 1984.
Monroe, James T. "The Striptease That Was Blamed on Abū Bakr's Naughty Son: Was Father Being Shamed, or Was the Poet Having Fun? (Ibn Quzmān's Zajal No. 133)." In Wright and Rowson 1997, 94-139.
Montaigne. See Trechmann 1929.
Montrose, Louis Adrian. "*A Midsummer Night's Dream* and the Shaping Fantasies of Elizabethan Culture: Gender, Power, Form." In Ferguson, Quillian, and Vickers 1986, 65-87. This is an abbreviated version of Montrose (1988).
———. "'Shaping Fantasies': Figurations of Gender and Power in Elizabethan Culture." In Greenblatt 1988, 31-64. This essay first appeared in 1983 in the journal *Representations*.
Moulton, Ian Frederick. "'Printed Abroad and Uncastrated': Marlowe's *Elegies* with Davies' *Epigrams*." In White 1998, 77-90.
Muhibbī [Sultan Süleyman]. *Dīvān-i Muhibbī*. Istanbul: Matba'a-ı 'Osmānīye, 1890/91.

Muir, Edward. *Civic Ritual in Renaissance Venice*. Princeton: Princeton University Press, 1981.

Mullaney, Stephen. "Strange Things, Gross Terms, Curious Customs: The Rehearsal of Culture in the Late Renaissance." In Greenblatt 1988, 65–92.

Murphey, Rhoads. *Ottoman Warfare, 1500–1700*. New Brunswick: Rutgers University Press; London: Taylor and Francis, 1999.

Necipoğlu, Gülru. "Süleymân the Magnificent and the Representation of Power in the Context of Ottoman-Hapsburg-Papal Rivalry." *Art Bulletin* 71 (1989): 401–27. Reprinted in İnalcık and Kafadar 1993, 163–94.

———. *Architecture, Ceremonial, and Power: The Topkapı Palace in the Fifteenth and Sixteenth Centuries*. Cambridge, Mass.: MIT Press, 1991.

———. "The Suburban Landscape of Sixteenth-Century Istanbul as a Mirror of Classical Ottoman Garden Culture." In Petruccioli 1997, 32–71.

Neuwirth, Angelika, Judith Pfeiffer, and Börte Sagaster, eds. *Ghazal as World Literature: From a Literary Genre to a Great Tradition*. Istanbuler Studien 5. Istanbul: Orient-Institut; Würtzburg: Ergon, in press.

Nicholson, Reynold A., ed. and trans. *The Mathnawí of Jalàlu'ddín Rúmí*. 8 vols. Gibb Memorial New Series, no. 4. London: Luzac, 1925–40.

Nims, John Frederick, trans. *The Complete Poems of Michelangelo*. Chicago: University of Chicago Press, 1998.

Oberhelman, Steven M. "Hierarchies of Gender, Ideology, and Power in Medieval Greek and Arabic Dream Literature." In Wright and Rowson 1997, 55–93.

Okuyucu, Cihan. *Cinânî: Hayatı, eserleri, Dîvânının Tenkidli Metni*. Ankara: Türk Dil Kurumu, 1994.

Onay, Ahmet Talât. *Eski türk edebiyatında mazmunlar ve izahı*. Edited by Cemal Kurnaz. Ankara: Türk Diyanet Vakfı, 1992.

Orgel, Stephen. "The Subtexts of *The Roaring Girl*." In Zimmerman 1992, 12–26.

Ortaylı, İlber. "Anadolu'da XVI. Yüzyılda evlilik ilişkileri üzerine bazı gözlemler." *Osmanlı araştırmaları* 1 (1980): 33–40.

Ozment, Stephen E. *Mysticism and Dissent: Religious Ideology and Social Protest in the Sixteenth Century*. New Haven: Yale University Press, 1973.

Öztekin, Dilek. "'Şehrengizler ve Bursa: edebiyat ve eşcinsel eğilim." *Kuram* 14 (May 1997): 37–41.

Padgug, Robert. "Sexual Matters: Rethinking Sexuality in History." In Duberman, Vicinus, and Chauncey 1989, 54–64.

Pakalin, Mehmet Zeki. *Osmanlı tarih deyimleri ve terimleri sözlüğü*. 3 vols. Istanbul: Millî Eğitim Basımevi, 1971.

Pala, İskender. *Ansiklopedik dîvân şiiri sözlüğü*. 2 vols. Ankara: Sevinç, 1989.

Pamuk, Şevket. *A Monetary History of the Ottoman Empire*. Cambridge: Cambridge University Press, 2000.

———. "The Price Revolution in the Ottoman Empire Reconsidered." *International Journal of Middle Eastern Studies* 33 (2001): 69–89.

Panofsky, Erwin. *Studies in Iconology: Humanistic Themes in the Art of the Renaissance*. New York: Harper and Row, 1960.

Parker, Alexander A. *Luis De Gongora, "Polyphemus and Galatea": A Study in the Interpretation of a Baroque Poem.* Verse translation by Gilbert F. Cunningham. Austin: University of Texas Press, 1977.

Peçevi [Peçuyī], İbrāhīm. *Tārīh-i peçuyī.* Facsimile ed. Istanbul: Enderun, 1980.

Peirce, Leslie P. "Seniority, Sexuality, and Social Order: The Vocabulary of Gender in Early Modern Ottoman Society." In Zilfi 1988, 169–96.

———. *The Imperial Harem: Women and Sovereignty in the Ottoman Empire.* New York: Oxford University Press, 1993.

———. "Politicizing Sex: Bodies, Honor, and the State in 16th Century Ottoman Anatolia." Paper at the meeting of the Middle East Studies Association, San Francisco, November 2001.

———. *Morality Tales: Law and Gender in the Ottoman Court of Aintab.* Berkeley and Los Angeles: University of California Press, 2003.

Pekin, Nermin Suner, ed. and transcriber. *Lâtifî: Evsâf-ı İstanbul.* Istanbul: Baha Matbaası, 1977.

Penzer, N. M. *The Harem.* 1936. London: Spring, 1966.

Petruccioli, Attilio, ed. *Gardens in the Time of the Great Muslim Empires: Theory and Design.* Leiden: Brill, 1997.

Pflugfelder, Gregory M. *Cartographies of Desire: Male-Male Sexuality in Japanese Discourse, 1600–1950.* Berkeley and Los Angeles: University of California Press, 1999.

Piterberg, Gabriel. *An Ottoman Tragedy: History and Historiography at Play.* Berkeley and Los Angeles: University of California Press, 2003.

Prochazka-Eisl, Gisela, ed. *Das Sūrnāme-i hümāyūn: Die Wiener Handschrift in Transkription, mit Kommentar und Indices versehen.* Istanbul: Isis, 1995.

Pullan, Brian, ed. *Crisis and Change in the Venetian Economy in the Sixteenth and Seventeenth Centuries.* London: Methuen, 1968.

———. "Wage Earners and the Venetian Economy, 1550–1630." In Pullan 1968, 146–74.

Refik, Ahmet. *On altıncı asırda İstanbul hayatı (1553–1591).* Istanbul: Devlet, 1935.

Repp, Richard. "Some Observations on the Development of the Ottoman Learned Hierarchy." In Keddie 1972, 19–32.

Rocke, Michael. *Forbidden Friendships: Homosexuality and Male Culture in Renaissance Florence.* New York: Oxford University Press, 1996.

———. "Gender and Sexual Culture in Renaissance Italy." In Brown and Davis 1998, 150–70.

Rogers, Michael. "The Arts under Süleymân." In İnalcık and Kafadar 1993, 257–94.

Rosenthal, Franz. "Male and Female: Described and Compared." In Wright and Rowson 1997, 24–54.

Rosenthal, Margaret F. *The Honest Courtesan.* Chicago: University of Chicago Press, 1992.

Rowse, A. L. *Sex and Society in Shakespeare's Age.* New York: Scribner's, 1974.

———, ed. *The Annotated Shakespeare.* 3 vols. New York: Clarkson N. Potter, 1978.

Rowson, Everett K. "Two Homoerotic Narratives from Mamlūk Literature: Al-Safadī's *Law'at al-shākī* and Ibn Dāniyāl's *al-Mutayyam*." In Wright and Rowson 1997, 159–91.

Ruggiero, Guido. *The Boundaries of Eros: Sex Crime and Sexuality in Renaissance Venice*. Oxford: Oxford University Press, 1985.

———, ed. *A Companion to the Worlds of the Renaissance*. Oxford: Blackwell, 2002.

Russell, Rinaldina, and Bruce Merry, eds. and trans. *Tullia d'Aragona: Dialogue on the Infinity of Love*. Chicago: University of Chicago Press, 1997.

Sahillioğlu, Halil. *Studies on Ottoman Economic and Social History*. Translated by Engin Akarlı and William Tobin. Istanbul: Organisation of the Islamic Conference Research Centre for Islamic History, Art and Culture, 1999.

Salter, Thomas. *The Mirrhor of Modestie*. See Holm 1987.

Saslow, James M. *Ganymede in the Renaissance: Homosexuality in Art and Society*. New Haven: Yale University Press, 1986.

Schick, Irvin Cemil. *The Erotic Margin: Sexuality and Spatiality in Alteritist Discourse*. London: Verso, 1999.

Schimmel, Annemarie. *Mystical Dimensions of Islam*. Chapel Hill: University of North Carolina Press, 1975.

———. "Eros—Heavenly and Not So Heavenly—in Sufi Literature and Life." In al-Sayyid-Marsot 1979, 119–41.

———. *As through a Veil: Mystical Poetry in Islam*. New York: Columbia University Press, 1982.

Sedgwick, Eve Kosofsky. *Between Men: English Literature and Male Homosocial Desire*. New York: Columbia University Press, 1985.

Sehī Beg [Edirneli]. *Heşt bihişt*. Edited, with a critical study, by Günay Kut. Facsimile ed. Cambridge: Harvard University Press, 1978.

Şeker, Mehmet, ed. *Gelibolulu Mustafa 'Âlî ve Mevâ'idü'n-nefâis fî-kavâ'idi'l-mecâlis*. Ankara: Türk Tarih Kurumu, 1997.

Şentürk, Ahmet Atillâ. *Osmanlı şiiri antolojisi*. Istanbul: Yapı Kredi, 1999.

Sevengil, Refik Ahmet. *İstanbul nasıl eğleniyordu?* Edited by Sami Önal. Istanbul: İletişim, 1985.

Sevgi, Ahmet, ed. *Latifî'nin iki risalesi: Enîsü'l-fusahâ ve evsâf-ı İbrâhim Pâşâ*. Selçuk Üniversitesi Yayınları 14, Eğitim Fakültesi Yayınları 1. Konya: Selçuk Üniversitesi, Eğitim Fakültesi, 1986.

Shakespeare, William. See Rowse 1978.

Sharma, Sunil. "Poetics of Court and Prison in the 'Divan' of Mas'ud-e Sa'd-e Salman." Ph.D. diss., University of Chicago, 1999.

———. "Generic Innovation in Sayfî Bokharaî's Shahr-ashub Ghazals." In Neuwirth, Pfeiffer, and Sagaster, in press.

Sidney, Sir Philip. *The Poems of Sir Philip Sidney*. Edited by William A. Ringler Jr. Oxford: Clarendon, 1962.

———. *An Apology for Poetry*. In *Critical Theory since Plato*, ed. Hazard Adams, 155–77. San Diego: Harcourt Brace Jovanovich, 1971.

Silay, Kemal. "Singing His Words: Ottoman Women Poets and the Power of Patriarchy." In Zilfi 1988, 197–213.

———, ed. *An Anthology of Turkish Literature.* Bloomington: Indiana University Turkish Studies, 1996.

Smith, Bruce R. *Homosexual Desire in Shakespeare's England.* 1991. Chicago: University of Chicago Press, 1994.

———. "Making a Difference: Male/Male 'Desire' in Tragedy, Comedy, and Tragi-Comedy." In Zimmerman 1992, 127–49.

Southgate, Minoo S. "Men, Women, and Boys: Love and Sex in the Works of Saʻdi." *Iranian Studies* 17 (autumn 1984): 413–541.

Spenser, Edmund. *The Faerie Queene.* With an introduction by J. W. Hales. 2 vols. Everyman's Library, no. 444. London: Dent, 1910.

Sphrantzes, George. *The Fall of the Byzantine Empire.* Translated by Marios Philippides. Amherst: University of Massachusetts Press, 1980.

Sprachman, Paul. *Suppressed Persian: An Anthology of Forbidden Literature.* Costa Mesa: Mazda, 1995.

———. "*Le beau garçon sans merci*: The Homoerotic Tale in Arabic and Persian." In Wright and Rowson 1997, 192–209.

Stallybrass, Peter. "Patriarchal Territories: The Body Enclosed." In Ferguson, Quilligan, and Vickers 1986, 123–42.

———. "Transvestitism and the 'Body Beneath': Speculating on the Boy Actor." In Zimmerman 1992, 64–83.

Stehling, Thomas. "To Love a Medieval Boy." In Kellogg 1983, 151–70.

———, trans. *Medieval Latin Love Poems of Male Love and Friendship.* The Garland Library of Medieval Literature, vol. 7, ser. A. New York: Garland, 1984.

Stetkevych, Suzanne Pinckney. "Intoxication and Immortality: Wine and Associated Imagery in al-Maʻarrī's Garden." In Wright and Rowson 1997, 210–32.

Stewart-Robinson, James. "A Neglected Ottoman Poem: The Şehrengiz." In Bellamy 1990, 201–11.

Stortoni, Laura Anna, ed. *Women Poets of the Italian Renaissance: Courtly Ladies and Gentlewomen.* Translated by Laura Anna Stortoni and Mary Prentice Lillie. New York: Italica, 1997.

Strocchia, Sharon T. "Gender and the Rites of Honor in Italian Renaissance Cities." In Brown and Davis 1998, 39–60.

Strong, Roy. *Portraits of Queen Elizabeth I.* Oxford: Clarendon, 1963.

Süleyman [Sultan]. *Dīvān-i Muhibbī.* See Muhibbī 1890/91.

Sümer, Faruk, Ahmet E. Uysal, and Warren S. Walker, trans. and eds. *The Book of Dede Korkut.* Austin: University of Texas Press, 1972.

Suner, Nermin. See Pekin 1977.

Talattof, Kamran, and Jerome W. Clinton, eds. *The Poetry of Nizami Ganjavi: Knowledge, Love, and Rhetoric.* New York: Palgrave, 2000.

Tanpınar, Ahmet Hamdi. *XIX asır Türk edebiyatı tarihi.* Istanbul: Ibrahim Horoz Basımevi, 1956.

Tarlan, Ali Nihat, ed. *Hayâlî Bey dîvânı*. Istanbul: Bürhaneddin Erenler Matbaası, 1945.
———, ed. *Necatî Beg divanı*. Istanbul: Millî Eğitim Basımevi, 1963.
———, ed. *Zatî divanı*. Vols. 1–2. Istanbul: Edebiyat Fakültesi, 1967–70. This edition of Zati's divan appears in three volumes. For vol. 3, see Çavuşoğlu and Tanyeri 1987.
Terzioğlu, Derin. "The Imperial Circumcision Festival of 1582: An Interpretation." *Muqarnas: An Annual on Islamic Art and Architecture* 12 (1995): 84–100.
Tietze, Andreas, ed. and trans. *Muṣṭāfā ʿĀlī's Counsel for Sultans of 1581*. 2 vols. Vienna: Verlag der Österreichischen Akademie der Wissenschaften, 1979–82.
Traister, Barbara Howard. *The Notorious Astrological Physician of London: Works and Days of Simon Forman*. Chicago: University of Chicago Press, 2001.
Traub, Valerie. "The (In)Significance of 'Lesbian' Desire in Early Modern England." In Zimmerman 1992, 150–69.
Trechmann, E. J., trans. *The Diary of Montaigne's Journey to Italy: In 1580 and 1581*. New York: Harcourt, Brace, 1929.
Tripp, C. A. *The Homosexual Matrix*. New ed. New York: New American Library, 1987.
Tuan, Yi-Fu. *Segmented Worlds and Self: Group Life and Individual Consciousness*. Minneapolis: University of Minnesota Press, 1982.
Uluçay, M. Çağatay. *Osmanlı sultanlarına aşk mektupları*. 1950. Istanbul: Ufuk Kitapları, 2001.
Uzunçarşılı, İsmail Hakkı. *Osmanlı devletinin ilmiye teşkilâtı*. Ankara: Türk Tarih Kurumu, 1965.
Valensi, Lucette. *The Birth of the Despot: Venice and the Sublime Porte*. Translated by Arthur Denner. Ithaca: Cornell University Press, 1993.
Veinstein, Gilles, ed. *Soliman le Magnifique et son temps*. Paris: La Documentation Française, 1992.
Veyne, Paul. "Homosexuality in Ancient Rome." In Ariès and Bejin 1985, 26–35.
Wall, Allison. *Power and Protest in England, 1525–1640*. London: Arnold; York: Oxford University Press, 2000.
Waller, Marguerite. "Usurpation, Seduction, and the Problematics of the Proper: A 'Deconstructive,' 'Feminist' Rereading of the Seductions of Richard and Anne in Shakespeare's Richard III." In Ferguson, Quilligan, and Vickers 1986, 159–74.
Warner, Jayne L., ed. *Cultural Horizons: A Festschrift in Honor of Talât S. Halman*. New York: Syracuse University Press; Istanbul: Yapı Kredi Yayınları, 2001.
White, Paul Whitfield, ed. *Marlowe, History, and Sexuality*. New York: AMS, 1998.
Wiesner, Merry E. "Spinsters and Seamstresses: Women in Cloth and Clothing Production." In Ferguson, Quilligan, and Vickers 1986, 191–205.
Woolf, S. J. "Venice and the Terraferma: Problems of Change from Commercial to Landed Activities." In Pullan 1968, 176–203.
Wright, J. W., Jr. "Masculine Allusion and the Structure of Satire in Early ʿAbbāsid Poetry." In Wright and Rowson 1997, 1–23.

Wright, J. W., Jr., and Everett K. Rowson, eds. *Homoeroticism in Classical Arabic Literature*. New York: Columbia University Press, 1997.
Yahya. *Şah u geda*. See Candaş 1941.
Yılmaz, Fikret. "XVI. yüzyıl osmanlı toplumda mahremiyetin sınırlarına dair." *Toplum ve Bilim* 83 (winter 1999/2000): 92–110.
Yourcenar, Margaret. *Memoirs of Hadrian*. Translated by Grace Frick. New York: Noonday, 1990.
Zati. See Çavuşoğlu and Tanyeri 1987; and Tarlan 1967–70.
Zilfi, Madeline C. *The Politics of Piety: The Ottoman Ulema in the Postclassical Age (1600–1800)*. Minneapolis: Bibliotheca Islamica, 1988.
——. "Sultan Süleymân and the Ottoman Religious Establishment." In İnalcık and Kafadar 1993, 109–20.
——, ed. *Women in the Ottoman Empire*. The Ottoman Empire and Its Heritage: Politics, Society, and Economy, vol. 10. Leiden: Brill, 1997.
Zimmerman, Susan, ed. *Erotic Politics: Desire on the Renaissance Stage*. New York: Routledge, 1992.

Manuscript Sources

ʿĀşık Çelebi. "Meşāʿiru üş-şuʿarā." Süleymaniye Kütüphanesi, Aşir Efendi 268.
Caʿfer Çelebi [Tācızāde]. "Hevesnāme." Konya Koyunoğlu Müzesi ve Kitaplığı 13955.
Fevrī. "Dīvān." Topkapı Sarayı Kütüphanesi, Revan 763.
Latīfī. "Tezkīre-i şuʿarā." Süleymaniye Kütüphanesi, Halet Efendi 342.
"Mecmūʿatü'n-nezāʾir." İstanbul Üniversitesi Kütüphanesi, TY 739.
Sānī. "Şehr-i Edirne'den Sāʿyī Beg merhūm gönderdügi mektūba Sānīʿnün yazub irsāl eyledügi cevābdur." İstanbul Üniversitesi Kütüphanesi, TY 1532, fols. 150b–151a.
Sāʿyī Beg. "Şehr-i Edirne'den Sāʿyi Beg merhūm İstanbul şuʿarāsına irsāl eyledügi mektūbdur." İstanbul Üniversitesi Kütüphanesi, TY 1532, fols. 149b–150a.
Yahyā [Dukaginzāde]. "Kitāb-i usūl." İstanbul Üniversitesi Kütüphanesi, TY 1800.
Zātī. "Edirne şehrengizi." Süleymaniye Kütüphanesi, Lâlâ İsmail 443, fols. 161b–167b.

INDEX

'Abdu'r-Rahman III, 2
Abou-El-Haj, Rifa'at, 24–25, 304, 363n.44
absolutism: in England, 322–23; literary economy in Ottoman Empire and, 312–16, 382n.25; modernization and, 338; in Ottoman Empire, 303, 322–24
Abu'l-'Ala al-Ma'arri, 157
Abu'l-Kasim Ferdevsi, 165
adultery *(zina)*, Islamic legal theory and, 271–74, 377n.5; legal decrees concerning, 276–88
Affectionate Shepherd, 128, 366n.31
Age of Beloveds: Andalusian culture and, 386n.16; consummated and unconsummated love in, 55–58, 84; economic breakdown and decline of, 316–24; historical evolution of, 22–31; law and religion during, 270–303; lesbianism in, 173–87; literary economy in, 311–16; love and power in Ottoman Court during, 237–50; love and violence in, 251–69; modernization of language during, 331–38; monarch in literature of, 231–32; Ottoman Empire as, 19; position of slaves in, 46–49; religion in, 288–303; Renaissance and, 22–31, 306–7, 329–53, 380n.5; role of women in, 163; socioeconomics of, 304–5; tale of Me'ali and, 217–28; in Venice, 116–17; waning of, in sixteenth century, 80–81, 316–24; women and society in, 187–93

agricultural development, breakdown of Ottoman Empire and, 316–24, 383n.50, 384n.53
Ahmet (Prince), 216
Ahmet Pasha, 180
Alexander VI (Pope), 116
'Ali, Mustafa, 44, 69–70, 81–82, 88, 362n.16; Age of Beloveds and, 351–52; on beautiful boys as beloveds, 137–38, 140–42, 178, 284; on cultured conversations *(sohbet)*, 365n.40; historical changes in Ottoman Empire described by, 306; imagined women in literature of, 167–68; on literary economy and state, 311; on Ottoman patronage, 143–44; poet biographies of, 286–87, 307; social role of women in work of, 190–93
'Ali Pasha, 103–4
Allen, Bridge, 127
Allen, John, 127
Amazon women, 163–65
Amores, 134
Anadolu Hisar district (Istanbul), 66–67
anagrams, in Ottoman poetry, 93–94
Anatomie of Abuses, 68, 76
Andalusian culture, 351–52, 386n.16
Andrews, Walter G., 228–30
androgyny: of beloveds, 39, 177–87; in Ottoman love poems, 21; transvestitism and, 375n.25; women's sexuality and, 43–58, 172, 177–87

antinomian orders, 303, 380n.67; decline of Ottoman Empire and, 319–20
Anti-Unionists, Notaras's mediation with, 2
Aretino, 338
Ariosto, Ludovico, 74, 165, 172
'Aşık Çelebi, 35–36; Age of Beloveds in work of, 351–52; anecdotal poetry of, 101–3, 105–6; on Ayyas and Rüstem Pasha, 326–28; on bathhouse culture, 285; on cultured conversation (sohbet), 107–12; on female beloveds, 179–87; on Hayali and Yahya, 324–25, 385n.71; as historical source, 307, 309n.10; on male beloveds, 49–51; poet biographies of, 39, 286; tale of Ferdi by, 251–53; tale of Me'ali by, 54, 217–28; on woman poet 'Ayişe, 208–16; on woman poet Mihri Hatun, 201–8
'askeri administrators, 307; breakdown of Ottoman Empire and, 317–24; Ottoman economic power and, 314–16
astrology, in Ottoman court, 242
Astrophel and Stella, 129, 168, 229–37, 266–67, 289
As You Like It, 22
'Atayi, Nev'izade, 59–63, 69, 72, 74–84, 361n.1
'Ayişe, 201–2, 208–16
Ayyas Pasha, 325–26
'Azizi Mısri, 44–48; women and society in literature of, 188; women as lovers in literature of, 54

Baba Ali (Persian Drunkard), 138–40
Bahşi, Sirkeci, 107–9, 365n.35
Bakhtin, Michael, 333
Baki (jurist and scholar), 81, 210, 293, 340–44
Bali, Turak, 232
Bali Çelebi, 73
Bandinelli, Baccio, 121
banditry, breakdown of Ottoman Empire and rise of, 320, 384n.58
Barbaro, Francesco, 194
Bardakçı, Murat, 358n.18
Barkan, Ömer Lutfi, 309
Barkey, Karen, 320, 384n.58
Barnfield, Richard, 128, 366n.31

Baroque era, mannerism and, 339
Bartolomé de Las Casas, Fray, 331
bathhouses, in Ottoman Empire, laws concerning, 284–85, 378n.29
Baudri of Bourgueil, 176
Bayezit II, 35, 66, 131, 217; dervishes supported by, 302–3; laws on sexual behavior of, 378n.19; mysticism of, 335; poetry patronage of, 103–4
beardless youths (emred), in Ottoman culture, 63, 285–86
beautiful boys: in beloveds poetry, 39–43; gendered space for, 51–52, 360n.29; in Italian culture, 51–52; love and power of, in Ottoman court, 237–50; in Ottoman literature, 137–47; poems about poetry and, 92–106; as prostitutes, 48–49; sexual violence and, 257–58; spirituality and divinity of, 290, 292–93, 300; in tale of Me'ali, 217–28; tavern culture and, 70–73; unconsummated love for, 55–58; violence by, 264–69; women's sexuality expressed in, 177–87
"beautiful souls," Italian concept of, 291, 379n.42
Beier, A. L., 233, 280, 374n.13, 375n.6
Bektaşis dervishes, 73, 303, 380n.66
Bellocchio, Isabella, 338
beloveds: as beautiful boys, 39–43; in courtly poetry, 229–37; gender ambiguity in Ottoman references to, 38–39; history of, 307; law and, 271–74; mercenary tendencies of, 308; public display of, 151–56; religion and, 288–303; as social category, 147–56; violent love and, 253–64; women as, 43–58, 163–216
Bembo, Pietro, 118, 291, 332
Bezen, Bald, 110
biology, cultural scripting concerning, 38
Birgili Mehmet, 80, 336
Black, Nejaat, 372n.82
boatman, segregation of sexes by, 189
Bocaccio, Giovanni, 59, 194
Book of Desire (Hevesname), 68–69, 180–87, 196, 361n.14
Book of the Courtier (Il cortegiano), 65–66, 111–12, 133–34, 244

412   Index

Borgia, Cesare, 116
Borgia, Lucrezia, 116
Boundaries of Eros, The, 117, 270
Bourdieu, Pierre, 215-16
Brackett, John, 273
Braudel, Fernand, 25, 339, 381n.17, 382n.30
Bray, Alan, 70, 128, 301-2, 362n.19, 366n.31, 367n.33
Brookes, Douglas S., 362n.16
Brown, Georgia, 87-89
Brown, Judith C., 172, 370n.20, 380n.3
Brummett, Palmira, 314
Bruto, Giovanni, 195
Burchard, Johann, 116
bureaucracy, growth of, in Ottoman Empire, 321-24, 384n.64; religious bureacracy, ascendancy of, 336-38

Ca'fer, Tacızade, 68-69, 73, 180-87, 196, 361n.14
Carr, Robert, 127-28
Castagno, Paul C., 340, 386n.17
Castiglione, Baldessar, 66, 111-12, 133-34, 244
Castilian of Nebrija, 331
Catena, Emilia, 338
Catholic Church, modernization of language and, 333-38
Causa-Steindler, Mariangela, 194
cavalry *(sipahi)*, 317-18
Çavuşoğlu, Mehmed, 210, 349-50
Celali revolts, 320, 384n.58
Celalu'd-din (Djelaluddeen) Rumi, 73, 302; *Mesnevi* of, 131-32
Cellini, Benvenuto, 37, 121-25, 164, 255-56, 288, 299, 366n.16
Ccm (Djem/gem) (shah of Iran), 64, 66
Çeşti Bali, 239-40
Cevdet, Ahmed, 307, 380n.7
Charles V, 26, 232
Charles VI, 116
chastisement *(ta'zir/te'dib)*, 273, 287
Chinese artists, in Perso-Ottoman culture, 33
"ching-a-ling" lover, of Gazali, 142, 264
Christianity: homoeroticism condemned by, 80-84, 301-2; Islam in relation to, 16; modernization of language

and, 333-34; Ottomans as threat to, 11; restrictions on women in, 43-44; rise as religious and political power, 14-15; slavery in, 241; spirituality and mysticism in, 297-98
chronogram poetry, 254
Cinani (poet), 254
circularity, in Ottoman literature, 37-38
city quarters *(mahalle)*, legal decrees concerning, 275-88, 303, 380n.62
class structure: among Ottoman males, 52-54, 75, 143-44, 368 n.53; ascendancy of puritanism and, 82, 363n.44; in 'Atayi's Seven Stories, 59-63; beloved as social category, 147-56; in beloveds literature, 40-43; breakdown of Ottoman Empire and, 317-24; coffeehouse culture and, 70-71; dervish sects and, 73-74, 379n.57; impact on poets of, 321-24; legal system in Ottoman Empire and, 287-88, 378-n.35; literary economy in Age of Beloveds and, 311-16; love and power of slaves in Ottoman Court and, 237-50; love in Ottoman literature and, 74-84; Ottoman garden party and role of, 77-78; perceptions of high officials and, 321-24; pleasure spots of Istanbul elites and, 63-73; poems about poetry and, 94; portrayal of beloved women and, 43-46; role of court setting in poetry and, 228-37; spirituality and love and, 291-94, 297-99; tavern culture and, 69-70, 362n.19; violence and love and, 255-58; women in Age of Beloveds and, 187-93; women Ottoman poets and, 195-96; women's sexuality and, 184-87
coffeehouses: cultural role of, 70-71, 81-82, 362n.20; laws concerning, 283-88; puritanical attacks on, 320
commedia crudita, sexual violence in, 262
convents, as alternative to prostitution, 200, 372n.72
conversation, cultural importance of, 111-12
Cook, M. A., 309, 381n.17

Corbaccio, 194
corporal punishment (*siyaset*), 273, 287
cortegiane oneste culture, 116–18
Coryat, Thomas, 111, 117, 174, 366n.6
Cosimo I de' Medici, 121, 281, 291
Council of Ten, 120
Council of Trent, 336
couplets, in Ottoman poetry, 92–95; beloveds portrayed in, 151–56; mannerism in, 340–53; women poets portrayed in tezkire with, 204–16
courtly settings, love poetry in, 228–37; literary economy and, 311–16; love and power in Ottoman Court and, 237–50, 315–16; sexual violence and, 266–69
creation, Ottoman concept of, 294
Crompton, Louis, 370n.20
culture: literary tradition in Ottoman culture, 156–62; literature about love and biases in, 8–10, 86–90; social context of, 56–58
cultured conversation (*sohbet*): Ottoman poetry and, 106–12; women poets' participation in, 204–8, 372n.77
Cupid, sexual violence and image of, 266
currency: debasement of, during Ottoman Empire, 309–10, 381n.19, 382n.22; literary references to, 73, 362n.24

Dafiʿü'l-gumum ve rafiʿü'l-humum (Repeller of sorrows and removers of cares), 130–32, 144–47, 168, 358n.17, 367n.34; 367n.39
Dante Alighieri, 119, 134, 194, 289
d'Aragona, Tullia, 196, 213, 290–92, 298, 332, 378n.40
Darling, Linda T., 385n.3
Davis, Robert C, 52, 360n.32
de Bourges, Clémence, 213
De Busbecq, Ogier Ghiselin, 367n.54
Decameron, 59
de Certeau, Michel, 337–38
De claris mulieribus, 194
Deleuze, Gilles, 38
Della Valle, Pietro, 189–90
Demir, Yavuz, 375n.31
De re uxoria, 194

Derrida, Jacques, 24
dervishes (Islamic mystics), 82; class structure and, 73, 379n.57; mendicant dervishes, 319–20; popularity among elites of, 298–303; role of young men in, 138–40; social life of, 321, 384n.66
desire, natural history of, 10–18
despots. *See* absolutism; monarchy
d'Este, Alfonso, 116
destination for outings (*mesire*) in Ottoman culture, 67
Devereux Rich, Penelope, 128, 135, 229
Dialoghi d'amore, 291
Dialogo della infinità d'amore (Dialogue on the infinity of love), 290–92, 378n.40
"Ditchley portrait" of Queen Elizabeth I, 312–13, 382n.26
Divan şiirinde sapık sevgi, 18–19
double entendres, in Ottoman poetry, 65
Doukas, 1, 357n.1
dream visitor, in Ottoman literature, 83, 363n.46
du Guillet, Pernette, 204, 207
du Moulin, Antoine, 207

earthquakes, during Ottoman Empire, 107–8
Ebreo, Leone, 291
Ebu's-suʿud (Ottoman jurist), 53, 258, 283, 285–88, 337, 378n.19
Economic Life in Ottoman Europe, 309
economics: breakdown of Ottoman Empire and, 316–24; demographics of Ottoman Empire and, 309–10; impact on poetry of, 321–24; of love, in Ottoman Empire, 307–8
education, in Ottoman Empire, 287–88, 340, 379n.57
Efe Meyhanesi tavern, 69
Elegies, 134, 244
elegies (*mersiye*) of Ottoman poets, 247–48
Elegy of Lady Fiammetta, 194
Elizabeth I (Queen), 199; court intrigues of, 242; "hypervirginity" of, 312–13, 382n.26
Emirek (Little Prince), 325–26

England: court intrigues in, 242; courtly settings in poetry of, 229–37, 374n.13; dangerous women in, 164; economics and demographics in, 309–10, 315–16, 318, 382n.34; end of Renaissance in, 380n.5; gardens and banquets in, 77–79; importance of conversation in, 111–12; leisure activities in, 68; modernization of language in, 332–38; Orientalist stereotyping in, 129–30; peasant unrest in, 318, 384n.55; power and hierarchy in, 312–16, 322–23; puritanism in, 320; sex and sexuality in, 125–29, 301–2; sexual violence in, 257, 266; standing army and, 255, 375n.6; tavern life in, 70, 362n.19; women's chastity in, 53–54; women's sexuality and, 173–87; young males in, 75, 362n.25. *See also* London
Enlightenment philosophy: influence of Renaissance on, 329–30; love and spirituality in, 290
Epicoene; or, The Silent Woman, 129, 367n.33
epyllion poetry, 87–90; mannerism and, 386n.19; sexual violence in, 259–64
Erasmus, 333
Erotic Margin, The, 28
Erünsal, İsmail E., 381n.11
Essay in Description of Istanbul, 67, 147–48, 307
essentialism: bias about Ottoman poetry and, 87; bias about sex and love and, 9–10
European culture: mannerism in, 339–53; Ottoman closeness to, 65–66; Ottoman historical rupture in context of, 306–7, 329–31
Evliya Çelebi, 189
Eyuboğlu, İsmet Zeki, 18

Faerie Queene, 164–65, 369n.6
faithfulness (*vefa*), in Ottoman poetry, 267–68
false accusation of zina (*kazf*), 272
Faroqhi, Suraiya, 47–48, 315; economic and demographic data of, 320, 381n.17
Feast in the House of Levi, 338
Feldman, Walter, 321, 352–53

female beloveds (*mahbube*), in Ottoman culture, 178–87
Ferhad narrative, in Ottoman literature, 136
festivals, role of women at, 190–92
Fevri (poet), 99–100, 135, 264–66
Ficino, 291, 375n.3, 376n.30
Figani, 240, 249
fines (*kesim*), for legal infractions, 280
Fleischer, Cornell, 25–27, 232, 338, 359n.27, 362n.16
Flemming, Barbara, 232
Florence: homoeroticism in, 75, 320; intellectual elites in, 291–92, 379n.42; law and punishment in, 273, 281, 291, 299, 384n.61; sex and sexuality during Renaissance in, 121–25, 244
Fondaco dei Turchi, 115, 118
food: breakdown of Ottoman Empire and shortages of, 316–24; economics and shortages of, 314–16, 318, 383n.36, 383n.39; love and spirituality in relation to, 289–90
Forbidden Friendships, 122, 366n.16
Forman, Simon, 37, 76, 126–28, 242, 257
Foucault, Michel, 11–12
Fra Fillipo Lippi, 123
Francis I, 26
Franco, Veronica, 118, 135, 193, 196, 204, 213–15, 332, 336
fratricide, Ottoman practice of, 317
friendship, ancient Greco-Roman concepts of, 14
Fumerton, Patricia, 77–78
Fuzuli (poet), 348, 372n.67

Gagnon, John H., 37–38
Galata district (Istanbul): as elite pleasure spot in Ottoman culture, 63–67, 69; legal decrees concerning, 275–88
Ganymede image: as literary device, 368n.56; magian boy as parallel to, 159–62; sexual violence in, 259–64, 266
Ganymede in the Renaissance, 159–60
gardens: cultured conversation (*sohbet*) set in, 107–12; in Ottoman literature, 75–84, 352–53; sexual violence in poetry using, 265

Index 415

Gazali, Deli Birader, 76; bathhouse of, 284–85; courtly intrigue in literature of, 244; on Ibrahim Pasha, 239–40; on kadi legal decrees, 279–80; mercenary tendencies of, 308; pornographic literature of, 131–32, 135–37; prostitution in literature of, 142–44; on sexual violence, 257–58, 264; women in literature of, 168, 171–73, 177–78
gazel, poems about poetry and, 91–106
"Gazels and the World," 114
Genç, Mehmet, 383n.36
Genç the Young (Osman II), 322
gendered space, women beloveds and, 51–52
gender roles: ambiguity of beloveds' identity and, 38–39, 54–58; in English poetry, 129; love and power in Ottoman state and, 247–50; of Ottoman women poets, 202–8; sexual violence and, 261–64; women's sexuality and, 177–87
Germany: merchants in Venice from, 116; peasant unrest in, 384n.55
Gheeraerts, Marcus, 312–13
Gibb, E. J. W., 87, 363n.2
Gli asolani, 291
Goffman, Daniel, 314, 320
Goldstone, Jack A., 384n.61
Gösku river (Istanbul), 66–67, 76
gossip: about beloveds, 106; role of, in Ottoman culture, 79–80
Great Schism, 2
Greek culture: influence on Renaissance of, 329; role of women in, 163–64
Greenblatt, Stephen, 173, 229–30, 292, 333–34
Greville, Fulke, 375n.31
Grimeston, 173
Gritti, Alvise, 66, 115, 314
Gritti, Andrea, 66, 115
Guattari, Félix, 38
Gülbahar (Rose Spring), 242–44, 248
Gülfem (Rose Mouth), 242
Gülistan (Rose garden), 100
Gülşeni order of dervishes, 73–74, 298, 338
Gülşen-i ş'ara, 201

hadd/hudud (limit/limits) crimes, law and religion and, 271–74
hadith (prophetic tradition), 136, 367n.46
Hafez, 158–59, 195
hairstyles in Venice, rules concerning, 120
hakkiki (real) love, 120, 124, 181; spirituality and, 290
Halperin, David, 13
Halveti dervishes, 73, 303, 338
hamse (pentad of poems), 59, 361n.1
Hanbali legal theory, 377n.2
harem: gendered space for women in, 53; political power and intrigue in, 244–45, 247, 317–18, 327–28, 375n.29; status of women in, 358n.16
Hasan ibn Thabit, 297
Hasbi, tale of, 240
Hashihal (Recounting of woes), 148–51
Hattox, Ralph S., 362n.20
Hauser, Arnold, 347, 350–51, 387n.34
Hayali, 36, 138–40, 158; courtly references in poetry of, 230, 232; decline of Ottoman Empire and poetry of, 324–28, 385n.71; Ibrahim Pasha and, 240; on love and violence, 256; mannerism in poetry of, 345–53; sexual violence in poetry of, 265, 267; spirituality in poetry of, 295–98
Heft han (Seven Stories), 59–84, 361n.1
Heilbrun, Carolyn, 21
Helaki, 253–54; divan of, 64, 361n.7
Henri III of Valois, 118
Hero and Leander, 87, 89, 259–64
Heşt behişt (Seven Paradises), 197
heterosexuality: in Florence, 124–25; in modern culture, 21; in Ottoman poetry, 56–58; in Venetian poetry, 119–21
Heyd, Uriel, 272–73, 287, 377n.4
Hidāyah, 377n.2
Hidden from History, 358n.13
historiography, research on Ottoman Empire and, 305, 380n.2–3
History of Ottoman Poetry, 87, 364n.2
homoeroticism: in epyllion poetry, 87–90; in European culture, 57–58;

416   Index

in Florence, 75, 122–25; in Greco-Roman antiquity, 11–12; historical evolution of, 24; literary economy in Ottoman Empire and, 311–16; in London, 127–29; in Muslim culture, 17–18; Neoplatonic argument for, 134–35; in Ottoman literature, 159–62; in Ottoman love poetry, 18–22; Ottoman morality concerning, 80; in Renaissance Venice, 119–21; spirituality and love and, 301–3; violence and, 259–64, 268–69; women's sexuality and, 172–87

Homoeroticism in Classical Arabic Literature, 358n.17
Honest Courtesan, 117–18
Howard, Frances (Lady), 128
Hubbi. See 'Ayişe
Hurrem (wife of Süleyman I), 238, 242–50, 327, 368n.60
Hurşid and Cemşd, 212
Hüseyn Baykara, 40
hüsn-i-ta'lil (beauty of cause), 341–42
Husrev, Amir, 97–98, 296–97, 348
Husrev u Şirin (Husrev and Shirin), 56, 136, 165–66
hyperbole, in Ottoman poetry, 342–43

Ibrahim Pasha, 88, 115, 140, 151; death of, 241, 244, 306–7, 325; jewelry financed by, 314; letters to wife Hatice, 368n.60; Süleyman's love for, 238–50
identity: Renaissance concept of, 333–34; sexuality and, 13
Imber, Colin, 287–88
İnalcık, Halil, 309, 381n.17
Industrial Revolution, 329–30
inflation, in Ottoman Empire, 310, 313, 315–16, 381n.19, 382n.20, 383n.36
intisab networks, cultured conversations (*sohbet*) and, 111
İpekten, Halûk, 362n.15
İsen (Mesleki konumları), 378n.35
İshak Çelebi, 98–100
Iskender Çelebi, 140, 314, 325
Islam: evolution of, 16–18; law and religion in, 270–303; legal practices of, 17; literary tradition in, 156–62; love and spirituality in, 290–94;

modernization of language and, 333–38; as religion of love, 83–84; views on sodomy in, 303, 379n.61
Istanbul: economic development of, 312–13, 383n.36; pleasure spots of, in Ottoman literature, 63–73; sex and sexuality in, 129–47; Venice compared with, 115–16
Italy: "beautiful souls" concept in, 291, 379n.42; Counter-Reformation in, 335–36; economics and demographics and, 309; end of Renaissance in, 380n.5; homoeroticism in, 81–82, 320; importance of conversation in, 111–12; law and punishment in, 273–74; mannerism in culture of, 351; protectiveness of women in, 43–44, 53; puritanical suppression in, 320; during Renaissance, 213; stereotypes of, 129–30; ties with Ottoman Empire in, 66–67; women and society in, 189–92; young males in, 51–52, 75

Jacobean courts, 242
James I (King of England), 127–28, 313
janissary corps, 317–18
Jardine, Lisa, 51–52, 360n.29
Javich, Daniel, 365n.44, 373n.3
Jinn (genie), 49
Jones, Ann Rosalind, 112, 193, 229–34, 372n.77, 373n.8
Jonson, Ben, 129, 367n.33

kabadayı class, 52
kadi, legal decrees by, 274–88
Kadizadeli movement, 81, 320, 336
Kadizade Mehmet, 81, 320
Kafadar, Cemal, 78, 324
Kağithane (Istanbul), 67–69, 76
Kalenderi order, 303
Kandi (the Candyman), 240
Kaplan, Mehmet, 369n.73
kaside poetry, 90, 229–30
Kava'idu'l-mecalis (etiquette of gatherings), 69, 137, 140–44, 284, 362n.16; imagined women in, 167
Kemal Pashazade, 325
Keuls, Eva, 12–13
Kınalızade Hasan Çelebi, 307, 351–52

Index 417

Kitab-i Dede Korkut (Book of Dede Korkut), 166
Kitab-i usul, 169–71
knife imagery, in Ottoman poetry, 266, 376n.34
Korkut (Prince), 131
Kortantamer, Tunca, 361n.1, 375n.1
köşk, 78–79, 363n.34
Kubad Pasha, 287
külhanbeys class of male youths, 52
kuls (elite slaves), 46–49, 317–24, 383n.45
Künhü'l-ahbar, 307
Kunt, Metin, 317–18
Kuru, Selim, 130–32, 367n.34, 367n.39, 378n.29

Labé, Louise, 193, 196, 204, 213, 215
La calandria, 262
La institutione di una fanciulla nata nobilmente, 195
Lami'i, 105–6
Lami'i (poet), 298–99
language: mannerist poetry and, 350–53; modernization of grammar during Renaissance and, 331–38
Last Judgment (Michelangelo), 338
Last Supper (Veronese), 338
Latifi, 32–35, 38; Age of Beloveds in work of, 351–52; on beloveds, 147–51; on European women, 65; on Helaki, 253–54; on Ibrahim Pasha, 239, 245–47, 306–7, 374n.21, 380n.6; Kağithane described by, 67–68; on literary economy and state, 311; on mercenary tendencies of beloveds, 308; on Rüstem Pasha, 326; tezkire of, 88–89, 307, 364n.5, 381n.9; on wine consumption, 82; women poets in tezkire of, 197–201, 206, 216
Lawbook of the Gypsies in the Province of Rumelia, The, 280
law in Ottoman Empire: during Age of Beloveds, 270–303; on distribution of food and goods, 315–16, 383n.39; legal opinions *(fetva)* and, 65; practice of, 274–88; social behavior and, 79–80, 82–84; status of women and, 188–92
Layla vu Majnun (Leyla and Mejnun), 56

La Zafetta, 375n.12
League of Cambrai, 116, 121
Le'ali, 28
Lee, Henry (Sir), 313
legal opinions *(fetva)*, 65; on women in society, 188–92
legal status, social behavior and, 79–80, 82–84
lesbianism, women's sexuality and, 172–74, 370n.20
letayif (amusing anecdotes), in Ottoman literature, 93
levend class of male youths, 52, 63, 75–84, 189
Leyla and Mejnun, 348–49, 372n.67, 386n.28
literary sources, for Ottoman poetry, 37–38, 85–90
literature, sex and love in, 1–10
London: economic development of, 315, 382n.34; sex and sexuality in, 125–29
love: ancient Greco-Roman concepts of, 14; in courtly settings, 228–37; culture of, in Christianity, 14–15; disorderliness of, in Ottoman literature, 74–84; economy of, 307–8; Islam as religion of, 83–84; law in Ottoman Empire and, 270–303; in literary fiction, 2–10; motives of, in elite cultures, 365n.44; Muslim cultural norms concerning, 16–18; Ottoman poetry on, 10–22, 113–62; and power, in Ottoman Court, 237–50; religion and, 288–303; role of women in, 163–216; spirituality and, 289–303; violence and, in Age of Beloveds, 251–69. See also *hakkiki* (real) love; *mecazi* (metaphoric love)
Luther, Martin, 26, 333

magian boy, Ottoman literary tradition of, 157–62
Mahzenü'l-esrar (Treasury of Secrets), 97–98
male beloveds: adult males as, 50–56; life stages of, in Ottoman culture, 63, 74–84
male dominance, as power relation, 13
male life stages, in Ottoman culture, 50–52, 244

male youths: in Florence, 122–25; love and violence among, 253–58; Ottoman literary tradition of, 157–62, 244; in Ottoman love poetry, 136–47; Ottoman populations of, 52, 63, 75–84, 280–88, 319–24; in Venice, 120–21

Mannerism, 350

mannerism, Ottoman poetry and, 338–53, 386n.17

Manuel II Palaelologus, 1

Marbod of Rennes, 175–77

Marghīnānī, 'Alī ibn Abī Bakr, 377n.2

Marlowe, Christopher, 87, 89, 134, 244, 259–64, 333, 351

marriage: law and religion and, 271–74; in Ottoman literature, 132–47

mastery and masterless, in English poetry, 233, 374n.13

Mas'ud Sa'd Salman, 40

Matla'u'l-envar (Dawn of Illuminations), 97

Me'ali, tale of, 54, 217–28; court etiquette in, 232–37; sexual violence in, 260–61

mecazi (metaphoric love), 124, 290

medieval literature: clash with modernism during Renaissance of, 331–38; homoeroticism in, 175–77, 370n.28

Mediterranean and the Mediterranean World in the Age of Philip II, The, 25

Mediterranean Apocalypse, A, 25–26

medrese (religious schools), career mobility through, 52

Mehmet III, 316–17

Mehmet the Conqueror, 247, 302–3; economic policies of, 310; mysticism of, 335; story of Lukas Notaras and, 1–10

Meisami, Julī, 160, 369n.72

melancholy, in love poetry, 292–94

Menaechmi, 262

Meninski, Franciscus à Mesgnien, 63

Menocal, María, 331–32

menstrual fluid *(hayz)*, references to, in Ottoman poetry, 205

mental health, sexuality in context of, 15–16

Meredith-Owens, G. M., 359n.3

meretrice (European prostitutes), 48

Merry Wives of Windsor, The, 53–54

Meşa'irü'ş-şü'ara (Stations of the poets' pilgrimage), 35–36. 307

Mesihi: parallel poems of, 92; şehrengiz of, 40

Mesnevi, 131–32

mesnevis (narrative rhyming poems), 56, 59, 198, 211, 335, 372n.67

Messiah, monarchs in image of, 232

Meva'idu'n-nefa'is fi kava'idu'l-mecalis (Exquisite appointments in the etiquette of gatherings), 69

Mevlānā Şemsüddin Kāmī, 365n.40

Mevlevi dervishes, 73, 302–3, 338

Michelangelo Buonarroti, 56–57, 123–24, 290, 336, 378n.39

Midsummer Night's Dream, A, 38, 164, 200

Miftahü'l-hidaye, 131

Mihri Hatun, 197–208, 216, 372n.65; patronage received by, 381n.11

military: decline of Ottoman Empire and breakdown of, 317–18; eroticization of, in Ottoman literature, 138–40

Mirek-i-Tabib, 325–26. See also Emirek

Mirollo, James V., 339, 386n.17, 386n.19

Mirror of Modestie, The, 195

misogyny, women's sexuality and, 174–87, 194

modernism, clash with medievalism during Renaissance of, 331–38

monarchy: breakdown of Ottoman Empire and decline of, 316–17, 321–24; in courtly poetry, 231; development of Ottoman state and role of, 245; in England, 322; kul administrators of, 317–24; literary economy and role of, 312–16, 382n.25; masculinization of, 312–16, 382n.27; modernization and, 338; sexual violence and role of, 268–69

Montaigne, Michel de, 111, 173

Montrose, Louis, 38, 164, 200–201; on court behavior, 237, 374n.17

More, Thomas (Sir), 333

Moryson, Rynes, 53

Mosque of Eyüp, college at, 207, 277–88

Moulton, Ian, 134

Index 419

mücerred/ergen (unmarried adult males), 63
Much Ado about Nothing, 116–17, 174–75
Mü'eyyidzade, 205, 216
mufti: kadi decrees and, 274–88; on Ottoman love poetry, 299–302
muhaddere class of women, 53
Muhibbi (Süleyman's pen name), 243
Muhitler, 362n.15
Mullaney, Steven, 332–33
Murat III (Sultan), 151
musahibs, at cultured conversations (*sohbet*), 110
musk, in Ottoman poetry, 68
Musli, Selimi, 232
Muslims: cultural stereotyping of, 130–31; fictional moral inferiority of, 2; law and religion concerning, 272–74; literary tradition of, 87; relations with Christians in Venice, 115–16; slavery among, 47–49; women's sexuality and, 173–87
Mustafa (Süleyman's heir), 242–45, 247–50, 322–23, 327, 375n.31
Mustapha, 375n.31
mysticism: modernization of language and, 334–38; in Ottoman literature, 73–84, 97–98, 345–46, 350, 386n.31; spirituality of Ottoman love poetry and, 296–303

Na'ili (poet), 352–53
name references, in beloveds' poetry, 42–43; of Ottoman women poets, 202–8; for slaves, 47–48
narrative tradition, absence of, in Ottoman literature, 37–38
Nasihatu's-selatin (Counsel for Sultans), 81–82, 88
natural history of desire, Ottoman love poems and, 11–18
Navigations into Turkey, 173–74
Necati (Nedjatee): beloveds named in poetry of, 39; court etiquette in poetry of, 234–36; cultured conversation (*sohbet*) and, 107, 110; patronage received by, 381n.11; sexual violence in poetry of, 265; on women poets, 206
Necipoğlu, Gülru, 231

Neoplatonism: courtly love and, 229–30, 234–37; love and spirituality and, 299–300, 378n.39; Ottoman literary tradition and, 160–62; in Renaissance literature, 134–35, 207
Nevayi, 50, 348
Nev'i, 71
Nicolay, 173–74
Nihali Ca'fer Çelebi, 39–40, 110
Nims, John Frederick, 56–57
Nişani (Mustafa or Mehmet), 91–92
Nisayi (Ottoman woman poet), 210, 248–49, 373n.89
Nizami of Ganja, 59, 97–98, 348
Notaras, Lukas, story of, 1–10
"Novel of the Amazones," 164

Oğuz Turks, oral literature of, 166
oral literature, strong women in, 166–67
Orientalism: bias about Ottoman poetry and, 87–90, 363n.2; bias about sex and love and, 9–10; history of Ottoman Empire and, 329–31; Ottoman sexuality in terms of, 129–31; women's sexuality in context of, 173–74
Orlando Furioso, 74, 165, 172, 262
Osman II, 322, 385n.67
Osmanlı'a seks, 358n.18
Osman line, 237
Ottoman Empire: in Age of Beloveds, 23–31; economic breakdown and decline of, 316–24; economy and demographics of, 309–10; as enemy of Christianity, 11; European culture and, 65–66; historical rupture in, 305–7, 380n.4; law and religion in, 270–303; love and power in court of, 237–50; modernization of language in, 331–38; monarchs' behavior during, 231–32; pleasure spots of Istanbul elites and, 63–73; religion in, 288–303; sex and sexuality in, 43–58, 79–84, 124; sexual violence in, 257–64; standing army in, 255
Ottoman Gentleman, 362n.16
Ottoman literature: critical interpretations of, 18–22; cultural biases about, 9–10, 85–90; cultural tradition of, 156–62; decline of empire and, 320–

24; dominance of male gender in, 54; economy of, 311–16; as historical resource, 305–6, 380n.2–3; imagined women in, 167–87; love poems and natural history of desire in, 10–18; mannerism and, 338–53; patronage system in, 103–4, 143–44, 306–7, 380n.8; as Renaissance, 329–53; social context for, 37–38; strong women in, 165–67; women poets in, 57–58, 195–216; women's sexuality in, 172–87. *See also* poetry in Age of Beloveds
outings *(mesire)* in Ottoman culture, 67
Ovid, 134

Painter, William, 164
Palace of Pleasure, 164
Pamuk, Şevket, 310, 362n.24, 383n.36
papacy, Venetian culture and, 116
parallel poems *(nazire)*, 92–106
particularism, Ottoman literature in context of, 24–25, 330–31
patriarchy: love and sexuality and, 49, 75–84; masculinization of power and, 313–16, 382n.27, 382n.29; Ottoman women poets and, 204, 372n.78; as power relation, 13
patronage, in Ottoman literature, 103–4, 143–44, 306–8, 380n.8; literary economy of, 311–16
Paul III (Pope), 256
Peçevi, İbrāhīm, 71
Peirce, Leslie: economic and demographic data of, 381n.17; on Elizabethan culture, 199; on gender and sexuality, 187, 375n.29; on Ottoman legal system, 270, 273–74, 280–81, 286, 378n.19; on Ottoman social mores, 79; on Ottoman women poets, 216; on politics of Ottoman Empire, 316–17
Pekin, Nermin Suner, 359n.1
pen names, of Ottoman poets, 32
perverted love, in Ottoman literature, 18–22
Petrarch, 118–19, 134, 194, 348; courtly poetry and influence of, 229–30, 234, 373n.8; influence on Renaissance of, 329, 331–32

phallocracy: in ancient Greece, 12–13; development of Ottoman state and, 244–45; masculinization of power and, 312–16, 382n.27; Ottoman literature and, 21; women poets and, 214–16, 373n.96; women's sexuality and, 168–72, 370n.11
phallus, in shadow-puppet theater, 189, 371n.49
Pilgrimage of Grace, 318
Piyale (Bey), 131
Plato, 375n.3; Florentine sexual mores and, 124–25; spirituality and love in philosophy of, 291, 379n.42
Plautus, 262
poems about poetry: in Ottoman literature, 90–106; women poets in, 202–16, 372n.77. *See also* tezkire (poet biographies)
poetry in Age of Beloveds: beautiful boys in, 39–43; class structure and, 321–24; courtly settings in, 228–37; cultured conversation *(sohbet)* and, 106–12; decline of Ottoman Empire and, 320–24; Ibrahim Pasha in, 237–50; literary economy and, 311–16; love in, 18–22, 113–62; mannerism and, 338–53; moralists' attack on, 88–90, 364n.7; name references in, 42–43, 47–48; Ottoman/Venetian poetry, comparisons of, 119–21; Persian court poetry, 160–62; poetry about, 90–106; poetry in the world and, 85–90; religion and, 288–303; Renaissance influences on, 329–53; sexuality in, 113–62; sexual violence in, 264–69; spirituality in love poetry of, 292–303; in Venice, 118–21; violence and love in, 251–69; Western critiques of, 87–90; women as writers of, 193–216; women in, 43–58. *See also* tezkire (poet biographies)
police officials, in Ottoman literature, 80–83
Pompeo de Capitaneis, 255–56
population growth, in Ottoman Empire, 187, 309–10, 371nn.40–41, 381n.17; economic breakdown and, 319–20

Index   421

pornography: in Ottoman literature, 131–47, 367n.36; sexual violence and, 257–58; women's sexuality in, 168–87
postmodernism, Renaissance and, 331
Potiphar, 44
power and love: eroticism and, 312–16; in Ottoman Court, 237–50; sexual violence and, 259–64
"powerful virginity" literary concept of, 199–201
Present State of the Ottoman Empire, 173
price revolution, in Ottoman Empire, 310, 314–16, 381n.19, 382n.20, 383n.36
"Printed Abroad and Uncastrated," 134
Priuli, 120–21, 281, 378n.22
Prose della vulgar lingua, 118–19
prostitution: in Age of Beloveds, 187–93; of beloved boys, 48–49; in Florence, 124–25, 281, 336, 378n.23; laws and punishment concerning, 276–88; in Ottoman literature, 142–47; sexual violence and, 257; slavery and, 47–48; in Venice, 115–21, 336, 366n.6
public celebrations, in Ottoman culture, 151–56, 368n.63
public space: gardens as, 76; masculine dominance of, in Ottoman culture, 51–54, 57–58; role of Ottoman women in, 51–53, 188–92, 360n.32
Pulci, Luigi, 123
punishment: class structure and impact of, 287; law and religion regarding, 272–74; Ottoman cultural attitudes concerning, 83, 363n.45
Purchas, 173
puritanism: ascendancy of, in post-Ottoman era, 80–84; decline of Ottoman Empire and, 320–24, 336–38, 384n.61

Qur'an: modernization of language and, 334–38; Ottoman literary tradition and, 156–62; Ottoman love poems and, 100–101

Rabelais and His World, 333
racism: bias about Ottoman poetry and, 87; bias about sex and love and, 9–10
rakib (guardian), at cultured conversations (sohbet), 109

rape: legal opinions concerning, 272–74, 285–88; love and violence in context of, 257, 376n.12
reason-for-writing *(sebeb-i-te'lif)* in poets' preface, 212–13
re'aya class, Ottoman containment of, 318–19
redif, in Ottoman poetry, 91–106
relationships, eroticization of, in Ottoman literature, 28–29, 359n.7
religion: bureaucratization of, in Ottoman Empire, 321; class structure and, 287–88, 378n.35; law in Ottoman Empire and, 270–74, 288–303; modernization of language and ascendancy of, 333–38
Renaissance: Age of Beloveds and, 22–31, 306–7, 329–53, 380n.5; clash of medievalism and modernism during, 331–38; cultural biases concerning, 87; debate over end of, 380n.5; in England, 301–2; in Florence, sex and sexuality during, 121–25; as global event, 329–31, 385n.4; homoeroticism during, 75, 82, 134–35; Italian culture during, 213; mannerism and, 338–53; modernization of language during, 331–38; restrictions on women during, 43–44, 53; sexual violence during, 259–64; in Venice, sex and sexuality in, 114–21; women's sexuality during, 173–87; women writers during, 193–216, 372n.78
Revani, 65; on cultured conversation *(sohbet)*, 107, 110
reversal: of love and power, in Ottoman court, 241–50; love and power of slaves in Ottoman Court and, 237–50; sexual violence and reversal of power, 266–69; in tale of Me'ali, 217–28, 233–37
rhetoric: rules in Venice of, 118–19. See cultured conversation *(sohbet)*
Risalat al-gufran (Essay on forgiveness), 157
Risale-i evsaf-ı (Istanbul), 32, 358n.1
Rocke, Michael, 43–44, 75, 122, 257, 280
Romano, Giulio, 338

422 Index

Rosenthal, Margaret, 117–18
Rowse, A. L., 76
Rudaki, 40
Ruggiero, Guido, 117, 257, 270–71
Rumi, 335. *See* Celalu'd-din (Djelaluddeen) Rumi
Russell, Rinaldina, 292
Rüstem Pasha, 247, 314, 325–27
Rycaut, 173

Sa'di, 100
Safavi, Isma'il (Shah), 303, 335
Safi, 148–51
Sahillioğlu, 47
Saint Pelagius, cult of, 2
salons, in Ottoman culture, 69–70, 144–47, 362n.16
Salter, Thomas, 195
Samanid court, poetry in, 40
Sandys, 173
Sani, 71, 81, 92, 145–46
Sanuto, Marin, 117, 366n.6
Saslow, James M., 159–60, 350
Savonarola, Girolamo, 26
Sayfi, 40
Sa'yi, 71–72, 145–46
Scève, Maurice, 207
Schick, Irving, 28, 357n.4
scripting: of beloveds, 151–56; love and power in Ottoman state and, 247–50, 323–24; in Ottoman literature, 37–38, 59–63, 77–84; in Ottoman poetry, 37–38; of Ottoman women poets, 196, 206–7; of pleasure seeking, in Ottoman literature, 73–84; of sexual violence, 259–64; spirituality in love poetry and, 299–303
scrounging, in Ottoman culture, 52–54, 143–47, 368n.56. *See also* patronage, in Ottoman literature
sebkhan (musketeers), 317–19, 384n.57
seduction: in courtly poetry, 230–37; in tale of Me'ali, 217–28
Sehı Beg, 197, 372n.63; tezkire of, 307
*sehl ü mümteni*ʿ (simple and complex) concept, 343–44
sekban (*segban*) (musketeers), 317–19, 384n.57
selamık (male part of home), 44

Selim I (Sultan), 110, 131, 216, 243, 249, 335
Selim II (Sultan), 281–82
semiotic universe, literary economy and, 312–16
sex and sexuality: Christian norms concerning, 14–15; cultural scripting and, 37–38, 359n.5; cultural stereotyping of, 129–31; in Florence, 121–25; in Istanbul, 129–47; law and religion in Ottoman Empire concerning, 270–303; life stages of Ottoman males and, 63, 75–84, 244, 361n.3; in literary fiction, 2–10; in London, 125–29; morality in Ottoman culture regarding, 79–84; Muslim cultural norms concerning, 16–18; natural history of, 11–18; in Ottoman poetry, 113–62; restrictions on women in Ottoman culture and, 43–58; sexual relations with slaves, 47, 360n.22; stereotyping of women and, 168–87; tavern culture and, 70; in Venice, 114–21; violence and, 256–64
Shakespeare, William, 53–54, 86–87, 116–17, 126, 178, 261–62, 332
Shards of Love, 331
sharia law, 271–303
Shiite Islam, modernization of language and, 334–35
Sidney, Philip, 89, 128–29, 229, 234, 289–90, 366n.31
Sihri, 92
Sihrī-i Sānī, 286–87, 378n.32
Silay, Kemal, 214
Simon, William, 37–38
Sipahi, parallel poems of, 92
slash fiction, 358n.21
slaves: in Age of Beloveds, 46–49; love and power in Ottoman Court and role of, 237–50; sex and sexuality in relation to, 143–44, 368n.56
Smith, Bruce, 44, 127, 376n.25
Social History of Art, 350
societal behavior: in courtly poetry, 231–37; eroticization of, in Ottoman culture, 140–47; importance of conversation in, 111–12; legal decrees

societal behavior (*continued*)
  concerning, 276–88; legal status and, 79–80; life stages of, in Ottoman culture, 63, 361n.3; in Ottoman literature, 37–38; of Ottoman littérateurs, 69–70, 308, 361n.15, 381n.11; women in Age of Beloveds and, 187–95
Society and the Sexes, 358n.17
socioeconomic conditions, in Age of Beloveds, 304–5
sodomy laws: in Florence, 121–25, 281, 299, 384n.61; German terminology and, 122, 366n.16; historical evolution of, 15; in London, 127–29; in Venice, 119–21, 281; violence and, 257; women's sexuality and, 172–73, 370n.20
Spanish Reconquista, 2
Spenser, Edmund, 164–65, 369n.6
spirituality, love and, 289–94
Spivak, Gayatri, 24
Şahname (Book of Kings), 135–36, 165
Şahname literature, women in, 165–66
Şah u geda (Shah and the beggar), 56
şehraşub ("city disturber"), beautiful boys represented in, 40
şehrengizes ("city thriller") literature: beautiful boys represented in, 40–43, 359n.10; beloved women in, 43–58, 188–93
Şentürk, Atillâ, 295
Şeyhi, 180
Stallybrass, Peter, 112, 229–34, 373n.8, 376n.25
Star Trek, 358n.21
state: growth and development of, in Ottoman Empire, 244–45; literary economy and, 311–16; personal relations and decline of, 321–24
Stations of the Poets Pilgrimage, 201
Stehling, Thomas, 175–76, 370n.28
Stetkevych, Suzanne, 156–57
stoning *(recm)*, punishment by, 272–73
Stuart monarchy, in England, 313, 384n.61
Stubbes, Phillip, 68, 76
Sufism: modernization of language and, 334–38; pornographic literature of, 131–32, 367n.37; rise of, 81, 384n.61; spirituality of Ottoman love poetry and, 299–300, 302–3, 380n.67
suhtes class of male youths, 52, 319
Süleyman I (Süleyman the Magnificent), 26, 35, 81, 88; courtly etiquette in reign of, 231–32; cultured conversation *(sohbet)* during reign of, 107; economics and population growth in reign of, 309–10; Hurrem's letters to, 368n.60; legal code of, 286, 378n.19; love and power of slaves in court of, 238–50; mysticism of, 335; paid appointments by, 321; patronage of literati during reign of, 308, 340, 381n.11
Sultan Mehmet II. *See* Mehmet the Conqueror
Sultan Murat II, 1
Sunni Islam, modernization of language and, 334–35
Suppressed Persian, 358n.17
sūrnāmes (festival books), 190
Symposium, 291, 375n.3, 379n.42

Tamburlaine, 351
Tanpınar, Ahmet Hamdi, 230
tavern culture, in Ottoman Empire, 69–73, 361n.15; ascendancy of puritanism and waning of, 81–82; laws and decrees concerning, 281–88; love and violence and, 256–57; puritanical attacks on, 320; role of women in, 189–92; sexual mores and, 143–44
taxation, Ottoman policies of, 317–19, 383n.50
tezkire (poet biographies), 35, 88–89, 364n.5; female sexuality in, 179–87; as historical source, 307, 326–28, 381n.9–10; of Latifi, 88–89, 307, 364n.5, 381n.9; mannerism and, 351–53; women poets in, 197–208
theft, Islamic law regarding, 273, 377n.4
Theory of Profane Love, 358n.17
timar (prebend) system, 317–24, 383n.47, 383n.49
Timurid period: modernization of language and, 333; *şehraşub* literature and, 40

töhmetlü/töhmetsiz (suspicion/without suspicion): legal decrees concerning, 276–88; legal status in Ottoman society and, 79–80
Tophane district (Istanbul), 69
tradesman and craftsman: beloveds as, 40–43; beloved women as daughters of, 46; laws concerning, 283–88
transvestites: in Ottoman culture, 178–87; sexual violence and, 375n.25
Traub, Valerie, 173
trees, in Ottoman poetry, 104
trentuno (gang rape), 375n.12
tropes, in Ottoman literary tradition, 158–59
Turkic languages, revival of, 333–38
Turkish Republic, recent history of, 11
Tuti (Hanım), 210
Twelfth Night, 53, 261–62
Tyndale, William, 333

Ufficiali di Notte, 122
ulema class, in Ottoman Empire, 287–88, 300–301, 307, 378n.35; breakdown of, 320
Unionists, Notaras' mediation with, 2
"universal intelligence/universal soul," Ottoman concept of, 294
Urania, 213–14

Valensi, Lucette, 26, 232, 387n.36
Varchi, Benedetto, 291, 299, 379n.42
Vasari, 352
Vasfı, 103–4
Venice: discourse about Ottoman Empire in, 380n.4, 387n.36; economics and demographics in, 309, 315–16, 383n.39; law and punishment in, 270–74, 281, 320; public celebrations in, 368n.63; sexual mores in, 114–21, 336; sexual violence in, 257; women's sexuality in, 174
Venier, Lorenzo, 375n.12
Venus and Adonis, 87
Veronese, 338
Veyne, Paul, 11
Villiers, George, 127, 313
violence, love in Age of Beloveds and, 251–69

virginity: "hypervirginity" of Queen Elizabeth I and, 312–13, 382n.26; Muslim and Christian preoccupation with, 43–44; women poets and cult of, 204–5, 216

Wall, Allison, 323
weak nominalism, sexual orientation and, 14
Western culture, role of women in, 163–66
wine parties, in Ottoman culture, 144–47; literary tradition and, 156–57
women: art of love and, 163–216; in beloveds poetry, 43–58; fear of, in Western cultures, 163–66; Florentine sexual mores and, 124–25; gendered space for, in Ottoman culture, 51–53, 360n.29, 360n.32; imagined images of, 167–87; Islam and rights of, 16; as Ottoman poets, 57–58, 193–216; as poets in Venice, 118–21; public role and activities, 189–92; sexuality of, in Ottoman literature, 132–47; as slaves, 46–49; tezkire writers and, 197; as writers and poets, 193–216
wool production, English and Ottoman comparisons, 318, 384n.53
Wroth, Mary, 213–15
Wyatt, Thomas (Sir), 229

Yahya, 42, 56, 106, 169–71, 184; decline of Ottoman Empire and poetry of, 324–28, 385n.71
Yani Meyhanesi tavern, 69

Zati, 35; androgyny of beloveds in literature of, 39; 'Aşık's anecdotes about, 101–2; beloveds named in poetry of, 39; Ibrahim Pasha and, 240–41; letayif (anecdotes) of, 93–94, 97–98; love poems of, 86; parallel poems of, 92–97; patronage refused by, 308; poetry about, 101–3; şehrengiz of, 40–42; spirituality in love poetry of, 294–95
Zelzele-i Sugra (Lesser Quake), 107–8
Zeynep Hatun, 197, 200–201, 204, 216
Züleyha, 44

WALTER G. ANDREWS is Research Professor of Near Eastern Languages and Civilization at the University of Washington. He is the author of *Poetry's Voice, Society's Song: Ottoman Lyric Poetry* (University of Washington Press, 1985) and *An Introduction to Ottoman Poetry* (Bibliotheca Islamica, 1976). He is the editor of *Intersections in Turkish Literature: Essays in Honor of James Stewart-Robinson* (University of Michigan Press, 2001) and co-translator and co-editor (with Najaat Black and Mehmet Kalpaklı) of *Ottoman Lyric Poetry: An Anthology* (University of Texas Press, 1997).

MEHMET KALPAKLI is an assistant professor and chair of the history department and director of Ottoman studies at Bilkent University. He is the co-translator and co-editor (with Walter Andrews and Najaat Black) of *Ottoman Lyric Poetry: An Anthology* (University of Texas Press, 1997).

Library of Congress Cataloging-in-Publication Data

Andrews, Walter G.
The age of beloveds : love and the beloved in early-modern Ottoman and European culture and society / Walter G. Andrews and Mehmet Kalpaklı.
p. cm.
Includes bibliographical references and index.
ISBN 0-8223-3450-x (cloth   ) — ISBN 0-8223-3424-0 (pbk.   )
1. Love—Turkey—Social aspects. 2. Love—Europe—Social aspects. 3. Turkish poetry—History and criticism. I. Kalpaklı, Mehmet, 1964- II. Title.
GT2630.A53   2004
306.7′09561—dc22   2004019577

www.ingramcontent.com/pod-product-compliance
Lightning Source LLC
Chambersburg PA
CBHW061341300426
44116CB00011B/1942